Texts in Philosophy
Volume 31

The Labyrinth of Infinity
or the Enigma of Existence

Volume 21
The Road Not Taken. On Husserl's Philosophy of Logic and Mathematics
Claire Ortiz Hill and Jairo José da Silva

Volume 22
The Good, the Right & the Fair – an introduction to ethics
Mickey Gjerris, Morten Ebbe Juul Nielsen, and Peter Sandøe

Volume 23
The Normative Structure of Responsibility. Law, Language, Ethics
Federico Faroldi

Volume 24
Karl Popper. A Centenary Assessment. Volume I. Life and Times, and Values in a World of Facts
Ian Jarvie, Karl Milford and David Miller, eds

Volume 25
Karl Popper. A Centenary Assessment. Volume II. Metaphysics and Epistemology
Ian Jarvie, Karl Milford and David Miller, eds

Volume 26
Karl Popper. A Centenary Assessment. Volume III Science
Ian Jarvie, Karl Milford and David Miller, eds

Volume 27
Unorthodox Analytic Philosophy
Guillermo E. Rosado Haddock

Volume 28
Quantum Heresies.
Kent A. Peacock, with a foreword by James Robert Brown

Volume 29
Carrollian Notes
George Englebretsen

Volume 30
Problems from Hume
David Bostock

Volume 31
The Labyrinth of Infinity or the Enigma of Existence
Stathis Livadas

Texts in Philosophy Series Editors
Vincent F. Hendriks   vincent@hum.ku.dk
John Symons   jsymons@utep.edu
Dov Gabbay   dov.gabbay@kcl.ac.uk

The Labyrinth of Infinity
or the Enigma of Existence

Stathis Livadas

© Individual authors and College Publications 2022
All rights reserved.

ISBN 978-1-84890-390-6

College Publications
Scientific Director: Dov Gabbay
Managing Director: Jane Spurr

http://www.collegepublications.co.uk

Original cover design by Laraine Welch

All rights reserved. No part of this publication may be reproduced, stored in a retrieval system or transmitted in any form, or by any means, electronic, mechanical, photocopying, recording or otherwise without prior permission, in writing, from the publisher.

Endorsements

"The ontologist Stathis Livadas writes on the irreducible subjectivity in the foundations of mathematics and the natural sciences and, with the sensibilities of the poet that he also is, on the difficulties offinding the right language to describe this. His detailed analyses, in and of the phenomenological tradition, but with an eye also on analytic philosophy, will reward close study and stimulate further developments."

Mark van Atten, Husserl Archive, Paris

"After decades of having been ostracized by analytic philosophers, the interest in Edmund Husserl's views on logic and mathematics was revived at the end of the last century and continues in this one. The present collection of papers by Dr. Stathis Livadas on the foundations both of mathematics and of physics, though partially continuing that tradition, seems to be influenced more by Hermann Weyl's much older rendering of Husserl's transcendental phenomenology as a foundation of physics and mathematics, on which Livadas develops his own philosophical views."

Dr. Guillermo E. Rosado Haddock
Retired Professor of Philosophy,
University of Puerto Rico at Río Piedras

Author's foreword

The subject matter of this book is in a certain sense a follow up to the content of my previous book under the title *Contemporary problems of epistemology in the light of Phenomenology* published also in the College Publications (2012). Both books are in fact collections of published articles in various established journals of the fields concerned, with the present book including an extra introductory chapter as a kind of global reference to the content presented in the chapters that follow.

Even as the appearance of a spate of new published articles in one book would probably make someone reserved as to the homogeneity of the subject matter touched, the fact is that both in the present book and the previous one the objective and the great picture is essentially the same. This is to offer a consistent interpretation of major epistemological issues of our time in the light of phenomenological philosophy with a special focus on the Husserlian phenomenology. On this account a major undertaking was always to show how phenomenological philosophy can be illuminating in the face of fundamental epistemological questions, more concretely in the fields of contemporary mathematics and physics, and offer insights that may not lead to naturalist, reductionistic descriptions normally associated with the narratives of concerned sciences themselves.

Yet while being aligned in the general orientation above, the present book has certain differences with regard to the *Contemporary problems of epistemology in the light of Phenomenology*. Two major ones are that, first, this book expands the field of philosophical reference and argumentation to include continental philosophy in general and consequently the Heideggerian and Sartrean views and the way they can be helpful in clarifying epistemological issues of our time and, second, it engages a philosophical discussion on issues philosophical, or rather ontological, on their proper account which means independently of their presumptive influence in the shaping of the discussion within the epistemological domain. Therefore key ontological issues like the concept of absolute being in contradistinction with that of existence in mundane terms, the concepts of transcendence within the world, of individuality, of unity and plurality, of totality and infinity, etc., are dealt with as such in purely philosophical-ontological terms in the general phenomenological perspective of the author and of course in the relevance they may have with the contemporary epistemological context.

Accordingly, the contents of *The Labyrinth of Infinity or the Enigma of Existence* are arranged into two parts, the first one (PART A) being more epistemologically relevant with a special emphasis on addressing questions of recent and relatively recent research in the mathematical foundations, and the second one (PART B) more philosophically oriented involving an articulated discussion of philosophical matters mentioned above per se. Yet as, at least according to the author's view, even the most purely transcendental ontological inquiry is not innocuous of mundane epistemological concerns and vice versa, such approach renders a wide-open horizon of convergence and mutual illumination between the philosophical-ontological and epistemological narratives, the latter being in constant fruitful feedback with day to day hard science.

The journey into the interminable, luring odyssey of bringing into the light of a subjectively founded and yet non-reductionistic philosophy the great issues of the epistemology of our time, by inquiring into the foundations of this brand of philosophy, cannot stop insofar as there is a persisting non-eliminable residuum of meaning of the world itself vis-à-vis the world as objectified and expressible sense. Hopefully this will be the motivation for a next book.

Closing, the author feels obliged to express his deep gratitude to professor Dov Gabbay, scientific director of College Publications, Jane Spurr managing director and the technical staff of the publishing house for making this publication possible.

Stathis Livadas
February 2022

VITA

Dr. Stathis Livadas is an independent scholar in the fields of the philosophy, logic and the foundations of mathematics as well as of the phenomenology and continental philosophy. He has earned his M.Sc. degree in theoretical mathematics and his PhD in the philosophy of mathematics from the Department of Mathematics of the University of Patras, Greece.

He has published numerous research articles in the fields of his expertise and has actively participated in many international conferences and workshops. He is currently working on a research project focused on a subjectively based approach to mathematical and quantum mechanical foundations as well as on a purely philosophical one on the questions of absolute being, existence and transcendence within the world.

He is also a poet (5 publications in Greek), a multilinguist art connoisseur and an amateur historian.

Contents

Introduction 1

Part A

Objects as Limits of Experience and the Notion of Horizon in Mathematical Theories 11

The Subjective Roots of Forcing Theory and Their Influence in Independence Results 29

What is the Nature of Mathematical-Logical Objects? 53

Weyl's Conception of the Continuum in a Husserlian Transcendental Perspective 87

The Transcendental Source of Logic by way of Phenomenology 113

Extending the Non-extendible: Shades of Infinity in Large Cardinals and
     Forcing Theories 13

The Plausible Impact of Phenomenology on Gödel's Thoughts 15

Talking about Models. The Inherent Constraints of Mathematics 18

Why is Cantor's Absolute inherently inaccessible? 20

Abolishing Platonism in Multiverse Theories 23

Is there an Ontology of Infinity? 25

Part B

Some Platonic Ontological Claims Under a Phenomenological
     Point of View 28

The Transcendence of the Ego in Continental Philosophy - Convergences
     and Divergences 29

Husserl's Sachhaltigkeit and the Question of the Essence of Individuals . . 32

The Relevance of Phenomenological Analysis with Current Epistemology . 35

The enigma of 'being there'. Choosing between ontology and epistemology 37

Is Existence an Ontologically Sound Term? 40

1. INTRODUCTION

As was almost the case with my previous book *Current Problems of Epistemology in the Light of Phenomenology*, published also in College Publications, the content of the present book can be said to stand in the interface of ontological philosophy, of continental philosophy with a special focus on phenomenology, the philosophy of mathematics and in a more general perspective the philosophy of science.

Yet while finding itself in the same field at large, this book may be evaluated as a further and deeper look into key philosophical questions traditionally considered the stuff of ontology, as e.g., the question of the ontological being-in-itself or the notion of platonic unity in contrast with multiplicity, both as such and also and foremost in relation to epistemological issues. These latter primarily concern the logic and the foundations of mathematics and to a certain extent aspects of quantum mechanics theory both in their current state of progress. This is exactly what the originality of this approach consists of, with regard to the classical and secondary literature, in that the whole undertaking deals with ontological issues with due philosophical *rigueur* while at the same time trying to find and highlight the thread-like connection that would make this kind of discourse relevant with issues touching on the ontology of mathematics, in the sense of a formal axiomatic science, and further with ontological aspects of quantum theory.

To make my point more clear, I start from some aspects of the epistemology of quantum mechanics which point inevitably to a reduction of an ontology of self-standing physical reality to an ontology of relations of reciprocity and co-belonging between an independent reality itself (not to be confused with empirical reality) and an embodied subjectivity which in a supplementary radical reduction can reach the transcendental sphere, this latter meant as a pure subjectivity whose essence may be thought precisely as its enactment in the present now of reflection (cf. with the Husserlian *nunc stans*). Moreover this kind of transcendental subjectivity may not be reducible to the phenomena of physical reality studied in the normative context of a physical theory and may not be expressible even in some kind of loose linguistic form. Of course there is no proof, at least in the sense implied by the physical or scientific realism, that vindicates the assumption of a radical reduction to the sphere of immanence[1] in absolute terms, however there is a strong indication *in rem* toward a non-eliminable subjective factor eluding the purely physicalistic context of quantum theory and from a certain viewpoint underscoring the approximative idealization of the corresponding mathematical metatheory. Thus according to B. D' Espagnat physical realism may be refuted to the extent that the ensemble of principles and notions elaborated in terms of actual life, further refined in reflection and applicable in physics in a way that forms a coherent theory, are not susceptible of an interpretation in a strong sense of objectivity which would be moreover unique and therefore non-arbitrary. Even in a newtonian universe, as simplistic as it may look in today's standards of physics, a scientific object would be in fill rigor a construction of the mind and the certitudes placed by a physicist in his science just as those placed in the world by any layman are certitudes concerning what is implied by the active presence of thinking and communicating beings in the world, and not at

---

[1]Immanent or immanence, a key term of continental philosophy, can be roughly explained as referring to what is or has become correlative (or 'co-substantial') to the being of one's own consciousness in contrast to what is 'external' or transcendent to it.

all of an independent reality.[2] In consequence the deficiencies, mostly evident in the physicalistic context of quantum mechanics, associated with the way physical realism views the (physical) world as a self-standing, independent reality imposes the need to find a conceptual foundation of at least positive science on a notion of weak objectivity that renders a primary role to such conscious acts as the preparation and measurement of a quantum state-of-affairs or the disentanglement of a state of quantum superposition, etc. In this view and in the light of quantum inseparability there seems hardly to be place for a naive notion of particles and fields as multiple, localized, ontologically self-standing realities in the absence of a consciousness-in-act on account of which D' Espagnat goes as far as to state that particles themselves (and fields for that matter) are no more than "simple properties (deceptively localized) of a reality not situated in space" (ibid., pp. 140-141).

In a more concrete sense the language of science and *a fortiori* common language has no way to represent reality other than in distinct macro-objects by 'cutting out' the same reality something that implies a constituting subjectivity, and it is precisely due to this latter factor that language fails to capture what is the quintessence of reality, namely the continuity as form of its existence, in other words the mode of being of reality as an unbreakable whole whose essence is being constantly in the form of a continuous 'flux'. In fact this de facto situation seems to underlie, for instance, the difficulty to interpret Young's double slit experiment in ignoring the non-eliminable role of consciousness and sticking either to the field or the supplementary variables (i.e., hidden variables) point of view, with the latter acquiring a mysteriously superior ontological status than that of a quantum field. Any attempt to remedy this state-of-affairs and banish the extra-theoretical 'intrusion' of the subjective (constituting) factor has led up to this time to arbitrary theoretical modifications that have not been experimentally confirmed (ibid., pp. 106-107). In consequence the linguistic tools underpinning quantum reality cannot be applied otherwise than in the description of the preparation of quantum states-of-affairs and the measurement of quantum observables, this one in particular meant only as an objectifying act in the present now 'extrinsic' to the being itself of the quantum situation.

It is well known to theoretical physicists that the question of quantum measurements has at least an ambivalent epistemological content. The persisting question of what happens to a quantum state between two successive measurements ('observations'), it comes as a plausible claim that may ultimately pertain to the subjective-transcendental and not the physical part of the observation. This question was epistemologically dealt with by Heisenberg in his aristotelian-inspired theory of potentia and in strictly theoretical terms by von Neumann's reduction postulate which assigns to the eigenvector of the physical state $s(t)$ of a quantum quantity Q upon a first-kind measurement at time t the same value as to the state $s(t_1)$ of the same quantity at time t_1 soon after the measurement. Yet both approaches are from different contextual standpoints both deficient in coming to terms with the being of the state-of-affairs between the measurements as being-in-itself, a situation that highlights the shakiness of physical realism founded on the notion of an independent reality in the absence of a consciousness irreducible to a physicalistic context.

---

[2]See, B. D' Espagnat: *À la Recherche du réel*, (2015), Dunod: Paris, pp. 140-141.

Introduction

Accordingly it is noteworthy that Bitbol has claimed in *L'Aveuglante Proximité du Réel*[3] that what is missing in the domain of the theory of quantum mechanics is the plurality of criteria of epistemological mimesis and to a lesser degree those of ontological projection (ibid., p. 108). This means that there can be no assumption of a pre-determined architecture of reality insofar as, disregarding the approximative description of the macroscopic world, the 'blinding' excess of proximity (think, e.g., of the non-commutativity of the algebra of observables, a conspicuous demonstration of which are Heisenberg's uncertainty principles) stands as a 'covering veil' to a complete knowledge on the part of a subject endowed with an irreducible to purely physical terms consciousness. In these terms, that is, in reference to an empirical yet veiled reality that is totally at odds with a notion of (ontological) independence, the specific architecture of human beings within nature plays, for D' Espagnat, a crucial role even as this must be read more as an epistemological statement rather than an ontological one.

There can be no doubt, in any case, that progressing research in quantum mechanics will bring more and more into the fore the question of the ontological foundation of the quantum mechanical edifice as a whole and the way it may lead the way to a 'residuum' of reality inherently associated with a subjective factor in absolute sense immune to any kind of eliminative reductionism, positivism or physical realism. And it is in this vein that one can also raise certain doubts on the possibility of consistently applying the language and the conceptual machinery of mathematics, fraught with the platonic-idealist charge of centuries of social and cultural evolution, toward a positivistic approach to the world of phenomena.

Much more than undertaking an interpretation of the expressional capacity of mathematics as a metatheoretical system of knowledge in connection with physical theories, one may sooner or later come across an ontology of mathematics in its own right. For if one is disposed to divest mathematics of their centuries-old platonistic cocoon and recalibrate them as a systematic science essentially and irrevocably associated with a constituting embodied consciousness within the world at large, one may establish a whole new 'ecosystem' in which a mathematical theory conditions and at the same is conditioned by the world of phenomena. At the same time it may lay its ontological foundation not in some vague platonic realm of ideas but in the constituting capacities of being-in-the-world in general in whatever particular subjective-transcendental character one may attribute to being-in-the-world. In these terms and due to the intrinsic trait of mathematics to project mathematical experience well beyond the finitistic and mundane, a whole new field opens up for inquiring into the way a vast array of fundamental mathematical ideas as the finiteness/infinity, discreteness/continuity, part/whole, etc., may be reducible to subjective attributes, often of an a priori character, of which (inner) temporality may prove a defining one. And to the extent that these subjective attributes underlie a meaning of well-defined objects as mental appearances of objects-in-the-world, naively considered as belonging to the pre-phenomenological (or pre-constitutional) reality, they ground by this measure a sense of subjectively based correlation of physical and mathematical objects in the modes, for instance, of presence-in-person in the actual now, of positability, of eidetic preservation,[4] of indefinite projection, etc.

---

[3] See, Bitbol, M.: *L' Aveuglante Proximité du Réel*, (1998), Paris: Flammarion.

[4] In *Thing and Space*, (*Ding und Raum*, Hua XVI, (Claesges, U., ed.), (1973), The Hague: M. Nijhoff, p. 166), Husserl thought of thing-like (*sachhaltige*) 'points' as 'visual atoms' in a process of fragmentation that ultimately leads to minima visibilia. He pointed out the essential similarity of the visual field to

Introduction

Further, if a sense of non-physical realism becomes the guiding principle of an epistemology that views the essence of absolute being as eluding the descriptive terms of objective reality, then one could well initiate a holistic discussion by means of which he would be able to talk about such notions as non-locality and instantaneity in terms that would take account both of their physical and mathematical content. In such case such mathematical and physical 'pathologies' as these above could by non-physical reductivism be, at least partly and yet non-eliminably, due to the mode of being and modes of constituting of an ever in-act subjectivity whose absolute origin would be reached only by logical necessity (and not de facto) out of this world. Just bring to the mind that Gödel's incompleteness results might be epistemologically accounted for by the lack of a rigorously defined notion of finitistic in metatheory and the well-known *Continuum Hypothesis* undecidability by the mathematically deficient translation of the 'fluidity' of events in the real world as continuity. It may have been essentially the latter view of non-denumerable infinity as continuity that prompted W. W. Quine [in the 'Reply to Charles Parsons' in: *The Philosophy of W. V. Quine*, (1986)] to deny to higher than the first uncountable ordinal (ω_1) infinities any ontological rights except for being forced on us 'by the simplest known systematizations of more welcome matters'. Understandably, if taken ontologically at face value, this statement would make fool of several decades of set-theoretical prowess in advancing the levels of infinity by consistent enlargements of models mainly through various forcing techniques.[5] A few more words are in order on the matter.

In Husserl's transcendental phenomenology ideal mathematical objects and associated truths (in terms of the meaning of judgements referring to them) are omnitemporal and acausal entities, meant as constituted invariants of acts of cognition. In this respect, they may be associated with the subjective unity of consciousness insofar as they can eventually become idealizations on the condition of first being fulfilled objects of intentionality in the present now of temporal consciousness, constituted as noematical objects and further as well-defined formal ones in abstraction. Moreover, the meaning-fulfillment of mathematical objects as original givennesses in temporal actuality would be essentially associated with such categorial objectivities as those expressible in a formal language by fundamental syntactical relations, e.g., the relation of ordering, the relation of transitivity (of ordinals), the absoluteness of syntactical individuals, etc. For instance, the fundamental syntactical properties of being transitive and well-ordered by the relation of set-inclusion $\in$ of ordinal numbers may be seen as idealization of fulfillments of intention-meaning towards a concrete mathematical object generated by a potentially indefinite colligation of content-free formal individuals.

However a claim to be made is that the idealization involved in the next to $\aleph_0$ cardinality, i.e., the cardinality $\aleph_1$ which by Cantor's continuum hypothesis is presumably equal to the cardinality of the continuum **c**, must be of a radically different character as it cannot be derived by abstraction of *ad infinitum* performable present-now intentional

---

itself, on a large and small scale and explained that it is obviously this immanent similarity which, as evident generic similarity, justifies the transposition of the eidetic relationships discovered in the macroscopic universe to the microscopic 'atoms' beyond divisibility. Of course this kind of eidetic interpretation is well beyond a strictly physical or (for that matter) formal-mathematical context, yet it may affect both.

[5]See chapter "*The Subjective Roots of Forcing Theory and Their Influence in Independence Results*" in the present book.

Introduction

acts toward an each time content-free 'general something', but seems to be founded in the constituting source of temporal unity which makes an indefinite colligation of formal individuals positable in the form of completed whole in original presentation and in the present now of reflection. It follows that there is no way to account for the constituting source of temporal unity, which by this token would be also the source of meaning-giving within-the-world, except by postulating a subjectivity whose essence would be its mode of being as transcendence within-the-world irrespectively of clinging to the particular credo of the Husserlian transcendental ego or the Heideggerian Dasein.

As paradoxical as it may seem to deduce a transcendence in the objectivity of the world out of epistemological concerns, yet it seems hardly possible to make a case for a constituting subjectivity that would not be in need of a pre-reflective, transcendental origin of its very self as objectified and therefore subjected to the necessities of objective reality; for otherwise one would end up entrapped in an endless sequence reflecting-reflected at least by logical necessity. Furthermore, an ontology of being reducible to the mode of being of absolute subjectivity as the 'incompressible' residuum after the presumed annihilation of the world (as physical objectivity) could possibly account for a notion of simultaneity independent of temporal constraints. This could pertain, to cite some concrete instances, on the formal-mathematical level to the positability of various levels of infinity as objective wholes in actuality and, on the quantum level, to the Bohrian notion of the non-objectivity of the state vector, as implying non-locality, and the wave packet reduction situations in quantum mechanics.

Concerning the mathematics of large infinities and the relevant research the argumentation presented in detail in the chapter '*Why is Cantor's Absolute inherently inaccessible?*' tries to show that the proof-theoretical machinery of the various model-theoretic approaches that, to our day, aspire to accede to the Cantorian absolute, in other words to the cardinality of an all-encompassing set-theoretical universe **V** that would consistently contain every other large cardinal, is conditioned, often in an implicit but fundamental way, on set-theoretical concepts and principles, the concept of absoluteness, the axiom of choice (**AC**) and the well-foundedness axiom being such examples, that depend metatheoretically on a notion of infinity belonging to the level of intuitive continuum. This, in turn, may be argued to be actually the continuous fluidity of the being of the objective world, re-presentable in the level of immanence by the 'flux' of temporal consciousness as irreducible, self-constituting unity. By following this kind of subjective reduction, such unity must be the extra-theoretical foundation for any kind of infinity irrespectively of the power of elements of the domains of corresponding formal structures and in this sense may serve as a non-reductionistic foundation for the mathematical continuum. In fact this is a unity by which causality in the absence of an objective real-world infinity may be ultimately reducible to a priori forms of absolute consciousness and to the possibility of correlation of objects-positings due to the unity itself as presentable in the now of each one's reflection. To the extent that the continuum of the real numbers may be conceptually associated with such kind of subjectively founded unity may offer a rationale along these lines to Feferman's claim that the *Continuum Hypothesis* is an inherently vague statement and that "the continuum itself, or equivalently the power set of the natural numbers, is not a definite mathematical object"[6].

---

[6] See, Feferman, S., Friedman, M. H., Maddy P., Steel, J.: Does Mathematics Need New axioms?, *The Bulletin of Symbolic Logic*, 6, 4, (2000), p. 405.

Introduction

In fact the ways to ever stronger infinite cardinalities by the known standard methods are very much dependent on performing consistent projections of well-founded mathematical acts in accordance with the finitistic intuitions of our natural experience indefinitely preserved against a continuous unity in the sense described above. Consequently one may put the question of whether can be indeed justified an ontological foundation of an infinity greater than the power of the continuum insofar as any known process of establishing large cardinals is circularly conditioned on assumptions associated with the acceptance of an indefinite continuous unity of a lower rank formally identifiable with the cardinality of the mathematical continuum.

In all these matters mentioned above and in the corresponding contexts, e.g., the non-locality of quantum states-of-affairs and the assumed non-objectivity of the state vector in quantum theory or the mathematical infinity as reducible to the immanent unity-in-the-flux and unconstrained by spatiotemporal and causal limitations, etc, there seems to be a non-objective residuum of being which, on rejecting any platonistic or idealist inclination, may be translatable to a transcendence of being as absolute subjectivity within-the-world. Yet a next question will be inevitable: if, out of epistemological concerns, we reach by a radical transcendental reduction the absolute ego in the Husserlian sense or settle for the transcendental modes of the Heideggerian Dasein's 'unwinding' itself in encountering the world, how can one establish transcendence in terms of acting in the world and yet ontologically 'being' out of the world? Moreover, how can absolute subjectivity be temporality constituting and yet unfettered by temporality concerns itself or else seeking its non-temporal *prima causa*? In other words, how can absolute being become a being-there and thus be relevant with the world in the being of the physical world while preserving identically itself? The risk of falling into circularities or generating an endless sequence of absolute subjectivities is more than evident.

One may then say that the question of being in absolute sense may be ontologically reformulated into a question of a subjectively founded 'being-there-in-actuality', which means, into each being's temporal particularity and the foundation of its very individuality for that matter. In that case a sense of individuality in purely subjective terms and in the specific 'being there', as transposable in objective terms, would be the ultimate foundation of the definiteness of a situation/state-of-affairs in the actual present. We can cite *a propos*, in quantum theory terms, the disentanglement of a quantum state upon 'observation', absolving the non-definiteness of the quantum situation to well-meant objective definability.[7] This kind of being-there-in-actuality pertains then to a relation of subject-object which far from transtemporal, metaphysical assumptions, pointing to an ideal universe of classical ontology, is a relation lived out and put in evidence due to the 'architecture' of individual beings we are, that is, embodied beings endowed with a constituting consciousness whose essence, if by this term we conceive its mode of being as pre-reflective and ever-in-act, is irreducible to objectivist reductionistic considerations. It is noteworthy that the temporal particularity in the sense of the awhileness

---

[7]The question of 'thingness' individuality or, in abstract terms, of formal individuality is a key issue itself both in ontological and epistemological terms. The chapter dedicated to a detailed discussion, of course in the guiding spirit of the book which is in a broad sense phenomenologically inclined, is "*Husserl's Sachhaltigkeit and the Question of the Essence of Individuals*". Further, the way Gödel's view of mathematical objects, in his own brand of conceptual realism, may be accountable by the presumed influence of his Husserlian readings in the later stages of his research life is discussed in the chapter "*The Plausible Impact of Phenomenology on Gödel's Thoughts*".

Introduction

(*Jeweiligkeit*), as the definiteness of being of Dasein's transcendence toward the world, may be thought in parallel terms with the Husserlian conception of the actual presence as original mode of being of absolute consciousness in virtue of living streaming ego.[8] At least it seems that one may inquire, following these clues, into the enigma of 'being there' both in ontological and epistemological sense without falling into the trappings of a realist driven reductionistic explication.

However, as this is not a smooth turf to tread on, new difficulties may arise as 'being there' in virtue of an essential state-of-affairs of being (as existence) might only be eliminable to a consciousness as consciousness-of, which is obviously not consciousness as absolute subjectivity independently of any reference 'alien' to itself, and yet consciousness without reference to a 'being there' as its necessary projection to the world is unthinkable. In the same vein, inner temporality as temporality-in-constituting in purely subjective terms may be subsumed to the necessity of the 'being there' for otherwise would reduce to the vacuous transcendence of an a-temporal subjective origin whose relevance with the world would be only reduced to an arbitrary logical supposition.

To search a way out of the impasse would amount to clarifying, beyond any possible relapse to circularities and indefinite regressions, the delicate dividing line between the transcendental and the mundane in terms of a purely ontological discourse and of a further elaboration and sharpening of our 'observational' machinery vis-à-vis the world, on the one hand, and, on the other, of a further search into the scope and bounds of the expressional capacity of formal mathematical language in virtue of metatheory of the physical situations and also as axiomatical theory in itself. This quest, in the spirit defended throughout the present book, would push *in extremis* the possibility of reducing the epistemological aspects of grand physical theories that aspire to project human observation toward and beyond the horizon of the life-world in the sense of Husserl's *Crisis*,[9] i.e., quantum theory and general relativity, together with the semantical and syntactical breadth and depth of corresponding formal mathematical theories, to their ontological foundation. In turn that kind of ontological discussion would imply a more acute regard into the question of being in virtue of absolute subjectivity, as absolutely self-standing and ultimate guarantor of the validity (*Geltung*) of the world at large, and also in relation to the world as the necessary field of its 'being there', in other words of its mundane existence.

At present, the blurring lines between the transcendental and the mundane spheres make the discourse about the transcendental subject be utterly the same as though it were existent "since the language of being constituted anonymously in the mundane realm before the performance of the reduction is the only language that is available to us"[10]. In a sense the 'as though' qualification to the being of the transcendental subject, in the preceding phrase, may in fact serve to show that natural language is the irreducible intermediary to any sort of transcendental insights, yet natural language knows only the

---

[8] A detailed account of Husserl's attitude on the primary importance of the living present as mode of being of the transcendental ego is found in the original Husserlian texts published in the Husserliana Materialien vol. VIII, under the title *"Späte Texte über Zeitkonstitution, Die C-Manuscripte"*.

[9] I refer, of course, to Husserl's *The Crisis of European Sciences and Transcendental Phenomenology*, (1970), transl. Carr, D., Evanston: Northwestern University Press.

[10] See, McGuirk J.: Phenomenological reduction in Heidegger and Fink: On the problem of the way back from the transcendental to the mundane sphere, *Philosophy Today*, (2009), p. 250.

Introduction

vocabulary of (objective) being, consequently it must be 'extraneous' to what Husserl's disciple Eugen Fink characterized as pre-being.

If substantial progress in clearing out these matters, preferably in a holistic sense, would come into effect in some future generations they would probably see in a new glaring light, and most probably far from any metaphysical or objective-physical realist prejudices, such key controversial issues of present day epistemology as quantum non-locality, wave packet reduction, non-causal interactions, etc. and, on the formal mathematical level, such key questions as finiteness vs infinity, the absoluteness of individuals and associated formulas, the limits of definability, etc. For then, they would have previously resolved the issue of coming to terms with the residuum of the transcendence of being with regard to its mirroring as 'being there' in the world of phenomena.

Part A

OBJECTS AS LIMITS OF EXPERIENCE AND THE NOTION OF HORIZON IN MATHEMATICAL THEORIES

Abstract. The present work is an attempt to bring attention to the application of several key ideas of Husserl's *Krisis* in the construction of certain mathematical theories that claim to be alternative nonstandard versions of the standard Zermelo-Fraenkel set theory. In general, these theories refute, at least semantically, the platonistic context of the Cantorian system and to one or the other degree are motivated by the notions of the life-world as the pregiven holistic field of experience and that of horizon as the boundary of human perceptions and the de facto constraint in reaching limit-idealizations. Moreover, I try to give convincing reasons for the existence of an ultimate constitutional 'vacuum' of a subjective origin that is formally reflected in the application of a notion of actual infinity in dealing generally with the mathematical infinite.

1. INTRODUCTION

In this article I try to provide a solid argumentation on the relevance of key phenomenological notions, namely that of the life-world and that of (phenomenological) horizon with the philosophical motivation of certain alternative versions of standard set theory that have sprouted in the last 40 years mostly out of the impact that bore in foundational mathematics Gödel's incompleteness theorems, P. Cohen's proof of the independence of key infinity assertions (i.e., the Continuum Hypothesis, **CH**, and the Axiom of Choice, **AC**) and A. Robinson's classical *Nonstandard Analysis*. Among these alternative theories, the Alternative Set Theory (AST) of the Prague School of around the last quarter of 20th century explicitly claimed, by the words of one of its main representatives P. Vopěnka, its motivation as being based on Husserl's ideas in *Die Krisis der Europäischen Wissenschaften und die Transzendentale Phänomenologie*, ([2]). Criticizing the rigidity and dogmatic acceptance in Cantor's theory of the notion of actual infinity associated, for instance, with the declaration that all objects capable of successive, infinitely extending construction have already been constructed, P. Vopěnka claimed that: 'Thus we deal here with a construction extending the real world and surpassing qualitatively the limits of the space of possibilities of our observation. Assertions about infinite sets thus lose their phenomenal content [...] One possible way out of the crisis of contemporary mathematics may be through an attempt to reconstruct mathematics on a phenomenal basis

Objects as Limits of Experience

[...] But a purely phenomenal conception of mathematics would considerably impoverish mathematics [...] Mathematics is a means for surpassing the horizon of human experience [...] In reconstructing mathematics we are thus obliged to accept also basic principles for surpassing the horizon of evidence.' ([15], p. 6 & p. 10).

A more detailed review of the phenomenologically 'relevant' content of AST theory will be undertaken in section 3. Also, in section 4 the same will be done with respect to another non-Cantorian and nonstandard theory thought of, under a certain semantical interpretation, as having a certain conceptual proximity with the notion of 'observable' horizon, namely, the Internal Set Theory (IST).

In my general approach a main purpose, next to pointing to the phenomenological affinities of the content of the theories above, is to present a strong argumentation for the assertion that infinity in general, in terms of a constituted whole surpassing the limits of evidence based on human experience, may be only embedded in the kind of mathematics conceived in the sense of a Husserlian mathematical natural science by means of infinity principles of *ad hoc* nature incorporating an implicit, at least, notion of actual infinity.[1] This means that in case we consider the horizon as the ever shifting limit of concatenations of human experience, to 'reach' or even 'transcend' the bounds of horizon we are set to fall into the same circular maze one is caught in Cantorian mathematics with regard to infinite objects in actuality. That is, we have to accept a disguised form of actual infinity principle to make the 'leap' from the ever advancing path of hereditary countability, in other terms from the progressing succession of concatenations of experience in implementing any 'observation' within the life-world, to the 'vagueness' of continuous unity upon or even beyond the horizon.

In section 2, I deal to some extent with certain core ideas of Husserlian *Krisis* especially in connection with my professed scope above and set about to propound the main pillars of Husserl's scheme to mathematize nature on condition of experiencing the world as being already there but, all the same, as being there for us awake to the world, directly (without any mediation) conscious of the world and of oneself, 'as living in the world, actually experiencing and actually effecting the ontic certainty of the world' ([2], p. 143). The world, in the sense of a world-horizon cannot be made a thematic object of phenomenological attitude as an object or entity but presupposes every act of positing objects within-it and consequently implies fundamentally different correlative types of consciousness with respect to them. This is a notion of the world as essentially an eidetic horizon conditioning the exact determination of mathematical objects as limit-idealizations in the construction of a mathematics based on the normativity of natural 'appearances' with regard to all carriers of a constituting consciousness in intersubjective coincidence. As such it stands as a key concept, naturally in relation to at least one consciousness intentionally oriented within it, of Husserlian *Krisis*.

It is true, though, that Husserl had made several important remarks on the broad notion of life-world as the possible world of experience that depends on the possibility of experience, in 'being' itself already and primordially there (thus avoiding the pitfalls of solipsism), already at the time of publication of *Ideas I*. It is notable that he had also used

---

[1] The term actual infinity here and throughout the text is taken as somehow stronger than its usual connotation, i.e., the conception of infinite (mathematical) objects as completed wholes with a typical instance the conception of the set of natural numbers as a whole in actual presence. My view of actual infinity is more focused on the conception of uncountable infinity as the immanent unity of a whole in presentational immediacy.

the term horizon to describe the 'correlate of the components of undeterminateness essentially attached to experiences of physical things themselves; and those components - again, essentially - leave open possibilities of fulfillment which are by no means completely undetermined but are, on the contrary, motivated possibilities predelineated with respect to their essential type'. In the same passage he went on to clarify that any actual experience points to a potentially infinitely extending concatenation of experiences which are effected 'involving species and regulative forms restricted to certain *a priori* types'; moreover, 'Any hypothetical formulation in practical life or in empirical science relates to this changing but always co-posited horizon whereby the positing of the world receives its essential sense' (engl. transl. [5], p. 107; [4], pp. 101-102). He even presaged the key to understanding his idea of life-world notion of intersubjectivity by referring to the 'existence' of an actual ego 'as a demonstrable unity relative to its concatenations of experience', to ground the validity and the essential possibility of determination of something transcendent to the world of real experience; in this position, what is cognizable by one ego must be by essential necessity be cognizable by any ego in the sense that there exist essential possibilities that the separated worlds of experience corresponding to each particular ego are in fact joined by concatenations of actual experience to identically make up the one intersubjective world as a correlate of the unitary world of human mental lives (engl. transl. [5], p. 108; [4], pp. 102-103).

In subsection 2.1, to strengthen my arguments on the essential necessity to recourse to some *ad hoc* actual infinity principle to shift the bounds of an ever advancing hereditarily finite horizon to the impredicative nature of continuous unity, I refer to some fundamental features of the phenomenology of consciousness. This is done in holding to the position that the possibility of the world is conditioned in intersubjective fashion on the possibility of each and every experience (in the essential mode it is carried through) constituting the world. In addition, one has to keep in mind that the universal a priori of the logical-mathematical sciences, generally the objective-logical a priori, is founded on the universal a priori 'which is in itself prior', that of the pure life-world ([2], p. 141). As a matter of fact my reference to the phenomenology of temporal consciousness in subsection 2.1, to the extent that infinite mathematical objects or notions, e.g. a transfinite recursion or an infinite well-ordering, may be thought of as purely mental constructions, may be justified in an almost reverse sense to that of G. Longo in [10]. He claims there that 'infinitary constructions in mental space and time may be understood as the subjective traces of intersubjective extensions of the objectivity of the phenomenal world, i.e. they are the 'mental marks' of the objectivity we constructed in intersubjective, historical praxis, over basic regularities. The concept of actual infinity is the result of many historical conceptual constructions [...] Its objectivity is obtained as an integration of 'metaphors' ([..] but they are not linguistic metaphors) and by the normative structuring of mathematics, well beyond phenomena and leaves traces in our minds;' ([10], pp. 24-25). My own approach is that there is a purely subjective origin associated with the constituting and, ultimately, self-constituting modes of consciousness that makes possible the establishment of infinite totalities as completed wholes in the present now independently of spatio-temporal and causal constraints and yet 'motivated' by the modes of experiencing within the life-world.

Finally in subsection 2.2, I refer to a simplified mathematical model (by J. Petitot) in which kinesthetic descriptions are also ultimately conditioned, in the processional continuous limit, on a notion of actual infinity in the general sense of a completed whole in presentational immediacy.

2. Outline of the relevance of certain key notions of Husserl's *Krisis* with alternative mathematical theories

In *Krisis*, which eventually came to be Husserl's last published work (lasting from 1934 to 1937), the founder of phenomenology inquired about the possibility of attaining what is in itself true of nature by means of what he termed a mathematical natural science. On this account, he drew a distinction between an ontology of nature 'in itself', meaning the necessary forms for a determination of the ideal essence of nature as such and of every individual which *idealiter* and 'in itself' can belong to nature, (something that can be accomplished by the pure mathematics of nature), and an a priori methodology of a possible knowledge of nature in itself in taking nature as experienced by experiencing beings. This latter possibility, that is, the possibility of the knowledge of nature in itself through nature experience begets the a priori possibility of a mathematical natural science, or 'the science of the method of natural-scientific determination of nature through the data of experience' ([2], pp. 305-306).

In this respect, Husserl devoted a significant part of this work to develop the notion of mathematical natural science as a new mathematics bearing its origin in Galileo's mathematization of nature in the sense that nature may be idealized by means of a new mathematics marking the rift with classical Greek mathematics that dealt only with finite tasks and thus referred to a finitely closed a priori body of (mathematical) knowledge. In contrast, the dawn of modern era saw mathematics becoming a rational universal science which can master the infinite totality of what in general may be taken as a rational all-encompassing unity, including also natural science insofar as it can be idealized by the new mathematical norms ([2], pp. 22-23). Husserl saw as the factually 'imposed' link to infinity the concept of geometrical space and geometry as the science belonging to it. To the ideal space, in his claim, belongs 'a universal, systematically coherent a priori, an infinite, and yet- in spite of its infinity- self-enclosed, coherent systematic theory which, proceeding from axiomatic concepts and propositions, permits the deductively univocal construction of any conceivable shape which can be drawn in space' ([2], p. 22). Generalizing the notion of infinite totality to that one attained by formal mathematics as a rational science proceeding apodictically through axioms, propositions, inferences, proofs, etc., Husserl described an infinite world of idealities whose objects are reached by a rational, systematically coherent method where in its infinite progression every object is ultimately attained in its full being-in-itself. However, he was eventually reserved concerning this last assertion, as in a subsequent part of *Krisis* he drew attention to the fact that the perceived being, the experienced as such, always stands 'under the essential law of a certain gradation of perfection which always exists as an ideal possibility' ([2], p. 309). Moreover he pointed out that correlatively to the differentiation of perfection are to be associated free 'can'-possibilities of approximation to the absolutely perfect, that is, the true in-itself of the object, even though he regarded it as forever receding. In this approach, the absolute in-itself of an object, in Husserl's view the identical self of the object through its multiplicity of appearances, together with its true characteristics are to be considered as limits of a possible gradation. It follows that insofar as mathematical characteristics are the only 'true' ones, true mathematical characteristics are utterly mathematical limits.

Overall, Husserl outlined an exact determination of mathematical objects by means of a limit-idealization which is conditioned on subjectively changing 'modes of appearance'

Objects as Limits of Experience

of the objects in question and therefore entails the possibility of their re-identification as identical in-themselves and of their 'truthfulness', by virtue of being contents of a determinative thinking (e.g., of general judgements, inferences, proofs, etc.), as subjectively conditioned. In Husserl's words 'A certain idealizing accomplishment is what brings about the higher-level meaning-formation and ontic validity of the mathematical and every other objective a priori on the basis of the life-world a priori' ([2], p. 140). In this sense, all the laws of mathematics to the extent that they apply to the real world are particularizations of the laws of formal ontology insofar as this latter was described in earlier Husserlian works (primarily in *Formale und transzendentale Logik*) as a pillar of formal mathematics (in Husserl's theory of manifolds) and as generally referring to objects as registered by (intentional) experience. In such approach, a notion of absolute equality may be seen *idealiter* as the limit of converging processes something that in an approximation process presupposes a conception of an unchanging magnitude that is taken as an absolute measurement unit and which is moreover always identical with itself. Consequently in consistency with Husserl's original characterization of phenomenology as a kinematical science in contrast with classical ontology's 'static' attitude, fixedness and categorial properties of formal objects were defined as limit idealizations of kinetical processes that founded formal objects' ontology on an ever continuing subjectively conditioned synthesis. In view of this position, ideal objects (e.g., ideal spatial shapes) admit of an exact determination which means that in that case the law of excluded middle is valid, whereas empirically experienced objects do not admit of such determination since they can only be determined as being experienced in the present now independently of being objects of sensible or mental experience. As Husserl rightly pointed out, the experienced object I reflect upon now is not the 'same' with itself being experienced a moment earlier, consequently for empirically experienced objects does not hold the law of excluded middle ([2], p. 314).

Given the Husserlian claim for the need of a new sort of thinking, or a peculiar method, to extract objectivity and truth in itself as subjectively conditioned through experiencing within-the-world, I will attempt in the following to bring out the axiomatical structure and the semantical content of certain mathematical theories allegedly finding their philosophical motivation in several key concepts of Husserl's *Krisis* (AST theory) or having, under a proper interpretation, a certain relevance with these very concepts (e.g., IST theory and certain nonstandard theories, including intuitionist theory, dealt with in the next sections). More specifically, a special attention will be given, (**1**): to the notion of phenomenological horizon inasmuch as this may be conceived as the ever expanding boundary of experience within the life-world (the latter meant as the original and unconditioned 'ground' of every possible experience) and consequently as the foundation of the possibility of attaining a limit idealization of mathematical objects and ultimately of a rational infinite totality of being, and (**2**): to the notion of the shift of the horizon of natural intuition with its associated categorial objectivities by some extension principle which nevertheless is conservative with regard to the pre-horizontal 'environment' and (**3**): to the constraints put upon the possibility of an exact determination of the objects of a mathematical natural science by the subjective and 'local' character of the observations of corresponding subjects in intersubjective coincidence.

Concerning the capital notion of horizon, Husserl described it in *Krisis* in a way that is generally consistent with his longtime endeavor in transcendental phenomenology, namely the constituting role of consciousness after phenomenological *Epoché*. In this

Objects as Limits of Experience

view, every perception (whatever might be its meaning) of an object is associated with a horizon of the object in question with regard to a consciousness. This is further clarified as, for example, a given object of perception[2] is as such never what it was a moment earlier, in the sense that is is given in a multiplicity of profiles corresponding to the multiplicity of its appearances in each present now of consciousness and yet it is constituted as identically one and the same through the continuous flux of consciousness. The perspectives of the 'exhibiting of' of each object 'combine in an advancing enrichment of meaning and a continuing development of meaning, such that what no longer appears is still valid as retained and such that the prior meaning which anticipates a continuous flow, the expectation of what "is to come", is straightway fulfilled and more closely determined. Thus everything is taken up into the unity of validity or into the one, the thing.' ([2], p. 158). Moreover, in the particular perception of a thing corresponds a whole horizon of nonactive and yet co-functioning modes of appearance and syntheses of validity which inescapably make that in the unfolding of the correlation we bear as constituting subjects to things, e.g. on the physical level on a closer inspection of an object at a certain distance, we realize that 'unnoticed limitations, horizons which have not been felt, push us on to inquire into new correlations inseparably bound up with those already displayed' (ibid. 159). This is a point of a special importance regarding the aforementioned mathematical theories inasmuch as it establishes a notion of 'internal horizon', referring in particular to non-finitistic mathematical objects (or processes), that reflects the possibility of unfolding properties in a systematic multiplicity of all possible 'exhibitings of' or yet inherent limitations in the unfolding of all possible 'appearances' of the objects in question. However, the 'internal horizon' cannot but be tied up to the 'external horizon' establishing any individual thing within a field of things and ultimately to the whole world as perceptual world and universal horizon of experience. Moreover, the notion of an 'internal horizon' of things-in-the-world is based on a correlation of the unfolding profiles of a thing within horizon with corresponding kinestheses of an 'acting' subject in a way that there may be a 'stable' consciousness of one and the same thing in actual presence exhibiting itself in a multiplicity of modes of 'appearance'. The simplest case of an intentional analysis of perception through the kinesthetic capacities of a subject is that of a thing remaining at rest and being qualitatively unchanged.

As I will show in the next, there will be need of some form of actual infinity notion to mathematically represent an exact determination of a mathematical object meant as a definite whole. Further, as it will also be seen in the exposition of the underlying semantical content of certain key notions of the mathematical theories to be dealt with, some form of actual infinity principle (e.g., the Prolongation Axiom in AST theory) is applied to 'bridge' the countable path to infinity with uncountable infinity, the latter concept serving as a set-theoretical foundation for the notion of mathematical continuity in being conceived as a completed whole in the present now of reflection. In terms more close to their phenomenological content in *Krisis*, the application of an actual infinity principle may serve to tie up the path of multiplicity of 'appearances' of an mathematical

---

[2]It should be noted here that Husserl regarded mathematical objects, in the sense of objects of mathematical theories, as close yet distinct to perceptual objects on the constitutional level. He termed the intuition of mathematical-syntactical objects as categorial intuition in their most fundamental sense of 'empty-somethings' in general, devoid of any content whatsoever, and as transformations of these 'empty-somethings'; see, *Ideen I* and *Formale und transzendentale Logik*, resp. [4], pp. 33-34 & [8], pp. 91-92.

object (or concept)[3] toward the bounds of its 'horizon', with its limit-idealization upon the 'vagueness of horizon'. In essence, this notion of horizon marks the limits of our intuitional capacities in intersubjective coincidence within-the-world, at least of our possibility as performers of the intentional correlation *original impression-retention-protention* to further constitute in noetical-noematical fashion well-defined objects in phenomenological perception (*Wahrnehmung*). As a matter of fact, in a kind of circular play, an actual infinity principle in the form of an *ad hoc* extension (prolongation) axiom is warranted to shift the horizon of countably infinite processes to the 'vagueness' of continuous unity conceived of as the ultimate qualitative shift of a horizon beyond which possibly collapse all our intuitions ([16], p. 123).

In the immediately following sections I'll draw attention to certain concepts in Husserl's description of the phenomenology of consciousness and, next, to certain features of a simple mathematical modelization of the notion of phenomenological kinesthese to point to the inherent necessity to turn to some 'higher-order' actual infinity principle to 'accede' to the horizon of limit-idealization of (mathematical) objects themselves in the sense of their constitution as complete totalities in the present now of reflection. In this concern it is essential to take account that the possibility of the world of experience for Husserl is conditioned on the possibility of experience itself which gives the world its reality and sense; in short, it is the experience of a subject that constitutes the world in intersubjective coincidence ([4], pp. 102-103). Moreover, it must be noted that Husserl never retreated from his long-standing position on the reduction of the being of the world and of every possible object within-the-world to the ultimate subjective origin of their constitution as such which is the transcendental ego of consciousness.

2.1. Temporal aspects of the radical phenomenological reduction.
According to Husserl's claim in *Ideas III*, the phenomenological analysis is of a kinetical (*kinetisch*) and not of a catastematical (*katastematisch*) character.[4] Moreover the conviction to an objective reality in an absolute sense is put in suspense - the corresponding well-known term is *Epochë* - by a constituted reality approach which is fundamental in phenomenological analysis. The constituted objects become immanent[5] to the constituting flux of conscience in which they are immanentized in a certain mode, that is, in terms of certain retentional forms of the constituting flux; for instance, in the *vor-zugleich* (anterior-simultaneous) mode of retention which generates a continuous sequence of retained phases trailing behind an original impression each of which is a retentional

---

[3]A mathematical object (or concept), e.g. a topological surface, is taken here as the formal counterpart of its 'real' existence in the act of 'observation' of a locally interacting and intentionally oriented embodied consciousness within the bounds of the life-world.

[4]The meaning of the term catastematical should be taken here to be the same as ontologically hypostasized. The following Husserlian quotation helps to better comprehend the difference between the aforementioned terms: "The mode of ontological consideration is, so to say, catastematical. It takes the unities in their identity and with regard to their identity as something fixed. The phenomenological and constitutive consideration takes such a unity in the flux, which means in terms of a unity of the constituting flux; it is attached on the movements, on the flows in which such a unity and every component, aspect or real property of this unity is correlate of the identity." (*transl. of the author*, [7], Beil. I, p. 129).

[5]This is a phenomenological term attributed to an object which is no more transcendent to an intentional consciousness, i.e. an object of 'external' reality, but has been modified to a noematical correlate of the constituting flux of consciousness.

consciousness of the preceding one, and this way for each new original impression ([6], pp. 29-33).

The temporal consciousness of immanent objects is the unity of a whole, an all encompassing unity of retentions of original impressions apprehended in actuality which modifies continuously the multiplicities of original impressions into a trailing sequence of just-passed-by retentions together with the retentions of these retentions just-passed-by and so on, in a way that one can talk about a double or longitudinal intentionality (*Längstintentionalität*) of the constituting flux of conscience. By this specific intentional form, Husserl meant the retention of an immanent object as such in consciousness, e.g. a sonorous effect in the present now, and also the consciousness of the retention of this sonorous effect as such, constituting by this token its immanent unity with the sequence of all former phases preceding this effect in terms of a continuous whole within the homogenous flow of the flux ([6], pp. 80-81). In Husserl's words: "The totality of the group of original impressions is bound to this law: It transforms itself into a constant continuum (*in ein stetiges Kontinuum*) of modes of consciousness, of modes of being-in the flow and in the same constance, an incessantly new group of original impressions taking originally its point of depart to pass constantly (*stetig*) in its turn in the being-in the flow. What is a group in the sense of a group of original impressions remains in the modality of being-in-the flow." (*transl. of the author*, [6], p. 77).

Consequently, by appealing to the double intentionality of the absolute flux of consciousness Husserl posited the immediate retention of an immanent object in the flux of conscience (the sonorous effect of a sound, for example), on the one hand, and the constitution of a 'descending' sequence of retentions of the original impression of this object, on the other, as a continuous unity always in the anterior-simultaneous mode of the flow; "Thus, the flux is traversed by a longitudinal intentionality which, in the course of flux, overlapps continuously with itself." ([6], *transl. of the author*, p. 81).

However, in the retentional-protentional and longitudinal[6] mode of the self-constitution of the flux there is no irreducible definition of the term continuity used by all accounts in a somehow circular sense in terms of the constituted (by the intentional modes) unity of the flux. Moreover, the self-constitution of the flux as a phenomenon in itself is not but an objectification of what is thought to be the ultimate subjectivity, the absolute ego, in other words the absolute subjectivity of the flux of consciousness. This is a supplementary and most radical phenomenological reduction, probably the key to comprehend the inherent vagueness of the notion of continuity even in the kinetical terms of the constituted reality in Husserlian sense. For, Husserl himself claimed that it is impossible to extend the phases of the absolute subjectivity of the flux in a continuous succession, to transform it mentally in a way that each phase 'extends' identically on itself, a certain phase of it belonging to a present that constitutes or to a past that also constitutes (not constituted), to the degree that it is an absolute subjectivity beyond any predication and whose retentional continuity in the constituting flux is not but its objectification, its ontification by its 'mirror' reflexion ([6], pp. 73-75).

---

[6]The retention (or primary memory) and the protention are phenomenological terms which are meant as specific intentional modes of consciousness; respectively, as an *a priori* in character immediate conservation in memory of the immanence of an original impression and the a-thematic attendance toward a not-yet-perceived impression. These are described by Husserl in terms of the transversal intentionality (*Querintentionalität*) of consciousness, in the a priori scheme original impression-protention-retention. For details the reader may consult the Husserlian texts in [6], (resp. pp. 29-33 and pp. 52-53).

18

It is clear that what is being intuited as a continuous flow in the temporal constitution of a group of simultaneities and corresponding retentions is irreducible in terms of an ontological deconstruction to constituent non-durating parts as it is essentially the objectification of an inherently elusive process which is always 'on the go', and where every attempt to simply reflect on it produces its 'mirror' objectification. The underlying role of this ultimate irreducibility within the flux of temporal consciousness which, in my view, is reflected in the inherent impredicativity of intuitive continuum and even further (under a certain interpretation) of mathematical continuity, I'll try to put in evidence in the axiomatical foundation of Alternative and Internal Set Theories as non-Cantorian versions of nonstandard theories in sections 3 and 4.

More to the point, I argue that there must ultimately be an immanent subjective root within each one's consciousness to account for the possibility to reach continuous unity of non-finite mathematical-logical objects as definite wholes solely through limit-idealizations (e.g., by applying some sort of actual infinity principle). Let us keep also in mind what H. Weyl stated in *Das Kontinuum*, namely that 'as basic a notion as that of the point in the continuum lacks the required support in intuition. It is to the credit of Bergson's philosophy to have pointed out forcefully this deep division between the world of mathematical concepts and the immediately experienced continuity of phenomenal time ("la durée").' ([17], p. 90).

From the unfolding of my arguments in the next sections, it will also become clear how the theories above offer a more natural mathematical approach to real processes in life, as at least P. Vopěnka claimed that AST theory does. In general, AST tries to imitate real processes in a witnessed and mutually interacting universe by following the unfolding of hereditarily finite multiplicities of phenomena to the horizon of 'observability' and by postulating, through *ad hoc* axiomatization, vagueness beyond the horizon of 'observability'. It is more or less along this general conceptual approach that non-Cantorian theories as well as intuitionistic ones follow an alternative path to the notion of continuum.

2.2. Vagueness in phenomenological kinesthesia. The problem of the kinesthetic control of perception belongs to "the great question [..] of penetrating as deeply as possible into three-dimensional phenomenological 'creation', or, in other words, into the phenomenological constitution of the identity of the 'body' of a thing through the multiplicity of its appearances" ([3], *transl. of the author*, p. 154). It also points, as will be seen in a specific case below, to a possible interpretation of the passage from empirically experienced spatial shapes to ideal ones as referred in Husserl's *Krisis* (p. 314).

The kinesthetic control of perception is not only a presupposition for the effective identity of an appearing object, thus founding logical identity upon continuous variability and synthetic *a priori* laws to a continuous synthesis (which is, in fact, a kinetical synthesis); it also "rules phenomenologically temporal series corresponding to three classes of movements, namely, those of the eyes, of the body and of objects" ([12], p. 354). Kinesthetic control is essential too, in interpreting phenomenologically the source of each movement as something 'internal' to the Husserlian kinesthetic sensations. As I will proceed now with the kinesthetic analysis of the simplest situation, which is that of a body (subject) being fixed and the object/s remaining at rest, it will be shown at least on the formal level, that 'vagueness' in the continuous limit underlies the unity of the constituted movements even though it is based on the temporal discreteness of the correlations

$k_1 \leftrightarrow i_1,.., k_n \leftrightarrow i_n,...$ The particular situation consists in the purely ocular kinesthetic sensation schematized by the correspondence $k \leftrightarrow i$ between the space of kinesthetic controls K and the space of visual images F in applying a temporal parametrization through reciprocally corresponding paths k_t, i_t.

In [12], J. Petitot refers to an elementary model from the theory of (geometrical) manifolds, to discuss the nature of the association between k_t and i_t (the temporal paths of kinesthetic sensations and those of image variations) and also that of the 'fixed association' of the space of kinesthetic controls K with the visual field M, the latter modelized as a simple domain D (a two-dimensional disk). We may imagine the domain D as a geometrical square S with end-points a, b, c, d, where to each end-point $p = a, p = b, p = c, p = d$ corresponds a 'slice' Dp of the field D as a way of interpreting the focusing on each such point.

Quoting from Jean Petitot: "If the figure i_a filling in D_a can 'refer' to the figure i_b filling in D_b, it is because D_a and D_b overlap and are glued together through their intersection $U_{ab} = D_a \cap D_b$. This means that there exists a local gluing isomorphism $\varphi_{ab} : U_{ab} \subset D_a \longrightarrow U_{ab} \subset D_b$ identifying the intersection U_{ab} viewed as a subdomain of D_a with the same U_{ab} viewed as a subdomain of D_b. In the continuous limit, there exists a temporal series D_t with gluing operators $\varphi_{tt'}$ for t and t' sufficiently near. This spatiotemporal series is filled in by the image series i_t. To say that the 'pointing' of each i_t to another $i_{t'}$ is intentional or that intentions 'go through' the series i_b, is to say that intentionality corresponds to gluing operators identifying different points of the visual flow as the same [...] More precisely, intentionality corresponds to the realization in consciousness of the gluing operators. Once again, it is essential here not to confuse, as the natural attitude does, the constituting level and the constituted one [...] This is the main role of kinesthetic controls: the k_t are gluing protocols." ([12], pp. 356-357).

The formalization of the kinesthetic constitution of movement, purely ocular in our instance, by means of gluing operators k_t realized in consciousness for t, t' sufficiently near, may be seen as a representation in a mathematically meaningful language of the concept of intentionality of the constituting flux of consciousness. As it was the case with the retentional modes of consciousness, namely the transversal and longitudinal intentionality, it is also clear that in the phenomenology of movement through kinesthetic controls one cannot avoid the circular introduction of the notion of continuity in the description of a constituted unity out of the multiplicity of kinesthetic controls. In the present case, the continuity factor conditioned on the implicit acceptance of an actual infinity, is represented by the local gluing isomorphisms $\varphi_{t,t'}$ for t and t' sufficiently near that 'glue' together the temporal series D_t filled in by the image series i_t as a continuous whole of constituted reality. Concerning the gluing isomorphisms $\varphi_{t,t'}$ in the mathematical model above, I draw a parallel in the pure phenomenology of consciousness with the 'conjunction' of a sequence of immanences of original impressions in the flux of consciousness (with the descending tail of retentions in-between) constituted as a continuous unity by the intentional modes of the constituting flux and ultimately by its non-objectifiable subjective origin (pure ego).

At this point, prior to dealing with indiscernibility or vagueness from the standpoint of Alternative and Internal Set theories in sections 3 and 4, it is important to refer to the Husserlian idea of scale invariance, as evident generic similarity which can lead to minima visibilia as point-like ultimate minimalities bearing the same eidetic relationships 'discovered' in the macroscopic universe, ([3], p. 166).This idea seems to have a profound effect on a shift of the horizon principle embodied in AST theory.[7]

3. THE PHENOMENOLOGICAL RELEVANCE OF THE AST APPROACH

The Alternative Set Theory (AST), as it happens with other nonstandard and (so-called) non-Cantorian versions of standard (**ZF**) set theory, was born out of the theoretical doubts raised in foundational mathematics during the 20th century and especially in the fermentation that followed Gödel's incompleteness results and the attempts to develop alternative formal theories that were willing to dispense with 'sacred' Cantorian principles. What makes, however, AST relevant to the scope of this article is that its conceptual motivation, as it is represented in the axiomatical construction, is explicitly based on the core ideas of Husserl's *Krisis*. As the main representative of the Prague School of this theory P. Vopěnka stated in describing the notion of countability in terms of AST: 'Our capacity for observation and distinction is limited by the horizon in all directions. Needless to say, this applies not only to optical observation; the horizon is understood in the sense of E. Husserl's *Krisis der Europäischen Wissenschaften und die Transzendentale Phänomenologie.*' ([15], p. 39). Yet, as it happens with standard set theory in the context of its own formal-predicative universe, at some point AST has to face the question of the axiomatical 'incorporation' of the transcending of the horizon beyond the limits of well-meant perceptional capabilities within the the life-world. As it will be shown below this is done in taking recourse to a general extension principle (i.e., the Prolongation Axiom) that is basically conditioned on the acceptance of a certain notion of actual infinity and is conservative in character in that it leaves intact the essential character of the entities 'existing' beyond the horizon with respect to their restriction in advance of the horizon.

One of the key features of AST's alternative theoretical approach is the reduction of the continuity of topological shapes and motions to the extension, by the application of the axiom of prolongation, of finite segments of the class of natural numbers to class infinities transcending the 'horizon of observation'. In this sense, a topology can be defined relying basically on the notion of countable classes in the extended universe of sets and on the principle of prolongation. Therefore, one need not adopt the traditional approach of topological openness, connectedness, etc. fundamentally based on the inner structure and generated continuity of the real numbers system.

The Alternative Set Theory, as exposed in its fundamentals by P. Vopěnka in [15], determines a universe of sets formed by sets constructed iteratively from the empty set together with some axioms subjecting the sets of this universe to laws valid in Cantorian set theory for finite sets, excluding 'abnormal' circularities like the set of all sets. The universe is extended by the inclusion of classes of the form $\{x;\ \varphi(x)\}$ where $\varphi(\mathrm{x})$ is a property of sets from the universe of sets; classes that are not sets are called proper classes such as the universal $\prod$-class of the theory. On the formal-syntactical level, AST basically deals with sets and classes as objects. Sets are definite (may be very large), sharply defined and finite from the classical point of view, taking into account that in its

---

[7]This generic similarity justifies the transposition of the eidetic relationships 'discovered' in the universe of common intuition to that beyond the horizon. It is remarkable, though, that P. Vopěnka seems to deny this principle in [16], (p. 123), where he insists that all ideas held hitherto could collapse beyond some genuinely qualitative shift of the horizon.

universe of sets AST accepts the axioms of Zermelo-Fraenkel theory with the exception of the axiom of infinity. Classes, on the other hand, represent indefinite clusters of objects (possibly found inside very large sets) such as the class N of natural numbers in the classical sense. Therefore, the extended universe of the theory includes some extra axioms, in addition to those of the well-known universe of sets V, which are not set-theoretical formulas and are presented below (p. 13). It is remarkable that countability in the sense of hereditary finiteness is closely related to the notion of 'observation' toward the 'horizon'.[8]

In giving a formal definition of AST-countability below, we need know in advance that: Segment of a class A is called a subclass of the original class with respect to a linear ordering which contains with each of its elements all its predecessors.

Formally one has two definitions:

– *A pair (A, ≤) of classes is called an ordering of type ω iff:*
(1) *(1) ≤ linearly orders A*
(2) *(2) A is infinite and*
(3) *(3) for each $x \in A$, the segment $\{y \in A; y \leq x\}$ is finite.*

– *A class X is called countable iff there is a relation R such that (X, R) is an ordering of type ω. A class is uncountable iff it is neither countable nor finite.*

In case we go beyond the horizon of countability, in other terms beyond the 'horizon of observability' in a sense close to the notion of horizon in *Krisis*, AST theory adopts the following Prolongation (or shift of the Horizon) Axiom:[9]

For each countable function F there is a set function f such that $F \subseteq f$.

In a phenomenologically motivated interpretation, a remarkable consequence of the Prolongation Axiom is this: If a perceived (think of it as definable inside a intersubjective universe including at least one 'observer') state of affairs φ holds of every element of a sequence (x_n), $n \in \omega$, (where ω is the cardinality of countable infinity in AST) progressing toward the horizon, then (x_n), $n \in \omega$, is extensible to a sequence (x_β), $\beta \leq \alpha$ which crosses the horizon and its members also satisfy φ ([13], p. 394).

Put in a somewhat less formal language, any collection of elements perceived in a phenomenological sense as an aggregate of individuals-substrates of intentional observation 'in front of the horizon' (of AST countability) can extend beyond the horizon preserving the essential characteristics of its elements (e.g. individuality, ordering).

It is important to point out that P. Vopěnka made a fundamental distinction between the class of all finite natural numbers FN proved to be a countable class and the set-theoretically definable proper class N of all natural numbers which is uncountable. In a witnessed universe, i.e., one that adopts the viewpoint of an observer of an extensible 'horizon' incorporated in it "The classical natural numbers correspond to the elements of N, whereas FN forms a canonical representative of the way to the horizon." ([15], p. 63).

---

[8] By the words of P. Vopěnka, 'If a large set x is observed then the class of all elements of x that lie before the horizon need not be infinite but may converge toward the horizon. The phenomenon of infinity associated with the observation of such a class is called countability' ([15], p. 39).

[9] As Vopěnka's claimed: 'People have always tried to go beyond the horizon; this is a typical human aspiration. The aim not merely to shift the horizon further away but to transcend it in the mind. Mathematics is one of the most important instruments for this; it formulates exact statements which transcend the framework of perception. We shall incorporate a typical principle of transcending the horizon into our theory in the form of an axiom (*author's note: the Prolongation Axiom*).' ([15], p. 41).

As aforesaid, the extended universe of sets of AST theory includes two extra axioms which are not set-theoretical formulas:

The axiom of existence of classes:
For any property $\varphi(x)$ of sets in the universe of sets the extended universe contains the class $\{x;\ \varphi(x)\}$

The axiom of existence of proper semi-sets:
There is a proper semi-set. In AST language,

$(\exists X)\ (\text{Sms}(X)\ \wedge\ \neg\text{Set}(X))$

Proper semi-sets play a very important role in the axiomatical construction of AST as they are thought of to represent classes inside sets and, roughly, blurriness and non-surveyability in the 'observation' inside very large sets.

In this formal-axiomatical context one can define a topology by the Kuratowski closure operations which are not taken as primitive as it is the case in general topology, but they are instead defined in terms of an indiscernibility equivalence, $\doteq$, which underlies every topological definition and is fundamentally based on the principle of the shift of 'countability horizon', that is, on the prolongation axiom in the AST sense. The underlying idea in the definition of an indiscernibility equivalence is that in each infinite set of 'observed' objects there must be at least one pair (x, y) of mutually indiscernible elements; in mathematical form $x \doteq y$. As a matter of fact, a topology may be defined in the extended AST Universe with the notion of indiscernibility as a conceptual and formal foundation for all subsequent topological constructions, including the definition of a formal notion of motion ([15], pp. 87-88 and pp. 98-108). In short, indiscernibility relations in AST formalize vagueness or 'blurring of the vision' in topological structures occurring as we transcend, e.g., the horizon of countability of finite natural numbers to the uncountability (beyond the 'horizon') of the infinite proper class of natural numbers.

As it is already claimed AST, even in its *Krisis*-themed conceptual approach and its original insight in formally treating infinite mathematical objects (or state of affairs), cannot dispense with the inherent need to abridge the 'vague residuum' in-between the discrete, progressing succession of perceptual acts within the bounds of horizon and the unity conditioning limit-idealizations beyond the horizon (the latter in its universal *Krisis* sense). This constraint is met by incorporating the axiom of prolongation (together with those of the existence of proper classes and of semi-sets) as essentially *ad hoc* meta-axiomatical statements in the AST universe of sets. Nevertheless, it points to a question of a deep meta-theoretical significance that also concerns standard set theory and whose content can well be a subjectively rooted one, possibly referring to the constitutional capacities of each individual consciousness in intersubjective coincidence. But this is a wider discussion concerning also transcendental phenomenology and the phenomenology of temporal consciousness which, (even though some hints were given in section 2.1), goes deep enough to 'transcend' the limits of this article.[10]

4. THE INTERNAL SET THEORY'S APPROACH TO CONTINUITY-VAGUENESS

In this section I set out to outline the main conceptual and axiomatical characteristics of Internal Set Theory (**IST**), concerning in particular the key ideas of continuity and

---

[10] On this account, expect a forthcoming article of the author.

Objects as Limits of Experience

vagueness, in view of its adoption of an external to **ZFC** Set theory[11] undefined predicate *standard* involving indirectly the presence of an observer within classical Cantorian universe. As a matter of fact, the intensional development of a large part of nonstandard analysis mainly coincides with E. Nelson's Internal Set Theory (IST) appropriately interpreted, along with other nonstandard and non-Cantorian theories such as the Alternative Set Theory (AST) dealt with in the previous section, ultrafinitist theories (J. Hjelmslev, S. Lavine & A. S. Yessenin-Volpin), and more recently Nonstandard Class Theory and the Theory of Hyperfinite Sets. We must have clear that in the intensional development of nonstandard analysis, infinitesimals and infinitely large numbers do not exist in an objective way as in the extensional case (e.g. A. Robinson's nonstandard theory), but their existence has a rather subjective meaning and is related to the observational limitations of an interacting 'observer'. As a matter of fact, the introduction of the undefined predicate *standard* in Nelson's theory is metatheoretically associated with a factor of vagueness with regard to a series of 'observations' carried out in a discrete mode. It is suggested, for instance, that: 'finiteness' + 'vagueness' = 'unlimited', where 'unlimited' is a non-Cantorian equivalent to infinity.

In general, we define a vague predicate R with regard to a series of 'observations' $O_0, O_1, ...O_n$ as following:

(1) (i) $R(O_0)$
(2) (ii) $R(O_i) \Leftrightarrow R(O_{i+1})$, $i = 0, 1, ..., n-1$, that is, O_i and O_{i+1} are indistinguishable with respect to R, and,
(3) (iii) $\neg R(On)$

By applying the Transfer Principle of IST and appropriate theorems within the IST extended axiomatical system one can prove that the predicate *standard* - abbreviated as *st* - is a vague predicate within the set N of natural numbers, ([1], pp. 295-296).[12]

From a syntactical point of view, E. Nelson introduced in the classical **ZFC** theory the new unary undefined predicate *standard* together with three axioms, the Transfer (T), the Idealization (I) and the Standardization (S) principles ([11], pp. 3-11). The *ad hoc* axiomatical machinery of the new predicate *standard* consists precisely of these three axioms, which in spite of their syntactical role in the theory induce *in rem* a nonstandard extension in the domain of 'fixed' objects. The term 'fixed' (in a broad sense finitistic) can be used as the intuition of the new predicate *standard* in informal mathematical discourse and it is implicitly associated with a domain of concrete 'observations' on the way to the horizon.

At this point it is important to refer to the intuition behind the idealization principle which alongside the transfer and standardization principles are the three extra axiomatical pillars of Internal Set Theory: 'The intuition behind the idealization principle is that we can only fix a finite number of objects at a time. To say that there is a y such that for all fixed x we have property A, is the same as saying that for any fixed finite set of x's there is a y such that A holds for all of them'; A is an internal predicate formula, that is, one that does not involve the 'unknown' predicate *standard* even indirectly

$$\forall^{stfin} x' \; \exists y \; \forall x \in x' \; A \longleftrightarrow \exists y \forall^{st} x \; A$$

---

[11]The abbreviation stands for: Zermelo-Fraenkel Set Theory with the Axiom of Choice.

[12]In the proof of this theorem it is applied a straightforward result of the idealization principle of IST theory with vast semantical consequences, namely that every infinite set contains a nonstandard element. In particular, there exists a nonstandard natural number ([11], pp. 5-6).

([11], p. 5).

As it stands, we can deduce vagueness along infinity with respect to the set of natural numbers, in terms of the predicate *standard*, by relying on the idealization principle. Therefore we can point to a common conceptual underlying basis between the idealization and transfer principles of IST theory, on the one hand, which induce nonstandard elements[13] and the prolongation principle of AST theory, on the other, in the sense of an axiomatic means to 'shift' the horizon of phenomenological observability to the vagueness of continuum. It is to be noted here that although E. Nelson insisted that the predicate *standard* has a syntactical rather than a semantical role in the theory, it may be de facto taken as having a semantical content by the adoption of the three extra axioms. The convergence in the conceptual motivation is all the more evident to the extent that while in AST one may define topological notions with indiscernibility equivalences taken as primitive, in IST infinitesimality and unlimitedness (and hence continuity and openness) are defined by taking as primitive the predicate *standard* together with the I,T and S principles. This means that continuity and topological openness are not necessarily associated to the real number system as standardness and nonstandardness are not describable solely within the real model R. As a matter of fact, the novelty of the IST approach to topological continuity and openness stands in that it treats these fundamental ideas of analysis and topology by enriching the existing **ZFC** axiomatical system with the undefined and implicitly related to the local horizon of an 'observer' external predicate *standard* along with the appropriate axiomatical equipment with no reference, by necessity, to any particular mathematical model. In a certain sense, both the transfer and idealization principles may be viewed as axiomatizing the 'passage' either way from the the 'fixedness' associated with abstractions of life-world experiences carried out in progressing multiplicities of meaning-acts to the indefiniteness associated with constituted unity within the immanence of consciousness.[14]

In conclusion, there seems to be a common ground in the conceptual foundation of AST and IST theories that consists in the 'shift' of the bounds of hereditarily finite countability (AST) or of standard fixedness (IST) to the vagueness of infinity by the adoption of certain *ad hoc* axioms or predicates that may be thought of as 'external' to their first-order axiomatical system. This is essentially the case with the intuitionistic view, too. In both L.E.J. Brower's and H. Weyl's approach, the continuum is formally postulated by axiomatizing the shift to an indefinite horizon in terms of *ad hoc* extension principles beyond the natural bounds of the finite and discrete which, in the case of choice sequences, is represented by their initial segments. This axiomatization is primarily expressed by intuitionistic continuity principles such as L.E.J. Brower's *Continuity Principle for Universal Spreads* and H. Weyl's *Principle of Open data* ([14], pp. 220-224).

Lastly, we should take into account that in the standard Cantorian mathematics the deeper impredicative nature of vague 'beyond the horizon' infinity manifests itself, for instance, in the independence of certain key infinity statements such as the *Continuum*

---

[13]The Transfer Principle essentially states that if something is true for a fixed but arbitrary x, then it is true for all x: $\forall^{st} t_1 .... \forall^{st} t_n \ [\forall^{st} x \ \mathbf{A} \leftrightarrow \forall x \ \mathbf{A}]$, where $\mathbf{A}$ is an internal formula (i.e., one that does not contain the 'unknown' predicate standard among its variables) whose only free variables are $x, t_1, t_2, ..., t_n$.

[14]For more details on the phenomenological relevance of nonstandard theories theory see: [9], (pp. 124-134).

Hypothesis (**CH**) and the Axiom of Choice (**AC**) from the other axioms of **ZF**, something that is still a topic of hot theoretical debate among set theorists. In any case one has to appeal to actual infinity assumptions in one or other form, e.g. by performing second-order quantification on all subsets of the set of natural numbers N as completed wholes in the proof of the consistency of the negation of **CH**, to do meaningful mathematics in dealing with infinite structures. Only that in Cantorian mathematics and in a sense of platonistic realism, mathematical objects are taken as complete idealizations with no reference to their sources in real life processes and consequently as standing there in a realm inaccessible in its entirety to the human mind. In contrast, the alternative nonstandard theories I dealt with above are to one or other degree grounded on the admission of a notion of 'observation' on the part of a knowing and locally interacting subject within the bounds of the life-world in the sense this latter is provided as a pregiven carrier of a transposable horizon of intentions and meaning-acts.

5. CONCLUSION

In this article, I tried to bring out the conceptual foundation of certain mathematical theories based, on the one hand, on the phenomenological notion of the immanentization of multiplicities of appearances in the self-constituting unity of consciousness and, on the other, on the notion of an indefinitely extensible phenomenological horizon with respect to the intuition of discrete multiplicities of concatenating experiences. The extra axiomatization of these theories to describe the transcending to the vagueness of continuous unity stands essentially in the adoption of certain *ad hoc* 'external' axioms or predicates in addition to the standard axiomatical machinery of the classical Cantorian system.

Each of the theories mentioned in the sections above, with Alternative Set Theory in a more manifest way, attempts to formalize the vagueness inherent in the subjective constitution of an ideal 'reality' in the 'upper' limit of concrete real-world perceptions, by adopting a phenomenologically motivated attitude in the description of the horizon toward vague continuum and its underlying indiscernibility. As it turns out, they bear a measure of vagueness inherent in the intuition of infinity concepts in the field in which they become meaningful, that is, the field of our intersubjective life-world (*Lebenswelt*) in its ever shifting horizon. This is about a vagueness that reflects our inherent limitations to describe continuity in analytical terms and handle it mathematically in the same first-order language (without adding extra *ad hoc* axioms or undefined predicates) as that describing a hereditarily finite countability in our witnessed universe. More, this article also offered some clues to a deeper subjective origin of our capacity to create the unity of an ideal mathematical-logical 'world' out of the regularity of real world experiences. As G. Longo put it in [10], (p. 22): 'As for geometry, and following Riemann, Poincaré, Weyl, we referred to symmetries, isotropy, continuity and connectivity of space, regularities of action and movement, as "meaningful properties". They are meaningful as they are embedded in our main intentional experience as hinted above: life.'

REFERENCES

[1] Drossos, A. C.: (1989), Foundations of fuzzy sets: A nonstandard approach, *Fuzzy Sets and Systems*, 37, pp. 287-307.

[2] Husserl, E.: (1970), *The Crisis of European Sciences and Transzedental Phenomenology*, (transl. D. Carr), Evanston: Northwestern University Press.
[3] Husserl, E.: (1973), *Ding und Raum: Vorlesungen*, Hua Band XVI, hsg. U. Claesges, The Hague: M. Nijhoff.
[4] Husserl, E. (1976), *Ideen zu einer reinen Phänomenologie und phänomenologischen Philosophie, Erstes Buch*, Hua Band III/I, hsgb. Karl Schuhmann, Den Haag: M. Nijhoff.
[5] Husserl, E. (1983) *Ideas pertaining to a pure phenomenology and to a phenomenological philosophy: First Book*, Transl. F. Kersten, The Hague: M. Nijhoff Pub.
[6] Husserl, E.: (1985), *Texte zur Phänomenologie des inneren Zeitbewusstseins (1893-1917)*, Text nach Husserliana Band X, hsgb. R. Bernet, Hamburg: Felix Meiner Verlag.
[7] Husserl, E.: (1986), *Die Phänomenologie und die Fundamente der Wissenschaften*, Text nach Husserliana Band V, hsgb. K.-H. Lembeck, Hamburg: Felix Meiner Verlag.
[8] Husserl, E.: (1992), *Formale und Transzendentale Logik*, Hua Band XVII, hsgb. E. Ströker, Hamburg: Felix Meiner Verlag.
[9] Livadas, S.: (2005), The Phenomenological Roots of Nonstandard Mathematics, *Rom. Jour. of Information Science and Technology*, 8, 2, pp. 115-136.
[10] Longo, G.: (2005), The reasonable effectiveness of mathematics and its cognitive roots, in: *Geometries of Nature, Living Systems and Human Cognition*, (L. Boi, ed.), World Scientific, pp. 351-382.
[11] Nelson, E.: (1986), *Predicative Arithmetic. Mathematical notes*, Princeton: Princeton Univ. Press.
[12] Petitot, J.: (1999), Morphological Eidetics for a Phenomenology of Perception, in: *Naturalizing Phenomenology*, (eds. J. Petitot et al.), pp. 330-372, Stanford: Stanford University Press.
[13] Tzouvaras, A.: (1998), Modeling vagueness by nonstandardness, *Fuzzy sets and systems*, 94, pp. 385-396.
[14] Van Atten, M., van Dalen, D. and Tieszen, R.: (2002), Brower and Weyl: The Phenomenology and Mathematics of the Intuitive Continuum, *Philosophophia Mathematica*, 10, 3, pp. 203-226.
[15] Vopěnka, P.: (1979), *Mathematics in the Alternative Set theory*, Teubner-Texte zur Mathematik, Leipzig: Teubner Verlag.
[16] Vopěnka, P.: (1991), The philosophical foundations of Altenative Set Theory, *Int. J. General Systems*, 20, pp. 115-126.
[17] Weyl, H.: (1991), *The Continuum*, transl. Pollard, S. & Bole T., New-York: Dover Pub.

The Subjective Roots of Forcing Theory and Their Influence in Independence Results

Abstract This article attempts a subjectively based approach, in fact one phenomenologically motivated, toward some key concepts of forcing theory, primarily the concepts of a generic set and its global properties and the absoluteness of certain fundamental relations in the extension to a forcing model **M[G]**. By virtue of this motivation and referring both to the original and current formulation of forcing I revisit certain set-theoretical notions serving as underpinnings of the theory and try to establish their deeper subjectively founded content and also their influence in reaching relative consistency results by the forcing method. In this perspective, the present approach may be seen as offering an alternative view of the consistency results of K. Gödel and P. Cohen in mathematical foundations reaching a subjective level that may be taken as ultimately conditioning the non-decidability of key infinity statements (such as the *Continuum Hypothesis*) on the level of formal theory.

1 Introduction-Preliminaries

As it is known the theory of forcing was originally developed by P. Cohen as an ingenious mathematical technique to establish certain independence results in the foundations of mathematics, notably the independence of the Axiom of Choice

The Subjective Roots of Forcing Theory

(**AC**) and of the Continuum Hypothesis (**CH**) from the rest of the axioms of commonly accepted Zermelo–Fraenkel (**ZF**) Theory. These fundamental results were presented by P. Cohen in a series of lectures given at several prestigious American universities back in 1963 and their far-reaching influence pointed to the depth and richness of the corresponding method of forcing. As a matter of fact, forcing theory was further elaborated to its current form by mathematicians of the likes of R. Solovay, R. Shoenfield and W. Easton, among others, and was established as a new powerful theory in itself further transforming set theory into a rigorous discipline with many interconnections to other mathematical disciplines.

Before entering the core matter of this article it will be useful, at this point, to summarize the main points of Cohen's original approach.

(**1**) P. Cohen introduced a ramified language in a ground (base) model **M** with ranked terms with the purpose of denoting sets in the generic extension. The ramified language uses ordinals of **M** as indexes of quantifiers $\exists_\alpha$ and $\forall_\alpha$. Cohen founded the existence of a countable, transitive model **M** for the axiom system **ZF** on his **SM** Axiom; specifically, there is a set **M** bearing the standard $\in$-relation which is a model of theory **ZF** (**M** Axiom) and moreover it is transitive in the sense that if the relation R is of the kind $\{<x,y> \,;\, x \in y \wedge x \in M \wedge y \in M\}$, then **M** is a model for **ZF** under R (**SM Axiom**) (Cohen 1966, p. 78). It was easy, next, to prove that **M** is a unique and minimal model for **ZF** whose countability is derived from the Skolem–Löwenheim Theorem.[1]

(**2**) A partially ordered set (henceforth poset) $(P, \leq)$ is devised within **M** ordered by the relation $\leq$ which is put in intuitive terms according to the increasing 'amount of information' held by its elements. This poset eventually helps define a generic set A.

(**3**) The forcing relation 'p forces φ' between conditions (members) p of P and formulas φ of the ramified language is defined within **M** with the scope of eventually specifying the truth of formulas φ in the forcing extension model.

(**4**) Assuming the ground model **M** to be countable, Cohen devised a complete sequence $p_0, p_1, p_2, \ldots$ of ever stronger (by $\leq$) conditions in a way that every formula or its negation is forced by some member of the sequence, introducing this way a generic set having the desired properties to establish relative consistency of various statements. As a matter of fact, the proof of existence and the properties of the complete sequence above is considered a Baire category argument[2] as it is carried out of **M** (Kanamori 2008, p. 361) and for that reason even if it seemingly refers to a countable set of conditions, actually it is founded on an actual infinity assumption. Let it be noted here that the actual infinity assumption refers to the possibility of assuming infinite mathematical objects as

---

[1] These two statements are unprovable in **ZF** since by Gödel's incompleteness theorem they would imply that **ZF** is consistent. In the face of it, Cohen considered them as stronger than consistency of the system and most probably 'true' on intuitive grounds, in the sense that if we believe in actual sets then it should exist in the 'real' world a model M bearing the standard $\in$-relation of inclusion and whose objects are such sets (Cohen 2002, p. 1081).

[2] A Baire space is defined to be a topological space with the property that each countable collection of open dense sets has dense intersection. The Baire category theorem can then be basically stated as follows: Every complete metric space and generally every completely metrizable topological space OR every locally compact Hausdorff space are Baire spaces.

completed wholes even if they are not constructible as such in an exhaustive way by, let's say, a recursively defined formula. A characteristic example of such objects is the set of real numbers; a more profound discussion of this concept will follow in later sections.

(5) The resulting forcing extension $\mathbf{M}'$ consisting of the interpretations of the terms of $\mathbf{M}$ through the generic set G is proved to be a model of $\mathbf{ZF}$ theory, a fact based on the completeness of the sequence $p_0, p_1, p_2, \ldots$, and also on the definability of the forcing relation within $\mathbf{M}$ and on $\mathbf{M}$ being a model of $\mathbf{ZF}$ (Kanamori 2008, pp. 359–361).

A key factor in the original forcing approach is the notion of a complete sequence of forcing conditions which was formulated out of Cohen's basic intuition that we can make conjectures about properties of sets as completed totalities in the new extended model based on a partial 'information' obtained by a finite number of elementary, non-contradictory statements (conditions) of the form $n \in A$ or $\neg n \in A$ for a generic set A. But how can this seemingly paradoxical conception be made intuitively apprehensible in the first place? A first step would be to create a partially ordered sequence of ever stronger members (conditions) p of $\mathbf{M}$ in terms of 'informational content' and a second would be to ensure that this sequence proceeds in 'upward' consistency, that is, for every condition p of the sequence and every statement S, there should be a stronger condition q than p such that it would imply *a fortiori* (in the forcing sense) either S or its negation $\neg S$. Closer to common intuition, the key forcing concept might be said to be that one which settles questions arising in a certain domain of (mathematical) reality by consistently setting up 'checking witnesses' in a new extended domain whose objects may be essentially irrelevant as to their exact mathematical character to the 'inhabitants' of the initial domain of reality.

On this account, P. Cohen's basic insight was to make sure at first that no new ordinals (an absolute concept) would be added to the original ground model so as to keep check on the intended number of new reals introduced for proving each time the desired relative consistency result. Then, his intention was to establish the existence of the above mentioned complete sequence of forcing conditions in the ground model by appropriate definitions (originally in terms of a ramified logic of formulas of $\mathbf{M}$) leading to a crucial lemma in the sense mentioned in the preceding paragraph, namely, that for all conditions p and statements S, there is an extension q of p such that q forces either S or its negation $\neg S$ (Cohen 2002, pp. 1094–1095). Another major question arising in the process was whether the generic set A is really a new set of integers not already contained in the ground model $\mathbf{M}$. At this point the ingenuity of the forcing method comes into play: For any A' and poset P of forcing conditions in $\mathbf{M}$ we can force $A' \neq A$ by choosing an integer n not already specified and extending P by the elementary statements $n \in A$ or $\neg n \in A$ so as to make $A' \neq A$. As one may see this common forcing trick depends very much on the properties of the complete sequence of forcing conditions or, alternatively in today's forcing language, on the properties of generic filters and dense sets.

To provide some insight to non-experts and also make more clear the evolution of corresponding notions here are the main features of forcing theory in its present common formulation:[3]

(i) Based on **M** and **SM** axioms (Sect. 1, par. 2) there is fixed a countable transitive model (c.t.m.) **M** for the Zermelo–Fraenkel with the Axiom of Choice (**ZFC**) axiomatical system. To avoid the pitfalls of Gödel's incompleteness results we rather choose to say that we fix a model **M** appropriate for just enough axioms of **ZFC** to carry out any intended consistency argument. We also specify a poset P with a largest element **1**, i.e. $\forall p \in P$ $(p \leq 1)$, whose elements are called forcing conditions and exist in the ground model **M**. Based on the definition of a filter of the poset P we define a set **G** as P-generic over **M** iff **G** is a filter in P and for all dense sets $D \subset P$ and $D \in M$ we have that $\mathbf{G} \cap D \neq \emptyset$. Generally the P-generic set **G** is not a subset of **M**.

(ii) A P-name τ in the ground model **M** is the definition by transfinite recursion of a 'label' corresponding to an object τ_G in the extended forcing model **M[G]**. A P-name τ is defined as the binary relation τ where

$$\forall <\sigma, p> \in \tau \; [\sigma \text{ is a } P\text{-name} \wedge p \in P]$$

'Inhabitants' of the countable ground model **M** can, in principle, comprehend a P-name τ, while probably they will not comprehend its corresponding object τ_G in **M[G]** as it requires knowledge of the generic set **G** which is generally not a subset of **M**. The generic model **M[G]** is defined by:

$$\mathbf{M[G]} = \{\tau_G; \; \tau \in M^P\}$$

where M^P is the set of P-names in **M**, and τ_G (or equivalently val(τ, G)) are members of **M[G]** corresponding to certain definite names τ in **M**;

$$\tau_G = \{\text{val}(\sigma, G); \; \exists p \in G \; (<\sigma, p> \; \in \tau)\}$$

The extended model **M[G]** is proved to be a model of **ZFC** (Kunen 1982, pp. 201–203).

(iii) People in the ground model may figure out certain properties of the generic set **G** and of the generic objects τ_G of extension model **M[G]** based on the knowledge they have acquired in **M** by means of the combinatorial properties of the poset P and the definitions and lemmas posited in **M**. More generally, people in the ground model **M** can construct a forcing language by using P-names and the rules of predicate calculus in **M** to assert something about respective generic objects in the forcing model **M[G]**. The key step in reaching these assertions is to have defined an appropriate generic set **G**. For instance, if we have defined a function f and names for its arguments in the ground model **M** then the sentence $\psi: f(\widehat{0}) = \widehat{1}$ is true in **M[G]** if we know that $<0, 1> \; \in \mathbf{G}$ for some generic set **G**.

---

[3] There is a host of other formulations of forcing theory mainly in terms of complete Boolean algebras and the theory of topoi, see e.g., Moore (1988) and Lawvere (1971). My approach based on the 'mainstream' version of forcing theory, i.e., the one principally involving the notion of generic filters, holds in its general conclusions for all versions.

The Subjective Roots of Forcing Theory

(iv) We write in the forcing language $p \Vdash \psi$ (p forces ψ) to mean that for all generic sets **G** over M whenever $p \in G$, then ψ becomes true in M[G]. For a formula $\varphi(\tau_1, \ldots, \tau_n)$ within a countable transitive model **M** of **ZF** and a partial order P in **M** with $p \in P$ the corresponding **Truth Property** (which is in fact a theorem) is as following:

$$p \Vdash_{P,M} \varphi(\tau_1, \ldots, \tau_n) \text{ iff}$$

$$\forall P\text{-generic } \mathbf{G} \text{ over } \mathbf{M} \wedge p \in G \to \varphi^{M[G]}(val(\tau_1, G), \ldots, val(\tau_n, G))$$

(v) Two key forcing properties, **Definability** and **Coherence**, are proved respectively representing the possibility to define the forcing relation $p \Vdash \psi$ within the ground model **M** and the possibility to consistently 'drag' upwards the forcing relation; that is:

Definability: $p \Vdash_{M,P} \varphi(x_1, \ldots, x_n)$ is definable in **M** and
Coherence: If $p \Vdash_{M,P} \varphi(x_1, \ldots, x_n)$ and $q \leq p$ then $q \Vdash_{M,P} \varphi(x_1, \ldots, x_n)$ (Kunen 1982, pp. 195–201).

(vi) An essential part of a major result of forcing theory, namely the proof of the consistency of the negation of **CH** with the rest of axioms of **ZFC** (that is, the proof of $2^\omega = \omega_2$) consists in adjoining ω_2 distinct, new Cohen reals in the forcing model **M[G]**.

My following arguments on the subjective origins of key forcing concepts will essentially refer to the current formulation of forcing theory prevalent since the 1970s and mainly due to R. Solovay's and R. Shoenfield's work in which Cohen's initial construction[4] was reformulated along the more general and inclusive framework of dense sets and generic filters (see, Shoenfield 1971; Solovay 1970).

Given the scope of this article it is important to note that a key issue to forcing theory is the possibility to construct a generic set as an indefinite whole bearing consistent global properties whose existence is conditioned on the prior acceptance of the metatheoretical notions of completed wholes and of second-order quantification over completed wholes. This means that in establishing a generic set **G** either through a Baire category argument or through a general form of Martin's Axiom (e.g., in the proof of the consistency of $\neg$ **CH** by introducing $\aleph_2$ new reals in the generic model **M[G]**), we have to rely on some form of actual infinity assumption to reach the genericity of **G**.[5] The deeper content of the notion of actual infinity in

---

[4] An excellent presentation of the motives and the stages in reaching the original formulation of forcing theory was given by P. Cohen himself in his later years in a conference at the University of Hawaii (2001) whose proceedings were published in the Rocky Mountain Journal of Mathematics; see Cohen (2002).

[5] As a matter of fact, the proof of the existence of a generic set **G** relies on the countability of the ground model **M** by means of the Rasiowa-Sikorski lemma. However in most cases **G** does not belong to **M** (it cannot be enumerated within **M**), therefore its generic properties are rather associated with the actual infinity statements mentioned above.

The Subjective Roots of Forcing Theory

connection with forcing theory as well as that of the notion of absoluteness[6] will be discussed in a subjectively and more specifically phenomenologically motivated context in the following sections.

2 The Main Underpinnings of Forcing Theory

If one was to present the key points of Cohen's approach in the development of the theory he would have to refer mainly to the following conceptual steps:

(i) The exhibition of models, in particular standard ones, in which the axioms of **ZF** theory as well as other statements hold, including of course the desired independence results, rather than the classical proof-theoretic approach involving proofs as strings of sentences derived from certain axioms according to specified rules. Cohen had a strong conviction about the possibility of establishing a standard model for set theory on intuitive grounds, taking naturally into account certain formal restrictions due to Gödel's incompleteness theorems, that eventually reach to the experience of sets and of the standard membership relation $\in$ in the 'real' world. This must be the underlying reason for Cohen's opting for the transitivity of the standard model **M** for **ZF** which is based on the well-foundedness of $\in$-relation and it is further indicative of the irreducible character of the membership relation of a formal individual with regard to a higher-level entity. A question arising here is whether the irreducibility of the inclusion relation in general and especially that of a formal individual in the sense of a lowest-level substrate of an analytical expression with regard to a higher-level entity (i.e., a set), refers to a mental abstraction corresponding to real world instantiations or whether it rather refers to an a priori form of intentionality directed toward an empty of 'thingness' content 'something-in-general'. In this case this 'general-something' (or 'something-anyhow'; '*Etwas-überhaupt*' in the Husserlian terminology of *Formal and Transcendental Logic*) cannot 'exist' but only in reference to the intentional consciousness directed to it and moreover only through a priori 'attached' derived forms such as in relation to, part to whole, in order to, etc. (Husserl 1992, p. 82). The nature of an existing object in logic or mathematics as receiving its sense of being from the intentionality of consciousness in a non-arbitrary way and certainly not one contradicting sense perception will be further dealt with in the following.

(ii) The unalterable character of ordinals in the construction of the generic extension of a ground model of **ZF** and the application of the notion of absoluteness next to the transitivity property over generic extensions to preserve the invariability

---

[6] The notion of absoluteness in set and generally model theories appeared first and was applied in a substantive way in Gödel's construction of the constructive universe **L**. Intuitively, it establishes the invariability of certain properties of mathematical objects in extensions of mathematical systems provided with a sound notion of well-foundedness. A general definition of the absoluteness of formulas is this: If φ is a formula of a structure X with free variables $x_1, \ldots, x_k$ and $X \subseteq Y$, then φ is absolute between X and Y if:

$$\forall x_1, x_2, \ldots, x_k \, (x_1 \in X \wedge x_2 \in X \wedge \cdots \wedge x_k \in X \Rightarrow (\varphi^X \Leftrightarrow \varphi^Y))$$

where φ^X and φ^Y are the relativizations of the formula φ to sets or classes X and Y respectively.

of fundamental predicative formulas, e.g. of $\in$-predication formulas, as well as the invariability of formulas involving set-theoretical operations such as subset inclusion, union, successor operation, etc., in the construction of generic models. These latter operations are essentially reduced to bounded quantifier formulas involving atomic formulas of the form $x \in y$ and Boolean connectives. Absoluteness of ordinals as an intrinsic means to assign numerical labels to any aggregate of objects independently of the formal hierarchy, is critical both in Cohen's original approach, e.g. in the use of labeled terms F_α in the ramified forcing language, as well as in the current definition by transfinite recursion of P-names. It is notable that Gödel ascribed a philosophical content to the concept of absoluteness, a view seemingly shared to a certain extent also by Cohen.

On a closer look what is fundamental in the concept of absoluteness is the possibility to preserve the invariability of a well-meant membership relation, that is, of the inclusion relation $\in$ in the atomic formula $x \in y$ (founded on real world experience), something that entails that one of the members of $\in$-relation is *in extremis* an atom with no inner structure. It is equally fundamental the preservation of the individual character of atoms x through the existential formula $\exists x\, \varphi(x)$ in transitive extensions of the original model in making also sure that there is a sufficient supply of such atoms in the language of the theory to carry out any desired arguments. The preservation of the essential identity of syntactical individuals in the unfolding of either recursively defined member sets of the universal class **V** or of corresponding transitive subclasses of Gödel's **L** class, is meant both in terms of preservation of their individual identity as such and also as preservation of their a priori and in principle empty-of-content categorial properties as those mentioned in (**i**) above. In this sense the notion of cardinals of a mathematical theory is contrasted to the absoluteness of individuals modeled in the notion of ordinals to the extent that their definition hinges on the existence of bijective correspondences between sets of a given class or model and by this token is conditioned on the possibility of enumeration even within models where this operation might be de facto impossible (see Skolem's paradox). In this view, the non-absoluteness of cardinals may be ultimately due to the irreducible character of the uncountable cardinality of the set(?) of reals R when it comes to applying absolute enumerating procedures.

(**iii**) The possibility of deriving the truth of statements by enforcing global properties reducible to a finite number of elementary non-contradictory statements of the form $n \in A$ or $n \notin A$ meant as forcing conditions over a new set A of integers (these considered formally as new individuals) which is adjoined to the original ground model **M**. In the words of P. Cohen, the whole approach is reduced to the possibility of adding a set A of integers which may not be determined completely, yet the properties of A should be completely determined on the basis of very incomplete information about A (Cohen 2002, p. 1092). The notions of a generic set and of its properties implied by Cohen's complete sequence of forcing conditions were later generalized by R. Solovay and J. Shoenfield to the currently standard notions of a generic filter and of a dense set of conditions, thus loosening genericity from being associated with a complete sequence and hence the countability of the ground model (Kanamori 2008, pp. 368, 371).

The Subjective Roots of Forcing Theory

(iv) The possibility of talking about uncountable ordinals within the countable ground model **M** of **ZF** which is an apparent paradox known as the Skolem paradox and it is further linked with the Skolem–Löwenheim Theorem. This latter landmark theorem which Cohen valued as analogous in importance and a kind of precursor to Gödel's incompleteness theorems is directly applied to secure a countable transitive ground model for **ZF** theory. The Skolem–Löwenheim Theorem essentially states that any model of a finite formal language contains a submodel which is countable and satisfies exactly the same first-order sentences; put in another way by Skolem himself in Skolem (1970), 'the theorem states that every first-order expression is either contradictory or already satisfiable in a denumerably infinite domain'. This result which excludes the uniqueness of a model for a first-order axiomatical theory and thus provides for the theoretical possibility of interesting new models for set theory (something that was indeed materialized by the forcing method), seems *prima facie* quite paradoxical and made Skolem to raise doubts as to whether axiomatization in terms of sets would be a satisfactory ultimate foundation of existing mathematics. It looks paradoxical for the simple reason that based on the Skolem–Löwenheim Theorem we can consider for any set of axioms of set theory a countable subset of the universe of all sets in which the axioms of set theory hold. But since we know that uncountable sets exist by the power-set axiom this assertion leads to an obvious contradiction. The standard way out of the impasse, known as the Skolem paradox, is to make clear that asserting a set A to be uncountable in a countable model M it is to say that there is no enumeration of this set within M, that is, the model M hasn't got any means to enumerate A.

Moreover and on account of my general approach, the proof of Skolem–Löwenheim Theorem in one or other version relies on such actual infinity assumptions as the *Axiom of Choice* or certain logically equivalent sentences (see, Cohen 1966, p. 82; Kunen 1982, pp. 139–140).

(v) The possibility of deciding within ground model **M** whether or not $p \Vdash \psi$ holds, something that is formally established by defining another relativized (to **M**) forcing relation $p \Vdash^* \psi$ and showing that for all formulas $\psi(\tau_1, \ldots, \tau_n)$ holds that:

$$p \Vdash \psi(\tau_1, \ldots, \tau_n) \leftrightarrow (p \Vdash^* \psi(\tau_1, \ldots, \tau_n))^M$$

This is a key part of the general forcing method and ensures that we may define generic sets and properties within the countable environment of **M** without even knowing the precise form of them and generally that of generic objects. An essential part in obtaining this result is due to the absoluteness of atomic formulas involved in the recursive definitions of P-names in transitive models **M** (Kunen 1982, pp. 195–200).

(vi) The notion of generic sets as completed wholes and the performance of a second-order quantification over these sets, an indicative statement of which is the Truth Lemma (Sect. 1, par. 12):

The conception of infinite sets as completed wholes is a centerpiece of mathematical activity in foundational theories and generally in pure mathematics and has deeper philosophical aspects. In the present case and due to the fact that generic sets normally do not belong to the countable model **M** there is raised the general issue of the character of non-denumerably infinite sets and the possibility of their grasping in intuition as well-meant objectivities. Besides, another question that may be raised is whether there is some subjectively founded reason to account for the difference between countable and uncountable infinity. In Tieszen (2011), R. Tieszen draws a line between countably infinite sets for which there is an idealization of the finite capacities of the mind due to the successor operation so as to have a complete grasp of such sets in their totality and uncountably infinite (or transfinite) sets whose structure transcends the possibility of acquaintance with the totality of their members by some analogous idealization. In this connection, Tieszen asks whether there exist complete infinite sets in actuality in the sense of mind-independent abstract infinite objects (Tieszen 2011, p. 91). In the next I will further deal with the character of transfinite sets in the sense of completed wholes in presentational immediacy. I will also refer shortly to S. Feferman's views of (uncountably) infinite sets as completed wholes in the beginning of next section (see, Feferman 2009, 2012).

(vii) The reliance on actual infinity principles in the process of reaching certain independence results. For instance, the process of proving the consistency of the negation of **CH** through the introduction of $\aleph_2$ Cohen reals hinges in part on an assertion implying the use of the *Axiom of Choice*. As a matter of fact, in the proof of the consistency of **CH** with the existing axioms of **ZF** Gödel also relied on certain forms of impredicativity (e.g., in the construction of the classes of constructible universe **L**), as well as on **AC** and the notion of ordinals which in the case of limit ordinals presuppose a notion of a completed infinite whole. It is remarkable what he had stated a propos in a draft letter dating back to 1962 and referring to the philosophical implications of his incompleteness results: "[..] it does not follow from my theorems that there are no convincing consistency proofs for the usual mathematical formalisms, notwithstanding that such proofs must use modes of reasoning not contained in those formalisms. What is practically certain is that there are, for the classical formalisms, [...], no consistency proofs that use only concepts referring to finite combinations of symbols and not referring to any infinite totality of such combinations." (Feferman et al. 2003, pp. 176–177).

The concept of actual infinity has a deeper philosophical content and I will try to show in the next that this concept may be regarded as based on a subjective level on our inner faculty to form objective wholes as instantaneous immanent[7] unities in our consciousness.

3 Revisiting Some Key Forcing Concepts

I have just referred to S. Feferman's views on the notion of infinite sets as definite wholes in particular concerning such sets as the set of all subsets of natural numbers N, $\mathcal{P}(N)$, its set of all subsets $\mathcal{P}(\mathcal{P}(N))$, etc. Arguing for his alternative doctrine of conceptual structuralism Feferman views as problematic the meaning of 'all' in the

---

[7] The meaning of the term immanent may be roughly explained to a non-expert in phenomenology as considering an object or state-of-affairs to be co-substantial to consciousness, this latter meant as a self-constituting temporal flux.

description of the power set $\mathcal{P}(N)$ which is considered in the standard set-theoretical view as a definite totality so that quantification over it is well-determined and may be used to express definite properties (Feferman 2009, p. 15). He further states that the proof of a number of theorems in second-order Peano arithmetic such as those involving the Comprehension Principle[8] hinge on the assumption of the set of subsets $\mathcal{P}(N)$ as a definite totality. This assumption is, in his words, 'a purely hypothetical and philosophically problematic one' and 'requires on the face of it a platonist ontology and in that respect goes beyond conceptual structuralism' (Feferman 2009, resp. pp. 16 and 15). Moreover, the issue of the acceptance of $\mathcal{P}(N)$ as a definite totality comes up anew in a higher-type level in the formulation of Cantor's *Continuum Hypothesis*, in considering the structure $(N, \mathcal{P}(N), \mathcal{P}(\mathcal{P}(N)), \in_1, \in_2)$, where $\in_1$ is the membership relation of natural numbers to sets of natural numbers and $\in_2$ is the membership relation of sets of natural numbers to sets of sets of natural numbers. Even if the definition of the continuum as the set of function values from the set of natural numbers N to the two-point set $\{0, 1\}$ looks in his view as intuitively more clear than the definition of it as the set of subsets of $\mathcal{P}(N)$ - in that our conception of what it means to be an arbitrary infinite path through the full binary tree is somewhat clearer than what it means to be an arbitrary subset of N - in neither case do we have a mathematically clear conception of the totality of such paths, resp. sets. This means that in spite of the fact that we can reason by some kind of Cantor's diagonal argument that there is no enumeration of all infinite paths through the binary tree or of all subsets of N, yet we have to recourse to a platonistic idealism (at least naively) to accept the respective sets as definite totalities all the more so in formulating the *Continuum Hypothesis* (**CH**) as we need to go one step further and appeal in a further loss of clarity to the set $\mathcal{P}(\mathcal{P}(N))$.

The discussion concerns not only the formulation of **CH** as such but also certain proof-theoretic means by which it was proved by P. Cohen to be ultimately independent of the axioms of **ZFC**. As already mentioned the fundamental Truth Property of forcing theory involves a second-order quantification over all generic sets **G**, these latter taken as completed wholes in the extended model **M[G]**, while it is true that even the notions of filters, generic filters and dense sets involve an existential-universal quantification over an indefinite horizon.[9] It can be seen then that universal quantification over an unbounded horizon is conditioned on the assumption of the domain of the universal quantifier as a completed whole

---

[8] This involves taking the formula **P** in.

$\exists X \, [\forall n \, (n \in X \leftrightarrow \mathbf{P}(n)]$

(where $\mathbf{P}(n)$ is a definite property of the members of the set of natural numbers N) as a formula of full second-order logic in the language of arithmetic.

[9] The two conditions satisfied if G is a filter in a partially ordered set P are:

(i) $\forall p, q \in G \, \exists r \in G \, (r \leq p \, \wedge r \leq q)$

and

(ii) $\forall p \in G \, \forall q \in P \, (q \leq p \rightarrow q \in G)$

In addition, for G to be a P-generic filter one has to perform a second-order quantification over all dense sets of the ground model **M**. In turn, defining a dense set of the poset P involves also an existential-universal quantification over an indefinite horizon; see Sect. 1, par. 9, 12.

something that turns again to the discussion above on the need to recourse to some kind of platonistic realism[10] to philosophically accommodate the notions of a completed infinite totality and generally of transfinite sets that are so common in mathematical practice. Indeed, the application of the notions of a completed whole as such and that of a universal (second-order) quantification over completed wholes is pivotal in obtaining an ω_2-sequence of distinct functions from ω into **2** within the forcing model **M[G]** which is a key step in finally getting the consistency of the negation of *Continuum Hypothesis*, i.e., that $2^\omega = \omega_2$ in **M[G]**. More specifically, the proof partly hinges on the postulation of an uncountably infinite class of dense sets $D_{\alpha\beta}$ and a second-order quantification over all these sets such that $\mathbf{G} \cap D_{\alpha\beta} \neq \emptyset$, in accepting the existence of $D_{\alpha\beta}$ as completed definite wholes; it is notable that by the very construction of the sets $D_{\alpha\beta}$ the second-order quantification is in fact a quantification over $\mathcal{P}(\mathcal{P}(N))$ (Kunen 1982, pp. 205, 206). As it happens, the non-empty intersection of a generic set **G** with all dense sets of the ground model is the way to see that generic properties are globally forced in the extended model and stands as a common 'test' in proving genericity in all kinds of forcing up to iterative forcing techniques.

Here I turn again to the key concept originally applied by Gödel in the construction of the constructible universe **L** and the subsequent proof of the consistency of the *Axiom of Choice* and of the *Continuum Hypothesis* with the rest of axioms of ZF. This is the notion of absoluteness whose importance is vital to show, for instance, that certain structural properties of the collection Def(*X*) of all subsets of a set X which are first-order definable over $<X, \in>$ [11] remain unaltered when applied to recursively defined subclasses $\mathbf{L}_\alpha$ of **L** with quantifiers restricted to **L** or to these subclasses. As already mentioned this notion was characterized by P. Cohen as a kind of new philosophical concept in the newly established context of Gödel's inner model **L** of constructibility (Cohen 2002, p. 1086). The concept of absoluteness plays a pivotal rule in forcing theory too in making sure that 'people' living in the ground model **M** can establish all nice facts in the extended forcing model **M[G]** without even knowing the generic set **G**, for instance, in establishing ¬CH ($2^\omega = \omega_2$) or any other versions of it (e.g., $2^{\omega_1} = \omega_4$) in **M[G]**.

As already stated, one of the key preliminary steps in acceding to independence results in the extended model **M[G]** is to make sure that 'people' living in the ground model **M** can label objects in **M** by their *P*-names, let's say τ, which will act as recognizable 'signs' for corresponding objects (sets) τ_G in **M[G]**, even though beings in **M** might not be in a position to decide those objects τ_G since they are constructed by means of the generic set **G** which is usually not in **M**. A main part of this kind of 'accessibility' is actually due to the absolute concepts applied in the definition (by

---

[10] There is a broad discussion opened among philosophers, logicians and set-theorists as to the nature of mathematical-logical objects and to the accompanying philosophical doctrines. The position of the author clearly does not side with the proponents of platonic rationalism in mathematics; it rather converges toward R. Tieszen's position of constituted platonism in Tieszen (2011) which can be roughly described as an attempt to accommodate platonic rationalism with transcendental phenomenology. A lengthier reference to the philosophical issue at hand will be made in the last section.

[11] A set $Y \subseteq X$ is first-order definable over $<X, \in>$ if there is a first-order formula $\varphi(v_0, v_1, \ldots, v_n)$ with $a_1, \ldots, a_n$ all in X such that $Y = \{z \in X; \varphi^X(z, a_1, \ldots, a_n)\}$.

transfinite recursion) of the forcing objects τ_G of **M[G]** and of the corresponding P-names of the ground model **M** (Sect. 1, par. 10), thus making possible to invariably 'reflect' their fundamental structural properties in the extension to the model **M[G]**. We can see that the absoluteness of these definitions is essentially due to the absolute character of the standard $\in$-relation in $<\sigma,p> \in \tau$ which together with the well-foundedness of $\in$ predication makes it possible for witnesses in **M** to 'keep an eye' on the properties of the forcing objects τ_G essentially by virtue of the invariable character of the atomic formulas $<\sigma,p> \in \tau$.

I go one step further into certain proof-theoretical technicalities in the proof of consistency of $\neg$ **CH** by the introduction of $\aleph_2$ Cohen reals to point to the instrumental role of the notion of absoluteness in achieving relative consistency results. It is known that a standard forcing technique in proving the relative consistency of $\neg$ **CH** is to posit a poset of conditions $\mathrm{Fn}(\kappa \times \omega, 2)$ consisting of finite partial functions from $\kappa \times \omega$ into 2, where κ is an uncountable cardinal in the ground model **M**. Then one devises a generic function $\bigcup \mathbf{G} = \kappa \times \omega \to \mathbf{2}$ and a dense set D of distinct conditions in **M**, which by the generic property of $\bigcup \mathbf{G}$ in **M[G]** establish an α-sequence of generic functions f_α from ω into **2** ($\alpha<\kappa$) which are all distinct. Taking $\kappa = \omega_2$, it is then easy to see that $2^\omega = \omega_2$ in **M[G]** and a major part of the consistency of $\neg$ **CH** has been completed (Kunen 1982, p. 205). Why absoluteness is so pivotal in obtaining the result above at this point? First, it makes sure that the generic function $\bigcup \mathbf{G} : \kappa \times \omega \to \mathbf{2}$ lies in **M[G]** by absoluteness of the operation of union and second, it ensures that the dense sets $D_{\alpha\beta}$ (for infinite cardinals $\alpha \neq \beta$) defined in the ground model **M** are preserved by absoluteness of the notion of density in the forcing model **M[G]**. This way, $\kappa = \omega_2$ distinct functions $f_\alpha(n) = (\bigcup G)(\alpha, n)$ ($\alpha<\kappa$, $n<\omega$) are introduced in **M[G]**, or equivalently ω_2 new reals.[12]

Let's now turn for a moment to the absoluteness of the density of sets $D_{\alpha\beta}$ in **M**. Generally, density of a set D taken as a subset of a poset $(P, \leq)$ within a transitive model **M** is by definition bound to the condition:

$$(\forall p \in P)(\exists q \leq p)(q \in D) \quad (1)$$

Here lie two fundamental conditions of the absoluteness of density which tend to be overlooked by the everyday working mathematician. These are the absoluteness of formula **(1)** due to its structure and the transitivity of the model **M** in which it becomes true. The former condition is ultimately conditioned on the absoluteness of the bounded formula $(\exists x \in y) \varphi$ which is essentially the possibility of invariably intuiting individuals (serving here as bounded variables of formula φ) together with the categorial property of inclusion $\in$ independently of the universe of discourse,

---

[12] The α-sequence $f_\alpha(n)$ in **M[G]** is, in fact, an α-sequence of generic functions from ω into **2**; this way, taking $\kappa = \omega_2$ for $\alpha<\kappa$, ω_2 new reals are introduced in **M[G]**.

whereas the latter condition ensures a well-meant treatment of predicate ∈ within the c.t.m. **M**.[13]

In a sort of non-reductionistic thinking we can say that what is originally the source of absoluteness is the possibility to think of formal individuals as invariably preserving some kind of a priori 'outward directed' relation (e.g., the non-logical predicate ∈) in any extension of their original domain in such a way that, for instance, ordinals of a certain domain may be treated as fixed and their classes as impredicatively specified. Concerning the critical importance of the preservation of the individuality of syntactical atoms both in terms of their 'ontological self' as formal individuals and of their inherent categorial properties in any recursively defined class we need only consider the impasse in which a theory would be left in case where, for instance, the atomic formula $x \in Y$ would not be absolute between classes ordered by set inclusion. In that case it would be simply impossible to project the formula $x \in Y$ of a class Y to an inclusive one Z and vice versa. In other words there would be no guarantee that we would have the same formally posited (irreducible) individual-names x preserved in each class extension, given a well-foundedness of the classes, consequently one would have no guarantee of the existence of fixed ordinals in the recursive definitions of sets and classes.

It is notable that Husserl referred in his later work *Experience and Judgment* to the concept of absolute substrates in these terms: "[..] a 'finite' substrate can be experienced simply for itself and thus has its being-for-itself. But necessarily, is at the same time a determination, that is, it is experienceable as a determination as soon as we consider a more comprehensive substrate in which it is found. Every finite substrate has determinability as being-in-something, and this is true *in infinitum*." (Husserl 1973, p. 137). In a comprehensive sense individual objects of external sensuous perception, as simply and originally given, and generally objectivities founded in objects capable of being simply and straightforwardly given can be designated as absolute substrates. In a deeper view an absolute substrate is characterized as "completely indeterminate from the point of view of logic" and is meant in the sense of individual 'this here' (*Dies-da*), that is, of the ultimate material (or immaterial) substrate of all logical activity. On this account, absolute substrates lack all logical formation and exclude by themselves everything that may be called forth as their determination by a logical activity of a higher level (ibid., pp. 139–140). Anyone who can admit to a reduction of absolute notions to constructions bound by logical connectives of atomic formulas of individuals-substrates (together with their fundamental categorial properties), can read in the quotations above the vestiges of a subjectively founded notion of absoluteness unconstrained as such by a logical-mathematical theory.

However, even if dense sets are absolute for a countable transitive model **M** their enumeration within **M** is not absolute (cardinality is not absolute) and takes place

---

[13] In the same approach one can interpret the absoluteness of the operation of union mentioned above by virtue of its definition as the union of a family $\mathcal{A}$ of sets, i.e.,

$$\bigcup \mathcal{A} = \{x : \exists Y \in \mathcal{A} \, (x \in Y)\}.$$

out of **M**. This is straightforwardly reflected in the fact that generic sets **G** do not belong to the countable transitive model **M**. Therefore since the generic character of **G** is proved on account of the countability of the base model **M** and the absoluteness of notions such as 'partial order' and 'dense' in **M** and yet **G** may not belong to **M**, it may need by virtue of its definition the countable chain condition (**c.c.c.**)[14] of the partial order P in order to eliminate an uncountable number of incompatible conditions $p \in P$.

I take the opportunity to make a comment concerning the application of the **c.c.c.** in proving the consistency of $\neg$ **CH** by forcing techniques including its more generalized versions. This is done in view of the meta-theoretical[15] interpretation of key forcing concepts which will be done in Sect. 4.

In a kind of circular meta-theoretical play one can see that the application of the **c.c.c.** condition to prove $2^\omega \geq \omega_2$ involves the Delta-system lemma which is, in turn, implicitly conditioned on the *Axiom of Choice*. This is an indication of the ways (explicit or implicit) in which certain forcing techniques are ultimately conditioned on the endorsement of actual infinity principles of which the *Axiom of Choice* or its logical equivalents are common cases. The dependence on the one or other form of actual infinity assumptions may also be seen in the implementation of forcing techniques involving partial functions of larger than ω cardinality. For instance, in case we want to violate the *General Continuum Hypothesis* (**GCH**) at any desired cardinal in **M[G]** we must restrict to regular cardinals whose definition involves the notion of a completed infinite whole and also implicate a stronger than ω **c.c.c.** condition for the poset P of forcing conditions (Kunen 1982, pp. 211–217).[16]

The **c.c.c** condition is the necessary constraint to be satisfied by the poset P of conditions of **M** to preserve cardinalities between the ground model **M** and the extended forcing model. Indeed, the imposition of the **c.c.c.** constraint for the partially ordered set of finite partial functions $\mathbf{Fn}(\kappa \times \omega, 2)$, where κ is an uncountably infinite cardinal, results in the 'projection' of uncountably infinite possibilities in the domain of conditions $\mathbf{Fn}(\kappa \times \omega, 2)$ to countably many compatible extensions of these conditions. In the context we discuss this means that by eliminating the uncountability factor in the domain of forcing conditions **Fn** one takes eventually advantage of an open-ended class of countably many compatible extensions; in fact, this is what the **c.c.c.** condition is all about in forcing

---

[14] A partial order $(P, \leq)$ has the *Countable Chain Condition* (c.c.c.) iff every antichain (any family of pairwise incompatible elements) of the poset P is countable. Letting $P \neq \emptyset$, the elements $p, q \in P$ are defined as compatible if,

(for $p, q \in P$) $\exists r \in P \, (r \preceq p \wedge r \preceq q)$

that is, r extends both p and q in the usual intuition of extension. For example, if p, q are finite partial functions from ω to $\mathbf{2}$ and $p \preceq q$ iff $q \subset p$, then p and q are compatible iff they agree on $\text{dom}(p) \cap \text{dom}(q)$, in which case $p \cup q$ is a common extension of p and q.

[15] This term with a dash after meta is meant by the author as pointing to some subjectively rooted origin of the corresponding concept.

[16] It should be also noted that proving 2^ω to be exactly equal to ω_2 in **M[G]**, on the supposition that the ground model **M** is a model of **GCH** and **AC**, requires not only the application of the **c.c.c.** condition for the poset P but also Zorn's lemma which is considered an actual infinity assumption (Kunen 1982, pp. 208, 209).

techniques: it eliminates an uncountable number of incompatible conditions p, meaning that even in the case of uncountable numbers in the domain or range of such conditions we can nevertheless proceed with countably many compatible extensions and on this account define a fairly generic set G. One can point here, except for the meta-theoretical content ascribed to the notion of completed infinite wholes, to the possibility of talking about an open-ended class of countably many compatible extensions in terms of a phenomenologically motivated discourse. For what is ultimately involved here is the possibility of extending ideally *ad infinitum* the determinations of a formal mathematical object, say in the present case of some member of the poset of finite partial functions $\mathbf{Fn}(\kappa \times \omega, 2)$ under extension order, in view of its horizon of indeterminate determinability which is "always pregiven with it and can also be cothematized" (Husserl 1973, pp. 218, 219). To the extent that these compatible extensions are grasped in the corresponding thematic interest of a certain intentional consciousness in a successive order, even if there is not an objective temporal succession of determinations and consequently no individual temporal positions, entails that these compatible extensions can be only thought of as of a countable cardinality as this is necessarily implied by the discrete character of the predicative activities of the mind. These mathematical acts, e.g., carrying out compatible extensions of finite partial functions in the sense of footnote 14, are meant as realized in successive order in objective time to the extent that they correspond to concrete predicative activities of the mind, even if they are to be idealized in the way to infinity, and thus may not be associated as such with any passive aspects of the intentional activities of consciousness.

4 The Subjective Origins of Forcing: A General Discussion

Generally, the model-theoretical wisdom of forcing is that we can produce a completely finitistic relative consistency proof, e.g., for the statement $\mathbf{ZFC} + \neg\mathbf{CH}$, by forging a generic extension $\mathbf{M}[G]$ of a countable, transitive model $\mathbf{M}$ for which enough (but not all) of $\mathbf{ZFC}$ axioms are satisfied in the following schematic procedure. Assume we want to prove the consistency of $\mathbf{ZFC} + \neg\mathbf{CH}$ given the consistency of $\mathbf{ZFC}$, that is

$$\text{Con}(\mathbf{ZFC}) \to \text{Con}(\mathbf{ZFC} + \neg\mathbf{CH})$$

Then assuming that we can derive a contradiction from $\mathbf{ZFC} + \neg\mathbf{CH}$, there will be a finite list of axioms $\varphi_1, \ldots, \varphi_n$ of $\mathbf{ZFC} + \neg\mathbf{CH}$ such that for some or any χ holds:

$$\varphi_1 \ldots \varphi_n \vdash \chi \wedge \neg\chi$$

Then by the forcing method we can produce a new generic model N such that

$$\mathbf{ZFC} \vdash \exists N \, (\varphi_1^N \wedge \cdots \wedge \varphi_n^N)$$

therefore,

$$\mathbf{ZFC} \vdash \exists N \, (\chi^N \wedge \neg \chi^N)$$

and **ZFC** is proved inconsistent.

If this straightforward procedure can strike a typical formalist's eye as a perfectly finitistic relative consistency proof describing in a pretty simple way how to construct the consistency of **ZFC** + ¬**CH** given that of **ZFC**, yet it presupposes certain assumptions primarily concerning the construction of the generic extension model N that implicitly at least imply the acceptance of non-finitary concepts more precisely of actual infinity notions such as those discussed in the previous sections.

Next to my arguments on a possible subjective foundation of key forcing concepts I must state that throughout this article I take the notion of actual infinity as somewhat 'stronger' than the often encountered content of the term referring to any infinite collections of objects including therefore the set of all natural numbers. Indeed there exists a qualitative difference, taking the human mind as finite and of finite capacities, between the idealization of the totality of the collection of natural numbers made possible by the grasp of each natural number due to the intuitively clear successor operation and the constitution of a transfinite set on the basis, for instance, of infinity, replacement and power-set axioms of **ZFC** theory. In this regard there is a notable dysanalogy with regard to the intuition of natural numbers (Tieszen 2011, p. 91). In contrast, the conception of an uncountably infinite and generally of a transfinite set requires a kind of idealization that is not based on the possibility of grasping each particular element by a definite predicative activity as it happens with the case of natural numbers and may demand a kind of idealization that has to do with constitution of unities in consciousness as objective temporal wholes. In other words, one has to proceed from an operation in iterative succession to a deeper constitutional process making possible the constitution of immanent continuous unities in consciousness as objective wholes thereby possibly involving a notion of self-constituting inner temporality. Therefore, I take actual infinity as an infinity of a higher order than that of the set of natural numbers meant as the completed totality of a definite iterative process or of any other infinite collection of objects admitting of some prescribed form of enumeration and apprehended as a completed whole. This means that I regard actual infinity as pointing to a stronger form of infinity, namely an infinity which cannot be enumerated and yet it may be regarded and it is indeed taken as referring to a completed object in common mathematical practice something that presupposes its conception as a completed whole in the present now of reflection.

Given this assumption one may have, in the context of forcing theory, an interpretation of generic sets, dense sets, filters, etc., as completed objects whose 'global' properties can be derived based on finitely many elementary statements concerning, e.g., the generic sets through statements of the form $n \in A$ or $\neg n \in A$ in original Cohen formulation. Moreover, their elements may not be in principle enumerable and this is clearly the case of a generic set **G** which is proved not to belong to the countable ground model **M**. Therefore the actual infinity involved here is of a higher order than an actual infinity associated with countably infinite sets. This is an argumentation valid *a fortiori* concerning second-order quantification

The Subjective Roots of Forcing Theory

over generic sets or dense sets which is a common practice in forcing proofs and is obviously conditioned on the acceptance of these sets as completed wholes.

Before going on with the discussion of the subjective origin of the concept of actual infinity I take advantage to refer briefly to the concerns raised by P. Cohen as to the content and role of the general notion of a completed whole in the foundations of mathematics.[17] In the last part of *The Discovery of Forcing* (Cohen 2002), Cohen summarized his view on the notion of infinite sets as completed wholes swinging between empirical realism and formalism and ultimately opting for a subjectively based version of the latter. Arguing that someone who rejects sets as 'completed wholes' existing in some ethereal fluid beyond all direct human experience would have the formidable task of explaining from where comes the beauty of simplicity and scope of set theory, he went on to choose an alternative option of realism in that "The only reality we truly comprehend is that of our own experience. But we have a wonderful ability to extrapolate. The laws of the infinite are extrapolations of our experience with the finite. If there is something infinite perhaps it is the wonderful intuition we have which allows us to sense what axioms will lead to a consistent and beautiful system such as our contemporary set theory". He even went on to comment that "The ultimate response to **CH** must be looked at in human, almost sociological terms" (Cohen 2002, p. 1099). In another equally contemplative mood Gödel expressed, in refuting Carnap's syntactical program by his second incompleteness theorem, his own doubts as to the possibility of treating infinite concepts as mathematically eliminable : "The mathematical essences we intuit could not be linguistic conventions. There are constraints on them that we do not freely invent or create. One might also say that this content or meaning will be "abstract" relative to the rules of syntax. Mathematical intuition will therefore not be eliminable. In Husserl's language, categorial intuition will not be eliminable. Thus, instead of clarifying the meaning of abstract and non-finitary mathematical concepts by explaining them in terms of syntactical rules, abstract and non-finitary concepts are used to formulate the syntactical rules." (Tieszen 1998, p. 193).

Concerning my argumentation on the possibility of reduction of the content of (mathematical) actual infinity to a subjective origin a main point is that we cannot have in a consistent way the intuition even of an indefinitely proceeding sequence of formal objects let alone of an uncountable set as a completed whole without at the same time having the intuition of the 'just-passed by' and also of the 'in attention-of' and the 'already-there' of its elements. In fact, independently of the content one might give to these notions they seem to be de facto preconditions not only of the intuition of a completed whole as such but also of the act of enumeration as a mental process carried out in actual present. In this connection one may find as properly motivated L.E.J. Brouwer's axiomatization in the intuitionistic approach to mathematics in which, among other primitive notions, he described the primordial intuition of mathematics as "the substratum, divested of all quality, of any perception of change, a unity of continuity and discreteness, a possibility of thinking together several entities, connected by a 'between', which is never exhausted by the insertion of new entities" (Brouwer 1907, p. 17). In addition, Brouwer considered

---

[17] I have referred to S. Feferman's view of the matter in Sect. 3, par. 1.

the generation of natural numbers and generally of indefinitely extendible sequences as based on a primordial intuition of succession of discrete objects, divested of all quality, termed by him a 'two-ity' intuition. Brouwer described these mathematical intuitions in a way that has considerable affinities with Husserl's phenomenological description of the internal consciousness of time. We may think, for instance, of the generation of natural numbers by means of the intentional forms of temporal consciousness based on an original impression in actual presence in which we pass instantaneously from this concrete perception into another next one ('two-ity' intuition) while establishing by this very intentional act natural numbers as durationless abstractions in the mode of 'just-passed by', 'original impression', 'in attention-of'. Real numbers, on the contrary, are viewed as 'incomplete' or 'unfinished' objects by virtue of being associated with a notion of temporal duration that ultimately points to the stream of time consciousness as a continuous fabric in which Brouwer ascribed certain intentional-type qualities described in the original Husserlian writings (i.e., the transversal and longitudinal intentionalities) (see: Husserl 1966, pp. 80–83; Van Atten et al. 2002, pp. 207, 208). It is important to point out that in his *Logical Investigations* Husserl described immanent infinity in terms of a completed whole in actual presence independent of any spatio-temporal or causal constraints, in fact as a freely generating infinity in imagination in the present now of reflection. In this respect, this kind of infinity does not prove the relative 'foundedness' of bits of space and time, that is, the dependence of time-stretches or of bits of space with respect to more inclusive spatio-temporal wholes and so does not prove space and time to be really infinite, nor even that they can really be so (Husserl 1984, pp. 299, 300). It seems rather to be originally reducible to a time-constituting subjectivity capable of 'apprehending' infinity as its correlate in the form of an objective whole by constituting its objective self. In this view actual infinity in the sense attributed to it in mathematical infinity assumptions such as those used in certain forcing statements and generally in various assertions of foundational mathematics[18] is subjectively founded and may not be characterized by the causal and objective boundary constraints inherently associated with spatio-temporality of physical experience. Moreover, insofar as actual infinity can be taken as subjectively founded and associated with the constitution of continuous unity as an objective form within the immanence of consciousness it would be a kind of unity founding *eo ipso* the possibility of positing and enumerating denumerable collections. One should be careful here not to confuse the description of immanent infinity referred to in Husserlian writings above as 'a freely generating infinity in imagination in the present now of reflection' with the character of transfinite mathematical-logical objects as such in which case their infinity may be

---

[18] The recourse to actual infinity assumptions proves to be an inescapable necessity in the construction of foundational theories such as Gödel's constructible universe **L** and Cohen's introduction of the forcing model **M[G]**. One may mention, for instance, the introduction of impredicatively specified sets up to limit ordinals and also the application of the Axiom of Choice in Gödel's proof of the consistency of **CH** with the other **ZF** axioms; while in forcing theory one may note the implicit application of the higher-infinity statement $MA(\kappa)$, $(\kappa > \omega)$, as this latter ensures the global properties of the generic set **G** out of the countable 'environment' of ground model **M**, as well as the application of second-order quantifications over generic sets.

subjectively founded in the sense described, yet they cannot be taken as arbitrarily generated in imagination without taking into account the constraints imposed by our mathematical-logical practices within the world as primitive ground of experience.

Another key notion that was initially employed by Gödel to secure the unalterable character of properties of classes of definable sets in-between the stages $\mathbf{L}_\alpha$ in the recursive definition of the constructible universe $\mathbf{L}$ and it is also broadly applied in forcing methods is the notion of absoluteness to which I referred at some length in the previous sections. A large part of the proof machinery in both Gödel's and Cohen's construction of suitable models of $\mathbf{ZFC}$ would be missing in the absence of the notion of absoluteness. For instance, without the application of the notion of absoluteness it would be impossible to decide the forcing relation $p \Vdash \psi$ within the ground model $\mathbf{M}$ and further to be able to structurally 'project' it in the extension model $\mathbf{M}[\mathbf{G}]$ without even knowing all the details of $\mathbf{M}[\mathbf{G}]$. Further the fundamental role of absoluteness can be more appreciated to the extent that this notion is intimately associated with that of ordinals. Cohen, for instance, even went as far as to note that "The ordinals remain a kind of mystery in that we do not know how 'far' they extend, but we must allow all of them if we are to assign ranks to sets" (Cohen 2002, p. 1082). I remind that the absoluteness of the notion of ordinals is critical in Cohen's proof of the existence of a unique transitive countable model of the axiomatical system $\mathbf{ZF}$.

Given the discussion above, the quest leads in the final count to the nature of mathematical-logical objects and the corresponding philosophical views formed in the historical development of mathematics starting with platonic idealism and reaching up to contemporary positions influenced to one or the other degree from logical positivism, holistic empiricism, scientific realism or phenomenology. Since my purpose is not to enter in the broad field of these topics, I only refer here as relevant with my own intentions to R. Tieszen's phenomenologically influenced approach to mathematical-logical objects by virtue of objects constituted by a constituting ego in a rational and non-arbitrary way as ideal or abstract and non-mental ones. In a somewhat 'technical' sense Tieszen categorizes them as being mind-dependent$_1$ and mind-independent$_2$ in a way that tends to do justice both to the platonistic aspects of mathematical-logical objects as abstract and atemporal ones and their constitutional aspects referring to the intentional capacities of a subject's consciousness (Tieszen 2011, p. 16 and pp. 114, 115).

Motivated by a phenomenologically influenced view one can then raise the question of whether the ontology and invariability of formal individuals meant as a priori bearers of empty of content categorial properties is a properly mathematical intuition originating in the objects themselves or whether it is rather a subjectively founded one that refers in a certain sense, as Gödel claimed, to a relationship of a special kind we bear with objects themselves one that goes beyond the world of senses. Gödel insisted, in particular, on "the idea of the object itself [...] Evidently, the 'given' underlying mathematics is closely related to the abstract elements contained in our empirical ideas [...] Rather they, too, (*auth. note:* the abstract elements) may represent an aspect of objective reality, but, as opposed to the sensations, their presence in us may be due to another kind of relationship between ourselves and reality." (Feferman et al. 1990, p. 268). Individuality of objects meant in its most extreme and irreducible sense may not be a property of objects themselves since any physical or generally 'thingness substance' individuals may be at least potentially decomposable as bearers of some objective content. Rather it must be a sort of subjectively founded intuition that presents in imagination upon instant reflection immanent individuals as pure forms with no content whatsoever. Moreover, except for their appearance in imagination as such they appear also by a priori necessity with proper to them categorial properties to the extent that they are not apprehensible but through 'a host of relations as referred to', the most fundamental of which is the inclusion with regard to a more comprehensive form formalized by the non-logical predicate $\in$. However, this is not to say that objects of mathematical theories are possible to know only on the basis of pure imagination as they are more constrained by mathematical-logical experience constituting their sense in a non-arbitrary way as objects within temporality, e.g. in finding necessities among pure possibilities (Tieszen 2011, pp. 154, 157). One can think as a case in point the generation of nonstandard numbers whose immanent existence as individuals is constrained by means of a universal-existential quantification over formulas involving standard numbers in the intuitive sense that one may extend in consciousness indefinitely but non-arbitrarily the internal horizon of a series of 'naturally' appearing individuals.

On this view what is given as an existing object in mathematics or logic is considered to have received its whole sense of being (intersubjectively) from each one's intentionality, this latter meant as an object and sense constituting activity of a temporal consciousness which is itself self-constituted within the world of immediate and non-reflective experience. To make it more intuitive, we cannot imagine an abstract mathematical-logical object than as an intentional invariant susceptible of being identified uniquely as such and such with such and such essential properties without admitting at the same time to the continuous unity of a consciousness in terms of which it appears as the unity of the multiplicity of its instantaneous profiles with a proper to it 'horizon' of categorial properties. In this approach, a subjective (in fact, phenomenologically motivated) meaning that may be given, for instance, to the notion of absoluteness of atomic formulas is the preservation of the possibility of identifying an individual of a theory and its essential categorial properties in the sense of an irreducible 'general-something' bearing no 'thingness' content in the unfolding of consistent extensions of the domain of transitive structures (see Sect. 2, par. 1, also Husserl 1992, pp. 91–93). Insofar as transitive structures by the property of transitivity and also by the foundation axiom may preserve a well-meant sense of individuality regardless of any attributes relative to a content they can also generate a sound definition of ordinals within their domain. Moreover, the domains of transitive structures provided with the property of well-foundedness can be seen to be subjectively founded on a formal-ontological unity in the Husserlian sense of a collective form of unity, that of assemblage, providing the basis for formal relations and thus making meaningful such mathematical-logical acts as a universal-existential quantification. This means that formal-ontological unity as a genetically temporal unity extends to all possible objects and further makes possible that objects may 'appear' in it in the present now of consciousness and in continuous apprehension one by one and also as a totality. This kind of unity in whose level, in Husserl's words, formal relations in general first appear is essentially not founded on material elements. Even the essence of things 'appearing' in it is not taken into consideration except insofar at it makes differentiation (*Unterschiedenheit*) possible which reasonably implies a well-meant notion of individuals and of their essentially attached relational properties (Husserl 1973, pp. 188–189). On this account infinities higher than that of the cardinality of continuum may be taken, lacking a foundation linked to subjective-constitutional states, as merely mathematical artifacts[19] or in the more modest opinion of P. Cohen as not only incapable of leading to a resolution of open questions in 'lower'-order theories, e.g. in number theory, but also as creating a sense of loosing contact with reality (Cohen 2005, pp. 2416–2418).

In the preceding discussion the notion of a mathematical completed whole was taken, on the subjective level, as essentially reflecting the possibility of constituting the objective totality of a whole in the present now of consciousness independently of any causality concerns associated with spatiotemporality, while even deeper it might be associated with an infinite regression constituting-constituted of mental states.[20] Further elaborating on this notion, I point out that Husserl founded in *Experience and Judgment* the concept of a set on an act of thematic apprehension, possible at any time, making what is preconstituted by a colligating consciousness as a plurality of objects, e.g. A then B in retaining A, then C in retaining A and B, etc., into a thematic object-substrate, that is, a set meant in the sense of plurality as unity. The colligating act is a polythetic operation through which a collection of objects is preconstituted whereby by completion of the act of colligation and by what Husserl called an act of retrospective apprehension (*rückgreifendes Erfassen*) the collection as plurality becomes the unity of an identifiable object known as set uniquely appearing to the ego. This means that in Husserlian approach even the notion of a finite set as a definite object, let alone talking of infinite ones, is conditioned on a sort of intentional act on the part of the constituting ego carried out in the present now of retrospective apprehension (Husserl 1973, p. 246).

On the other hand formal individuals as irreducible substrates of 'lowest-level' analytical sentences and bearers of a sense by virtue of their very existence as last resorts of meaning were considered by Husserl to be as to their possibility and essential structure beyond any analytical description even beyond possession of a temporal form, that is, of a duration and a qualitative plenitude of duration. As such they only acquire their sense with regard to the evidence of 'things' and in accordance with preceding syntactical effectuation (Husserl 1992, p. 211). In a certain way this approach may open a path to a mathematical intuition that is far broader than perceptual intuition, indeed a kind of intuition extensively presented as categorial intuition in *Formal and Transcendental Logic*. However, the conception

---

[19] Quine stated in (1986, p. 400), in response to the views of Ch. Parsons, that non-denumerable infinities are acceptable to him insofar as they are the only known systematizations of more welcome matters whereas anything beyond them, (e.g. inaccessible cardinals), should be considered as a mathematical recreation with no ontological rights.

[20] For a subjectively founded interpretation of universal sentences of Predicate Calculus by means of an infinite regression of mental-constitutional states in the process of constitution expect author's *The Metaphysical Source of Logic by way of Phenomenology*.

of most fundamental substrates of analytical formulas as intentionalities of the 'lowest degree' deprived of any inner (pre-phenomenal) temporality could pose a circular problem, namely the question of whether intentionality toward a 'general-something' precedes temporal objectification or it just happens the reverse way around.[21] The whole question relates to the question of temporality of mathematical-logical objects, if there is indeed assumed one, in taking them as intentional invariants in the unity of consciousness and ultimately as commonly identifiable through intersubjective coincidence. There is a deep enough discussion here specifically oriented to key phenomenological questions such as the constitution of time that may take us far afield and consequently it is not within the scope of the present article to develop it further. It is however my intention to do so in a future article.

In this last section I tried to argue, in view of the meta-theoretical questions raised by certain key notions in the foundation and structure of forcing theory, for the possibility of a subjective-constitutional origin of the corresponding mathematical objectivities. These notions primarily were those of absoluteness, of ordinals, of genericity with the accompanying notion of infinitely many compatible extensions and that of a completed infinite whole. I also entered into a somewhat more general discussion, motivated throughout this article by a phenomenological inclination, that led from the specific issues above pertaining to forcing theory as such to the character of mathematical-logical objects and the role of a temporal-constituting consciousness in establishing them as abstract and transtemporal ones. This was done on the belief that the possibility of a subjective reduction of the theoretical principles of forcing theory could be further clarified and invigorated by a wider angle view of the constitution and ontology of mathematical objects in general. The whole issue of the nature of mathematical objects and the ontological status of mathematical-logical theories still is and perhaps will be well into the future a major point of theoretical divisions. I remind that one of the contemporary theoretical disputes is whether set theory refers to an existing reality or it is essentially a theory whose prevalence is mainly due to the beauty and elegance of its concepts and methods. This has been known as a major source of dispute between formalist and realist approaches of mathematics and in a certain sense underscores the inescapable reference of mathematical theories to their most original foundation in the all encompassing world-for-us and in the intersubjectively identical constitutional capacities of all intentional subjects.

References

Brouwer LEJ (1907) Over de grondslagen der wiskunde, quoted from the English translation: on the Foundations of Mathematics, In: Heyting A (ed) Collected works I. (1975). North-Holland, Amsterdam, pp 13–101

---

[21] For an indirect reference to this 'obscure' point see, e.g., J. S. Churchill's introduction in *Experience and Judgment*, (Husserl (1973), p. xix) and K. Michalski's *Logic and Time* in (Michalski (1997), pp. 136–138).

The Subjective Roots of Forcing Theory

Cohen P (1963) The independence of the continuum hypothesis. Proce Natl Acad Sci 50:1143–1148
Cohen P (1966) Set theory and the continuum hypothesis. W.A. Benjamin, MA
Cohen P (2002) The discovery of forcing. Rocky Mt J Math 32(4):1071–1100
Cohen P (2005) Skolem and pessimism about proof in mathematics. Philos Trans R Soc 363:2407–2418
Feferman S (2009) Conceptions of the continuum. Intellectica 51:169–189
Feferman S (2012) Is the continuum hypothesis a definite mathematical problem? In: EFI Project, Harvard 2011–2012, Draft 9/18/11, pp 1–29
Feferman S et al (eds) (1990) Kurt Gödel: collected works II. Oxford University Press, Oxford
Feferman S et al (eds) (2003) Kurt Gödel: collected works V. Oxford University Press, Oxford
Husserl E (1966) Vorlesungen zur Phänomenologie des inneren Zeibewusstseins. In: Hua, Band X, hsgb. R. Boehm, Den Haag: M. Nijhoff
Husserl E (1973) Experience and judgment, transl. In: J.S. Churchill & K. Americs. Routledge & Kegan Paul, London
Husserl E (1984) Logische Untersuchungen, Hua XIX/1, herausg. In: U. Panzer. M. Nijhoff, The Hague
Husserl E (1992) Formale und Transzendentale Logik, Hua Band XVII. In: hsgb. E. Ströker. Felix Meiner Verlag, Hamburg
Kanamori A (2008) Cohen and set theory. Bull Symb Logic 14(3):351–378
Kunen K (1982) Set theory. An introduction to independence proofs. Elsevier, Amsterdam
Lawvere FW (1971) Quantifiers and sheaves, actes du congrès international des mathematiciens, vol 1. Gauthier-Villars, Paris, pp 329–334
Michalski K (1997) Logic and time. Kluwer, Dordrecht
Moore HG (1988) The origins of forcing, logic colloquium '86. In: Drake F, Truss J (eds) Studies in logic and the foundations of mathematics. North-Holland, Amsterdam, pp 143–173
Quine VW (1986) Reply to Charles Parsons. In: Hahn L, Scillp PA (eds) The philosophy of W.V. Quine. Open Court, La Salle, pp 396–403
Shoenfield J (1971) Unramified forcing. Axiomatic set theory. In: Scott D (ed) Proceedings of symposia in pure mathematics, vol 13. AMS, Providence, pp 357–381
Skolem Th (1970) Selected works in logic by Th. Skolem. In: Fenstak JE (ed) Scandinavian University Books, Oslo
Solovay R (1970) A model of set theory in which every set of reals is Lebesgue measurable. Ann Math 92:1–56
Tieszen R (1998) Gödel's path from the incompleteness theorems (1931) to Phenomenology (1961). Bull Symb Logic 4(2):181–203
Tieszen R (2011) After Gödel. Oxford University Press, New York
Van Atten M, van Dalen D, Tieszen R (2002) The phenomenology and mathematics of the intuitive continuum. Philos Math 10(3):203–226

What is the Nature of Mathematical–Logical Objects?

Abstract This article deals with a question of a most general, comprehensive and profound content as it is the nature of mathematical–logical objects insofar as these are considered objects of knowledge and more specifically objects of formal mathematical theories. As objects of formal theories they are dealt with in the sense they have acquired primarily from the beginnings of the systematic study of mathematical foundations in connection with logic dating from the works of G. Cantor and G. Frege in the last decades of the nineteenth century. Largely motivated by a phenomenologically founded view of mathematical objects/states-of-affairs, I try to consistently argue for their character as objects shaped to a certain extent by intentional forms exhibited by consciousness and the modes of constitution of inner temporality and at the same time as constrained in the form of immanent 'appearances' by what stands as their non-eliminable reference, that is, the world as primitive soil of experience and the mathematical intuitions developed in relations of reciprocity within-the-world. In this perspective and relative to my intentions I enter, in the last section, into a brief review of certain positions of G. Sher's foundational holism and R. Tieszen's constituted platonism, among others, respectively presented in Sher (Bull Symb Log 19:145–198, 2013) and Tieszen (After Gödel: platonism and rationalism in mathematics and logic, Oxford University Press, Oxford, 2011).

What is the Nature of Mathematical-Logical Objects?

1 Introduction

A major question that can be raised concerning the essential nature of mathematical–logical objects is their relation to objective reality, to the capacities of the mind and ultimately to temporality conceived in the dual sense of both a 'real world' factor underlying spatio-temporal phenomena and as an intrinsic property of a self-constituting temporal consciousness. On the one hand, they can be regarded in terms of the 'external' objective temporality as immutable objects occupying each time an absolute temporal position with regard to the reality of objective world and on the other hand as temporally constituted re-identifications of appearing profiles with regard to the inner temporality of consciousness. In the following, I will consider the term 'mathematical-logical objects' as identical in meaning to 'mathematical objects' insofar as these are taken in the sense of objects of a formal axiomatical theory, their sense bearing a certain affinity with the one attributed to them, for instance, in Gödel's *Is mathematics syntax of language?* (Feferman et al. 1995, pp. 334–363), and, more closely, in Tieszen's *After Gödel* (Tieszen 2011). In this respect, I will talk about mathematical–logical objects primarily as objects of formal theories, consequently not in the sense of objects of sensuous observation within objective reality, e.g., as geometrical figures in plane or space or space-filling graphs in a digital screen, etc. On account of this general position one is confronted with a host of philosophical attitudes that range between pure platonism in which mathematical objects are perfect, immutable objects of an ideal world transcending human experience and naive empiricist approaches in which mathematical–logical objects are merely elaborated representations in our mind of what physical experience brings to us through our sense organs. In-between there are quite a few theories more inclined either to the platonistic-idealist attitude or to the empiricist-'real world' one going as far back as to the Aristotelian description of mathematical objects as being between (μεταξύ) immutable forms (εἴδη) and perishable (φθαρτά) things (Aristotle 1989, p. 78 and p. 110). Among these theories there exist those which try to incorporate elements of empiricist approaches into a holistic view of the constitution of knowledge taking into account also the role of language (W.v. Quine's holistic empiricism), those which blend platonic rationalism with the constitutional character of transcendental phenomenology (R. Tieszen's constituted platonism) and those which attempt to found logic on veridical facticity (G. Sher's foundational holism). Of course there exist many other variants in the approaches to the nature of mathematical objects and to the content of mathematical theories, e.g., Feferman's conceptual structuralism in Feferman (2009) and C. Parson's eliminative structuralist view of mathematical objects in Parsons (2008), influenced to one or other degree by the the main trends in the philosophy of mathematics that followed the foundational crisis in the beginning of the twentieth century and further marked by the impact of Gödel's philosophical quests after his incompleteness theorems. However in this article except for my own phenomenologically influenced position on the nature of mathematical–logical objects, I will primarily refer (in the last section), in founding my arguments, to certain positions of G. Sher and R. Tieszen on the matter. I also include references and comments on articles relevant to the question of the possible role of transcendental phenomenology in providing a subjective foundation to mathematical–logical objects; namely those of Hauser (2006), da Silva (2013) and Ortiz-Hill (2013).

My main objective is eventually to establish a view of mathematical–logical objects as each time temporally constituted and yet transtemporal and intersubjectively identical ones, and further as conditioned on the intentional modes of an embodied consciousness living in reciprocal terms with the world of experience as its primitive soil. In this task, my primary motivation will be the Husserlian position on mathematical–logical objects as it evolved over time to accommodate Husserl's espousing of transcendental phenomenology and the phenomenology of temporal consciousness while at the same time not rigidly adhering to the tenets of this theory in their entirety and mainstream interpretation. I rather feel free at least in certain points of specific mathematical interest to invigorate and develop my own argumentation trying all the same to consistently follow a subjectively founded mode of reasoning. Let it be stated that concerning the Husserlian writings a key source of reference, though not the only one, will be his late work *Erfahrung und Urteil* (*Experience and Judgment*), [almost exclusively in its english translation (Husserl 1939)], which, in my view, reflects the whole evolution of Husserl's thought with regard to the concepts of pure logic and mathematics starting from the early years of the *Philosophie der Arithmetik* (*Philosophy of Arithmetic*) (Husserl 1970).

2 Objectivities of Sense as Irreal Objects and the Origin of Their Substrates

A basic step of a deeper inquiry into the nature of mathematical–logical objects is to make clear the distinction between what may be taken as real, in talking about objects of knowledge, and what irreal objectivities[1] this latter term mindfully distinguished from the linguistically opposite to real (unreal). Having this in mind I'll use the term real in the rest of the article to describe perceptual objects taken as 'external' to consciousness and existent in an absolute sense in objective space–time, whereas I will reserve the term immanent for those objects which are correlates of a constituting consciousness either as 'appearances' of corresponding real objects of perception or as pure creations of imagination possibly constrained by the modes of re-presentation (*Veranschaulichung*) of, e.g., specific mathematical objects (sets, classes of sets, mappings of classes, free topological transformation of figures, etc.). Talking generally about objectivities as carriers of sense one can add new dimensions to the previous distinction between real and immanent objects along the lines proposed by Husserl in *Experience and Judgment* (Husserl 1939, §

---

[1] In Husserlian terminology these objectivities are referred to as *irrealen Gegenständlichkeiten*.

65). In this approach one can talk about real objectivities as objectivities which are not intended contents, that is, objectivities of outward 'observation' before any spontaneous activity of the mind and irreal objectivities as intended contents, that is, objectivities of sense or yet objectivities emanating from other intended contents. To the extent that sense is inherently tied to an object which means that a certain sense derives from an object and, vice versa, a sense is an object or at least can be made one, we may be faced to an infinite regression as the sense of a sense (which 'lies' in an object) 'lies' consequently itself in an object and therefore can be made to one, then it may have sense by being an object and so on in the regression scheme: sense—sense of sense (as objectified)—sense of [sense of sense [as objectified (as objectified)]]— ....Therefore, objectivity as intended sense is an irreal objectivity in that by virtue of the infinitely proceeding regression above it cannot be a real (*reelles*) component of an object (Husserl 1939, pp. 268–269).

It is noteworthy that Husserl drew a distinction, concerning irreal objectivities as intended 'sense-of', between the objective sense in the sense of predication through which we are directed toward an object as the identical pole of its various self-givings and sense as the determination of an object. This latter determination is considered as something 'more' than mere predication insofar as predication is associated with simple receptivity of objects in their spatiotemporal occurrences while sense as object determination or generally as intended content is considered as a sense of sense (a second-level sense) and is the identical pole of a multiplicity of intentions referred to an object by means of a spontaneity producing and reproducing them at will. To cite an example, a sentence or a text as a collection of sentences have their objective sense as real linguistic-grammatical agglomerates of words, while taken as a theme and further elaborated by various acts of intention, e.g., free variation in imagination, abstraction, parallel comparison, idealization, etc., they acquire the possibility of a second-level sense, a sense as object determination (ibid. pp. 268–269).

A major question arising here is that of the temporality of irreal objectivities or objectivities of understanding, as Husserl termed them in *Erfahrung und Urteil*, in the context of judicative propositions referring to individual sensuous objects, including also in the specific case of mathematical predicative formulas (or generally predicative formulas of a formal language) formal individuals in their modes of being as such, e.g. being a member of, ordered with respect to, being identical with, etc.).[2] This given, I'll try to show that mathematical objects of a 'lower' or 'higher' order, even propositions to which there is ascribed a meaning and consequently a truth value in accordance with that of their constituent parts bound by quantifiers and logical connnectives, share a temporality which is, in fact,

---

[2] Husserl already drew in the *Lessons for a Phenomenology of Inner-Time Consciousness* a clear distinction between objects-substrates of mathematical judgments which are temporal in nature as (mathematical) objects and the relevant states-of-affairs in the sense of meanings assigned to such objects which are brought to judgment within time but are not themselves temporal objects. In other words it appropriately belongs to objects as such to be objects of a temporal consciousness in virtue of their appearances in front of it but not to states-of-affairs associated with them. For instance, a (physical) temporal object may be smooth in touch, dense, compact, etc. as object, but smoothness, density, compactness, etc. are properties reflected within time which are not themselves temporal objects (Husserl 1966, pp. 96–98).

an omnitemporality in a specific sense. They have an objective temporal duration each time as being 'created' anew by a subject, consequently they possess a temporal form in their noematic mode of givenness,[3] yet they are identically the same at all times at any place and for any subject to the extent that their original being-in-itself is that of their constitution. I go a step further from the Husserlian position to claim that while the temporality of an objectivity of understanding in the sense of the unity of a meaningful whole in the actual now may be the same for all subjects, yet the application of various intentional faculties on the part of each subject, for instance, the apprehension of formal individuals as such and the mode in which they are apprehended, the act of colligation or quantification over individuals or collections of individuals make that mathematical objects, propositions, theorems, etc., be in principle not eternal and immutable. Instead they are conditioned at least in part on the (albeit identically the same) constitutional modes of each intentional subject possessing a potentially open intentional horizon within the life-world.[4]

Husserl had pointed out the difference in the signification of temporalities associated with sensuous individuals, on the one hand, and objectivities of understanding, on the other. Sensuous individuals are individualized by their appearance at an objective temporal point which presents itself in the immanence of temporal consciousness, while irreal objects in the sense of objectivities of understanding are not considered individuals and consequently may not share the objective time in which individual sensuous objects are themselves individualized. This is what may be asserted even as a judicative proposition can be immanently simultaneous, that is, constituted in the same givenness-time as that of its constituent substrates which may be immanent 'appearances' of sensuous individuals. However, one may argue that insofar as judicative propositions and in particular predicative formulas and logical–mathematical sentences have as substrates formal individuals (that is, a kind of quasi-individuals termed so by Husserl in distinction to real individuals) they are always and everywhere the same to the extent that their substrates are the same always for every subject in the sense of pure intentionalities which may not even refer to existing causally related objects. In this sense objectivities of understanding as intended senses are as irreal as their

---

[3] A certain ambivalence exists as to whether temporality may be considered an underlying factor in the being of noematic objects as such, something reserved at least by some phenomenologists only for noetic ones. I myself tend to consider inner temporality as underlying also noematic objects insofar as they are constituted as identically the same in the multiplicities of their immanent appearances over time. In *Ideas I* Husserl underlined the difference between noetic-noematic in the following epigrammatic phrase: The noematic is the field of unities (*Einheiten*), the noetic that of 'constituting' multiplicities (Husserl 1976a, p. 231). A few lines farther a noematic object is characterized as identical in literal sense, whereas the consciousness of it in the various segments of its immanent duration is characterized as not identical but only a conjunct, continuous one. The unity of the noema (i.e., an 'appearing' object and its predicates) is set in contradistinction to the multiplicities of constituting mental processes of consciousness, that is, the concrete noeses (ibid., p. 231).

[4] The phenomenological notion of life-world is originally conceived to be an indefinitely extensible horizon of our special reduction-performing co-presence in the world, this latter meant as the primitive soil of our experience. A major later work of Husserl's in which this notion is further elaborated is the well known to phenomenologists *Crisis of European Sciences and Transcendental Phenomenology* (Husserl 1976b).

quasi-individual substrates, these latter ones having their own immanent time of individuation which does not correspond, however, to an absolute temporal position in the 'real' objective world.

The individuation in the phenomenological attitude is meant as an a priori intentional act independent of causality not even of the necessity of presence of a concrete 'thingness' individual. Husserl thought of formal-mathematical individuals as a special case of quasi-individuals in contrast to 'real' individuals of physical perception, even though he considered that in both cases the individual essence of corresponding objects encompasses both the identical temporal duration of each one and the identical distribution of temporal fullness over this duration. This individual essence tends toward unity in their perfect likeness (of 'real' and quasi-individuals) and, even more, one may assume that in the noematic stock of each lived experience there is always one individual essence (Husserl 1939, App. I, p. 382). In contrast, the constitution of sets as collections of individuals and also the constitution of sets of a higher order (classes) as collections of sets, etc. is conditioned on the possibility of their constituting as completed wholes in the immanence of consciousness and in the actual now of reflection irrespectively of whether infinite sets, in particular, are formally postulated as denumerable or non-denumerable ones. For Husserl, in the case of sets or classes of sets one should distinguish between the act of colligation or drawing together of a sequence of objects and the act of constitution of sets as thematic objects in actual presence. In this view a set as an original objectivity is preconstituted by an act of colligation which links disjunct objects to one another and is 'complemented' by what he called a retrospective apprehension (*rückgreifendes Erfassen*), an act whose content is that of the thematization by the constituting ego of a collectivity preconstituted through the polythetic act of colligation into an identifiable and re-identifiable object possibly posited as a substrate of judgments (Husserl 1939, pp. 246–247). This latter act of thematization in terms of immanent unity should be associated with the possibility of infinity as generated freely in imagination without any spatiotemporal and causal constraints. The modes of temporality involved respectively in the act of individuation of objects as 'appearances' in front of the intentionality of consciousness and the act of a non-receptive apprehension of a collection of immanent objects in the form of a completed whole will be more lengthily discussed in the next section.

Given that objectivities of understanding as intended senses have no real content just as their most fundamental substrates taken as formal individuals (bound to certain constraints in case we talk about substrates of mathematical–logical formulas), the question that may arise, inasmuch as their existence is not conditioned in an absolute sense to that of their 'real world' counterparts, is whether there could possible be a refinement of our intentional apprehension of objects in a way that objectivities of sense that look as being always and in a transtemporal sense the same could for that reason change over time. For that matter Husserl referred to the concept of internal and external horizon of objects taken either as appearances in consciousness of corresponding real-world ones or as pure objects of imagination. In this respect one may in principle elaborate and further refine his 'regard' inside the noematic horizon of mathematical objects. For instance, one can have the intuition of nonstandard objects as existing within the

What is the Nature of Mathematical-Logical Objects?

internal horizon of standard ones by 'projecting' his intentional faculties in a non-arbitrary and relevant to acquired mathematical experience way, e.g. in the formal definition of a nonstandard number x: x is nonstandard in case

$$\forall \text{ standard } \epsilon \ \ |x| < \epsilon$$

(I present this view in some technical detail in "Appendix 1").

To discuss another issue pertaining to the the foundation of existential and universal quantifications as a priori possibilities, I choose the formal theory of forcing in the mathematical foundations where one can introduce sets with generic properties essentially based on the notion of filters as upwardly closed sets with respect to their (partial) order, on the notion of density with respect to this partial order and the operation of intersection these two latter presupposing the existence and invariability of individuals bounded by existential and universal quantifiers. It is important to note that Husserl viewed existential ($\exists$) quantification as an a priori possibility of existence which, we may further claim, combined with universal quantification points to a constraint 'imposed' by our mathematical activity (meant as an activity-within-the world) on mathematical individuals-substrates of formulas which is that of introducing necessities out of possibilities. The a priori possibility of existence together with the possibility of an indefinite repetition of this 'act' of existence cannot be otherwise construed but as linked to mental faculties, in fact linked to the intentional modalities of consciousness to the extent that these can found the existence of individuals independently of a material or generally 'thingness' content, even of an objective spatio-temporal existence. Moreover, prior to the application of a universal quantification as an act of an ideally ad infinitum repetition we must cling to the possibility of preserving individuality as such over indefinite extensions (e.g. in bounded by $\exists$ and $\forall$ quantifiers formulas), something that may be fundamentally regarded as an act of preservation of individual essence over constituted time no matter if the time segment could just be an instant in actual reflection. This means that the process of constitution of an intended sense (i.e., of an objectivity of understanding) as an irreal objectivity in actual presence involves a temporality in the mode of constituted, whereas the receptive-passive apprehension of individuals as such without any reference to an objective-real existence may involve a temporality in the mode of constituting. I'll come back to this question in the next.

I turn for a little while to the notion of genericity of sets to make a point as to the essence of individuals in the form of substrates of objectivities of sense, in particular of mathematical–logical formulas acquiring an ontological status as necessities out of possibilities, which is a status basically implemented by the application of $\forall$ and $\exists$ quantifiers. In applying these quantifiers in the aforementioned sense of a priori possibilities linked in turn to an intentional directedness toward individuals independently of 'thingness' content, we must stick to the necessity of preservation of the essence of these individuals in constituting the objectivity in question as intended sense and preserving it as identically the same in the unity of a whole.

I remind in rough terms the formal definition of a generic set **G** in forcing theory: Based on the definition of a filter of the partially ordered P of forcing conditions p, we define a set **G** as *P*-generic over a countable transitive model **M** iff **G** is a filter in *P* and for all dense sets $D \subset P$ and $D \in \mathbf{M}$ we have that $\mathbf{G} \cap D \neq \emptyset$. Generally the *P*-generic set **G** is not a subset of **M**.[5] It is important to note a second order universal quantification over all dense sets in **M** and also the implementation of the intersection operation which must yield a non-empty content ideally ad infinitum, that is, one has to find at least a common element of both **G** and the dense *D*. In this respect, one must not only presuppose the existence and the invariability of formal individuals over time but also a sort of discernibility of them to the extent that we must find within the range of a universal quantification over the class of all dense sets of **M** at least a pair of individuals identically the same, one belonging to a dense set *D* and the other to the generic set **G**. This is clearly associated with the possibility of invariably preserving individuality of lowest level elements in iterated acts of reflection and in posing thematically the respective sets as completed wholes and also the possibility of 'recognizing' at least two elements-individuals as identical and in principle discernible only on account of their 'ontological' being as individuals (perhaps lowest level ones) equipped with the non-logical predicate $\in$.

An interesting question that may arise here is whether this kind of 'discernibility' is an inner property of formal individuals, that is, a property of being attached with a distinctive 'ontological label' in an implicit but unique way in the process of their appearing as immanent objects in instantaneous reflection or whether it should be solely referred to the modes of their intentional constitution. This is a question that may be associated with the definition of ordinals as transitive and well-ordered by $\in$ relation sets something that implies their 'fixedness' as individuals with regard to any enlargement of a structure. On this ground, urelements (roughly irreducible individuals) of an extended Zermelo–Fraenkel universe (ZFU, $\in$) taken as not identical yet indiscernible elements by means of the definition of $\mathcal{A}$-indiscernibility within a relational structure, can be made discernible by associating to any collection of them an ordinal number so that it is possible to talk about a collection e.g., σ_0, σ_1, σ_2, ..., σ_{n-1} of such objects. This is a result of the simple proof that any ordinal as a well-ordered structure $\langle A, < \rangle$ is a rigid structure, i.e. the only automorphism in this structure is the identity function (Krause and Coelho 2005, p. 201). In other words in a rigid structure $\mathcal{A}$ the notion of non-identical elements and $\mathcal{A}$-discernible elements coincide.

My position inasmuch as we refer to mathematical–logical objects, in the sense of non-arbitrarily constituted objects of consciousness, is that 'discernibility' of individuals in objectivities of sense (with an eye to non-finitistic in content formulas bounded by existential-universal quantifiers) is due to the intentional modes of a consciousness orienting itself in an a priori and causality-independent way toward individuals-substrates as such and in the modalities of this intentional orientation. This claim points to the modes of phenomenologically perceiving formal individuals as 'general somethings', irrespective of any objective spatio-temporality constraints, which are moreover constituted with a noematic nucleus thought of as their essential and unique way to be a 'something' in general with respect to, in

---

[5] For a detailed presentation of these and relevant mathematical notions in the context of the theory of forcing one may consult Kunen (1982, pp. 53–54 and pp. 186–187).

relation to, in colligation with, etc. It was in *Formale und Transzendentale Logik* (Husserl 1929), that Husserl faced squarely the question of grounding mathematical science in these terms as a formal-ontological discipline, namely a discipline in a fully comprehensive sense whose universal domain is delimited as the range of the highest form-concept, the 'anything-whatsoever' (*Etwas-überhaupt*), that is, the field of the (thought of in the emptiest generality) 'something-in-general' with all in this field a priori generated and derived forms which always give new forms in an ever reiterable construction (Husserl 1929, p. 68).

3 A Subjectively Founded Conception of Set-Theoretical Aggregates

A remarkable divergence from the tradition of a purely logical definition of sets started with Frege's *Begriffschrift* is found in Weyl's *Das Kontinuum*, in 1918, which is generally considered as one of the most strongly influenced from phenomenological analysis foundational works in the mathematics of the twentieth century.

In the section on sets Weyl noted that "[..] how two sets (in contrast to properties) are defined (on the basis of the primitive properties and relations and individual objects exhibited by means of the principles of §2) [*note of the author: by means of the six principles of the combination of judgments* (Weyl 1994, pp. 9–14)] does not determine their identity. Rather an objective fact, which is not decipherable from the definition in a purely logical way is decisive; namely, whether each element of the one set is also an element of the other, and conversely.". The same objective factor holds for relations and their judgment schemes (i.e. the multidimensional sets in Weyl's parlance), which means that their identity is determined by their objective range of applicability rather than their form of definition; in other words their extensional rather than their intensional 'content' determines their identity. Further, by means of what Weyl called a mathematical process (essentially consisting of the six judgment combination schemes plus the principles of substitution and iteration) one can build from the primitive category of objects, i.e., from the category of natural numbers with the successor relation, a new derived system of ideal objects, for instance, those sets which are "altogether different from the primitive objects; they belong to an entirely separate sphere of existence." (ibid., p. 22).

Another important point in Weyl's remarks about infinite sets is that 'inexhaustibility' is essential to the infinite, in the sense that the notion of an infinite set as an aggregate of elements brought together by infinitely many individual acts assembled and then surveyed as a completed whole by consciousness is utterly nonsensical. This is a position that may ultimately be taken as having to do with a conception of infinite mathematical objects as associated, on the one hand, with the mental capacities of a thinking subject standing in terms of reciprocity with the world of experience and, on the other, as conditioned on the intentional-constituting modes of a consciousness in intersubjective coincidence. In consequence, infinite mathematical objects are open to further elucidation, readjustment of form, content clarification even to the possible emergence of hidden underlying insights and regularities possibly uncovered by new intuitions thus leading de facto to the refutation of the notion of mathematical objects as immutable and atemporal ones. In sum, Weyl's position on the matter is that the "transition from the 'property' to the 'set' (of those things which have the property) signifies merely that one brings to bear the objective rather than the purely logical point of view, i.e., one regards objective correspondence (that is, 'relation in extension' as logicians say) established entirely on the basis of acquaintance with the relevant objects as decisive rather than logical equivalence." (ibid. p. 23). In view of this position, Weyl regarded the concepts of set and function espoused in analysis since Dirichlet as completely vague, and while he acknowledged the huge advances of nineteenth century analysis due primarily to the likes of Dedekind, Cantor and Weierstrass, he was still doubting the clarity and unassailability of its ultimate principles, with particular reference to the obscure nature of irrationals and the ensuing vagueness of the notion of continuity. For that reason he called for the attainment of a solution based on objective insights in view of the fact that more or less arbitrarily axiomatized systems cannot be of much help regarding, for instance, continuity "given to us immediately by intuition (in the flow of time and motion) (which) has yet to be grasped mathematically as a totality of discrete 'stages' in accordance with that part of its content which can be conceptualized in an 'exact' way." (ibid. p. 23). In any case and in spite of the obvious indescribability of continuum by any analytical means, Weyl thought that any further refinements of the concepts of set and function should be based on the prior intuitions of iteration and, primarily, that of the sequence of natural numbers.

Although Weyl made explicit references to the underlying intuition of time and motion as immanently constituted in consciousness, in particular in section 6 of Ch. 2 of *Das Kontinuum*, he did not enter into any detailed description of how these phenomenological notions could affect the apprehension in the first place and then the formal definition of such notions as number, element, set, class, etc. However especially after Frege's strictly logical foundation of these concepts in *Begriffshrift* and the *Grundlagen der Arithmetik*, had already appeared an attempt to involve the temporal factor in the articulation of the general notion of aggregates of objects as formations in simultaneity in Husserl's *Philosophy of Arithmetic* [*Philosophie der Arithmetik*, Husserl (1970)], first published in 1891. Giving as an example the particular tones of a melody as temporally interconnected in the formation of a simultaneous whole, Husserl pointed to the general formation of an aggregate of objects as constituted through the succession of simultaneities of its particular objects (which demand particular reflections) to achieve the simultaneity in the mental representation of the aggregate. This is considered as an indication of the role of inner experience and, in any case, as excluding the possibility of description of a collective ensemble of objects as a temporal simultaneity (Husserl 1970, p. 24).

However, at this stage Husserl was still influenced by his psychologistic preoccupations in a way that considered the role of time in these concept formations as a psychological precondition in a double mode: (1) It is essential that in the representation of an aggregate of elements forming the concept of a number its associated parts are given simultaneously in our consciousness and (2) almost all representations of aggregates and in any case all number representations are results of processes meaning that they are constituted from successive wholes corresponding to elements insofar as each element 'carries' with it a particular temporal definiteness (ibid, p. 32). In other words one can put forth the claim: because enumeration requires a temporal succession of representations, number is the collective form of successiveness in abstracto, while temporal succession leads to a complete whole in all cases of aggregates and for that reason provides the ground for the abstract concept of an aggregate (ibid, p. 29). Yet Husserl remarked that neither simultaneity nor successiveness in time occur somehow in the content of aggregates and thus in the content of number representations. In fact, he was wondering of the meaning one would give to the notion of the coincident content of an aggregate in which case the meaning of a temporal co-existence would seem an incomprehensible conundrum (ibid, p. 29). It is noteworthy, however, that even though Husserl was still far from ridding himself of psychological preoccupations and well before entering his properly meant phenomenological phase he nonetheless claimed that the interconnection of the colligated contents in an aggregate or of those enumerated in the (formation of) number is not a spatial nor a temporal one. In that case the synthesis of notions such as that of an aggregate of objects lies not in the colligation of contents but in certain synthetic acts through which they can be brought to presentifying reflection (ibid, p. 42).

Later of course he entered into a more systematic, and related to his eidetic intuition, attitude toward the formation of mathematical objects in founding the conception of mathematical objects as formal-ontological ones in *Formal and Transcendental Logic* (from now on *FTL*) until reaching the later mature stage of *Experience and Judgment* (from now on *EU*). Nevertheless, the temporality of mathematical objects taken, for instance, either as formal individuals or as aggregates of formal individuals within the structure of formal theories was always one of Husserl's preoccupations even when he was shifting the focus to the discussion of a properly mathematical (categorial) intuition or generally to an eidetic one. In *FTL* Husserl thought of the object-in-general (or 'object-whatsoever'; *Gegenstand überhaupt*) as the unifying concept of both apophantic mathematics (as derived from aristotelian apophantics) and non-apophantic mathematics (the traditional formal mathematical analysis, set theory, the theory of cardinals and ordinals, etc.) in a most general formal sense that leaves out of account any relation whatsoever to a 'thingness' content. In such a view, set and number theories as well as all other formal mathematical disciplines are formal in the sense that they have as fundamental domain certain derived forms (*Ableitungsgestalten*) of the formal 'anything-whatsoever' (or 'something-whatsoever'; *Etwas überhaupt*). These derived forms are, next to finite or infinite sets and numbers, various relations, combinations, sequences of, relations of parts and whole, etc., in the context of a universal science of logic (termed *Mathesis Universalis*). This way the whole mathematics can be characterized as a formal-ontological discipline insofar as it can be evaluated as an ontology in the sense of an a priori theory of objects in general and moreover a formal one in the sense of a theory associated with the pure forms of 'anything-whatsoever' (Husserl 1929, p. 68). It follows that this way mathematics can be considered as a theory of pure forms referring to an non-eliminable 'nucleus', the 'object'- or 'something-whatsoever' whose origin is external to the formal structure as such and consequently must be searched in the sphere of the objective, that is, in the real objective universe with which we have some form of (ultimately) a priori relation. Consequently if all judgments, and all sentences of predicate calculus in particular, may be reduced to most elementary ones bearing a direct reference to last objects-substrates, these latter in the sense of individuals devoid of any 'inner' analytically describable content, one transcends the realm of analytical logic and gets into the realm of evidence as objectivity within-the-world and yet independent of the constraints relating to a material or generally 'thingness' and (therefore) spatiotemporal substance. This means that one is faced here with a kind of directedness to individuals-substrates which is of an a priori nature and brings again to the forefront the question of temporality with respect to these irreducible individuals. Given that analytical sentences are reducible to lowest-level sentences referring to last objects-substrates which take their plenitude of sense from the 'things' as pure objectivities corresponding to these substrates, one deals in the level of evidence with individuals as such irrespective of a 'thingness' content whose possibility and essential structure are beyond the limits of analytical logic. Husserl even claimed that these individuals do not appropriate of a temporal form, a duration and a qualitative plenitude of duration, being rather known by a sort of evidence that refers to 'things', while being only possible to penetrate their sense through a prior syntactical effectuation (Husserl 1929, p. 181). In any case, here can be raised the question of temporality as a self-constituting process leading back to an original subjectivity that constitutes temporal objectivity (by constituting itself) and temporal objects either as representations of existing in the objective world counterparts or as products of constrained imagination (e.g., generally mathematical–logical objects). In these terms it is questionable whether one can talk, as Husserl claimed above, of 'lowest-level' objects of intentional directedness such as individuals-substrates in virtue of pure forms that lack any 'inner' temporality insofar as nothing can be brought into actual reflection but as objectively and therefore temporally existing. In short, any discussion of temporality as objectivity-constituting reduces to the origin of temporality as a non-objectifiable subjectivity that is self-constituting which is a concept generating, though, an infinitely regressing sequence of reflecting-reflected.

I complete this section with Husserl's conception of certain objectivities of understanding, in particular of sets and classes, as contained in the posthumous publication of *EU*. In this work Husserl referred far more explicitly than in *FTL* and previous works to the role of the unity of consciousness and also to the sense-giving 'ground' of the life-world in shaping a genealogy of logic as essentially a logic of predications reducible to the cognitive acts of a constituting consciousness within the life-world. In this broadened view "It is an essential peculiarity of every thematically unitary process, grounded most deeply in the internal structure of consciousness, that no matter how many objects may affect thematically and join together in the unity of a theme, still, a satisfaction of interest is possible only by [the mediation of] concentrations in which, at any given time, one object becomes a substrate and thereby a subject of determination" (Husserl 1939, p. 213). It is remarkable though that Husserl's departure from psychologistic preoccupations and his transition to a purely phenomenological attitude toward formal logical objects in general and formal-mathematical ones in particular is not a discontinuous evolution.

What is the Nature of Mathematical-Logical Objects?

In fact, the *Philosophy of Arithmetic* in spite of its immaturity in his own confession as a first book, was in many ways a phenomenological-constitutional investigation seeking for the first time to make categorial objectivities of the first level and of higher levels (sets and cardinals of a higher ordinal level) understandable on the basis of 'constituting' intentional activities in whose effectuations they appear *originaliter* and accordingly in the full originality of their sense (Husserl 1929, p. 76). Further, to better comprehend Husserl's conception of elements of sets, sets, sets of a higher order etc., I point below to certain of his views concerning the nature of mathematical–logical activity as a fundamentally genetic-constitutional activity involving primarily the predicative activity of the ego. (1) The universal significance of the core-form of substantivity becomes clear to us from its genetic origin, that is, as based on the universality of the concept 'object-in-general' by virtue of its corresponding original sense belonging to every object already preconstituted in passivity and at the same time as something a priori explicable 'possessing' a horizon of indeterminate determinability. (2) The concepts of a multitude in general and the concept of number (a species concept) have their origin in concrete phenomena yet the presentation of multitudes as (immanent) objectivities of understanding are such that the individual characteristics of their determinate contents are ignored and taken as 'objects-in-general' or 'objects-whatsoever'. Moreover, to experience the relations of more or less presupposing an intuition of cardinality of elements at least within the limits of an authentic presentation in consciousness, the related terms have to be presented in a single act of consciousness so that, for example, the original and the expanded totality are present to us simultaneously and in one act. These Husserlian theses were already expressed in a more 'primitive' sense in the *Philosophy of Arithmetic* (see also: Hartimo 2006, pp. 330–331). (3) Just as an object in receptivity is the identical pole of the various apprehensions intentionally directed to it and eventually constituted in the form of the unity of its profiles and modes of givenness, so what is identical in predicative determination is identical as the unity of the predicative actions on the part of a subject and of the evolving logical sense. What is more these objects are nothing that could be apprehended in simple receptivity; rather they are higher level objects being the result of a judicative operation of predication and were termed by Husserl syntactical or categorial objectivities (Husserl 1939, p. 239). They are the product of predicative spontaneity on the part of a subject yet they ultimately refer, in (intentional) receptive apprehension, to objects-substrates with an 'attached' noematic nucleus of a priori relational forms, i.e. part or member of, unity vs multiplicity, greater or less than, etc. (4) Concerning the apprehension of a collection of objects as sets, as long as we carry out a merely collective assemblage (colligation) in the way of turning the regard toward one object, then to another while holding on to the apprehension of the first, then to a third while holding on to the apprehension of the first two in togetherness and so on, we have only a preconstituted object, a 'plurality', which only in the turning of 'regard' by a single act of consciousness, termed by Husserl a retrospective apprehension, can become a thematic object in the sense of plurality as unity, that is, what we may call an aggregate of objects in the form of a set. It is therefore in terms of retrospective apprehension that a set as a re-identifiable thematic object can enter, for instance, as object of a second-order quantification or as a syntactical substrate in various mathematical–logical formulas, something that entails that it somehow retains in semantical content the 'traces' of the modes of its constitution as above. It can be also further explicated in an ever renewed identification (as 'possessing' a priori a horizon of indeterminate determinability) and this act of explication in its turn is always an act of colligation and retrospective apprehension (ibid. p. 246).

This way sets can also be colligated in their turn with other sets in disjunction and become sets of a higher order (i.e., classes of sets) and so on, which can again be thematically objectified in a single act of consciousness. Given any set as an objectivity-substrate within a judgment or a combination of judgments after retrospective apprehension, there is already present a pregiven multiplicity of particular affections in the mode of colligation of its elements, at least as finitely many 'authentic' presentations, and next a repetition ideally ad infinitum in the mode of so on. It is not precluded though, and this is of a special importance concerning the approach toward mathematical-logical objects in this article that in accordance with the above mentioned idea of a horizon of indeterminate determinability, new affections may come into play by an 'approaching' intuition in a way that intended unities (as elements of a set taken in the sense of a thematic object) can be again resolved into pluralities. In this eventuality, every set "must be conceived a priori as capable of being reduced to ultimate constituents, therefore to constituents which are themselves no longer sets" (ibid. p. 247). This is a position that can be seen as parallel to Husserl's earlier idea in *FTL*, namely that any analytical sentence can be ultimately reduced to last individuals-substrates with no 'inner' analytical content not even a possession of temporal form (see Sect. 3, par. 6).

In short, as Husserl evolved from the psychologistic stage of the *Philosophy of Arithmetic* toward the intentional, ego-founded stage initiated to some extent with *Logical Investigations* (from now on *LI*) and further pursued with *FTL* and *EU*, the possibility of existence of no further reducible formal individuals can be founded on the sole evidence of a subject's intentional directedness toward 'something-in-general' irrespectively of any material content, not even a spatiotemporality and causality associated one. In this view, elements of sets as ultimate constituents which cannot be themselves sets may be founded independently of 'real' world objectivities corresponding to an absolute temporal position, in fact their existence should be rather reduced to the absolute evidence of the corresponding enactment of an intentional regard toward a general empty-of-content 'anything-whatsoever'. Put in this way the members of a set are not related to the set the way the parts of a sensuous whole are related to the whole itself as partial coincidences conditioned on relations of homogeneity (e.g. of like and unlike), something that holds for the intuition of sensuous objects as unities in apprehension. On the contrary, they remain 'exterior to one another' by being simply colligated in the sense of being primarily objects of distinct intentional orientations with accompanying forms of retention in consciousness. Consequently, to the extent that they are merely collections brought together through colligation and retained as thematic unities by retrospective apprehension, they acquire the form of a syntactical connection and not of a 'sensuous' one. This further means that while in sensuous intuition of material objectivities the corresponding likenesses and similarities determine the

What is the Nature of Mathematical-Logical Objects?

degree of homogeneity of sensuous community between parts and whole, in formal communities (e.g. set—members of the set) the homogeneity of formal community goes back to similarities of form as form and further to the modes of intentional-constituting activities as described above.

4 The Question of Universal-Existential Quantification in Formulas with Ontological Claims

W.V. Quine sought to justify in Quine (1947) the existence of universals mainly through the dual form of quantification (universal-existential) as well as through the concept of classes and the notion of the identification of indiscernibles. In terms of the dual form of quantification, the quantifiers $\exists$ and $\forall$ are taken as assigning an attribute (or attributes) to an entity x, i.e. $\exists x$ means 'there is an entity x such that..' and $\forall x$ means 'for every entity x such that..'. Consequently and in contrast with quantification over variables taken as simple schematic letter variables bounded by a universal-existential quantification these are construed as variables requiring attributes or classes as range of values. In such an approach a theory dealing solely with concrete objects in a nominalist sense can be reconstrued as one dealing with universals basically through the application of the dual form of quantification to bounded variables having a definite range of values and in a weaker sense simply through identification of indiscernibles, i.e. treating objects as identical to one another when they differ in no respect expressible within the formal theory (Quine 1947, pp. 75–77). The main point here is that by relying on universal quantification over bounded variables ranging over the whole domain of which the theory treats, we are set to assign to these variables corresponding entities as values whose truth-functions or propositions could be considered as their names. In other words syntactical variables of a theory that might be hitherto taken as mere schematic letters can be henceforth associated with ontological commitments, thus opening a field of discussion reaching beyond an apparently presumed platonistic status. In the above sense of universals as abstract entities susceptible of attributes and in what can be taken as a unifying perspective with respect to their factual or formal sense I point, on the one hand, to what has already been referred to as ultimate syntactical individuals of analytic sentences in the sense of empty of content 'somethings-in-general'; that is, as abstractions of lowest-level intentional orientations toward a general immaterial concrete 'something' (something akin to the Aristotelian τόδε τι) which is moreover *a priori* associated with derived and devoid of content categorial forms.

On the other hand, I point to what seems to be a fundamental difference between universals as formal individuals in the sense of 'empty-somethings' whose existential evidence is completely reduced to the intentional directedness of a reflecting subject (thus made in principle free of any spatiotemporal constraints) and individual sensuous objects which are individualized by their appearance as original impressions at an absolute temporal point and are presented in the now of consciousness. This distinction can be founded on the possibility of a distinct view of universals taken in abstraction as either necessities out of essential possibilities reducible to the evidence of the presence of at least one reduction performing ego or as 'real world' sensuous individuals occupying an absolute spatio-temporal position and turned to corresponding immanent presentations. In EU Husserl referred generally to a universal as the eidos 'residing' in an object, e.g. in the predicative sentence S is p, p is taken not as just the individual moment of the individual object S but as something totally different, namely the general eidos p characterizing S in a way that just as well one could state that the individual moment p' is of the kind p. In these terms, I regard individuality of an object as a universal inasmuch as one may take it in the sense of a content "which is capable of being seen as identical, which, as 'complete sense', lies both in the experiencing consciousness, or rather in its noema, and there has the experiential character (the correlate of experience 'actual'); and, in the corresponding imaginary consciousness of quasi-experience, it has the character 'imagined' (the correlate of quasi-experience 'quasi-actual'.)" (Husserl 1939, App. I, pp. 381–382). In a certain sense, this concept of individuality may be characterized as the noematic essential 'stock' within consciousness that is identically the same in a positing of experience as 'actual' and also in a positing of quasi-experience as 'quasi-actual'. To the extent that this essence may be disjoined in the possible coincidence of an object posited as 'actual' and another one posited as 'quasi-actual', while tending to unity in the case of their perfect likeness (in passive coincidence), there is in fact always one individual essence in the noematic 'stock' of each lived experience. It is in this sense that individuality of an object in the sense of individuality as such , be it an 'actual' or 'quasi-actual' one according to an exact parallelism, can be considered as a universal possibly treated in a formal approach according to Quine's notion of universals in Quine (1947).

In sum, one can provide an ontological justification of individuals of formal mathematical theories as universals in universal-existential formulas along the following lines:

a. Starting from a finite closed experience of individuals as immanent counterparts of 'real world' ones, one can open a horizon of individuals as irreal objectivities bound to the original ones by perfect coincidence of likeness, while in the apprehension of a whole in terms of constitution of a unity in the present now of consciousness new elements of likeness are immediately recognized as particularizations of the same universal in a process that can be ideally extended ad infinitum. In Husserl's words, "As soon as an open horizon of like objects is present to consciousness as a horizon of presumptively actual and really possible objects, and as soon as it becomes intuitive as an open infinity, it gives itself as an infinitude of particularizations of the **same** universal. The generalities individually apprehended and combined then get an infinite extension and lose their tie to precisely those individuals from which they were first abstracted." (Husserl 1939, p. 328). In this sense a universal is not bound to any particular instance in actuality.

b. The formation of formal-mathematical individuals as universals is ultimately independent of their positing as objects of actual ('real world') experience for they can be generated as objects of imagination. This latter possibility is bound to certain specific constraints associated with formal-mathematical objects as such taken as appearances in consciousness which are not free products or unconstrained variations of imagination. Generally everything which can occur either as an actuality of experience or as a pure possibility (associated with a corresponding intentionality) can be a term in relations of comparison and further be conceived through the activity of eidetic identification and subsumption in terms of a universal. In this sense a universal as an ideal concept has a purely ideal being which does not presuppose the actual existence of corresponding particulars; it can be what it is even if the corresponding particulars are pure possibilities. Husserl notably characterized the being of the pure possibilities as correlative to the pure being of the universal in which they 'participate'. These pure possibilities "must be constructed as its bases and as an ideally infinite extension of the bases of the pure abstraction giving access to the universal" (ibid., pp. 329–330).

Consequently, one can provide a proper foundation to a universal quantification of the general form $\forall x\, Q(x)$ in regarding the variable x as a universal-individual whose essential being does not presuppose by necessity the actual existence of corresponding particulars but rather the existence of individuals bound to an ontological commitment as pure possibilities of intentionality toward a general 'anything-whatsoever' which can be ideally extensible to infinity. Further, these individuals as pure possibilities remain identically the same through all alteration pertaining to the flux of the multiplicities of their possibly instantiated appearances within consciousness. It should be reminded that generally in Husserl's theory of eidetic intuition the concept of a mathematical–logical object as pure eidos can be attained through pure variations in the mode of a non-arbitrary mathematical experience produced in the realm of imagination and in an ideal extension while co-positing the world as an underlying assumption too.

c. The question of existence in mathematical propositions may be reduced to an a priori possibility of existence in the following sense: every actuality of experience must first comply with the a priori conditions of its possible experience, that is, with the free of 'real world' contingencies conditions of its pure possibility, its representability and positability as an objectivity of a uniformly identical sense (ibid., p. 353). Consequently, existential and universal quantification in logical-mathematical formulas should be reducible to the application of the a priori intentional mode of positing formal individuals as pure possibilities in imagination (in a non-arbitrary way) and ideally extending them ad infinitum in retaining their identity as pure $eid\bar{e}$ in the unity of an actual immanent whole. In this way, quantifying over universals in logical–mathematical theories is freed from the finitistic constraints and the contingencies associated with 'real world' particulars and is ultimately conditioned on the a priori modes of positing a concrete, empty-of-content 'anything-whatsoever' as a pure possibility in the actual now of intentional apprehension with the ideal possibility of re-iterating this act indefinitely while retaining as identically the same the essential being of the particular 'anything-whatsoever'. In fact, all existential judgments of mathematics as a priori existential judgments are judgments of existence about possibilities with the accompanying attention to the fact that such possibilities are not considered arbitrary products of imagination but are constrained by proper mathematical intuitions, e.g. the intuitions of order, of symmetry, of permutability, of conservative extension, etc. In a parallel sense, universal judgments also emerge from acts in the sphere of actuality (not necessarily a 'real-world' actuality) and then proceed from each particular object e.g., a X having a property Y to an open horizon of X's, as concrete possibilities having this property Y, each new one considered as a non-arbitrary 'anything-whatsoever' added anticipatively from the chain of X's. At this point, I refer to Gödel's platonistic position regarding existential assertions in mathematics motivated by his general (and to a certain extent phenomenologically influenced) view of mathematical–logical objects as 'existent' in a separate realm from that of space–time reality and yet accessible to us through a relation of a special kind we bear with objects themselves independently of sensuous experience. Claiming that the ideas of transfinite objects or operations "cannot be known to be meaningful or consistent unless we trust some mathematical intuition of things completely inaccessible to (*add. of the author:* physical) experience" he characterized the existential statement 'there exists' as a transfinite (i.e., non-constructive) concept insofar as this phrase means objective existence regardless of actual producibility in objective spatio-temporality (Feferman et al. 1995, p. 341, fn. 20). Gödel also offered an indirect clue as to an existing ontology of existential assertions in mathematics by pointing out that the fact that they are not taken as a mere 'way of talking' is due to the fact "that they can be disproved (by inconsistencies derived from them) and that they have consequences as to ascertainable facts" (ibid., pp. 355–356).

d. In regarding self-constituting temporality as the ultimate common ground of all phenomenologically motivated analysis of logical–mathematical concepts and meanings (which is my position), the issue of the inverse procession, namely that of passing from a general pure concept to its pure possibilities as its particularizations is also conditioned on the phenomenological notion of time. More specifically the logical requirement of individuality in the sense, for instance, of positing an object-individual as the identical substrate of predicates and logical truths is not just a particularization of the universal concept individual in general but may be bound to the conditions of temporal constitution. This means that in particularizing a formal individual from a universal sentence of a general form in order to fulfill another predicative sentence or formula we may be subject to the requirement of confirmation by a continuous connection of actual and possible intuitions. In turn, the possibility of a continuous connection of actual and possible intuitions is conditioned on the existence of a subjectively generated continuous unity and is associated with a sense of inner temporality, one that is not rooted in the 'external' objective temporality. For instance to check that a subset A of a partially ordered space $(X, \leq)$ is dense in X we must take a random element $x \in X$ and prove the existence of another element y, possibly fulfilling some other property, to satisfy the formula $(\forall x \in X)\, (\exists y \leq x)\, [y \in A]$ (**1**). In case such an element y is a free or bounded variable of a second formula its identification as the particular element that fulfills the definition formula (**1**) of density presupposes the confirmation of all actual and possible intuitions relative to its place in the second formula which is conditioned in turn on the continuous (immanent) unity of all possible connections establishing its prior ontological status (see for some technical details "Appendix 2").

I complete this section with a review of the role of universal-existential quantification over an indefinite horizon in formulas with ontological claims, in particular, in the proof-theoretic process of generation of Gödel's incompleteness results. In fact, universal quantification over an indefinite horizon plays a major part in the proof of almost all significant infinity results in foundational mathematics, e. g., in certain well-known independence results as it is the *Continuum Hypothesis* (**CH**) and its generalized form **GCH**. In this case one has to go a step further and apply a second-order universal quantification over all subsets of the power-set of the set of natural numbers $\mathcal{P}(N)$, a process considered as presupposing a concept of completed totality for the uncountably infinite set $\mathcal{P}(N)$ and therefore as losing contact with 'real-world' intuition.[6] Any statement (or relation) expressed by applying universal quantification over sets such as $\mathcal{P}(N)$ or even $\mathcal{P}(\mathcal{P}(N))$ is normally taken as a definite one with legitimate ontological claims which is evidently a circular interplay since any universal quantification over such sets, regardless of any temporal or constitutional concerns for this quantification, already establishes their de facto acceptance as completed totalities.[7]

Consequently any universal–existential quantification over an indefinite horizon, and *a fortiori* a second-order one clearly presupposes a notion of complete totality for the intended scope of its quantifiers which, in view of the previous discussion at the level of constitutional–temporal processes, reduces to the constitution of infinite sets of any order in the form of the continuous unity of completed wholes in presentational immediacy. In turn, this kind of actual infinity far from being a spatio-temporal and causality-generated one, insofar as it is immanent to the self-constituting temporal consciousness, conditions in one way or another not only the already established key foundational results of K. Gödel and P. Cohen but also certain more recent attempts to achieve enlargements of inner models so as to be consistent with all known large cardinal axioms. I refer, in particular, to H. Woodin's proposed construction of a special enlargement L^{Ω} of Gödel's constructible universe L to provide among other things a better understanding of the transition to large and very large cardinal axioms as well as an elimination of all large cardinal axioms known to contradict the Axiom of Choice (Woodin 2011a, p. 470). Yet, to the extent that this construction is structurally associated

---

[6] The acceptance of the existence of $\mathcal{P}(N)$ (or equivalently of the set 2^N of functions from the set of natural numbers N into the set $\{0,1\}$) as a definite totality requires in S. Feferman's view a platonist ontology, that is, the acceptance of its objective existence independently of human conceptions something that in a certain sense runs contrary to his alternative foundational position of conceptual structuralism (Feferman 2009, pp. 14–15).

[7] A second-order quantification of this kind establishes, for instance, that there exist ω_2 distinct functions from N into $\{0,1\}$ (or equivalently ω_2 distinct subsets of $\mathcal{P}(N)$), in an extended forcing model of standard **ZF** set theory, leading to the proof of the negation of **CH**; see: Kunen (1982, pp. 204–206).

with Woodin's Ω-conjecture it is circularly conditioned on a notion of actual infinity by the very definition of the Ω-completeness which is ultimately based on topological continuity notions (e.g., the property of being universally Baire) (Woodin 2011b, p. 108).

Concerning Gödel's incompleteness results, quantification over an indefinite horizon within the realm of arithmetic is a critical factor in the generation of both incompleteness theorems by formally representing, through the application of universal quantifiers, the non-finitistic content of meta-mathematical statements within arithmetical calculus.[8] In the general view of this article the non-finitistic meta-mathematical content of certain expressions and properties in formal arithmetical calculus can be associated with the kind of actual infinity freely generated through the continuous unity of temporal consciousness and presented as an objective whole in acts of reflection.

As it is known as main pillars in achieving Gödel's incompleteness results stand: (a) Gödel's complete arithmetization of formal (predicate) calculus (b) the complete arithmetization of meta-mathematical statements referring to expressions in the formal calculus and (c) the notion of the mapping of sets of meta-mathematical statements turned to expressions of the formal calculus onto arithmetical ones.

Accordingly, the formula $(\forall x)(\exists y) \neg \text{Dem}(x, y)$ is the arithmetical representation of the meta-mathematical statement 'for every x the sequence of formulas with Gödel number x is not a proof of the formula with Gödel number y'. By an ingenious technique Gödel constructed a universally quantified arithmetical formula (in S.C. Kleene's notation $A_p(\mathbf{p})$) which asserts of itself that it is not demonstrable (even though it is true) and corresponds to the meta-mathematical statement: 'For every x the sequence of formulas with Gödel number x is not a proof of the formula whose Gödel number is the Gödel number of the formula which is obtained by substituting in the place of numerical variable y the Gödel number of the formula $(\forall x) \neg \text{Dem}(x, \text{sub}(y, 13, y))$'. This latter represents in turn the meta-mathematical statement: 'The formula with Gödel number $\text{sub}(y, 13, y)$ is not demonstrable'.[9]

In a definite sense by relying on the mapping of meta-mathematical statements onto arithmetical ones, in other words by arithmetizing a 'non-rigorous' discussion about mathematical objects Gödel essentially transposed meta-mathematical 'pathologies' of a non-finitistic content (those whose range of application is an indefinite horizon) onto arithmetical ones by means of a universal quantification over variables x with x being a Gödel number belonging to a certain (infinite) subset of N.

I note that in Gödel's original presentation it was proved that if the formal arithmetical system is (simply) consistent then $A_p(\mathbf{p})$ is not demonstrable and if the system is ω-consistent[10] then $\neg A_p(\mathbf{p})$ is not demonstrable (ω-consistency implies

---

[8] A simple meta-mathematical statement about natural numbers is the following: 'For every natural number x either x or its successor is odd'.

[9] For an expository presentation of the structure of the incompleteness proofs the reader may look at Nagel and Newman (1958), Ch. VII.

[10] A formal system is said to be ω-consistent if for no variable x and formula $A(x)$ are all of the following true: $A(0)$ is demonstrable, $A(1)$ is demonstrable, $A(2)$ is demonstrable,...,$\neg (\forall x)A(x)$ is demonstrable.

simple consistency). Consequently, if the arithmetical system is ω-consistent then it is incomplete with $A_p(\mathbf{p})$ an example of an undecidable formula (Kleene 1980, pp. 207–208). At this point it is noteworthy that the notion of ω-consistency points indirectly to the views presented in earlier sections, namely those bearing to the fact that mathematical objects or relations in general possess an 'inner' horizon which is open to new insights, new possibilities of intuitive elaboration, even to a mental reconfiguration of apprehended objects with regard to all existing and possible interrelations referring in a significant part to the capacities of a subject's categorial intuition. Technically this has to do here with the fact that a system may be ω-inconsistent without being inconsistent. This means that while formula $(\exists x)\, P(x)$ and some member of the infinite set of $\neg P(0), \neg P(1), \neg P(2), \ldots$ should be both demonstrable by ω-inconsistency definition, the formula $(\forall x)\, \neg P(x)$ may nonetheless not be demonstrable in which case the system in question is not inconsistent since in that case $(\exists x)\, P(x)$ and $(\forall x)\, \neg P(x)$ should be both demonstrable (Nagel and Newman 1958, p. 91). This formal result clearly shows that even though we may have an infinitely proceeding series of identical formulas 'indexed' by corresponding values of variables (these formulas being demonstrable), yet a universal quantification over these values may not yield a demonstrable formula.

In fact, one can hardly interpret this paradoxical situation at the subjective meta-theoretical level than by admitting to some infinity factor underlying universal quantification over an indefinite horizon which is non-eliminable by a discrete 'stepwise' approximation. Moreover, one can hardly proceed to an objectivity of understanding such as $(\forall x)\, \neg P(x)$ through a generation of objectivities like $\neg P(0), \neg P(1), \neg P(2), \ldots$ which correspond to 'real-world' or immanently induced apprehensions, than by admitting to some kind of temporal unity that makes up for the deficiency between the temporal moments of objectifying acts $\neg P(0), \neg P(1), \neg P(2), \ldots$ going on ideally ad infinitum and the temporal moment in which the expression $(\forall x)\, \neg P(x)$ becomes an objectivity of understanding in immediate presentation.

As a matter of fact, both Gödel's incompleteness results in the various forms of their proof can be seen from a certain angle as essentially due to the insufficiency of finitistic arithmetical means to represent meta-mathematical statements incorporating a non-rigorous finitistic content. As meta-mathematical statements are mapped **onto** corresponding arithmetical ones a possible means to formally express the non-finitistic meta-mathematical content is by the application of universal quantifiers with an indefinite scope in the intermediate stage of predicate calculus. In my approach, any universal quantification of an indefinite scope even one concerning the set of natural numbers in its entirety may be taken as ultimately conditioned on the assumption of an actual infinity in the present now independently of any spatiotemporal constraints and at the same time as conditioned on a stepwise enactment of mathematical intuitions (concerning formal individuals or generally 'concrete' mathematical objects) progressing ideally *ad infinitum*. It is thanks to these subjectively founded conditions that there exists a possibility of extending indefinitely the scope of concrete mathematical acts in preserving the essential invariability of corresponding mathematical objects. On these grounds, for instance, we can construct the undecidable formula $A_p(\mathbf{p})$ in a way that the (universally quantified) variable b does not stand with $\mathbf{p}$ in the arithmetical relation $A(\mathbf{p}, b)$, where $\mathbf{p}$ is the Gödel number of the formula $(\forall b) \neg (a, b)$. In the particular case this formal possibility is implemented by applying Cantor's diagonal method which is known to presuppose a meta-theoretical notion of an 'infinite' objective whole in presentational immediacy.

5 Conclusion: A Look at G. Sher's Foundational Holism, R. Tieszen's Constituted Platonism and Other Relevant Views

In the main part of the concluding section I'll sum up the main clues of my position on the nature of mathematical–logical objects and at the same time point to some similarities and divergences in the approaches of G. Sher and R. Tieszen, respectively in Sher (2013) and Tieszen (2011), with some emphasis on R. Tieszen's thesis of constituted platonism which bears a host of common traits with my own position.

Concerning the views of G. Sher, I will refer almost exclusively to certain of her positions on the foundations of logic which form part of the general thesis of foundational holism. Although her views concern basically logic as a normative science appealing to all branches of knowledge yet it is due to the osmotic relation of logic with the research and breakthroughs in the foundations of mathematics that make a review of her position relevant to the scope of this article.

Sher's position is largely an attempt to reconcile the seeming conflict between the need to ground logic in the faculties of the mind and at the same time in the world as its foremost veridical grounding. The grounding in the world is not meant, though, in a naively naturalistic way but rather in the sense that "...there are certain (highly specific) features of the world that logic is grounded in (where 'world' is understood in a relatively broad way), and our task is to explain why logic is grounded in the world at all, what specific features of the world it is grounded in, and how these features ground it. In pursuing this task we will use the foundational-holistic method." (Sher 2013, pp. 15–16). In a certain sense this reasoning may be seen as a further elaboration of her thesis in Sher (2000) on the logical roots of indeterminacy, in particular the view that logical notions themselves "obtain their meaning through the abundance of models and referents (i.e., through the indeterminacy of their extralogical counterparts)" (Sher 2000, p. 118). This approach is clearly distinct from both traditional foundationalist theories which impose a rigid ordering requirement in their methodology and thus reach the impasse of having to justify the grounding of basic units of knowledge to resources out of the system of knowledge and also from coherentism where the coherence of internal relations between various theories and beliefs is the prime factor in securing knowledge at the expense of grounding-in-reality justifications. Foundational holism has a firm inclination toward a justification of logic by factual considerations citing the characteristic though controversial case of quantum logic to present a situation in which a logic is created to conform to the factual data of quantum observations. This way logical relations are conditioned on the way things are-in-the-world in a way that, for instance: "a sentence σ is a (logical) consequence of a set of sentences Σ iff there is an appropriate connection (which ensures truth-preservation with the requisite modal force) between things being as the sentences in Σ say and things being as σ says." (Sher 2013, pp. 19–20).

Therefore, a correct theory of logical consequence must conform to the connections (or to the lack of them) between certain conditions in the world so that the world limits *eo ipso* the scope of logical theories. Husserl in a comparative reference described the eidetic laws of mathematics (meant as axioms) having always in mind that the world is co-posited [his view culminating in the *Krisis* (Husserl 1976b)], even when he characterized the field of categorial intuition in mathematics as the 'empty' field of content-free, general 'somethings-whatsoever'. Yet this conditioning of logic to originating state-of-affairs within the world, in spite of its importance per se, seems to be the only affinity of G. Sher's approach with corresponding Husserlian views started with *LI* and pursued further on in *FTL* and *EU*. To cite an example, Feferman (1999) criticised the Tarski–Sher thesis by claiming that logic in foundational holism is unduly committed to set-theory and the expressibility of mathematical entities within set-theory, whereas "if logical notions are at all to be explicated set-theoretically, they should have the same meaning independent of the exact extent of the set-theoretical universe" (Feferman 1999, p. 38). He further claimed that foundational holism notions such as the logicality criterion[11] for logical constants cannot successfully couch such robust notions as that of absoluteness by citing as an example of logical constant the quantifier *'there exist uncountably many x'* which satisfies the logicality criterion but fails to be absolute and thus qualify for being characterized as logical. However, Feferman himself seems to have an understanding of absoluteness that is 'sensitive to a background set-theory' (ibid. p. 38), while moreover Sher claims that as a feature of the background vocabulary of a formal theory absoluteness is by all accounts not centrally relevant to the foundational problem of logic (Sher 2013, p. 36). Concerning the latter position, even if the notion of absoluteness may be judged as not of primary importance in foundational questions of logic, yet the prominent role attributed to it by Gödel in the proof of the consistency of *Continuum Hypothesis* with **ZFC** and later by Cohen in the proof of the consistency of the negation of *Continuum Hypothesis* with **ZFC** attest to the major if somewhat indirect influence of this notion in shaping the interconnection of mathematical foundations with logic. Moreover, to the extent that absoluteness is taken as sensitive to a background set-theory there is little room left for a more radical, a priori (in fact phenomenologically motivated) reduction of this formal notion that may be ultimately referred to an intentional directedness toward devoid of thingness content distinct formal individuals, their definable collections and categorial properties. In this viewpoint, Husserl proposed a new understanding of the concept of absolute substrate in which "a 'finite' substrate can be experienced simply for itself and thus

---

[11] The Logicality Criterion for logical constants as posited by Sher (2013, p. 33) is concisely as follows: A constant is logical iff:

i. it denotes a formal operator
ii. it is a rigid designator, its meaning is exhausted by its extensional denotation, it is semantically fixed and defined over all models, etc.

has its being-for-itself. But necessarily, is at the same time a determination, that is, it is experienceable as a determination as soon as we consider a more comprehensive substrate in which it is found. Every finite substrate has determinability as being-in-something, and this is true *in infinitum*." (Husserl 1939, p. 137).

In consequence absolute substrates may be notably characterized as completely indeterminate from the point of view of logic, inasmuch as they are taken as individuals in the sense of 'this here' (*Dies-da*), that is, as ultimate material or immaterial substrates of all logical activity. On this account they exclude by themselves everything that may be their determination by a logical activity of a higher level (ibid., pp. 139–140). Anyone who can admit to a reduction of absolute notions to atomic formulas of individuals-substrates bound by logical connectives together with their fundamental categorial properties (e.g. those of of inclusion, order, permutability, etc.), can read in the passages above the vestiges of a subjectively founded and unconstrained by a strictly logical context description of the notion of absoluteness.

One can also point to Sher's thesis on the non-existence of formal individuals[12] to argue that while her logical approach gives to the world and the states-of-affairs within the world (as 'primitive soil') their due in shaping the foundations of logic, her treatment of formal individuals is fairly distinct from a phenomenologically motivated or even simply a subjectively based approach. More specifically, the way she construes individuals is strictly within the context of the formal theory with no concerns about their origin and sense as immanent objects corresponding to 'real-world' or imaginary (quasi) individuals that may be further treated as formal-ontological ones in view of formal mathematics as the field of a formal ontology [see, Husserl (1929) and Husserl (1939), resp. pp. 81–82 and p. 27, pp. 382–383].

In short, while Sher's foundational holism excellently takes into account the world (as a reality of things in the way these are referred to this original 'ground') as a key factor in the foundation of logic, yet she does not seem to consider the possibility of subjectively originating modes of constitution of objects-in-the-world. The outcome of this is a world-grounded logic that is inevitably led from certain veridically justifiable positions to a subsequent 'self-reproducing' formalism. Moreover, she does not consider the possible influence of the inner temporality factor in shaping a well-defined universe of mathematical–logical objects, which is, of course, no mainstream quest even for logicians with some subjective or specifically phenomenological inclination.

I now enter a limited review of R. Tieszen's position of constituted platonism in Tieszen (2011) which is to a considerable extent phenomenologically influenced and close to my own outlook of mathematical–logical objects. The main issues touched by Tieszen are: (i) the acknowledgement of phenomenology as the

---

[12] G. Sher is led to the claim that there are no formal individuals by showing that individuals of a theory cannot fulfill the following Formality Criterion: An operator is formal iff it is invariant under all isomorphisms of its argument-structures (Sher 2013, p. 33).

Firstly, since individuals have no arguments they cannot be differentiated according to what features of their arguments they take or not into account. Secondly, the identity of individuals is not invariant under isomorphisms, that is, given any individual α and a structure $<A, \alpha>$, there is a structure $<A', \alpha'>$ such that $<A', \alpha'> \cong <A, \alpha>$ and yet $\alpha \neq \alpha'$ (ibid. p. 40).

descriptive science, in fact a universal eidetic ontology, of all phenomena proper to subjectivity and intersubjectivity which amounts to its recognition as an a priori science of all possible existence and existences (Tieszen 2011, p. 25), (ii) the foundation of each a priori concept or act on subjective processes reaching the level of intentional constitution engendered by the ego (monad), (iii) the possibility of interpreting mathematical–logical sciences in the sense of a priori ones by founding their methods and premises on phenomenological analysis, (iv) the foundation of ideal objects and generally of idealities, in sharp contrast with rational platonism, on a subjectively based intuition of essences which is a process of ideation termed in Husserl's later works as *Wesenschau*. Except for the origin of ideal objects in our sense-constituting processes another issue that may be raised is the possibility of constitution of the meaning of beings in the world through the intentionality of the full concreteness of ego, (v) the a priori directedness of intentionality associated not only with sensory objects but also with immanent ones (temporal in nature and generated by 'inner' mental processes) and even ideal ones (non-spatial and 'atemporal' objects such as numbers, elements of sets, aggregation of elements, etc.). This way, intentional orientation is not necessarily bound to objective spatiotemporality and causality insofar as intentional directedness is not conditioned on the existence of its objects in absolute spatio-temporal terms but rather on the 'content' or 'meaning' associated in each occurrence with intentional acts, (vi) A characterization of mathematical–logical objects as mind-dependent$_1$ and mind-independent$_2$ (where mind-independence$_2$ falls under mind-dependence$_1$), in the sense that they are intentional objects not constrained by material and causal preoccupations and yet not arbitrary ideal 'counterparts' of appearances in front of consciousness or pure constructs of imagination (ibid., p. 115). This schematic classification is in fact founded on Tieszen's phenomenologically rooted view of mathematical–logical objects as taken their whole sense of being from a subject's intentionality. In his words, "There is no way that life of consciousness could be broken through so that a transcendent mathematical or logical object might have some other sense than that of an intentional unity (invariant) making its appearance in the subjectivity of consciousness." (ibid., p. 109).

Tieszen's general approach is meant as an attempt, on phenomenologically motivated grounds, to do also justice to Gödel's preoccupations on the foundation of abstract concepts and meanings in mathematics especially in the light of his incompleteness results and the subsequent independence of the *Continuum Hypothesis* and the *Axiom of Choice* from the rest of the axioms of **ZF** theory. On this account, a main concern of Tieszen's constituted platonism is related to Gödel's and platonists' question over how it is possible for human reason (or human mind) to know about transcendent objects like large transfinite sets or strongly inaccessible cardinals that do not belong to the physical world. Tieszen's proposed answer is that the transcendental ego (or monad) constitutes in a rationally motivated manner the meaning of being of mathematical–logical objects as ideal or abstract and mind-independent$_2$ in the sense of being non-arbitrary products of the intentional capacities of consciousness in accordance with what is experienced as mathematical practice in terms of a predicative activity within the world. Yet one should be careful enough to the content that may be given to the Husserlian notion of intentionality taking into account that originally this concept is referred to as the a priori directedness of consciousness to objects standing 'in person' in front of it irrespectively, in principle, of material or immaterial content and also of spatiotemporal and causal constraints. Further, in the Husserlian texts especially after the time of *LI* intentionality and generally intentional forms of consciousness as a priori forms of 'awareness' are largely meant as passive features of the constituting activity of consciousness[13] Therefore certain concerns might be raised as to what extent intentionality or intentional forms of consciousness can be associated with predicative activities of the mind, e.g., with the being and meaning of mathematical objects, propositions, proofs of theorems, etc. This is what Tieszen seems to propose by making reference to the 'intentionality of human reason', while indicating at the same time that "The way to bridge the gap between human subjectivity and mathematical objectivity is to fill in the account of the kinds of founded intentional acts and processes that make the constitution of the meaning of being of mathematical and logical objects possible" (ibid., p. 80). Elsewhere he claims that "knowledge involves intentionality, and our mathematical intentions can be (partially) fulfilled (in intuition), frustrated, or neither fulfilled nor frustrated" and that "Constituted platonism is concerned with the kind of directedness (intentionality) involved in thinking and problem-solving in the practice of mathematics and logic" (ibid., p. 104).

Yet, intentional forms of mathematical–logical activity may be present only as passive co-constitutive factors in the constitution of mathematical objectivities of various levels. Therefore their assumption in Tieszen's sense as shaping the status and meaning of mathematical entities seems to contradict the a priori nature of intentionality in the first place. Husserl described in *FTL* and *EU* in a certain way and partly in terms of the intentionality of consciousness the formation both of lowest-level mathematical objects (e.g., formal individuals, absolute substrates) and higher-level ones (e.g. sets, classes, infinite wholes, etc.) as essentially noematic objects on the constitutional level. For example, quite apart from his early psychologistic preoccupations Husserl founded in *EU* the concept of a set on an act of thematic apprehension, possible at any time, making what is preconstituted by a colligating consciousness as a plurality of objects into a thematic object-substrate, that is, a set meant in the sense of plurality as unity (see Sect. 3). It is quite interesting to see that after this apprehending act, a set can be possibly further elaborated by a closing-in intuition and by new hitherto unknown affections brought into play so that previously intended unities are decomposed as pluralities and so on until one reaches ultimate constituents which are themselves no longer sets (Husserl 1939, p. 247). Evidently this is a position that considers intentional features of consciousness as co-constituting factors of mathematical–logical objects of various levels in the form of well-meant transtemporal objectivities. However this may not associate intentional features as a priori ones with any further meaning as part of a post-constitutional predicative activity.

---

[13] This is meant in the sense that consciousness cannot but exhibit each moment intentionality toward an object irrespectively of a material or formal content.

What is the Nature of Mathematical-Logical Objects?

In general, constituted platonism to a significant extent meets my own view of mathematical-logical objects, for instance, in categorizing mathematical and logical objects as mind-dependent$_1$ and mind-independent$_2$ with the meaning given to these terms (Sect. 5, § 8). I would like to add, though, that Tieszen's denying of Hilbert's approach to objects or constructions of mathematical theories as reducible to immediate sensory perceptions of sign tokens and the proposition of categorial intuition and certain intentional forms of consciousness to accede, for instance, to 'second order' mathematical concepts such as the transfinite sets enters us more generally into some tricky questions with regard to the fundamentals of Husserlian approach. For example, it is not very clear how it is possible to talk, e.g., about formal individuals as objects of a 'lowest-level' intentionality which are not necessarily causally related to the subject, namely about those individuals generated non-arbitrarily in imagination and yet not possessing an absolute 'real-world' temporal position. What I want to say is that one may propose the a priori directedness of intentionality to account for the possibility of grasping and reflecting on mathematical objects-individuals (and generally on collections of such objects and their categorical properties) and yet we have no means to describe this a priori directedness but in terms of the contents of its enactments considered as already objectified. However, in being objectified the intentional contents in question are already constituted as real objectivities and 'spatio-temporal like'.

This is yet another issue that goes deep enough to the endless circularity reflecting-reflected and consequently to the dubiously non-objective character of intentionality in the sense that there is posed the circular question of whether intentional directedness precedes objectification upon its enactment or it is the reverse way around. This means that positing an intentional enactment as a priori referred to a 'something-whatsoever' independently of any spatiotemporal constraints is in a certain sense self-contradictory by the simple fact that even in passively reflecting on the intentional act causes the objectification of its content in the present now as an already real spatio-temporal objectivity even if it does not correspond to an absolute 'real world' time and place.[14]

I do not leave without notice Tieszen's distinction of the notion of transfinite sets from that of the denumerably infinite sets in that in the latter case we have a way, e.g., through a recursion formula, to grasp the totality of the elements of the corresponding sets while the same does not happen in the case of non-denumerably infinite sets. This is a view that seems consistent with a phenomenological perspective and also with Tieszen's specific description of mathematical objects as ideal, abstract and mind-independent$_2$. My own view is that transfiniteness (generally non-denumerable infinity of any scale) to the extent that it is associated with the notion of mathematical continuum may be based in turn on that of the intuitive continuum and founded in a radical non-reductionistic approach on the original source of the continuous unity of temporal consciousness. Ultimately, I think that the absolute flux of temporality objectified as a continuous, homogenous unity (thematized upon reflection) and its absolute subjective origin may hold the key to comprehend non-denumerable infinity

---

[14] I refer in this regard to J. S. Churchill's introduction in *Experience and Judgment* (Husserl 1939, p. xix) and K. Michalski's *Logic and Time* in Michalski (1997, pp. 136 and 138).

as an abstracted completed whole in the immanence of consciousness. In this respect, I find the canonical scaling of non-denumerable infinities following $\aleph_1$, and generally the talk about inaccessible or strongly inaccessible cardinals as rather a mathematical recreation with no corresponding 'real world' or purely immanent intuitions. To what extent inner temporality affects our conception of mathematical–logical objects is a great and rather murky issue per se, and, it is true, constituted platonism gives it a due attention although it does not enter into further consideration of the founding role of temporality as such in constituting mathematical–logical objects. For instance, Tieszen refers to the temporal character of mathematical–logical objects, characterized by Husserl as omnitemporal in the sense of being identically and intersubjectively the same across places and times (by virtue of their immanent appearances), and also to the non-reductionistic phenomenological investigation of human consciousness as standing in the background of mathematics and logic without further dealing with the matter on the level of temporality (Tieszen 2011, p. 110 and p. 225).

These issues have been also the focus of recent research work of other people oriented in the interface of phenomenology with mathematics and logic especially those taking into account Husserl's gradual evolution toward transcendental phenomenology. I refer in particular to the articles of Ortiz-Hill (2013), da Silva (2013) and Hauser (2006). Hauser (2006) reviews K. Gödel's version of mathematical realism on account of phenomenological analysis given the fact that Gödel had started a systematic reading of Husserl's main works (*Ideas I* and *Logical Investigations* among them) from the early 1960s onward. What comes out is that the kind of mathematical realism defended by Gödel, even though it bears an imprint of phenomenological influence, e.g. when talking about the epistemic non-eliminability of mathematical intuition or "the fundamental property of the mind to comprehend multitudes into unities. Sets are multitudes which are also unities. A multitude is the opposite of a unity.[...]It is a seemingly contradictory fact that sets exist. It is surprising that the fact that multitudes are also unities leads to no contradictions: this is the main fact of mathematics." (Wang 1996, p. 254), it cannot actually be defensible in a consistently phenomenological and more generally subjectively founded approach.

From a phenomenological standpoint one cannot conceive the fundamental property of the mind to comprehend multitudes into unities and correspondingly provide a foundation to the concept of set without associating this property of the mind with the temporality factor to the extent that mathematical objects become objects in immanence. For Husserl this kind of unity within the immanence of consciousness is the objective form of the self-constituting source of inner temporality, i.e., what he called the absolute ego of consciousness from as early as the time of the *Lessons on the Phenomenology of Inner Time Consciousness* and the *Cartesian Meditations*. There is nowhere in Gödel's writings any hint on the possibility of specifically founding unity, e.g., with regard to infinite mathematical collections (taken as completed wholes) on the subjective temporality factor,[15]

---

[15] As a matter of fact, there is a relevant Gödel hint as described by Wang (1996) but there he refers generally to time as the only natural frame of reference for the mind; there is also an allusion to the fact that our intuitive concept of time is not objective or objectively representable (p. 319).

especially in view of the fact that for a phenomenologist Gödel's orientation toward a mind-independence of mathematical objects turns out to be a 'transcendence in immanence', irrespectively whether we talk about real or ideal objects (Hauser 2006, p. 578). In this regard, it is highly questionable, from a phenomenological point of view, Hauser's claim that the idea of sets as categorial objects (experienced as mental representations in a higher-order act) constituting themselves 'within' the stream of consciousness is compatible with the view of mathematical objects existing independently of our mental acts and dispositions which is a core matter of Gödel's mathematical realism (ibid., p. 559).

It is not pointless to refer here to da Silva's view in da Silva (2013), that genetic phenomenology presents an alternative to the "misleading and utterly preposterous view that the mathematical realm of sets has an independent existence, just like the empirical world.". Both, for da Silva, as objects of the Ego require complex processes of intentional constitution in which case concerning the empirical reality this rests on a 'given formless hyletic material' while concerning mathematical sets these are considered as pure forms existing only as intentional correlates even in the absence of a direct intuition (da Silva 2013, p. 97). With regard to da Silva's approach toward set constitution and his position (from a phenomenological vantage point) that the transcendental ego constitutes the domain of mathematical sets and its theory through the intermediate stage of what he calls empirical sets (in contradistinction with finite collections of material objects naively conceived), my main argument against is that he downplays the role of the temporality factor in attributing to the otherwise atemporal ego meaning-giving acts that cannot be conceived but within temporality. While he refers, for instance, interestingly enough to the notion of well-foundedness of sets as emanating from the intentional activity of the ego toward constituting empirical sets by making the process of set constitution no longer associated with the sequence of natural numbers but instead "insofar as the well-ordering of all well-orderings allows", yet the fundamental property of the mind to apprehend multitudes into unities which ultimately provides the foundation to the concept of set (especially a transfinite one) cannot be properly explained without engaging the temporality factor, more precisely the self-constituting inner temporality.[16] Da Silva's position on the role and the attributes of the transcendental ego in the constitution of mathematical objects deserves a lengthy discussion per se which would however come down to its essential nature and the legitimacy of linguistic conventions referring to it, something that would take us too far astray. My main point is that one cannot have a properly meant view of the constitution of mathematical objects without involving the temporality factor in the sense it acquires in the phenomenology of temporal consciousness,

---

[16] For example, the acts of collection of objects and their 'subsequent' unification to an (empirical) set seem to be separate intentional acts of the ego (ibid., p. 90), whereas in my own view they are two distinct aspects of the same constituting process insofar as a collection cannot be meaningfully comprehended but in terms of a temporal instantaneity in which distinct intentional acts are conceived as one in the present now of consciousness, something that obviously demands the joint availability of all the elements of a set at once (be it an infinite one) at least for those sets in the same stage of a certain hierarchy. However reflecting on a plurality in temporal instantaneity presupposes already an act of unification temporally constituted.

irrespectively of the 'second order' question of the origin of inner temporality itself which ultimately enters the question of an atemporal ego.

A position that mainly derives its argumentation from earlier texts of Husserl (around the time of the *Logical Investigations* and the *General Theory of Knowledge* (*Allgemeine Erkenntnistheorie*), both between 1900 and 1908), is defended by Ortiz-Hill (2013), where she tries to delineate a border line between the ideal objectivities of pure logic and mathematics, e.g., the concept of number as such, and purely subjective processes belonging to the field of transcendental phenomenology even in rejecting any trait of psychologism in this respect. On this account, she refers to Husserl's early views on what is and what is not phenomenology (Ortiz-Hill 2013, p. 67) barring, among others, natural sciences and also mathematics and formal logic from being characterized as belonging to phenomenology, while referring also to his claim in 1902–1903 that pure logic is the science of the form concepts to which "the objective content of all logical, all scientific thinking in general is subject". In view of these Husserlian theses, Ortiz-Hill strongly supports that all mathematical concepts are purely logical and at some point ties the proposed ideal objectivity of the mathematical and purely logical universe to Husserl's (subsequent to the *Logical Investigations*) espousing of the notion of a general, vacuous of content, 'anything-whatsoever' whose domain is the field of formal ontology which is further considered in abstraction as the field of pure arithmetic (ibid., pp. 69–70). Arguing against Ortiz-Hill's tendency to defend a strict incompatibility between the purely ideal character of objects and meanings of formal logic, consequently leading to their reduction to the field of analyticity, and the acts of a subject exhibiting intentional characteristics, one can reasonably claim the following:

In *Experience and Judgment*, that is, essentially in his genealogy of logic and first time in a systematic fashion, Husserl accepted and highlighted the role that transcendental phenomenology has to play into securing a (partially) subjectively based foundation for mathematical–logical concepts, thus distancing himself from his earlier rigidity with regard to the purely ideal character of mathematical–logical objects; this Ortiz-Hill acknowledges on pp. 76–77 while pointing to Husserl's own admission of the vagueness existing in the boundaries between the ideal objectivity of logical structures and the constitutive, subjective dimension (p. 79). Further given Husserl's later views, the fact that the domain of arithmetic is taken *in abstracto* to be the domain of the 'anything-whatsoever' and of its modalities should not be thought of as introducing (even indirectly) any kind of objective idealism with regard to logical-mathematical objects and the associated truths. For, evidently, the vacuous of content 'anything-whatsoever' cannot be thought of otherwise but as an intentional correlate of a consciousness, something clearly compatible with the view of an intentional correlate being existent solely in terms of referring to an intentional consciousness (whose 'possession' it is) without necessarily having a material content and a causal relation to the subjectivity. At least with regard to this latter assertion both Tieszen and Hauser seem to have taken the same position.

In conclusion, phenomenologically talking, the mind independence of mathematical objects espoused by Gödel turns out to be a 'transcendence' in immanence which is further reducible to the ultimate source of a transcendental subjectivity to which world and objective reality as phenomena refer to. This means, taking also into account Husserl's idea of eidos as freed of all metaphysical interpretations, that his position is not reducible to any kind of ideal objectivism therefore standing in obvious opposition, e.g., with Gödel's view of a set in the expression 'a set of x's' or of any other paraphrased one as something that exists in itself "no matter whether we can define it in a finite number of words" (Feferman et al. 1990, fn. 14, p. 259).

In view of all that was argued in this paper, mathematical and in a wider sense mathematical–logical objects established as such within formal theories are largely shaped by the constitutional-intentional capacities of each one's consciousness in intersubjective coincidence in a way that their formation is constrained by each one's specific presence in the world (as the soil of primitive experience) and also by the mathematical intuitions associated with this kind of presence. These intuitions corresponding to such features of reason as abstraction, idealization, invariability in transformation, the sense of symmetry, permutation, uniformity, etc., are not intentional capacities of consciousness, at least in a pure reality-independent sense, as they are not conceivable without reference to a reality transcendent to a self-constituting subjectivity, even non-conceivable without reference to a reality impregnated with a sort of historicity with respect to the existence of all conscious beings as its co-constituting and reduction performing factors. Given that mathematical–logical objects, as long as we go up the level of abstraction and complexity, acquire a widening inner horizon of content and properties, an interesting question to raise is the extent to which a further quest on the character of inner temporality of consciousness might further clarify the inner horizon especially of transfinite objects. For what is an undeniable fact reducible to the evidence of cogito is the non-eliminable 'superfluity' of an objective whole in actual reflection, be it in extreme cases a transfinite set or a huge cardinal on the level of constituted, with regard to the generating predicative activities of the mind in discrete steps within objective time. This kind of 'deficiency' in subjective constitution that ultimately seems as temporal in nature can be partly accountable for a characterization of mathematical–logical objects within the context of formal theories as intersubjectively identical, transtemporal ones and yet provided with an 'inner' and 'outer' horizon open to potentially new insights and clarifications corresponding to possible further refinements in the future to come of the intentional-predicative capacities of the mind. In this view the non-eliminability of the mathematically transfinite and the associated meanings of non-finitistic objects might be seen as a question pointing to the need for a further clarification, if feasible at all on the constitutional level, of the notion of a self-constituting temporality and the way it underlies the meaning-giving acts of the mathematical mind.

Appendix 1

A convenient reference to the possibility of introduction of nonstandard elements by means of the notion of an 'internal horizon' of (standard) objects is E. Nelson's axiomatical foundation of Internal Set Theory (IST) (Nelson 1986, pp. 4–14). More specifically, a key part of the syntax of the theory stands the undefined predicate

What is the Nature of Mathematical-Logical Objects?

standard which is the formal equivalent, so to say, of the notion of a fixed object in informal mathematical discourse. Though this new predicate has a syntactical rather than a semantical content it acquires by three *ad hoc* postulated axioms (the transfer (T), the idealization (I) and standardization axioms (S)) a metatheoretical sense of the 'fixedness' of individuals, these latter possibly conceived as either corresponding to real-world counterparts or as pure products of imagination acting, e.g., as substrates of objectivities of understanding. In the present case these objectivities of understanding may be represented by predicate formulas of classical mathematics whose variables are standard (classical) ones. The following two axioms may be taken as corroborating the claim that the introduction of nonstandard individuals can be associated on the constitutional level with the notion of an 'internal horizon' of standard ('fixed') objects.

The Transfer Principle (**T**):

$$\forall^{st} t_1 ... \forall^{st} t_n \; [\forall^{st} x \, A \leftrightarrow \forall x \, A]$$

where A is an internal formula (i.e., one of classical mathematics which does not include the new predicate *standard*) whose only free variables are $x, t_1, t_2, ..., t_n$

The intuition behind (T) is that if something is true for a fixed, but arbitrary x, then it is true for all x.

The Idealization Principle (**I**):

$$\forall^{stfin} x' \; \exists y \; \forall x \in x' \, A \leftrightarrow \exists y \; \forall^{st} x \, A$$

where A is again an internal formula.

In loose terms, to say that there is a y for all fixed x such that we have A, is the same as saying that there is a y for any fixed finite set of x's such that A holds for all of them. Put more naively, we can only fix a finite number of objects at a time.

Now we can prove by means of these principles that any infinite set includes a nonstandard element, in other words it includes an element that might be larger or smaller than any standard one. The formal proof is very easy and straightforward (ibid. pp. 7–8). Let the classical mathematical formula (internal formula) be $x \neq y$. Then by the (**I**) principle for every standard finite set x' there is an element y such that for all $x \in x'$, $x \neq y$ and this is equivalent to saying that for every standard x we have $x \neq y$. Further, if we take x and y to range over infinite sets we deduce that in every infinite set there is at least a nonstandard element. In particular, there exists at least a nonstandard natural number.

To come up to this result we have first to assume a notion of 'fixedness' for those objects termed as standard, expressed as such by syntactical means, which cannot be meant otherwise than by taking these objects in a lowest-level sense as concrete individuals of intentionality possibly presentified any time at will in reflection. Next, they can be thought to possess a horizon of 'fixedness' ideally extensible to indefinite bounds by means of universal or universal-existential quantifiers respectively in the principles (T) and (I). Referring to the principle (I) in particular, one may 'keep track of the fixedness' of standard elements as concrete individuals and each time verify the existence of an element distinct from those fixed ones apprehended thus far. To the extent that we can project this kind of intuition from

What is the Nature of Mathematical-Logical Objects?

the finitary level to any 'fixed' level extending it indefinitely, we can say that it may exist a nonstandard element whose existence is conditioned on the possibility of applying ideally *ad infinitum* intentional acts performed within the 'internal horizon' of standard objects in a non-arbitrary way; that is, in accordance with the syntactical–logical structure of the corresponding predicate formula. In this view, **T** and **I** principles are irreal objectivities as intended senses which are always the same (being intersubjectively identical) and whose substrates are formal individuals, i.e., individuals not necessarily corresponding to 'real-world' counterparts, having an 'internal horizon'. A further elaboration of this horizon by means of the intentional faculties of a subject's ego may lead, and indeed does on the formal level in the case at hand, to new mathematical entities/states-of-affairs.

Appendix 2

Here is an easy example from forcing theory of how a particularization of a formal individual from a universal sentence of a general form to fulfill another predicative sentence is subject to the requirement of 'confirmation' by a continuous connection of actual and possible intuitions. I will skip some subtleties of relevant definitions which are too technical for a philosophical reader (or even for a mathematician not knowledgeable of forcing theory) and moreover do not have a special significance for my arguments. Let's start with the definition of a set A that is dense below an element p:

If P is a partial order and $p \in P$ then the set A is dense below p iff:

$$\forall q \leq p \; \exists r \leq q \; (r \in A) \quad \textbf{(I)}$$

Let $p \in P$ and $\varphi(\tau_1,..\tau_n)$ a formula whose free variables $x_1,..,x_1$ have been replaced by P-names $\tau_1,..,\tau_n$ which may be roughly thought of as individuals of forcing theory (for further details see: Kunen 1982, pp. 186–204).

The forcing relation $p\Vdash_{P,M}\varphi(\tau_1,..,\tau_n)$ relative to a base model M of the standard set theory **ZFC** is defined by a certain logical equivalence which notably involves a second order quantification over generic sets G (Kunen 1982, p. 194). Then it holds that the following relation **(1)** implies **(2)**:

(1) Given that $p\Vdash\varphi(\tau_1,..,\tau_n)$ holds, then $\forall r \leq p \; [r\Vdash \varphi(\tau_1,..\tau_n)]$
(2) The set $\{r; \; r\Vdash \varphi(\tau_1,..\tau_n)\}$ is dense below p

The almost trivial proof, given the definition **(I)** and and relation **(1)**, is as follows: Let $A = \{r; \; r\Vdash \varphi(\tau_1,..\tau_n)\}$. By definition **(I)** we must prove that

$$\forall r \leq p \; \exists w \leq r \; (w \in A)$$

Then by relation **(1)** given any r there is always a $w \leq r$ such that obviously $w \in A \; \diamond$.

The point here is that the element w satisfying the density below p property of A is confirmed as such after first being identified as the one that fulfills the universal quantification formula $\forall r \leq p \; [r\Vdash \varphi(\tau_1,..\tau_n)]$ of **(1)** which further means that we must have previously formed in actual unity the formula $\forall r \leq p \ [r \Vdash \varphi(\tau_1, .. \tau_n)]$ as an objectivity of understanding implying the continuous connection of all possible intuitions. All the more so as here is involved a universal quantification formula over bounded variable r which presupposes a notion of a completed infinite whole, the scope of the bounded variable r, in presentational immediacy.

References

Aristotle (1989) Aristotle XVII. Metaphysics I-IX (trans: Treddenick H). The Loeb Classical Library. Harvard University Press, Cambridge
da Silva J (2013) How sets came to be: the concept of set from a phenomenological perspective. In: Hopkins B, Drummond J (eds) The new yearbook for phenomenology and phenomenological philosophy, vol 13, pp 84–101
Feferman S (1999) Logic, logics, and logicism. Notre Dame J Form Log 40:31–54
Feferman S (2009) Conceptions of the continuum. Intellectica 51:169–189
Feferman S et al (eds) (1990) Kurt Gödel: collected works II. Oxford University Press, Oxford
Feferman S et al (eds) (1995) Kurt Gödel: collected works III. Oxford University Press, Oxford
Hartimo M (2006) Mathematical roots of phenomenology: Husserl and the concept of number. Hist Philos Log 27:319–337
Hauser K (2006) Gödel's program revisited part I: the turn to phenomenology. Bull Symb Logic 12 (4):529–590
Husserl E (1929) Formale und Transzendentale Logik. Max Niemeyer Verlag, Halle
Husserl E (1966) Vorlesungen zur Phänomenologie des inneren Zeibewusstseins, Hua, Band X, hsgb. R. Boehm. M. Nijhoff, Den Haag
Husserl E (1970) Philosophie der Arithmetik, Hua Band XII, hsgb. L. Eley. M. Nijhoff, Den Haag
Husserl E (1939) Erfahrung und Urteil, hsgb. L. Landgrebe, Prag: Acad./Verlagsbuchhandlung. Engl. translation: (1973) Experience and judgment (trans: Churchill JS, Americs K). Routledge & Kegan Paul, London
Husserl E (1976a) Ideen zu einer reinen Phänomenologie und phänomenologischen Philosophie, Erstes Buch, Hua Band III/I, hsgb. K. Schuhmann. M. Nijhoff, Den Haag
Husserl E (1976b) Die Krisis der Europäischen Wissenschaften und die Transzendentale Phänomenologie, Hua Band VI, hsgb. W. Biemel. M. Nijhoff, Den Haag
Kleene SC (1980) Introduction to metamathematics. North-Holland Pub, New-York
Krause D, Coelho AMN (2005) Identity, indiscernibility, and philosophical claims. Axiomathes 15:191–210
Kunen K (1982) Set theory. An introduction to independence proofs. Elsevier Sci. Pub, Amsterdam
Michalski K (1997) Logic and time. Kluwer Academemic Publishers, Dordrecht
Nagel E, Newman J (1958) Gödel's proof. New York University Press, NY
Nelson E (1986) Predicative arithmetic. Mathematical notes. Princeton Univ. Press, Princeton
Ortiz-Hill C (2013) The strange worlds of actual consciousness and the purely logical. In: The new yearbook for phenomenology and phenomenological philosophy, vol 13, pp 62–83
Parsons C (2008) Mathematical thought and its objects. Cambridge University Press, Cambridge
Quine VW (1947) On universals. J Symb Log 12(3):74–84
Sher G (2000) The logical roots of indeterminacy. In: Sher G, Tieszen R (eds) Between logic and intuition. Cambridge University Press, Cambridge, pp 100–124
Sher G (2013) The foundational problem of logic. Bull Symb Log 19:145–198
Tieszen R (2011) After Gödel: platonism and rationalism in mathematics and logic. Oxford University Press, Oxford
Wang H (1996) A logical journey. From Gödel to philosophy. MIT Press, Cambridge
Weyl H (1994) The continuum (trans: Pollard S, Bole T). Dover Pub, New York
Woodin HW (2011a) The transfinite universe. In: Baaz M et al (eds) Kurt Gödel and the foundations of mathematics. Cambridge University Press, NY, pp 449–471
Woodin HW (2011b) The realm of the infinite. In: Heller M, Woodin HW (eds) Infinity, new research frontiers. Cambridge University Press, NY, pp 89–118

Weyl's Conception of the Continuum in a Husserlian Transcendental Perspective

This article attempts to broaden the phenomenologically motivated perspective of H. Weyl's *Das Kontinuum* (1918) in the hope of elucidating the differences between the intuitive and mathematical continuum and further providing a deeper phenomenological interpretation. It is known that Weyl sought to develop an arithmetically based theory of continuum with the reasoning that one should be based on the naturally accessible domain of natural numbers and on the classical first-order predicate calculus to found a theory of mathematical continuum free of impredicative circularities (such as the standard definition of the least upper bound of a set of real numbers) only to stumble, to cite a key question, in the evident lack of intuitive support for the notion of points of the continuum. In this motivation, I set out to deal from a Husserlian viewpoint with the general notion of points as appearances reducible to individuals of pre-predicative experience in contrast with the notion of an interval of real numbers taken as an abstraction based on the intuition of time-flowing experience. I argue that the notions of points and of real intervals in the above sense are not by essence related to objective temporality and thus their incompatibility in mathematical terms is ultimately due to deeper constituting reasons independently of any causal and spatio-temporal constraints.

1. Introduction

This phenomenologically motivated article is primarily based on Hermann Weyl's famous monograph *Das Kontinuum* (henceforth *DK*), first published in 1918, and still remaining the broadest known mathematical text in foundations taking into account Husserl's phenomenology of inner time-consciousness in the problematic of mathematical continuum. I note here that

Husserl's student Oscar Becker had also published mathematical-philosophical texts influenced by the Husserlian phenomenology (Becker 1914; Becker 1927) and has been lately found to have had an interesting correspondence on these matters with Weyl himself.[1]

As J. da Silva has put it, the strict adherence of Weyl's arithmetical theory to what had been disclosed in the phenomenological analysis of intuitive continuum, most notably the acceptance of everything originally given as given in its "bodily" form in the modes and the bounds presented therein, makes it possible that phenomenological ideas can help us achieve a deeper insight into the mathematical theory of DK (Da Silva 1997, 281). Not to weigh less in the overall evaluation of the content of DK is H. Weyl's general scientific formation and his fundamental work in the theory of relativity[2] which made him especially apt in grasping the fundamental questions that a deeper analysis of spatiotemporal continuum generates, especially in the face of certain theoretical deficiencies with regard to a predicative foundation of continuum in taking into account the nature of the system of real numbers. It should be added that interest in Weyl's program for the arithmetical foundation of mathematics initiated with *Das Kontinuum*, originally overshadowed by Hilbert's finitistic foundations program in mathematics and L.E.J. Brouwer's intuitionistic theory, has been to a certain extent revived thanks to a considerable research work that has helped underline its significance for a viable predicative theory in mathematics (Feferman 1998, 249).[3] It is notable, though, that in the years following the first publication of DK and possibly due to insurmountable difficulties in eliminating, among others, an impredicative definition of the least upper bound principle for reals as well as certain measurability results, Weyl abandoned the phenomenological motivation of the original system of DK to espouse Brouwer's intuitionistic model of choice sequences. Later on he even went so far as to deny the relevance of phenomenological analysis altogether with regard to classical mathematics, especially in taking the latter as an objectifying metatheory for physics, on the assumption that Hilbert's formalism prevails over intuitionism. Of course it is known that Hilbert's formalism and his finitistic consistency program for mathematics suffered a serious blow just a few years

---

[1] On the correspondence between Weyl and Becker see the work of T. Ryckman and P. Mancosu in (Ryckman and Mancosu 2002; Ryckman and Mancosu 2005). The reader is also referred to (Ryckman and Mancosu 2002) for details on Weyl's first exposure to phenomenological analysis dating back to his graduate years between 1904 and 1908. In Weyl's own confession it was around 1912 in Göttingen that he "owed to Husserl's influence a liberation from his previous positivistic allegiances" (Ryckman and Mancosu 2002, 132).

[2] See, for instance, his *Space-Time-Matter* (1922), first published in the same year as DK.

[3] Among the recent literature on the subject one can cite (Feferman 2000), (Feist 2002) and (Feist 2004).

ahead with Gödel's incompleteness results.[4] However, I will leave out of discussion Weyl's subsequent estrangement from Husserlian phenomenology and try instead to offer a deeper phenomenological perspective to certain key concepts of the *DK* system with regard to the mathematical vs intuitive continuum.

Generally Weyl's approach in *DK* may be viewed in the wake of the theoretical discussions provoked by Cantor's introduction in the late 19th century of the theory of infinite ordinals and cardinals as well as the notion of transfinite sets in the foundations of mathematics, and the subsequent attempts to secure a sound foundation of set theory excluding apparent antinomies such as the set of all sets. In this general setting Weyl was largely influenced by Poincaré's definitionist approach of mathematics which implied the acceptance of the following general positions:

(i) the concept of a natural number sequence as an irreducible minimum of any abstract mathematical thought and the ensuing acceptance of the principle of induction as a key proof-theoretic tool; (ii) the acceptance that all other mathematical concepts, e.g., those of sets and functions, are to be introduced by an explicit definition founded on the acceptance of position (i); (iii) the thesis that there are not in principle completed infinite totalities; and (iv) the claim that definitions which single out a definite mathematical object by implicit or explicit reference to an assumed complete totality of which the defined object is a part should be excluded altogether from mathematics. Position (iv) is apparently the predicativist position in mathematics which in later years provided for many theoretical discussions and also for alternative approaches in the mathematical foundations (Feferman 1998, 254). Except for those properly espousing the definitionist-predicativist approach of mathematical theories, the acceptance of the domain of natural numbers as the most fundamental domain of mathematical intuition is to be found also in Kurt Gödel's writings suggesting that arithmetic in mathematics is the domain of elementary indisputable evidence that may be most fittingly compared with sense perception in the case of sensory knowledge (Tieszen 2011, 176). In a certain sense this view is reflected in Husserl's writings too with reference, for instance, to the determination of thematic objects (including perceptual ones) in the form of "*and so on*" in which every object-substrate of determination is always passively pregiven with an original horizon of indeterminate determinability "beyond the succession of actually constituted determinations and open to new properties which must be expected" (Husserl 1939, 217–218).

---

[4] A discussion of Weyl's later objections to phenomenological analysis in relation to mathematics, as presented by him in the mathematics seminar of the university of Hamburg in 1927, is undertaken by J. Toader in (Toader 2013a) and (Toader 2013b).

On this account, Weyl's three major theoretical positions can be summed up as follows: (i) definitionism as the conditioning of the introduction of any ideal entity on the explicit relations linking its constituent elements; (ii) intuitionism implying a mathematical universe in which all entities are assumed to be generated by logical principles from a basic category of objects given intuitively as primitive objects and relations irreducible to anything semantically more fundamental. In contrast to Brouwerian intuitionism, Weyl's original version admits of a definite truth-value for every well-built proposition involving only primitive objects and consequently does not contradict the Excluded Middle Principle; (iii) predicativism as the rejection of every impredicative definition, that is, of every definition that presupposes the knowledge of the totality of objects among which the object to be defined is taken. This position is materialized by restricting the scope of quantifiers to primitive entities alone which are taken in the terminology of the ramified type theory of *Principia Mathematica* as objects of Level 1. Weyl was particularly attentive to avoid the *circulus vitiosus* of impredicative definitions by restricting the use of quantifiers in the set-theoretic comprehension scheme and was attentive as well to avoid the pitfalls of set-theoretical antinomies by subjecting the $\in$ relation to type restrictions.

In view of the three positions above implying the existence of a basic category of primitive objects and relations and the additional condition of completeness of the number system involved, Weyl conceived of natural numbers as intuitively the most proper such category. The completeness of the basic category involved here is taken in the sense of existence of a definite totality generated by an indefinite iteration, this latter thought in turn as a homogeneous relation of its elements, i.e., of the successor relation starting from the element named 1 (Bernard 2009, 161). The intuition of iteration makes it possible to apply the notion of completeness of natural numbers to every totality of ideal objects isomorphic to it.

What is more, this structure not only guarantees a well-defined meaning to the logical expressions "there is a natural number n such that..." or "for every natural number n such that..." to define a new entity, but it also helps found the possible definition of a new entity by extending these expressions to include a sequence of sets iterated by a homogeneous functional relation $\Phi(X_i, X_j)$, where the X_is are sets of the same category. One may then define a new entity, e.g., by virtue of the existential formula "there is some set among the sequence $< X_1, X_2, \ldots, X_n, \ldots >$ such that...." As we will see in the next sections in spite of the intuitive clarity due mainly to the natural intuition of natural numbers as an ontological-categorial domain, Weyl was sooner or later to be faced with the difficulty of applying his arithmetical-predicative scheme to capture the inherent impredicativity of mathematical continuum.

The present paper as rather philosophically oriented will not enter into the mathematical technicalities of Weyl's proposed arithmetical theory of continuum, at least no more so than what is thought to be enough to comprehend the mathematical content of the issues raised in relation to the nature of continuum. Given Weyl's orientation toward interpreting the incompatibility between the intuitive continuum as associated with a continuous flow of time and the durationless character of (natural) numbers (meant as temporal points) in terms of the phenomenology of internal time, I will be mostly focused on elucidating the character of points as appearances in their most abstract form of "empty-of-content" individuals-objects of intentionality and as noematical[5] objects within a constituted, immanent[6] continuous unity. This unity is not, in principle, identifiable with the real-world spatio-temporal continuity. In this level of discourse it will be seen that Weyl's undertaking to describe the continuum of mathematical analysis based on the basic ontological-relational domain of natural numbers is bound to reach the impasse of an inherent incompatibility whose origin is well beyond the formal-mathematical realm, which is to say that it may be taken as ultimately founded on the subjective origin of the self-constituting inner temporality. To this goal an in-depth analysis will be undertaken of points as intentional individuals and of actual infinity (in the sense of a completed totality) as rooted in the continuous immanent unity of each one's consciousness.

2. A critical review of Weyl's treatment of the dialectical opposition of points vs. continuum

In a first reading of Weyl's foundation of mathematical continuum in *DK* (Weyl 1994, Ch. 2, §6) one may note a distinct view between, on the one

---

[5] A noematical object, a phenomenological term, is constituted by certain modes as a well-defined object immanent to the temporal flux of a subject's consciousness possibly transformed, in the sense of a formal-ontological object, to a syntactical object of a formal theory. It can then be said to be given apodictically in experience inasmuch as: (1) it can be recognized by a perceiver directly as a manifested essence in any perceptual judgement (2) it can be predicated as existing according to the descriptive norms of a language and (3) it can be verified as such (as a re-identifying object) in multiple acts more or less at will. For more details on this concept and the general meaning of noema the reader may consult Husserl's *Ideas I* (1976, §87–§94).

[6] The term immanent which is widely used in Husserlian and generally phenomenological texts can be roughly explained as referring to what is or has become correlative (or "co-substantial") to the being of the flux of consciousness in contrast to what is "external" or transcendental to it. For instance, a tree is external as such to the consciousness of an observer while its appearance as the image of it within his consciousness is immanent to it.

hand, real numbers in terms of an abstract scheme representing ever embedding parts within a definite whole (with continuous functions as uniquely defined dependencies of overlapping "continua") and, on the other, time- and space-points as "non-existent" individuals within an ever in-act temporal flow which are eventually considered as abstractions of what is immediately given in experience. In Weyl's view, "the exhibition of a single point is impossible" and further "as points are not individuals they cannot be characterized by their properties," in contrast to the formal treatment of the elements of the continuum of real numbers considered as genuine individuals. In fact, there is a clear distinction in the way points may be treated as "individuals" in a theory of synthetic (without co-ordinates) homogenous space and the way they are treated in terms of the arithmetico-analytic concept of a real number which belongs to the purely formal sphere where "...those ideas thoroughly crystallize into full definiteness."

Further, in a next level, there is little evidence that time- or space-points as individuals of an arithmetized theory of time and space correspond to what is immediately given in (intentional) experience, in other words, there is a separation *in rem* of mathematical and intuitive continuum (Weyl 1994, 93). In Weyl's approach if we have to talk about continuity, e.g., in the geometry of straight lines, then space-points may be only meant as *functions of*, referring to a coordinate system which unavoidably "fulfills" the underlying act of a pure sense creating ego (Weyl 1994, 94). This way, a space-point is taken as associated with a "motion" corresponding to a coordinate system in terms of which it "moves," its motion being actually an abstract scheme to represent its constitution as "being-in-the-flow" within an immanent self-constituting unity.

On this account, the principle that to each (temporal) point belonging, e.g., to a unit time-span interval, corresponds a real number and vice versa is merely a kind of conventional continuity axiom that stands in contrast to the intuitively evident "being-of-the-flow." Yet it is established as a cornerstone of a pure arithmetical analysis which is necessitated by the need of an extra axiomatical principle, extraneous to first-order logic, to accede to a description of continuous processes originating in a time or space theory. As it may be already seen Weyl shifted his theoretical focus to the discrepancy between an intuitively given continuum and the concept of number as a time or space point, primarily turning his attention to the temporal continuum as the most fundamental one. He claimed that this discrepancy would cease to exist if the following conditions were met:

(1) Insofar as a certain intuition is associated with temporal duration, a temporal expression of the kind "during a certain period L, I see this man

crossing the street," might be replaced by the expression "in every time-point which falls within the time span L, I see this man crossing the street."

(2) If P is a time-point and OE is a certain time span, supposing that we have constructed an elementary theory of time on the assumption of a time-point as a basic category and the relations "earlier" and "equal" defined accordingly in a natural way, then the domain of rational numbers to which the number ϵ belongs so that $OL = \epsilon OE$ for a time-point L arbitrarily "earlier" than P, can be constructed arithmetically in pure number theory based on certain principles of definition set by Weyl to define a real number. Further, on this assumption and taking OE as a unit time span to every time-point P corresponds a definite real number and conversely to every real number corresponds a definite time-point; [*Continuity Principle*] (Weyl 1994, 89).

On the supposition that a pure theory of time can be founded by the postulation of a time-point as a basic category and the relations of "earlier" and "equal" defined in a natural way compatible with the intuition of time, Weyl claimed in the first place that the very intuition of time might suffice to determine the one-to-one correspondence between time-points and real numbers. Obviously such a correspondence not only cannot be demonstrated, it is even intuitively unthinkable and Weyl considered this talk as utterly nonsensical to the extent that a "theoretical clarification of the essence of time's continuous flow is not forthcoming" inasmuch as continuum fails to satisfy certain features of first-order calculus described in the first chapter of DK. Moreover the notion of "a point in the continuum lacks the required support in intuition" (Weyl 1994, 90). Further, pointing implicitly to the Husserlian description of the inner time-consciousness by the claim that to every temporal point corresponds a definite experiential whole, he tried to strengthen his argument on the discrepancy of mathematical and intuitive continuum by referring also to the retentional schemes of the temporal flux of consciousness. On this account, having an original impression at some instant A necessarily implies that one has already in place and in an a priori mode except for the primary memory[7] of A the primary memories corresponding to the original impressions for all instants B_i occurring

---

[7] The primary memory is well-known to phenomenologists to be the a priori associated "imprint" within consciousness of each original impression which should not be confused with the actively re-produced memory (rememoration) in the actual now of consciousness. This sentence is difficult to understand. Also, maybe we should aim for avoiding word repetition here? "known [...] to phenomenologists," "well known to phenomenologists." Also, here and elsewhere, maybe "a priori" should be in italics for the sake of clarity?

an arbitrarily short time earlier than A. These instants B_i are constituted in consciousness as a descending continuous degradation of retentions.[8]

At this point already came to Weyl's attention the inherent circularity in the description of the intuitive continuum in terms of the flux of temporal consciousness. The infinite sequence of point-like moments of experience fitting endlessly into one another in the progression of time and in the form of a continuous unity apprehended as such at any moment of reflection ultimately seemed to him as an absurdity. He was intuitive enough to note that abstracting each temporal now from its being-in-the-flux as part of a changing experiential content and treating it as an object of reflection, it would then instantly become a being-in-the-flux in its own right in which one could place new points possibly associated with new original impressions. In fact, this may be taken as a first step in facing the tantalizing question of an endlessly regressing sequence of reflections which the ego of temporal consciousness may bear on its objectified self. Ultimately Weyl landed in questioning the nature of continuity, in other words the flowing from point to point as ever eluding us, "in other words, the secret of how the continually enduring present can continually slip away into the receding past" (Weyl 1994, 92).

Of course the original Husserlian approach to the modes of constitution of temporal consciousness is far more articulate than Weyl's brief reference to the absurdity of passing from an infinite series of moments of perceptual experience to the apprehension of a continuously progressing experiential whole. In his main treatise on the phenomenology of time consciousness *Vorlesungen zur Phänomenologie des inneren Zeibewusstseins* (*Lessons on the Phenomenology of Inner-Time Consciousness*) (1966), Husserl dealt with the issue of the apparent incompatibility of the point-like character of each time perceptual experiences registered by an intentionally oriented consciousness as original impressions and the constitution of a temporal duration as a definite immanent whole by primarily appealing to two diverse intentional forms, the transversal (*Querintentionalität*) and the longitudinal intentionality (*Längstintentionalität*) of consciousness (Husserl 1966, §38, §39).

It is notable, though, that in the Husserlian phenomenology the ultimate step to reach the *prima causa* of the continuous unity of the temporal flux in the present now of reflection, involves a quite obscure notion which is the absolute (or pure) ego of consciousness, a notion Husserl was trying to clarify till his latest years only with limited success almost certainly due to the essentially transcendental character of this kind of subjectivity. It is

---

[8] The reader interested in a more detailed description of the intentional forms of the flux of consciousness (namely the transversal and the longitudinal intentionality) should consult the original Husserlian texts in (Husserl 1966, §11, §12, §38, §39).

noteworthy that although Weyl did not enter into the deep waters of the transcendence of the absolute ego, yet he was reserved enough to note that

> Each one of us, at every moment, directly experiences the true character of this temporal continuity. But, because of the genuine primitiveness of phenomenal time, we cannot put our experiences into words. (Weyl 1994, 92)

One may apply similar argumentation with regard to any intuitively given continuum, in particular to the continuum of spatial extension (Weyl 1994, 92). In fact, in original Husserlian view spatial continuum is considered as an objective form of temporal fulfillment. More specifically, Husserl referred to temporal extension as "fraternal" (*verschwistert*) to the spatial one. He pointed out that

> Like temporality, spatiality pertains to the essence of the appearing thing. The appearing thing, whether changing or unchanging, endures and fills a time; furthermore it fulfills a space, its space, even if this may be different at different points of time. If we abstract from time and extract a point of the thing's duration, then to the time-filling content of the thing there belongs the thing's spatial expanse. (Husserl 1973, 55)

As a matter of fact in view of the phenomenologically founded incompatibility between mathematical and intuitive continuum Weyl was eventually totally dismissive of the validity of the notion of an individual point as an independent, self-standing object. Concerning objectively constituted time he came to conclude that:

> (1) An individual point in it [constituted inner temporality] is non-independent, i.e., it is pure nothingness when taken by itself and exists only as a "point of transition" (which, of course, can in no way be understood mathematically); (2) it is due to the essence of time (and not to contingent imperfections in our medium) that a fixed time-point cannot be exhibited in any way, that always only an approximate, never an exact determination is possible. (Weyl 1994, 92)

On these grounds one may not be entitled to a formalization of the continuum based on the exact concept of a real number in that, ontologically speaking, there exists a kind of redundancy which is left "untreated" in the mathematical definition of real numbers by rational or non-standard approximations e.g. by approximating rational sequences or by ad hoc non-conventional entities in the form of infinitesimals. At this point Weyl seemed to resort to some kind of ultimate subjectivity referred to as "*Logos dwelling in reality*" (Weyl 1994, 93), which is reminiscent of the phenomenological pure ego, yet avoided any further descent into these murky waters.

Weyl's Conception of the Continuum

In the bottom line, in Weyl's view, one should settle for a theory of continuum that establishes its reasonableness the way a physical theory does. One could cite, for instance, quantum-mechanical theory which establishes its authority by seeking a rational justification provided by its interpretative and predictive power in the derived "exact" physical world subjected to certain idealizations with regard to its pre-predicative experiential origins. Consequently the abstract scheme of real numbers associated with the possibility of infinite embeddings of possible parts into a presupposed completed whole and that of functions as uniquely-valued correspondences of "overlapping" continua are rationally justified in the context of an objective reality which is of a constitutive sense; meaning one that is "meaningful" only in the presence of at least one phenomenological reduction performing consciousness.[9] In this sense a real analysis, as we know it, can give an exact account of various physical phenomena within an idealized objective world e.g., in the description of the motion of a point along a surface. Yet, it is unreasonable to construct a space-time theory as a formal-mathematical discipline without conceding to the impossibility of existence of a single time- or space-point as a self-standing individual of experience solely characterized by its properties insofar as time-space points are apprehended solely within the continuous flow of immanent temporality. This is a major impediment to the possibility of a space-time theory construed as a formal-axiomatical one by postulating a continuity axiom which guarantees that given a unit time span OE to every point P of OE corresponds a real number and vice versa. This impredicativity-generating incongruence is also implicitly in place in Weyl's subsequent proposal (which he did not elaborate further) to provide a higher-order analysis, termed by him hyperanalysis, in which real numbers are admitted as a basic category like naturals and where certain sets are introduced in whose definition the existential quantifiers refer to real numbers.[10]

Ultimately Weyl saw the points of a space-time theory only relative to a coordinate system, that is, essentially as functions of a "meaning-providing something" in the understanding that they cannot be construed as self-stand-

---

[9] In rough terms one can refer to the phenomenological attitude in contrast to the natural attitude as the performance of the phenomenological reduction by an intentionally directed consciousness in which things of the objective world are put into "parentheses" in absolute ontological terms and taken as only valid in their appearance as such and such within consciousness. (Considering that this is a clarificatory footnote, for the sake of clarity I would also consider slicing this sentence up into shorter sentences.) This includes the possibility of consciousness to reflect on itself.

[10] As a matter of fact more sets of real numbers are generated in hyperanalysis than in standard analysis. In this case the totality of points of spaces, surfaces, lines, etc., can be constructed arithmetically as three-dimensional sets of real numbers (Weyl 1994, 95–96).

ing entities but only relative to a coordinate system which is thought of as the "residue" of the objectifying ego after its eradication in the geometrical-physical world. Yet they are thought to be grounded all the same on the world of experience as primordially given and susceptible to the objectification process originating in the sense-giving ego (Weyl 1994, 94).

In short, Weyl admitted even indirectly to insurmountable obstacles, pertaining to the subjective foundation of the continuum, in achieving its formalization in a way that real numbers as well-defined individuals would represent time- or space points while staying clear of any sort of circularity in the construction. This led him to point out that

> both contemporary analysis and its principles are left hanging in a nebulous limbo half-way between intuition and the world of formal concepts - even though, under the mask of its vague presentations of set and function, analysis is able to pass itself off as a science operating in the formal-conceptual sphere. (Weyl 1994, 96)

This is an argumentation that may also apply against his proposed version of hyperanalysis to the extent that it claims to introduce sets by quantifying over real numbers in the place of basic-category objects. More specifically, the "filling-in" and the "there is" principles[11] as principles arising from the three major theses of Weyl's approach, namely from definitionism, intuitionism and predicativism, essentially refer to natural numbers in the sense of primitive objects (and relations) given straightforward to us by intuition which moreover, taken as a basic category of entities, form a complete system of definite self-existent objects. Accordingly, Weyl's proposed hyperanalysis

---

[11] The "filling-in" and the "there is" principles are respectively established in (Weyl 1994) as follows:

> If, for instance, $U(xyz)$ is a judgment with three blanks and a is a given object of our [basic] category, then the judgment $U(xya)$, which is produced by the operation of "filling in," is one with only two blanks. In particular a closed judgment (i.e., one without blanks), a judgment in the proper sense, which affirms a state of affairs, arises from a judgment scheme when all its blanks are filled by certain given objects of our category.

> Let[...]$U(xyz)$ be a judgment with three blanks. Then we can form the judgment $U(xy*) = V(xy)$, which means "There is an object z of our [basic] category such that the relation $U(xyz)$ obtains." Similarly, we can form $U(*y*)$, meaning "There is an object x and an object z such that $U(xyz)$ is true." The number of blanks of a judgment scheme will be reduced by application of this scheme too. If no blanks at all are left, then here again a judgment in the proper sense arises, about which it is appropriate to ask whether it is true or not. (Weyl 1994, 10–11)

must at least admit to a conception of real numbers as well-defined individuals possibly identifiable with points of a space-time span by the *Continuity Principle*,[12] (even in discarding the possibility of their generation by a homogenous iteration operation), so as to rightfully claim the introduction of new sets by quantifying over real numbers in the place of basic-category objects. In short, one is about to be faced again with the "vague" nature of real numbers as presumed individuals of an axiomatical form of space-time theory by reproducing a circularity on the level of hyperanalysis.

However the constraints of Weyl's *restriction principle*, namely his predicativist rejection of the notion of a set as a definite totality to quantify over, can be partly overcome by the (so-called) arithmetism which is considered a way to legitimize quantification over sets on the condition of a partial application of abstraction on their elements (Bernard 2009, 158, 162–163). More specifically, one can imagine a totality of sets in which at least one variable $n \in N$ is left independent as an enumerator of the sets within the totality, producing in effect a function $R(n)$ which may generate a set as a totality without infringing on Weyl's *restriction principle*. For example, one can define a real number as a set of rationals by leaving as an independent (not abstracted) variable the natural number n enumerating the sequence of its rational approximations. Yet even Weyl's *iteration principle*[13] for partially abstracted functions is not exempt of the possibility of quantifying over objects greater than Level 1 (in the sense of a ramified type theory) in order to introduce new entities or relations. On this account one may refer without entering into more technical details to S. Feferman's introduction of a formal system W, proved to be a conservative extension of the Peano Arithmetic, to accommodate Weyl's mathematics in *DK* where there is no obvious definability model of W in which the class of all total functions of natural numbers $(N \to N)$ consists of arithmetical functions (Feferman 1998, 279).[14] Consequently, and in view of the existing (equivalent) characterizations of hyper-

---

[12] See, page 105.

[13] In less technical terms the *iteration principle*, which "expands" the iterative structure of natural numbers and in a certain sense the intuitive accessibility of naturals toward totalities of sets, claims that a totality of objects obtained by successive iterations of a homogenous one-to-one set-theoretical operation $\Phi(X)$ between objects of the same category can be regarded as a complete totality available in turn for the definition of new entities.

[14] Feferman, based on Kleene's ^2E computable functionals over N, has introduced a system W whose definability model makes that the class of all total functions $(N \to N)$ consists of the hyperarithmetic functions and the Π_1^1 partial ones (Feferman 1998, 278–279). There is also a certain controversy regarding the capacity of the theory W to accommodate all scientifically applicable mathematics, in particular its capacity of consistently incorporating a host of mathematical aspects of quantum mechanics. Yet Feferman thought that the matter can be properly treated by pure mathematical-topological means and does not seem to pose a major "ontological" challenge for the theory W (Feferman 1998, 281–283).

Weyl's Conception of the Continuum

arithmetical sets, involving e.g., set-quantification of formulas of second-order arithmetic or transfinite recursion based on so-called Turing jumps, a part of the intuitive clarity of the basic category of natural numbers which would vindicate Weyl's predicativist program seems to be missing.

In sum, Weyl sought to talk about sets as totalities of objects insofar as this is done in the secure stepwise way of a definitionist predicative approach, providing as a basic category the set of natural numbers whose iterative generation lays *eo ipso* the heuristic significance of their inductive character. On this motivation, and mainly on account of the iteration principle, he tried to provide explicit and predicative definitions of subsets and functions within classical logic while seeking to evade impredicative traps by substituting the general definition of sets with that of definable sequences of reals. Yet, he was plainly admitting that

> the continuity given to us immediately by intuition (in the flow of time and in motion) has yet to be grasped mathematically as a totality of discrete "stages" in accordance with that part of its content which can be conceptualized in an "exact" way. More or less arbitrarily axiomatized systems [...] cannot further help us here. We must try to obtain a solution which is based on objective insight. (Weyl 1994, 24)

In other words Weyl's predicativist definitions of sets and functions up to the introduction of ideal elements through the new approach, was ultimately faced with the imposition *in rem* of the incompatible concepts of points and intervals as fundamental structures of a space-time continuum. Further, this means that one had to reconcile the intuitively accessible means provided by a theory founded on the conception of natural numbers as a basic category of objects with the essential nature of intuitive continuum as an ever changing state-of-affairs, associated moreover with an inner temporality and thereby rendering the notion of space-time points as immutable individualities a meaningless notion.

It should be reminded that Weyl's choice to restrict attention to definable sets of the first level, that is, essentially to the category of natural numbers as the absolute operational domain meant giving up the general least upper bound principle for the real number system. This kind of restriction also brought out certain problems concerning Weyl's iteration principle[15] by producing a relation of the type $R *_\Phi (\frac{p}{n}, N)$ over the set of natural numbers

---

[15] Weyl's principle of iteration, presented in three different forms, can be summarily defined in its simplest form as the recursive relation $R_{n+1}(\frac{xx'}{X}) = R_n(\frac{xx'}{F(x)})$, $R_1 = R$, where relations $R_1, R_2, R_3,\ldots$ arise from a single original one $R(n; \frac{xx'}{X})$ which has the blank n affiliated with the category "natural number" and filled in successively by 1, 2, 3,... The relation $R(\frac{xx'}{X})$ gives rise to the function $F(X)$ and has its blanks divided into the dependent variables x, x' and the independent X with the latter affiliated with the category of two-dimensional

N which is not arithmetical in N (due to the diagonalization argument) and hence not definable at level 0; for further details see: (Feferman 1998, 264–265).

3. A phenomenologically motivated approach of the mathematical continuum

Weyl's attempt to do justice to his main positions of definitionism, predicativism and his own version of intuitionism, led him to establish a predicatively founded mathematics which would be ultimately divergent from both Frege's logicist approach and Russerl's approach in the theory of logical types, while preserving fundamental features of respective positions. In at least one crucial point, he distanced himself from Frege, Russell and Poincaré, namely in that the principles of definition must be used to give "a precise account of the sphere of the properties and relations to which the sets and mappings correspond" (Weyl 1994, 47).

He rejected, in particular, the Fregean definition of natural numbers as equivalence classes as well as the reducibility axiom in Russell's *Principia* which he thought were incompatible with his "narrower" procedure associated with the conception of sets and functions founded on the *iteration principle*. In fact his meaning of the concept of a set lent a substantial content to the following assertion: "To every point of a line (given an origin and a unit of length) corresponds a (distance measuring) real number (= a set of rational numbers with the properties a), b) and c)[16] and vice versa" (Weyl 1994, 49). This noteworthy assertion establishes a connection between something given by space intuition (points in space) and something (the set of real numbers) generated by a logical conceptual way. Yet, Weyl conceded to the insufficiency of this assertion with respect to what is given us by intuition, more specifically the assertion above does not offer a morphological description of what is given to our intuition as a constant temporal flow. It rather does so by giving an exact "representation" of an immediately given reality in the actual now of reflection while missing at the same time the grasp of the intuitive evidence of a homogenous flow and further the possibility to describe in exact logical-theoretical terms what is by its nature inexact.

---

sets whose blanks are filled in with the same categories of objects as the dependent x, x' in R.

[16] In Weyl's definition of a real number as a one-dimensional set α of rational numbers the following properties hold: a) if r is an element of α, then so is every other rational r' such that $r - r'$ is positive; b) for every element r of α there is a rational number r^*, also belonging to α, such that $r^* - r$ is positive c) α is non-empty, but not every rational number is an element of α (Weyl 1994, 31).

This constant temporal process, Weyl stressed, is vital to all exact knowledge of physical reality and through this very process mathematics becomes relevant as a metatheory of natural science. In a definite sense Weyl's reconstruction of the intuitive continuum within a "symbolic universe" ought to establish its reasonableness beyond strict formal consistency in the same way a physical theory does and its direct evidence should formally result as faithfully as possible as presented in intersubjective identity. Ultimately, as discussed already, Weyl was unable to overcome the inherent incompatibility generated by the vague nature of continuum, as subjectively constituted, in contrast with the "exact" nature of formal mathematical objects something that ultimately led him to put in doubt the objective existence of the "points" of continuum (Weyl 1994, 90).

It is noteworthy that Weyl had the insights, well before Gödel's incompleteness results, to sense the restrictions posed by formalism/conventionalism to the meaning-content of mathematics for which certain determinations should be implemented other than those taking its objects/state-of-affairs as simply the result of logical inferences derived from a prescribed set of axioms. In this respect, he argued against the position that mathematical statements as, for instance, Fermat's Last Theorem, are mere consequences of arithmetical axioms by citing an example in which the arithmetical axioms cannot guarantee a sound meaning to the existential predication "there is," therefore putting into doubt the consistency and completeness of Peano's axiomatical system of arithmetic and Dedekind's completeness of the real numbers system. Prompted by his definitionist-predicativist approach and Cantor's proof of the non-denumerability of reals, he had also the mathematical acuteness to foresee the independence of the Axiom of Choice by proposing that "naturally there is no reason at all to assume that every infinite set must contain a denumerable subset - a consequence from which I certainly do not shrink" (Weyl 1994, 28).[17]

In view of these positions one can reasonably argue that Weyl was not only preoccupied with the incompatibility between the spatiotemporal continuum, founded on the intuition of the continuous flow of temporality, and the existing mathematical analysis, but he was also concerned with the sterility of strictly formalist approaches of mathematics. This attitude, to the extent that it recognized a sort of objective reality of mathematical objects originating in the categories of primitive objects and their relations and

---

[17] Weyl's point in the quoted assertion is that the infinity of a set does not guarantee by itself that there will be a constructive pairing function whose domain is the set of natural numbers and whose range is a subset of the infinite set in question; in other words one has to postulate the possibility of choice as an axiom independently of the meaning-content of infinity in general.

insofar as it refuted the notion of infinite sets as definite totalities by the *restriction* and *iteration principles*, distanced itself as a matter of fact from both later Hilbertian finitistic formalism and Carnap's logical-syntactical program for mathematical theories. More than this, Weyl converged in a certain sense to Gödel's critical attitude toward the respective theoretical positions in recognizing that there is some kind of deficiency of mathematical theories, originating in their formal-axiomatical structure, with respect to the objective existence of mathematical entities. These latter entities taken as evidences knowledgeable by primitive world-experience and consequently conditioned at least partly by the modes of constitution of that experience.

It turns out that a more profound and phenomenologically motivated analysis of intuitive continuum, taken in Weyl's monograph as intimately associated with the notion of space-time continuum, should concentrate on the deeper meaning of points as individuals-objects of intentional experience in contrast with the meaning of intervals as impredicatively defined totalities bearing subtotalities of the same genus and embodying the notion of duration. On this account, it seems quite problematic how one can possibly build a space-time theory by defining space-time points as individuals represented by real numbers when there is no intuition of a durationless time point in the flow of any (within-the-world) experience. Moreover, it seems doubtful whether one can have the intuition of a set of points (these latter taken as set-theoretical individuals) without conceding to the existence of a non-eliminable temporal factor conditioning by the underlying (impredicative) unity of temporal consciousness the very act of colligating an indefinite collection of formal objects in the form of definite wholes in the present now of consciousness.[18]

One faces, in fact, the challenge of building a theory of the most primitive entities and their essential relations while being constrained at the same time by intuitions deeply rooted in a constituted and subjectively generated temporality which cannot be apprehended in reflection but as the "ever-changing" homogenous unity of immanent objects with the modalities of being such and such.

Therefore, one may raise the question of how we can have a proper interpretation of the essential distinctness between points and the intervals of the continuum, indeed of how we can have a proper theory of space-time continuum, without taking into account what is originally given to us as non-mediated experience. That is, without doing justice at the same time

---

[18] The act of colligating a definite or indefinite collection of formal objects in the form of completed wholes and as such turned to thematic objects "in front of" the intentionality of the ego of consciousness is termed in Husserl's *Experience and Judgment* a retrospective apprehension (*rückgreifendes Erfassen*) (Husserl 1939, 246).

to the intuition of a temporally founded continuum annulling by its own non-eliminability the definability of any object—be it a material or formal one—as a durationless immutable object within the world. At this point it is of primary importance to have in mind the content that may be given to the concept of mathematical objects and their relations in general. Are they to be regarded in the commonly shared view of many platonistic logicians and philosophers of mathematics as atemporal, unalterable objects (and for that reason mind-independent) or rather as subjectively constituted objects of intentionality enjoying "artificially" by virtue of their intersubjective verification within the world of experience the status of immutable transtemporal entities retrievable any time at will in the form of well-meant objects in actuality?

My own position tends to side with the second option on the following grounds: even in regarding mathematical objects as atemporal ones and mind-independent, think for instance of the function $z = tan\pi(x-\frac{1}{2})$ which helps prove the non-denumerability of a real interval, at the very instant they become objects of the intentional directedness[19] of a self-constituting temporal consciousness by this very fact they are being "nullified" as atemporal objects as they instantly become *objects-in-front-of* (a consciousness) adumbrated moreover by the modes of being *objects-in-front-of* a consciousness. This means that an *object-in-front-of* is given as such in original presence together with its "inner" and "outer" horizon in reference to an intentional consciousness which has grasped it as an unambiguous verification of its enactment in the actual now and it is moreover susceptible of every possible modality in having become part of its immanence. This means a further elaboration of the *object's-in-front-of* inner horizon is possible by free variation in imagination, abstractive ideation, comparative reflection, formalization, etc. It follows that mathematical objects as objects of axiomatized theories are each time potentially open to further clarification, further accession to possible hidden properties or relations insofar as they are made objects of the intentional and further explicative regard of at least one subject performing concrete intentional-cognitive acts within-the-world.

A view of mathematical-logical objects as receiving their whole sense of being within the world from each subject's intentionality is given by R. Tieszen in *After Gödel: Platonism and Rationalism in Mathematics and Logic* (2011). More specifically, Tieszen points out that

---

[19] The key terms intentional or intentionality are fully taken in this article in their phenomenological connotation, that is, roughly as meaning the a priori tendency of consciousness toward "something in general" independently of a material or a general "thingness" content.

Taking our lead from Husserl's comments in *The Idea of Phenomenology, Ideas I, Formal and Transcendental Logic*, and elsewhere, we can say that ideal objects are also constituted as such by consciousness, by the monad. [...] whatever things are, mathematical objects or logical included, they are as experienceable things. It is experience alone that prescribes their sense. [...] Nothing exists for me otherwise than by the actual and potential performance of my own consciousness. Whatever is given as an existing object in mathematics or logic is something that has received its whole sense of being from my intentionality. There is no conceivable place where the life of consciousness could be broken through so that we might come upon a transcendent mathematical or logical object that had any other sense than that of an intentional unity (invariant) making its appearance in the subjectivity of consciousness. (Tieszen 2011, 97)

4. Points as empty-of-content substrates of intentionality

Can we have formal "lowest-level" individuals (think possibly of the "points" of the formal space-time theory) as immanent objects independently of an absolute temporal position, the latter state-of-affairs implying their existence as spatio-temporal and therefore "real world" objects? In view of Weyl's inquiry in *DK* discussed in the previous sections about the possibility of interchanging the notion of space-time points with that of real numbers and further the relation of both to spatiotemporal and phenomenological continuum this question is of crucial importance.

In this connection it is important to see that even though Husserl denied in *Erfahrung und Urteil* (*Experience and Judgment*) the status of genuine individuals to the objects of imagination, thus depriving them of the possibility of founding their identification, he nevertheless ascribed an ambivalent status to such individuals; in fact he termed them quasi individuals and the associated identities quasi-identities. He claimed that there is a notion of time that may be associated with these quasi-objects in terms of a broader intuitive unity allotted to them by virtue of being "there" in the uniform stream of consciousness (Husserl 1939, 174–175).

In view of what has been said so far my position concerning mathematical individuals can be summed up as follows: to the extent that mathematical individuals are essentially taken as syntactical atoms of a formal-mathematical theory assigned with a certain ontological sense, for instance those bounded by universal-existential quantifiers in a first-order predicate formula of the kind $(\forall x)(\exists y)Q(x,y)$, they can be logically founded irrespective of their possible spatio-temporal "mirror-image," that means, solely by virtue of the intentionality of a subject's "regard" free of any causality constraints. This means that they can be founded as content-free fulfillments of intentional acts which should not be by necessity causally related with objects-individuals existing in objective spatio-temporal terms. This is a view shared also by Tieszen in (Tieszen 2011), in which he refers to the possibility of the non-existence of an object in real terms even though our (intentional) awareness may be directed to it as if there were indeed such an object. Precisely by virtue of their nature unconstrained by spatio-temporal or causal determinations and also due to their intersubjectively founded identity over time, mathematical-formal individuals can serve as universals of formal-axiomatical theories bearing an ontological sense through bounded predicate formulas.

In these terms the question of the possible existence and the modes of existence of objects as fulfillments of concrete intentional enactments is "freed" from the constraints of their absolute existence as real spatio-temporal objectivities. Husserl had thought of quasi-individuals and generally of quasi-objects, taken as objects of imagination,[20] as united in a most inclusive unity of intuition which cannot be a unity of objectivities in absolute world-time to the extent that objects of imagination and generally objects in the sense of mere intentional enactments have no temporal connection either with objects of perception or among themselves (in real-world terms). This kind of unity is not a unity of objectivities; "it can only be a unity of the lived experiences that constitute objectivities, of lived experiences of perception, of memory, and of imagination" (Husserl 1939, 175).

Consequently and inasmuch as the unity of lived experiences is evidently bound by Husserl to the continuous flow of inner-time consciousness, the connection that might be established with these quasi-objects on the intentional level cannot in principle be causally grounded one.

An individual in purely formal abstraction can therefore be thought of as founded on the a priori enactment of the intentional direction of consciousness, this latter being totally inconceivable without orienting itself toward "anything-whatsoever" (*etwas überhaupt*). In fact an individual in this sense can be brought upon into evidence as intuitively self-given each time of reflection.[21] A "lowest-level" individual as an abstract individual is impene-

---

[20] Objects of imagination might be thought of as a general category of objects immanent to the consciousness and freed of real-world constraints among which one can think, as a "subspecies" enjoying a special status, mathematical or logical objects. Tieszen thinks of the objects of mathematics and logic as mind-independent in the sense of immanent to the consciousness objects of intentionality which are nonetheless constituted in a rational motivation throughout our experience in mathematical practice (Tieszen 2011, 104–105).

[21] Think, for instance, in extreme introspection as emptying yourself of any contemplative thought, pushing beyond any kind of focusing on whatever imaginable object or state-of-affairs; then you can see that you are by necessity oriented *in extremis* to a vague, indefinite, boundless and yet non-eliminable "something-there."

trable in terms of a thingness content since we cannot bring into reflection something "internal" to it in the form of a new concrete something-there and in the contemplative relation part-of. In other words, the content of each vacuous intentional act, eliminating any possible higher-level distraction, may be taken as founding the notion of an irreducible individual (including quasi-individuals in the sense attributed in *Experience and Judgment*), appropriating a host of categorial properties by virtue of being objectified as a general *Dies-da* (this-here) through the enactment of intentional orientation. This kind of impenetrability in reflection may be thought of, at this level of evidence, as founding individuality *in rem* independently of any reference to a really existing object-counterpart, while the single act of seizing it in the present now of consciousness may be thought of as founding meta-logically its uniqueness.

One may note that Husserl was careful to clarify that "individuation and identity of the individual, as well as the identification founded on it is only possible within the world of actual experience, on the basis of absolute temporal position" (Husserl 1939, 173–174). Consequently imagination, in general, does not generate individuals as irreducible objects associated with a fixed temporal position and spatial content but only quasi-objects and quasi-identities in the broadly conceived unity of intuition. In this approach, such individuals may not serve as ultimate self-evidences in laying the foundation of a theory of judgments, even though in Husserl's earlier texts (in *Ideen I*) "lowest-level" substrates of analytical sentences in the sense of ultimate phenomenological evidences, that is, as noematical nuclei-forms (*Kerngebilde*) deprived of any "inner" analytical content, even of a temporal form, and consequently not necessarily associated with the world of real experience are thought of as establishing the foundation of such objects of mathematical theories, as numbers, sets, classes, functions of sets or classes, Euclidean or non-Euclidean domains, etc., (Husserl 1976, 33–34). Consequently the above Husserlian view in *Ideen I* does not contradict the possibility of founding formal-mathematical individuals as fundamentally intentional objects (of a special status) not necessarily associated with a subject in causal terms within objective spatio-temporality.

Individuals such as those associated with actual experience and quasi-individuals of imaginary intuition (also individuals of memory) can be "embedded" in the unity of intuition only insofar as they are encompassed within the unity of constituted time, this way conditioning the unity of a plurality of various objects brought to the immanence of consciousness on self-constituting inner temporality.²² Indeed, all immanent objects, together with actual relations (concerning objects of actual experience) or quasi-relations concerning objects of memory or imagination, including mathematical objects as objects of categorial or eidetic intuition are ultimately conditioned on the intuition of the unity of time reduced in turn to the phenomenology of absolute temporal consciousness and its pure ego (Husserl 1939, 182).

Ultimately as the possibility of existence of "lowest-level" individuals of a mathematical theory is not necessarily associated with a spatio-temporal position founded on real-world objectivity one may get as a consequent result the ontological "suspension" of Weyl's proposed continuity principle (Weyl 1994, 6) insofar as it seeks to establish a one-to-one correspondence between the points of a time span and real numbers in taking time-points as individuals in objective time.

5. The possibility of a causality-free infinity

The present approach to the notion of formal-syntactical individuals as independent of spatio-temporal constraints can possibly extend to a notion of infinity also made free of spatio-temporal and consequently causal constraints. This kind of infinity is grounded in the immanence of consciousness and vestiges of this position are recognized from as early on as Husserl's *Philosophie der Arithmetik*. In this early work, generally considered as rather belonging to the psychologistic phase of Husserl's evolving phenomenological formation, Husserl referred to the inner experience as the evident factor for the possibility of representing a multiplicity of objects as an instantaneous lived experience (Husserl 1970, 24).

In later works, Husserl elaborated the conception of an immanent whole of multiplicities of appearances in terms of the continuous unity of a self-constituting temporal consciousness. In fact the foundation of continuous unity, as thematically presented in reflection, was to ultimately rest on the modes of constitution of temporal consciousness and more radically on its self-constituting origin. At the time of *Logische Untersuchungen* (*Logical Investigations*) he conceived of a kind of actual infinity in presentational immediacy in these terms:

> The fact that we freely extend spatial and temporal stretches in imagination, that we can put ourselves in imagination at each fancied boundary of space or time while ever new spaces and times emerge before our inward gaze—all this does not prove the relative foundedness (*Fundierung*) of bits of space and time, and so does not prove

---

²² One can construe an extension of relations of actuality subsisting between real individuals to quasi ones and make them appear in the quasi mode "precisely as far as the unity of an intuition of imagination and a world of imagination extends" (Husserl 1939, 187).

space and time to be really infinite, or even that they could be really infinite, nor even that they really can be so. This can only be proved by a law of causation, which presupposes, and so requires, the possibility of being extended beyond any given boundary. (Husserl 1984, 45)

Later in *Experience and Judgment* (which incorporated most of the key ideas of previous works), after having been engaged in the search for the essential structure of temporal consciousness in the *Phenomenology of Inner-Time Consciousness* and in the *Bernau Manuscripts*, Husserl referred to

> a special kind of constitution of unity which provides the basis for special relations, for the formal relations. It is the formal-ontological unity, which neither rests on the actual connection of the objects united nor is founded on their essential moments or their entire essence. (Husserl 1939, 188)

The objects and the relations referred to here are also thought to include, in the broad sense of formal-ontological ones, such mathematical objects as sets, classes, elements of sets or classes, functions and their domains, Euclidean or non-Euclidean manifolds, etc.

In an apparent reference to his conception of formal ontological objects in *Formal and Transcendental Logic*,[23] Husserl described this formal-ontological unity as a collective form of unity extending to all possible objects individual or not individual. Further the unified "whole" of collection becomes objective, as thematized, if a continuous apprehension of these objects one by one and in their totality takes place through a presentation in the actuality of consciousness. This collective unity is essentially neither founded on real space-time objectivity nor on material elements to the point that even the essence of things is not taken into consideration except insofar as it makes differentiation (between them) possible. By virtue of this unity we may be provided with a subjective foundation to universal-existential predicative forms in such a way that a proposition of the kind: "each and every thing (everything possible and hence everything actual...such that)...is capable of being intuited as actual or possible in the actual present of one consciousness" may be taken as equivalent to the proposition: "each and every thing...(such that)...is in principle capable of being colligated" (Husserl 1939, 189).

In these terms one may have a notion of actual infinity independent, as it is the case with formal individuals-substrates, of spatiotemporal constraints

---

[23] For a detailed description of the meaning of formal-ontological objects the reader is referred to Husserl's *Formale und Transcendentale Logik* (*Formal and Transcendental Logic*) (Husserl 1929, §24, §25, §37).

and consequent causal concerns. In fact, this kind of immanent "infinity," objectified as a completed whole in the instantaneous now of reflection, is what makes mathematics such an effective and inexhaustible tool in describing real world processes while by this token and in a certain holistic approach may be seen as de facto establishing the non-decidability of key questions in the foundations of mathematics (Livadas 2013; Livadas 2015). This kind of non-causal infinity to the extent that it may be, according to Gödel, linked with "the psychological fact of the existence of an intuition sufficiently clear to produce an open series of extensions of the axioms of set theory" (Gödel 1990, 268) may pertain also to the conception of transfinite sets in general as definite totalities and further to the ontological status of large cardinals, e.g., of measurable or supercompact cardinals, and consequently underlie the intelligibility of strong infinity axioms.[24]

6. Conclusion

As already stated, Weyl sought to provide in *DK* an arithmetical foundation of the mathematical continuum, taken as essentially associated with the continuum of space-time, on the assumption of the field of natural numbers as the most basic ontological-categorial domain. In doing so, he was convinced that arithmetical assertions, that is, those whose variables are exclusively restricted to the domain of natural numbers (or to any isomorphic structures) may have a definite truth-value attached to them in virtue of the fact that the arithmetical theory pertaining to the naturals is most fitting to a straightforward sense perception.

On the other hand, transfinite assertions whose variables range over domains of higher-level and not "self-standing" objectivities, i.e., those which do not correspond to direct sensory intuition, may not have a definite truth-value attached to them. In view of this, he espoused the restriction principle to allow for expressions whose variables range solely over the basic domain for which he offered the following justification:

> Clearly we must take the other path—that is, we must restrict the existence concept to the basic categories (here, the natural and rational numbers) and must not apply it in connection with the system of properties and relations (or the sets, real numbers, and so on, corresponding to them). In other words, the only natural strategy is to abide by the narrower iteration procedure. (Weyl 1994, 32)

In his own elaboration of a Husserlian perpective to Weyl's *DK*, J. Da Silva refers to ultimate syntactical substrates of any analytical sentence which

---

[24] There is a broad discussion in foundational mathematics concerning the implicit role of actual infinity in determining infinite mathematical objects as completed wholes which cannot be dealt with further here; see, for instance, (Feferman 2009) and (Livadas 2017).

are admittedly syntactically irreducible on pain of an infinite regression and thought of as corresponding to evidences of experience, as naturally represented in Weyl's analysis by the natural numbers (Da Silva 1997, 288). On this account, ultimate individuals-substrates of formal mathematical expressions given as evidences of pre-predicative experience (meant as prior to the predicative act of making judgments) may be taken, in a revisiting of Weyl's analysis, as underlying the concept of the points-individuals of continuum by virtue of being non-causally generated individuals of intentional experience independently of any spatiotemporal concerns.

On this ground and on the evidence of the unity of constituted temporality a new light may be shed to the lack of support in the intuition of a durationless point in contrast to the immediately experienced continuity of phenomenal time.

In this perspective I undertook a re-evaluation of the notion of the points of a space-time meta-theory as reducible to vacuous (with no-"thingness" content) individuals of intentional experience whose original givenness can be, in an alternative phenomenologically motivated approach, dispensed with causal and spatio-temporal constraints. At the same time I have tried to bring about the possibility of an immanent "infinity," also independent of any causal constraints pertaining to real-world experience, which is founded instead on the continuous unity of inner-time consciousness to account for the concept of completed wholes in the postulation of infinity assumptions and also of transfinite objects in the mathematics of continuum.

In view of the incompatibility between space-time points, in the sense of lowest-level individuals of a formal theory and time-intervals, founded on the notion of an immanent "infinity" ultimately reducible to a subjective temporal origin, Weyl's attempt to a description of the real continuum by purely arithmetical means was eventually doomed to fail on the phenomenological grounds discussed in this paper.

Bibliography

Becker, O. (1914). Beiträge zur Phänomenologischen Begründung der Geometrie und ihrer physikalishen Anwendungen, *Jahrbuch für Philosophie und Phänomenogische Forschung* **6**: 385–560.

Becker, O. (1927). Mathematische Existenz, *Jahrbuch für Philosophie und Phänomenogische Forschung* **8**: 439–809.

Bernard, J. (2009). Notes on the first chapter of Das Kontinuum: Intension, Extension and Arithmetism, *Philosophia Scientiae* **13**: 155–176.

Da Silva, J. J. (1997). Husserl's phenomenology and Weyl's predicativism, *Synthese* **110**: 277–296.

Feferman, S. (1998). *In the Light of Logic*, Oxford University Press, Oxford.

Feferman, S. (2000). The significance of Weyl's "Das Kontinuum", *in* V. F. Hendricks, S. A. Pedersen and K. F. Jorgensen (eds), *Proof Theory: History and Philosophical Significance*, Kluwer, Dordrecht, pp. 179–194.

Feferman, S. (2009). Conceptions of the continuum, *Intellectica* **51**: 169–189.

Feist, R. (2002). Weyl's appropriation of Husserl's and Poincaré's thought, *Synthese* **132**: 273–301.

Feist, R. (2004). Husserl and Weyl: Phenomenology, mathematics and physics, *in* R. Feist (ed.), *Husserl and the Sciences*, University of Ottawa Press, Ottawa, pp. 153–172.

Gödel, K. (1990). *Collected Works II, Publications 1938–1974*, Oxford University Press, Oxford. S. Feferman et al. (eds).

Husserl, E. (1929). *Formale und Transzendentale Logik*, Max Niemeyer Verlag, Halle.

Husserl, E. (1939). *Erfahrung und Urteil*, Acad./Verlagsbuchhandlung. hsgb. L. Langrebe.

Husserl, E. (1966). *Vorlesungen zur Phänomenologie des inneren Zeibewusstseins*, M. Nijhoff, Den Haag. hsgb. R. Boehm.

Husserl, E. (1970). *Philosophie der Arithmetik*, M. Nijhoff, Den Haag. hsgb. L. Eley.

Husserl, E. (1973). *Ding und Raum*, M. Nijhoff, Den Haag. hsgb. Claesges, U.

Husserl, E. (1976). *Ideen zu einer reinen Phänomenologie und phänomenologischen Philosophie, Erstes Buch*, M. Nijhoff, Den Haag.

Husserl, E. (1984). *Logische Untersuchungen*, M. Nijhoff, Den Haag. hsgb. U. Panzer.

Livadas, S. (2013). Are mathematical theories reducible to non-analytic foundations?, *Axiomathes* **23**: 109–135.

Livadas, S. (2015). The subjective roots of forcing theory and their influence in independence results, *Axiomathes* **25**: 433–455.

Livadas, S. (2017). What is the nature of mathematical-logical objects?, *Axiomathes* **27**: 79–112.

Ryckman, T. and Mancosu, P. (2002). Mathematics and phenomenology. The correspondence between O. Becker and H. Weyl, *Philosophia Mathematica* **10**: 130–202.

Ryckman, T. and Mancosu, P. (2005). Geometry, physics and phenomenology: The correspondence between O. Becker and H. Weyl, *in* V. Peckhaus (ed.), *Die Philosophie und die Mathematik: Oskar Becker in der mathematischen Grundlagendiskussion*, Wilhelm Fink Verlag, München, pp. 153–228.

Tieszen, R. (2011). *After Gödel: Platonism and Rationalism in Mathematics and Logic*, Oxford University Press, Oxford.

Toader, I. (2013a). Concept formation and scientific objectivity: Weyl's turn against Husserl, *HOPOS: The jour. of the Intern. Soc. for the History of Philosophy of Science* **3**: 281–305.

Toader, I. (2013b). Why did Weyl think that formalism's victory against intuitionism entails a defeat of pure phenomenology?, *History and Philosophy of Logic* **35**: 198–208.

Weyl, H. (1922). *Space-Time-Matter*, Dover Pub, New York. transl. Brose, H.

Weyl, H. (1994). *The Continuum*, Dover Pub, New York. transl. Pollard, S. and Bole T.

The Transcendental Source of Logic by Way of Phenomenology

Abstract In this article I am going to argue for the possibility of a transcendental source of logic based on a phenomenologically motivated approach. My aim will be essentially carried out in two succeeding steps of reduction: the first one will be the indication of existence of an inherent temporal factor conditioning formal predicative discourse and the second one, based on a supplementary reduction of objective temporality, will be a recourse to a time-constituting origin which has to be assumed as a non-temporal, transcendental subjectivity and for that reason as possibly the ultimate transcendental root of pure logic. In the development of the argumentation and taking into account W.V. Quine's views in his well-known *Word and Object*, a special emphasis will be given to the fundamentally temporal character of universal and existential predicative forms, to their status in logical theories in general, and to their underlying role in generating an inherently non-finitistic character reflected, for instance, in the undecidability of certain infinity statements in formal mathematical theories. This is shown also to concern metatheorems of such vital importance as Gödel's incompleteness theorems in mathematical foundations. Moreover in the course of the discussion the quest for the ultimate limits of predication will lead to the notions of separation and intentional correlation between an 'observing' subject and the object of 'observation' as well as to the notion of syntactical individuals taken as the irreducible non-analytic nuclei-forms within analytical discourse.

The Transcendental Source of Logic

1 Introduction

Someone could be probably tempted, on account of the title of this article, to raise serious doubts as to the possibility of deriving a transcendental source of logic in terms of a phenomenologically motivated approach. After all, phenomenology is widely known to have suspended the conviction to the 'legitimacy' of the objective world as such let alone the belief to a possible transcendental foundation of logic, the latter considered in phenomenological credo as being a science fundamentally reduced to a theory of meaning-acts conditioned on the intentional-cognitive faculties of an acting subject within-the-world. However convincing might sound this kind of argument, yet it seems not to take into account Husserl's gradual evolution from the time of *Logical Investigations* (1900–1901) on toward transcendental phenomenology and, among other quests, to the possibility of a (partial at least) reduction of logical objects and meanings to a priori features of consciousness, a key factor being his description of the inner temporality of consciousness. It is well-known to phenomenologists that Husserl's description of temporality leads ultimately to the subjective origin of constituted temporality, in other terms to a transcendental ego-pole often referred to as the absolute ego of consciousness. As it will be noted in the sections that follow, Husserl left this notion quite obscure and vague to the end of his longtime efforts to elucidate its nature in view of the capital question of temporality.[1] The transcendental source of self-constituting temporality is, by all accounts, of such primary importance that it underlies also the possibility of a transcendental intersubjectivity in establishing the world of our empathetic presence as the world-for-us, that is, the life-world (*Lebenswelt*) described in Husserl's *Krisis* (Husserl 1976a, pp. 187–190). It is evident that the extent to which the transcendental source of temporal consciousness (left over after a radical phenomenological reduction) might have an indirect influence to the foundations of formal logic and of axiomatical mathematical theories is intimately associated with the relevance of phenomenological analysis as such with the structure of logical forms and theories. In this concern one might refer to the view of a philosopher of no less authority than Ludwig Wittgenstein for whom phenomenology is the name given "to the investigation into the nature of phenomena which is required in order to determine the logical syntax of the clarified notation" (Noe 1994, p. 8). In fact, even after changing his mind on the idea that phenomenological and grammatical investigation are in fact one, Wittgenstein continued to regard phenomenology as critical to the comprehension of logical-grammatical forms (ibid. p. 25).

The question of the absolute subjective origin of all temporality will be actually the *leit motiv* of my undertaking to provide convincing reasons for a transcendental source of logic by way of phenomenology. This task, carried out in the next sections, is firmly conditioned on the possibility of a subjective reduction of logic in its own right and also as a formal metatheory of science. This subjective reduction

---

[1] Husserl's *Späte Texte über Zeitkonstitution* (*Late Texts on Time Constitution*), Husserl (2001b), edited by D. Lohmar and published in 2006, offer to the interested reader many insights to Husserl's tantalizing efforts to reach a proper foundation for a timeless ego while doing justice all the same to its 'self-reflexion' as an absolute temporal flux; see, for instance, pp. 198–199.

sets the stage for a discussion of the fundamental role of temporality, thought in terms of the self-constituted absolute flux of each subject's consciousness, to generate a meaningful discourse referring to well-meant objects. On the level of predication as the most fundamental form of meaningful discourse this discussion takes mostly place in Sect. 2 in which I try to show that the constituent parts of a predicative form are fundamentally conditioned on the notions of identification, co-existence and invariability over time, where time is basically meant here as the temporality of the absolute flux of consciousness with its specific constitutional modes. It should be reminded at this point, and in view of logic as intimately linked with formal mathematical theories, that for Husserl pure logic embraces all the concepts and propositions without which science would not be possible and would not have any sense or validity. In particular, the mathematical disciplines of the purely logical sphere proceed from given purely logical concepts and axioms which are grounded in the essence of purely logical categories (Ortiz-Hill 2013, pp. 69–70).

Further in Sects. 3 and 4 I deal with the fundamentally temporal character of the universal sentences of logic pointing to the implicit role of universal–existential quantifiers in establishing ontological commitments within a purely logical context. This is a discussion that hopefully addresses some nominalist concerns mainly by means of W.V. Quine's theory of universals in Quine (1947). In Sect. 4 I try to bring about the extent to which universal–existential quantification over an indefinite 'horizon' may influence well-known results in foundational mathematics such as certain independence results and Gödel's incompleteness theorems. In view of my general approach the semantical content of universal–existential quantification in the context of a formal theory can be primarily associated with the preconditions and the constitutive modes of a subjective temporality in leading along the way to the reasons to recourse to an a-temporal subjective origin of the unity of the domain of discourse.

Lastly in Sect. 5, I present a holistic approach toward both objects of an empirically verifiable sentence having a factual meaning and those of an analytic one having a formal meaning with the purpose of demonstrating the possibility of establishing a 'metaphysical' foundation of pure logical forms by means of the phenomenological description of inner temporality. Except for the original Husserlian texts cited in the bibliography I was also considerably motivated by W.V. Quine's general approach of the semantics of predication in the context of his pragmatic holism as presented in Quine (1960).

Overall the Husserlian approach meant a shift from the established view of logic, as the exact pure science of idealized objectivities, to its reassessment as fundamentally referring to the experience of the life-world, this latter notion essentially conceived as it is well known to phenomenologists to be an indefinitely extendible horizon of our special reduction-performing co-presence in the world. In this approach a genealogy of logic understood as an ultimate clarification of its origins and focused in elucidating its development as an apophantic discipline should inevitably view predicative judgements as the essential foundation of logic. This, in turn, calls for a further reduction of predication on the level of unambiguous evidence, based on the fact that the world is the universal ground of all possible substrates of predicative judgements, of all that is made, in intersubjective fashion, knowable and logically posited. It is remarkable that the life-world as the universal horizon of all meaning-acts was considered by Husserl as related not only to the meaning attributed to the objects as objects of possible knowledge but also to everything the natural sciences (of his time) had rendered valid as determination of beings (Husserl 1972, p. 39). Further, the objective-logical self-evidences (e.g. the mathematical insight or the natural-scientific one) are thought to lead back to the path of the prime self-evidence in which the life-world is ever pregiven; that is, rendering ideas intuitive in the way of mathematical or natural-scientific models is thought as hardly enacting intuitions of the objectivity itself but as rather enacting life-world intuitions suitable to elucidate the conception of the objective ideals in question (Husserl 1976a, p. 132).

In this view and taking into account that objects of formal mathematical theories are viewed in complete abstraction as objects of a categorial intuition in the sense of general 'empty-somethings' or modifications of 'empty-somethings', a mathematization of nature is essentially possible by positing objects of mathematical theories (such as those of mathematical analysis) in the broader context of a pure logic as *mathesis universalis*,[2] that is, as formal-ontological ones rooted in turn in our intentional–constitutional capacities as conscious beings-in-the-World and bearers of a self-constituting inner temporality.

2 An A Priori Rooted Reduction of Predicative Forms

In the discussion of this section I enter first the question of reaching a fundamental level of meaningful discourse either in terms of a formal language provided with a set of axioms and syntactical rules or in terms of a loose common vernacular. In this sense we can hardly imagine of a more fundamental meaningful linguistic form, indeed a more protean form of discourse, than a sentence of predication in which we connect a general term to a singular one in a way that we can form a sentence which is true or false according to whether the general term is true or false of the object, if there is one, to which refers the singular term; e.g., we may think of the form of the predication '*a is F*', where '*a*' is a singular term and '*F*' is a general term. It is notable that for E. Husserl in *Erfahrung und Urteil* (*Experience and Judgement*) (Husserl 1972), language as an object of investigation reduces to the investigation of most fundamental predication which is thought of as a mode of pre-linguistic thought in the understanding that language (especially a scientific one) simply represents meaning-bestowing acts and their generated meaning (Husserl 1972, *Nachwort*, p. 483). In W.V. Quine's view the form of predication thus posed is the most fundamental linguistic form in which general and singular terms find their contrasting grammatical roles while leaving the other grammatical contrasts, namely, those between the substantival, adjectival and verbal forms as having little bearing on questions of reference (Quine 1960, p. 96).

---

[2] See Husserl (1976b, pp. 33–35).

The Transcendental Source of Logic

It can be said that substantives, adjectives and verbs can be simply viewed as grammatically variant forms of general terms essentially leaving intact the ontological commitment of a general term as being what is predicated of the singular term, this latter occupying the place of the subject in the form of predication. In this sense the predicative forms 'Hussain Bolt is a runner', 'Hussain Bolt is ultrarapid' and 'Hussain Bolt turbo-accelerates' run in a parallel sense in predicating to the singular term (personified here by the super-runner H. Bolt) definite attributes expressed respectively by a substantive, an adjective and an (intransitive) verb. In Quine's view the verbal form can even be considered as a more fundamental one by entering the predication without the auxiliary 'is' or 'is an', considered then as a simple prefix serving to convert a verbal form in the predicative position to a substantival or adjectival one. In fact, the interchangeability of the forms 'runs', 'is running', and 'is a runner', taken as fundamentally verbal ones, points to an inherent common characteristic of these forms going as far as the presumption of an ontology of the verbal form 'to be'. For as long as someone is willing to discard a platonistic static realm grounding existential statements, naturally including the fundamental form of predication, and adopt instead a constitutional-temporal approach then all three forms above can be taken as equivalent not by virtue of simply adjoining the auxiliary verbal form 'is a' or 'is' to the substantive or adjectival forms, but by inquiring deeper into their common origin as essentially motion terms reflecting the constitutive modes of an embodied subjectivity. In this sense the verbal character of the syntactical predicate can be taken as an 'inherent' kinetic state of affairs inasmuch as one is willing to accept on a deeper subjective level the constituting presence of a subject of discourse who is a priori provided with certain modes of apprehending the world of phenomena and restituting its objects as well-defined noematic ones. For example, a noematically[3] constituted object like a painting in a wall is commonly experienced as unambiguously identical to itself, however the consciousness of it in the various stages of its immanent duration is non-identical; it is only a 'continuously' connected unity (Husserl 1976b, p. 231). In this approach the ontological content of existential statements referring to well-meant predicable objects of 'observation' is further reducible, on a kinetic-constitutional level, to objectivities within the world which are each time conceived as the unique objectification of ideally infinitely extendible kinetic stages (i.e., the multiplicity

---

[3] The meaning of the phenomenological terms noetic and noematic are mainly described in E. Husserl's *Ideen I* [see: Husserl (1976b, pp. 230–231)]. A noematic object is constituted by certain modes as a well-defined object immanent to the temporal flux of a subject's consciousness and it is possibly abstracted, in the sense of a formal-ontological object, as a syntactical object of a formal theory. A noematic object can be said to be given apodictically in experience inasmuch as: (1) it can be recognized by a perceiver directly as a manifested essence in any perceptual judgement (2) it can be predicated as existing according to the descriptive norms of a language and (3) it can be verified as such (as a reidentifying object) in multiple acts more or less at will. In contrast, a noetic object can be only characterized in terms of the multiplicities of real moments of a hyletic–noetic perception intentionally directed to it by its sole virtue of being given as an absolute evidence.

The Transcendental Source of Logic

of their profiles) within the immanence[4] of consciousness. Even in the case where one refers in a meaningful discourse to his own self as an object of 'observation' he must have already objectified his own subjectivity (in the unity of its temporal profiles) prior to any reference to himself as the singular term of a predication. It is naturally raised then the question of the origin of an ontology of being in general (including the being of logical objects) in accepting that 'being' as an object of reflection is the re-identification[5] within the immanence of consciousness of the multiplicity of its kinetic-temporal profiles.

In the next it will be made further clear that the constituting origin of 'being' cannot be conceived but as an absolute subjectivity non-objectifiable without alternating its very essence and ultimately what Husserl described painstakingly to the end as the absolute ego of consciousness. By essentially eluding any kind of objectification within the real world of phenomena this absolute subjectivity as an ever constituting (and never constituted) *'prima causa'* within the immanence of each one's consciousness may be reasonably claimed to stand as the transcendental origin of logic insofar as logic is considered as inalienable to the subjective constitution of reality within an all-encompassing life-world of experience.

Turning back to to the fundamental form of predication, it is important to take into account that a significant part of a meaningful discourse is based on taking mass terms, for instance the term water, as concrete definite objects both in the role of singular terms before the copula and that of general terms after the copula; e.g., consider the simple examples of predicative sentences: 'The water is fluid' and 'that swamp is water'. In these cases in which the mass term water is taken respectively as the singular and the general term of predication there is no way to assert anything meaningful of the subject of predication 'The water is fluid' or render a host of attributes being true of the subject in 'that swamp is water', except by taking a scattered physical object like water as a concrete and definite totality (Quine 1960, p. 97). The instance then of a scattered object, e.g. of liquid water in the example, being taken as a unique sprawling mass term (singular or general) in a

---

[4] The terms immanent and intentional, among others, which are used very often in this text are very common in phenomenological analysis and familiar to any reader with a minimum of knowledge of phenomenology. Yet for the sake of self-sufficiency of the content of this article I enter hereby a very brief description.

1. Intentionality is a phenomenological notion which is not to be understood as a relation of a psychological character towards the objects of experience. To a non-expert in phenomenology it can be roughly described as grounding the a priori necessity of orientation of a subject's consciousness towards the object of its orientation.
2. An immanent object and generally immanence is thought of as a correlate of intentional consciousness in contrast with a transcendent to the consciousness common physical object whose objectivity is anyway put by phenomenology into brackets.

[5] Concerning the meaning of identity in logic and the underlying ambivalence relative to this concept one should take into account a persisting confusion in positing under the same terms the identity between the signs of a language and the identity of corresponding physical objects. In any case, Quine's reference to the Heraclitean flux, Hume's claim of the non-identity of physical objects and also Whitehead's and Wittgenstein's essential refutation of the notion of the identity of objects can be taken as pointing, in a proper interpretation, to a notion of temporal-kinetic foundation of the concept of identity (Quine 1960, pp. 116–117).

sentence of predication may be put under the same predicative norms with those of a real, concrete object even in the case where this latter might well be a motionless enduring object as a tree or a building. To the extent moreover that we take real objects as temporally constituted, in taking into account that they are initially apprehended as hyletic–noetic perceptions,[6] that is, in the sense of multiplicities of intentional acts 'in advance' of their noematic objectification, there is raised the question of the possibility of constituting in objective time a particular real object/state-of-affairs as a unique self-standing objectivity. In this view without the possibility of transforming within the immanent unity of temporal consciousness the multiplicities of phenomenological perceptions (*Wahrnehmungen*) into a unique, re-identifying-in-the flux object we would be deprived of the possibility to conceive even of apparently motionless objects, as those referred to above, as unique noematic objects in objective time. Consequently in the absence of the intuition, e.g. of a tree, as a concrete, self-standing 'immutable' object it would be hardly possible for it to stand as a well-meant syntactical object taken as a singular or general term in sentences of predication. In short, both singular and general terms of predication, respectively taken in the place of syntactical subjects and syntactical predicates (predicating certain attributes to the subject), seem to be essentially motion terms by virtue of being abstractions of temporal re-identifications of multiplicities of intentional acts of (phenomenological) perception toward objects in a most general sense.

In the next section, I'll try to show the key role of universal–existential quantification in general predicative discourse and in building formal logical sentences over an indefinite domain. At the same time I'll try to demonstrate the relevance of a phenomenologically motivated approach in view of the fact that universal sentences may be associated with ontological commitments.

3 A Phenomenologically Motivated Reduction of Universal Quantification in Predicative Discourse

In *Word and Object* (Quine 1960, § 36), W.V. Quine made a strong claim for the acceptance of a time factor in categorial formulas bounded by universal or existential quantifiers.[7] His position was partially reminiscent of a phenomenologically motivated one in that physical things are events (or processes) in the sense of temporal fulfillments-contents of some portion of space–time, with the further insight that each specific time interval be as long as one may wish is a temporally thick slice of the four-dimensional material world exhaustive spatially and

---

[6] The hyletic–noetic perception described in terms of corresponding moments of intentionality based on sensory (hyletic) data is not by necessity conditioned on a temporal-noematic constitution, this latter considered by Husserl as 'posterior' to noetic perception. For instance, the figure of a tree trunk, as a noematic object, is the invariably one and the same immanent object of a temporal consciousness constituted through a multiplicity of real hyletic–noetic moments of the concrete experience intentionally directed to the particular tree trunk in its various angles, adumbrations, etc. (Husserl 1976b, p. 226).

[7] As well-known the universal–existential forms of quantification are logically interconnected since $\forall x\, P(x)$ is equivalent to $\neg \exists x\, \neg P(x)$.

The Transcendental Source of Logic

perpendicular to the time axis. Then letting t indicate any position on the time axis and letting x be a spatiotemporal object, the expression 'x at t' indicates the common part of x and t (Quine 1960, p. 172). Therefore Quine could treat temporal postulations such as 'now', 'then', 'before t', 'after t', 'at t' as referring to slices of space–time taken as well-meant objects susceptible of quantification, e.g. the common expression 'x catches up y before t' is transformed into the more formalized one:

$$(\exists u)\ (u \text{ is before } t \text{ and } x \text{ at } u \text{ catches up } y)$$

As a matter of fact, the time parameter t in the form of a variable bounded by universal or existential quantifiers in logical formulas, e.g. of the kind '$(\forall t)$ (if t is less than one nanosecond then t is measured by a non-conventional device)', is taken as a constant objective factor irrespective of being associated with a Newtonian or relativity theory leaving aside the question of its constitutive subjective origin. However, in phenomenological view the range of values of the time parameter t represent (in abstraction) possibilities of instantaneous temporal fulfillments upon objective reflection on the part of any conscious subject in intersubjective coincidence. Consequently temporal values insofar as they are taken as representing instantaneous objectifications in the present-now of reflection would be 'non-existent' within objective temporality before the act of reflecting upon them in the present-now of intentional consciousness. In this sense any application of temporal qualifiers such as those of 'before t', 'after t' and 'at t' is inescapably caught in the circular maze of reflecting (subjectivity of consciousness)—reflected (temporal objectivity) to the extent that, for instance, in stating that 'at time t, the velocity $u(t)$ of a particle reached its maximum', we have to objectify at the value t the temporal 'slice' at which the velocity $u(t)$ was supposedly maximum, therefore letting vary *in extremis* the velocity of the particle at the fraction of the time in advance of or in the aftermath of its 'observation'.

In spite of the questions of metatheoretical content[8] raised above concerning the totality of the range of values of a variable (or variables) bounded by universal quantifiers in sentences implying an ontological commitment, e.g., of the form 'Every F is an object x such that... x ..', it is often the case that a meaningful application of ideal objects in mechanics is implemented through universal conditionals: $(\forall x)$ (If x is a mass point then, ...). It seems that even if such ideal statements may be vacuously true *in infinitum* by sheer lack of counter-instances, it is nevertheless a concrete fact that certain of these conditionals rather than others impart useful scientific knowledge (Quine 1960, p. 249). In Quine's view, which seems to generate a circularity on account of my metatheoretical concerns above, this kind of statements alongside similar ones concerning infinitesimals find their meaningful answer in the theory of limits. Talking, for instance, of mass points as behaving in a certain way under 'observation' should be understood as saying that corresponding real mass particles behave more nearly that particular way the

---

[8] The term metatheoretical as applied here and elsewhere in the text should be taken in a broad sense as referring to a theory pertaining to and yet transcending the bounds of formal theory in the first place, and further as ultimately associated with a subjective constitution within the world of phenomena.

The Transcendental Source of Logic

boundlessly smaller their volumes are. Or, in another case, saying that an isolated system of particles behaves in a certain way it is meant that a system of particles behaves more nearly that way the 'infinitely' smaller the exchange of energy between that system and the outside world is. In this regard any Newtonian sentence may be paraphrased as a symbolic truth with regard to a relativistic sentence in a Weierstrassian sense,[9] in such a way that, e.g., physical bodies behave more nearly thus and so the smaller their relative velocities are. This can also happen with geometrical Euclidean objects relative to the corresponding 'real' objects of 'true' non-Euclidean geometry, the former objects serving as limit myths formally explicable by paraphrasing the sentences involved in a Weierstrassian sense (Quine 1960, pp. 248–249 and 253–254). In essentially the same sense one may apply a Weierstrassian formula in the common definition of a nonstandard number x:

$$\forall \text{ standard } \epsilon > 0 \, \exists x \text{ such that } |x| < \epsilon$$

An objection could be possibly raised here by a nominalist concerning quantification over universals to the extent that these are meant as transtemporal abstract objects instantiated each time by their physical counterparts. On this account one should be careful enough to distinguish between quantification over signs taken as abstract nontemporal objects and quantification over physical objects named after the signs. By a certain measure the nominalist argument on the 'illegitimacy' of the use of numbers as values of variables of quantification strongly impairs the work of mathematicians whereas, on the opposite, an uncritical acceptance of a purely formal view of numbers as reducible to the notion of a class of abstract objects (as in the Fregean definition of a natural number n) is not exempt of logical paradoxes such as those generated by the notion of the class of all classes. On the other hand, the impairment to the nominalist program can be easily seen in citing the following sentences: 'there are n objects x such that Fx for each specific n' and 'there are just as many IDs as individuals'. In the first sentence one has simply to apply on the formal level the equality sign = and an existential quantifier which is an intuitively clear task for each specific finite value of n, whereas in the second sentence one is required to quantify in terms of $(\forall n)$ (there are n IDs and just as many individuals), which obviously demands taking the numbers n as (indefinite) values of quantified variables. In the latter case, a nominalist would find himself almost helpless because he would have to presuppose the n objects as abstract ones prior to quantifying over them as values bounded by a universal quantifier or else he could lose all mathematical equipment in view of the need to treat the physical objects, 'ID' and 'individual' as entities-members of an indefinite collection linked by a certain extensive relation.

In his article *On Universals* (Quine 1947), W.V. Quine sought to justify the existence of universals, in the sense of irreducible abstract entities in a logical–mathematical context, mainly through the concept of classes and the notion of the identification of indiscernibles. In this approach the quantifiers $\exists$ and $\forall$ are taken as

---

[9] By Weierstrassian sense I basically mean the application of some form of the well-known (ϵ, δ)-Weierstrass formula which is a universal–existential quantification formula initially intended to dispense with the need of introducing infinitesimal numbers in coping with the subtleties of differential calculus.

assigning an attribute (or attributes) S to an entity x, i.e. $\exists x$ means 'there is an entity x such that..' and $\forall x$ means 'every entity x is such that..'. Consequently and in contrast with pure quantification over variables taken as simple schematic letters, variables in Quine's sense bounded by universal–existential quantifiers are construed as variables demanding attributes or classes as range of values. In such view a theory dealing solely with concrete objects in a nominalist sense can be reconstrued as one treating universals by the application of the dual form of quantification to bounded variables having a definite range of values and in a weaker sense simply through identification of indiscernibles, i.e. treating objects as identical to one another when they differ in no respect expressible within the formal theory (Quine 1947, pp. 75–77).

The main point to focus here is that by relying on a universal quantification over bounded variables ranging over all entities which the theory treats we are constrained to assign to these variables corresponding entities as values whose truth-functions or propositions would be considered as their names. In other words syntactical variables of a theory which might be hitherto taken as mere schematic letters would be henceforth associated with ontological commitments, thus opening a field of discussion reaching beyond an apparent platonistic status. In the above sense of universals as irreducible abstract entities susceptible of attributes and in what could be considered as a unifying perspective with respect to their factual or formal sense, I refer to what Husserl described in *Formale und Transzendentale Logik* as ultimate evidences of real individuals taking the form of syntactical individuals of analytic sentences in the sense of empty of content 'somethings'-in-general. These syntactical individuals as abstractions of lowest-level intentional orientations toward a general concrete 'something' (something akin to the Aristotelian τόδε τι), independently of any spatio-temporal and for that reason causal constraints, are also a priori associated with devoid of content categorial modifications[10] (Husserl 1976b, pp. 33–34; Husserl 1974, pp. 81–82).

In the next sections I set out to present a phenomenologically oriented approach, possibly considered as a holistic one, by which to regard the objects of universal–existential quantifications as abstractions of intentional 'lowest-level' objectivities which are further constituted as noematic ones within objective temporality and are therefore associated with a temporality factor underlying every predicative form and ultimately leading to a transcendental-like source of logic.

---

[10] Let it be noted here that predication in the Aristotelian *Categories* is associated with the definition of the primary and secondary substances where the former ones as substances in the strictest and primary sense of the term are defined to be those which are neither asserted of nor are present in the subject of a predication form. For instance, such primary substances can be regarded a particular man or a particular horse, which in their most abstract sense of a certain 'something' [τόδε τι], can be regarded as grounding the irreducible character of syntactical individuality (Aristotle 1983, pp. 18 and 28).

4 The Place of Universal Sentences Within Formal Mathematical Theories

In *Word and Object* W. V. Quine recognized the central role of universal and existential quantifiers within predicative discourse characterizing these quantifiers as prefixes known for 'unobvious but traceable reasons' (Quine 1960, p. 163). Moreover he pointed out that they may never be encountered except followed by the words '*is an object x [..] such that*'; indeed, the entire category of indefinite singular terms can be reduced to '*Every F is an object x such that ... x ...*' and '*Some F' is an object y such that ... y ...*'. In a compound form these can be put: '*Every F is an object x such that ... some F' is an object y such that ... y ...*'.

Yet to the extent that there are traceable reasons for affirming the sound articulation of this statement these must be reasonably conceived of as indirectly associated with a temporality factor underlying the statement. And insofar as we can affirm the unique existence each time of the object x representing the indefinite singular term F, this existence should necessarily refer to the 'traceable history' of F. But how can a 'traceable history', here formalized by the application of a universal–existential quantification with ontological committments, be thought of except by being the abstraction of an indefinite extension of discrete cognitive acts, possibly taken of an intentional character, and considered sufficient in generating a complete formal object, e.g. a choice sequence in its entirety as a complete mathematical object in accordance with the intuitionistic continuity principles (Atten et al. 2002, pp. 214–215). On this account, even though these cognitive acts are meant as an immanent finiteness yet by extending indefinitely within the continuous unity of consciousness they 'impart' a certain non-finitary character to the object specified by the attribute/-s provided by the corresponding predicate form (in accepting, of course, the extensionality axiom).

It must be noted though that this kind of infinity has nothing to do with spatio-temporal infinity, bound to causality constraints, since it may be only conceived of as the result of a mental activity of free generation within the immanence of consciousness of an unbounded extension toward the constitution of well-meant infinite objects/states-of-affairs. Indeed this may be considered as a kind of actual infinity in presentational immediacy within the immanence of temporal consciousness. In this connection, Husserl referred in *Logische Untersuchungen* (*Logical Investigations*) to the essential difference between spatio-temporal extensiveness and the free mental extension of any conceivable spatial and temporal stretches within imagination: "The fact that we freely extend spatial and temporal stretches in imagination, that we can put ourselves in imagination at each fancied boundary of space or time while ever new spaces and times emerge before our inward gaze - all this does not prove the relative foundedness (*Fundierung*) of bits of space and time, and so does not prove space and time to be *really* infinite, or even that they could be *really* infinite, nor even that they really can be so. This can only be proved by a law of causation, which presupposes, and so requires, the possibility of being extended beyond any given boundary" (Husserl 1984, Engl. transl., p. 45).

Moreover, this actual infinity can never be actually traceable and expressible in a predicative form which would eliminate a reference to 'every F_i ..such that..' or generally to 'every-thing ..such that ..', for that would presuppose the annulment of the 'distance' (in terms of constitution) between a reflecting subjectivity and the reflected objectivity. For as long as we intentionally perform a meaning-giving act that acquires its meaning through the content of this very act and which moreover can be only reflected upon as an already formed objectivity, it must have for that reason overlapped upon its very enactment performed 'in advance' of its reflection in a constant mirror-interplay of reflecting-reflected. This means of course that it could be generated an infinite regression, in terms of reflecting-reflected, of a priori intentional cognitive acts 'in advance' of their reflection and of their resulting objectification. And yet this infinite regression is taken as a complete process in generating the unique existence of an object x through the application of a universal–existential quantification $\forall - \exists$ by essentially putting within ontological brackets the 'vacuous distance' between reflecting self and reflected 'image'. This is done, to cite some instances, in establishing the weak continuity principle for numbers in intuitionistic theory, in applying the Weierstrassian (ϵ, δ)-criterion in the definition of the continuity of a function and, notably, in the definition of a nonstandard number x (see: par. 3).

Put in a schematic way if we symbolize, in the 'observation' of an intentional object, an intentional enactment by G_i, $i \in I_1$, and the corresponding objectification by $T(G_i)$,[11] then for a definite i and its successor, be it j (suc$(i) = j$), we would have a new corresponding objectification $T(G_{ij})$, $j \in I_2$, next for j and its successor k we would have a new objectification $T(G_{ijk})$, $k \in I_3$ and after n successors we would have for the n-th successor l a corresponding objectification $T(G_{\underbrace{ijk....l}_{n}})$ and this way *ad infinitum*. Based though on the evidence of real world experience this infinite regression of successive objectifications, generated by an ideally infinite series of intentional enactments toward a concrete 'something'-in general, is annulled by a certain kind of fulfillment bridging, in effect, the still non-reflected enactment acting in the present-now with its objectification upon reflection. This kind of fulfillment in full generality was meant by J. Patočka as a form of retention in general, ultimately establishing itself as 'being' interposed between the reflecting pure ego of consciousness and its inward gaze on itself (Patočka 1992, p. 166). This retention to the extent that fulfills the 'distance' between the pre-reflectively acting ego and its self-image apprehended in reflection is the presupposition of any possible reflection that establishes objectivity. It is, in fact, the retention that 'covers the distance' between the acting-constituting ego taken in an absolute sense and its objective identical self upon reflection. But obviously this is a quite obscure state of affairs for then we might face the circularity of considering this originally interposed retention between the pure subjectivity of ego (in other terms the pre-reflective ego) and its objective self as a datum in itself of intentionality and thus

---

[11] We take each I_i to be a countable set having as elements parametrized temporal instants corresponding to original impressions with the exclusion in each phase of instants corresponding to previous objectifications.

enter a new endless interplay of reflecting-reflected. It is worthwhile, concerning the ultimately transcendental character of the subjective foundation of temporal objectivity, to compare at this point with A.N. Whitehead's notion of genetic division in the process of forming actual entities toward the stage of complete actualization in view of the ontological elusiveness and, for that matter, the impossibility of a first-order analytic discourse with regard to the process of genetic division (see: Whitehead 1978, pp. 283–284; Livadas 2013, p. 133).

Leaving aside for the moment the discussion on the possibility of an inherently temporal character of predicative statements applying universal–existential quantification over an indefinite horizon, I turn toward more specific logical–mathematical questions within the broadly meant scope of this article.

One of the great questions in the foundations of mathematics still remaining open to various theoretical and even philosophical approaches is the question of the mathematical continuum and its cardinality. A standard set-theoretical conception of the continuum is the one that defines it as the set 2^N of all functions from the set of natural numbers N onto the two-member set $\{0, 1\}$. In this representation and as long as rules in the form of definite statements are thought of as specific procedures to carry out concrete evaluations, they can define a function in a way that each definite statement between natural numbers n, m (e.g., in the form $(\forall n)\,(\exists !\, m)\, P(n,m)$) determines a function $F : N \to \{0, 1\}$ by the equivalence

$$F(n) = m \longleftrightarrow P(n,m) \quad (I)$$

(In the predicative formula above the punctuation mark ! means that for each n there is a unique m).

The question that could be raised here is what sort of statements P can be actually considered as definite. For instance, it is clear that the relation $P(n, m)$ between arbitrary $n \in N$ and $m = 0, 1$ for which $m = 1 \leftrightarrow n$ is odd (1), is a definite one at least from a conventional point of view. But what about the statements below:

$$m = 1 \leftrightarrow n \text{ is the number of primes such that } \frac{\pi(n)}{\frac{n}{\ln(n)}} < 100{,}001 \cdot 10^{-5} \quad (2)$$

and the one given by Feferman (2009, p. 14),

$$m = 1 \leftrightarrow n \text{ is the number such that } \mathbf{GCH} \text{ holds at } n \quad (3)$$

which are at least ambivalent in terms of our current mathematical knowledge.[12] Concerning statement (3), even in acknowledging that the independence of Generalized Continuum Hypothesis (**GCH**) from the rest of the axioms of the Zermelo–Fraenkel theory with the Axiom of Choice (**ZFC**) obviously generates its

---

[12] The statement (2) makes an assertion about the cardinality of prime numbers up to a certain bound, something that is dependent on the asymptotic character of the Prime Number Theorem and the inherent vagueness of the particular distribution law which is moreover associated with the intricacies of the still unsolved Riemann hypothesis. The Prime Number Theorem states that the limit of the quotient of the following two functions: $\pi(x)$ (the function that gives the number of primes less than or equal to a real number x) and $\frac{x}{\ln(x)}$, as x approaches infinity, is 1; this is expressed by the formula $\lim\limits_{x \to +\infty} \frac{\pi(x)}{\frac{x}{\ln(x)}} = 1$.

vagueness, there exists already some kind of inherent vagueness due to the application of the universal quantification formula $(\forall n)(\exists! m)$ P (n, m) (something that happens also with statement (2)) which generates a certain measure of indefiniteness by universally quantifying over the whole set of natural numbers N and even beyond over the realm of infinite cardinals. As a matter of fact, the implicit application of a universal quantification over an indefinite horizon in statements (2) and (3) generates an inherent difficulty in construing a well-meant function F by means of equivalence (**I**) and clearly shows the impasse one may get in in case he lets a universal quantification over an indefinite horizon generate a supposedly well-defined mathematical object. In fact, an unconditional acceptance of a universal quantification over N is straightforwardly associated with the acceptance of a well-determined meaning for the sentence 'all arbitrary sequences of 0s and 1s' and consequently a well-determined meaning for the set 2^N of all subsets of N considered as a definite totality.

Obviously the difficulty concerning the postulation of the set 2^N of all functions from N onto the set $\{0, 1\}$ as a definite totality also concerns the definition of the set $S(N)$ of all subsets of N.[13] As S. Feferman admitted, the acceptance of the existence of the sets 2^N or $S(N)$ as definite totalities requires a platonist ontology which means the acceptance of their objective existence independently of human conceptions, something that runs contrary to his alternative position of conceptual structuralism (Feferman 2009, pp. 14–15). In accepting their existence as definite totalities, any statement (or relation) expressed by applying universal quantification over 2^n or $S(N)$ is taken as a definite one which is evidently a vicious circle interplay since any universal quantification over 2^n or $S(N)$, regardless of any temporal or constitutional concerns for these quantifications, clearly reproduces new and more intricate definite totalities increasingly at odds with natural intuition. On this account "both intuitionists and predicativists reject the assumption of any completed infinite totality of uncountable cardinality, and in particular the set-theoretical conceptions of 2^n and $S(N)$ as definite totalities" (Feferman 2009, p. 20).[14]

In view of the inherently vague character of a broad class of infinite sets taken as definite totalities Feferman held view that key questions such as Cantor's *Continuum Hypothesis* (**CH**) should be rather considered on their own merits and in particular as making sense within the realm of some kind of set-theoretical platonism and not as being structurally founded on the concept of the set of real numbers. Such independent questions of mathematical foundations clearly demonstrate the analytic limits of formal logical predication concerning in particular the tool of universal–existential quantification over a boundless vague horizon in quantifying, for instance, over all subsets of $S(N)$ with regard to the **CH** question. On a deeper level and on account of my phenomenologically motivated approach the **CH** question might be in fact associated, partially at least, with the 'ontological

---

[13] The equivalence between the two descriptions can be easily seen by associating with each function F from N to $\{0, 1\}$, the subset X of all naturals n such that $F(n) = 1$; inversely, each member X of $S(N)$ determines a function F given by the equivalence $F(n) = 1 \leftrightarrow n \in X$.

[14] Nonetheless one can say that even in intuitionistic analysis one has to resort *in rem* to some implicit sense of completed infinite totality. One may cite, for instance, the continuity of functions in intuitionism founded on the notion of choice sequences taken as complete objects (Heyting 1966, pp. 42–46).

vacuum' generated in the constant interplay of reflecting subjectivity—reflected objectivity in the process of constituting infinite objective wholes in presentational immediacy out of distinct intentional acts ideally extendible *ad infinitum*.[15]

The far-reaching consequences of a universal quantification in connection with predicate formulas representing definite (in a first reading) statements that involve formal objects of set-theory can be also seen in the course of the proof of Gödel's incompleteness theorems. More specifically, one may refer to the proof of the first incompleteness theorem which essentially states that if T is any recursive, consistent set of axioms extending **ZF** theory then it is incomplete in the sense that there might be a sentence φ such that $T \not\vdash \varphi$ and $T \not\vdash \neg \varphi$. As it is known a key step in the original proof was Gödel's idea of arithmetizing, in terms of the so-called Gödel numbers, the constructs of a formal theory. Complex formulas are inductively constructed based on the possibility of a unique prime factorization of each positive integer and on the general rule that whenever $\mathbf{x_0}, \mathbf{x_1}, \ldots, \mathbf{x_s}$ are entities to which respective numbers $x_0, x_1, \ldots, x_s$ have already been assigned then to the successor entity $(\mathbf{x_0}, \mathbf{x_1}, \ldots, \mathbf{x_s})$ it is assigned by prime factorization the unique number $p_0^{x_0} \cdot p_1^{x_1} \cdot \ldots \cdot p_s^{x_s}$ (Kleene 1980, pp. 254–255, see also: Nagel and Newman 1958, pp. 69–97).

The metatheoretical content of formal objects, introduced in a theory through extension by definitions of its set of sentences, is primarily expressed by means of two kinds of predicate formulas, the Level-1 and Level-2 formulas; for instance, a Level-1 formula may be one of the form $\mathcal{X}_{\text{even}}(x) \equiv \exists y \in \omega \, (x = \ulcorner 2 \urcorner y)$ and a Level-2 formula one of the form $\forall x \in \omega \, (\mathcal{X}_{\text{even}}(x) \vee \mathcal{X}_{\text{even}}(x + \ulcorner 1 \urcorner))$. In the case of the Level-1 formula above we can easily check whether for example, $\mathbf{ZF} \vdash \mathcal{X}_{\text{even}}(10)$ or whether $\mathbf{ZF} \vdash \mathcal{X}_{\text{even}}(11)$. Moreover it is generally proved, in metatheoretical terms, that any recursive set A of natural numbers is formally representable (in **ZF** theory) in the sense that:

$$n \in A \rightarrow (\mathbf{ZF} \vdash \mathcal{X}_A(\ulcorner n \urcorner)) \text{ and } n \notin A; \rightarrow (\mathbf{ZF} \vdash \neg \mathcal{X}_A(\ulcorner n \urcorner))$$

Level-1 formulas, indeed, formally reflect the finitistic character of the metatheoretical objects involved which are intuitively conceived as such by their very construction. In contrast an issue concerning the finitistic character of corresponding metatheoretical objects may be raised in dealing with Level-2 assertions as the aforementioned one, i.e. $\mathbf{ZF} \vdash \forall x \in \omega \, (\mathcal{X}_{\text{even}}(x) \vee \mathcal{X}_{\text{even}}(x + \ulcorner 1 \urcorner))$. In this case there is a non-rigorously defined notion of finitistic which is generated on the formal level by means of a universal quantification over the set of all natural numbers (taken as a definite whole). It is known that Level-2 formulas are critically involved in the proof of both incompleteness theorems and Tarski's undefinability of truth lemma in endorsing assertions of the form:[16]

---

[15] On details of this interpretational approach the reader may consult Livadas (2012, pp. 260–265, 2015).

[16] In this assertion the predicate $\mathcal{X}(u, w)$ formally represents a recursive map of finite sequences. The application of this assertion is a key part in the proof of the general form of Tarski's undefinability of truth lemma (Kunen 1982, pp. 40–41).

$$\text{ZF} \ \vdash \ \forall u \ \exists! w \ \mathcal{X}(u, w)$$

generated through a universal quantification over an indefinite 'horizon' and for that reason implying a vagueness as to the finitistic character of corresponding metatheoretical objects.

There is no substantial difference with the argumentation above regarding the original form of Gödel's first incompleteness theorem. In this case it turns out that we have to rely on Cantor's diagonal method to substitute the numeral **p** for the free variable a in the formula $A_p(a) : \forall b \ \neg A(a, b)$, where p stands for the Gödel number of the formula $A_p(a)$ and b stands for the Gödel number of a proof of this formula. In other words we must rely on Cantor's diagonal method[17] so that for any Gödel number b (by universal quantification) we can find a numeral **p** such that the sentence $A_p(\mathbf{p})$ essentially asserts its own unprovability (Kleene 1980, p. 208). Three remarks here are worthy of attention:

First, Cantor's diagonal method presupposes the acceptance of a set consisting of all infinite sequences of 0s and 1s as a definite totality which means that we face again here the conceptual ambivalence concerning the sets $S(N), S(S(N)),..$ taken as definite totalities. Indeed, the diagonal method helps to reason that there is no enumeration of all infinite paths of 0s and 1s (or what amounts to be the same, of all subsets of N) through the full binary tree representing the natural numbers but this is done on the implicit acceptance of an idealized conception of the sets 2^N (resp. $S(N)$) as definite totalities (Feferman 2012, p. 21).

Second, even in accepting that universal quantification over successor entities (e.g. successive natural numbers) may be in a sense intuitively clear, there remains the fact that Gödel numbering preserves the order relations but destroys the relations of immediate succession.

Third, an essential part of the proof of the first incompleteness theorem relies on the ω-consistency of a number-theoretic formal system. This kind of consistency essentially states that we can be led through the provability of formulas $A_0, A_1, \ldots$ to the provability of the formula $\forall x \ A(x)$, therefore introducing an (indefinite) universal quantification of number-theoretic formulas and for that reason generating a non-finitistic character of the ω-consistency assumption (Kleene 1980, p. 207).[18]

In conclusion, the brief reference to Gödel's incompleteness result above serves to show that statements formally involving a universal quantification of a Level-2 type are prone to intrinsically generate a non-rigorous notion of finitistic with regard to the object/s they help define, this latter notion of finitistic conceived as a metatheoretical one possibly reaching far enough to be associated with a subjective state of actual infinity.

---

[17] Cantor's diagonal argument (method) is a simple but ingenious technique introduced by G. Cantor to prove the existence of sets that cannot be put onto one-to-one correspondence with the set of natural numbers; in other words, it proves the existence of uncountable sets. The method essentially consists in constructing a set whose elements do not belong to any conceivable list of sequences of 0s and 1s, yet this is implicitly conditioned on the concept of an infinite set as a completed totality.

[18] There is a slightly more complicated instance in Rosser (1936, p. 15) of an undecidable formula dispensing with the ω-consistency assumption, yet the form of the new proposed undecidable formula is such that my remarks concerning the application of Cantor's diagonal argument are still valid.

5 A Holistic View of Formal Discourse as Pointing to the Transcendental Character of Absolute Ego: Conclusion

So far I have tried to show, mainly focused on a logical–mathematical context, that predication as a protean form of meaningful formal discourse can be reduced in a phenomenologically grounded approach to an intersubjectively defined form of judgement conditioned on the intentional-constituting presence of at least one embodied temporal consciousness within the life-world. In this approach the syntactical objects of predication in the modes they are logically joined in predicate formulas, taken as abstractions of either physical objects or objects of imagination, are essentially temporally constituted immanences within consciousness pointing to a constituting subjectivity, irrespectively of the fact that we may refer to an empirically verifiable sentence having a factual meaning or to an analytic one having a formal meaning.

Concerning certain empirically verifiable sentences, the kind of separation between the subjective presence of an 'observer' and the 'observed' state-of-affairs existing in the quantum realm is being carried out in the macroscale of our common physical experience in a loose decontextualized way through the implicit imposition of a Boolean logical context to generate a meaningful discourse about well-defined objects in the world of phenomena. The common foundation, however, underlying both contextualized and decontextualized states-of-affairs should be a temporal-constituting one in the sense that all mental states including the formation of judgements as objects of reflection are constituted within the same inner temporality, indeed that one in which also make their appearance all objects of perception including logical–mathematical ones. Moreover meanings considered as subject-meanings, predicate-meanings, or relation-meanings, etc. of various sentences, may be thought of as fundamentally associated with intentional acts (or moments) of experience the contents of which determine these very meanings as identically the same possibly through repeated acts of representation or judgement by any person. In this respect, the identity of meanings is in fact the identity of a species which is essentially constituted as the unity of a multiplicity of meaning-acts, namely of meaning-intentions (*Bedeutungsintentionen*), in a way that each meaning corresponds to respective acts-of-meaning, each logical judgement to respective acts-of-judgement, each logical inference to respective acts-of-inference (Husserl 1984, pp. 105–106).[19]

It turns out, by the argumentation above, that in addition to conditioning a meaningful predication to a separation of a special kind between a constituting subject and the general objects of discourse there is also introduced as a subjective origin of predication the constituting-temporal faculties of any embodied consciousness-in-the-world positing intersubjectively identical objectivities. The present approach tends also to loosen the tight difference between signs and significations, in other words the difference between the semiotic and semantic

---

[19] In this sense, redness as a species is associated, for instance, with the same redness of certain here and there lying red paper ribbons where their individual 'rednesses' are put next to other concrete constituting act-moments (extension, form, etc.).

function of linguistic signs in the sense that linguistic signs cannot be solely taken as referring to a close system of signs-as such but they should be rather considered at the same time as irreducible syntactical building blocks of words and expressions with reference to a special status of intentional, empty-of-content individuals as such associated with meanings as referent to concrete communicative situations in the world of phenomena and ultimately reducible to meaning-acts on the part of an intentionally oriented subject.

My approach from a certain viewpoint (not a properly meant Husserlian one) does also partially justice to the view attributed to J.S. Mill that the laws of logic are extremely highly confirmed empirical generalizations, while at the same time bringing out the core issue of a subjectively constituted temporality and its absolute non-reflective origin termed by Husserl the absolute ego. For insofar as we refer to meanings in the sense of a 'species' generated by the same-content multiplicities of corresponding meaning-acts we have to take into account the subjective forms by which we turn from a multiplicity of appearances as distinct temporal profiles (with regard to a concrete intentional object) to the unity of one and identically the same noematic object. Also we must take into account the subjective temporal factor in shaping well-defined objects-individuals of a formal logical system as abstractions of concrete noematic objects constituted in turn as temporally identical ones out of multiplicities of hyletic–noetic moments of intentionality. Consequently we have to inquire into the inner temporal structure that allows for the possibility of co-existence, invariability and thus transtemporality of formal logical objects and object-meanings and relations, that is, essentially for the possibility to constitute (and therefore conceive) steadiness within incessant change.

Indeed, anything we can conceive of within objective temporality cannot but exist in terms of a changing duration, even in reflecting thematically on our own instantaneous flux of consciousness. In virtue of this it would seem that constancy of objects, meanings, relations, etc. over time would be beyond our reach. In fact almost everything meaningful in natural or formal discourse over millennia of civilization would have been already lost in case we had not been provided with the inner faculty of preserving invariability and further transtemporality within temporal duration, constancy within change. Based, among others, on the evidence of invariability within change one can turn to the concept which Husserl termed absolute flux of consciousness with its specific a priori constituting modes, i.e. forms of retention–protention, that make possible the unity of well-meant objects within the homogenous temporal flux (Husserl 1966, § 12, § 14, § 24). This opens the way for yet another deeper reduction that of reflecting on the absolute flux itself which points to yet another self-constituted 'temporality', that one originating in its own purely subjective self.

Following this line of thought we would be led to a pure subjectivity beyond the absolute flux which would be turned into an objectivity solely by reflection and this way enter a regression of subjectivities *in infinitum*. Husserl answered to this capital question by appealing to the absolute ego of temporal consciousness which he virtually introduced in his *Phenomenology of Inner Time-Consciousness* and left as an obscure and vague notion in his later Bernau Manuscripts (Husserl 2001a) up to his *Late Texts on Temporal Constitution* (Husserl 2001b). My point is that what

Husserl termed as the absolute (or transcendental) ego of consciousness (also referred to as the primary process, *Urprozess*), whose transcendental nature was later criticized by certain philosophers as a back-door entrance of the transcendence of external world into the immanence of consciousness, can reasonably be considered as a transcendental source of logic this latter meant either as a theory in itself pertaining to objects within the world at large or as a metatheoretical support of physical theories winding down to even simple forms of meaningful predicative discourse. The absolute ego may be knowable as an 'image' of itself within temporality, that is, as an identical living-ego in the world, origin of all synthetic immanent processes and in various temporal forms (present, past, future), yet it 'is' nevertheless as such extraneous to the world meant as temporally existing (Husserl 2001b, pp. 30–32 and 120). In short, one is led to ground any objectivity either real or (rationally) imaginable on temporality and yet in order to be able to lay the foundation for temporality itself one has to appeal to a non-objectifiable subjectivity. Based on my arguments so far this is a claim that can be also founded on the essential need to take recourse to an a-temporal non-reflective subjectivity of consciousness in order to break the potentially infinite chain of reflecting-reflected in the constitution of well-meant objects of predicative discourse, establishing therefore an ever being-in-constituting source of the unity of objects and of corresponding meanings as generated from intentional acts. Following my argumentation in previous sections this claim is also founded on the role of inner temporality in shaping invariable over time mathematical–logical objects within meaningful predicate formulas whose variables may be possibly bounded to quantifiers whose scope may be an indefinite one. As I tried to show in Sect. 4 universal quantification over an unbounded horizon can have a very significant metatheoretical role in generating a non-rigorous notion of finitistic in key foundational questions of mathematics.

In view of the above and based on the Husserlian belief that logic has its origin in predicative judgements (Husserl 1972, Engl. transl., p. 11), one can reasonably defend the claim that the transcendence of the absolute ego 'casts its shadow' as an underlying unity-constituting factor in any predicative universe of discourse. In the final count, a conception of logic as originally associated with fundamental predicative judgments rests also upon the notion of life-world as an original ground of experience in whose bounds objective temporality as the common form of all subjective temporalities of lived experiences may constrain in a certain sense the content and range of logical–mathematical concepts referring either to abstract objects of a formal theory or to concrete objects of a physicalistic language.

References

Aristotle (1983) Categories, on interpretation, prior analytics (trans Cooke HP, The Loeb Classical Library)

Feferman S (2009) Conceptions of the continuum. Intellectica 51:169–189

Feferman S (2012) Is the continuum hypothesis a definite mathematical problem? In: EFI Project, Harvard 2011–2012, Draft 9/18/11, pp. 1–29

Heyting A (1966) Intuitionism: an introduction. North-Holland Pub, Amsterdam
Husserl E (1966) Vorlesungen zur Phänomenologie des inneren Zeibewusstseins. Hua Band X, hsgb. R. Boehm, Den Haag: M. Nijhoff
Husserl E (1972) Erfahrung und Urteil. hsgb. L. Landgrebe, Hamburg: Felix Meiner Verlag (Engl. trans (1973) Experience and judgment, trans Churchill JS, Americs K, Routledge and Kegan Paul, London)
Husserl E (1974) Formale und Transzendentale Logik. Hua Band XVII, hsgb. P. Janssen, Den Haag: M. Nijhoff
Husserl E (1976a) Die Krisis der Europäischen Wissenschaften und die Transzendentale Phänomenologie. Hua Band VI, hsgb. W. Biemel, Den Haag: M. Nijhoff
Husserl E (1976b) Ideen zu einer reinen Phänomenologie und phänomenologischen Philosophie, Erstes Buch. Hua Band III/I, hsgb. K. Schuhmann, Den Haag: M. Nijhoff
Husserl E (1984) Logische Untersuchungen. Hua Band XIX/1, hsgb. U. Panzer, The Hague: M. Nijhoff Pub (Engl. transl (2001) Logical investigations, trans Findlay JN, Routledge, New York)
Husserl E (2001a) *Die Bernauer Manusckripte über das Zeitbewusstsein* (1917/18), hsgb. R. Bernet and D. Lohmar, Kluwer Acad. Pub, Dordrecht
Husserl E (2001b) Späte Texte über Zeitkonstitution, Die C-Manuscripte. Hua Materialien Band VIII, hsgb. D. Lohmar, Springer, Dordrecht
Kleene SC (1980) Introduction to metamathematics. North-Holland Pub, New-York
Kunen K (1982) Set theory: an introduction to independence proofs. Elsevier, Amsterdam
Livadas S (2012) Contemporary problems of epistemology in the light of phenomenology. College Publications, London
Livadas S (2013) The notion of process in nonstandard theory and in Whiteheadian metaphysics. Manuscr Rev Intern Filos 36:103–137
Livadas S (2015) The subjective roots of forcing theory and their influence in independence results. Axiomathes 25(4):433–455
Nagel E, Newman J (1958) Gödel's proof. New York University Press, New York
Noe AR (1994) Wittgenstein, phenomenology and what it makes sense to say. Philos Phenomenol Res 54(1):1–42
Ortiz-Hill C (2013) The strange worlds of actual consciousness and the purely logical. In: Hopkins B (ed) The new yearbook for phenomenology and phenomenological philosophy, vol 13. Routledge, Abingdon, pp 62–83
Patočka J (1992) Introduction à la Phénoménologie de Husserl (trans Abrams ER, Ed. Millon, Grenoble)
Quine VW (1947) On universals. J Symb Log 12(3):74–84
Quine VW (1960) Word and object. MIT Press, Cambridge
Rosser B (1936) Extensions of some theorems of Gödel and Church. J Symb Log 1:87–91
Van Atten M, Van Dalen D, Tieszen R (2002) Brouwer and Weyl: the phenomenology and mathematics of the intuitive continuum. Philos Math 10(3):203–226
Whitehead NA (1978) Process and reality: an essay in cosmology. Free Press, New York

Extending the Non-extendible: Shades of Infinity in Large Cardinals and Forcing Theories

Abstract
This is an article whose intended scope is to deal with the question of infinity in formal mathematics, mainly in the context of the theory of large cardinals as it has developed over time since Cantor's introduction of the theory of transfinite numbers in the late nineteenth century. A special focus has been given to this theory's interrelation with the forcing theory, introduced by P. Cohen in his lectures of 1963 and further extended and deepened since then, which leads to a development and further refinement of the theory of large cardinals ultimately touching, especially in view of the discussion in the last section, on the metatheoretical nature of infinity. The whole undertaking, which takes into account major stages of the research in large cardinals theory, tries to present a defensible argumentation against an ontology of infinity actually rooted in the notion of subjectivity within the world. This means that rather than talking of a general ontology of infinity in the ideal platonic or in the aristotelian sense of potentiality, even in the alternative sense of an ontology of the event in A. Badiou's sense, one can argue from a subjective point of view about the impossibility of defining cardinalities greater than the first uncountable one $\aleph_1$ that would correspond to a distinct existence in real world terms or would be supported by a mathematical intuition in terms of reciprocity with experience. The argumentation from the particular standpoint includes also certain comments on the delimitative character of Gödel's constructive universe L and the influence of the constructive approach in narrowing the breadth of an 'ontology' of infinity.

1 Introduction

The main purpose of this article is to deal with the possibility of acceding to and representing other levels of infinity, beyond those associated with the natural and real numbers systems, by means of the theory of large cardinals especially as this theory has evolved after the consistency results of K. Gödel in 1939 and the independence results of P. Cohen in 1963. In assessing the overall capacity of large cardinals theory to decide open problems in the foundations of mathematics a review of its interconnection with the forcing theory will be undertaken in order to forge a defensible argumentation on the necessity of an implicit acceptance of a subjectively founded level of reality as the condition *sine qua non* to establish a formal-axiomatical approach to higher levels of infinity.

A question that can be raised in the study of large cardinals theory is the extent to which the assumption of a subjectively founded level of reality, in particular the conception of the intuitive and formal-mathematical continuum, influences in one way or another the formal-axiomatical development of the theory. One may ask whether this level of reality must be implicitly assumed in extending *ad infinitum*, for instance, the field of application of quantifiers in first-order or second-order formulas in the various stages of the construction of a large cardinal, as it is the case with the definition of κ-complete filters and ultrafilters for $\kappa > \omega$ (ω the first infinite countable ordinal). One may even put into question the ultimate origin of the aforesaid level of reality, that is, whether it can be taken as a broadly conceived version of the intuitive continuum we perceive in our objective experience in real world terms or whether it can be eventually reduced to an immanent[1] continuous unity constituted in temporal consciousness independently of causal and spatio-temporal constraints.

According to Hauser and Woodin in the *Strong Axioms of Infinity and the Debate about Realism*, (2014), strong infinity axioms are a systematic attempt of contemporary set-theorists to quantify and understand the open-endedness of the iterations implemented in the counting of infinite collections by means of two Cantorian principles: The first one, is the transition from any number α to its immediate successor $\alpha + 1$ and the second one yields for a given infinite sequence of numbers its least upper bound, e.g. the infinite cardinal $\omega \cdot \omega = \omega^2$ is the least upper bound (lub) of the infinite sequence $\omega \cdot n$ corresponding to n of ω, with the latter being characterized as the smallest transfinite number which is the lub of the sequence of integers in their canonical enumeration (Hauser and Woodin 2014, pp. 397–398). A primary example of strong infinity axioms are the large cardinal axioms implying the existence of sets of a large size whose size is defined in terms of other infinite

---

[1] The term immanent, widely used in Husserlian and generally phenomenological texts, can be roughly explained as referring to what is or has become correlative (or 'co-substantial') to the being of the flux of one's consciousness in contrast to what is 'external' or transcendental to it. For instance, a tree is transcendental as such to the consciousness of an 'observer' while its appearance in the modes of its appearing within his consciousness is immanent to it.

set-theoretic notions, e.g. for inaccessible cardinals those of limit and regular cardinals, or set-theoretic operations like the closure under the power set operation.

Concerning the large cardinals theory a key part of my discussion will be the place of large cardinals within the context of **ZFC** theory (standard Zermelo–Fraenkel Set Theory with the Axiom of Choice). On this account a special attention will be given to D. Scott's fundamental result of 1961, namely that if there is a measurable cardinal then $V \neq L$, where V is the set-theoretical universe and L is Gödel's constructible universe (Kanamori 2009, p. 49). This result seemed at the time to vindicate K. Gödel's prediction, marginally put in the updated version of his initial *What is Cantor's Continuum Problem?* (1947), that large cardinal axioms might offer in the future a solution to the open questions of formal set theory, including the *Continuum Hypothesis* (**CH**). More specifically for Gödel it was a plausible conjecture that, given P. Mahlo's axioms of infinity, the axiomatic system of set theory was at the time incomplete yet it could be supplemented "without arbitrariness by new axioms which only unfold the content of the concept of set [..]". He noted, further, that "In recent years great progress has been made in the area of axioms of infinity. In particular, some propositions have been formulated which, if consistent, are extremely strong axioms of infinity of an entirely new kind. Dana Scott has proved that one of them implies the existence of non-constructible sets. That these axioms are implied by the general concept of set in the same sense as Mahlo's has not been made clear yet. However, they are supported by strong axioms from analogy, [..]" (Feferman 1990, fn. 20, pp. 260–261).

As a matter of fact the main tool for introducing new and ever more powerful infinite cardinals over the last decades is by means of elementary embeddings,[2] that is, through truth-preserving injective mappings from the set-theoretical universe V into inner models M^3 equipped with structural properties associated each time with an ascending scale of infinity and reflected in the increasing resemblance between V and M. It turns out that through elementary embeddings a sense of connection with Cantor's Absolute can be obtained by increasingly enhancing the 'simulation' of M toward V thus vindicating Gödel's later position that 'every axiom of infinity should be derived from the (extremely plausible) principle that V is indefinable, where definability is to be taken in [a] more and more generalized and idealized sense" (Wang 1996, p. 285). As it happens Scott's result on measurable cardinals obtained by the elementary embeddings approach opened a way of transcending Gödel's delimitative universe of constructibility by contradicting the constructibility axiom $V = L$ through the postulation of existence of a measurable cardinal. Later, Vopěnka and Hrbáček generalized Scott's result by proving that if there is a strongly

---

[2] For structures $\mathcal{M}_0 = <M_0, ...>$ and $\mathcal{M}_1 = <M_1, ...>$ of a language $\mathcal{L}$, an injective function $j : M_0 \longrightarrow M_1$ is an elementary embedding of $\mathcal{M}_0$ into $\mathcal{M}_1$ ($j : \mathcal{M}_0 \prec \mathcal{M}_1$) iff for any formula $\varphi(u_1, ..., u_n)$ of $\mathcal{L}$ and $x_1, ..., x_n \in M_0$

$$\mathcal{M}_0 \vDash \varphi[x_1, ..., x_n] \text{ iff } \mathcal{M}_1 \vDash \varphi[j(x_1), ..., j(x_n)].$$

[3] A class M is an inner model iff M is a transitive model of **ZF** under the $\in$ predicate and contains the class of all ordinals, i.e., $ON \subseteq M$.

compact cardinal then $V \neq L(A)$ for any set A.[4] It is characteristic that both results are conditioned on the existential postulation of a κ-complete ultrafilter over $\kappa > \omega$ which is by itself associated with set-theoretical operations on infinitely many elements above $\aleph_0$ as well as universal quantifications on scales above $\aleph_0$.

A significant part of the present article will be also concerned with the relation of large cardinals to the forcing theory given that since the introduction of forcing theory by P. Cohen in the spring of 1963 there has been an osmotic relationship of the research on large cardinals as such and the further development and expansion of forcing theory. Although very large cardinals were to a significant extent by-products of the research on the possibilities of elementary embeddings and were soon to develop an elegant theory of their own, it was some new forcing results in the 1970s and 1980s that highlighted their potentialities, especially with regard to supercompactness, to establish new relative consistencies of assertions low in the cumulative hierarchy (Kanamori 2011, p. 383). It is widely admitted by set-theorists that part of the influence of very large cardinals in modern set theory is due to the possibilities they give to applications of the method of forcing in view, for instance, of the capability of forcing models to expand the 'width' of a given ground set-theoretic model without changing its 'height' (meaning in rough terms expanding at will its supply of cardinals without adding new ordinals). As it is known this latter technique was applied by P. Cohen in the proof of the negation of the Continuum Hypothesis, **CH**, through the extension of a countable, transitive model of **ZFC** to include $\aleph_2$ new reals.

My whole approach fits with a general outlook concerning the ontological status of formal-axiomatical theories and the ways mathematical platonism may cede its place to an approach that takes mathematical objects as outcomes of a constitution process, 'created' each time anew in the mind and yet taken as intersubjectively invariant and atemporal. This is an approach that has considerable affinities to R. Tieszen's constituted platonism,[5] Tieszen (2011), while taking clear distances from both mathematical platonism and the proponents of mathematical realism having in mind, for the latter case, Hauser's and Woodin's positions in Hauser and

---

[4] There are mathematical notions and definitions in the text for which it would be cumbersome and inconvenient to add an explanatory footnote for each one of them. The interested reader can consult accordingly A. Kanamori's *The Higher Infinite* and K. Kunen's *Set Theory. An Introduction to Independence Proofs*, resp. (Kanamori 2009; Kunen 1982). For a given set A the constructive closure $L(A)$ is defined in Kanamori (2009, p. 34).

[5] Two key positions of R. Tieszen's constituted platonism, a sort of blend of phenomenological analysis with platonic idealist positions refer to: (a) the a priori directedness of intentionality associated not only with sensory objects but also with immanent ones (temporal in nature and generated by 'inner' mental processes) and even ideal ones, that is, non-spatial and 'atemporal' objects such as numbers, elements of sets, aggregation of elements, etc. (b) the characterization of mathematical-logical objects as mind-dependent$_1$ and mind-independent$_2$ (where mind-independence$_2$ falls under mind-dependence$_1$), in the sense that they are intentional objects not constrained by material and causal preoccupations and yet not arbitrary ideal 'counterparts' of appearances in consciousness or pure constructs of imagination (Tieszen 2011, p. 115). This schematic classification is in fact founded on Tieszen's phenomenologically rooted view of mathematical-logical objects as taking their whole sense of being from a subject's intentionality within the world at large.

Woodin (2014).[6] Yet, I share in principle their view that the unexpected convergence of widely varying incentives for strengthening the standard axioms of infinity suggests that all axiomatic extensions of this kind describe different aspects of the same underlying reality.

In the following section I will start with some preliminaries that include definitions of the mathematical notions dealt with in this article, more precisely those deemed necessary for a (philosophically inclined) mathematical reader with a limited knowledge of the field to follow the argumentation. I will devote the next two sections to overview and comment some key points in the structuring of the theory of large cardinals as such and in their feedback with the forcing theory, while dedicating the last section to an extensive discussion of the possibility of a non-reductionistic interpretation of the corresponding theories by espousing a metatheoretical,[7] in fact subjectively founded, approach of strong infinity axioms and consequently of large cardinals. This is an approach that may indeed justify the title of the article and from a certain point of view vindicate W.V. Quine's position about large and very large cardinals as essentially mathematical recreations.

The last section contains, among others, a brief reference along these matters to A. Badiou's epistemology of the event as presented in Badiou (2005). I considered a short discussion of Badiou's approach of the 'technical' mathematical concepts (e.g., generic extensions of sets, large cardinals and the constraints of the forcing method) dealt with in my paper as especially relevant given the non-analytic character of the French philosopher's approach. Besides, although brief for obvious reasons in extent, my discussion of Badiou's ontology of the event and his more mathematically oriented approach helps to better understand my own phenomenologically motivated view toward infinite mathematical objects.

Overall my intention is to provide strong arguments for defending the idea that no matter how high up on the large cardinals scale we may ascend due to ever stronger infinity assumptions there are in fact two non-eliminable kinds of infinity, the one out there in the real world of phenomena which is an ever shifting horizon of finiteness (a nice formalized version of this infinity is the countability of classes in Vopěnka's AST sense; see Vopěnka 1979), and the one subjectively generated by consciousness as an immanent unity in temporal actuality indefinitely extending at will (yet according to certain 'internal' eidetic laws[8]) and totally unhinged by the constraints of causality and spatiotemporal objectivity. This immanent infinity is brought into evidence in subjective terms as a temporal fulfillment that entails the re-presentation of infinite mathematical objects as complete ones in actual

---

[6] Hauser's and Woodin's positions (Hauser and Woodin 2014) can be summed up as proposing in favor of mathematical realism examples in which strong axioms of infinity are demonstrably incomparable thus refuting the anti-realist thesis that the convergence of methods toward higher infinity is a mere artefact of set-theoretical language.

[7] The term metatheoretical used in this text, in a wider and deeper sense than the one referring to a (formal) theory from the 'outside', points to an ultimately subjective foundation.

[8] By an eidetic law in the world of phenomena one can roughly communicate to a non-phenomenologist what is implied by essential necessity and not by mere facticity. The interested reader may consult Husserl's *Ideas I* (Husserl 1976, *Engl. transl.*, pp. 12–15).

presentation. As will be shown throughout my arguments, immanent infinity as such conditions on a fundamental metatheoretical level the conceptual and often technical groundwork relative to the introduction of ever stronger cardinals while generating occasional circularities due to its inherently impredicative character.

2 Some Critical Remarks on the Development of Large Cardinals Theory

My main goal in this section is to run through the development of large cardinals theory and present certain arguments for the fact that this theory, irrespectively of whether it is motivated by internal open questions or evolving in connection with the developments in other research fields, ultimately hinges on concepts that may be reducible on a metatheoretical level to a subjectively founded content. In particular, there seems to be a non-eliminable notion of a 'background' infinity through which to be able to talk about indefinitely extending quantifications bearing existential claims along with maximality principles, well-orderings and transitive collapses which imply on their part the application of some form of the Axiom of Choice (**AC**). This is what I set out to do in the following by referring in some detail to various key issues in the conceptual construction of the theory.

A first remark to be made is that none of the large cardinals can be proved to exist by means of **ZFC** theory alone, assuming that **ZFC** is consistent. They have to be introduced as extra infinity axioms to **ZFC** for which we must settle with the sole condition of not being inconsistent with the rest of **ZFC**. More specifically, to take the case of weakly and strongly inaccessible cardinals,[9] one can easily prove that the **ZFC** system of axioms is consistent with both the existence of these cardinals and its negation. For, taking the universal set V as a model of **ZFC** then either V does not contain any strongly inaccessible cardinal or if it contains we can define a submodel V_κ[10] of **ZFC** for κ the least strongly inaccessible cardinal which obviously contains no strongly inaccessibles. Therefore, the consistency of **ZFC** implies the consistency of **ZFC**+ 'There are no strongly inaccessible cardinals'. In a similar fashion either V contains no weakly inaccessibles, or taking κ the least ordinal which is weakly inaccessible relative to any standard submodel of V, then the constructive class L_κ is a model of **ZFC** which contains no weakly inaccessible cardinals, therefore the consistency of **ZFC** implies the consistency of **ZFC**+ 'There are no weakly inaccessible cardinals'. This means that **ZFC** is consistent with the negation of existence of both kinds of inaccessible cardinals.

On the other hand the consistency of **ZFC** implies that V_κ is a model of **ZFC** whenever κ is strongly inaccessible, whereas the consistency of **ZF** implies that the

---

[9] A cardinal κ is weakly inaccessible iff κ is a regular limit cardinal and it is strongly inaccessible iff $\kappa > \omega$, κ is regular and $\forall \lambda < \kappa$ ($2^\lambda < \kappa$).

[10] In the cumulative hierarchy the submodel V_κ is defined to be the collection of all sets whose von Neumann rank is less than κ and is a model of ZFC. The constructive class L_κ is the class recursively defined for the ordinal κ within Gödel's constructive universe L; see for details: Kunen (1982, pp. 166–167).

Gödel class L_κ is a model of **ZFC** whenever κ is weakly inaccessible. Consequently, the consistency of **ZFC** implies the consistency of **ZFC**+ 'There exists a strongly inaccessible cardinal' and of **ZFC**+ 'There exists a weakly inaccessible cardinal'. This has as an obvious result that the existence of these two low hierarchy large cardinals is independent from the rest of the axioms of **ZFC**, in other words **ZFC** has not the proof-theoretic means to prove or disprove the existence of inaccessible cardinals.[11]

It happens that a significant part of the theory of large cardinals is about the concept of measurable cardinals[12] largely brought out of the quest to expand the notion of Lebesgue measure to all sets of real numbers. In somewhat different formulations than current ones, measurable cardinals along with two other classes of large cardinals, the weakly and strongly compact ones, were thoroughly studied in the Keisler–Tarski, Tarski and Erdös–Tarski seminal papers, (resp. in: Keisler and Tarski 1964; Tarski 1962; Tarski and Erdös (1943), and thought to establish a properly large cardinal character in the sense that: (a) they introduce the existence of a large cardinal which is essentially larger than low-hierarchy cardinals, i.e. the inaccessible and other 'smaller' ones, and moreover they are represented as critical points of 'thinning' procedures narrowing the universal set to more flexible and susceptible to definability constraints inner models and (b) they provide new strength to set theory for the provability of open formal statements (e.g. the truth or falsity of **GCH**[13]) while enriching the structure of the cumulative hierarchy itself with new combinatorial properties. Concerning, in particular, the settling of the **CH** question it must be said that a formative result was Martin's Maximum implying $2^{\aleph_0} = \aleph_2$, something that heated up a discussion on the possibility of forcing axioms to determine the size of the continuum. Yet the strong forcing axioms implicated in this quest (Proper Forcing Axiom and Martin's Maximum) are conditioned on strong cardinal assumptions, namely the assumption of supercompact cardinals[14] (Kanamori 2011, p. 394 and 397). However the existence of these latter cardinals cannot be conceived independently of the assumption of existence of normal ultrafilters (generated by κ

---

[11] It is interesting to note in connection with the independence of the existence of inaccessible cardinals, that the 'conventional' axiom of infinity in **ZFC** theory has the notable characteristic that its truth implies its independence of the other axioms essentially due to the fact that the infinite set of hereditarily finite sets forms a model of the other axioms in which there is no infinite set. Therefore as the assertion of the truthfulness of the infinity axiom implies its independence we are forced to introduce it as a new axiom and moreover one should expect that the postulation of existence of ever larger cardinals to have this character, as it indeed has. Solovay et al. (1978, p. 73).

[12] A major concept of large cardinals theory, associated with a generalization of Lebesgue's measure, is that of measurable cardinals whose definition is this: For a cardinal $\kappa > \omega$, κ is measurable iff there is a κ-complete (non-principal) ultrafilter over κ (Kanamori 2009, p. 26).

[13] As a matter of fact this particular question is left unanswered by adding to the **ZF** axioms the large cardinal axiom of existence of a measurable cardinal (Lèvy and Solovay 1967, p. 1). In another paper Jensen has proved by forcing techniques that **GCH** (*Generalized Continuum Hypothesis*) is consistent with the existence of large cardinals, in particular with the existence of measurable and Ramsey cardinals (Jensen 1974, pp. 175–177).

[14] A cardinal $\kappa > \omega$ is defined as supercompact iff for all ordinals $\lambda \geq \kappa$ there is an elementary embedding $j : V \longrightarrow M$ with critical point κ (i.e. the least ordinal 'moved' by j) and $\lambda < j(\kappa)$ such that any sequence of elements from M with length λ belongs to M.

-ultrafilters with $\kappa > \omega$ by a simple 'projection' operation) which in a circular turn are conditioned on the metatheoretical assumption of a completed infinity on which to perform logical-mathematical acts, e.g. universal-existential quantifications, over an indefinite extension. A further discussion on this kind of infinity will be undertaken in the last section.

A dominant option of generating new strong axioms of infinity is the one in which one may use the same guiding idea (think of the 'thinning' procedures narrowing the universal set V to more flexible and susceptible to definability constraints inner models) to get stronger and stronger axioms in which case if the strong infinity axioms are given as a recursively enumerable sequence it must be incomplete (due to Gödel's results) and therefore let the guiding idea 'continue' forever. Yet Kunen's result in *Elementary Embeddings and Infinitary Combinatorics*, Kunen (1971), has set an upper limit to this ascending procession by obtaining, with the indirect application of the Axiom of Choice, that there is no non-trivial elementary embedding of the set-theoretical universe V into itself. Further he established that if there were such a case it would be inconsistent with the Axiom of Choice. While still pending an answer to the question of whether in **ZF** without **AC** can be proved the existence of a non-trivial elementary embedding of the set-theoretical universe V into itself, Kunen's result can be seen anyway as placing a 'natural' bound to our efforts to (elementarily) embed the universe V into too 'spacious' an inner model, while by the same token highlighting the influence the Axiom of Choice may generally have on foundational questions (Solovay et al. 1978, pp. 82–83). In this view, one should not be "troubled by the fact that what appeared to be the 'ultimate' strong axiom of infinity - the existence of an elementary embedding of V into itself - turned out to be inconsistent with the Axiom of Choice" (Hauser and Woodin 2014, p. 407, fn. 41). Even though this argument may show the mathematical intuition's inherent deficiency, in accepting as naively obvious the existence of such an ultimate infinity axiom, my view is that Kunen's result also vindicates the claim that placing an order in whatever logical-mathematical system one might think of ultimately 'suppresses' its universality with the tacit assumption that these notions even in their most abstract sense are reducible to purely mental constructions. For instance, the Axiom of Choice may refer to the mental state of an intentionally oriented subject in which he reserves himself the possibility of selecting each temporal instant, in a discrete and unique fashion, a mathematical object taken in the sense of a lowest-level element of a transitive class under $\in$.

More generally on questions of methodology I point to the following principles, where a subjectively founded interpretation follows below, as instrumental in the formulation of large cardinal properties: (1) **generalization**, in the sense of attributing certain properties of countable limit ordinal ω to uncountable cardinals in the case of the definition of κ-complete ultrafilters, or in founding the existence of strongly compact cardinals to a generalization of the Compactness Theorem of lower predicate calculus to infinitary languages $\mathcal{L}_{\kappa\kappa}$, (2) **reflection**, as a generalization of the ordinary reflection principle generating e.g., the indescribable cardinals, (3) **resemblance**, closely related to the reflection principle and the structure of the cumulative hierarchy generating along with reflection the extendible cardinals and (4) **restriction**, as a weakening of known assertions to get sharpened implications, e.g., in the definition of Rowbottom and Ramsey cardinals from measurable ones (Solovay et al. 1978, p. 75).

It is important to note that while the reflection principle is provable as a statement in **ZF** theory (without the Axiom of Choice) insofar as first-order parameters are allowed in the reflecting formulas, yet it is conditioned on the well-ordering and transitivity property of ordinals which may metatheoretically mean that it is dependent on the preservation of individuals as 'content-free' elements in cumulative transitive structures. However if second-order parameters are allowed in reflecting formulas the reflection principle is a strong axiom of infinity which is unprovable in **ZFC** theory. As a consequence the ordinals indexing segments of V, in case the reflecting formulas contain higher order parameters, are taken to generate the indescribable cardinals (Hauser and Woodin 2014, p. 400).

A concept critically involved in the development of the theory of large cardinals is that of inner model roughly conceived as a way to refine the concept of the set-theoretical universe V in terms of the transitivity property and the supply of ordinals. This way one may restrict the power-set operation to definable sets of a certain level V_α of V to produce the elements of the next level $V_{\alpha+1}$ and thus generate the Gödel constructible universe **L** which is regarded as the smallest inner model. As a matter of fact, inner models are directly involved in questions asking about the 'height' and 'width' of the set-theoretical universe V, the 'height' associated with new infinities arising on top of existing ones and the 'width' with the breadth of the power set operation in the individual levels V_α.

As it turned out the concept of inner models coupled with the notion of elementary embeddings proved to be a new radical method and a high-powered tool to recast large cardinals in a way that a class of strong infinity principles arising from concrete mathematical problems found a fairly homogenous context to be dealt with. A prominent case in point is that of measurable cardinals whose postulation of existence, as already mentioned, was an outgrowth of the efforts to extend the Lebesgue measure to all sets of reals. It was indeed by means of the notions of a κ-complete ultrafilter and of an elementary embedding of the universe V to an inner model M, that D. Scott reached the key result that measurability is unconstrained by constructibility limitations ($V \neq L$), while new and stronger cardinals were introduced in the process by further elaborating and expanding the range of inner models M toward the scope of V. These cardinals are generally defined to be the critical points of the respective elementary embeddings, i.e., the least ordinals moved by such elementary embeddings j, $j(\kappa) \neq \kappa$. Further, it is proved for measurable cardinals κ that any 'slice' $V_{\kappa+1}$ of V is found in M as also happens with any κ-sequence of elements of M. The definition of supercompact cardinals (fn. 14) is an even stronger one in this sense and moreover it is proved that the existence of supercompact cardinals does not entail the existence of still larger cardinals. The characterization of λ-supercompactness in terms of the existence of normal ultrafilters over $\mathcal{P}_\kappa(\lambda)$ and the fundamental notion of an elementary embedding of the universe V into inner model M are indicative of the power and scope of the particular method in engendering large cardinals.

In the next I will show, basically in connection with measurable cardinals, that the whole concept of elementary embeddings of which measurable cardinals are critical points rests in a fundamental way on the implicit acceptance of principles which are conditioned on a pre-existing notion of actual infinity as a completed whole in actuality and also on constitutional a priori capacities on the part of a mathematically performing subject.

For the moment I note that the aforesaid Scott's result ($V \neq L$) enlarged the field of possibilities for reaching Cantor's Absolute by transcending Gödel's delimitative universe $V = L$ while undermining at the same time Gödel's effort to provide the minimum possibility for the construction of a model of **ZF** in the way of the ramified hierarchy of *Principia Mathematica* applied in an entirely non-constructive way. What is more, the fact that measurable cardinals contradict $V = L$ inspired research that was to establish further the intrinsic need of large cardinals for transcending such hypotheses. Indeed the generalizations of constructibility to accommodate measurability led to elaborate theories of minimal models for large cardinal hypotheses demonstrating de facto, through an ample host of results, the success of large cardinals in settling a large variety of questions (among them many about definable sets of reals) and thus vindicating Gödel's professed hopes about large cardinals stated in his well-known 1947 article *What is Cantor's Continuum Problem?*: "First of all the axioms of set theory by no means form a system closed in itself, but, quite on the contrary, the very concept of set on which they are based suggests their extension by new axioms which assert the existence of still further iterations of the operation 'set of'. These axioms can also be formulated as propositions asserting the existence of very great cardinal numbers..." (Feferman 1990, p. 181).

Yet from a metatheoretical point of view Scott's result as well as several propositions involving measurable cardinals are based on the concepts mentioned already, namely on the construction of elementary embeddings coupled with ultrapower constructions Ult (V, U),[15] conditioned in turn on a 'non-contextual' notion of actual infinity serving to perform quantifications of an indefinitely large order and also the possibility of application of independent from the theory **ZF** axioms as it is the Axiom of Choice or its logical equivalents. More specifically, the κ-completeness of an ultrafilter U except for the notion of a completed infinity on which to perform a quantification of order $\kappa > \omega$, it is also fundamentally associated with a notion of well-foundedness of the corresponding order relation $\leq_U$ between its equivalence classes which is critical in engendering its transitive collapse to an inner model M. The very construction of an ultrafilter, at least, is well-known to be based on the assumption of maximality principles logically equivalent to the Axiom of Choice.

As stated in the Introduction a reason large cardinal propositions have a widely osmotic relation with the theory of forcing is due to the possibilities they offer for applications of forcing, a special case of which are the equiconsistency results, namely the derivation of logical equivalences between large cardinal hypotheses and combinatorial propositions about low levels of the cumulative hierarchy essentially

---

[15] The ultrapower Ult (V, U) is constructed as a quotient space on the basis of a κ-complete ultrafilter U over the set-theoretical universe V which is subsequently transformed into an inner model M by Mostowski's transitive collapse.

achieved by application of the Levy collapse.[16] On a fundamental theoretical level Cohen's forcing techniques showed how relative the Cantorian concept of cardinality can be by adjoining any infinite number of distinct bijective functions to the forcing model while making sure that cardinals are preserved between the base and the forcing model. Of course such manoeuvering takes advantage of the fact that cardinals have the fundamental distinction with regard to ordinals of not being absolute mathematical objects due to their very definition as representatives of numerical equivalences. Therefore set-powers like $2^{\aleph_0}$ can be made arbitrarily large, while large cardinals may be found to satisfy substantial propositions of a lower hierarchical level after they are Levy collapsed to ω_1 or ω_2. Conversely such lower level propositions were found to entail in an L-like inner model the very same large cardinal hypotheses initially assumed.

A characteristic example of a large cardinal assumption generating lower-level properties by means of the forcing method is a nice result of R. Solovay reached shortly (1964) after Cohen's public communication of his independence results through forcing:

> If there is an inaccessible cardinal, then in a **ZF** inner model of a forcing extension the principle of Dependent Choices (DC) holds and every set of reals is Lebesgue measurable, has the Baire property and also has the perfect set property (Solovay 1970, p. 1).

With an eye to the philosophical discussion of the last section, one should pay attention to the fact that Solovay's transitive $\in$-model cannot prove the existence of non-Lebesgue measurable sets of reals without assuming the Axiom of Choice, a fact already known in reverse sense by G. Vitali's earlier construction of a non-Lebesgue measurable set of reals from a well-ordering of the reals. Even the weaker assumption of the Dependent Choices Principle which establishes a sense of order by allowing countably many consecutive choices does not suffice to construct a theory strong enough to prove the existence of a non-measurable set.

If the universality and strength of the forcing method[17] is an underlying factor of R. Solovay's result above, it may be nevertheless argued that the forcing method has been proved insufficiently effective to resolve the *Continuum Hypothesis* even under the assumption of a 'conventional' strong infinity assumption, namely the existence of an inaccessible cardinal. The case is also a reminder of the inherent limitations of strong infinity assumptions to influence the decidability of **CH** in view of the fact

---

[16] The collapsing of cardinals is an ingenious forcing technique primarily founded on the notions of genericity and absoluteness. Thus an uncountable cardinal in a base model M can be made to collapse to a countable cardinal in the forcing model $M[G]$ thanks to the generic property of an onto function $\bigcup G$ over $M[G]$, where G is a P-generic set over a partially ordered set P in M (in this case the poset P can be the set of finite functions from the infinite countable cardinal ω to an uncountable cardinal κ). The Levy collapse is a generalization of the technique involving a regular cardinal κ and a cardinal $\lambda > \kappa$ which can be made to collapse to κ in the generic extension. For details, see Kunen (1982, p. 205) and Jech (2006, p. 237).

[17] For a discussion of the metatheoretical foundations of forcing theory the reader may look into Livadas (2015).

that traditionally strong axioms of infinity did not have any effect on the number of subsets of a given set with the partial exception of the assumption of existence of a measurable cardinal which, as already said, entails the existence of non-constructible sets (via $V \neq L$). Yet while it has been proved, thanks to research by Rowbottom, Gaifman, Silver and Solovay, that on the assumption of the existence of measurable cardinals there exist many non-constructible subsets of ω, the answer to the question of whether there exist more than $\aleph_1$ subsets of ω, in which case the *Continuum Hypothesis* is refuted, is still elusive. Instead, Levy and Solovay have proved that on the hypothesis that **ZF+** 'there is a measurable cardinal' is a consistent theory then both the *Continuum Hypothesis* and its negation can be consistently added to **ZF** (Lèvy and Solovay 1967, p. 235). This is an argument generalizable to other large inaccessible cardinals.

3 A Phenomenologically Motivated Subjectivism as Alternative to Realist versus Antirealist Positions Toward Infinity

In his well-known article *Is mathematics syntax of language?*, (Feferman 1990, pp. 334–356), Gödel set out to refute R. Carnap's systematic attempt at a reduction of mathematics into a syntax of language generating its objects through combinations of finitely many symbols. In a certain sense, in defending his version of mathematical realism Gödel was arguing against nominalism and conventionalism with the content these philosophical positions had acquired early on in the positivistic circle of Vienna (R. Carnap, H. Hahn, M. Schlick, O. Neurath, *et al*). Given his grasp of the key foundational questions of mathematics and his evolving philosophical background it can be said that Gödel's conceptual realism cannot be properly assessed without taking into account his views on epistemology and the ways in which, under the influence of Husserl's readings in later years, he shaped his position on intuition, mathematical reason and his particular approach of an ontology of mathematical-logical objects. From a certain viewpoint Gödel's conceptual realism may well be considered itself as a peculiar kind of objective idealism (Hauser 2006, p. 542). In fact, Gödel's evolving philosophical stance may be thought of as part of the ever pertinent philosophical debate between the camps of realists and anti-realists which was heated up in the subsequent years amid the ongoing research in mathematical foundations and the generation of a host of theories and results leading to ever stronger infinity assumptions and consequently ever larger infinite cardinals.

Arguing for the non-eliminability of abstract and transfinite concepts of mathematics by considerations based on finite combinations of symbols in a purely syntactical context, Gödel argued that "instead of clarifying the meanings of the non-finitary mathematical terms by explaining them in terms of syntactical rules, non-finitary terms are [used] in order to formulate the syntactical rules; and instead of justifying the mathematical axioms by reducing them to syntactical rules, these axioms (or at least some of them) are necessary in order to justify the syntactical rules (as consistent)" (Feferman 1995, p. 342). Further, Gödel cited Ramsey's ideas that "necessitate admitting propositions of infinite (and even non-denumerable) length" and Carnap's use of non-finitary syntactical rules and arguments (ibid., p. 343) to point to the impossibility of a syntactical-finitistic reduction of mathematics which is generated, as a matter of fact, by the non-eliminability of the mathematical content of an axiomatic system by a syntactical interpretation. Yet Gödel, and it is in this sense that he may be branded as a special case mathematical realist, did not entirely banish empirical induction from formulating mathematical truths to the extent that for certain mathematical axioms "there exists no other rational (and not merely practical) foundation except either that they [..] can directly be perceived to be true (owing to the meaning of the terms or by an intuition of the objects falling under them), or that they are assumed (like physical hypotheses) on the grounds of inductive arguments, e.g., their success in the applications" (ibid., pp. 346–347). However, he adamantly insisted that mathematical reason is different from sense perception insofar as with the latter we know particular objects and their properties and relations, while with the former we perceive the most general (namely the formal) concepts and their relations, going as far as to suggest that these formal concepts are separated from space-time reality to the extent that this reality is completely determined by the totality of particularities of experience without necessitating a reference to the formal concepts.

Gödel's brand of rational platonism bordering to an elaborate realism with regard to mathematical concepts in general and to existential assertions in particular, was motivated by his general (and to a certain extent phenomenologically influenced) view of mathematical-logical objects as 'existent' in a separate realm from that of space-time reality and yet accessible to us through a relation of a special kind we bear with objects themselves independently of sensuous experience. Claiming that the ideas of transfinite objects or operations "cannot be known to be meaningful or consistent unless we trust some mathematical intuition of things completely inaccessible to (*author's add.:* physical) experience" he characterized, for instance, the existential statement 'there exists' as a transfinite (and in a sense non-constructive) concept insofar as this phrase means objective existence regardless of actual producibility in objective spatio-temporality (ibid., fn. 20, p. 341).

Research over the last decades in the new and fruitful fields of forcing theory and large cardinals has provided the motivation and the theoretical ground for new dimensions in Gödel's arguments and has generally further contributed to the debate between the realist and anti-realist positions in mathematics. In the *Strong Axioms of Infinity and the Debate about Realism*, Hauser and Woodin argue for the realist position against the anti-realist one on account of the philosophical significance of the regularities (e.g., the observed linearity) found in the system of strong axioms of infinity, even though to their admission there is not as yet an established mathematical 'explanation' (Hauser and Woodin 2014, fn. 22). As realists they feel that the 'astonishing convergence' found in the plethora of the strong axioms of infinity would remain a mystery unless one admits that they represent different aspects of an independent reality, whereas for an anti-realist the observed linearity of the large cardinal hierarchy means nothing 'extrinsic' to the theory and moreover comparability between infinity axioms is ubiquitous and is the natural outcome of the principles and structure of the theory unless it is deliberately encoded in the respective definitions.

Ultimately for the anti-realist side the explanation offered for this ubiquitous comparability between (strong) infinity axioms is justified either on logical-syntactical grounds or on intuitions founded in human psychology. In any case for the anti-realists there is no question of granting an ontological status to some kind of higher infinite reality amounting for them to no more than syntax or psychology. Defending the realist view and standing against reductionist schemes in general, Hauser and Woodin acknowledge in effect that the 'true jump' in mathematical reality is from the finite to the infinite while presenting at the same time a case of strong axioms of infinity which are intuitively plausible and yet demonstrably incomparable (ibid., pp. 10–11). Although the authors do not regard such examples as construed to support mathematical realism per se, yet these examples may be useful just to show possible deficiencies of the realist position in mathematics to the extent that this position does not give to the constitutive role of the subject its due, that is, to the role played by an intentionally[18] oriented consciousness of a mathematically performing subject. In the following I will argue for this view by discussing their technical in nature argument in some greater detail.

The argument hinges on the possibility of construction of two theories T_1 and T_2 which have incorporated two large cardinal axioms, the first one stating the existence of two measurable cardinals and the other one the existence of a measurable cardinal. For these theories it is proved that even though they are both intuitively plausible they are incomparable, i.e., neither the implication $Con(T_1) \longrightarrow Con(T_2)$ nor the implication $Con(T_2) \longrightarrow Con(T_1)$ are provable in Peano Arithmetic.

Formally the basic idea of the proof of incomparability, working in the theory $ZFC + Con(ZFC + MC^2)$ (where MC^2 is the statement: 'there exist two measurable cardinals' and MC the statement: 'there exists one measurable cardinal'), is to show that there are (nonstandard) models $\mathcal{M}_1, \mathcal{M}_2$ such that $\mathcal{M}_1 \vDash Con(T_1) \wedge \neg Con(T_2)$ and $\mathcal{M}_2 \vDash Con(T_2) \wedge \neg Con(T_1)$ (Hauser and Woodin 2014, pp. 409–411).

In view of deeper meta-theoretical concerns associated with a subjectively based interpretation, my two major arguments against this proposed counter-example in Hauser and Woodin (2014) are these:

(1) The proof of the proposition relies on Gödel's Second Incompleteness Theorem whose proof, in turn, is partially conditioned on the assumed validity of Level-2 assertions (that is, essentially of Π_1^0 sentences) of the kind, e.g., $ZF \vdash \forall x \in \omega \, (\mathcal{X}_{even}(x) \vee \mathcal{X}_{even}(x + \ulcorner 1 \urcorner))$. With Level-2 assertions, however, there is a non-rigorously defined notion of finitistic on the metatheoretical level which is formally reflected in the representing formulas of the language of **ZF** theory by the application of a universal-existential quantification over infinite sets taken as completed wholes. Evidently, this is a way to transpose metatheoretical 'pathologies' to the language of **ZF** (holding also in reverse sense) which raises a question as to how a completed infinity, even the one of the first limit ordinal ω, can influence formal results through the representing formulas something that touches also *a tergo*

---

[18] The term intentional is taken in its phenomenological connotation, that is, roughly as meaning the a priori tendency of consciousness toward something-in-general independently of a causality and spatio-temporality context and also independently of the object's material or general 'thingness' content.

on the nature of infinity in general on the metatheoretical level. This is a discussion that seems to highlight the diverging approaches, on the one hand of Gödel's mathematical realism taken as espousing a certain kind of extra-physical objective reality concerning at least infinitary mathematical objects, and on the other, of a phenomenologically motivated subjectivism for which infinity in the logical-mathematical sense has ultimately its roots (in rejecting a spatiotemporal origin belonging to objective reality) in a subjective and temporality constituting origin within intentional-constituting consciousness.[19]

(2) The proof makes also use of the existence of nonstandard models $\mathcal{M}_1$, $\mathcal{M}_2$ such that $\mathcal{M}_1 \vDash \mathrm{Con}\,(T_1) \wedge \neg\, \mathrm{Con}\,(T_2)$ and $\mathcal{M}_2 \vDash \mathrm{Con}\,(T_2) \wedge \neg\, \mathrm{Con}\,(T_1)$. More specifically, it is assumed that in $\mathcal{M}_2$ there exists a nonstandard integer α and a proof of length α of a contradiction in $ZFC + MC^2$. Yet, the existence of nonstandard models of Peano arithmetic or of the higher order real number system is conditioned on the application of the Skolem-Löwenheim theorem which requires, at least in its original strong form, the application of the Axiom of Choice or of logically equivalent principles (Van Dalen 2004, pp. 112–113).

In these terms any first-order universal-existential quantification over an indefinite horizon, and *a fortiori* a second-order one, clearly presupposes a notion of completed totality for the intended scope of its quantifiers which, on a subjectively founded level, reduces to the constitution of infinities of any order in the form of the continuous unity of a whole in presentational immediacy. In turn this kind of actual infinity far from being a spatio-temporal and causality-generated one, insofar as it is immanent to the self-constituting temporal consciousness, underlies (on the metatheoretical level) in one way or another not only the already established key foundational results of K. Gödel and P. Cohen but also certain more recent attempts to achieve enlargements of inner models so as to be consistent with all known large cardinal axioms. I refer, in particular, to H. Woodin's proposed construction of a special enlargement L^{Ω} of Gödel's constructible universe L to provide among other things a better understanding of the transition to large and very large cardinal axioms as well as an elimination of all large cardinal axioms known to contradict the Axiom of Choice (Woodin 2011a, p. 470). However to the extent that this construction is associated with Woodin's Ω-conjecture it is circularly conditioned on a notion of actual infinity by the very definition of the Ω-completeness which is based on topological continuity notions (e.g., the property of being universally Baire) (Woodin 2011b, p. 108). At least one can put into doubt the eligibility of applying topological notions, insofar as they implicitly refer to the system of real numbers for which there

---

[19] A further description of this kind of immanent infinity free of spatio-temporal and, for that matter, causal constraints can be found in Husserl's *Logical Investigations*. At some point Husserl cautioned that the free extension of space and time stretches in imagination is not really a proof of the relative 'foundedness' of bits of space and time and therefore does not prove the real infinity of space and time which is anyway subject to the natural laws of causality (see: Husserl 1984, pp. 299–300). This kind of actual infinity freely generated in terms of the continuous unity of temporal consciousness is presented as an objective whole in acts of reflection in the actual now.

is a reasonable objection as to whether it is a set, to resolve purely set-theoretical questions.[20]

4 In What Sense Subjectivity Relates to Infinity Questions?

Given that developments in the theories of the higher infinite have acquired a significantly accelerated pace over the last decades with no corresponding breadth of literature in the philosophy of mathematics, I enter below a brief reference to A. Badiou's postmodernist approach toward an ontology of the mathematical event insofar as it touches (or possibly interacts with) on my own intentions in this article.

A major question arising in Badiou's ontological-categorial system, as described in his magnum opus *Being and Event* (Badiou 2005), is, on the one hand, whether the possibility of existence of large cardinals is inherently associated with a general ontology whose basic categories include the category of the event as transcendent to the possibilities of a subjective intervention. And on the other, whether the existence of large cardinals is influenced by the expressional breadth of a constructive universe in which event and subjective intervention are reduced to necessary conditions of a situation prescribed by the constraints imposed by the constructibility axioms.

One may also bring to the fore the possible connection between the existence of inaccessible cardinals in terms of a general ontology and the nature of intervention in an eventual situation[21] in which a subject consciously performs mathematical acts in the way they may be performed over objective time. In a parallel situation in forcing theory Badiou proposes to consider the generation of a generic set G as an indiscernible multiple out of finitistic conditions belonging themselves to the particular situation as arising in terms of a sort of intervention at the evental site. Put in other words an indiscernible and unnameable whole, the generic set G, is generated by means of subjective acts performed over a set of finitistic conditions. In view of this apparent incompatibility which from my own standpoint can be reducible to the sphere of subjectivity, Badiou wonders how "an ontological concept of the pure indiscernible multiple exists" (ibid., p. 358). He concludes in the face of the incompatibility concerning the nature of a generic set as a pure indiscernible multiple, that "at base its sole property is that of consisting as pure multiple, or being. Subtracted from language, it makes do with its being." (ibid., p. 371).

This is, in fact, a state of affairs which is the outcome of Badiou's particular ontology in which the subjectivity factor stands 'opposite' to the transcendence of the (mathematical) event and is deprived of the essential property of being co-constitutive to the event, be it a physical or mental one, in the modes in which it can be

---

[20] Concerning Woodin's ongoing research in deep foundational questions and the quest for what has been called the Ultimate L-Conjecture (V = Ultimate-L), I note the difficulties encountered, in his own words, in the construction of a weak extender model witnessing the Ultimate L-conjecture which validates also consistency claims beyond the level of one supercompact cardinal (see Woodin 2017).

[21] For instance, a cardinal κ is defined as measurable through the existence of a non-principal, κ-complete ultrafilter over κ, which is considered as a statement of existence and not a procedure of inaccessibility, e.g., by means of closedness under the taking of the power-set of all smaller cardinals.

co-constitutive of an event within-the-world. However on accepting the latter supposition of co-constitutivity what are thought to be essential properties of genericity, i.e., the filter and generic properties proper, are not mere subtracts of the formal language for they can be seen as abstractions generated by mental acts presupposing subjectively founded meaning-acts as those of set formation (in terms of passive and retrospective apprehension; see Husserl (1939, pp. 246–247), of ordering relation, of the conservative extension of a set-theoretical structure over an indefinite horizon, etc. These can be considered as mathematical acts performed within the immanence of consciousness independently of any spatio-temporal and causal constraints, being only subjected to certain eidetic, a priori norms of the intentional-constitutive consciousness and also mediated by previous mathematical experience in reference to the world as ground of experience.

The fact that a generic set G retains the property of being indiscernible (in Badiou's sense), even though it does not introduce any new ordinals in the extended forcing model M $[G]$, can be seen as a concrete case, among others in the mathematics of the infinite, where one can think of an infinite set in excess of constructivist steps as having a host of desired properties even if they are not generated by definability formulas associated with Gödel's constructive universe **L**. In this sense Badiou sets a dividing line between the subject on the one side and the event on the other, in the sense that "situated in being, subjective emergence forces the event to decide the true of the situation" (ibid., pp. 429–430). Infinities as meant in Badiou's ontology are associated to one or the other extent, as happens with the extrinsic indiscernibility of a generic set G, with the transcendental character of the event which is generally thought of to be a major prerequisite of truth.

A phenomenologically motivated view, however, should dismiss an artificially made distinction between subject and event with the meaning that the event in the sense of implementation of a mathematical act carried out in objective time and endowed with the appropriate noematic[22] content cannot be conceived independently of the self-evident presence of a constituting consciousness. In this sense, referring again to the method of forcing, the subject cannot force the event to 'decide' the truthfulness of a situation existing on the ground level (by its presumed veracity in the extended model) on the supposition of existence of a generic indiscernible part of the ground model M, a position that seems to me a rather superficial interpretation of the subjective influence in shaping mathematical truths. Rather one should assume that the existence of the indiscernible part G of the ground model with the presumed generic properties represents the capacity of the mathematical consciousness to construct within its immanence mathematical objects with specific combinatorial properties and to extend or restrict them indefinitely in a consistent way eventually granting them global desirable properties always in the fond of a

---

[22] A noematic object, a phenomenological term, is said to be constituted by certain modes as a well-defined object immanent to the temporal flux of a subject's consciousness. It can then be said to be given apodictically in experience inasmuch as: (1) it can be recognized by a perceiver directly as a manifested essence in any perceptual judgement (2) it can be predicated as existing according to the descriptive norms of a language and (3) it can be verified as such (as a reidentifying object) in multiple acts more or less at will. More in Husserl's *Ideas I* Husserl (1976, Engl. transl., pp. 240–243).

continuous unity which is not as such part of the predicative universe of the formal system in question.

On this subjective condition any objects in the extended universe retain their sense of completed wholes in actual presence even though they may be formally endowed with various degrees of infinity most probably not the one of the model of the ground universe. If one could view combinatorial properties of objects in the ground model as implementations of mathematical acts corresponding to absolute mathematical notions, e.g., to set formation, pairing, ordering, etc., then the constitution of sets bearing generic properties, in a way that they do not only contradict the original properties but 'spill' them over to extended new models, may be reasonably argued to be precisely the outcome of a kind of constituting and meaning-giving activity of consciousness. This said, one may take as an essential 'passive' feature of consciousness the possibility of embedding independently of various formal constraints mathematical-logical objects, be finite or infinite ones, in a continuous unity which is always metatheoretical in the sense that it is not part of the formal theory, being essentially a subjective condition associated with the a priori modes in which consciousness is at once self-constituted and constituting.

On this account the 'passive' feature of consciousness to embed any formal-mathematical object in a subjectively generated continuous unity seems on the level of evidence to be irrelevant to the intuition we have of finite or countably infinite mathematical objects thought of in terms of concrete mathematical acts carried out in actuality or ideally extensible in actuality. However this seems not to be the case with uncountable and further inaccessible cardinalities of ascending power. In particular, such axioms or properties as the well-foundedness and well-ordering principles, the axiom of choice, the transitivity property and the notion of ordinals with their consequences, cannot be as intuitively evident as in the case of finite or countably infinite sets since in the simplest situation one has to accept the power set $\mathcal{P}(N)$ of the naturals as a completed mathematical object even though we cannot have *in rem* a complete intuition of the enumeration of its elements. The situation becomes more complex of course in case one continues to apply the power-set operation to ever emerging infinite totalities or in case one faces the possibility of the existence of a set which is not definable in Gödel's sense.

In fact there is hardly a proof-theoretic situation in a meaningful mathematics of the infinite and *a fortiori* of the theory of large cardinals in which there is not found some kind of application of a notion of completed infinity in actuality along with the notion of preservation of ordering and set-inclusion of zero-level elements among V or L classes. In this view the endowment of inner models with an intrinsic sense of order may ultimately imply a measure of 'restrictiveness' of the breadth of the inner model in which the universal set V can be elementarily embedded. As already mentioned it was formally shown by Kunen, on this account, the non-existence of a non-trivial elementary embedding $j : V \longrightarrow V$. On such grounds it seems that these inherent restrictions place an upper limit to the possibility of a sequence of very large cardinals which would subsume the existence of lower-level ones and at the same time would not contradict the Axiom of Choice. In turn one could raise the question of whether such features of the mathematics of large infinities are part of the expressional means of the corresponding formal theory or whether they are extra-theoretical, in fact subjectively rooted constraints imposed 'externally' to the theory.

My argumentation so far points to the second option and this is in accordance with my phenomenologically motivated view of mathematical-logical objects, even though I do not intend to engage in the specifics of a phenomenological description relevant to the issue (one may see for details: Livadas 2016; Hauser 2006; Tieszen 2011).

In any case my central position is that, in a subjectively founded perspective, the performance of mathematical acts pertaining to the infinite, taking also into account the reality of mathematical experience within-the-world, is constrained in a two-fold way:

First, a necessary condition for any conception of infinite set (or class) as a completed totality in actual presence is the possibility of an infinity objectifiable as such within the immanence of consciousness. This can be taken as a 'passive' feature of consciousness and it is particularly evident in the conception of any greater than the first limit ω cardinality. In a deeper level of reduction this kind of immanent infinity is nothing relative to objective spatio-temporality and consequently nothing pointing to conditions of causality. Therefore one does not talk here about an infinity inexhaustible in real world terms and bound to physical laws, in fact one may go a step further and argue that this kind of infinity within immanence is not really an infinity at all, at least not one in the conventional sense. It seems rather to be a continuous unity by which consciousness, among other a priori forms, can present in reflection any imaginable non-finitistic object of a formal theory as a completed whole. By this token any conceivable scale of ever stronger than ω_1 infinities (and of ever larger cardinals for that matter) can be regarded as a formally generated mathematical 'recreation' which in a kind of circular game is conditioned through prerequisite definitions or assumptions on a notion of 'background' immanent infinity which is actually the continuous unity of reflecting consciousness.

Second, all notions of order in the implementation of mathematical acts are ultimately reducible on the subjective level to intentional features of consciousness, e.g., the intentional orientation to unities as such bearing no 'thingness' content and a priori associated with some kind of relation to other unities or classes of unities (as wholes in instantaneity), with further possibility of an indefinite, consistent extension with no spatio-temporal constraints. Yet there is no way these intentional features might be conceivable without the assumption of existence of 'passive' features of consciousness like its self-constitution as a continuous temporal unity.[23] In this sense any predicative 'intervention' with regard to the objects of a formal mathematical theory by necessity restricts its 'ontological breadth', a fact whose evidence may be taken to be, for instance, the delimitative character of Gödel's constructive

---

[23] Think, for instance, of a sequence of natural numbers or of elements of any other isomorphic structure as associated with intentional acts of a consciousness performed in a perfectly distinct and finitistic mode (called the two-ity intuition in Van Atten et al. 2002, pp. 206–208). These are not conceivable but as performed in an ideally infinite iterative fashion against the background continuous unity of the immanence of consciousness.

universe L. Ultimately on the subjective grounds presented in this article there seems to be no possibility of obtaining a pure ontology of mathematical infinity unconstrained from the restrictive notion of a predicative intervention that limits its scope.

Said roughly in general terms, a pure ontology of infinity, if this term has indeed a meaningful content, is 'spoiled' in response to the scope and depth of a subjective predicative intervention. On these grounds one may put up serious counter-arguments as to the feasibility of existence of cardinals possibly realizing the ambitions of Cantor's absolute.

Appendix I: The Notion of Actual Infinity as a Precondition for the Separability of Space Points

To strengthen my arguments about formal infinity taken as the abstract form of a subjectively founded continuous unity, I present the example (which may be skipped by the mathematically uninterested reader) of a special topology in which the uncountability and separability of the points of the corresponding topological space is not by essence associated with infinity in objective real world terms. To formally ground my claim I will be based on a well-known mathematical space proved to be homeomorphic to the set of irrational numbers, this latter set provided with the subspace topology inherited from the standard Euclidean topology of the real line. The space in question, the Baire space N^ω, is taken to be the set of maximal elements of the cpo[24] of finite and infinite sequences of natural numbers equipped with the subspace topology of the Scott topology.[25] This topology has as a base the collection of sets of the form $\uparrow s \cap N^\omega$, where by $\uparrow s$ is denoted the upper set of the finite sequence of digits s, that is, $\uparrow s = \{\xi; s \leq \xi\}$ where the order relation $\leq$ is defined by: $\xi \leq \xi'$ iff ξ' extends ξ (or ξ is a prefix of ξ'); that is, ξ' starts with exactly the same digits as ξ and possibly has infinitely more. Usually this partial order is called in the mathematical literature a prefix ordering and is the key to the definition of several order-induced topologies of computational interest.

The interesting thing about the space N^ω as a Scott space is that it can be turned into a Stone space by taking as basic open sets except for the basic Scott opens of the form $\uparrow s$ (s finite) also their complements $N^\omega \setminus \uparrow s$. Generally it is proved that in this refined topology the base B of the clopen sets as above is a sub-Boolean algebra of the power-set of the original space N^ω and that every ultrafilter of B is a B-neighborhood filter $\mathcal{N}_B(x)$ for a unique point x of N^ω, where $\mathcal{N}_B(x)$ is the set $\{U \in B; x \in U\}$ (Smyth 1992, pp. 734–735). Moreover, by Stone's representation theorem one has

---

[24] A cpo is defined to be a dcpo with a least element. A dcpo, in turn, is a partially ordered set in which every directed subset has a least upper bound. Most technical definitions in this section are not deemed as absolutely necessary to comprehend the intended argument, therefore they may be skipped. In any case one may look for relevant stuff in Smyth (1992) and Porter and Woods (1988, Ch. 3).

[25] A subset O of a dcpo X is taken as open in the Scott topology of X if:
    (i) $x \in O$ then $\uparrow x \in O$
    (ii) $\sqcup_\uparrow S \in O \Rightarrow S \cap O \neq \emptyset$ where $\sqcup_\uparrow S$ is the least upper bound of a directed subset S;
for details, see Smyth (1992), pp. 642–650.

that the Stone space N^ω is a Hausdorff, compact, zero-dimensional and totally disconnected space (Porter and Woods 1988, pp. 171–172). What is of a special importance here, given my intention, is the Hausdorff property of N^ω, namely the fact that for any two distinct points x, y of N^ω (which are actually infinite sequences of natural numbers) it can be proved that there are neighborhoods U_x and Y_y belonging respectively to the $\mathcal{B}$-neighborhood filters $\mathcal{N}_B(x)$ and $\mathcal{N}_B(y)$ such that: $U_x \cap Y_y = \emptyset$.

This means that the way to separate any two distinct points x, y of N^ω (which as homeomorphic to the space of irrational reals is a space of uncountable cardinality), is by generating at least two disjoint open neighborhoods of them. Further and to the extent that the points of N^ω can be thought of as corresponding to infinite decimal expansions of irrationals, it follows that however close any two distinct points can be in terms of proximity of their decimal expansion they can still be separated by disjoint open sets. Put more intuitively, the possibility of discerning between any two points of N^ω regardless of their proximity ad infinitum is conditioned on the formation of two disjoint neighborhoods to which they respectively belong, these latter ones meant as non-finite (by virtue of their topological openness) yet definite wholes in presentational immediacy. Essentially, the possibility for distinguishing space points in the form of infinitely extending sequences of natural numbers (or of binary digits) ordered by prefixing is ultimately conditioned on the possibility of forming at once their disjoint neighborhoods as definite continuous wholes in the present now of consciousness. In turn, completed wholes as actual 'infinities' freely generated in reflection independently of any spatio-temporal and causal concerns point to a concept of infinity constituted as the objective form of the continuous unity of each one's temporal consciousness.

Consequently there is a case to be made here for the fact that, in shifting the focus of discussion to a fundamental constitutional level, the notion of continuity as such is not necessarily connected with the mathematical notion of uncountability. In fact, conventional uncountability is underdetermined with regard to its subjective origin in all classical proofs (e.g., think of Cantor's diagonal proof of the uncountability of real numbers) to the extent that it is circularly conditioned on a pre-existing notion of 'infinity' in the sense of a subjectively generated and completed totality non-eliminable within a formal logical-mathematical universe.

References

Badiou A (2005) Being and Event, transl. O. Feltham, London: Continuum
Feferman S et al (eds) (1990) Kurt Gödel: collected works, vol II. Oxford University Press, Oxford
Feferman S et al (eds) (1995) Kurt Gödel: collected works, vol III. Oxford University Press, Oxford
Hauser K (2006) Gödel's program revisited part I: the turn to phenomenology. Bull Symb Log 12(4):529–590
Hauser K, Woodin HW (2014) Strong axioms of infinity and the debate about realism. J Philos 111(8):397–419
Husserl E (1939) Erfahrung und Urteil, hsgb. L. Landgrebe, Prag: Acad./Verlagsbuchhandlung. Engl. translation: (1973), *Experience and Judgment*, transl. J.S. Churchill & K. Americs, London: Routledge & Kegan Paul
Husserl E (1976) Ideen zu einer reinen Phänomenologie und phänomenologischen Philosophie, Erstes Buch, Hua Band III/I, hsgb. K. Schuhmann, Den Haag: M. Nijhoff. Engl. transl.: (1983), *Ideas*

pertaining to a pure phenomenology and to a phenomenological philosophy: First Book, transl. F. Kersten, The Hague: M. Nijhoff

Husserl E (1984) Logische Untersuchungen, Hua XIX/1, herausg. U. Panzer, The Hague: M. Nijhoff

Jech T (2006) Set theory. Springer, Berlin

Jensen BR et al (1974) Measurable cardinals and the GCH. In: Jech T (ed) Axiomatic set theory, proceedings of the symposium in pure mathematics of the AMS. Amer. Math. Soc, Providence, pp 175–179

Kanamori A (2009) The higher infinite. Springer, Berlin

Kanamori A (2011) Large cardinals with forcing. In: Kanamori A (ed) Handbook of the history of logic: sets and extensions in the twentieth century. Elsevier BV, Amsterdam

Keisler JH, Tarski A (1964) From accessible to inaccessible cardinals: results for all accessible cardinal numbers and the problem of their extension to inaccessible ones. Fundam Math 57:119

Kunen K (1971) Elementary embeddings and infinitary combinatorics. J Symb Log 36:407–413

Kunen K (1982) Set theory. An introduction to independence proofs. Elsevier Sci. Pub, Amsterdam

Lèvy A, Solovay R (1967) Measurable cardinals and the continuum hypothesis. Israel J Math 5(4):234–248

Livadas S (2015) The subjective roots of forcing theory and their influence in independence results. Axiomathes 25(4):433–455

Livadas S (2016) What is the nature of mathematical-logical objects? Axiomathes 27(1):79–112

Porter J, Woods R (1988) Extensions and absolutes of Hausdorff spaces. Springer, New York

Smyth BM (1992) Topology. In: Abramsky S, Gabbay D, Maibaum T (eds) Handbook of logic in computer science. Clarendon Press, Oxford, pp 641–761

Solovay R (1970) A model of set-theory in which every set of reals is lebesgue measurable. Ann Math 2nd Ser 92(1):1–56

Solovay R, Reinhardt W, Kanamori A (1978) Strong axioms of infinity and elementary embeddings. Ann Math Log 13:73–116

Tarski A (1962) Some problems and results relevant to the foundations of set theory. In: Nagel E, Suppes P, Earski A (eds) Logic, methodology and philosophy of science. Proceedings of the 1960 international congress. Stanford Univ. Press, Stanford, pp 125–135

Tarski A, Erdös P (1943) On families of mutually exclusive sets. Ann Math 44(2):315–329

Tieszen R (2011) After Gödel: platonism and rationalism in mathematics and logic. Oxford University Press, Oxford

Van Atten M, van Dalen D, Tieszen R (2002) The phenomenology and mathematics of the intuitive continuum. Philos Math 10(3):203–226

Van Dalen D (2004) Logic and structure. Springer, Berin

Vopěnka P (1979) Mathematics in the alternative set theory. Teubner, Leipzig

Wang H (1996) A logical journey. From Gödel to philosophy. MIT Press, Cambridge

Woodin HW (2011a) The transfinite universe. In: Baaz M et al (eds) Kurt Gödel and the foundations of mathematics. Cambridge University Press, New York, pp 449–471

Woodin HW (2011b) The realm of the infinite. In: Heller M, Woodin HW (eds) Infinity, new research frontiers. Cambridge University Press, New York, pp 89–118

Woodin HW (2017) In search of ultimate-L: the 19th Midrasha mathematicae lectures. Bull Symb Log 23(1):1–109

The Plausible Impact of Phenomenology on Gödel's Thoughts

Abstract: It is well known that in his later years Gödel turned to a systematic reading of phenomenology, for the founder of which, Edmund Husserl, he reserved a high esteem as a philosopher who sought to elevate philosophy to the standards of a rigorous science. For reasons purportedly related to his earlier attraction to Leibnizian monadology, Gödel was particularly interested in Husserl's transcendental phenomenology and the way it may shape the discussion on the nature of mathematical-logical objects and the meaning and internal coherence of primitive terms in mathematics. This article, which is less interested in historical facts that are amply presented in other scholars' accounts, rather tries to point to the mostly indirect influence that the ideas of transcendental phenomenology, including Gödel's reported reference to the notion of (inner) time, had on his philosophy of mathematics, especially with a view to key independent questions of mathematical foundations. A main source for Gödel's philosophical-epistemological views (of course in addition to his own published material) will be his recorded discussions with H. Wang and S. Toledo, as well as various articles and drafts found in his *Nachlass*.

1. Introduction

IT IS COMMONLY ACCEPTED that Gödel started systematically reading Husserlian phenomenology, from around 1959, from the then existing editions of Husserl's works, studying mostly Husserl's *Logical Investigations* (Husserl, 1984a, 1984b), *Ideas I* (Husserl, 1976b), *The Idea of Phenomenology* (Husserl, 1973a) and the *Cartesian Meditations* (Husserl, 1973b). Gödel also highly praised Husserl's article *Philosophy as a Rigorous Science* which he associated with what he believed was Husserl's critical turn in 1909 to the phenomenological investigation of time (Toledo, 2011, p. 200). There is ample evidence, though, cited by van Atten et al. in the article "On the Philosophical Development of Kurt Gödel" (van Atten, 2015, ch. 6), that Gödel, at this stage seemingly not particularly interested, had only loose contact with phenomenology from the pre-war years in Europe, presumably, among other occasions, through his presence at meetings of the Vienna circle. In fact, as he himself confessed, he did not become acquainted with Husserl's writings until many years after his emigration to the US (van Atten, 2015, p. 97).

Yet the fact remains that it is after 1959 that there is concrete evidence of Gödel's reading and attraction to phenomenology, attested by his comments in various articles (published in his lifetime or unpublished), recorded discussions and scholarly references. It is also a hard fact that Gödel did not leave a paper or essay of his own applying his acquired knowledge of phenomenology to questions of logical-mathematical interest, nor is there any recorded in-depth discussion of matters pertaining to transcendental phenomenology with someone who was either an authority on phenomenology or at least a distinguished mathematics scholar well versed in it (see also the remark by van Atten, 2015, p. 8). However, it is possible to form a view of the influence of phenomenological ideas on his philosophical positions concerning logic and mathematics, judging from his insights in the philosophically oriented articles preceding 1959 and those following in the next two decades, not to mention his expressed approval of the possibilities left open by the emerging science, as he characterized phenomenology, which he also recommended as a development of the core of Kantian philosophy in his article, "The Modern Development of the Foundations of Mathematics in the Light of Philosophy" (Feferman, 1995, pp. 383–387). The present article intends to do just this: to review the extent to which phenomenology, or at least phenomenologically influenced ideas, helped shape Gödel's mathematical philosophy along the way taking into account his own evolution in mathematics and the twentieth-century evolution of the disciplines of set theory and mathematical foundations which he mastered and helped shape. However, caution is necessary – as Husserl did not leave an explicit and systematic account of the integration of phenomenological ideas into his purely foundational mathematical research, any assessment of the influence these ideas had on his views, while being somehow speculative at base, should nevertheless be based on his own writings or on reliable sources that have registered his thoughts and are properly interpreted in accordance with each historical context. This given, I will also pay special attention to the question of time, in the phenomenological sense of the inner time of consciousness, in shaping a meaningful predicative discourse about mathematical-logical objects, in particular about infinite ones, a question Gödel touched on almost in passing in his recorded discussions with Wang (1996, pp. 319–320) and Toledo (2011, p. 200).

As a matter of fact, Gödel was gradually led to his settled philosophical approach, in later years, regarding mathematical objects and concepts, an approach that is a peculiar blend of rational platonism and objective realism. A case in point is the distinction Gödel draws between objects and concepts about objects, in taking the instance of sets as objects and the filter or ultrafilter properties as concepts about particular sets. This distinction is drawn in epistemological terms along the lines of sensuousness and understanding, with the former referring to objects and the latter referring to concepts, with the aim of arriving at the primitive concepts of our thinking and the inborn intuitions that thinking is based on (Hauser, 2006, p. 544). An example of these "inborn intuitions" could be the fundamental property of the mind to comprehend multitudes into unities, which Gödel called "the main fact of mathematics".

Gödel even talked about something more general besides reason and sense perception "which comes from the outside psychologically but not physically", an obscure third element like an objective mind which "does represent an aspect of, and may be a plan of, objective reality" (Wang, 1996, p. 149). Yet one may remark that certain aspects of Gödel's mathematical realism, even though they bear an imprint of indirect phenomenological influence, e.g., when he talked about the epistemic non-eliminability of mathematical intuition or the fundamental property of the mind to comprehend multitudes into unities,[1] cannot actually be defensible in a consistently phenomenological and particularly in an inner temporality founded approach. For instance, Gödel is quoted by Wang as saying that he disliked the whole field of set theory in its (then) present state as lacking a well-established plausibility and finding itself in a certain state of fluidity. In Wang's words, "He was not in favor of the temporal or the fluid. He found the talk about possible sets objectionable only because of their fluidity; he would not mind if they were fixed". Further, Gödel considered sets as a limiting case of objects (just as general mathematical objects were being thought of as abstract objects lying between the ideal world and the empirical one) analogous to physical objects in space for which the laws of nature are non-facticious but rather analytic in that they do not change, and moreover they are the determining reason behind any physical change (Wang, 1996, pp. 148–149). For the specific case of sets I point to Gödel's dissatisfaction with the way the operation *"set of x's"* is defined, as presented in footnote 14 of his supplement to Cantor's continuum paper (1964), which can only be paraphrased by expressions like *"multitude of x's"*, *"combination of any number of x's"*, *"part of the totality of x's"*, involving again in a circular fashion the concept of set as something existing in itself no matter whether we can define it in a finite number of words (Feferman, 1990, p. 259). We have no evidence that Gödel had read Husserl's description in *Erfahrung und Urteil* (*Experience and Judgment*) (Husserl, 1939), of the concept of the set as a thematic object comprising a plurality of elements in original presence to the consciousness. Husserl, referring there to sets as syntactical

---

1 Gödel's relevant view of sets is recorded by Wang (1996, p. 254) as follows: "Sets are multitudes which are also unities. A multitude is the opposite of a unity ... It is a seemingly contradictory fact that sets exist. It is surprising that the fact that multitudes are also unities leads to no contradictions: this is the main fact of mathematics".

objectivities, by virtue of being collections of representations of well-meant objects in consciousness, stated that it was not only due to a colligating act of consciousness that sets as collective assemblages of objects become thematic objects in their own right, but also due to an act of retrospective apprehension (*rückgreifendes Erfassen*) by which sets as object-pluralities are given to the ego as object-unities in the form of re-identifiable objects and possibly substrates of judgements (Husserl, 1939, Engl. transl., p. 294). Apparently this is a way to reduce sets, as syntactical objectivities, to unique thematic objects generated by the noetic-noematic[2] structure of consciousness and in the final count by the essential character of consciousness to constitute unity as temporal unity. There is no indication that Gödel followed this line of thought anywhere by entering the constitutive structures of consciousness and "backdoor" the question of time in the discussion of the constitution of sets as syntactical objectivities.[3]

Gödel was above all inclined in his philosophy of mathematics to a peculiar kind of rational platonism and the consequent belief that concepts are sharp in an objective sense, in spite of all the influences he had been subjected to in the long years following the incompleteness results. This is perhaps nowhere more evident than in his apparent espousing of fixedness toward mathematical objects and also in his belief in some kind of objectively existing relation between ourselves and the realm of mathematical objects (these latter in the sense of limit-case objects) that lies beyond sense perception and rational reasoning. Accordingly, in his critique of Carnap's syntactical programme in the article "Is Mathematics Syntax of Language?", he referred to the possibility of possessing an additional sense "that would show to us a second reality completely separated from space-time reality

---

2 The meaning of the phenomenological terms noetic and noematic are mainly described in Husserl's *Ideen I* (see Husserl, 1976b, pp. 230–231). A noematic object is constituted by certain modes as a well-defined object immanent to the temporal flux of a subject's consciousness and it is possibly abstracted, in the sense of a formal-ontological object, as a syntactical object of a formal theory. A noematic object can be said to be given apodictically in experience inasmuch as: (1) it can be recognized by a perceiver directly as a manifested essence in any perceptual judgement; (2) it can be predicated as existing according to the descriptive norms of a language; and (3) it can be verified as such (as a re-identifying object) in multiple acts more or less at will. In contrast, a noetic object can only be characterized in terms of the multiplicities of real moments of a hyletic-noetic perception intentionally directed to it by its sole virtue of being given as an absolute evidence.

3 Hauser, in Gödel's *Program Revisited Part I: The Turn to Phenomenology* commenting on Husserl's view of the constitution of sets as immanences and taking account of the fact that sets are not collections of objects but of representations of objects, maintains that "the idea of sets constituting themselves 'within' the stream of consciousness is compatible with the view of mathematical objects existing independently of our mental acts and dispositions that lies at the heart of Gödel's mathematical realism" (Hauser, 2006, p. 559). I do not share this point of view to the extent that Husserl's description of sets as categorial objectivities is purely constitutive and sets (or classes of sets) as formal mathematical objects are taken precisely as syntactical-categorial objectivities immanently constituted in the first place.

and moreover so regular that it could be described by a finite number of laws" (Feferman, 1995, p. 353).

According to Gödel, we know with mathematical reason (counted as an additional sense) the most general concepts, objects and their relations "which are separated from space-time reality insofar as the latter is completely determined by the totality of particularities without any reference to the formal concepts", in contrast to sense perception through which we know particular objects and their properties (Feferman, 1995, p. 354). Here one might argue against Gödel's platonistic tendency that in case formal concepts and objects of mathematics in their most general sense were thought to be separated from space-time reality then they would be inaccessible, at least in an absolute sense, to a mathematical subject whose mathematical reason, not to say anything of sense perception, cannot be conceived but as a chain of synthetic mental (not necessarily intentional) acts carried out within space-time reality. Further, going *a tergo* and in a recursive fashion to the ultimate subjective origin of intentionality and reason, the transcendental ego, to which Husserl conferred, although in a way leaving room for serious ambiguities, a temporal essence at least as a self-reflecting ego, one can hardly talk about mathematical concepts or objects residing out of space-time reality while at the same time being potentially objects apprehended and elaborated by an intentionally structured temporal consciousness.

For Husserl, the kind of unity within the immanence of consciousness is the objective form of the self-constituting source of inner temporality, namely, what he initially called the absolute subjectivity of consciousness at the time of the *Lessons on the Phenomenology of Inner Time Consciousness* and later associated, in the course of his espousing of transcendental phenomenology, with the idea of transcendental ego in the *Cartesian Meditations*. Nowhere in Gödel's writings is there an elaboration on the possibility of specifically founding unity, e.g., with regard to infinite mathematical collections (taken as completed wholes), on a subjective temporality factor,[4] especially in view of the fact that, for a phenomenologist, Gödel's orientation toward a mind-independence of mathematical objects turns out, in fact, to be a quest for a "transcendence" within the immanence of consciousness irrespective of whether we talk about real or ideal objects (Hauser, 2006, p. 578). Consequently it is highly questionable, from a phenomenological point of view, as to whether Hauser's claim that the idea of sets as categorial objects (experienced as mental representations in a higher-order act) constituting

---

4 As a matter of fact there exists a relevant hint of Gödel's, described by H. Wang in *A Logical Journey. From Gödel to Philosophy*, but there he refers generally to time as the only natural frame of reference for the mind. There is also an allusion to the fact that our intuitive concept of time is not objective or objectively representable (Wang, 1996, p. 319).

themselves "within" the stream of consciousness is compatible with a view of mathematical objects existing independently of our mental acts, something that is a central feature of Gödel's mathematical realism. I will comment on these matters in more detail in the next section.

Sources for inquiring into Gödel's level of phenomenological expertise and the way it impacted his conception of a possible ontology of mathematical objects include his *Collected Works* and Wang's account of his conversations with Gödel in his books *Reflections on Kurt Gödel* and *A Logical Journey. From Gödel to Philosophy.* There is a further account by Toledo (2011) of her conversations with Gödel between 1972 and 1975 which is commented on by Franks (2011). In Toledo's interesting though brief account, we should note a hitherto little-noticed reference by Gödel to the question of time, by all accounts in relation to Husserl's conception of inner time.

2. Gödel and the Question of Temporality: A Challenge Left Unanswered

Given that Gödel did not make any further clarification or comments on Husserl's investigation of time with the purpose of elucidating the system of primitive terms and their relationships (e.g., including such central notions as object, existence, property and relation), we can only draw attention to certain of his views by which he might have been motivated to point to the need for "repeating" Husserl's investigation of time in his recorded exchanges with Toledo (2011, p. 200). As mentioned earlier, Gödel is quoted by Wang (1996) as claiming that the main fact of mathematics is the fundamental property of the mind to comprehend multitudes, such as sets or classes, into unities in spite of the fact that multitudes are the opposite of unity. He also found surprising the fact that although the concepts of multitude and unity are contradictory, nevertheless sets exist in the mathematical universe without leading to contradictions. This claim is also found in Gödel's supplement to the second edition of *What is Cantor's Continuum Problem?* (1964), where he pointed to a close relationship between the concept of set (according to which a set is something obtainable from the integers or any other well-defined objects by iterated application of the operation "set-of") and the categories of pure understanding in Kant's sense. The core of this relationship, for Gödel, stands in a kind of "synthesis", namely, the generation of unities out of manifolds with particular reference to Kant's idea of one object out of its various aspects (Feferman, 1990, p. 268, n. 40). Yet, for all the importance Gödel ascribed to this kind of synthesis, nowhere in his published writings has he dealt with the character of this synthesis in the first place, that is, in case we stick to a phenomenological approach, whether it is of an essential-eidetic character whose realization each time is a space-time instantiation, or whether it is a process realized *in rem* in terms of the intentional-constituting capacities of an embodied consciousness.

Another issue raised frequently in Gödel's writings is the nature of mathematical concepts in general and, if we take the terms as conceptually equivalent in the context of formal theories, the nature of primitive concepts and primitive relations within logical syntax. For instance, in his article "Is Mathematics Syntax of Language?", he emphatically pointed to the role of primitive terms in mathematics (as reduced to logic) as follows:

If mathematics is reduced to logic (in the sense of the Frege-Russell system), then axioms about the primitive terms of logic must be assumed, some of which are so far from trivial that they are rejected as false or meaningless by many mathematicians. If the mathematical axioms are replaced by syntactical rules, one needs axioms of the same power about the primitive terms of syntax or about abstract or transfinite concepts to be used in the syntactical considerations. (Feferman, 1995, p. 350)

He further argued, making use of the consequences of his second incompleteness theorem and of the existence of propositions expressing new and independent mathematical facts irreducible to symbolic conventions on the basis of the axioms of the system, that the content of mathematics is unlimited in relation to the "closed" universe implied by the standard axioms. Gödel also accounted the wrong (in his view) claim that the conclusion in logical inferences contains no further information beyond that of the premises to the neglect of the conceptual content of sentences as being objective (non-psychological). Moreover, he accounted the fact itself of the conclusion implied by the premises as being objective and due (in part) to the primitive terms of logic occurring therein (Feferman, 1995, p. 350, n. 40). Gödel, in an obvious display of the strong influence that platonism always exerted on him, even went as far as suggesting that formal concepts and their relations as perceived by mathematical reason are separated from space-time reality[5] "insofar as the latter is completely determined by the totality of particularities without any reference to the formal concepts" (Feferman, 1995, p. 354).

In an article entitled "On an Extension of Finitary Mathematics which Has Not Yet Been Used" (appearing in *Dialectica* in 1958 and in a reworked version in Gödel's *Nachlass* in 1972), Gödel described abstract concepts in logical-

---

[5] It should be noted, however, that the time when Gödel elaborated on the article refuting Carnap's position on the reduction of mathematics to a syntax of language, in which this specific platonistic claim is made, precedes his beginning of a systematic study of Husserl's works. Incidentally, it might be of some importance to note that at one point in his life Carnap studied under Husserl, and Gödel, in turn, began to undertake serious studies in logic after a seminar by Carnap which he attended in the summer of 1908 in the environment of the Vienna Circle (Goldfarb, 2005, p. 185).

mathematical terms as essentially those of a second or higher level, that is, as those which do not have as content properties or relations referring to mathematical objects in the sense of concrete spatio-temporal symbols (or their combinations). Instead they are taken to be such abstract mental structures as proofs, meaningful propositions, etc., where in the proofs of propositions about the mental objects involved are required insights beyond anything relating to the space-time properties of the symbols representing them, but rather pertaining to the underlying meanings (Feferman, 1990, pp. 272–273).

Judging from Gödel's views as cited above, one may be reasonably inclined to say that in Gödel's sense abstract concepts and meanings in the context of formal-axiomatical theories, while pointing to some "extra-logical" or at least partly non-empirical content possibly inaccessible by purely logical-syntactical means, are nevertheless not taken up as constituted idealities or eidetic states-of-affairs in Husserl's sense (at the time of *Logical Investigations* and later). To a far lesser extent they are taken as reducible to a subjective constitutive procedure originating in a temporality founded intentional consciousness, the latter notions being a predominant theme in Husserl's later turn to transcendental phenomenology.

It is quite indicative of the role ascribed to the source of inner temporality relative to abstract concepts that Husserl talked, in a collection of his later texts on time constitution,[6] about the comprehension of an "open" general concept comprising objective unities not in terms of a collection-of but as a global unity, that is, as a subjectively founded co-positioning of objects under any transformation in the mode of givenness which endure as unities of appearances in changing themselves in their own right or as a result of someone's action (Husserl, 2001b, p. 216). Further, the foundation of knowable objects, of the predicative truth for everyone and consequently of the being of a real-scientific truth, presupposes the possibility, in terms of a spatial and time-succession postulation, of identification, explication and determination of the temporal "content" through which each individual (object or state-of-affairs) is defined (Husserl, 2001b, p. 217). A series of inferences identified as inferences, global inferences taken as global inferences together with their "size", intermediate intervals and their 'size', all these presuppose a constitutional process referring to the primordiality of an ego and also to an intersubjective world, based on relations of reciprocity, meant as the primitive soil of experience (Husserl, 2001b, p. 219). However, it is only through a possibility of co-existence and temporal succession meant necessarily in terms of an inner temporality that any predicative sentence (or groups of sentences) can be

---

6 Edited in Husserliana Materialien by D. Lohmar as *Späte Texte über Zeitkonstitution* (*Late Texts on Time Constitution*) (Husserl, 2001b).

taken as a whole and as an "externally" independent bearer of a meaning generated by virtue of the meanings and interrelations of its constituting members.

It is noteworthy that at another point in the supplementary volume to *Logical Investigations* (first part), Husserl referred in general terms to the difference between the static and dynamic fulfillment in knowledge acts, in the sense that in the dynamic relationship the parts of the relationship and the related act of knowledge are tied up in a phenomenological temporal fashion and are thus unfolded in a phenomenological temporal form, whereas in the static relationship which stands as the remaining result of this temporal process they are in a temporal and thingness cover (*Deckung*) (Husserl, 2002, p. 40). While Husserl at this stage of his phenomenological evolution had not yet been deeply immersed in the question of temporality as a constitutional prerequisite, he still referred on various occasions in his texts to the underlying origin of the unity of expressional forms, namely, to the unity of consciousness, even to its temporal form of continuous duration.

It is also from this perspective that we should view his subsequent claim that the motivated synthesis of knowing acts, as mentioned above, is nothing else than the implementation within the unity of consciousness of the causal connection between different "theses" and of their articulation in accordance with this causal motivation. Overall, syntheses in their various forms are meant as unities of consciousness and as connected through acts which in their "lowest-level" form may be non-synthetic (Husserl, 2002, pp. 208–209). In the second part of the supplementary volume to the *Logical Investigations*, Husserl argued that insofar as sentences, propositions, logical propositions and parts of them belong to a thematic consciousness, they are conditioned on the realization of the corresponding acts of the thematic consciousness, while the *a priori* horizon associated with each proposition (statement) in its realization belongs not to the process of sentence articulation itself but to the process of consciousness in which the proposition is constituted (Husserl, 2005, p. 63). In short, the logical constructs of a language (either a formal or an informal one) are invariably reduced to processes within consciousness in accepting, for the most part implicitly at this stage, the temporal character of the constitutive process of consciousness.

In the recorded exchanges with Toledo, next to Gödel's allegation that the best way to understand primitive terms and their relations would be to repeat Husserl's investigation of time, there is his noteworthy allusion to the existence of a 500-page Husserl manuscript on the investigation of time which Gödel believed at the time had been lost[7] (Toledo, 2011, p. 200). The issue of the purportedly

---

7 Details of the case of the manuscript referred to above – Husserl's most profound work on time, according to the statement of his former student R. Ingarden – can be found in editor J. Kennedy's annotation of Toledo's exchanges with Gödel (Toledo, 2011 n. 1, pp. 200–201).

lost work on time raised by Gödel is also mentioned by Wang in *A Logical Journey. From Gödel to Philosophy* alongside a remark on Gödel's belief that Husserl had done instructive work on our idea of time and also that the understanding of the idea of time is very difficult and of central importance to philosophy (Wang, 1996, pp. 168, 319–320). As a matter of fact, this manuscript had never been lost and was finally published in 2001 under the editorship of Bernet and Lohmar, with the title *Die Bernauer Manuskripte über das Zeitbewusstsein* (*The Bernau Manuscripts on Temporal Consciousness*, Husserl, 2001a).

In what follows, I will argue that some parts of Husserl's work in the Bernau manuscripts, had they been read, might have convinced Gödel how treacherous a turf the question of the origin of time may prove in case one seeks an ultimate foundation for the concept of unity within multiplicity, as well as for the concept of unity as an underlying and non-eliminable factor of such primitive notions as "object", "existence", "relation", "property" (or species), etc.

In the Bernau manuscripts Husserl tried to clarify more meticulously than ever before the role of the absolute ego of consciousness in view of his interest in properly characterizing the temporal streaming of the ego, especially on account of his assertion in *Cartesian Meditations* that time is the form of all egological genesis. In the Bernau manuscripts he mostly used other terms for the transcendental ego of *Cartesian Meditations*, such as primary process (*Urprozess*), primary lived experience (*Urerleben*) and others, presumably in an effort to reach the most radical answer to the question of the constitution of time by appealing to a notion of irreducibly primary constitution as such. Ultimately he was left with essentially no answer to the open question of the clarification of the meaning of the constituting subjectivity of temporal unity.

What turns out to be certain, though, is that anything that becomes an object of reflection, even the ego itself, has to be in a temporal form and also has to be identically the same in the flux of the multiplicities of its givennesses. But here one may raise the following issue: if primary process (or primary lived experience) is temporal, then we can turn our "reflecting glance" to the givenness of its phases, which is a temporal continuum in the scheme original impression-retention-protention, and as the experience of these phases as givennesses would also be a time sequence to which we could turn anew our reflection as givennesses and so on *in infinitum*, we would end up with an endless regression of reflections meant as consciousness-of and in this way as unities of temporal consciousness in infinite series. Therefore, one may possibly wonder how primary process could be meant as "being" in preceding reflection.

Husserl suggested at this point the concept of a primary flux (*Urstrom*) perceived as a temporal flux which nonetheless cannot be consciousness of a temporal flux nor a phenomenological perception in the proper Husserlian sense of

Wahrnehmung[8] (Husserl, 2001a, p. 197). In the face of these grave difficulties, Husserl proposed to consider phenomenological time and events taking place in it as given by means of phenomenological perception (*Wahrnehmung*). In that case a process could take place as a unity within the unity of phenomenological time without this particular unity having a special "qualification" to become the object of phenomenological perception (Hosserl, 2001a, p. 198). This would in turn beg the question: can a transcendental, time-constituting process be known by any other means except by reflection? Isn't it necessarily a givenness in reflection?

Evidently Husserl's pains to provide a more elaborate foundation for the circularity-generating concept of a primary origin of temporality, meant also as the origin of all immanent[9] unity, ended up in a quite vague description of a primary process whose essence could be that of "being as such" while eluding at the same time any possibility of intentional seizure and reflection in real-world terms. In conclusion, if underlying unity makes meaningful any talk about abstract concepts and objects in logical-mathematical theories and *a fortiori* about infinite aggregates of formal elements in the form of sets and classes taken as completed wholes, then this unity, if considered as subjectively founded in terms of a time-constituting consciousness, ultimately leads to an extra-logical (in fact a transcendental) impasse, at least concerning the foundation of the unity of abstract mathematical objects irreducible to processes of concrete, finitistic meaning-acts.

Returning to Toledo's account of Gödel's views, it is indicative of Gödel's loose yet tangible relation to the core notion of transcendental phenomenology, i.e., that of the transcendental (or absolute) ego, that he referred to the statements of intuitionism as allowing greater clarity of our actual intuitions by relying on the sense-bestowal role of a mathematician's ego. He claimed that "meaning must be completely within the ego", while noting that the statements of intuitionism are psychological statements not of empirical psychology but of an essential *a priori* psychology, this latter "discipline" being one of Husserl's basic arguments in *Philosophy as a Rigorous Science* against the naturalistic tendencies of modern experimental psychology (Husserl, 1976a, Engl. transl., pp. 118–120). On this account, Gödel contrasted the classical and intuitionistic approaches, in view of

---

8 The Husserlian term *Wahrnehmung*, commonly rendered in English translation as phenomenological perception, roughly refers to a kind of perception of objects that are either immanent or transcendental to consciousness which bears an original, unmodified intentional character. It is primarily taken as the *a priori* directedness to an object as content irrespectively of being a purely formal or a 'thingness' one.

9 The term immanent, widely used in phenomenological texts, can be roughly explained as referring to what is or has become correlative (or 'co-substantial') to the being of the flux of one's consciousness in contrast to what is 'external' or transcendental to it.

the place allotted to mathematical intuitions as primitive elements of mathematics, reaching the conclusion that intuitionism is perfectly meaningful and intuitionistic statements more readily susceptible to self-analysis (in opposition to the critical stance of a classical mathematician for whom the hunt for axioms implies the use of extra-mathematical ideas), thus leading to more clarity in our intuitions (Toledo, 2011, p. 206). However, Gödel's stance toward intuitionism was fundamentally a critical one and at times openly negative, especially on ontological grounds. Gödel considered, in particular, the intuitionistic subject as a psychological and thus a mundane one, a condition that would deprive it of time-constituting and therefore of noesis-noema constituting capacities; this latter view is challenged by van Atten (2004, pp. 66–68).[10]

3. Gödel's Proposal of New Infinity Axioms in the Light of Phenomenology

Gödel had on various occasions expressed the view that phenomenology as an existing body of thought, and also as an evolving philosophical programme enriched by new experiences and breakthroughs in the field of epistemology at large, and in the field of logic and mathematics in particular, would help clarify and possibly decide questions concerning the soundness of primitive terms in logical-mathematical theories and their associated axioms in a completely convincing manner.[11] Moreover, at least at the stage of drafting the 1964 supplement to his famous 1947 paper on Cantor's continuum problem, Gödel maintained that if the meanings of the primitive terms of set theory (e.g., the meaning of sets as definable by the properties of their elements or as arbitrary multitudes regardless of the possibility of their definition) are accepted as sound:

it follows that the set-theoretical concepts and theorems describe some well-determined reality, in which Cantor's conjecture must be either true or false. Hence its undecidability from the axioms assumed today can only mean that these axioms do not contain a complete description of that reality. Such a belief is by no means chimerical, since it is possible to point out ways in which the decision

---

10 It is noteworthy that certain drafts of Gödel's work for the so-called Dialectica paper, *On a Consistency Proof Based on the Notion of Computable Functions of a Finitary Type* (Feferman, 1990, pp. 217–241, 271–281), published for the first time and commented on by van Atten (2015, pp. 205–222), are quite demonstrative of Gödel's view of intuitionism in relation to his later phenomenological turn. In addition, a group of notes pertaining to this work, kept in a separate folder at Princeton Library, are Gödel's marginal but as yet the closest found application of phenomenological notions to concrete mathematical acts (van Atten, 2015, pp. 220–222).

11 The view associating in a straightforward way the development of phenomenology with the decision of questions relative to primitive terms and axioms of mathematics is found explicitly stated in an unpublished part of Gödel's supplement to the 1964 reprint of his Cantor paper, as referred to in van Atten's *Essays on Gödel's Reception of Leibniz, Husserl and Brouwer* (van Atten, 2015, p. 5).

of a question, which is undecidable from the usual axioms, might nevertheless be obtained. (Feferman, 1990, p. 260)

In his 1961 (posthumously published) article "The Modern Development of the Foundations of Mathematics in the Light of Philosophy", Gödel gave unreserved praise for the positive influence phenomenology might have on mathematics as presumably possessing a systematic method for the clarification of the meaning of abstract mathematical concepts themselves and of the fundamental relations subsisting among them, and consequently into the axioms that hold therein. He specifically claimed that phenomenology is not a science in the same sense as other sciences, echoing Husserl's thesis that phenomenology is a descriptive eidetic theory of essences, to the extent that it turns its attention to our own acts in making use of the abstract concepts in question and in the *a priori* subjective modes in carrying out those acts, etc. Phenomenology as a procedure or technique is, in Gödel's view, what makes possible a clarification of the meaning of the basic concepts used thus far and the possible grasp of other basic concepts hitherto unknown to us by producing in us a new state of consciousness (Feferman, 1995, p. 383).

Motivated by this argument, Gödel went on to claim that in spite of the negative results generated by his incompleteness results with regard to Hilbert's proposal of a finitistic formalism, every clearly posed mathematical yes or no question may be solvable insofar as new axioms which do not follow by formal logic from those previously established become evident on the "basis of the meaning of the primitive notions that a machine cannot imitate" (Feferman, 1995, p. 385). Yet in terms of the progress in foundational mathematics at that time, Gödel could not but be very reserved as to their ability to solve the *Continuum Hypothesis* (*CH*), and this was made explicit in the 1964 version of his *Cantor's Continuum* article by citing highly implausible consequences of the *CH* (e.g., the existence of subsets of a straight line of the power of the continuum which are covered up to denumerably many points by every dense set of intervals) and by referring to many results in point-set theory obtained without using the *CH* which are also highly unexpected and implausible (Feferman, 1990, pp. 263–264). Reasonably, a short time before Cohen's communication of his independence results, Gödel came to believe that, out of these indications, the undecidability of Cantor's conjecture is the most likely outcome and the difficulties of the problem may not be purely mathematical. However, he stressed again that the continuum problem cannot be solved on the basis of the axioms set up so far, but could possibly be solvable with the help of some new axiom that "would state or imply something about the definability of sets" (Feferman, 1990, p. 262). Gödel referred at this point to his own Constructibility Axiom ($V = L$), by which he postulated that every set can be logically definable by means of predicate formulas representing concrete logical operations within classes constructed along transfinite ordinals. On the basis of the Axiom of Constructibility he was able to prove both the *Axiom of Choice* and the *Continuum Hypothesis*; however, this was done with the restrictive condition that sets could be accepted only insofar as they are definable by formal-logical properties, in other words insofar as they are extensions of definable properties excluding in principle all sets in the sense of arbitrary multitudes deprived of any possibility of predicative definition.

In the same article Gödel made the prediction that there is little hope of solving the continuum problem by means of those axioms of infinity based on Mahlo's principles,[12] leaving the door open for new axioms based on different principles (he referred to them as extremely strong axioms of infinity of an entirely new kind) as well as other hitherto unknown axioms of set theory "which a more profound understanding of the concepts underlying logic and mathematics would enable us to recognize as implied by these concepts" (Feferman, 1990, p. 261). It is quite interesting that Gödel, who was knowledgeable about developments in the fields of set theory and mathematical foundations at that time, bore in mind, in referring to extremely strong axioms of infinity, the works of Keisler and Tarski (1964) and of Scott (1961), known for applying new methods and ideas to generate cardinals stronger than weakly or strongly inaccessible ones, for instance, by applying the notions of α-complete ideals or filters, elementary embeddings, inner models, etc.

Following on from this, I discuss at this point the impossibility of deciding the continuum problem (in the simple or generalized form) insofar as the infinity concept is taken in a phenomenological, metatheoretical perspective as subjectively founded and ultimately associated with inner time constitution while being at the same time integrated into the predicative universe of a formal theory in the form, for instance, of complete well-meant infinite mathematical objects (e.g., infinite sets or classes). The main points of my argumentation are as follows.

In the 1964 version of *Cantor's Continuum* (Feferman, 1990, p. 262, n. 23), Gödel made the prediction that the negation of Cantor's *Continuum Hypothesis* could perhaps be derived from an axiom opposite in a certain sense to his own Axiom of Constructibility which, as already mentioned, roughly states that every set is definable by certain logical-mathematical operations in a classification scheme in terms of ordinal numbers. He went on to state that this axiom (similar to Hilbert's completeness axiom in Geometry) would state some maximum property of the system of all sets, having in mind that in contrast the Constructibility Axiom states a minimum property. If we keep in mind that the Constructibility

---

12 In his own proof of the undisprovability of the *Continuum Hypothesis* based on the Axiom of Constructibility Gödel had passed through them all.

Axiom $V = L$ by its restrictive nature, excluding sets in the sense of arbitrary multitudes, represents a minimum property of the system of all sets, then its negation $V \neq L$ would normally be expected to represent a maximum property of the system of sets as it allows for consideration both classes of sets: those definable by means of predicative formulas by the properties of their elements and those taken in the sense of arbitrary multitudes, among these latter ones the generic sets of forcing theory on account of which Gödel had said, as recorded by Wang (1996, p. 252), that "forcing is a method to make true statements about something of which we know nothing". As is well known, Cohen had proved by a finitistic relative consistency proof the axiom $V \neq L$ to be consistent with the rest of the axioms of Zermelo-Fraenkel plus the Axiom of Choice system (**ZFC**), and on these grounds he eventually derived the negation of Cantor's continuum conjecture in accordance with Gödel's aforementioned anticipation.

Scott proved in 1961 on the assumption of the the existence of a special kind of large cardinal, i.e., the measurable cardinal, the validity of the axiom $V \neq L$. In turn, Levy and Solovay proved in 1967 that if **ZFM** is the Zermelo-Fraenkel set theory **ZF** together with an axiom that asserts the existence of a measurable cardinal, then if **ZFM** is consistent it is consistent with both the *Continuum Hypothesis* and its negation (Levy and Solovay, 1967, p. 234). By and large, the above chain of results shows the subtleties of the question of determining the size of the continuum and indeed how Gödel's expectations about the possibility of resolving it by new axioms based on extremely large infinity assumptions ultimately proved to be fruitless.[13] Indeed after his proposal to decide *CH* by applying large cardinal axioms did not succeed, and even before knowing Levy and Solovay's result, Gödel proposed a host of new axioms or axiom schemas (four in number), the first of which is now called Gödel's square axiom (see Feferman, 1990, p. 173), in order to resolve the *CH*. In what remains in his *Nachlass* as his last attempt to resolve the *Continuum Hypothesis*, there are three versions of a paper written in 1970 (abbreviated in his *Collected Works*, V. III, as *1970_a, *1970_b, *1970_c) in the first of which he allegedly disproved *CH* (i.e., he proved that $2^{\aleph_0} = \aleph_2$), a result he had envisaged from the time of the 1964 version of Cantor's continuum, while paradoxically proving *CH* in *1970_b by means of some of the (four) axioms mentioned in *1970_a (Feferman, 1995, pp. 405–422).

Taking into account that even today the *Continuum Hypothesis* remains an unresolved major foundational question, one can plausibly claim, even without

---

13 In the updated postscript to the 1964 version of Cantor's continuum problem, Gödel conceded that the axioms of infinity he mentioned in fn 20 of the same version (i.e., Keisler-Tarski's and Scott's results), in their precise formulation by then, were not sufficient to resolve Cantor's continuum hypothesis (Feferman, 1990, p. 270).

any background phenomenological or other philosophical motivation, that, as Gödel stated in the 1964 version of *Cantor's Continuum* paper, the difficulties of the problem may not be purely mathematical. In fact, in all subsequent attempts to resolve the continuum question using inner models coupled with extremely large cardinal approaches, there is not a single case in the proof-theoretical machinery in which a concept of actual infinity, arguably rooted in a subjective temporally founded constitution, does not implicitly condition the existence of formal objects of infinite cardinality as complete, set-theoretical ones upon which a host of logical-mathematical operations may be carried out.

In these terms any first-order universal-existential quantification over an indefinite horizon, and *a fortiori* a second-order one, clearly presupposes a notion of completed totality for the intended scope of quantifiers as well as for the infinite cardinals themselves as substrates of formulas and objects of quantification which, on a subjectively founded level, may reduce to the constitution of infinities of any order in the objective form of the continuous unity of a whole in presentational immediacy. In turn this kind of actual infinity, far from being a spatio-temporal and causality-generated one,[14] insofar as it is immanent to the self-constituting temporal consciousness, underlies (on the metatheoretical level) in one way or another not only the already established independence results of the *Continuum Hypothesis* and the *Axiom of Choice* but also certain more recent attempts to achieve enlargements of inner models in order to be consistent with all known large cardinal axioms. I refer, in particular, to Woodin's proposed construction of a special enlargement L^Ω of Gödel's constructible universe L to provide, among other things, a better understanding of the transition to large and very large cardinal axioms, as well as an elimination of all large cardinal axioms known to contradict the Axiom of Choice (Woodin, 2011a, p. 470). However, to the extent that this construction is associated with Woodin's Ω-conjecture, it is circularly conditioned on a notion of actual infinity by the very definition of the associated notion of Ω-completeness based on topological continuity notions, e.g., the property of being universally Baire (Woodin, 2011b, p. 108).[15]

---

14 A further explanation of this kind of immanent infinity free of spatio-temporal and, for that matter, causal constraints can be found in Husserl's V. II of *Logical Investigations*. At some point Husserl cautioned that the free extension of space and time stretches in imagination is not a proof of the relative foundedness of bits of space and time and therefore does not prove the real infinity of space and time, which is in any case subject to the natural laws of causality (see Husserl, 1984a, pp. 299–300). This kind of actual infinity freely generated in terms of the continuous unity of temporal consciousness is presented as an objective whole in acts of reflection in the actual now.

15 In recent research, Woodin has tried to accommodate the ultimate global conjecture V=Ultimate-L with the existence of very large cardinals, namely supercompact ones, with no full success at this point. As a result the structural generalizations of the constructive universe L he realizes cannot resemble the set-theoretical universe V beyond the level of Σ_2-sentences (see Woodin, 2017, and the links:

Eventually, one might even doubt the soundness of applying topological notions, inasmuch as they implicitly refer to the system of real numbers for which there is a reasonable objection as to whether they constitute a set, at least in the sense of Gödel's definability constraints, to resolve purely set-theoretical questions.

There seems to be no way, also judging by Gödel's allusions to the primary importance of time in the understanding of the system of primitive terms and their relationships, to talk about infinite objects and relations in logical-mathematical theories and at the same time "remain" in the predicative universe of the theory, let us say the commonly accepted **ZFC** theory, so long as the notion of infinity taken as a continuous unity in actual presence implies an extra-theoretical, and more specifically a subjectively founded reduction to inner temporality. It is important to note in this respect that the unity originating in the being of consciousness as such not only underlies the possibility of reflecting on things in general as identical and enduring unities over time, but also grounds the possibility of reducing the concept of an ideal infinity in progression to an act of fulfilment and completion in the present now of consciousness. In this sense the unity of the physical thing:

stands over against an ideally infinite multiplicity of noetic mental processes of a wholly determined essential content and which can be surveyed despite the infinity, all of them united by being consciousness of the 'same thing'. This unification becomes given in the sphere of consciousness itself, in mental processes which, on their side, also belong again to the group which we have delimited here. (Husserl, 1976b, Engl. transl., p. 323)

To the extent that the transcendence of physical objects as immanent ones is reduced to the transcendence of consciousness, something that also happens with their unity founded in the unity of consciousness, the above statement also holds good for categorial objects in the sense of immanent objects corresponding to pure, content-free, object-forms with *a priori* associated, empty-of-content specific relational forms, a class that includes all objects of a formal-mathematical theory as states-of-affairs, i.e., all categorial forms, numbers or number-theoretical forms, functions of pure analysis and their Euclidean or non-Euclidean domains (Husserl, 1976b, p. 33).

4. The Phenomenological Influence in Gödel's View of Mathematical Objects

As with the question of time in relation to its underlying role in the constitution of mathematical concepts and objects, Gödel did not go to any lengths or to any

---

https://settheory.mathtalks.org/wp-content/uploads/2016/02/mm70.pdf and http://sms.victoria.ac.nz/foswiki/pub/Events/NZMRI2017/Slides/lectureIV-F.pdf). As mentioned previously, Woodin's scheme, to the extent that it largely refers to universally Baire subsets of the real numbers, entails, on the metatheoretical level, the circularity of entering large infinity assumptions while being conditioned on an actual infinity at least of the power of continuum on the level of topological definitions.

deeper level, at least in his published work or recorded exchanges, in discussing the influence of certain fundamental phenomenological ideas, e.g., those of categorial intuition, of the eidetic state-of-affairs, of categorial objectivity, etc., on our conception of logical-mathematical objects as immutable and transtemporal ones. Yet we may be able to see how some of his views on mathematical objects in the context of his peculiar brand of mathematical realism are to a certain extent influenced by his readings of Husserl's works, in particular of *Logical Investigations*, of *Ideas I* and of *Cartesian Meditations*. It is noteworthy that even though Gödel recommended to logicians in the 1960s "that they should study the sixth investigation in Logical Investigations for its treatment of categorial intuition" (Wang, 1996, p. 5), he himself left no detailed description of the ways categorial intuition might shape the constitution of logical-mathematical objects in an intersubjective fashion. Below I will examine several views expressed by Gödel on mathematical objects and their meanings, and try to bring out the extent to which they conform to Husserl's corresponding ideas, and ultimately to see in what sense they shape Gödel's particular version of mathematical platonism or objective idealism (as his philosophy of mathematics is termed by some logicians).

A clue is the following well-known passage from Gödel's supplement to the Cantor paper (1964) which may lend itself to an interpretation according to the theory expounded in the sixth logical investigation:

That something besides the sensations actually is immediately given follows (independently of mathematics) from the fact that even our ideas referring to physical objects contain constituents qualitatively different from sensations or mere combinations of sensations, e.g., the idea of object itself, whereas, on the other hand, by our thinking we cannot create any qualitatively new elements, but only reproduce and combine those that are given. Evidently the 'given' underlying mathematics is closely related to the abstract elements in our empirical ideas. It by no means follows, however, that the data of this second kind, because they cannot be associated with actions of certain things upon our sense organs, are something purely subjective, as Kant asserted. Rather they, too, may represent an aspect of objective reality, but, as opposed to the sensations, their presence in us may be due to another kind of relationship between ourselves and reality. (Feferman, 1990, p. 268)[16]

---

[16] Føllesdal (1995, pp. 441–442) has interpreted Gödel's statement above concerning the proposed idea of the object itself as pointing to such abstract features involved in the individuation of objects as identity and distinctness, which is a view I agree with. Yet he continues by stating, at which point I disagree, that these features, being principal elements studied in mathematics, are part of the same "package" as space and time. My own view, however, is that they cannot possibly be part of the same 'package' (as space and time) since they are *a priori* features of intentional perception unconstrained in principle by spatio-temporality.

This is preceded, concerning the objects of set theory, by his statement that "despite their remoteness from sense experience we do have something like a perception also of the objects of set-theory, as is seen from the fact that the axioms force themselves upon us as being true" (Feferman, 1990, p. 268).

It is reasonable to assume even with a basic knowledge of phenomenology that Gödel's statement above is (or at least could be) to a certain extent influenced by the Husserlian notions of intentionality, eidetic state-of-affairs and meaning-content. These are notions that are inherently interconnected and to the extent that they are reduced to *a priori* necessities involving objectivity as a constituted situation-of-affairs[17] they are by this token independent as such by spatio-temporal contingencies. Even though there are in Husserlian texts certain ambivalences concerning the temporal status of intentionality as a *directedness toward* act with no necessity of the actual existence of its object-content in real spatio-temporal terms, the primary reasons that make meaning-content, eidetic intuition and intentional apprehension parts of a unitary *a priori* based process that helps constitute the idea of an object, in the way Gödel may have thought of, are as follows.

In the supplement to the *Logical Investigations* (Part 2) Husserl stated that an object may be defined as: (1) the object thought of as such (*vermeinte Gegenstand*) and further as (2) the meaning-object, that is, the object with the "content" through which it is thought of therein. In this regard the former sense is the identical object which in any change of the meaning through which it is represented is preserved as such (Husserl, 2005, p. 285). In what is consistent with the description of non-self-standing forms (abstracta) in *Ideas I* and later with the description of the general meaning of an object regardless of any material content as "something anyhow" (*etwas-überhaupt*; also rendered as "anything-whatever") in *Formal and Transcendental Logic*, Husserl stated that the forms which are not self-standing ones and which can be made substrates of states-of-affairs are not themselves objects and also not states-of-affairs, as they are in need of a unitary "glance" to be shaped as objects. In the same vein, objects are distinguished as self-standing and not self-standing, with the latter referring to categorial forms, to the extent that they point to substrates whose form they are. In this sense substrate and form are interchangeable notions where the categorial form object as a purely logical form independent of all material objectivities is not a self-standing one. Husserl considered objects of a special kind the "empty of content"

---

17 The Husserlian term situation-of-affairs (*Sachlage*) is a broad concept subsuming the concept of state-of-affairs (*Sachverhalt*), and is thought of as a passively constituted foundation of states-of-affairs, a simple instance being: the situation-of-affairs of A is of greater size than B giving rise to the states-of-affairs A > B and B < A. More details can be found in Rosado-Haddock (1991).

substrates or pure forms, with all associated syntactical objectivities, as modifications of "empty-somethings" (*leer Etwas*), in the sense of states-of-affairs with all categorial objectivities from which they are built up, in which class he also included all states-of-affairs expressible through formal axioms or theorems (Husserl, 1976b, p. 33).

In no way was this class considered by Husserl an empty or deficient one with regard to the class of "thingness" substrates, the latter class meant as the class of substrates corresponding to concrete, well-meant objects of objective reality. The unifying link, so to say, between objects as "thingness" substrates and objects as "empty" substrates (with categorial objectivities proper to them) is attained at the "lowest" possible level of evidence, the level at which both lowest-level "thingness" substrates and "empty" substrates stand as nuclei of all associated syntactical structures that ultimately lead to the notion of individuality at the level of evidence since last "thingness" essence and the "this-there" as a pure, syntactically formless individuality become interchangeable notions. This gradual process of laying bare the essence of an object as such by withdrawing any constraint to a material or generally a "thingness" content culminated, concerning at least the objects of formal logic as a global science, in *Formal and Transcendental Logic*. There the idea of an object of formal mathematics in the Husserlian sense and the one Gödel referred to in the passage from his supplement to the Cantor paper seem remarkably compatible. Moreover, the particular sense attributed by Husserl in *Formal and Transcendental Logic* to logical-mathematical objects provides a proper foundation for the meaning of categorial intuition for the objects of the broad field of mathematics, this latter meant as an ontology by virtue of being an *a priori* theory of objects and a formal one inasmuch as it relates to the pure modes of "anything-whatever". In this way the domain of formal mathematics, in a fully comprehensive sense, is rigidly delimited as the sphere of the highest form-concept, the "object-whatever" in its emptiest universality with all the derivative formations conceivable as reiterable constructions in this field. Such derivative forms, besides sets and cardinal numbers (finite and infinite), were considered combinations (in the mathematical sense of the word), relational complexes, series, connexions, whole and parts, etc. (Husserl, 1992, Engl. transl., pp. 77–78).

If logical-mathematical objects are freed from the constraints of material and causal contingencies and insofar as in Gödel's mathematical realism they cannot be considered as purely platonic entities, by Gödel's reference to the presence in us of the idea of abstract objects themselves due to another kind of relationship between ourselves and reality, the next question should be about the modes in which they are apprehended in the first place and then become objects of knowledge in a temporally enduring, intersubjective fashion. The key concept employed

The Plausible Impact of Phenomenology on Gödel

by Husserl is of course intentionality, in whose place and in parallel meaning he frequently used the term *Wahrnehmung*, meant as an intentional act to be realized toward a specific "this-there" irrespective of a possible thingness content and prior to explication. The *a priori* directedness of intentionality is associated not only with sensory objects but also with immanent, temporal in nature (including imaginary objects) and even ideal ones (non-spatial and transtemporal objects such as numbers, elements of sets, aggregation of elements, etc.). In this way intentional orientation is not necessarily bound to objective spatio-temporality and causality insofar as intentional directedness is not conditioned on the existence of its objects in absolute spatio-temporal terms but on the "content" or "meaning" associated in each occurrence with corresponding intentional acts even in the absence of the object represented in real experience by the specific "content". Consequently intentionality is taken as an intrinsic feature of our conscious experience enacted independently of whether what is intended does exist as factuality. A general remark to be made here is that reducing the meanings of world, reality, object, horizon, etc. to intentional-explicative features of a consciousness and taking also account of the Epochë performed with regard to the being or non-being of the world does not all mean that the world is lost for phenomenology. What is left after phenomenological reduction is the world at large but in its every aspect as a correlate of consciousness which is on the noetic side the openly endless, always-in-act, life of pure consciousness and on the noematic side, as a correlate, the meant world purely as meant (Husserl, 1973b, pp. 36–37).

In *Ideas I*, which Gödel justifiably valued highly, Husserl elaborated the idea of objects as "post-intentional" noematic ones, stating that in noematic respect two sorts of objects-concepts are to be distinguished, the noematic object *simpliciter*, the pure "point" of unity, and the object in the how of its determinations (the sense attributed to the object by the noematic act) including undeterminatednesses which may be "open" at the time being but in the mode of constituting are co-meant (Husserl, 1976b, p. 303). This particular possibility of undeterminatedness as a co-meant and potentially susceptible to being uncovered property of objects in terms of the noema of the corresponding constitutive acts marks in a most obvious way the demarcation line between a pure mathematical platonism and Gödel's hybrid and (to a certain extent) phenomenologically influenced brand of platonism of his later years.

That said, I take Tieszen's interpretation of Gödel's position in *Some Basic Theorems on the Foundations of Mathematics and their Implications*[18] as a false

---

18 Tieszen (1998, pp. 226–227) attributed platonistic tendencies to Gödel to the extent that he went beyond the existential commitments of **ZFC** theory by arguing for the need for new axioms and also by

way to attribute to Gödel a vindication of pure platonism: in this article Gödel associated his view, namely that conceptual realism (as his sort of platonism is often characterized) seems to be supported by modern developments in the foundations of mathematics, with the second alternative of the disjunctive position that "Either mathematics is incompleteable in this sense, that its evident axioms can never be comprised in a finite rule ... or else there exist absolutely unsolvable diophantine problems of the type specified" (Feferman, 1995, p. 310). Concerning the second alternative, which is the existence of absolutely unsolvable diophantine problems in case the human mind does not surpass the powers of any finite machine, Gödel pointed out in *Some Remarks on the Undecidability Results* that problems like the absolutely unsolvable diophantine ones may be in fact not absolutely unsolvable owing to the existence of a still unexplored series of axioms which are analytic in the sense that they only explicate the content of the concepts occurring in them (Feferman, 1990, p. 306).

Motivated by a theorem conditioning the solution of Goldbach type problems of a certain degree of compilation, Gödel claimed that these axioms and even more complicated ones may appear in the development of mathematics and, in the particular case of the axioms of infinity, in a substantial development of set theory. Lest this process be interpreted as a purely formal outgrowth of new theorems or simply conjectures necessitating the postulation of new axioms, Gödel clarified that it is due to our mind's constantly developing capacity that we understand abstract terms more and more precisely as we use them, while more and more abstract terms enter into the sphere of our understanding. He went on to add that even though the number and precision of the primitive terms at our disposal may be finite, and accordingly Turing's number of distinguishable states of mind, both number and precision tend toward infinity in the process, for instance, of forming stronger and stronger axioms of infinity in set theory.[19] This may be taken as a kind of subjectively based process that seems to be in line with Gödel's view in his well-known 1961 article (Section 3) that phenomenology makes possible a clarification of the meaning of the basic concepts used thus far and the

---

sharpening our intuition toward the already existing "realm" of objects or truths, to express more of what already exists in the universe of abstract, mind-independent transfinite sets. Yet it seems to me the way he raised the issue by pointing to a pre-existing, platonic-like realm of mathematical objects and truths does not do justice to his conclusion elsewhere that phenomenology might help with the task of sharpening our intuition toward logical-mathematical objects or truths (Tieszen, 2011, p. 91).

19 It is true, however, that in his argumentation in favour of conceptual realism in *Some Basic Theorems on the Foundations of Mathematics and Their Implications*, Gödel was pessimistic about the developments in set theory, stating that in spite of an insurmountable degree of exactness in the development of mathematical foundations this had provided practically no help for the solution of concrete mathematical problems (Feferman, 1995, p. 314).

possible grasp of other basic concepts hitherto unknown to us by producing in us a new state of consciousness.

What is noteworthy about Gödel's view of the objects of mathematics and the associated meanings is that even before his systematic reading of Husserlian texts, starting by all accounts from 1959 onward, one can still find in his philosophically inclined texts insights that can be reasonably taken as at least susceptible to a phenomenological interpretation. I refer to Gödel's indication in his well-known Gibbs lecture of the characteristic feature of mathematical objects to be "known (in principle) without using the senses (that is, by reason alone) for this very reason, that they don't concern actualities about which the senses (the inner sense included) inform us, but possibilities and impossibilities" (Feferman, 1995, p. 312, n. 18). Van Atten (2015, pp. 81–82) has aptly suggested in *Essays on Gödel's Reception of Leibniz, Husserl and Brouwer* that so long as mathematical objects are taken as purely categorial objects, as indeed Husserl considered them to be at the time of *Logical Investigations* and after, they are studied not as factually given but with respect to their possibility or impossibility. Accordingly he quotes, quite to the point, a passage from *Logical Investigations* (V. II, part 2) in which Husserl asserted that the ideal conditions of the possibility of categorial intuition are correlated to the conditions of possibility of the objects of categorial intuition and of categorial objects as such.

One may also point to Gödel's notion of mathematical existence, in his well-known pre-1959 article "Is Mathematics Syntax of Language?", as admitting of an interpretation close to the corresponding Husserlian view in *Experience and Judgment*. Husserl viewed existential quantification as an *a priori* possibility of existence which (combined with universal quantification) points to a constraint "imposed" by our mathematical activity (meant as an activity-within-the world) on mathematical individuals which is that of introducing necessities out of possibilities (Husserl, 1939, Engl. transl., pp. 370–371). The *a priori* possibility of existence together with the possibility of an indefinite reiteration of this "act" of existence cannot be otherwise construed but as linked to mental faculties, in fact linked to the intentional modalities of consciousness to the extent that these can found the existence of individuals independently of a material or generally "thingness" content, even of an objective spatio-temporal existence. In this regard it is possible to find common ground with Husserl's position concerning existential assertions in terms of Gödel's view of mathematical-logical objects as "existent" in a separate realm from that of space-time reality and yet accessible to us through a relation of a special kind we bear with objects themselves independently of sensuous experience. Claiming that the ideas of transfinite objects or operations "cannot be known to be meaningful or consistent unless we trust some mathematical intuition of things completely inaccessible to experience", Gödel characterized the existential statement "there exists" as a transfinite (i.e., non-constructive) concept insofar as this phrase means objective existence regardless of actual producibility in objective spatio-temporality (Feferman, 1995, p. 341, nn. 19, 20). He also offered an indirect clue to an ontology of existential assertions in mathematics by pointing to the fact that they are not taken as a mere "way of talking", due to the fact that they can be disproved by inconsistencies derived from them and also by having consequences for ascertainable facts (Feferman, 1995, pp. 355–356).

5. Concluding Remarks

In the phenomenologically motivated argumentation of this article, Gödel's views on logical-mathematical objects as well as his position on the non-eliminability of abstract mathematical concepts by a concrete, finitistic intuition in Hilbert's sense may find a proper interpretational context, even though he himself did not choose to enter into a systematic discussion of the application of phenomenological ideas to his philosophy of mathematics. My intention was therefore mainly focused on pointing to several of his ideas either pertaining to technical aspects of his work in the foundations of mathematics or being outright philosophical positions associated with his overall philosophy of mathematics that can be seen as directly or indirectly phenomenologically influenced. However, his own insights and degree of mastery of the Husserlian theory of the constitution of inner time, as possibly founding on an absolute, subjective level the concept of infinity in mathematics and further as conditioning purely logical relations on the evidence of co-existence, coherence and causal necessity, will remain a riddle (judging by all that has been published in his lifetime or retrieved from his *Nachlass*) and will perhaps provide motivation for future research on the matter.

References

Feferman, S., Dawson, J. W. Jr., Kleene, S. C., Moore, G., Solovay, R., and van Heijenoort, J. (eds) (1990) *Kurt Gödel: Collected Works*, Vol. II. Oxford: Oxford University Press.

Feferman, S., Dawson, J. W. Jr., Goldfarb, W., Parsons, C., and Solovay, R. (eds) (1995) *Kurt Gödel: Collected Works*, Vol. III. Oxford: Oxford University Press.

Føllesdal, D. (1995) "Gödel and Husserl." In J. Hintikka (ed.), *From Dedekind to Gödel*, pp. 426–446. Dordrecht: Springer.

Franks, C. (2011) "Stanley Tennenbaum's Socrates." In J. Kennedy and R. Kossack (eds), *Set Theory, Arithmetic and Foundations of Mathematics*, pp. 208–226. Cambridge: Cambridge University Press.

GOLDFARB, W. (2005) "On Gödel's Way In: The Influence of Rudolf Carnap." *Bulletin of Symbolic Logic* 11(2): 185–193.

HAUSER, K. (2006) "Gödel's Program Revisited Part I: The Turn to Phenomenology." *Bulletin of Symbolic Logic* 12(4): 529–590.

HUSSERL, E. (1939) In L. Landgrebe (ed.), *Erfahrung und Urteil*. Prague: Acad./Verlagsbuchhandlung. English translation: *Experience and Judgment* (1973), transl. J. S. Churchill and K. Americs. London: Routledge & Kegan Paul.

HUSSERL, E. (1973a) *Die Idee der Phänomenologie. Funf Vorlesungen*, Hua Vol. II, ed. W. Biemel. Den Haag: M. Nijhoff. English translation: *The Idea of Phenomenology* (1966), transl. W.P. Alston and G. Nakhnikian. The Hague: M. Nijhoff.

HUSSERL, E. (1973b) *Cartesianische Meditationen und Pariser Vorträge*, Hua Vol. I, ed. S. Strasser. Den Haag: M. Nijhoff. English translation: *Cartesian Meditations* (1982), transl. D. Cairns. The Hague: M. Nijhoff.

HUSSERL, E. (1976a) "*Die Krisis des Europäischen Menschentums und die Philosophie*." *Die Krisis der Europäischen Wissenschaften und die Transzendentale Phänomenologie*, Hua Vol. VI, ed. W. Biemel, pp. 314–348. The Hague: M. Nijhoff. English translation: *Phenomenology and the Crisis of Philosophy* (1965), transl. Q. Lauer. New York: Harper & Row.

HUSSERL, E. (1976b) *Ideen zu einer reinen Phänomenologie und phänomenologischen Philosophie*, Erstes Buch, Hua Vol. III/I, ed. K. Schuhmann. Den Haag: M. Nijhoff. English translation: *Ideas Pertaining to a Pure Phenomenology and to a Phenomenological Philosophy: First Book* (1983), transl. F. Kersten. The Hague: M. Nijhoff.

HUSSERL, E. (1984a) *Logische Untersuchungen*, Hua XIX/1, ed. U. Panzer. The Hague: M. Nijhoff. English translation: *Logical Investigations*, V. I (2001), transl. J. N. Findlay. London and New York: Routledge.

HUSSERL, E. (1984b) *Logische Untersuchungen*, Hua XIX/2, ed. U. Panzer. The Hague: M. Nijhoff. English translation: *Logical Investigations*, V. II (2001), transl. J. N. Findlay. London and New York: Routledge.

HUSSERL, E. (1992) *Formale und Transzendentale Logik*, Hua Vol. XVII, ed. E. Ströker. Hamburg: Felix Meiner Verlag. English translation: *Formal and Transcendental Logic* (1969), transl. D. Cairns. The Hague: M. Nijhoff.

HUSSERL, E. (2001a) *Die Bernauer Manuskripte über das Zeitbewusstsein (1917/18)*, ed. R. Bernet and D. Lohmar. Dordrecht: Kluwer.

HUSSERL, E. (2001b) *Späte Texte über Zeitkonstitution, Die C-Manuscripte*, Hua Materialien Vol. VIII, ed. D. Lohmar. Dordrecht: Springer.

HUSSERL, E. (2002) *Logische Untersuchungen, Ergänzungsband, Erster Teil*, Hua Vol. XX/1, ed. U. Moeller. Dordrecht: Kluwer.

HUSSERL, E. (2005) *Logische Untersuchungen, Ergänzungsband, Zweiter Teil*, Hua Vol. XX/2, ed. U. Moeller. Dordrecht: Kluwer.

KEISLER, J. H. and TARSKI, A. (1964) "From Accessible to Inaccessible Cardinals: Results for All Accessible Cardinal Numbers and the Problem of Their Extension to Inaccessible Ones." *Fundamenta Mathematicae* 53: 225–308. Correct.: (1965), 57: 119.

LEVY, A. and SOLOVAY, M. R. (1967) "Measurable Cardinals and the Continuum Hypothesis." *Israel Journal of Mathematics* 5(4): 234–248.

ROSADO-HADDOCK, E. G. (1991) "On Husserl's Distinction between State of Affairs (*Sachverhalt*) and Situation of Affairs (*Sachlage*)." In T. Seebohm, D. Føllesdal and J. N. Mohanty (eds), *Phenomenology and the Formal Sciences*, pp. 35–48. Dordrecht: Springer.

SCOTT, D. S. (1961) "Measurable Cardinals and Constructible Sets." *Bulletin de l'Académie Polonaise des Sciences* 9: 521–524.
TIESZEN, R. (1998) "Critical Notice, Gödel's Philosophical Remarks on Logic and Mathematics." *Mind* 107(425): 219–231.
TIESZEN, R. (2011) *After Gödel: Platonism and Rationalism in Mathematics and Logic.* Oxford: Oxford University Press.
TOLEDO, S. (2011) "Sue Toledo's Notes of Her Conversations with Gödel in 1972–5." In J. Kennedy and R. Kossack (eds), *Set Theory, Arithmetic and Foundations of Mathematics*, pp. 200–208. Cambridge: Cambridge University Press.
VAN ATTEN, M. (2004) *On Brouwer*. Belmont, CA: Wadsworth.
VAN ATTEN, M. (2015) *Essays on Gödel's Reception of Leibniz, Husserl and Brouwer.* New York: Springer.
WANG, H. (1987) *Reflections on Kurt Gödel*. Cambridge, MA: MIT Press.
WANG, H. (1996) *A Logical Journey. From Gödel to Philosophy.* Cambridge, MA: MIT Press.
WOODIN, H. W. (2011a) "The Transfinite Universe." In M. Baaz, C. H. Papadimitriou, H. W. Putnam, D. S. Scott and C. L. Harper Jr. (eds), *Kurt Gödel and the Foundations of Mathematics*, pp. 449–471. New York: Cambridge University Press.
WOODIN, H. W. (2011b) "The Realm of the Infinite." In M. Heller and H. W. Woodin (eds), *Infinity, New Research Frontiers*, pp. 89–118. New York: Cambridge University Press.
WOODIN, H. W. (2017) "In Search of Ultimate-L: The 19th Midrasha Mathematicae Lectures." *Bulletin of Symbolic Logic* 23(1): 1–109.

Talking About Models: The Inherent Constraints of Mathematics

Abstract

In this article my primary intention is to engage in a discussion on the inherent constraints of models, taken as models of theories, that reaches beyond the epistemological level. Naturally the paper takes into account the ongoing debate between proponents of the syntactic and the semantic view of theories and that between proponents of the various versions of scientific realism, reaching down to the most fundamental, subjective level of discourse. In this approach, while allowing for a limited discussion of physical and positive science models, I am primarily focused on the structure and ontology of mathematical models, in particular Cohen's forcing models and to a lesser extent Gödel's constructible universe, to the extent that these were designed to answer questions bearing on the scope, the capacity and ultimately the ontology of models themselves (e.g., the question of continuum), therefore influencing in one or the other way the status of models in general. This status, it is argued, is largely defined by the way models subsume a set-theoretical structure whose constraints, reducible to an extra-linguistic level of discourse, may implicitly condition the epistemic status of models as representations of axiomatic theories. In the last section I deal extensively with the inner constraints of theories (or of corresponding models for that matter) as subjectively originated in a less technical philosophically oriented discussion with certain prompts from phenomenology.

1 Introduction

As already stated my intention is to give convincing arguments on the existence of certain inner constraints that condition the scope and ontological breadth of models in general, and mathematical models in particular, based on subjectively reducible and essentially a priori grounds. In my argumentation, taking into account the syntactic and semantic view of theories, I will try to show that inner constraints are imposed by the sole fact of the linguistic mediation of the 'internal' structure of theories and also by virtue of the nature of the objects of a metalanguage (e.g., a physicalistic one) as associated with respective models by means of a formal logical syntax. This entails a transition of the logico-linguistic universe to a level of discussion in which the following are accounted for: (a) the 'residua' left over in passing from registered experience to objectification and formal representation and (b) the 'residua' lying in-between formal objects and their aggregates as concatenations of discrete, finitistic sequences of signs with underlying meaning-contents. As it turns out one may be ultimately led to a review of these questions on a deeper, in fact, subjectively grounded level which is why I chose to call these subjectively founded conditions of an essential character as inner constraints. As my approach is to a certain extent phenomenologically motivated, I mention here Husserl's view in *Transcendental Psychology* that the foundational crisis affecting the positive sciences of his time (i.e., the first decades of the twentieth century) concerns most thoroughly the pure mathematical sciences underlying the exact physical sciences in the sense that the ground concepts of the latter are also the ground concepts of the former as a priori sciences (Husserl 1968, pp. 520–521). This is a discussion further left for the concluding section.

Given that a major preoccupation of this article is to inquire into the nature of theories and the corresponding models, a special attention will be given to the nature of logical-mathematical structures as pure forms expressible by formal axiomatic means and the ways in which the dialectical opposition linguistic-syntactical structure vs. associated meanings defines the scope and breadth of formal theories to the point of producing seemingly paradoxical situations within a first-order logical universe such as those implied by the Skolem–Löwenheim Theorem.

At this point it seems purposeful to make a brief reference to some ideas deemed necessary for a non-specialist to understand the mathematical relationship and the feedback between theories and models that help explicate to a large extent the difference between the so-called syntactic (pertaining to the internal structure of corresponding theories) and semantic (pertaining to models as representations of theories) view.

Theories are commonly said to have a standard formalization when they are formulated within first-order logic. Roughly speaking, first-order logic is just the logic of sentential connectives and predicates holding for one type of object usually taken to be variables as lowest-level objects of the theory. Yet when a theory assumes a logic higher than first-order it is not possible to formalize it this way, a common instance being theories involving the real numbers continuum as topological theories in mathematics are taken to be.[1] In Suppes' words "Theories of more complicated structure like quantum mechanics, classical thermodynamics, or a modern quantitative version of learning theory, need to use not only general ideas of set theory but also many results concerning real numbers. Formalization of such theories in first-order logic is utterly impractical." (Suppes 1967, p. 58). In consequence in such case it is much simpler to talk about things in models of the theory in terms of isomorphisms rather than to talk explicitly about sentences of the theory since the notion of a sentence of the theory may not be well established when the theory is not given in standard formalization. "Given an axiomatized theory of measurement of some empirical quantity such as mass, distance, or force, the mathematical task is to prove a representation theorem for models of the theory which establishes, roughly speaking, that any empirical model is isomorphic to some numerical model of the theory. The existence of this isomorphism between models justifies the application of numbers to things" (ibid., pp. 58–59).

Obviously then the transition to models ensures that, based on the key notion of isomorphism of structures, one may rid himself of the fetters of a first-order linguistic formulation and concentrate on applying the familiar knowledge of computational methods within the numerical model to infer facts about the isomorphic empirical model. The semantic view in contrast to the syntactic view is also well-suited to an extrinsic characterization of theories to the extent that instead of inquiring into the logical structure of the theory itself one may simply define the intended class of models of the theory and see that this class is exactly the class of models of the axioms in the initial axiomatization of the theory. However for anyone who would argue for the formal equivalence of the syntactic and semantic approaches on the basis of Gödel's Completeness Theorem, van Fraassen's response is that we cannot categorically (i.e., through isomorphism) designate the models we are interested in with regard to an axiomatical first-order theory because (as a result of Skolem–Löwenheim Theorem) of the existence of non-standard models which are generated as a formal outcome of the theory. Even in stipulating the *ad hoc* use of standard models as intended ones by discarding non-standard models altogether this would be a mathematical act that could not be generated syntactically (French 2010, p. 247).[2]

These questions associated on a fundamental level with the way theories and models are mediated by the capacity and expressional means of formal language are dealt with in the following Sects. 2 and (partially) 3 and in a philosophical, in fact a subjectively based, orientation in the concluding Sect. 5. In Sects. 3 and 4, essentially in the second part of this article, I focus my attention to questions arising in the constructions by K. Gödel and P. Cohen of respective mathematical models (especially of the latter one). These models were mainly built for the purpose of resolving

---

[1] Of course this has largely to do with the debated position that the real numbers system is beyond the expressional means of at least the standard set theory.

[2] Concerning the debated possibility of identification of models with theories which is a position discarded by the author, I point to van Fraassen's view that a scientific theory though not identifiable with, is still identifiable through a class of models properly conceived (Van Fraassen 1985a, p. 25).

the question of the size of the continuum which is a fact that by itself shapes our conception of models as carriers of a logico-linguistic machinery and further helps to clarify the limits of set-theoretical description. They are also directly involved with the question of the consistency with existing set theory of the Axiom of Choice which is a tool indispensable for the proof of the Model Existence Lemma among (many) other things. Not least, both models and associated theories have helped spawn new techniques and results (e.g., through the theory of inner models) in the search toward ever greater infinities potentially converging to Cantor's Absolute.

Talking about mathematical models it would be useful to remind that the set-theoretical models referred to above are not the sole achievement of mathematicians handling model-theoretical questions in terms of mathematical theories. There exists, for instance, F. W. Lawvere's categorical approach in the elementary theory of topoi and the associated functorial model theory which has not only affected pure mathematical constructions, take for instance some constructions of nonstandard analysis, but has also tried to refocus questions of physics in the formal context of categorical theory.[3] However given the scope and the meta-theoretical argumentation of the article and judging from the fact that foundational questions in mathematics are virtually independent from the formal-mathematical scaffolding one chooses to forge a meaningful discourse, I clearly find the set-theoretical framework more appropriate to deal with.

The discussion in the concluding section is primarily concerned, in the light of the preceding argumentation, with the defense of the claim that models as representational structures mediated by the formal language and determined by the axiomatic machinery of the corresponding theory are constrained as such by the essential (one could say eidetic[4] in phenomenological parlance) characteristics of a subjective constitutive presence within the world.

2 A General Assessment of Models Within a Predicative Universe

Van Fraassen asserts that if the theory as such is to be identified with anything at all, that is, if theories are to be reified, then a theory should be identified with its class of models (van Fraassen 1989, p. 222). In Da Costa's and French's view of models, "This brings the issue into sharp focus: whether the role of models is to be merely representational or to be constitutional, in the sense that the class of models actually constitutes the theory. The 'if' in van Fraassen's remark is a big if, and reification raises concerns that we do not intend to address here. Nevertheless, if models are granted a constitutional role in this sense, the question of how we are to understand the truth, or pragmatic truth, of theories becomes crucial" (da Costa and French 2003, p. 30). In a further corroboration of this position motivated by

---

[3] Some references to F. W. Lawvere's work are: Lawvere (1975, 2002, 2017).
[4] By an eidetic law in the world of phenomena one can roughly communicate to a non-phenomenologist what is implied as a regularity by essential necessity and not by mere facticity. The interested reader may consult E. Husserl's *Ideas I*, (Husserl 1976, *Engl. transl.*, pp. 12–15).

P. Suppes's insights that to present a theory we must define the class of its models directly, van Fraassen claimed that models are mathematical structures which may be called models of a given theory only insofar as they belong to the class defined as models of that theory, thus discarding a view of models defined as partially linguistic entities tied each one with a particular syntax (van Fraassen 1989, pp. 222, 366).

On this account the Completeness Theorem yields the equivalence of van Fraassen's approach with the traditional syntactic one which then due to Gödel's incompleteness results may fall prey to the inherent ambiguities associated with the deficiency of the syntactical structure of theories with regard to the meanings underlying the syntax. As already mentioned this pathological situation is actually brought to surface in case the real mathematical continuum is dealt with in terms of the theory, in which case we do not talk about an elementary set of models corresponding to a consistent set of first-order sentences where it is irrelevant whether the syntactic or the model-theoretic approach is adopted. However there is an argument, concerning physical theories, that this situation is in a certain sense productive to the extent that it may lead to a consistent enlargement of the prototheory: "Just as the system of real numbers is not closed, in the sense that one can formulate equations in terms of real numbers only whose solutions point outside the system, so a physical theory may show its lack of closure. The points at which a theory is open, or anomalous, provide a strong indication of the way in which the future larger theory is to be built." (Post 1971, p. 222).

In any case even in physical theories an open-endedness motivated, for instance, by points of inconsistency is not totally unconstrained in the sense that the heuristic criteria associated with the structure of theories and models are themselves not strictly algorithmic. This means that there is no prescribed set of rules so that what is simply needed to be done is to follow the rules and obtain a theory development; rather it seems that this development is suspended between the algorithmic and the totally free. Moreover continuity must be sought in structures generated in a bottom-up extension, something that may involve a series of 'free' and 'forced' moves, the latter resulting from what is established in the base model and the former from the intention of 'filling in' the gaps or inconsistencies by means of tentative choices among the indefinitely open spectrum of choices offered on account of conceiving the world at large as a primitive soil of experience.

Concerning the 'forced' moves this is partly characteristic of mathematical theories insofar as they are mediated by formal linguistic means especially concerning conservative extensions of standard mathematical theories (e.g. in the foundation of nonstandard theories either of an extensional or intensional flair), reaching up to the paradigm of forcing extensions in which the extended forcing models are at least partially founded on the possibility of consistent generic extensions of combinatorial properties holding in the base model.

Let's turn a little while to the case of physical theories and the corresponding models to come up with several arguments indicating the need to seek an 'internal' analysis of the theory or model in question. What it means in an epistemic sense to say an 'internal analysis' of the theory or model in question will be made clear in the development of the relevant arguments. At the moment on account of concrete cases relating to modelizations of quantum phenomena in group-theoretic terms, I point to da Costa's and French's claim that "(1) the space of possibilities might be drastically more limited than the sociologists of scientific practice seem to appreciate, once we accept that even apparently 'free' moves in pursuit are structured by objective considerations and (2) relatedly, it is the structure of the model itself that plays a crucial role in 'foreshadowing' which is chosen. This is not to deny the 'openness' of theories to further development [...]" (da Costa and French 2003, p. 121).

One could take as reasonable candidates of intrinsic, constraining characteristics of theories even in situations that are not explicitly epistemic, such as implied by the general correspondence principle, the simplicity and validity of universal invariance principles. However, there exist concrete cases in physical theories where these principles are broken on the level of observation (e.g., the violation of the principle of parity conservation) or, where in cases of non-observability of a physical situation where we might be tempted on aesthetic and even metaphysical considerations to adhere to the so-called superlaws of symmetry, they are proved, e.g., in the weak interactions of elementary particles, as susceptible to empirical revision as other less evidently intuitive laws of physics (Redhead 1975, pp. 78, 105). Another point of concern can be the ambivalent role of symmetries especially in the pursuit of successful quantum models in which the sort of appropriate symmetries is often the outcome of elaboration of the corresponding mathematical model and may not be implied by any explicitly empirical factors.[5] In a certain sense the meaning of the symmetry of a physical law is associated with invariant feature/s represented in the mathematical form of the law and the symmetry transformations are transformations affecting the variables in terms of which the law is formulated which leave the form of the law unchanged. As a matter of fact to discuss change in a system we must be able to identify what it is that is changing, and this identification of a system during change is only possible by specifying the set of invariants which remain unchanged during the transformation and thus lead to the possibility of definition of the identity of the system.

The bottom question is inescapably whether one can define identity by means of the system in question, in other words whether it can be taken as an intertheoretical notion or a notion transcending the logico-linguistic environment of the theory. Since from an intrinsic perspective theories as objects of epistemic attitudes are described by belief reports (i.e., as true, approximately true, empirically adequate, etc.) that are sentential in nature if one chooses to stay within the bounds of the purely logical-syntactical, then notions such as identity in transformation, co-existence and interconnectedness of the individual parts of a whole, reproducibility at will of formal counterparts of registered 'observations', etc., become problematic in a sense that may point to what Gödel considered as a missing 'residuum' of meaning of the logical-mathematical concepts by means of the exclusive use of the rules of logical syntax. The situation cannot be remedied by taking models themselves to act as objects of epistemic attitudes in the place of the theories, for in terms of

---

[5] This is the case of the color model (i.e., Quantum Chromodynamics, QCD) by which were not only compatibly elaborated the symmetry characteristics of quarks and their composites but was also found to be observably equivalent to the paraparticle counterpart (da Costa and French 2003, p. 117).

expressional means this is to inappropriately switch from one perspective to the other.

One may draw attention to the non-eliminable influence of the logico-linguistic structure in shaping concepts such as similarities and dissimilarities between models also by the way, not ignoring of course the ultimate empirical ground, these concepts are mathematized through partial isomorphisms holding between certain members of the families of the relations concerned. The formal characteristics of these notions can then be captured in terms of the number and kinds of relations included in the relevant subsets. In the case of Quantum Electrodynamics and Quantum Chromodynamics, for instance, it is in terms of the correspondence between certain members of the partial relations Ri,[6] which refer to the relationships between the particles expressed by the relevant Lagrangians, that we can say the theories are similar with respect to gauge invariance. I note that the relations Ri may not only apply to 'physical' relationships in this respect but also to mathematical ones so that the fundamental role of (mathematical) group theory can be accommodated on the physical level in a way that group-theoretic similarities can heuristically establish a bridge between domains in terms of physical observation and, formally, the partial isomorphism between models (da Costa and French 2003, p. 123).

General qualitative characteristics, such as similarity, dissimilarity, 'family' resemblance, etc., which arise on the empirical level and concern the domain of observation are in this way translated into partial isomorphisms holding between certain members of the families of relations modelized in the corresponding structure. Naturally partial isomorphisms are a key set-theoretical tool, in the explanatory hierarchy, to proceed to a justificatory 'descent' from higher-level to lower level models reaching 'raw' data models at the bottom. Even the openness of the 'field of evidence' of a theory as the set of possible empirical discoveries in support of its truth of falsity can be partially mapped via the partial isomorphisms holding between respective structures in the model-theoretic approach. In fact qualitative, non-mathematical, aspects of a theoretical structure can be represented through the resources of logic and set theory (topology is a case in point), pointing to the fact that logical-linguistic constraints and their underlying meaning-content may ultimately condition in an essential way theories in the syntactic and also the semantic view by means of models. I refer at this point to A. Chakravartty's view that the switch from the syntactic to the semantic view cannot satisfy the positions of scientific realism to the extent that the use of linguistic devices (e.g., of mathematical equations) in making correspondence relations between substantial model

---

[6] In a model-theoretic approach the notion of truth is rigorously defined by means of a formal language $\mathcal{L}$ and an interpretation of $\mathcal{L}$ in a mathematical structure $\mathcal{A}$. A 'simple pragmatic' structure is called a partial structure of the form $\mathcal{A} = <A, R_i, Q>_{i \in I}$ where A is a nonempty set, $R_i, i \in I$, is a partial relation defined on A for every $i \in I$, where I is an appropriate index set, and Q is a set of sentences of the language $\mathcal{L}$ having the same similarity type as that of $\mathcal{A}$. For some i, R_i may be empty and Q may also be empty. The R_i are called partial because any relation $R_i, i \in I$ of arity n_i is not necessarily defined for all n_i-tuples of elements of A. The set A is the domain of the individuals of 'observation' modeled in the structure $\mathcal{A}$ and the set Q of sentences may include observation statements referring to the individuals of the domain. See: da Costa and French (2003, p. 18).

descriptions and reality explicit "seems to run afoul of the semanticist aspiration for linguistic independence" (Chakravartty 2001, p. 327).

Concerning the semantic view it is important to emphasize that the definition of isomorphism, a concept crucial in the model-theoretic approach, depends only on the set-theoretical character of the models of a theory and not on any of the substantive axioms imposed. Thus, attesting to the non-eliminable place of the 'underlying' set-theoretical structure of models, "two theories whose models have the same set-theoretical character, but whose substantive axioms are quite different, would use the same definition of isomorphism" (Suppes 2002, p. 54). One may object, though, that in many cases within the philosophy of science, e.g., in general practices of measurement, the structural notion of isomorphism between, say, an empirical model and a numerical one proves inappropriate since distinct physical objects may be assigned the same number thus invalidating the one-to-one condition of isomorphism. By a simple extension however, on the formal level, of the notion of isomorphism to the more inclusive notion of homomorphism one can easily accommodate this awkward situation, while ensuring that the structural relations between the models remain the same. In cases where indistinguishability and identity of elements may not be equivalent, think e.g. of quantum cases, one may again remedy the situation by assigning to any collection of elements of the model an ordinal number so that it is possible to talk about a collection, e.g., $\sigma_0, \sigma_1, \sigma_2, \ldots, \sigma_{n-1}$ of such elements. This is a result of the simple proof that any ordinal as a well-ordered structure $\mathcal{A} = \langle A, < \rangle$ is a rigid structure, i.e. the only automorphism in this structure is the identity function (Krause and Coelho 2005, p. 201). In other words in a rigid structure $\mathcal{A}$ the notion of non-identical elements and of $\mathcal{A}$-distinguishable elements coincide.[7]

It should not be left unnoticed that van Fraassen has suggested, on account of the semantic view of theories, that the notion of embeddability of models suits better his notions of 'empirical adequacy' and 'empirical equivalence'[8] in which case this notion of embeddability cannot be defined syntactically. However Turney (1990) has claimed, to have refuted this position by defining a syntactic relation, the 'implantability', which corresponds to the semantic relation of embeddability.[9] This may, in fact, help my philosophical argumentation on the matter by a holistic, subjectively founded approach toward models in general and mathematical ones in particular.

---

[7] Krause and Coelho (2005) claim however, that the mathematical structure of quantum mechanics should have a non-trivial rigid expansion (i.e. not one obtained by trivially adjoining the ordinal structure) whose physical intuition is that quantum objects are somehow 'intrinsically' distinguishable.

[8] For definitions of empirical adequacy and empirical equivalence of theories one may look into van Fraassen's *The Scientific Image*; van Fraassen (1980, pp. 45, 64).

[9] In Turney's words, 'there is a symmetry between syntax and semantics, which makes it unlikely that one is better than the other for an account of science'. By this token van Fraassen's view that theory and observation cannot be distinguished by syntactic methods, in which case he makes up for this distinction by semantic methods, is undermined by Turney's alleged construction of a syntactic method which is equivalent to van Fraassen's semantic one (Turney 1990, p. 449).

3 Talking About Mathematical Models

3.1 Mathematical Aspects of the Debate on the Ontology of Models

As it is known a conception of models uniquely corresponding to the breadth of a logical-linguistic universe was shattered by the Skolem–Löwenheim Theorem which proved that any infinite set-theoretical model of a theory in first order logic is reducible to a countable one.

It is also known that the Skolem paradox is a direct outcome of the Skolem–Löwenheim Theorem (**SLT** henceforth), in the sense that one can prove the existence of a countable transitive[10] model M for any desired finite fragment of **ZFC** (The Zermelo–Fraenkel set theory with the *Axiom of Choice*) in which ordinal numbers of any infinite scale are defined as countable ones although not by the means available within M. Concerning this paradox the following consideration may make things a bit more clear. The only subsets of a set that a model is able to 'see' are the ones arising out of iterated applications (at most countably many) of set-construction operations permissible in the theory. Given the countable character of the expressional means of a formal theory there will be at most a countable number of formal-logical operations, consequently this process can generate at most countably many sets. "It is in this sense that the LST is an artifact of the countable nature of formal systems" (George 1985, p. 78).

Generally Skolem's later view of **SLT** was that it dealt a fatal blow to the theoretical plausibility that there are absolute and consequently language-transcendent mathematical truths to be captured or serving as foundations. On the contrary, "A consequence of this state of affairs [*auth. add.:* **the SLT**] is the impossibility of absolute categoricity[11] of the fundamental mathematical notions" (Skolem 1970, p. 635). It follows that all the notions of set theory, and consequently of all of mathematics, become in this way relativized to the extent that the meaning of these notions is not absolute as it is associated with the axiomatic model. Skolem argued that if one analyzes mathematical reasoning in such a way as to formulate the fundamental modes of thought as axioms, in an apparent revisiting of his recursive mode of thought, namely the espousing of inductive inferences and recursive definitions based on integers of his earlier years, 'then the relativism is inevitable because of the general nature of Löwenheim's theorem' (ibid., 468). Therefore, in Skolem's view, a relativist conception of the fundamental mathematical notions is more clear than the absolutist and platonist conception that dominates classical mathematics. And, on account of his former positive stance (in the early 20s) concerning the clarity, naturalness and absoluteness of recursive arithmetic, he still leaned in his later works for

---

[10] The transitivity property could be roughly described as the preservation under the inclusion relation $\in$ of the individuality of the zero-level elements of a theory, i.e., for any set A if $x \in A$ and $x \in y$ then $y \in A$.

[11] A formal system any two models of which are isomorphic is called categorical. It follows from the **SLT** that no formal system that has a non-denumerable model is categorical because this model is reducible to a denumerable one.

the kind of foundation based on a formalization of primitive recursive arithmetic (guided by some faculty of mathematical intuition) albeit on the acceptance of the axiomatic-formal systems as the meaningful way to fix the fundamental hypotheses and modes of mathematical reasoning.

Talk about models in the semantic view is largely shaped by the way a theory is presented in terms of models in the sense of relational structures for which all the sentences in a particular linguistic formulation of the theory express true properties about the model when this acts as an interpretation or a possible realization of the theory. In fact this seems to be a way to axiomatize a theory other than through the specification and elaboration of a first-order logical language. What is more, such axiomatization may have important consequences, both philosophical and epistemological, as exemplified by the result that including or deleting certain set-theoretical axioms, such as the continuum hypothesis or Martin's axiom, may produce definite physical results: A positive entropy shift, for example, becomes a zero-entropy shift (da Costa and French 2003, p. 26). Moreover it has been claimed that to define formally a model as a set-theoretical entity in the sense of an ordered tuple consisting of a set of objects, relations and operations on these objects, is not to rule out the physical model of the kind which is appealing to physicists for the physical model may be simply taken to define the set of objects in the set-theoretical model. One may have in mind, for instance, a model of the orbital theory of atoms or even, in more recent research, the possibility of modelizing quantum temporal histories, localized in space-time regions and causally related in some way, based on notions of set-theoretical topology.[12] Topological explanations, let it be pointed out, inherently tied with real continuum concepts, are currently beginning to stand as a growing research methodology in such diverse disciplines as cell biology, molecular genomics or neuroscience where "methodology is largely based on network analysis and the graph theoretical properties are treated as a kind of topological properties, as well as the pervasive use of landscape models for states of systems (inherited from physics, and now pervasive in population genetics, ecology or in the study of cell metabolism) are tokens of the fruitfulness of topological explanatory practices." (Kostić 2018, pp. 1–2).

These results relate, of course, to the inherent relationship between the theoretical and the observational terms of a theory and their interpretations in the metalanguage of the model. These may be ultimately reducible to the fundamental way objects as objects registered in by a constituting consciousness are transformed to well-meant objects of a formal discourse in an environment that hinges on the meta-linguistic conditions of co-existence, succession, continuity in succession, instant recall, etc.

A relevant question is the way the conception of models is influenced by the embedding of the real number continuum in theories of which the models are the representations. If following van Fraassen we identify a theory with a class of models or structures and suppose that the class of models in question is a so called 'elementary class', i.e., it contains precisely the models of some first order theory T, then the Completeness Theorem would immediately yield, as said before, the

---

[12] For such a case, see: Isham (1994, pp. 29–32).

equivalence of van Fraassen's account and the traditional syntactic account. Consequently on this supposition to every 'elementary' class of models corresponds a consistent set of first-order sentences, and it would be merely a matter of preference whether the model-theoretic or syntactic approach is employed unless this were not true for those classes of models of mathematical or generally scientific theories available for modeling the domain of the continuum of real numbers. In fact, there is no possibility of a categorical designation of models (in the sense that they are all isomorphic to each other) for any axiomatized first-order theory because of the inevitable existence of nonstandard models[13] in case we use the general approach of building a class of models in terms of which the axiomatical structure of the corresponding theory is satisfied. It follows that since almost all scientific theories will need the real number continuum, the class of models of such theories will not be an elementary class, and thus these models will not be specifiable by an axiomatization up to isomorphism. The crucial point here to be reserved for an extensive discussion in the next sections, along with other relevant questions, is whether and in what level of discourse the real number continuum is the underlying cause or the effect of the 'pathology' of the non-uniqueness of models taken as representations of formal theories.

Van Fraassen has offered a concrete argument in van Fraassen (1985b) against M. Friedman's assumption that a theory is to be identified with an elementary class by citing, in what is typically the semantic view approach, the example of a set N, in the form of a structure with a function that interprets its sentences, which may contain every structure of an original set M modeling the domain of a scientific theory. Supposing that the real number continuum is adjoined to the original theory properly formalized to a new extended axiomatized one, then the new class of models N satisfying the extended set of original axioms may well contain the original model M but according to the **SLT**, since the real continuum is something infinite, may also contain many structures not isomorphic to any member of M (van Fraassen 1985b, p. 302). This means that the addition of the real number continuum has not only put hurdles in the way of postulating a uniquely defined model to represent the extended system but has further 'blurred' the image by producing indefinitely many new non-isomorphic models of the extended system. In other words if N contains a more exact image M^* of M by including the structures in M (after its enlargement with the continuum) with their interpretations in the given syntax, then *ipso facto* M^* fails to be an elementary class.

Yet what comes out of this example as well as from other cases that espouse the model theoretic approach from the 'extrinsic' perspective in terms of which models can be treated as distinct 'objects' or individuals susceptible of mathematical manipulation, e.g., through the definition of ultra-power product of first-order structures, through isometry between metric spaces or the proof of a representation theorem

---

[13] This turns out to be the case in the proof of existence of nonstandard models for Peano arithmetic, (**PA**), where by the application of the Completeness Theorem and the upward **SL** Theorem, **PA** has been proved to have, except for the standard countable model, infinitely many non-isomorphic ones, i.e., it has models for every cardinal $\kappa > \aleph_0$; see van Dalen (2004, p. 113).

in the theory of groups and so forth, is, in general, the need to talk about models in some form of language which must contain a fairly significant amount of the language of set theory (da Costa and French 2003, p. 34). In this way we can develop a theory of classes of models, including partial ones, viewed as mathematical structures in their own right having in mind topological structures, algebraic and order structures considered as fundamental ones. However, even granted the point that description of a structure in terms of satisfaction of sentences is much less informative than 'direct' mathematical description of it, this latter must be made within set theory and hence must be subject to the same limitations. Furthermore, it is not clear that satisfaction can be dismissed altogether.

3.2 The Design of an *Ad Hoc* Mathematical Model

Given my argumentation on the reducibility of the discourse about models, irrespectively of the choice of the syntactic or semantic approach (at least in the Suppesian sense), to discourse about the set-theoretical concepts they subsume, I am going to deal next with the specific case of mathematical models. As stated in the Introduction I will focus primarily on the model designed by P. Cohen mostly to decide the question of the size of real continuum which is by itself the motivating reason for my choice.[14] The importance of the discussion about Cohen's forcing models derives from the fact that some key concepts in the construction of appropriate ground model derive, in his own avowal, by real world intuitions in contrast to Gödel's logical-syntactical approach. Doing so, I will discuss the way in which the postulation of a countable, transitive model to establish various infinity results in the generic extensions of the original model hinges on assumptions non-eliminable in the language of set theory as the underlying theory.

In *Set Theory and the Continuum Hypothesis*, Cohen (1966) introduced in **ZF** theory (Zermelo–Fraenkel theory) two axioms of a special status given his intention to construct an extended model of **ZF** in which he would ultimately prove, among other results, the independence of two key questions of mathematical foundations, namely the *Continuum Hypothesis* (**CH**) and the *Axiom of Choice* (**AC**). These are the **M** and the **SM** axioms establishing respectively the existence of a standard model of **ZF**, i.e., a model of **ZF** that satisfies the standard $\in$ relation, and the transitivity property of this relation. However to the extent that these axioms are unprovable in **ZF** (since in the reverse case this would imply the consistency of **ZF** not allowed by Gödel's Incompleteness Theorem), Cohen proceeded to an informal justification of their validity on intuitive grounds relating to the way we perform concrete mathematical acts within the world.

More specifically, the axiom **M** is justified in terms of its obvious validity if one has a clear intuition of sets, while the axiom **SM** which may ultimately lead to the establishment of a countable, standard model for **ZF** is justified by applying **SLT** in intuitive real world terms. This means, that since the universe of sets does not form

---

[14] If the exposition proves too mathematically demanding or cumbersome for the generally interested reader he may choose to follow the key steps of the argumentation skipping some technical details.

a set and accordingly we cannot prove the existence of a countable sub-model in **ZF**, we may take recourse to real world processes and accept as plausible the possibility of choosing successively and countably many times sets satisfying certain properties to yield finally a countable standard model for **ZF** (Cohen 1966, pp. 78–79). A first significant remark to be made here is that, with the exception of alternative mathematical theories claiming to be inspired by real world processes and the constituting capacities of a mathematically performing subject,—think for instance of the Alternative Set Theory of the Prague School or of certain ultrafinitist theories, - Cohen's justification of the axioms above on essentially intuitive real-world grounds is a rare occasion in the foundations of modern mathematics. Yet, it is not in dissonance with the so-called semantic approach toward models in which theories are represented by set-theoretical models where these theories can be true in the usual correspondence sense formalized by Tarski. The way, however, to escape identification of theories with the corresponding class of models and thus avoid circularities in the application of (the same) appropriately interpreted logico-linguistic formulations is to adopt a more moderate line and present a theory, as van Fraassen suggested, by defining its class of models directly (French 2010, p. 235). Then if it fits our natural intuition in real world terms the model, in mathematical terms, can be called a standard one as we may reasonably assess Cohen's approach to the axioms **M** and **SM** to be.

A second remark is that a satisfaction relation between a sentence and the 'world' can hold if the latter is taken in a representational sense, more specifically as a set-theoretical structure constructed in a set theory with urelements, where the representation of the world by the set-theoretical structure is itself problematic to the extent that it comes up against non-eliminable in logico-linguistic terms qualitative elements of the world as transcendent being.[15] It follows that the 'imitation' of real world processes to justify the existence of axioms **M** and **SM** and further found a countable, transitive model on the base level of a forcing theory, is undermined by the set-theoretical language used to construct and talk about the models. In the first place one can point to the fact that the **SLT** is conditioned in a substantial way, in Skolem's original stronger version, on the validity of the *Axiom of Choice* applied in its proof, which in turn is unthinkable without the subjectively founded constraint of an immanent[16] infinity thought of as an actually completed whole. More than that: *AC* is conditioned on the possibility of a unique definition each time of a mathematical object in terms of this infinity in an *ad infinitum* process which obviously presupposes a subjective factor with certain inner-time capacities applicable in a totally unrestricted mode relative to external spatio-temporal constraints.

---

[15] Da Costa & French state that this relation of representation remains problematic in their version of a semantic approach where broadly 'theoretical' structures are related via partial isomorphisms to equally broadly 'phenomenological' ones in which case the latter 'represent' the phenomena (da Costa and French 2003, fn. 46, p. 211).

[16] The term immanent, widely used in phenomenological and in a broader sense philosophical texts, can be roughly explained as referring to what is or has become correlative (or 'co-substantial') to the being of one's consciousness in contrast to what is 'external' or transcendental to it. For instance, a tree is transcendental as such to the consciousness of an 'observer' while its appearance in the modes of its appearing within his consciousness is immanent to it.

A key constraint in the process of constructing a minimal standard model for **ZF** is the possibility of stratification of constructible sets as models for **ZF** along the ordering of ordinals and the underlying assumption of ordinals as absolute notions relative to any standard, transitive model of **ZF** (Cohen 1966, p. 104). This, in turn, might raise the question of whether the existence of ordinals as absolute notions and consequently their application in defining accordingly a constructible hierarchy of sets, is an 'internal' constraint of the logical-linguistic universe of the theory or whether it is 'external' (extra-theoretical) constraint imposed by the ways a subject may constitute objective reality: for instance, an object in representational abstractness as an irreducible, invariant and unique individual in itself and also in co-existence and relation to other objects or agglomerations of objects within-the-world.

Another question worth discussing is the purpose metatheoretically served, in Cohen's construction of a countable, transitive, model M for generating forcing extensions which is moreover a minimal one. The answer on the strictly formal level is provided by Cohen (1966), in a theorem immediately following the proof of the unique existence of such model M. In formal terms the theorem asserts that for every element x in the model M there is a formula $A(y)$ in **ZF** such that x is the unique element in M satisfying the relativized formula $A_M(x)$. In simple words this theorem serves the critical metatheoretical purpose of showing that every element in M can be 'named'. To arrive at this result we need the minimality property of M, the **SLT** and the *Axiom of Choice*.

As a matter of fact if by $A_n(x)$ we enumerate all formulas with one free variable, the key to the proof is that the formula $B_n(x)$: '$A_n(x)$ and $\exists \alpha$ such that $x = F_\alpha$ and for all $\beta < \alpha$ $\neg A_n(F_\beta)$' picks out (thanks to **AC**) at most one set x and then thanks to **SLT** and the minimality of M this process can be made to happen in the minimal, transitive, countable model M (see details: ibid., pp. 105, 106). On the metatheoretical, subjectively founded level these properties of the base model M ensure the uniqueness of the choice of each element of M and of associated predicative statements in accordance with the act of 'naming' ahead of implementing forcing extensions (of the base model) constrained by filter and generic properties.

It is true that in the 60s Solovay and Scott developed the idea of re-forming forcing entirely in terms of Boolean-valued models in which case they showed that a countable standard model was not necessarily needed. This was done, though, by proving in **ZFC** that there is a complete Boolean algebra assigning to the negation of **CH** the Boolean value one something that implies that the more powerful semantic construction was replaced by a syntactic one that directly established relative consistency (Kanamori 2008, p. 369).[17] In any case we should bear in mind that the discrete, finitistic character of 'naming' in the original approach, which presupposes on the subjective level the uniqueness of choice of the corresponding object-content by the mere enactment of the act of choice is realizable only on the condition of acceptance of a pre-linguistic impredicative substratum reflected in the principles

---

[17] It is notable, however, that later Schoenfield showed that forcing on partial orders can catch the 'essence' of the Boolean approach in a straightforward way, while Boolean models proved also to be cumbersome and unintuitive in the search for new consistency results (Kanamori 2012, p. 56).

applied in the proof-theoretic process, e.g. by the implicit application of **AC** through the **SLT**. The nature and foundation of this substratum (for which I have given some clues in the previous page) and the extent to which it conditions, among others, the absoluteness of ordinals in contrast with the relative character of cardinals in varying the 'width' of set-theoretical models while leaving intact their 'height' will be further dealt with in the next.

4 Mathematical Models and Foundational Mathematics

In this section I intend to show how mathematical models as set-theoretical structures are intertwined with theories by means of the formal language machinery and also show the way this intermingling is subject to certain common constraints. I step back again for a while to the role of **SLT** insofar as it has largely shaped the discussion on the status of mathematical models in the context of a predicative universe and has also implicitly contributed to the proof of the independence of **CH** and **AC** from the rest of the axioms of **ZF** theory.

As already pointed out **SLT** essentially proves that purely set-theoretical means are unable to guarantee the uniqueness of models with respect to first-order axiomatical theories, the so-called categoricity of models; in fact, it proves that any infinite model is reducible to a countably infinite one. Moreover by generating Skolem's paradox it even made possible to introduce subjectively founded arguments in a strictly formal context of discussion, namely by justifying the paradoxical definition of the uncountable ordinal ω_1^M within a countable model M by the claim that 'inhabitants' of M lack the formal means to enumerate ω_1^M. The outcome led to Skolem's pessimism as to the viability of axiomatization in terms of sets as the ultimate foundation of mathematics. The outline below of the main steps of the proof of **SLT** and the accompanying comments will hopefully clarify my motivation relative to the scope and intentions of this article.

We know that **SLT** generates a countable set M of sets such that a statement in M is true precisely if the same statement is true in the universe of all sets V. It is possible to show that all statements can be regarded as starting with a sequence of quantifiers, i.e., existential and universal ones, including of course the case where this sequence is null.[18] Naturally all such statements can be enumerated, let's call this set A_n, and going through them all we pick out for each true existential statement a corresponding set in the universe of sets. Consequently on account of the countability of such statements we choose countably many elements of the universe V and place them in M. In the reverse sense we may form all existential statements from these sets in M and if they are true in the universe of sets we can pick out a set which makes them true and adjoin it to M. This is a process that can be repeated countably

---

[18] It happens that statements with universal and existential quantifier are not exempt themselves from opposing arguments regarding their status within a formal theory, especially with regard to the supposedly ontological claims attributed to the bounded variables. See: Quine (1947, pp. 75–77) and Feferman et al. (1995, p. 341, fns. 19 & 20).

many times and so finally the collection M of sets chosen this way is countable. It is clear that the true statements of the universe V are exactly the true statements of M by way of induction on the number of quantifiers at the beginning of each statement. This conclusion simply takes into account that by simple negation universal quantifiers can be turned into existential ones and statements with no quantifiers are taken as finitely many statements of the irreducible form $x \in y$ connected by Boolean operators (Cohen 2002, pp. 1076–1077).

This simple reasoning with a little more technical sophistication is what lies behind one of the most influential results in the foundations of mathematics, the Skolem–Löwenheim Theorem (**SLT**), which has wider repercussions in the way we view the construction of models as representative of theories. It is due to its prominent place in the foundations that I'll try to give some clues to its significance based on the lowest possible level of reduction beyond the formal logico-linguistic level. In the first place the proof of **SLT** is critically dependent on the **AC** whose subjectively founded meaning will be discussed in the last section. For the moment I note that it may be interpreted as associated with meaningful, though a priori founded, acts of a subject ideally extensible ad infinitum. Understandably these are acts carried out in the sphere of immanence which means they are carried out as pure acts of consciousness. Another critical step in the proof is that by the countability of statements of the formal language of M one can obtain the countability of corresponding sets of the universe placed in M.

It seems to me, however, that it would be naive to take the countability of the expressional means of a formal language (logical connectives, variables, logical and non-logical constants) to account for the countability of statements for then one may reasonably circularly ask about the origin of countability of the expressional means of the language themselves. Therefore a possible way out of this circularity is to consider a reduction to the level of subjectivity in the sense that any logical statement bearing a meaningful relation between fixed objectivities is the abstracted form of a conscious act of reasoning which as such is distinct (by the evidence of reflection) from any other act of its kind performed at any other temporal moment with regard to the same or other objectivities. It follows that the performance of such acts should by necessity be of a finitistic character by being carried out by a finitistic being which then by ideal extension can be regarded as of a denumerably infinite scope. In addition this is an assertion taken to hold irrespectively of the quantification form of respective predicate formulas, having in mind that existential and universal quantifications are interchangeable by simple negation.

In such view the domain of universal quantification may not be associated with a kind of infinity in a real world sense as the only constraint put to the bounded variable/s is that they 'fulfill' the meaning-content of the respective formula over an indefinite 'horizon' meant as an actually existing, completed whole. I refer in connection to Gödel's view about the ideas of transfinite objects or operations in that they "cannot be known to be meaningful or consistent unless we trust some mathematical intuition of things completely inaccessible to experience" (Feferman et al. 1995, p. 341). In this sense Gödel, in his peculiar brand of conceptual realism of later years, characterized the existential statement 'there exists' as a transfinite (i.e., non-constructive) concept insofar as this means objective existence regardless

Talking about Models

of actual producibility in objective spatio-temporality. Consequently there is, on these grounds, no cancellation of the finitistic, or countably infinite character (in idealization) of the multiplicity of predicative statements in the context of a formal language. This is true also with statements with no quantifiers at all insofar as they may be taken as finitely many statements of the irreducible form $x \in y$ connected by Boolean operators, with the understanding that the set-theoretic formula of $\in$ inclusion is a most fundamental, in fact an irreducible one in set-theory, possibly apt to an interpretation on the subjective level in its own right.

I proceed here and in the next section to extend the previous discussion of model construction in mathematical foundations, namely the construction of forcing models by P. Cohen considered also on account of Gödel's pre-existing concept of constructible sets, to a deeper subjectively founded level. My intention is to show how inner constraints on the formal theory influence and largely shape the structure and scope of corresponding models.

One can say that the most basic concepts behind the construction of forcing models are these:

1. The concept of ordinals which generally play a fundamental role within mathematical theories starting from Cantor's attempt to define a sequence of infinite cardinalities. This is a means of enumeration of objects which, in contrast to the notion of cardinals, invariably retains its validity regardless of other structural properties or extensions of the formal systems and moreover even if the assumption of their totality leads to the Burali-Forti's paradox one has to admit all of them if he has to assign ranks (i.e., a sort of 'definite' invariable numbering) to sets. In a certain sense ordinals 'masked' either as integer-atoms or as names for sets are crucial in the build up of forcing models or of any other mathematical models and may be reducible to a subjectively oriented, possibly phenomenologically founded, interpretation. I point out that ordinals, which are the only syntactic elements not in need of a predicative 'restriction', can be taken as abstractions of a (presumably) a priori tendency of a subject toward a 'something-in-general', possibly devoid of content, which is invariably preserved as 'indecomposable' unity in mental representation.

2. The concept of a generic set which, if metaphor is allowed, is a kind of trail blazer within a forcing model 'keeping watch', over forcing extension, of the preservation of desired properties established in the lower-level of the ground model. In Cohen's original formation a generic set is a set of integers-as atoms, let's say the generic set A of integers, and the forcing conditions are sequences of finitely many, non-contradictory, irreducible formulas of the type $n \in A$ or $\neg n \in A$, where n is an integer, through which one may inquire into the nature and properties of the set A. Accordingly one may define a well-meant notion of truth, based on a consistent application of these $\in$-formulas, without the need either to know the generic set A in its entirety in the classical sense nor its eventual belonging to the ground model.

3. The notion of absoluteness to which Gödel ascribed almost a philosophical meaning, a view seemingly also shared by Cohen. Actually absoluteness first appeared in set and generally model theories and was applied in a substantive way in

Gödel's construction of the constructible universe L.[19] Intuitively, it establishes the invariability of certain properties of mathematical objects in extensions of mathematical systems provided with a sound notion of irreducibility of individuals (i.e., of well-foundedness) and as such is inherently associated with the notion of ordinals. The application of the notion of absoluteness next to the set-theoretical property of transitivity over generic extensions ensures the invariability of fundamental predicative formulas, e.g. of $\in$-predication formulas, as well as the invariability of formulas involving set-theoretical operations such as subset inclusion, union, successor operation, etc., in the construction of extended forcing models. Absoluteness of ordinals as an intrinsic means to assign numerical labels to any aggregate of objects independently of the model hierarchy, is critical both in Cohen's original approach, e.g. in the use of labeled terms F_α in the ramified forcing language, as well as in the current definitions by transfinite recursion over forcing-induced names. It is also critical within Gödel's constructible universe L not only in the extension of the ramified hierarchy of constructible sets (i.e., the sets defined by logical operations) to include transfinite orders but also to make sure that the assertion that the constructible sets is all there is in the universe sets is context independent.

4. The countability and the standard character of the ground model. These properties have been discussed in Subsection 3.2. I add here that Cohen introduced the idea of standard models as actual (not fictitious) sets, whose objects are sets and the membership relation is the usual one, to circumvent the proof-theoretic postulation of models of such theories as **ZF**, whose existence cannot be proved within the theory due to the incompleteness results. Concerning the countability condition this is a formal implication of **SLT**, whereas on the intuitive level it is justified almost on the same grounds as **SLT** itself with the particularity that if one assumes the model M to be countable, then one can ask within it every question in sequence, deciding every one.[20] Ultimately on a subjectively founded level, one may again argue, predicative statements involving names-objects on the ground level correspond to conscious acts of predication on the part of a subject oriented in each specific instance to well-meant objects of predication.

---

[19] Gödel's constructible universe L can be roughly described as a subuniverse of the classical universe of sets V constructed in stages along a transfinite generation of ordinals where each stage contains sets definable by well-formed formulas of set theory in the previous stage. The universe L is a prototype of the broader concept of inner models developed in the last decades with the purpose of establishing ever larger infinities.

[20] A broader countability condition, the *CCC* (Countable Chain Condition), is also necessarily assumed in eliminating an uncountable number of incompatible forcing conditions in the completion of Cohen's disproof of **CH**. See: Kunen (1982, pp. 205, 206).

5 The Subjective Foundation of Inner Constraints

Given my argumentation as presented in earlier sections that either in the syntactic or semantic view of models one cannot overpass a possible reduction to the set-theoretical substructure through which models are represented, we may reasonably admit that the inner constraints on the logical-mathematical level should someway be reflected on the model-theoretic one. For instance, how could we have a sound notion of isomorphism or for that matter partial isomorphism of models if we could not have a prior intuition of atoms as irreducible unities, of invariability in variation properly possessed by ordinals, of the concept of actual immanent infinity as the indefinite scope of quantifiers in predicate formulas, etc.? Therefore my intention is precisely to discuss those constraints outlined as inner constraints of models on a yet deeper subjective level relying, as a matter of fact, on certain phenomenological ideas.

I set out by quoting from K. Hauser's *Is Choise Self-Evident?* in which he makes a noteworthy correlation of ordinals with **AC** to a certain extent inspired by Husserl's earlier positions in *Logical Investigations*. "Ordinals as originally conceived by Cantor serve as figural moments[21] for well-ordered sets. To this it may be objected that an ordered set is ontologically more complex than a bare set. However, the construal of ordinals as figural moments is fully in line with Husserl's overall approach [...]— that which is prior for us (in the epistemological sense)—when arguing that figural moments should be regarded as second-order qualities" (Hauser 2005, p. 249). Thus the concept of ordinals by this essential ordering property is thought to precede in ontological terms that of sets as bare collections, something that Hauser attributes also to Aristotle, while by being invariably persistent in all structural transformations ordinals lay down a significant part of what the notion of isomorphism consists of. This naturally includes those set-theoretical transformations (e.g., sum, pairing, one-to-one mapping, etc.) characterized as absolute that may be taken at least on the subjective level as correlative with the notion of ordinals. By this token absoluteness is the backbone of structural invariance under isomorphic or homomorphic transformations of models independently of the nature of the elements of the domain. In this sense "[...] we become aware of an identity that persists in all instances we could possibly imagine, and whereby they are variants of a paradigm rather than random individuals. What this yields, then, is essentially a 'rule' for generating further variants ad libitum, and it is this ad libitum character which indicates that we have grasped something universal. For ordinals qua species (i.e., as canonical representatives of types of well-orderings) that rule is in effect 'being isomorphic'." (ibid., p. 251).

The next question would admittedly relate to what it means beyond the formal level to be identical with itself as a vacuous of content individual and remain

---

[21] To explain the notion of figural moment Hauser refers to Husserl's views in as early as the *Philosophy of Arithmetic* where he proposed that in the intuition of a sensory set must lie immediately comprehensible signs by which the set character can be recognized. Husserl called these 'immediately comprehensible signs', e.g. of sethood, figural moments (Hauser 2005, p. 246).

invariably so in every consistent extension of the existing formal system independently of whether we talk about formal mathematical objects or physical objects as represented within a formal axiomatical theory. In the reduction to a subjectively founded level I have found quite appealing the phenomenological concept of 'something-in-general' (*Etwas überhaupt*) meant as an immanent, content-free object X in the sense of a pure form and carrier of predicates, which in elimination of any predicates is still the pure X in abstraction, which moreover in the synthetic progress of consciousness remains always the same even though it could be susceptible of any new predicates or any new determination-content. It is the central noematic nucleus of predicates that is distinct from them and yet indissociable from them, something that also holds in reverse sense (Husserl 1976, *Engl. transl.*, p. 313). In an apparent clue to the constituting role of the inner-time consciousness Husserl reduced the identity of objects in the inner time flow to unity of acts-noemata[22] 'joined together' to a unity in which the corresponding cores (of acts) are united into the intended identical 'something'. In a later stage, in *Formal and Transcendental Logic* he thought of the pure 'general-somethings' as the irreducible substrates of all logical-mathematical propositions, in a sense of logic as a universal theory of mathesis in the Leibnizian sense, reaching up on the level of evidence and in the lowest possible level of phenomenological perception to no further reducible individuals that lack any analytically describable content, even being deprived of a temporal form. In short, in his gradual descent into the murky waters of transcendental phenomenology Husserl came to see atoms-individuals as abstractions of intentional correlates toward a vacuous 'something' irreducible to anything more fundamental. Of course these atoms-individuals are by essence provided with a noematic content by which they cannot be conceived but as related to 'something else' which may translate in the formal-ontological and further purely formal level to the common ordering of ordinals as lowest-level individuals. Ultimately the identity of noematic objects (roughly meant as well-formed objects of consciousness), consequently that of lowest-level atoms-individuals, and accordingly the invariability of their noematic relations (think, e.g. of the formal $\in$-relation of zero-elements) is reducible to the continuous unity of their temporal profiles within consciousness, these latter not being themselves identical (ibid., *Engl. transl.*, p. 242).

As presented earlier the concept of ordinals on a par with the notion of absoluteness was a key tool in the stratified definition of Gödel's constructible universe L while being also necessary in Cohen's technique of manipulating the combinatorial properties of object-names in the ground level with the intention to inquire into the properties of the 'unexplored expanses' of the generic set and the generated

---

[22] The phenomenological term noema can be roughly considered as a generalization of meaning-giving to all acts, including also all linguistic activities, and is inherently associated with the meaning of a noematic object as intended. This latter object is constituted by certain modes as a well-defined object immanent to the temporal flux of consciousness and it is possibly abstracted, in the sense of a formal-ontological object, as a syntactical object of a formal theory. In Hauser and Öner (2018), Hauser offers a nice parallelism in that the the relation between noema and intentional object is to be construed in terms of satisfaction in the model-theoretic sense, while noema and noesis (i.e. the meaning-giving moment of an act) may stand in a relation of correspondence (Hauser and Öner 2018, p. 32).

forcing sets. Consequently a subjectively oriented discussion along the lines presented above must reasonably include the notion of absoluteness. In a sort of non-reductionistic thinking we can say that what is originally the source of absoluteness is the possibility to think of formal individuals as invariably preserving some kind of a priori 'outward directed' relation (e.g., in terms of the non-logical predicate $\in$) in any extension of their original domain in such a way that, for instance, ordinals of a certain domain may be treated as fixed and their classes as impredicatively specified. Concerning the critical importance of the preservation of the individuality of syntactical atoms both in terms of their 'ontological self' and of their inherent categorial properties in any recursively defined class we need only consider the impasse in which a theory would be left in case where, to cite an instance, the atomic formula $x \in Y$ would not be absolute between classes ordered by set inclusion. In that case it would be simply impossible to project the formula $x \in Y$ of a class Y to an inclusive one Z and vice versa. In other words there would be no guarantee that we would have the same formally posited (irreducible) individuals-names x preserved in each class extension, given a well-foundedness of the sets, consequently one would have no guarantee of the existence of fixed ordinals in the recursive definitions of sets and classes.

It is notable that Husserl referred in his later work *Experience and Judgment* to the concept of absolute substrates in these terms: "[...] a 'finite' substrate can be experienced simply for itself and thus has its being-for-itself. But necessarily, is at the same time a determination, that is, it is experienceable as a determination as soon as we consider a more comprehensive substrate in which it is found. Every finite substrate has determinability as being-in-something, and this is true *in infinitum*." (Husserl 1972, *Engl. transl.*, p. 137). Further an absolute substrate is characterized as completely indeterminate from the point of view of logic and is meant in the sense of an individual 'this here' (*Dies-da*), that is, of the ultimate immaterial substrate of all logical activity. On this account, absolute substrates lack all logical formation and exclude by themselves everything that may be called forth as their determination by a logical activity of a higher level (ibid., pp. 139, 140). Anyone who can admit to a reduction of absolute notions to constructions of atomic formulas of individuals-substrates (together with their fundamental categorial properties) bound by logical connectives, can read in the quotations above the vestiges of a subjectively founded notion of absoluteness non-eliminable as such in terms of a logical-mathematical theory.

The place of the countability constraint in mathematical and consequently any kind of models expressible through set-theoretical language has already been discussed to a considerable extent in Sects. 3 and 4. At this concluding stage I just want to point out my view that countability is in fact imposed extra-theoretically in logico-linguistic and more concretely set-theoretical constructions by the way the predicative (you may prefer to call it noematic) activity, pertaining to well-meant objects of a system, is carried through by the mental activity of a subject: that is, in finitely many steps ideally extensible in infinitum, an extrapolation that can also accommodate a universal quantification over an indefinite domain.

It may then be rightly said that it is fundamentally on this account that **SLT** proves that any infinite model of a first-order logic theory is reducible to a countable one, establishing in effect the non-uniqueness of models and thus dealing a blow to mathematical realism. However there is no way a a predicative activity of the mind may be otherwise a meaningful one but against the backdrop of an actual infinity construed as an indefinite and yet completed whole in performing logical and set-theoretical operations within a predicative universe. One might ask then whether this is really a subjectively founded constraint, as the identity of individuals and the absoluteness properties, that may be possibly associated with the way continuous unity is constituted as a self-generated essential feature of temporal consciousness in Husserlian phenomenology. This is a complex and highly controversial issue of philosophical as well as of epistemological dimensions worth dealing in a separate paper; here I only refer to Husserl's own view in *Logical Investigations*: "The fact that we freely extend spatial and temporal stretches in imagination, that we can put ourselves in imagination at each fancied boundary of space or time while ever new spaces and times emerge before our inward gaze—all this does not prove the relative foundedness (*Fundierung*) of bits of space and time, and so does not prove space and time to be *really* infinite, or even that they could be *really* infinite, nor even that they really can be so. This can only be proved by a law of causation, which presupposes, and so requires, the possibility of being extended beyond any given boundary" (Husserl 1984, *Engl. transl.*, p. 45). In this viewpoint the so convenient extrapolation from the finite character of predicative acts to an indefinite infinity 'existing' in actuality cannot have any foundation in objective spatio-temporality, otherwise the *Axiom of Choice,* just to state a key set-theoretical principle associated with the uniqueness of choice, would be meaningless. Moreover by admitting that the sense of noema is inseparable from the sense of being beyond space and time, then any mathematical activity should have its noetic correlate in the characteristic feature of such activity to be about something which is not individuated in consequence of a temporality or location belonging to it originally (Hauser and Öner 2018, p. 32).

Yet the possibility of the foundation of mathematical infinite, in particular the infinity of continuum, in terms of the unity of a self-constituting temporal consciousness is not but marginally addressed in the existing literature even though, being a thorny philosophical-epistemological issue per se, it seems to implicitly condition all meaningful mathematical activity dealing with the infinite in logico-linguistic terms and naturally with the construction of infinite models of any scale.[23] I only note here among various epistemological or purely philosophical views concerning infinity as an 'inconvenient' part of formal mathematics,[24] Badiou's position on the generic sets and the forcing extensions thought of as indiscernible (infinite)

---

[23] The reader may consult in Livadas (2015, 2016) an approach based on a reduction of the infinity of continuum and of any infinity beyond it to the mode of constitution of immanent continuous unity.

[24] A relevant case may be thought of the topological modelization of temporal processes in quantum evolution presented as quantum histories formalism. Again as in set-theoretical structures the issue is the incompatibility, translated in topological terms, between the distinct and the continuous, more precisely, between single-time and continuous-time projection operators. See: Anastopoulos (2001) and Isham (1994).

multiples knowable in part and only through the 'names' of the ground model taken as well-meant objects adduced to the generic procedure (Badiou 2005, Ch. 31, 33).

As it is evident my principal intention was, rather than engage in the debate among the various tendencies over the epistemological status of models either in the syntactic or semantic view and their nuances, to inquire into the origin of the constraints that bound the breadth and scope of models as mediated by the formal linguistic tool which also serves the corresponding formal theory. Following the way to the *ad hoc* construction of specific set-theoretical models to resolve questions ultimately touching on the ontology of models themselves, I tried to articulate an argumentation in favor of the existence of certain subjectively reducible 'inner' constraints that (implicitly at least) condition the ontological as well as epistemological character of models. In this kind of discussion the whole issue is far from being exhausted as ever new advances in foundational mathematics and generally positive science forge the need for new, enriched approaches toward the extra-theoretical underpinnings of models.

References

Anastopoulos C (2001) Continuous-time histories: observables, probabilities, phase space structure and the classical limit. J Math Phys 42(8):3225–3259

Badiou A (2005) Being and event, transl. O. Feltham. Continuum, London

Chakravartty A (2001) The semantic or model-theoretic view of theories and scientific realism. Synthese 127:325–345

Cohen P (1966) Set theory and the continuum hypothesis. W. A. Benjamin, Inc, Reading

Cohen P (2002) The discovery of forcing. Rocky Mt J Math 32(4):1071–1100

da Costa NCA, French S (2003) Science and partial truth. Oxford University Press, New York

French S (2010) Keeping quiet on the ontology of models. Synthese 172:231–249

Feferman S et al (eds) (1995) Kurt Gödel: collected works III. Oxford University Press, Oxford

George A (1985) Skolem and the Löwenheim–Skolem theorem: a case study of the philosophical significance of mathematical results. Hist Philos Log 6:75–89

Hauser K (2005) Is choice self-evident? Am Philos Q 42(4):237–261

Hauser K, Öner T (2018) Perception, intuition and reliability. Theoria 84:23–59

Husserl E (1968) Phänomenologische psychologie, Hua IX, hsgb. W. Biemel. Springer, Dordrecht

Husserl E (1972) Erfahrung und Urteil, hsgb. L. Landgrebe, Hamburg: Felix Meiner Verlag. Engl. transl.: (1973), Experience and judgment, transl. J.S. Churchill & K. Americs. Routledge & Kegan Paul, London

Husserl E (1976) Ideen zu einer reinen Phänomenologie und phänomenologischen Philosophie, Erstes Buch, Hua Band III/I, hsgb. K. Schuhmann, Den Haag: M. Nijhoff. Engl. transl.: (1983), Ideas pertaining to a pure phenomenology and to a phenomenological philosophy: First Book, transl. F. Kersten, The Hague: M. Nijhoff

Husserl E (1984) Logische Untersuchungen, Hua Band XIX/1, hsgb. U. Panzer, The Hague: M. Nijhoff Pub. Engl. transl.: (2001), Logical investigations, transl. J.N. Findlay. Routledge, New York

Isham JC (1994) Quantum logic and the histories approach to quantum theory. J Math Phys 35(5):2157

Kanamori A (2008) Cohen and set theory. Bull Symb Log 14(3):351–378

Kanamori A (2012) Set theory from Cantor to Cohen. In: Gabbay MD, Kanamori A, Woods J (eds) Handbook of the history of logic, 6. Elsevier B. V., Oxford, pp 1–72

Kostić D (2018) Mechanistic and topological explanations: an introduction. Synthese 195:1–10

Krause D, Coelho AMN (2005) Identity, indiscernibility, and philosophical claims. Axiomathes 15:191–210

Kunen K (1982) Set theory. An introduction to independence proofs. Elsevier Science Pub, Amsterdam

Lawvere WF (1975) Introduction to part I. In: Lawvere FW, Maurer C, Wraith GC (eds) Model theory and topoi. Springer, Berlin

Lawvere WF (2002) Categorical algebra for continuum micro physics. J Pure Appl Algebra 175:267–287

Lawvere WF (2017) Everyday physics of extended bodies or why functionals need analyzing. Categ Gen Algebraic Struct Appl 6:9–19

Livadas S (2015) The subjective roots of forcing theory and their influence in independence results. Axiomathes 25(4):433–455

Livadas S (2016) What is the nature of mathematical-logical objects? Axiomathes 27(1):79–112

Post HR (1971) Correspondence, invariance and heuristics. Stud Hist Philos Sci 2:213–255

Quine VW (1947) On universals. J Symb Log 12(3):74–84

Redhead MLG (1975) Symmetry in intertheory relations. Synthese 32(1–2):77–112

Skolem T (1970) In: Fenstad JE (ed) Selected works in logic. Universitetsforlaget, Oslo

Suppes P (1967) What is a scientific theory? In: Morgenbesser S (ed) Philosophy of science today. Basic Books Inc., New York, pp 55–67

Suppes P (2002) Representation and invariance of scientific structures. CSLI Publications, Stanford

Turney P (1990) Embeddability, syntax, and semantics in accounts of scientific theories. J Philos Log 19:429–451

van Fraassen BC (1980) The scientific image. Clarendon Press, Oxford

Van Fraassen BC (1985a) On the question of identification of a scientific theory. Critica 17:21–25

van Fraassen BC (1985b) Empiricism in the philosophy of science. In: Churchland P, Hooker C (eds) Images of science. University of Chicago Press, Chicago

van Fraassen BC (1989) Laws and symmetry. Oxford University Press, Oxford

van Dalen D (2004) Logic and structure. Springer, Berlin

Why is Cantor's Absolute Inherently Inaccessible?

Abstract
In this article, as implied by the title, I intend to argue for the unattainability of Cantor's Absolute at least in terms of the proof-theoretical means of set-theory and of the theory of large cardinals. For this reason a significant part of the article is a critical review of the progress of set-theory and of mathematical foundations toward resolving problems which to the one or the other degree are associated with the concept of infinity especially the one beyond that of the natural intuition of natural numbers. Naturally the review includes the foundation and development of the theory of large cardinals, especially after Cohen's revolutionary introduction of the forcing method, insofar as it paved the way toward a transcendence of the delimitative character of Gödel's constructible universe L and further toward ever stronger infinity assumptions. Given that Cantor in his theory of transfinite numbers defined the mathematical absolute in ontological rather than concrete mathematical terms, I proceed in the last section to a philosophical discussion with certain prompts from phenomenology regarding the transposability of the formal conception of the infinite to the level of subjective constitution and argue in these terms on the infeasibility of acceding to an 'absolute' infinite cardinality. Of course the argumentation is strongly based on a view of the set-theoretical universe V of von Neumann's cumulative hierarchy as a formal representative of the essential traits one would seek from a model of Cantor's Absolute. It is also based on the conclusions reached from the whole discussion within the context of formal-theoretical structures as such.

1 Introduction

In Cantor's enumerative conception of sets the well-ordering principle was inherently linked with the concept of well-defined sets even though this principle had to wait until its postulation as an axiom by E. Zermelo within the **ZF** system (1904) to be compatible with a conception of sets as arbitrary collections in the sense of unities. If sets are to be well-ordered then sets as such and their powers are susceptible in Cantor's structured version of the mathematical infinite to the assignment of transfinite numbers. However, Cantor having deep philosophical-metaphysical influences had left a place in the *Grundlagen* for a concept beyond anything incorporated in his canonical transfinite scale. This is the so-called Cantor's Absolute, clearly demarcated from all other transfinite infinities, which Cantor " eventually associated mathematically with the collection of all ordinal numbers and metaphysically with the transcendence of God" (Kanamori 2012a, p. 7). It was conceived as an absolute maximum, the true infinite identifiable as a divine attribute which does not permit any determination whatsoever (Hauser 2013, p. 162). Cantor in Cantor (1887) clearly demarcated the Transfinite from the Absolute in ontological terms in the following sense:

"The Transfinite with its wealth of formations and forms points with necessity to an Absolute, the 'veritable Infinite', whose greatness is not subject to any addition or subtraction and which therefore is to be regarded quantitatively as the absolute Maximum. The latter effectively transcends human comprehension and eludes in particular mathematical determination; the Transfinite, on the other hand, not only fills the vast range of what is possible in God's knowledge, but also provides a rich and continuously expanding field of ideal research, and [...] is realized in the world of the created to a certain extent in order to express the magnificence of the Creator [...]" (in: Hauser 2013, p. 164).

In more epistemologically appropriate terms if we take account of Cantor's second generation principle, namely the transition from a 'definite succession of numbers' (e.g., the sequence of integers) to its least upper bound by which the canonical scale of transfinite numbers was formed, then taking each such definite sequence to be a possibility the progressing scale of all transfinite numbers is considered an entity of a completely different ontological category. It may be conceived as a maximum where all possibilities are being realized while itself is not considered as being such a possibility (ibid., pp. 161–162).

Anyone knowledgeable with the fundamentals of the evolution of research in set theory and the foundations of mathematics since Cantor's introduction of the mathematical 'paradise' built for the generations of mathematicians to come, recognizes two landmark results in the field both appearing in the 20th century. As well-known, these are Gödel's conception of the Constructible Universe L as a model of the theory **ZF** (Zermelo-Fraenkel set theory) primarily motivated by the need to prove or disprove two of the most important questions in foundational mathematics, namely the *Continuum Hypothesis*, (*CH*), and the *Axiom of Choice* (*AC*), and Cohen's conception of the forcing theory by which he could construct by finitistic relative consistency considerations and the help of the idea of genericity alternative models to prove infinity results at will, at least those contradicting Gödel's results on the truth of *CH* and *AC* within *L*. Consequently the proof of the independence of these fundamental hypotheses and the importance of the notion of relative consistency, on the one hand, and, on the other, the fact that certain principles, e.g. the Suslin Hypothesis and the Borel Conjecture, behave differently in forcing extensions of the constructible model *L* or under the assumption of existence of large cardinals,[1] has forged an intensive research among set-theorists that has spanned almost the last five decades (essentially after Cohen's lectures on forcing theory back in 1963) with at least one common recognizable characteristic: the search for new stronger infinity axioms as a way to extend existing systems in order to resolve the aforementioned independent questions but also as a means to gradually approach or even become identical with the all-inclusive universal set *V* of von Neumann's cumulative hierarchy of sets and thus attain a status of Cantor's Absolute.

The set-theoretical universe $V = \bigcup_{\alpha \in ON} V_\alpha$, where *ON* is the class of all ordinals, can be indeed interpreted as encompassing the meaning attributed to Cantor's Absolute in the sense of an absolute maximum which includes all possibilities of set formation in a transfinite recursion scheme. It follows that *V* cannot be the first level V_{ON}, at the stage of the class of all ordinals, for in that case by the rules of set-level formation it would generate a next upward scale. Moreover out of this fact any set-theoretical formula holding in *V* must reflect, thanks to the absoluteness properties generated by the existence of levels along the ordinals, to some lower level V_κ, a property termed the reflection principle. In Hauser's view in Hauser (2013) the underlying heuristic of this principle " betrays a close connection with Cantor's Absolute and, therefore, with the metaphysical tradition to which this doctrine belongs" (Hauser 2013, p. 176). In the same vein " the phenomenon of reflection lends a definite sense to the totality of all sets functioning as a symbol for the Absolute in way that is analogous to the manner in which Cantor conceived of the open-ended progression of transfinite numbers as a symbol for the Absolute. The key to this analogy lies in conception of the Absolute Maximum that Cantor adopted from Cusanus." (ibid., p. 176).

Taking account of the ontological content Cantor gave to the Absolute and the epistemological aspects founded in his own work and further developed in the ensuing decades of remarkable achievements in set theory and mathematical logic, I'll try to argue in the next sections that Cantor's Absolute is unattainable at least on the level of a formal mathematical theory. This is an argumentation articulated both in terms of the formal theory with a special attention to its evolution after Gödel's incompleteness results and in terms of a philosophically oriented discussion (mainly

---

[1] The term large cardinals will be used to characterize those cardinals larger than 'small' large cardinals, e.g., those in the Mahlo hierarchies of inaccessible cardinals. These cardinals correspond to existence axioms based on extrinsic grounds, that is, on axioms not necessarily consistent with $V = L$, which is what happens with the axiom of existence of a measurable cardinal. Large cardinals are often termed in bibliography as 'large' large cardinals.

in the last section) that draws on the subjectively founded capacities of (temporal) constitution and meaning giving.

The universal set V is, in fact, viewed by some set-theorists as playing a conceptual role different from any other model of **ZFC** (Zermelo-Fraenkel + Axiom of Choice) theory plus additional axioms. It is claimed, in this respect, that it is not known at the outset what axioms, beyond the system **ZFC**, may hold in V (e.g, due to a corpus of of meta-mathematical results having also to do with Gödel's incompleteness theorems). This is associated with the axioms that are thought to reflect definite set-theoretic statements according to the current state of knowledge about sets, and perhaps our current state of mind about them in Gödel's sense, which makes that the universe V remains for that matter vague. In Arrigoni's view in Arrigoni (2011) it is reasonable to say that in " contemporary set theory appealing to V amounts to endorsing a specific heuristic assuming the overall goal of set theory to be the achievement of an ultimate extension of **ZFC**, which, once available, would be true for the universe (i.e., V)." (Arrigoni 2011, fn 9, p. 340).

In this quest a major orientation is the development of inner models[2] for large cardinals which started in the last decades of the 20th century and is still in evolving progress. In this direction there exist two central themes to pursue, the extension of Gödel's class L of constructible sets to obtain L-like (inner) models of **ZFC** capable of accommodating a host of larger cardinals existing in the universe V, and the development of core model theory, a relatively recently elaborated theory which provides the possibility of proving that the universe V is well approximated by a core model. Both questions involve an ongoing research that stumbles to the one or the other degree to technical difficulties, in spite of partial achievements, especially in the need for obtaining inner models for supercompact cardinals, these cardinals being thought of as a benchmark in an ascending scale of large cardinals consistency.[3] Judging from the viewpoint of this article the whole (quite perplexing) technical approach is very much dependent on the notions of ultrapowers in terms of elementary embeddings, on well-foundedness in non-linear iterations of ultrapower models, on the notion of extenders, on the notion of Woodin cardinals, etc. All these notions which depend on a lower-order level on more fundamental infinity notions, e.g., those of ultrafilters,[4] of unboundedness or well-foundedness in infinite iterability structures, of second or third-order quantification, etc., are conditioned, in the final count, on a circular notion of infinity which is that of assuming any infinite object independently of the scale of cardinality as a completed whole in actuality.

---

[2] A proper class M is an inner model iff M is a transitive $\in$-model of **ZF** with ON $\subseteq M$ where ON is the class of all ordinal numbers. A transitive set is intuitively a set that preserves the notion of $\in$-inclusion and is defined to be a set in which each of its elements is a subset of it.

[3] An extensive, though quite technical, look into the research results in inner models theory in the last decades of 20th century and a brief reference to prospective results in the beginning of 21st is found in Mitchell's *Inner Models for Large Cardinals*, Mitchell (2012).

[4] U is an ultrafilter over a set S iff it is a maximal filter over S, i.e. for any $X \subseteq S$ either $X \in U$ or else $S - X \in U$. Given that the paper includes quite a few technical mathematical terms I chose for reasons of cohesion and economy of space to be selective about definitions. The interested reader may in any case consult Kanamori's *The Higher Infinite* about relevant definitions, Kanamori (2009).

In other words, as a well-meant object of predication within the universe of a formal language susceptible to be treated under the same syntactical norms independently of the scale of cardinality.

Whatever specific method one chooses to advance to higher and higher infinity assumptions and the ensuing introduction of larger and larger cardinals, where the inner models approach often combined with forcing techniques is the predominant one, there are certain results along the way that testify to the inherent difficulties of attaining the universality of Cantor's Absolute in the formal-axiomatical level. My intention is to inquire into the origin of these difficulties, that is, into whether they are imposed by deficiencies found on the formal level and thus possible to be addressed by new radical methods or new hitherto undiscovered axioms in Gödel's anticipatory sense in Feferman (1995) (p. 385) or whether they are due, in a non-reductionistic approach, to subjectively founded constraints consequently unresolvable by purely formal-axiomatical means.

A special attention in the development of the whole argumentation is given also to questions associated with the maximality status one should seek from an all inclusive set-theoretical universe having in mind, in particular, the delimitative character of Gödel's constructible universe L and the possibilities of its transcendence by the introduction of an 'augmenting' sequence of large cardinals.

2 The Inherent Obstacles in Acceding to a Determinate Universal Set

In this section I set out by referring to some controversial points of the large cardinals theory in a context of discourse that refers primarily to the construction of *ad hoc* set-theoretical models and the relevant proof-theoretic methods. My intention is to comment on some specific weak points in the foundation and the breadth of corresponding theories so as to further ground my overall argumentation on the matter.

(A) In spite of the progress made in the development of the theory of large cardinals and the introduction of stronger and stronger infinity assumptions one key question of mathematics, holding in fact the key to a possible ontology of infinity, is still unresolved. This is the well-known *Continuum Hypothesis* which is proved not only independent from the commonly accepted **ZFC** theory but moreover independent " of all remotely plausible axioms of infinity, including MC,[5] that have been considered so far (assuming their consistency)" (Feferman 1999, p. 107). According to Feferman, " In fact, it is consistent with all those axioms - if they are consistent - that the cardinal number of the continuum is anything it 'ought' to be, i.e., anything which is not excluded by König's Theorem" (Feferman et al. 2000, p. 405). This is a situation essentially unchanged to date even if there have been approaches

---

[5] This is a reference to the statement of existence of a measurable cardinal, MC, which was proved back in the sixties by Lévy and Solovay, in Lévy and Solovay (1967), to have no influence on the decidability of CH. More precisely, it was proven that if ZFM is set theory with the axiom asserting the existence of a measurable cardinal, then if ZFM is consistent then it is consistent with both the continuum hypothesis CH and its negation.

via forcing axioms such as the *PFA* (Proper Forcing Axiom) or Woodin's Ω-conjecture which renders a negative answer to *CH* through Woodin's Ω-logic provability which is invariant under forcing. Relatively recently Woodin has embarked on the 'Ultimate-*L*' program which is more directly connected with large cardinals and their canonical models. If the whole program can be successfully worked out, one may obtain (as a corollary) that *CH* is true.[6] However, both of these latter programs are provisional insofar as they employ hitherto unproven major hypotheses.

It is notable that even those set-theorists, who like Steel argue against Feferman's claim that *CH* is an inherently vague statement (as all Σ_1^2 statements), are ready to admit that the solution to the Continuum Problem may " best seen as resolving some ambiguity" (Feferman et al. 2000, p. 432). This may involve finding conditional generic absoluteness theorems for mutually incompatible theories, each of them consistent with all the large cardinal axioms and adopt one such theory in an analogous fashion to speaking one of some family of intertranslatable languages. As a matter of fact, " At the moment, however, these are simply speculations, and the most important point is just that further investigation is needed." (ibid., p. 239)

(B) A major question concerning the introduction of large cardinal axioms is whether these axioms can make the set-theoretical universe more determinate, given the existence of mutually incompatible, successful extensions of **ZFC**, e.g., of **ZFC** + V=L and **ZFC** + $V \neq L$, and the allegedly 'restrictive' nature of V=L. A controversy persists among set-theorists as some cling to the view that even though large cardinals are shown to be preserved under forcing and hence to exist models of 'ZFC + large cardinal axioms' in which mutually exclusive propositions are true, somehow new correct (true) axioms will emerge to decide questions independent of 'ZFC + large cardinals'. On this account the set-theoretical universe could be made more determinate by finding suitable axiomatic extensions of '**ZFC** + large cardinals' (Arrigoni and Friedman 2012, p. 1362). Counterarguments as to the feasibility of such an undertaking based on the ambivalences of the implication '**success** (in Gödel's sense) $\longrightarrow$ **correctness (or) truth**' are presented by Arrigoni & Friedman in Arrigoni and Friedman (2012), and Arrigoni in Arrigoni (2011).[7] From a

---

[6] Woodin was able to show that if an inner model could be found compatible with supercompact cardinals, then, contrary to what holds for smaller large cardinals, this inner model would be compatible with all other large cardinals which are consistent with **ZFC**. This significant result could lead to a new kind of axiom, the axiom $V =$ Ultimate $- L$. In turn, this axiom would decide independent statements such as *CH*. However given that such an inner model has not yet been found, there has been a turn of Woodin's toward the idea of applying strategic extender models which in case they can accommodate a supercompact cardinal they can accommodate all large cardinals consistent with **ZFC**. These extender models are of the form HOD $^{L(A,R)}$ where A is a universally Baire set. Proving the existence of such models it would be, thanks to the axiom $V = L_S^\Omega$ (i.e., $V =$ Ultimate $- L$), possible to achieve the global consistency requirements of the model as above and the truth of *CH*. As a matter of fact there are no formal proofs as yet relative to the existence of such models and the ensuing conjecture. A more detailed technical exposition of these matters can be found in Rittberg (2015) (pp. 140–146).

[7] This is done in arguing for the *Inner Model Hypothesis*, an alternative infinity hypothesis essentially ensuring a concept of maximization based on qualitative rather than quantitative criteria. This is the following statement: If a statement φ without parameters holds in an inner universe of some outer universe of V (i.e., in some universe compatible with V), then it already holds in some inner universe of V (Arrigoni and Friedman 2012, p. 1364). See also Friedman (2006).

certain point of view due to Scott's result in 1961, namely that on the assumption of the existence of a measurable cardinal holds $V \neq L$, the expression 'the universe is maximal' took a concrete mathematical content implying that methodological principles like maximization based on the intuitive, iterative concept of set may not be sufficient, in conjunction with success, to produce truth or correctness in set theory (Arrigoni and Friedman 2012, p. 1363). Their arguments on the matter help to further invigorate my own arguments on the inherent inaccessibility of a fully determinate set-theoretical universe that may be consistent with all known large cardinal axioms and also decide CH and not contradict AC.

I note that 'maximization' meant as a principle based on a quantitative, extensional notion of sets fails to suggest a unique axiomatic extension of **ZFC**, taking into account that the existence of a nontrivial elementary embedding $j : V \longrightarrow V$ of the set-theoretic universe V into itself is proved to be incompatible with the *Axiom of Choice*, a key principle known to be associated with the iterative conception of sets and in line with maximality considerations. Further, 'maximization' conceived in terms of the *Inner Model Hypothesis, IMH,* as maximality in the sense of internal consistency of sentences in V is ultimately revealed an ambiguous concept. On the one hand, it implies a maximality property of the universe of sets in an intensional sense, that is, the maximality of the internal consistency of sentences of V with regard to an outer universe. On the other hand, it contradicts the existence of large cardinals in V which is against an idea of maximality of V in an 'extensional' sense, as large cardinals are naturally thought of as asserting a form of maximality of the universe of sets inspired by the iterative conception of sets, meaning that the universe of sets should be high (by the transfinite progression of ordinals) and wide (by the unfolding of infinite cardinals).[8] Of course this argument implies the possibility and the conditions of mutual translatability between extensional and intensional concepts in mathematical theories which is by itself another issue of concern at least in connection with their metatheoretical or even extra-theoretical (possibly subjective) origins. It is not my intention, though, to deal further with this in the present paper.

In any case one should be careful concerning alternative assumptions, such as *IMH*, to 'classically' conceived large cardinal axioms as to what kind of new axioms Gödel claimed would decide the existing undecidable statements within **ZFC**. Arrigoni & Friedman maintain, in connection to Gödel's statement in *What is Cantor's continuum problem?*[9] that some axiom stating a maximum property of the system of all sets could settle the *CH* conjecture, that " there is no implication in this quote that 'maximization' must be based on large cardinal axioms" (ibid., p. 1365). Yet in the same article Gödel made the prediction that there is little hope of solving the continuum problem by means of those axioms of infinity based on Mahlo's principles, leaving the door open for new axioms based on different principles (he referred to them as extremely strong axioms of infinity of an entirely new kind) as well as

---

[8] Let it be noted that while *IMH* has served to settle some independent questions of **ZFC** it still leaves the *CH* question unresolved (Arrigoni and Friedman 2012, p. 1365).

[9] See: Feferman (1990), fn 23, p. 262.

other hitherto unknown axioms of set theory " which a more profound understanding of the concepts underlying logic and mathematics would enable us to recognize as implied by these concepts" (Feferman 1990, p. 261). It is interesting that Gödel knowledgeable of the developments in the fields of set theory and mathematical foundations at the time, bore primarily in mind, in referring to extremely strong axioms of infinity, the works of Keisler and Tarski (1964) and Scott (1961) known for making use of new methods and ideas to generate cardinals stronger than weakly or strongly inaccessible ones by applying the notions of κ-complete ideals or filters, elementary embeddings, inner models, etc. Measurable cardinals had already been formulated by Stanislaw Ulam in terms of ultrafilters construed as two-valued measures while Jerome Keisler had the idea of taking the ultrapower of a measurable cardinal κ by a κ-complete ultrafilter to obtain that the completeness property led to a well-founded, and so in his case well-ordered, structure (Kanamori 2012a, p. 50).

In the bottom-line the ground-breaking method of acceding to large cardinalities by elementary embeddings from the universe V to *ad hoc* inner models was made possible by the construction of ultrapowers of V by ultrafilters U which ensured that the relation of satisfaction in the ultrapower is reduced to satisfaction over a large set of coordinates in accordance with the properties of the ultrafilter U. This in turn involved the Lós Theorem, proved by induction on the complexity of the formulas of satisfaction, due to the filter properties of U, the ultrafilter property for the negation step, and AC for the existential quantifier step.[10] In a final step to ensure that the relation E_U between the members of the ultrapower Ult (V, U) is a well-founded one and then apply the Mostowski collapsing theorem to reduce the ultrapower to a transitive structure, the condition of ω_1-completeness (a restriction of κ-completeness to the first uncountable ordinal ω_1) of U is necessary. I give a special importance to this brief description of the model-theoretic method to accede to larger cardinals insofar as it involves some fundamental set-theoretical concepts, primarily well-foundedness, transitive structure, AC, and the ulrtafilter properties, which I intend to discuss in the larger picture of the last section that deals with a philosophically based overview of the whole subject.

On this account even though Gödel did not exclude extensions of existing infinity axioms based on the concept 'property of set' (cf. with intensional approach), he seemed rather inclined to the view that they should be generated by extreme infinity axioms in the sense of the aforementioned ones. Accordingly he drew attention to the fact that " only a maximum property would seem to harmonize with the concept of set explained in footnote 14.".[11]

---

[10] The construction of the ultrapower of V (or generally of any inner model of **ZFC**) by ultrafilter U hinges principally on the following satisfaction formula and is based on Lós theorem:

$$<^S V/U, E_U > \vDash \varphi[(f_1)_U, \ldots, (f_n)_U] \text{ iff } \{i \in S; V \vDash \varphi[f_1(i), \ldots, f_n(i)]\} \in U$$

where S is a subset of the universal set V, U an ultrafilter over S and $<^S V/U, E_U>$ the ultrapower of V by U. For more details on these matters look into: Kanamori (2012b), pp. 365–367 and Kanamori (2009), pp. 47–49.

[11] Footnote 14 refers essentially to the intuitive, iterative concept 'set of x's', even though the operation 'set of x's' itself seemed to Gödel somewhat circular in that it can only be paraphrased by other expres-

(C) The outgrowth of progress in large cardinals theory has generated some ambiguities with regard to the real need for axioms of large cardinals, on the one hand, and the 'restrictive' character of $V = L$ on the other. Feferman has argued, citing concrete cases in Feferman et al. (2000), that certain large cardinal axioms needed for the proof of *ad hoc* combinatorial statements are equivalent to the ω-consistency of the corresponding formal theories restricted to Σ_1^0 sentences (i.e., to their 1-consistency). This means that in spite of the plausibility of 1-consistency in the relevant case, one should not accept these large cardinal axioms as 'first-class mathematical principles' (Feferman et al. 2000, pp. 406–407).

Steel has claimed that by Scott's result of 1961 any sentence φ of set-theory **ZFC** that includes a measurable cardinal can be relativized to a sentence φ^L of $V = L$ by $\varphi \longrightarrow \varphi^L$ and not vice versa, which obviously narrows the interpretative power of set-theory. Yet this argument has been contested by Jensen who stands by the view that the systems '**ZFC** + large cardinal axioms' and '**ZFC** + $V=L$' are of mutual interpretability. As a matter of fact, by Shoenfield's Absoluteness Lemma,[12] the constructible model L and the set-theoretical universe V are proved to have transitive countable models for the same large cardinal hypotheses; a brief outline of this proof can be found in Arrigoni and Friedman (2012), (fn 15, p. 1363). This may be meant, according to Jensen, as a kind of evidence that the relation between **ZFC** + $V = L$ and **ZFC** + 'large cardinals' should be more correctly understood as one of mutual interpretability than as one of contradictory existence, a view that tends to bridge the supposed incompatibility of the **ZFC** + 'large cardinals' system incorporating the maximum iterative concept of sets[13] with the **ZFC** + $V = L$ which restricts an arbitrary, non-predicative character of set formation. I point out *a propos*, however, that the proof referred to above implicitly needs the *Axiom of Choice* as it makes use of Skolem-Löwenheim and Mostowski's Collapsing Theorems.

However, this is a position disputed from a position of mathematical realism insofar as " realism is to underwrite the assumption that there is a real question to be decided here, that it isn't enough to say that ZFC + $V = L$ and ZFC + $V \neq L$ are equally acceptable because they are both equiconsistent with ZFC." (Maddy 1997, p. 110). In other words, there is a concrete matter-of-fact here according to which one of the statements might be true in the world of sets and thus established as a new axiom. Besides, there is a legitimate form of evidence in mathematics

---

Footnote 11 (continued)
sions involving again the concept of set, e.g., 'multitude of x's', 'combination of any number of x's', etc. (Feferman 1990, p. 263).

[12] The Shoenfield's Absoluteness Lemma states that all $\Sigma_2^1(\alpha)$ and $\prod_2^1(\alpha)$ relations are absolute for inner models M of ZF theory (plus the weaker dependent choice maxim) which contain the real number α as an element. In other words, Shoenfield's Absoluteness Lemma shows that in the analytical hierarchy, Σ_2^1 and $\prod_2^1$ sentences are absolute between the model V of **ZF** and the constructible universe L, when interpreted as statements about the natural numbers in each model or about sets of natural numbers as parameters from V.

[13] As commonly understood this term refers to a concept of the set of all subsets of a given set envisaging all possibilities in the iteration of this mathematical act irrespectively of how a set is defined, e.g. by a predicative definition or not.

beyond that associated with perceptual or intuitive evidence associated, in a Gödelian sense, with the positive impact a hypothesis might have in the type of theory it generates, e.g. the breadth, simplicity and elegance of the proofs it produces. This is what is called extrinsic evidence in contrast to the intrinsic one (perceptual or intuitive). In these terms, at least, **ZFC** $+ V \neq L$ is generally considered to have the edge over **ZFC** $+ V = L$, even though Maddy argues in Maddy (1997) against the latter in terms of the failed status of definabilism in mathematics for the delimitative character of which she gives an ample account in the historical progression of analysis. She also contrasts definabilism with her presumed endorsement of Bernay's combinatorialism which, notably, to the extent that it subscribes to a notion of set as constituted by finitely or infinitely many independent determinations perfectly accommodates the impredicative sense of *AC*. For, if a set is constituted in this sense then " the choice set for a family of disjoint, non-empty sets is constituted by independent determinations selecting one element from each of those non-empty sets" (ibid., p. 128). In Bernay's combinatorialism, therefore, one has to accept as a precondition the notion of a complete actual infinity in which to proceed through independent determinations and, through a 'leap of faith' in analogy from the finite to the infinite, to the concept of sets, choice sets, sequences, functions, etc. In other words, one has to deal with a formally non-predicative and perhaps, on a deeper subjective level of discourse, non-objectifiable residuum.

A key statement of infinitary mathematics associated with large cardinals which, this time, contradicts *AC* is the *Axiom of Determinacy*, *AD*, stating that J_x [14] is determined for each subset *X* of the real numbers. To remedy the situation one may take recourse to a weakening form *PD* (*Projective Determinacy*) of *AD* applied to projective sets of reals or to a strengthening of it, that is, the statement $AD^{L(R)}$, where $L(R)$ is the collection of all sets definable in the constructible hierarchy *L* relativized to the set *R* of reals. In both cases we reach a high point in the development of large cardinals theory (beyond the $V = L$ level), in the extension of 'nice' properties of Borel and analytic sets, such as Lebesgue measurability, the Baire property, and the perfect subset property, to arbitrary sets respectively in the projective or constructible hierarchy, yet only under the assumption of strong infinity principles. These are the existence of infinitely many Woodin cardinals in the case of *PD* and of infinitely many Woodin cardinals with a measurable cardinal above them in the case of $AD^{L(R)}$ (Feferman 1999, pp. 12–13), & (Feferman et al. 2000, p. 404). I note that, taking $X = \omega$ and noting that a strategy itself can be construed as a real, it has been shown that by diagonalizing through all strategies and on the assumption of *AC* there is an undetermined $A \subseteq \omega^{\omega}$, a natural consequence of which is that *AD* contradicts *AC*. This is a result forged,

---

[14] J_x is an idealized infinite game associated with each subset *X* of the set of real numbers, or what essentially amounts to the same thing, of the set 2^N of all infinite sequences of 0's and 1's. This game has two idealized players, I and II, where at each stage of the play, I plays first by choosing a 0 or a 1; player II responds in the same way. The play terminates with a sequence s in 2^N, for which player I wins if $s \in X$ and player II wins if not. The game J_x is said to be determined if one or the other of the players has a winning strategy, i.e. a rule for how to play at each stage in order to win no matter what choices are made by the opposite player. *AD* says that J_x is determined for each set *X* of reals.

though, by the essentially Cantorian method of diagonalizing over an indefinite complete whole (Kanamori 2012b, p. 381).

In view of the preceding discussion a special attention relative to the purpose of this article concerns the status of **CH** as a logical problem in the sense that there is a general agreement among mathematicians over the years that it is not a mathematical question borne out and treated within the bounds of a mathematical theory irrespective of its axiomatic foundation. Consequently, it can be considered as a definite logical problem relative to any specific axiomatic system or model. But one cannot say that it is a definite logical problem in some absolute sense unless the systems or models in question have been singled out in some canonical way. To cite a parallel case, one may argue that the notion of an arbitrary subset of the real numbers is inherently vague in the sense that there is no reasonable way the notion could be sharpened without violating the sense of arbitrariness inherent in it. If the assumption that all subsets of reals **R** are in Gödel's constructible universe L or even, for that matter, in $L(\mathbf{R})$, would be such a sharpening that violates the idea of 'arbitrariness', then it turns out that we would be faced with the ambivalent situation that if **ZFC** is consistent then so are both **ZFC** + $L=\mathbf{R}$ and **ZFC** + $L \neq \mathbf{R}$. In the other direction, in Feferman's view, " it is hard to see how there could be any non-circular sharpening of the form that there are as many such sets as possible" (Feferman et al. 2000, p. 411).

Objections can be also raised against the view that the notion universe of all sets can only be made determinate by finding axiomatic extensions of the theory '**ZFC** + large cardinal axioms' which successfully decide questions independent of it. In advancing this view, it is assumed that mathematical success provides evidence for the correctness or truth of large cardinal axioms which renders these axioms definitive set-theoretic principles that one can only 'extend' but not contradict. In assuming that success implies correctness (truth), however, one is either tacitly committed to Platonism or one faces the embarrassing situation that mutually exclusive and successful axiomatic systems for sets coexist. On the other hand, no a priori ground seems to exist for ruling out the possibility of making the notion of the universe of all sets more determinate through the introduction of new axiomatic proposals rather than existential postulations of new, ever larger cardinals. As pointed to earlier one such proposal is the *Inner Model Hypothesis* advanced by Arrigoni and Friedman whose approach is not to 'determine' the universe by directly postulating what sets exist in it but to state from a metatheoretical perspective what properties the universe of sets is supposed to possess.

Over the last decades two programs have received considerable attention claiming to be oriented, among others, to the aim of consistently extending the system '**ZFC** + large cardinal axioms'. The first is Woodin's approach via Ω-logic and the evolving aftermath of the Ultimate-L conjecture. The second one is the inner model program. Both take large cardinals to a considerable extent for granted and both have been pursued over a number of years with results of great technical complexity. I am going to primarily deal with the latter as it is currently the main field facing the possibility of reaching up to the power of Cantor's Absolute.

Cantor's Absolute

3 Are Large Cardinals the Key to Accede to Cantor's Absolute?

If the axiom of constructibility is considered as restricting the scope of the set-theoretic universe by specifying a notion of predicatively generated sets it turns out that neither inaccessible cardinals can be taken as an alternative to constructibility. This is principally due to their consistency with this axiom since if a cardinal κ is inaccessible in V, it is also in L. To fix this situation one needs a principle saying that the universe is not only 'high' by transfinite construction based on the ordinals but also 'wide'. The first such large cardinal axiom is the axiom of existence of a measurable cardinal proved by D. Scott in 1961 to imply $V \neq L$. This cardinal arose from the need to extend the notion of Lebesgue measurability to all subsets of reals and involves by definition the concept of a κ-complete, non-principal ultrafilter over the measurable cardinal κ, a fact that needs at some stage the application of AC. Formally a measurable cardinal κ is defined as follows:

Definition 3.1 The cardinal κ is measurable if and only if there exist M and function j such that

- M is an inner model.
- $j : V \longrightarrow M$ is an elementary embedding[15]
- κ is the critical point of j, that is, the least ordinal moved by j, (i.e., $j \upharpoonright \kappa = $ id, $j(\kappa) > \kappa$).

Over the last decades a spate of ever stronger cardinals has been produced by imposing additional closure conditions, among others, to the inner model M, e.g., the cardinal κ is α-strong iff $V_\alpha \subseteq M$, strong if it is α-strong for all ordinals α, and superstrong if $V_{j(\kappa)} \subseteq M$. More powerful cardinals followed suit with huge and supercompact cardinals being the main representatives of the upper echelons. Reinhardt cardinals, the definition of which implies $M = V$, were greeted initially as a means of realization of Cantor's Absolute by simulating V with M, yet their existence was refuted in the years to come by Kunen in his well-known proof (1971) on the non-existence of a non-trivial mapping $j : V \longrightarrow V$.[16]

If the process of ascending the large cardinal hierarchy is interwoven with consistent extensions of the theory '**ZFC** + large cardinal axioms', a key argument

---

[15] For structures $\mathcal{M} = \{M, ...\}$ and $\mathcal{N} = \{N, ...\}$ and a language L, an injective function $j : \mathcal{M} \longrightarrow \mathcal{N}$ is an elementary embedding of $\mathcal{M}$ into $\mathcal{N}$ denoted $j : \mathcal{M} \prec \mathcal{N}$, iff it satisfies the elementarity schema: for any formula $\varphi(v_1, ..., v_n)$ of L and $x_1, ..., x_n \in M$

$$\mathcal{M} \vDash \varphi(x_1, ..., x_n) \text{ iff } \mathcal{N} \vDash \varphi(j(x_1), ..., j(x_n))$$

[16] Kunen's proof is based on the Erdös-Hajnal theorem which is dependent in a substantial way on the application of the *Axiom of Choice* (Kunen 1971). The problem is open without this assumption. On the other hand, the question of whether a weaker version of Reinhardt cardinals is consistent with the axioms **ZF**, and thus not dependent on AC, proves to be a controversial issue too. This owes to the results of Woodin's, namely, the theory **ZF** + 'There is a weak Reinhardt cardinal' proves the formal consistency of the theory **ZFC** + 'There is a proper class of strongly $(\omega + 1)$-huge cardinals' with the latter cardinals being the strongest large cardinals not known to be refuted by the *Axiom of Choice* (Woodin 2011, p. 99).

raised by Moschovakis against accepting $V = L$ is that "the axiom of constructibility (or even $\mathcal{N} \subseteq L$)[17] appears to restrict unduly the notion of arbitrary set of integers" (Moschovakis 2009, p. 472). This argument is driven by the conviction that "there is no a priori reason why every subset of ω should be definable from ordinal parameters, much less by an elementary definition over some countable L_ξ. Some would go further and claim disbelief that the real line can be definably well-ordered on any rank - it is quite plausible that the only sets of reals which admit definable well-orderings are countable." (ibid., p. 472). This is a view that was in an indirect way endorsed by Feferman in claiming that the transfinitely iterated power set operation in the built up of the cumulative hierarchy of sets 'is even more so inherently vague' to the point that one cannot in general clarify what is the fact of the matter in that conception (Feferman et al. 2000, p. 405). The suggestion is that $V = L$ requires every set to be definable in a certain uniform way and this requirement is in perspective undesirable. Given that inaccessible cardinals are not an alternative to the axiom of constructibility, strong axioms of infinity, except for establishing that the set-theoretic universe V is not identifiable with L (proved by Scott in 1961), should also be expected to prevent the set-theoretic universe from being 'constructed from below' in the sense of L.

In this regard I sketch below Jensen's construction of an L-like model that presumably avoids 'construction from below', yet it is conditioned on fundamental assumptions presupposing a notion of sets as arbitrary completed wholes. More specifically, Jensen describes a process of acquiring an inner model L^U, by a measurable cardinal κ, which is very L-like in the following way. The measurability of κ means that there is a normal ultrafilter U[18] in $\mathcal{P}(\kappa)$. The hierarchy of L_α^U's can be essentially defined like that of L_α's in Gödel's constructible universe L in which case we have the class $L^U = \bigcup_\alpha L_\alpha^U$. By its definition L^U is an inner model. It turns out that κ is measurable in L^U since $U \cap L_\alpha^U \in L^U$ proves to be a normal ultrafilter in L^U. Jensen continues: "Silver and others have shown that L^U is thoroughly similar to L. It satisfies GCH (*auth. add.*: i.e., the Generalized Continuum Hypothesis). It has the combinatorial properties of L. (In fact, until now, no purely combinatorial difference between L and L^U has been discovered.) [...] Even the absoluteness of L has an analog: L^U has a definition (using κ as a parameter) that is absolute in every inner model M with $L^U \subseteq M$." (Jensen 1995, p. 402).

The model L^U cannot be built, by its definition, from below by well-understood operations insofar as the normal ultrafilter U involved in the construction of L^U is defined in the general case by impredicative, non-constructible means, e.g., by invoking a maximality principle (Zorn's lemma)[19] proved to be logically equivalent

---

[17] $\mathcal{N}$ is a common symbol for the Baire space ω^ω.

[18] For a filter F over cardinal λ, F is normal iff for any class $\{X_\alpha; \alpha < \lambda\} \in {}^\lambda F$ its diagonal intersection

$$\Delta_{\alpha<\lambda} X_\alpha = \{\xi < \lambda; \xi \in \cap_{\alpha<\xi} X_\alpha\} \in F$$

By setting $X_\alpha = \lambda$ for α sufficiently large it follows that normality subsumes λ-completeness. See: Kanamori (2009), p. 26 & pp. 52–53.

[19] By Zorn's lemma it is proved that any partially ordered set in which each chain (i.e., a linearly ordered subset) has an upper bound, has a maximal element. Historically, versions of what is known as Zorn's

with the *Axiom of Choice*. Indeed all ultrapower constructions in the large cardinals theory turned into inner models by Mostowski's Collapsing Lemma are inherently tied to such impredicative maximality assumptions which underly as a matter of fact the definition of generated large cardinals. However Jensen claims that a construction from below by well-understood operations is to a certain extent feasible thanks to the so-called core model theory (ibid., p. 402).

On this account, and without entering into the minute technicalities of the construction, I'll just point to some weak points to show how inherent pathologies of set theory, the impredicative character of actual infinity assumptions being most common, condition at some point or another seemingly well-defined predicative constructions.

In the specific case one may assume that not only V is not identifiable with L but also that there is a non-trivial elementary embedding $j : L \longrightarrow L$. This assumption turns out to be equivalent to the existence of a certain set, considered as a 'well-understood' mathematical object denoted by $0^\#$ (think of it as a non-constructible set of ordinal numbers),[20] that encodes a complete description of the structure of L and also of the canonical elementary embedding $j : L \longrightarrow L$. The set $0^\#$ regarded as the next larger construction step than L can generate the inner model $L[0^\#]$, the constructible closure of $0^\#$, defined from $O^\#$ the way L^U was defined from U. By the same assumption as above one is led to a set $0^{\#\#}$ encoding $L[0^\#]$ and the canonical embedding $j : L[0^\#] \longrightarrow L[0^\#]$. Continuing this way along all ordinal numbers α one may derive the set 0^∞ encoding the transitive closure $L^\sharp$ for all 0^α and all non-trivial elementary embeddings $j : L[0^\alpha] \longrightarrow L[0^\alpha]$ as before. Finally this generates the sequence: $0^\#, 0^{\#\#}, \ldots, 0^\alpha, \ldots, 0^\infty, 0^{\infty+1}, \ldots$. The terms of this sequence are called mice and they can define a class along a natural ordering much longer than ∞. The union of all transitive closures $L[m]$ such that m is a mouse is called the core model K. It is an inner model and moreover absolute in the sense that for every inner model $M \supseteq K$, $K_M = K$. K is L-like in the same way L^U was, except that U can be obtained fairly directly from the non-trivial elementary embedding $j : K \longrightarrow K$ as no new mice can be generated out of it as all are included in K (ibid., pp. 402-403).

Weak point 1: All $0^\#$s are defined as sets encoding non-trivial elementary embeddings of inner models of an 'immediately lower order', yet the limit step toward the definition of 0^∞ by the non-trivial elementary embedding $(L^\sharp \longrightarrow L^\sharp)$ of the constructible closure $L^\sharp$ for all $\alpha \in ON$ may not give a set in the sense of the recursively defined previous stages as, due to the Burali-Forti paradox, there is no set of all ordinals. As well-known the Burali-Forti paradox derives from the simple fact that one cannot have the intuition of a well-meant ordering of a set without the intuition of a set as a complete whole in actual presence and of a least part x of it as unit

---

Footnote 19 (continued)
lemma were given prior to Zorn by Haudorff in connection with the maximality aspect of the Well-Ordering Theorem (Kanamori 2012a, p. 23.)

[20] The existence of the set $0^\#$ has a significant role to play in the development of large cardinals theory and the quest for an ever closer approximation to the set-theoretic universe as due to Jensen's covering theorem it expresses a sense of closeness between V and L by its non-existence!

which is not a whole, i.e. $x \notin x$. In other words this paradox may be seen to reflect the growing tension in the historical development of set theory between establishing well-orderings in set constructions and admitting sets as constructively unspecified completed wholes, e.g., sets of arbitrary functions (or power sets). The controversial status of the Burali-Forti paradox is further highlighted if we consider the fact that Cantor used the Burali-Forti paradox argument to point out that the class of all ordinal numbers is an inconsistent multiplicity, i.e., a multiplicity which when taken as a unity leads to contradiction.[21]

The next question should be the reach of the aforementioned process in terms of stronger and stronger cardinals. In Jensen's account the difficulties of defining a core model for a strong cardinal (stronger than a measurable one) are great and some progress made in terms of the existence of such a model cannot go "much further without seriously modifying the program" (Jensen 1995, pp. 403–404). The case for even stronger cardinals becomes even more perplexed as the existence of a superstrong cardinal, a result due to Martin, Steel and Woodin, implies *AD* in the inner model *L*[**R**] (ibid., p. 404). Steel has also constructed an extended core model *K* to accommodate Woodin cardinals[22] but in order to carry this out needs third order set theory and measurability property for the class of all ordinals. The question as to how far one can go in the scale of large cardinals realizable within inner models and whether this question also subsumes a sort of linear ordering of strong infinity axioms in terms of relative consistency, which would be indicative of a kind of successive approximation toward an absolute universe, has still many open problems to resolve. My stated intention, I remind, is to show that Cantor's Absolute is unattainable for reasons whose origin eludes the formal-logical level and may, in fact, be reducible to a subjective constituting one conditioning precisely at this level any concept or implication of actual infinity.

Weak point 2: The existence of a superstrong cardinal implies *AD* in the inner model *L*[**R**]. As it is known *AD* contradicts the *Axiom of Choice* which in this case is a result equivalent to the non-existence of a well-ordering of the set of reals **R** in *L*[**R**], a serious default in doing much of meaningful mathematics in this context as, in particular, **R** is proved to have no well-ordering definable in second-order arithmetic. In fact a major deficiency of the core model program is the loss of a nicely definable well-ordering of **R**.

Weak point 3: Any attempted extension of the core model program by incorporating superstrong or Woodin cardinals defies absoluteness. As mentioned above a certain progress has been made by Martin, Mitchell and Steel toward an extended core model *K* accommodating Woodin cardinals, having a host of other important

---

[21] Cantor used the Burali-Forti paradox positively to give a mathematical expression to his Absolute. The 'totality of everything thinkable' was noted to be an absolutely infinite or inconsistent multiplicity (Kanamori 2012a, p. 18). An excellent exposition of the theoretical debate that followed the Burali-Forti paradox which is essentially reducible to the ambivalences of the well-ordering concept along infinite classes is presented in Moore's and Garciadiego's *Burali-Forti's Paradox: A Reappraisal of its Origins*, Moore and Garciadiego (1981).

[22] Call κ a Woodin cardinal if for each class $A \subseteq V_\kappa$ there exists a cardinal $r < \kappa$ which is strong with respect to A in V_κ. See also definition in Kanamori (2009), p. 360.

properties along the way, yet this needs third order set theory (an intuitively prohibitive level of complexity) and measurability property for the class of all ordinals (think of the well-known problem of the non-existence of the set of all ordinals). The notion of absoluteness, except for ensuring that 'well-understood' objects of the inner model remain so along any extension step, is a concept generally accepted as having a deeper, metatheoretical content. This was recognized to one or the other extent by both Gödel and Cohen. In fact one may even inquire into the possibility of a subjectively founded origin of this concept, more concretely into the subjective foundation of essential, invariant properties associated with lowest-level elements of sets taken in turn as complete wholes in actuality. This is a discussion that will be resumed in a wider, philosophically motivated scope in the last section.

Weak point 4: A distinctive feature of the research combining inner model methods with forcing theory and its techniques is the increasing strength of cardinality power along the increase of consistency strength. A major example of powerful large cardinals serving also as a consistency gauge are the classes of supercompact[23] and Woodin cardinals. These are cardinals motivated by concrete questions which except for the level of abstractness of respective definitions they are mostly, especially the latter, concept formations elaborated through method and intended purpose, therefore less supported by a kind of 'direct' intuition of infinity as cardinals like $\aleph_0$ and $\aleph_1$ are thought to be. In the case of supercompact cardinals their prominence in the large cardinals theory is primarily due to their construction compatible with the principles of generalization and reflection while by their consistency strength and their bordering to almost absolute infinity concepts (i.e., n-huge cardinals) delimited only by Kunen's inconsistency result they have become among set-theorists something like an absolute benchmark of infinity strength within inner models theory. However it seems that, at least on the technical side, supercompact cardinals contrary to expectations cannot resolve the question of an ultimate infinite cardinal consistent with all large cardinals of lesser strength, in particular, with regard to Woodin's efforts to construct an ultimate version of L by the axiom $V = $ Ultimate $- L$. More specifically, in Woodin's view " if one could extend the Inner Model Program to the level of one supercompact cardinal then subject to a very general condition on the relationship of the supercompact cardinal of the inner model constructed and supercompact cardinals in V, the inner model constructed must be an ultimate version of L. In particular the Scott effect (*auth. note:* $V \neq L$) would no longer apply" (Woodin 2017, p. 2). Yet, there is evidence that the inner model program cannot be extended to supercompact cardinals due to results that do not guarantee the reflection property of supercompactness into the HOD class (ibid., p. 3).

Leaving the technicalities aside there is no doubt that corresponding to the ascending scale of infinite cardinals, toward a supposed absoluteness, is the growing perplexity of the concepts and assumptions employed and of the interrelationships

---

[23] A cardinal κ is γ-supercompact iff there is an elementary embedding $j : V \longrightarrow M$ for some inner model M, with critical point κ, crit $(j) = \kappa$, and $\gamma < j(\kappa)$ such that $^\gamma M \subseteq M$, i.e. M is closed under the taking of arbitrary γ-sequences. κ is supercompact iff κ is γ-supercompact for every $\gamma \geq \kappa$ (Kanamori 2012b, p. 379).

forged by *ad hoc* methodological tools that stand as autonomous theories themselves, e.g., elementary embeddings coupled with forcing extensions or combinatorial principles. A key trick, to cite an instance, for proving the consistency strength of supercompactness is by implementing forcing extensions or by collapsing supercompact cardinals to cardinalities of a lower level in the cumulative hierarchy through collapsing techniques.[24] In turn collapsing and forcing techniques in general are constrained by the assumptions of a generic extension over an indefinite horizon, the preservation of ordinals, the implicit use of *AC* at least in the case of preservation of cardinals along forcing extensions, etc., in sort by all that presupposes a notion of sets as completed wholes in actuality closer to Zermelo's sense rather than Cantor's enumerative one.

In fact every concept applied in the gradual progression to ever larger cardinals toward an absolute, specified in the postulation of a non-identity elementary embedding $j : V \longrightarrow V$ (or $j : V_{\lambda+2} \longrightarrow V_{\lambda+2}$ for any cardinal λ), e.g., elementary embeddings, 'generic' elementary embeddings, uncountable cofinalities, stationarity, extenders, saturated ideals, etc, presupposes the implicit assumption of sets (and functions thereof) in a circular mode as arbitrary unities in the sense of actual completed wholes. In this approach order within sets is induced not by an 'internal' enumerative sense but instead may be thought of as imposed 'externally' by the constitutive capacities of a subjective factor (e.g., through *AC*) for which the sense of order ultimately applies to individuals as zero-elements without inner structure provided by essence with an absolute relation of inclusion within more inclusive wholes, i.e., the non-logical $\in$-predicate.

I stress at this point that either in the general form or in its weaker counterpart, i.e. the Axiom of Dependent Choices, the *Axiom of Choice* represents the possibility of the uniqueness of choice of ideal elements in conscious mathematical acts extensible ad infinitum something that originates in the uniqueness of the performance of these acts themselves as intentional in character and therefore spatiotemporally unconstrained and further on their objective reflection as such. In these terms in either case the choice set may be considered as impredicatively defined and it is presumably for this reason that Baire, Borel, and Lebesgue were among its fiercest critics even though it implicitly conditioned certain proofs, e.g., relative to the cardinality of Baire functions. The *Axiom of Choice* whose impredicative sense eludes anything even resembling a definition is presented by Maddy as a strong case against definabilism in mathematics in general and the restrictive, predicative nature of Gödel's constructible universe *L* in particular. This is part of her attempt to show that the axiom $V = L$, whose connection to definabilism is evident by the construction of the sets of the constructible universe *L* by a uniform, indeed predicative fashion, seriously impedes by its restrictive nature the development of mathematics. One

---

[24] Such instances are, to cite a few, Foreman's, Magidor's and Shelah's result that if there is a supercompact cardinal κ, then there is a forcing extension in which $\kappa = \omega_2$ and where Martin's Maximum holds, Kanamori (2012b), p. 398, the same set-theorists' result that the Levy collapse of a supercompact cardinal to ω_2 generates a $\aleph_1$-complete $\aleph_2$-saturated ideal over ω_1, ibid., p. 398, and Magidor's result that if κ is supercompact there is a forcing extension in which κ is $\aleph_\omega$ as a strong limit cardinal, yet it violates the Singular Cardinal Hypothesis, i.e. $2^{\aleph_\omega} > \aleph_{\omega+1}$, ibid., p. 387.

should also point out here that even though *AC* is consistent with **ZF** + $V = L$,[25] the constructible universe contradicts large cardinal axioms in general while failing on the practical level to satisfy Suslin Hypothesis, the Whitehead conjecture, the Borel Conjecture, and the existence of a Borel bijection between any two non-Borel analytic sets.

4 The Maximality Versus Minimality Debate in Modern Set-Theory. What It Fails to Capture

If Gödel's research in foundations was a precursor to modern day developments in set-theory, then a single assertion of his included as a footnote to the 1964 revised form of *What is Cantor's Continuum Problem?* continues to spark opposing arguments, on a purely mathematical and even on a more philosophically inclined level, in the current debate among set-theorists. Namely, " [...] from an axiom in some sense opposite to this one, (*auth. add.*: i.e., that every set is definable in the sense of the constructible universe *L*), the negation of Cantor's conjecture could perhaps be derived. I am thinking of an axiom which (similar to Hilbert's completeness axiom in geometry) would state some maximum property of the system of all sets, whereas axiom *A* (*auth. add.*: the formerly meant one) states a minimum property. Note that only a maximum property would seem to harmonize with the concept of set explained in footnote 14 (*auth. add.*: see fn. 11 in the text." (Feferman 1990, pp. 262–263). In the subsequent developments in set-theory and mathematical foundations, especially after Cohen's introduction of forcing method which proved de facto the existence of larger than *L* models and the consistency (relative to **ZFC**) of the enlarged system, the main contrasting views corresponding to the maximality and minimality concepts in set theory have settled around those who tend to justify Gödel's constructibility axiom and those who oppose it and espouse an extension of **ZFC** by a progression of even stronger cardinals. The former justify the axiom $V = L$ mostly based on its success in resolving key questions, among them *CH* and *AC* proved of course later to be independent, and the fundamental conviction that if mathematics is meant as a predicative, meaning-giving activity of the mind then it should construct a set-theoretical universe by well-defined logical operations securing its growth both in 'height' and 'width' in a way that leaves no space to impredicative redundancies.

Except for these set-theorists there are those who, while cautious for some reasons other than its presumed delimitative character, e.g., the ease by which extensions of *L* by forcing are subject to modifications, they are yet ready to fully or partially endorse *L* in the place of any cumulative hierarchy defined by 'unconstrained' power-set operation. There are also those who like Jensen, while acknowledging that **ZFC** with large cardinals has proved more successful than **ZFC**+ $V = L$ they nevertheless see in $V = L$ a clear statement about the mathematical universe, fruitful in

---

[25] Of course **ZF** + *AC* is also proved consistent with the negation of $V = L$ so there is no apparent contradiction concerning the consistency of *AC* with **ZF** + $V = L$, at least on epistemological grounds.

results and fertile in new concepts and methods which may also be seen as "philosophically attractive for adherents of 'Ockham's razor', which says that one should avoid superfluous existence assumptions." (Jensen 1995, p. 398). On the other hand, opponents of $V = L$ see in the constructible universe a restriction of the free outgrowth of mathematical concepts and generated objects and therefore see it as being incompatible with the platonist or realist belief that what eludes us in mathematical ontology is the residuum left between a mathematical object's being-in-itself and its predicative description. As it is known the majority camp of these set-theorists were further bolstered in their views by Scott's landmark result, that one can expand the $V = L$ universe by the existence of a measurable cardinal, and the ensuing pursuit of ever stronger large cardinals to accede as closely as possible to the set-theoretical universe V.

Except for those who like Moschovakis (Sect. 3, par. 4) bring up the argument that there is no a priori reason for accepting that all subsets of natural numbers should be definable, there are also those who, like Hao Wang, are against the axiom of constructibility by a positive motivation, that is, by appealing to the maximum iterative concept of set which presupposes a conception of sets as "arbitrary multiplicities regardless of how or if they can be defined. Hence, it is extremely unlikely that constructible sets, which are essentially the ordinal numbers only, give us all arbitrary sets" (Wang 1974, p. 196). This means that the definition of the cumulative hierarchy should imply the application of the power-set axiom without the restrictions posed by definability concerns (Arrigoni 2011, p. 339).

Further, Wang who was otherwise an admirer of Gödel's argued against the restrictiveness of the axiom of constructibility on the grounds of intuitive plausibility which goes against the pragmatic view that an axiom should be acceptable because of its simplicity and success in resolving open mathematical problems. In this respect the existence of a definable well-ordering of the real numbers and of fairly simple uncountable sets without perfect subsets implied by the axiom $V = L$ seem to be contrary to the intuition of ordinary mathematics. Moreover the reliance in a fundamental level on the ordinal numbers that constitute the backbone of the scaled construction of the universe L, to the extent that they can only afford at most an impredicative definition, in obvious 'contradiction' with the definable character of the sets in each subclass L_α of L, is presented by Wang as an additional argument against the plausibility of $V = L$. The point is that Gödel's iterative definition of sets as 'multitude of x's' or 'combination of any number of x's', etc., was in his own confession unsatisfactory due to the circularity in the application of the expression 'collection or multitude of'. This means, after all, that Wang's argumentation against constructibility on the grounds of the intuitive plausibility of the arbitrary concept of sets in the 'unfettered' iterative sense may be in fact deficient for that matter or conditioned on constraints that may stand beyond the reach of the expressional means of a formal system. I'll deal further with this question in taking into account the intellectual fermentation that followed Cantor's introduction of the concept of sets and the associated theory of infinite sets and transfinite numbers. The discussion will also show that Husserl's early intuitions on sets and meanings-of-sets in response to Cantor's metaphysical inclinations seem to be a precursor to the conception of sets evolved after several decades of foundational work and achievements, a fact that by itself weakens Arrigoni's statement that it was exactly through the technical developments in the mathematics of the end of 19th and the beginning of 20th century " that theorists got an idea of what sets are in mathematics, which they then began to render also in informal and non-strictly-mathematical terms" (Arrigoni 2011, p. 349). My approach, at this level, serves also to argue against the claim that if the maximum iterative concept is what " is mostly called upon in arguing for the 'immediate' intuitiveness of set theoretic notions, axioms and theorems [...] the maximum iterative concept [...] can be coherently understood as no pre-reflective belief of ours." (ibid., fn. 27, p. 348). Therefore it runs against the attempt to interpret at least 'immediate intuitiveness' as an epistemic feature that was not attached to the **ZFC** axioms at the outset of their formulation.

If by immediate intuitiveness in mathematics we refer to contents that are evocative of our implicit beliefs developed at a pre-reflective level, then the maximum iterative concept of sets, based on the intuition of sets conceived as a species in terms of the unity of their members (which are species of a lower-order, i.e., not sets), definitely can be understood as a pre-reflective apprehension of ours. Indeed, rather than taking recourse to platonistic metaphysics one may choose a subjectively founded interpretation for which we can apply Husserl's conception of sets as not mere aggregates of objects but, in a bold evocation of his transcendental leanings of his later period, as thematic objects of consciousness through an act of retrospective apprehension (*rückgreifendes Erfassen*) by which the collection as plurality becomes the unity of an identifiable object known as set uniquely appearing to the ego (Husserl 1939, *Engl. transl.*, p. 246).

For Husserl, in the case of sets or classes of sets one should distinguish between the act of colligation or drawing together of a collection of objects and the above act of constitution of sets as thematic objects in actual presence and consequently as potentially substrates of predicative formulas. This act of thematization in terms of an immanent[26] unity should be associated with the possibility of infinity as generated freely in imagination without any spatiotemporal and, for that matter, causal constraints.

Given that mathematical meaning-contents as intended senses have no real content just as their most fundamental substrates taken as formal individuals (bound to certain constraints in case we talk about substrates of mathematical-logical formulas), the question that may arise, insofar as their existence is not conditioned in an absolute sense to their 'real world' counterparts, is whether there could be possibly a refinement of our intentional apprehension of objects in a way that objectivities of sense that look as being always and in a transtemporal sense the same could for that reason change over time. This means that mathematical objects and their meaning-contents could be subject to refinement due to our intentional-explicative capacities taking into account the insights developed by mathematical practice and the fact that the world is by necessity co-posited. This is acknowledged by Husserl in *Experience and Judgment* and elsewhere in talking about the 'internal' and 'external' horizon

---

[26] Immanence or immanent object is roughly meant something correlative (or co-substantial) to the stream of consciousness and therefore not 'external' or transcendent to it.

of objects, with the former immediately co-awakened by the givenness of an object and proceeding through a 'streaming' of individual apprehensions, of individual acts in linear continuity bound internally to one another to " a polythetic unity of the individual theses" (ibid., p. 112). The 'external' horizon may be associated with the universality of the concept 'object in general' in a sense already pre-constituted in passivity yet possessing a horizon of indeterminate determinability (ibid., p. 222). However, mathematical objects as categorial objects susceptible to the judicative operation of predication in addition to passive receptivity as lowest-level objects-substrates must first comply as pure generalities to eidetic laws[27] meant as a priori conditions of all possible experience free from presupposition of any factual existence and yet " producible in an absolute identity for every conceivable exemplification of its pure concepts" (ibid., p. 351).

Keeping in mind this brief phenomenologically motivated clarification of the concepts of sets and mathematical objects in general one may get back to the epistemological aspects of the maximality concept. A key argument against the constructibility axiom, besides plausibility associated with the maximum iterative concept of sets is, as already said, the existence of large cardinals (i.e., those above inaccessible ones) whose existence contradicts $V = L$. Hauser states a propos " [...] the large cardinals not found in L furnish a combinatorial analysis of the transcendency of V over L", (Hauser 2004, p. 103), an example of its kind being the Silver indiscernibles and $0^\sharp$ which, along with the fact that L can be studied from within V under large cardinal hypotheses but not vice versa, leads many set-theorists to take as evident that $V = L$ is false. In fact Hauser's argumentation on an intrinsic plausibility against $V = L$ is intended to ultimately lead the way to an extra-mathematical, in fact a subjectively based treatment of the plausibility of an axiom as inextricably bound to the meaning of the primitive terms it contains, among them, the intended meaning of the concept of set.

Naturally the debate between those having a positive view of $V = L$, those outright opposing it, and those who, prompted by some technical results, subscribe to a mutual interpretability rather than a mutual exclusion of **ZFC** + $V = L$ and **ZFC** + 'large cardinals', brings manifestly into the fore the epistemic character of the maximum iterative concept of sets. In the first place, one can point to a circularity in the content of the maximum iterative concept since any metamathematical interpretation of this term must apply at this level the same set-theoretic contents that it is supposed to explain. Further, explanations of set theoretical notions and principles in terms of the maximum iterative concept taken as metaphorical are justified on the ground that such explanations hinge on a mathematical activity performed by a

---

[27] Here I must refer to some phenomenological concepts I apply, for which the reader may further consult Husserl's *Ideas I*, Husserl (1976), *Experience and Judgment*, Husserl (1939), as well as other Husserlian works. Summarily, a noematic object corresponding to the phenomenological notion of noema is an object as meant, said to be constituted by certain modes as a well-defined object immanent to the temporal flux of a subject's consciousness (Husserl 1976, *Engl. transl.*, pp. 240–245). By eidetic laws or eidetic attributes in the world of phenomena one can roughly communicate to a non-phenomenologist what relates to the existence of objects or states-of-affairs as regularities by essential necessity and not by mere facticity. One may also consult E. Husserl's *Ideas I*; Husserl (1976), *Engl. transl.*, pp. 12–15.

mind different from ours insofar it entails e.g., " running through an infinite multitude up to the point where its entire range is overviewed, completing the process of selecting different multitudes of integers from the set of all integers, etc." (Arrigoni 2011, p. 356). However if someone reduces the supposedly epistemic character of the maximum iterative concept of sets to the ways a mathematical mind performs definite mathematical acts, for instance in the process of forming subsets of ω given the unavailability of an exhaustive technique of omitting elements of ω in forming new and new subsets of it, it seems to be a direct means to enter the field of subjective constitution even if one may be superficially stuck to various versions of platonistic idealism as well as to the appeal to an idealized infinite mind. The latter concept may be thought of as contradicting *in rem* the notion of the construction of a universe of sets through stages along the ordinals as a time-evolving act.

It is notable that the talk of maximizing over $V = L$ has become over time, on the epistemological level, quite confusing to the point that theorists who argue against $V = L$ are not ready to accept a maximizing role for $V \neq L$ either. This is the case of Maddy who, motivated by naturalistic concerns,[28] regards the simple theory $V \neq L$ as 'nevertheless unattractive' " for it is too weak to settle any of the outstanding open questions, and though it does, strictly speaking, provide a new isomorphism type, it tells us nothing about that type, which makes it pretty much unusable.[...] If the only theory strongly maximizing over T is a non-starter like ZFC + $V \neq L$, it again seems that T is not restricting set theory from developing in any direction we might be inclined to take." (Maddy 1997, p. 230).

5 The Unattainability of Cantor's Absolute by Subjectively Founded Arguments

In the preceding sections my intention was to review Cantor's essentially philosophical-metaphysical conception of the Absolute,—as a maximum above and beyond the transfinite constructions implemented by the two generation principles,[29]—in terms of the set-theoretical universe V as it is commonly understood in set-theory especially after the introduction of von Neumann's cumulative hierarchy of sets. On these grounds I entered into a thorough review of certain questions in the evolving theory of large cardinals toward the goal of attaining an ultimate large cardinal whose consistency with the existing **ZFC** theory would entail its consistency

---

[28] Even though Maddy claims to be driven by naturalistic motivations in the general sense that "the entities to be admitted are just those posited by and studied in the natural sciences, and that the methods of justification and explanation are somehow continuous with those of the natural sciences", she argues against $V = L$ and in favor of the acceptance of various large cardinal axioms from a point to view that does not always conform to a conventional naturalistic attitude. I refer in particular to her claim that mathematics in general and set theory in particular are susceptible of interpretation in their own right independently of relationships to natural sciences (Feferman et al. 2000, p. 409).

[29] By the first principle of generation a given number γ is followed by its successor $\gamma + 1$. By he second principle to any given 'definite succession' of numbers, e.g. an integer sequence, is assigned a least upper bound. See also Sect. 1.

with all lower rank cardinalities. A key conclusion resulting from the discussion is that underlying the model-theoretic structures built in the process of achieving ever greater cardinalities (e.g., inner models, elementary embeddings, generic extensions, etc.) are logical assumptions or principles which are either impossible to be expressed (or derivable) by the formal language of a mathematical universe, think of the notion of an infinite set as a unity in the actual now, or are proved independent of the existing **ZF** axioms, think of the *Axiom of Choice*. One could say that without these assumptions one can hardly produce anything of value in infinitary mathematics.[30] One would even say that these assumptions (or their formal-logical implications) explicitly or implicitly are reproduced in a somewhat circular mode independently of the strength of cardinality and the consistency level attained, a fact that may be considered a de facto clue to their reduction to an 'extra-theoretical' level of discourse. One that is, as I will further argue, subjectively founded in a non-reductionistic, phenomenologically based approach. This owes mainly to the conviction that phenomenology as an eidetic-descriptive science is not only relevant with the epistemology of positive sciences[31] but furthermore has important things to say about a presumed 'ontology' of mathematics. To this end I present the following stepwise approach.

Prompt 1: Talking about the mathematical infinite one must have in mind that this is not about a spatio-temporal and consequently causally articulated infinity, otherwise one would simply not be able to deal with infinite objects as completed wholes in terms of a formal theory. Husserl had in *Logical Investigations* a clear idea of how infinity may be conceived of as an immanence in consciousness: " The fact that we freely extend spatial and temporal stretches in imagination, that we can put ourselves in imagination at each fancied boundary of space or time while ever new spaces and times emerge before our inward gaze - all this does not prove the relative foundedness (*Fundierung*) of bits of space and time, and so does not prove space and time to be *really* infinite, or even that they could be *really* infinite, nor even that they really can be so. This can only be proved by a law of causation, which presupposes, and so requires, the possibility of being extended beyond any given boundary" (Husserl 1984, Engl. transl., p. 45).

A notion of immanent infinity that is subjectively founded and re-presentable as a completed whole at any instant of reflection cannot, in Husserl's view, be a fully determined 'individual being' and as such is open to a noematic horizon which is eidetically pre-fixed yet susceptible to new clarifications and breakthroughs through acquired mathematical experience and categorial elaboration. Specified in a logical-mathematical context one can characterize as eidetic attributes those attributes invariably and irreducibly possessed by mathematical objects, e.g., the property of ordinals to be transitive sets under the set-theoretic inclusion $\in$ which in turn underlies

---

[30] Cantor remarked, in a letter to Hilbert in 1897, that a collection of well-defined, distinguished elements of our intuition or thought conceived as a whole is "only possible if a 'being together' is possible" without clarifying the conditions or laws under which the distinct elements can be united into a whole (Hauser 2013, p. 11). Given his metaphysically leaning attitude, however, one can safely assume that these conditions were taken to be of an ontological nature, therefore presumably not subjectively based.

[31] See e.g., Husserl (1973), pp. 205–206.

absoluteness properties of mathematical objects in set-theoretic extensions. In these terms a fairly large number of derivative notions (e.g., genericity, cofinality, regularity of cardinals, collapsing processes, ultrafilter properties, etc.) essentially hinge on a conception of infinity in this subjectively founded sense with an accompanying notion of preservation of eidetic properties of objects or states-of-affairs throughout.

Prompt 2: If spatio-temporality of infinity and causality are reciprocal terms how to explain notions of logical implication or contradiction, in general of all that is consequential on account of presupposed or pre-existing conditions in having gotten rid of a 'mundane' character of infinity? Furthermore, is there an 'internal' foundation to account for the co-existence and co-succession in establishing a predicative judgment especially in cases where universal and existential quantifiers are applied over arbitrary sets as domains? Husserl treated such questions by appealing to the factor that poses objectivity in terms of constituting temporality and that is what he described as the absolute flux of consciousness with its specific modes of constituting within the world of phenomena. Of course since it is not given for someone doing research in the philosophical-epistemological aspects of set-theory or of mathematical foundations to be well-versed about phenomenology especially across its particularly broad spectrum, I will restrict myself to arguing strictly in terms of the logical-mathematical questions posed.

Concerning the question of the foundation of an alternative form of causality in the absence of an objective real-world infinity, Husserl appealed to a priori forms of absolute consciousness by which each positing of an object or state-of-affairs refers, to the extent this is meant as intentionally applied, to a prior object or state-of-affairs within a past memory. This is a kind of correlation between an original present, a receding past and an awaiting future that is founded on a priori intentional forms of consciousness and as such is essentially different from causality as understood in objective-physical terms even though it does not preclude it as a *post a priori* state. Thus 'anterior' consciousness motivates possibilities for the 'succeeding' stage a priori and makes that the latter insofar as it has the character of an empirical positing is necessarily motivated in its facticity from the former, this motivation having the particularity of a rational act (Husserl 1973, pp. 356–357).

Then there is the question of a sound foundation for the possibilities of co-existence (or co-succession) of logical-mathematical objects and their meaning-contents, a pre-condition for the articulation of meaningful mathematical propositions, theorems, proofs, etc, more generally for the articulation of a meaningful mathematical discourse. Evidently there is no possibility of reduction to a unity founded on objective real terms for that would automatically eliminate the possibility of co-existence. For this reason one must concede that the underlying foundation must be of a temporality other than the objective one, a temporality that would make possible actual impression, immediate memory, (awaited) immediate future all re-presentable at once, at will or even passively, in a way that by the noema attributed to individual objects (or state-of-affairs) one could proceed to noemas of higher-order entities (e.g., of classes of objects), to relations, inferences, etc. This is, in fact, a way to proceed to a conception of a plurality of objects, physical or formal, real or imaginary ones in terms of the unity of a whole, insofar as they are re-presentable as immanent ones within consciousness, a fact that is only possible by reducing unity to its temporal essence and placing an absolute subjectivity as the constitutive origin of homogenous temporal unity. If Cantor's vague predicative condition of 'being together' to define a collection of well-meant objects as sets or Husserl's retrospective apprehension (*rückgreifendes Erfassen*), an act whose content is the thematization of a collectivity of objects as an objective whole by the constituting ego,[32] are going to have a real meaning and not be a mere *façon de parler* they have to be conditioned on a continuous unity susceptible to be reduced in turn to inner temporality. A unity which must be of the same species irrespectively of the power, in terms of the multiplicity of elements, of the domains of corresponding formal structures. In fact this is a unity which is 'extra-theoretically' ever present in the background so long as we talk about collections of objects in the sense of contents-meanings as unities, being all the more evident in case we proceed to the realm of non-denumerable infinity in which case this kind of unity may be taken as a non-reductionistic foundation[33] for the intuitive continuum and further the mathematical continuum in L. E. J. Brouwer's intuitionistic sense (van Atten et al. 2002, p. 205). To the extent that the continuum of the real numbers may be seen to be inherently associated with this kind of subjectively founded unity it might offer an alternative rationale to Feferman's claim that the *Continuum Hypothesis* is an inherently vague statement and that " the continuum itself, or equivalently the power set of the natural numbers, is not a definite mathematical object" (Feferman et al. 2000, p. 405). Further, the ways to accede to ever stronger infinite cardinalities by the mainstream methods reviewed in the previous sections are essentially reducible to performing consistent projections of well-founded mathematical acts in accordance with finitistic 'natural' intuitions[34] against a continuous unity in actual presence whose predicative postulation proves always elusive. Clearly on these grounds one may pose the question of whether there exists indeed on purely logical grounds an infinity greater than the power of the continuum as any known process of establishing greater infinities is circularly conditioned on assumptions associated with the acceptance of an indefinite unity of a lower rank as discussed above. Moreover on the supposition of the existence of an ultimate infinity in the sense of Cantor's Absolute, consistent with the existing 'lower-rank' axioms, someone would naturally raise the question, in accepting a phenomenologically motivated approach, of whether such an infinity would be compatible after all with the constituting and eidetic capacities of a subject's consciousness, therefore whether it could be positable in consciousness as an indisputable evidence and an 'ontologically' legitimate one.

Prompt 3: The question of infinity and its relation to mathematical concepts and methods both in epistemological and purely philosophical aspects has been a debated issue since Greek antiquity, think, e.g., of Platon's metaphysical view of

---

[32] See: Husserl (1939), pp. 246–247.

[33] This means that one does not perform a reduction of the intuitive continuum to a constitutive consciousness in terms of the biological-neuronic structure of the brain possibly down to the quantum level.

[34] In this sense I cite, for instance, the 'curtailing' of uncountable inconsistent conditions by the *Countable Chain Condition* restriction to preserve the power of cardinals along forcing extensions, (Kunen 1982, p. 205) or the diagonalizing through all strategies, in assuming *AC*, to prove that there is an undetermined set $A \subseteq \omega^\omega$ (Kanamori 2012b, p. 381).

infinity in *Timaeus* and Aristotle's concept of potential and actual infinite in *Metaphysics*. The possibility of arithmetization of infinity was an issue too, either on the scale of the infinitely grand or the infinitely small, and culminated after the great progress of the analysis of 19th century in Cantor's research results on the transfinite numbers. As a historical instance to be accounted for, a prime point of discord between Hilbert and Brouwer was the place of the infinite in the former's finitisctic formalism in which case Hilbert rejected the intuitionists' arguments on infinity as superfluous and dubious.[35] Yet as set-theory and foundational mathematics gained currency from early 20th century on at the same time battling over inter-theoretical consistency issues, the suspicion that something like a key piece of the puzzle was missing was hanging among set-theorists and logicians especially in view of Gödel's incompleteness results and his prolific *What is Cantor's Continuum problem?* The story afterwards, especially in view of Cohen's independence results, is more or less known and to some extent presented in this article. Even though significant research projects are in progress on the matter I am still of the opinion that the question of an absolute infinity in the form of an all-inclusive cardinality consistent with the whole 'ascending' context is not resolvable by the means of a formal theory without circular assumptions (referrable to some kind of impredicative continuum) or intermediate independent results. A favorable argumentation along this way is A. Badiou's *Being and Event* and his subsequent work where, by calling the entity that seems to bear certain common traits with infinity in the described sense an indiscernible multiple, he claims that: " The revolution introduced by Cohen in 1963 responds in the affirmative: there exists an ontological concept of the indiscernible multiple." (Badiou 2005, p. 355). He seems to disregard however the possibility of a temporal foundation of this kind of 'elusive' infinity, in the particular context of Cohen's forcing theory in which it is primarily treated in Badiou (2005), nor does he make any allusion to a possible subjective origin of the presumed ontology of an indiscernible multiple.

For Husserl unity as such as well as the re-identifying unity of objects as abstract representations within consciousness is temporally founded whereupon this kind of unity, being essentially the 'infinity' within consciousness, as a form of the absolute consciousness[36] is a pre-condition for the constitution of objective time and space, " the non-temporal ground for the constitution of endless time and an endless in the time extended world" (Husserl 1973, p. 16). If, in recurring fashion, we ask for the ultimate origin of the absolute consciousness and therefore of the immanent infinity we have to pass to the totally transcendental concept of the Husserlian pure ego. This is apparently the dead-end of any epistemological discussion about the origin of the mathematical infinite and the possibility of attaining the absolute infinite as an all encapsulating maximum.

---

[35] Prompted by this controversy Oskar Becker set out to argue in Becker (1927) that the indefinite even in the metamathematical assumptions of Hilbert's theory is not avoided and is not avoidable. See Becker (1927), pp. 485–494.

[36] For details on the being of absolute consciousness, as well as its temporal essence and its proper intentional forms the interested reader may look into Husserl's *On the Phenomenology of Inner-Time Consciousness*, Husserl (1966).

References

Arrigoni T (2011) $V = L$ and intuitive plausibility in set theory. A case study. Bull Symb Logic 17(3):337–360
Arrigoni T, Friedman D-S (2012) Foundational implications of the Inner Model Hypothesis. Ann Pure Appl Logic 163:1360–1366
Badiou A (2005) Being and Event, transl. O. Feltham. Continuum, London
Becker O (1927) Mathematische Existenz: Untersuchungen zur Logik und Ontologie mathematischer Phänomene. Jahrbuch für Philosophie und phänomenologische Forschung 8:439–768
Cantor G (1887/88) Mitteilungen zur Lehre vom Transfiniten, Zeitschrift für Philosophie und philosophische Kritik, 91 (1887): 81–125 and 92 (1888): 240–265
Feferman S et al (eds) (1990) Kurt Gödel: collected works, vol 2. Oxford University Press, Oxford
Feferman S et al (eds) (1995) Kurt Gödel: collected works 3. Oxford University Press, Oxford
Feferman S (1999) Does mathematics need new axioms? Am Math Monthly 106(2):99–111
Feferman S, Friedman MH, Maddy P, Steel J (2000) Does mathematics need new axioms? Bull Symb Logic 6(4):401–446
Friedman DS (2006) Internal consistency and the inner model hypothesis. Bull Symb Logic 12(4):591–600
Hauser K (2004) Was sind und was sollen neue Axiome? In: Link G (ed) One hundred year of Russel's paradox. De Gruyter, Berlin, pp 93–117
Hauser K (2013) Cantor's absolute in metaphysics and mathematics. Int Philos Quart 53(2):161–188
Husserl E (1939) Erfahrung und Urteil, hsgb. L. Landgrebe, Prag: Acad./Verlagsbuchhandlung. English translation, (1973), Experience and Judgment, transl. JS Churchill, K Americs. Routledge & Kegan P, London
Husserl E (1966) Vorlesungen zur Phänomenologie des inneren Zeibewusstseins, Hua Band X, hsgb. R. Boehm. M. Nijhoff, Den Haag
Husserl E (1973) Zur Phänomenologie der Intersubjektivität, Hua XIII, Erster Teil, (ed. I Kern). M. Nijhoff, The Hague
Husserl E (1976) Ideen zu einer reinen Phänomenologie und phänomenologischen Philosophie, Erstes Buch, Hua Band III/I, hsgb. K. Schuhmann, Den Haag: M. Nijhoff. English translation: (1983), Ideas pertaining to a pure phenomenology and to a phenomenological philosophy: First Book, transl. F. Kersten. M. Nijhoff, The Hague
Husserl E (1984) Logische Untersuchungen, Hua Band XIX/1, hsgb. U Panzer. M. Nijhoff, The Hague. English translation: (2001) Logical investigations (trans: Findlay JN). Routledge
Jensen R (1995) Inner models and large cardinals. Bull Symb Logic 1(4):393–407
Kanamori A (2009) The higher infinite. Springer, Berlin
Kanamori A (2012a) Set theory from Cantor to Cohen. In: Gabbay MD, Kanamori A, Woods J (eds) Handbook of the history of logic, vol 6. Elsevier B. V, Oxford, pp 1–72
Kanamori A (2012b) Large cardinals with forcing. In: Gabbay MD, Kanamori A, Woods J (eds) Handbook of the history of logic, vol 6. Elsevier B. V, Oxford, pp 359–415
Keisler HJ, Tarski A (1964) From accessible to inaccessible cardinals. Fund Math LIII:225–308
Kunen K (1971) Elementary embeddings and infinitary combinatorics. J Symb Log 36(3):407–413
Kunen K (1982) Set Theory. An introduction to independence proofs. Elsevier, Amsterdam
Lévy A, Solovay R (1967) Measurable cardinals and the continuum hypothesis. Isr J Math 5(4):234–248
Maddy P (1997) Naturalism in mathematics. Oxford University Press, New York
Mitchell JW (2012) Inner Models for Large Cardinals. In: Gabbay MD, Kanamori A, Woods J (eds) Handbook of the History of Logic, 6. Elsevier B. V, Oxford, pp 415–456
Moore HG, Garciadiego A (1981) Burali–Forti's Paradox: a reappraisal of its origins. Historia Mathematica 8:319–350
Moschovakis Y (2009) Descriptive set theory, mathematical surveys and monographs, vol 155. AMS, Providence
Rittberg JC (2015) How Woodin changed his mind: new thoughts on the Continuum hypothesis. Arch Hist Exact Sci 69:125–151
Scott D (1961) Measurable cardinals and constructible sets. BAPS 9:521–524
van Atten M, Van Dalen D, Tieszen R (2002) Brouwer and Weyl: the phenomenology and mathematics of the intuitive Continuum. Philosophia Mathematica 10(3):203–226

Wang H (1974) The concept of set. In: Wang H (ed) From mathematics to philosophy. Routledge & Kegan, London, pp 81–123

Woodin HW (2011) The Realm of the Infinite. In: Heller M, Woodin HW (eds) Infinity, new research frontiers. Cambridge University Press, New York, pp 89–118

Woodin HW (2017) In search of ultimate-L: the 19th midrasha mathematicae lectures. Bull Symb Log 23(1):1–109

Abolishing Platonism in Multiverse Theories

Abstract
A debated issue in the mathematical foundations in at least the last two decades is whether one can plausibly argue for the merits of treating undecidable questions of mathematics, e.g., the Continuum Hypothesis (CH), by relying on the existence of a plurality of set-theoretical universes except for a single one, i.e., the well-known set-theoretical universe V associated with the cumulative hierarchy of sets. The multiverse approach has some varying versions of the general concept of multiverse yet my intention is to primarily address ontological multiversism as advocated, for instance, by Hamkins or Väänänen, precisely for the reason that they proclaim, to the one or the other extent, ontological preoccupations for the introduction of respective multiverse theories. Taking also into account Woodin's and Steel's multiverse versions, I take up an argumentation against multiversism, and in a certain sense against platonism in mathematical foundations, mainly on subjectively founded grounds, while keeping an eye on Clarke-Doane's concern with Benacerraf's challenge. I note that even though the paper is rather technically constructed in arguing against multiversism, the non-negligible philosophical part is influenced to a certain extent by a phenomenologically motivated view of the matter.

1 Introduction

A key issue in the current debate among set-theorists about the concept of multiverse is the way one may assess the argumentation in favor or against multiversism in set-theory and the mathematical foundations. In a deeper sense this

Abolishing Platonism in Multiverse Theories

debate concerns the content and the terms in which the conflicting views about multiversism or universism are brought out to the fore. Of course the debate on the mathematical universe vs. multiverse approach has almost nothing to do with the corresponding debate among cosmologists regarding the single vs. multiple universes approach insofar as by mathematical universe one normally understands the conventional set-theoretical universe V in terms of which all meaningful mathematics can be done.[1] As to the multiverse approach the question of whether this term stands for a multiplicity of mathematical universes distinct from the conventional one V, the answer depends on the philosophical leanings one might have in terms of a presumed ontological (or other) content of mathematics, something that will be made clear concerning my own philosophical attitude in the next sections.

A key motivation in the setting and elaboration of the pro-multiversism arguments is the fact that some set-theoretical statements of fundamental importance, first and foremost the *Continuum Hypothesis* (**CH**),[2] whose independence in terms of existing mathematical models has puzzled set-theorists and logicians for decades, are thought to be better approached in an 'ontological' sense by multiverse theory. This means that that their independence would not be a de facto result owing perhaps to an insufficiency of the existing axiomatical machinery of the **ZFC+AC** (Zermelo-Fraenkel plus the Axiom of Choice) theory, something that reflected also Gödel's intuitions from the time of *What is Cantor's Continuum Hypothesis?* (1947), but it would rather reflect a situation in which, for instance, the statement of **CH** and its negation are 'ontologically' justified as being true in distinct universes belonging to a multiverse, the latter thought of as a determinate reality at least by ontological multiversism. My intention in this article is to show that key set-theoretical concepts such as absoluteness, countability, generic extension and continuity-as-unity employed with a purely logical content hinge on an irreducible 'affinity' of the multitude of universes inside a multiverse possibly interpretable in subjective-constitutive terms and thus making its conception a rather 'heuristic' tool for handling certain set-theoretical pathologies. Besides, if the set-theoretical quest for maximization and unification in the context of large cardinals theories and the convergence toward an all-encompassing set-theoretical universe V in the sense of Cantor's Absolute can be achieved by means of inner models and forcing extensions within the 'standard' universe V, why bother to enter into the complexities and, after all, the ontological subtleties of multiverse theories?

To be more concrete one may put up an argument against multiversism on account of the claim associated with the ontological multiverse view that "There is no absolute background concept of set and of other set-theoretic notions, such as set, ordinal, cardinal", a consequence of which is that the constructible universe L may not have the same ordinals as the set-theoretical universe V (Ternullo 2019, pp. 60–61). This is due to the fact that the concepts ordinal^L and ordinal^V are not the same

---

[1] I point out, however, that in adding 'almost' next to 'nothing to do' I reserve a clue to a possible interpretational connection between the mathematical and physical versions of universe - multiplicity of universes in this section (par. 5).

[2] The generalized version of the *Continuum Hypothesis* will be abbreviated in the text as **GCH**.

as there is no absolute background concept of ordinals. It follows in a multiversist sense, contrary to the mainstream view of most logicians and set-theorists including Maddy's account of mathematical naturalism in Maddy (2002), that Gödel's axiom $V = L$ is not inherently restrictive[3] in a context of discussion guided by the drive toward maximization and unification in the foundations of mathematics.

As it happens often with newly appearing trends in the philosophy of mathematics the multiversist approach has branched out in distinct versions depending on the particularities in the formal treatment of the subject matter and possibly on the epistemological or philosophical predilections of the researchers of the field. Far from being of a compelling character a categorization of the multiversist approach proposed by Ternullo could be as follows: **(a)** naive multiversism succinctly put as the idea that "no single model $\mathcal{M}$ of a theory of sets T, should be viewed as 'special', as being the universe of sets, the collection of all sets" **(b)** instrumental multiversism in which multiverses might be an important mathematical tool, yet their ontological as well as epistemological status could be irrelevant in view of their usability *in rem*. Research programmes in this specific category can be regarded Woodin's set-generic multiverse and Friedman's *et al* Hyperuniverse Programme (HP) **(c)** ontological multiversism which is the view that a multiverse is a determinate, independently existing reality "consisting of particular entities, the models of set theory". A major instance of such platonistic conception is Hamkin's version of multiversism (Ternullo 2019, pp. 47–51).

I will mostly address ontological multiversism, even if there is no such thing as a tight compartmentalization of the versions above, for the main reason that except for the elaboration of major questions having been made in line with this version it stands, regarding the multiverse story, as a showcase of the platonistic trend in the philosophy of mathematics. In view of my subjectivist philosophical inclination, more precisely one phenomenologically oriented, my argumentation against ontological multiversism will be accordingly calibrated in the next sections in favor of a subjectively founded approach both at the level of theory and at that of epistemological or ontological content. In terms of the latter it seems that such an approach might give a sense to the question of whether one can draw a parallel between the concept of a plurality of universes in cosmology and that of the mathematical multiverse. For, in the author's view, only on account of the constitutive-eidetic[4] capacities of a subject as invariably applied independently of context can this question be a meaningful one given that in the first place a material, spatiotemporal universe should have no relation whatsoever with the purely formal character of a mathematical universe. But this story sits in a different and rather uncharted territory to be told here in any further detail.

---

[3] Gödel's axiom $V = L$ essentially identifying the set-theoretic universe V with the constructible universe L is generally thought to be restrictive in the sense of imposing the predicative formation of sets across ordinals in L to the universe V. Notably $V = L$ has been proved consistent with **ZFC** theory if **ZFC** is. See for details Kunen (1982), Ch. VI.

[4] By eidetic laws or eidetic attributes in the world of phenomena one can roughly communicate to a non-phenomenologist what on subjective grounds holds of the existence of objects or states-of-affairs as regularities by essential necessity and not by mere facticity. One may consult a propos E. Husserl's *Ideas I*: Husserl 1983, *Engl. transl.*, pp. 12–15.

If my approach can be regarded as an argumentation against multiversism articulated mostly in subjectively founded terms, one may yet find arguments against (Hamkins') multiversism in purely logical-mathematical terms, even if in essentially metatheoretical ones. This is N. Barton's argumentation in Barton (2016) in which a sound ontology of universes associated with referent models (e.g., mathematical models correlated with set-theoretical concepts) can be refuted on the grounds of Skolem-Löwenheim Theorem. As known, the latter means that if a theory has an infinite model then it can have non-isomorphic models of every infinite cardinality including the countable one. It is known by this theorem that first-order theories are completely unable to uniquely determine their models up to isomorphism, consequently one cannot pick out a model (universe) in a unique fashion and after implementing whatever mathematical construction might choose move to another model-universe and thus vindicate Hamkins' multiversism in the first place. Furthermore, given that choosing a precise universe corresponding to a particular concept of set is impossible as one may only refer to models using concepts expressed as first-order axiomatisations, one can reach an infinite regression of set-theoretical backgrounds, an option out of which would be a genuine selection of particular set-theoretic backgrounds as more privileged than others. This would entail, contrary to ontological multiversism, that some key model-theoretic constructions should be absolute with respect to these models, which would in turn "require a stock of absolutely understood concepts, sufficiently rich in character that we can identify determinately a class of set-theoretic backgrounds" (ibid. pp. 197–198 and pp. 203–204).

As most set-theorists consider the *Continuum Hypothesis* (**CH**) an absolutely undecidable proposition, a major theme of discussion could be whether we may reasonably argue for an ontological foundation of **CH**, an assumption that might help impose a de facto plurality of universes and thus vindicate the strong ontological multiversism for which a multiverse is a determined reality consisting of actually existing distinct entities in the respective set-theoretical constructions. Indicative of the key influence absolutely undecidable statements like **CH** bear on the conception of the multiverse is Steel's attempt through his *MV* axioms to prescribe a collection of universes (sharing anyway **ZFC** and large cardinals theories) which would agree with each other on **CH**, resulting in a (presumably provisional) failure that has pushed him into searching the limits of expressibility of the multiverse language. Even if by an elementary forcing argument it can be shown that the multiverse may have a uniquely definable world included in all others, called the core of the multiverse, it is still true by Steel's confession that "Neither *MV* (axioms) nor its extensions by large cardinal hypotheses of the sort we currently understand decides whether there is a core to the multiverse, or the basic theory of this core if it exists" (Steel 2014, pp. 168–169).

It happens that **CH**, being a $\sum_{1}^{2}$ statement expressible in terms of second-order predicate calculus, presupposes a firm grasp of the concept of all subsets of an infinite countable set which is a persisting source of controversy over the epistemological aspects of the **CH** undecidability. Moreover it not only raises the question of whether second-order logic is in fact logic as it appeals to the concept of all subsets of an infinite set on which we do not have a firm grasp but also of "whether full second-order logical truth is a sufficiently determinate notion to be of interpretational use" (Horsten 2019, p. 87). On this account the **CH** undecidability and the general context in which it is brought about may be further seen as pointing to the subtleties of an extra-theoretical, indeed subjectively founded level of discourse for which more will be said in the epistemologically-philosophically oriented Sect. 6.

It should be made clear at this point that platonistic tendencies in multiverse theories and more generally in mathematical foundations are to be construed in the general sense conveyed by the term mathematical platonism which can be succinctly said to be the view that mathematics 'exists' independently of human beings 'out there somewhere' hovering in the realm of platonic eternal ideas. In this view the existence of mathematical objects is objective independently of our knowledge of them so that even the most abstruse of mathematical objects, for instance uncountably infinite sets, sets with larger than $\aleph_1$ cardinalities, space-filling curves and so on, lie 'somewhere' as definite objects, with definite properties available to get to be known if they are not already, in a way that even undecided (e.g., the *Continuum Hypothesis*) mathematical hypotheses have a definite answer waiting for the humans to find it out (Davis and Hersh 1982, p. 68, 318).[5] My own general view being at odds with mathematical platonism, I'll try to show in the next how the platonistic sense of multiversism can be weakened in intra-theoretical terms in favor of an approach that takes into account the constitutive capacities of a subjective factor and the kind of mathematical intuitions it implies. After all, even though the ordinary working mathematician would shun all talk about the epistemological or ontological content his purely mathematical work might have, and the same would go for a multiversist doing the hard mathematics of the subject, he would still hardly avoid the question of the epistemological-ontological implications of his results and the philosophical attitude that serves them better. For instance, Feferman's claim that the **CH** hypothesis "has ceased to exist as a definite problem in the ordinary sense and that even its status in the logical sense is seriously in question"[6] is indicative of the fact that specific philosophical preoccupations and their interpretational agility may underlie even *prima facie* pure mathematical stuff.

An option could be to deny the outright adoption of universes within the multiverse as really existing in a platonic sense and instead construe the ontological multiversism's use of concepts within the framework of a concept expansion, a view of M. Buzaglo in Buzaglo (2002). The main principles of this approach are the following:

---

[5] A kind of mathematical platonism is often attributed to Gödel, yet even if this has a solid base it is also true that Gödel especially in his later years was allured by Husserl's phenomenology and this was reflected in a certain sense in the view he held of mathematical objects as implying a special kind of intuition we have of them forced by mathematical objects upon us. For more details on this matter the reader may see Livadas (2019).

[6] See Feferman, S: 'The Continuum Hypothesis is neither a definite mathematical problem nor a definite logical problem', p. 2, a revised version of Feferman (2011).

"(1) concepts are flexible constructs; (2) the expansion of a concept is a law-like, forced process, that is, it is guided by the 'stretching' of some pre-established laws (axioms) which force the concept to evolve in a way which is unavoidable and, above all, (3) concept expansion gives rise to new objects.

I set out to comment on these principles, especially on (3), in view of the mathematical experience of the introduction of nonstandard entities within a standard system and further from a more philosophically oriented position with regard to the introduction of absoluteness in the context of formal-mathematical theories in the sense of a concept having a metatheoretical origin and having accordingly such kind of consequences.

2 Concept Expansion and Inter-Theoretical Constraints

It is true that after the Greeks' use of incommensurate magnitudes as a direct product of concrete mathematical practice, talk about nonstandard quantities took a more formal shape through the introduction and use of infinitesimals by Newton and Leibniz in the course of the systematic development of mathematical calculus. My attention will be primarily drawn to the formal introduction of nonstandard elements by axiomatical means, e.g., to A. Robinson's introduction of nonstandard numbers.

In this sense the extensional part of nonstandard analysis whose significant parts can be considered Robinson's axiomatical construction in Robinson (1966), and Zakon's nonstandard ultrapower constructs in Zakon and Robinson (1969), is thought to be fundamentally based on extensions of the classical Cantorian objects of mathematics, whereas the intensional part of non-standard analysis is based on the subjective observations of a potential 'observer' implemented in a local and non-Cantorian way inside an intersubjective universe.

Robinson's quest of ideal elements, in a model theorist's saturation approach, is implemented inside the domain of consistent enlargements of standard axiomatical structures in a way that is conceptually in accordance with both Leibniz's idea of an extended mathematical universe in the sense of the preservation of standard properties in the extended one and Husserl's idea of consistent enlargements of (relatively) definite formal-deductive systems developed in his Göttingen lectures of 1901 (Livadas (2005), p. 118–119). This means no proposition can be proved inside a B-model of the B-enlargement $H_B = K \cup K_B$ of a stratified set of sentences K which when restricted in all its variables to the domain of K cannot be decided in the model M of K (Robinson 1966, pp. 33–34). In fact from an ontological viewpoint Robinson's nonstandard numbers are by-products of theoretical constructions involving universal quantification formulas inside an indefinite horizon of finite sets of constants occurring in a stratified set of sentences K and may be accordingly intuited as exceeding any standard entity of common intuition.

However as a reminder that an extended theory generated by the 'stretching' of existing standard axioms may be essentially constrained by principles on the level of ground theory proven themselves undecidable, nonstandard theories rely in a substantial way on the *Axiom of Choice* or its logical equivalents or on certain *ad hoc* extension principles in other alternative nonstandard theories. For instance, the

Axiom of Choice or its logically equivalent Zorn's lemma are applied both in Robinson's introduction of nonstandard elements by the construction of B-enlargements of standard models and in Zakon's non-constructive version of equivalence classes of infinite sequences modulo an ultrafilter over the set of natural numbers (Livadas 2005, p. 125). In fact there is no concept or principle 'embedded' in a nonstandard theory that outright contradicts, at least on the ground level, the standard intuition of sets as well as the intuitions of well-ordering, of ordinals, of global choice, etc.

In the formal-deductive level, as Robinson conceded, nonstandard models are constructed within the framework of contemporary (classical) mathematics and "thus affirm the existence of all sorts of infinitary entities" (Robinson 1966, p. 282). Yet one is compelled to adjoin to their axiomatical system actual infinity principles, for instance the *Axiom of Choice* or its stronger forms, either in a direct fashion as, e.g. in Zermelo-Fraenkel-Boffa Set Theory with Choice (ZFBC), or indirectly in the details of proofs in the construction of ultraproducts and ultrapowers. The fact is that these axioms or principles presuppose a notion of actual, complete infinity non-eliminable in analytical terms in a sense that fits with natural intuition (Livadas 2005, p. 126). If this brief discussion on nonstandard theories has something to offer to our present reflection on multiversism it is precisely the view that the introduction of new (nonstandard) objects by concept expansion is not unconstrained with regard to standard concepts that eventually appeal to 'finitistic' subjective intuitions.

If Boolean modelization in the formal treatment of foundational questions of mathematics can be considered a concept expansion, then a special place in the current debate has Woodin's generic multiverse which is in fact the Boolean-valued multiverse V_α^B, and the way it is associated with Ω-logic (Woodin 2011, pp. 14–24). The use of the Boolean-valued multiverse or of what would become the set-generic multiverse seems to be an incisive method to elucidate statements of the complexity of **CH** by pointing to what such statements require in terms of solving resources. Even in disregarding that Woodin's assumptions are generally too strong in contradistinction to the naturalness of the *Continuum Hypothesis*, the fact that Ω-provability and consequently Ω-conjecture are conditioned on the introduction of a universally Baire set $A \subseteq R$ to account for the validity of a sentence φ, definitely weakens Woodin's multiverse approach to the truth or falsity of **CH** as it becomes bound to the specific topological structure of the subspace A of the space of reals R. In fact, Woodin's topological constraint put on Ω-provability is not a sole exception in terms of weakening a viable multiverse perspective by such metatheoretical ambivalences. One can even point to 'inner' contradictions in the proof-theoretic structure of multiverse arguments. Take, for instance, Hamkins' assertion that any transitive model M can in principle be 'continued' so that it may ultimately become a model of **ZFC**+ $V = L$, in support of the claim that the principle $V = L$ is not inherently restrictive; "More generally, for any transitive model, we may first collapse it to be countable by forcing, and then carry out the previous argument in the forcing extension. In this way, any transitive set M can in principle exist as a transitive set inside a model of **ZFC** $+ V = L$", (Hamkins 2012, p. 435). The assertion hinges on the conviction that the ontological multiverse is associated with a refutation of the concept of absoluteness for such fundamental set-theoretic notion as it is the concept of ordinals.[7] Yet absoluteness criteria are necessarily applied in all forcing methods including of course the one leading to the statement above.

A particular case against multiversism may be found in Steel's adoption of Weak Absolutism (WA), a compromising statement stating that a reference universe $\dot{V}$ not captured by *MV* axioms,[8] can still make sense as a definable world in its own right included in all other worlds of the multiverse. This means that the multiverse may be reducible to one of its members enjoying a 'preferred' reference status and thus possible to be termed as the core. However WA is dependable on other mathematical conjectures, in particular on the Woodin axiom H which is part of an argument in favor of the concept of a core of multiverse that leads in fact to certain inconveniences. More specifically the Woodin-proposed axiom (i.e., axiom H) roughly stating that the set-theoretical universe V looks like HOD^M for models M of the axiom of determinacy,[9] conducive in the multiverse language to the statement 'the multiverse has a core, and it satisfies Axiom H', can neither be proved as consistent with all large cardinal hypotheses nor as implying **GCH** (while implying **CH**) (Steel 2014, p. 171).

In the Appendix,[10] counting on axiom's H pedagogical value on the matter, I set out to show that the proof-theoretical machinery leading to the axiom $V = \text{HOD}$, and *a fortiori* to its stronger version $V \subseteq \text{HOD}^{V[G]}$, applies certain 'standard'[11] notions developed in the context of large cardinals and inner model theories without the need of taking recourse to radically different concepts which would in turn imply the need for alternative universes.

This will help further strengthen my claim that if 'standard' notions inherently linked with a sense of absoluteness are the gold standard of any meaningful and *a fortiori* insightful mathematical practice, then at least ontological multiversism to the extent that aspires to their 'undermining' may give credit to Ternullo's words that ontological multiversism, for all its professed merits, "is also the most controversial and problematic conception among those examined" (Ternullo (2019, p. 66). The conclusion can sound quite pessimistic having in mind that the other versions of multiversism (the naive and instrumental ones) fail to provide an alternative and supported 'in things themselves' ontological standing.

---

[7] Gödel had noted that there is no element of randomness in the definition of ordinals and hence neither in sets defined in terms of them. He found this particularly clear in von Neumann's definition of ordinals insofar as it is not based on any well-ordering relations of sets which may well involve some random element as applied to various ranks of infinity. See (Gödel 1965, p. 87).

[8] Steel's multiverse (MV) axioms in a two-sorted multiverse language are found in Steel (2014, p. 165).

[9] A set is ordinal definable, **OD**, if and only if it is definable over the universe of sets from ordinal parameters, and is hereditarily ordinal definable, **HOD**, in the case that itself and all members of its transitive closure are ordinal definable. The precise statement of a version of axiom H is found in Steel (2014, p. 171).

[10] The reader who wants to avoid Woodin's extremely technical proofs may well skip the Appendix without losing anything of the general picture.

[11] I use the term standard in quotation marks to refer to certain notions in set-theoretical constructions, like the transitivity of $\in$-inclusion or the well-foundedness, having some direct or indirect relation to the concept of absoluteness or to other concepts linked with natural intuition, to distinguish from the conventional term standard as used in non-standard mathematics.

3 Refuting Hamkins' Argumentation for Multiversism

I set off by drawing attention to Barton's claims that if the intent of Hamkinsian multiversism is to study the multiverse through analyzing models of **ZFC**, he has to stick to a determinateness of **ZFC** which is naturally preconditioned on a determinateness and a well-understanding of the notion of proofs and well-formed formulas, "indicative of the fact that certain notions need to be taken to be absolute. It has long been noted that certain mathematical concepts are necessary for the expression of metalogical definitions. By adhering to a very strong form of relativism, the Multiversist undercuts the very concepts required to properly express her own view" (Barton 2016, pp. 16–17). It turns out that Barton's view may be justly thought compatible with a key position of this article, namely the underlying necessity of absoluteness of certain notions, even though my own argumentation on the matter is justified primarily on subjectively founded grounds.

In the next my position on formal-mathematical grounds against Hamkins' multiversism will be primarily presented by a two-fold argumentation:

First, the refutation of Hamkins' (and generally the proponents' of ontological multiversism) position that one may identify a set concept with the model of set theory to which it gives rise, in other words the refutation of the position that a set concept has no self-standing content but it should be rather referred to the description of the set-theoretic universe in which it is instantiated. On this account a key argumentation of ontological multiversism, namely the discarding of the absoluteness of the concept of set, and further of ordinals, of well-orderings and well-foundedness of sets, can be critically weakened by a counter-argumentation articulated on subjectively founded grounds. This is a position that seems partly in resonance and partly in conflict with the view expressed by Hamkins himself, namely: "The assertion that there are diverse concepts of set is a metamathematical as opposed to a mathematical claim, and one does not expect the properties of the multiverse to be available when undertaking an internal construction within a universe. That is, we do not expect to see the whole multiverse from within any particular universe. Nevertheless, set theory does have a remarkable ability to refer internally to many alternative set concepts, as when we consider definable inner models or various outer models to which we have access" (Hamkins 2012, p. 417). However the fact is that by Skolem's paradox the metamathematical meaning attributed to the notions of inside and outside a universe in a certain sense runs in conflict with Hamkin's position above, namely in terms of the ways an 'inhabitant' of a countable model M, in contrast with someone 'living' outside M, thinks of the countable ordinal ω_1^M (ω_1^M, the first uncountable ordinal relativized to the countable model M) as an uncountable one insofar as there is no function in M from ω onto ω_1^M. Obviously this would not be the case if there was no absolute notion of ω (ω, the first limit countable ordinal) to alter the assumption of the hypothetical 'inhabitant' of M about ω_1^M with regard to that of an 'external observer' to the model M (see Kunen 1982, p. 141).

Second, by refuting a central argument of Hamkins' in defending the ontological multiversism, namely his belief that forcing extensions, for instance the forcing extension $V[G]$ of the universe V (this latter taken as just one universe within a multiverse), can have a real existence even though the generic filter G may not be found in V.[12] As the argument goes even in the non-existence of the generic filter G within V, the extension $V[G]$ can be simulated in V either by the forcing principles or by the Boolean-valued structure V^B. Of course Hamkins concedes to the impossibility of establishing an isomorphic copy of the forcing extension $V[G]$ into the ground model V but he argues that the forcing methods come "maddeningly close" to this and in any case one can have a high accessibility to $V[G]$ from the ground model due to the character of forcing methods (Hamkins 2012, p. 420).

I argue against the position that forcing extensions can have an (ontologically meant) self-standing existence, particularly on the naturalist account of forcing,[13] by a metatheoretical interpretation of the same arguments by which Hamkins defends his brand of multiversism with regard to forcing extensions.

More concretely: Hamkins proved[14] that for any forcing notion P one can have an elementary embedding of the universe V into a class model $\overline{V}$ for which there is a $\overline{V}$-generic filter $G \subseteq \overline{P}$ so that the forcing extension $\overline{V}[G]$ is a definable class in V and $G \in V$. Consequently the universe V may have full access to the model $\overline{V}[G]$ including the generic set G and the way V is mapped to $\overline{V}$ for they are all definable classes in V. The models $\overline{V}$ and $\overline{V}[G]$ are not necessarily transitive or well-founded which makes that their membership relation $\overline{\in}$ is not the standard one associated with transitivity and well-foundedness. However the proof of this theorem relies on the Axiom of Foundation, in virtue of appealing to Scott's trick concerning reduced equivalence classes[15] to form $\overline{V}$ as the collection of equivalence classes of names τ inside V, with the generic set G being the equivalence class $[\dot{G}]_U$ in V where U is an ultrafilter in V 'imitating' the role of the generic set in standard forcing (for details: Hamkins (2012), pp. 423–424).

The payoff for the proponents of (ontological) multiversism is that even though the extended universe $\overline{V}[G]$ may not actually exist, since the proof of Hamkins' theorem does not provide a concrete V-generic filter G, it behaves like it exists in the sense that it is definable in all stages of its construction within V. Yet it is questionable whether the extended model $\overline{V}[G]$ would qualify for an ontologically

---

[12] The case of forcing extensions on the set-theoretic universe V as presumably legitimate universes in their own right can be addressed by universism, on the one hand, as simply model-theoretic representations within V with nothing non-trivial added to the semantics of V, and, on the other hand, by easily accommodating this situation by appealing to the reflection theorem and the downward Skolem-Löwenheim Theorem to define a countable model on which to implement forcing (Barton 2016, p. 4).

[13] The naturalist account of forcing in Hamkins' approach is closely related to the Boolean valued model approach to forcing primarily in the sense that one can implement forcing entirely within **ZFC** without restriction to the kind of models, in particular the countable transitive models in the classical forcing techniques, or without the need to appeal to the metatheory in the proof-theoretic machinery.

[14] See (Hamkins 2012), p. 423.

[15] Scott's trick is a method for giving a definition of equivalence classes in a proper class by referring to the levels of the cumulative hierarchy $V_{\alpha \in ON}$. It is basically a way of assigning representatives to cardinal numbers in **ZF** theory without the Axiom of Choice using the fact that for every set A there is a least rank in the cumulative hierarchy when some set of the same cardinality as A appears. As such Scott's trick makes an essential use of the Axiom of Foundation (Axiom of Regularity).

existing universe given that firstly, it is entirely definable within V and secondly, in the naturalist account of forcing the definability in V is proved with the help of the Scott trick for defining equivalence classes which is conditioned in turn on the Axiom of Foundation. The Axiom of Foundation, however, is inherently linked with the absoluteness of well-ordering,[16] in the understanding of course that the notion of absoluteness of set-theoretical properties is radically denied by ontological multiversism.

At another point Hamkins argues that second-order categoricity arguments "requires one to operate in a context with a background concept of set" which as a matter of fact 'undermines' the absoluteness of the concept of finite natural numbers in terms of the natural procession '1,2,3,...' and *so on*. Hamkins goes as far as to wonder whether the scheme '1, 2, 3, . . .,' and *so on* is meaningful as an absolute characterization of natural numbers or whether there should be the other way round, namely a background concept of set would be *ante* to the concept of natural numbers, in the sense that two different concepts of sets need not agree even on the concept of the natural numbers. Following Hamkins' reasoning, Peano's categoricity proof and therefore the structure of the finite numbers as uniquely determined are conditioned on a background concept of set, and further on a vague understanding of which subsets of the natural numbers really exist, *a fortiori* on the vagueness of existence of the totality of the subsets of natural numbers. Hamkins asks therefore, "why are mathematicians so confident that there is an absolute concept of finite natural number, independent of any set-theoretic concerns, when all of our categoricity arguments are explicitly set-theoretic and require one to commit to a background concept of set?" (ibid., pp. 427–428). Consequently in Hamkins' view one might, just like in forcing methods, modify models of arithmetic by the invention of new technicalities and this would generate new models that would shake the confidence in a unique model of arithmetic, in analogy with the way forcing methods generate new forcing models in extension of ground-level ones.

However I find these arguments deficient for the following reasons: On the purely set-theoretical level one can have nonstandard models of arithmetic only as conservative extensions of the existing standard one. To the extent the axiomatical assumptions applied to generate the extended models are compatible with the existing ones over the standard domain, there can be in principle no reasonable claim to the existence of ontologically diverse models of arithmetic something that might shake our belief to a unique natural number structure.

On a metamathematical, in fact an extra-theoretical level, Hamkins' claim that set-theoretical concerns undermine the absoluteness of natural number statements by reducing them to set-theoretical ones, may fall short on subjectively founded grounds. By this I mean that the intuition of natural numbers and their procession in terms of '1, 2, 3, . . .' and *so on*, on the one hand, and the fixed concept of the set of all subsets of natural numbers, on the other, may be thought of as pointing to two diverse intuitions corresponding to distinct modes of object-constitution on the part of a subject. (**a**) The intuition of natural numbers as discrete enactments of a subject's consciousness (of an a priori intentional character in phenomenological

---

[16] See lemma 4.2, p. 124 in Kunen (1982).

terms), and **(b)** the intuition of a collection of objects, material or abstract ones as mental representations, in the form of a totality in the actual now. I point out that the intuition of a sequence of natural numbers is associated in Van Atten et al. (2002) with the phenomenologically motivated principle of two-ity applied in connection with the progression of choice sequences.[17]

On the other hand the intuition of a set as a totality may point, on phenomenological grounds, to Husserl's view of a set as an original objectivity pre-constituted by an act of colligation of disjunct objects-elements which is 'complemented' by what he called a retrospective apprehension, an act making possible the thematization of a collectivity of objects pre-constituted by the act of colligation into an identifiable and re-identifiable object possibly posited as a substrate of judgments (Husserl 1939, pp. 246–247). This latter act of thematization, in terms of the continuous unity of consciousness, points to the origin of the constituting temporal consciousness in the various denominations Husserl gave to this concept (absolute or pure ego among others). It is remarkable that well in advance of his properly meant transcendental phenomenology phase to which belong these views, Husserl had acknowledged that corresponding to the set-presentation is an objectivity proper to it (a position that probably influenced later Gödel's conceptual realism[18]), namely the set or the multiplicity, for which the "indefiniteness of the left-open continuation of concatenation still precedes the nominalization of the plural 'some' and then makes the transition to nominalization, where a multiplicity, a set, an aggregate results—all, properly understood, synonymous words" (Husserl 2019, p. 172).

In consequence it seems hardly convincing to argue in favor of an ontologically founded translatability between a concept of sets as potentially modifiable by the manipulation of corresponding universes and the concept of absoluteness (e.g., of natural numbers), in taking account that these concepts may be attributable to diverse intentional-constitutive capacities of a rational subject's consciousness. Naturally then Hamkins is led to the controversial assertion that "the multiverse view allows for many different set-theoretic backgrounds, with varying concepts of the well-founded, and there seems to be no reason to support an absolute notion of well-foundedness" (Hamkins 2012, p. 439).

In view of these arguments, Hamkins does not seem to me to have produced convincing grounds for an ontological need of multiversism neither in his metatheoretical arguments nor in his technical work on the modal logic of forcing and his (so-called) set-theoretic geology.

4 Why the Continuum Hypothesis Cannot be Resolved by Multiversism

Everybody in the community of set-theorists, not to say of mathematicians in general, knows that Cantor's *Continuum Hypothesis* is a virtually unresolved set-theoretical question since Cantor proposed his famous conjecture about it, $2^{\aleph_0} = \aleph_1$.

---

[17] See for details: (Van Atten et al. 2002, pp. 206–210).

[18] See for details (Livadas 2019).

Yet even though the question is still an undecidable one it has spawned, throughout decades of mathematical toil to assign it a truth value, a good deal of inspiring and innovative theories and results owing perhaps to the attractiveness and naturalness of the question given its claim to provide a link between the intuition of infinitely proceeding countability and that of the real-world or intuitive continuum. Of course one could go on and on with the philosophical discussions this question has raised, for instance, the view of Feferman that **CH** is an inherently vague question in Feferman (1999), or Martin's parallel view that "As long as no new axiom is found which decides *CH*, their case (*auth. note*: of those who argue that the concept of set is not sufficiently clear to fix the truth-value of **CH**) will continue to grow stronger, and our assertion that the meaning of *CH* is clear will sound more and more empty" (Martin 1976, pp. 90–91).

However as further discussion of this far-reaching matter is understandably not within the scope of this article, I will focus instead on some deficiencies of Hamkins' arguments for a non-bivalent position concerning the continuum question in the sense that it may have truth values acceptable within the context of the each time specific universe in which its proof is articulated. As with the main line of argumentation of this paper here also one may point to the fact that the existing proof-theoretic apparatus either for the consistency of the *Continuum Hypothesis* or of its negation with the existing **ZFC** theory is constrained to principles of a metatheoretical, in fact subjective foundation, that makes them determinately understood and absolute throughout any generic extension of a standard ground universe.

Hamkins argues that the mathematical knowledge of the universes in which **CH** or ¬**CH** statements hold would make hard to view these worlds as imaginary, in other words Hamkins expresses a common view among ontological multiversists that the **CH** question should not be characterized, as in standard terms, an undecidable question but as a question having a truth value corresponding to ontologically existing diverse universes of which we have abundant knowledge over decades of relevant mathematical experience especially after the introduction of the forcing method. For if by assuming Step 2 of the dream solution template[19] we have that $\Phi \implies$ **CH** or that $\Phi \implies \neg$**CH**, given a beyond doubt established sentence Φ, then for Hamkins either solution would mean that we nullify all those worlds in which the opposite case is true, and where we 'resided' and constructed the proof-theoretic machinery 'all those preceding years'. Hamkins' argument may be extended beyond the frame of the dream solution to include also Woodin's results though Ω-logic, in fact to any proof that decides the **CH** insofar as it would make illusory the experience gained so far on the matter.

As pointed out my arguments against the positions of multiversism in general, and on the question of **CH** in particular, are drawn primarily from the metatheoretical dimensions of the question. Having in mind that for Gödel the standard definition of a set through the impredicative expression of 'a collection or a

---

[19] Hamkins refers to the dream solution template in the following sense: Step 1: Produce a set-theoretic assertion Φ expressing an 'obviously true' set-theoretical principle and Step 2: Prove that Φ determines **CH**, i.e., $\Phi \implies$ **CH** or $\Phi \implies \neg$ **CH** (Hamkins 2012, p. 430).

multitude of elements x' already inserts a kind of vagueness to the semantics of **ZF** set theory, Feferman's concerns about the following problematic features of **ZFC** theory are even more telling:

"(i) abstract entities are assumed to exist independently of any means of human definition or construction; (ii) classical reasoning (leading to non-constructive existence results) is admitted, since the statements of set theory are supposed to be about such an independently existing reality and thus have a determinate truth value (true or false); (iii) completed infinite totalities and, in particular, the totality of all subsets of any infinite set are assumed to exist; (iv) in consequence of (iii) and the Axiom of Separation, impredicative definitions of sets are routinely admitted; (v) the Axiom of Choice is assumed in order to carry through the Cantorian theory of transfinite cardinals" (Feferman 1998, pp. 287–288).

As known the proof of the independence of **CH** is conditioned on at least the (ii), (iii), (iv) and (v) assumptions. The definition of a generic set in the forcing method is one obvious example of a non-constructive existence, while the totality of all subsets of the natural numbers must be assumed to exist to determine its cardinality. Even in proof steps where there is no explicit use of the assumption (v) of the *Axiom of Choice*, this latter is nonetheless implicitly applied through other statements or theorems conditioned in turn upon its acceptance.[20]

Besides, attempts to determine the **CH** question by other approaches are either dependent on set-theoretically ambivalent assumptions (Woodin's initial determination of the falsity of **CH** under Ω-conjecture) or on conjectures that need verification (Woodin's Ultimate-L hypothesis). Steel has the view that "None of our current large cardinal axioms decide CH, because they are preserved by small forcing, whilst CH can both be made true and made false by small forcing. Because CH is provably not generically absolute, it cannot be decided by large cardinal hypotheses that are themselves generically absolute" adding furthermore that there is no obvious way to state **CH** in the multiverse (MV) language he has laid down (Steel (2014), p. 163).

I have already provided some hints to the extra-theoretical, in fact subjectively founded (therefore not platonic) character of some guiding principles in the body of the established **ZFC** set theory such as those of set formation, absoluteness, the conception of infinities as complete totalities for which I enter into a more detailed discussion in the last section.[21] These principles are made part, in an explicit or implicit fashion, of the proof-theoretic machinery leading to the independence of **CH** in ways that would be 'immune' to the structural properties of another universe (within a multiverse) which by this reason alone weakens any claim to the ontological independence of universes. Consequently one cannot hope the **CH** to be placed in a radically new context by the multiversist approach to the extent that it is constrained by the same subjective-constituting principles as the universist one.

---

[20] See for instance the way by which the forcing conditions consisting of functions FN (I, J), with I arbitrary and J countable sets have, by the application of the Delta Lemma, the countable chain condition (*CCC*) so as to preserve cardinals among the ground and forcing model in the proof of the negation of **CH** (Kunen (1982), pp. 205–206).

[21] These concepts are discussed in more detail and in a phenomenological motivation in Livadas (2013); Tieszen (2005) and (Tieszen 2011).

5 Is There an Ontological Basis for a Multiverse Axiomatization?

A major motivation of the proponents of ontological multiversism is the possibility to resolve the question of absolutely undecidable statements in mathematics as it is the case with **CH** discussed in the preceding section. This will presumably provide a counterargument to Gödel's claim, namely that there should be a unique well-determined universe of mathematical objects where mathematical propositions would be true or false, by providing the alternative existence of 'parallel' universes working inside **ZFC** theory itself, hence not by a metamathematical approach nor as a consequence of Gödel's first incompleteness theorem. In the latter cases one would be led to an 'outside' view of **ZFC** theory, thus leading to ambivalences of reasoning to the extent that considering **ZFC** as referring to the standard universe V of our time everything should be in principle carried out within it.

In what follows I argue against the possibility of an 'ontological' axiomatization of multiversism, at least of the kind undertaken in Väänänen's work in Väänänen (2014). My primary arguments against this kind of axiomatization, which adds to the corpus of the known **ZFC** axioms some special axioms, termed multiverse dependent logic axioms, to ensure 'ontologically' diverse parallel multiverses, are again for the most part extra-theoretical and subjectively founded. These are the following:

(A) As it happened with Hamkins' approach, Väänänen assumes the domain of set theory as a multiverse of parallel universes in which variables of set theory simultaneously range over each parallel universe, thus pointing to the multiverse as a kind of Cartesian product of all its parallel universes (Väänänen 2014, p. 182). This assumption even as a mental image bears, in Väänänen's own admission, the deficiency of 'isolating' each universe from any other in the class and, what is more important from my point of view, is conditioned on the invariability of first-order logical propositions across the universes which would be unattainable if it weren't for the absoluteness of individuals and relations of individuals in terms of $\in$-inclusion in well-founded structures. Even if one discards any subjectively founded connection with the mathematical notion of absoluteness, still he might hardly interpret the intranslatability of the variables of set theory across the universes if the latter are to be thought of as ontologically distinct ones. All the more so, in case these variables are bound to quantifiers and by this token acquire, according to Quine, ontological claims insofar as they are construed as universals demanding attributes or classes as values (Quine 1947, pp. 74–77).

(B) Both the Axiom of Foundation and the Axiom of Choice, axioms of a strong metamathematical significance and susceptible of a subjectively founded interpretation, arise in multiverse theory for the same reasons as in a single universe theory. In the iterative concept of set-formation, sets are formed in stages and if these are going to be well-founded there must be an element x in each stage formed earlier than the actual set, so it is irrelevant whether this process will run, insofar as variables range simultaneously over universes, over one universe or over a multitude of universes. Further, as Väänänen concedes, the essence of the Axiom of Choice, that is, the act of choosing among an infinite class of sets is "problematic even in one universe when there are infinitely many sets to choose from [..]. The extra complication arising from choosing simultaneously in many universes is simply not part of the setup of multiverse set theory" (Väänänen 2014, pp. 190-191). Therefore, both at the level of **ZFC** theory itself and on metamathematical or further extra-theoretical, subjective grounds it makes no difference whether the act of choice in the specific sense is implemented over a unique universe or a multitude of universes. As known a standard practice of ontological multiversism is to apply first order logic in the structural conception of the multiverse which makes truth to be reflected in each structure of the multiverse.

(C) The way Väänänen chooses to establish a multiverse that would not be by metamathematical reasoning a trivial multiverse of all possible models of **ZFC** is the introduction of a team semantics described as a variation of ordinary Tarski semantics of first order logic.[22] This can be seen as essentially a means of formally expressing dependence and independence situations across the universes through a set of assignment functions defined on each universe M of a multiverse structure $\mathcal{M}$.

The critical step is to extend first order logic to multiverse dependent logic, i.e. the MD logic, by adding the dependence atomic formulas $= (\vec{y}, \vec{x})$ with appropriate axioms, which can be associated with the intuition: "the values of $\vec{y}$ functionally determine the values of $\vec{x}$ in the team." However the way it is applied by Väätänen, for instance, through the sentence

$$(\forall z)(\forall x)(\exists y)(= (y,x) \wedge \neg y = z)$$

which says that there is a one-one function from the universe to a proper subset, in other words the universe has infinite points, amounts in fact to an implicit application of a process of choice reducible, at least metamathematically, to the uniqueness of each act implied by the Axiom of Choice. This can be seen as yet another indication of the impossibility of 'transcending' the metatheoretical constraints that underlie and to a large extent determine a single universe theory. This is indirectly admitted by Väänänen in claiming that the semantics of dependent logic do not depend on either universe or multiverse set theory for the reason that "although dependence logic goes beyond first-order logic and dependence logic truth cannot be reduced to truth in all universes, we do not use dependence logic in metatheory. Our metatheory is just first-order logic" (ibid., fn 20, p. 198). This means that in effect Väätänen constructs the multiverse by adding new predicates through (single universe) first order logic in the metatheory.

(D) Although one of the main motivations of the multiverse theory is to provide a new context for resolving the question of **CH** once and for all, Väänänen's attempt to a metatheoretical approach through MD logic and the Boolean disjunction

$$\mathcal{M} \models_S \phi \vee_B \psi \text{ if and only if}$$
$$\mathcal{M} \models_S \phi \text{ or } \mathcal{M} \models_S \psi$$

---

[22] In team semantics the basic concept is not that of an assignment s satisfying a formula φ in a model M, but of a set (S) of assignments, called a team, satisfying the formula φ. See Väänänen (2014, p. 197).

leads again to an impasse (ibid., pp. 200–201). More concretely, given that the multiverse formula $= (\phi)$ is made to represent $\phi \vee_B \neg\phi$, then $\neq (\phi)$ would mean the sentence ϕ is absolutely undecidable over the multiverse. It follows that adopting $\neq$ (**CH**) as an axiom would mean that as such is beyond controversy which goes against the mathematical experience and of course against Hamkins' appreciation of the accessibility due to existing experience. On the other hand adding $=$ (**CH**) to the other first order axioms of set theory does not resolve the question either, since **CH** would then have a definite truth value, yet in the current state of affairs it may well have, by forcing techniques on the ground model, any truth value we might wish to assign.

If Väänänen's approach has, in spite of his primary goal of a multiverse axiomatization, a certain sense of leaning toward a single universe by 'smoothing the edges' of multiple universes, we can find approaches favorable to the single universe by indirect means and in a totally different context, as Clarke-Doane has done in Clarke-Doane (2019). Clarke-Doane's view is one of vindication of the single universe approach on account of Benacerraf's challenge.[23]

Clarke-Doane has undertaken to refute the view that set-theoretical pluralism rightfully answers Benacerraf's epistemological challenge, among them Hamkins' position on the abundance of set-theoretical possibilities offered by our experience working with different models of set theory, by naively arguing that the real existence of various models in set theory does not help to causally explain set theorists' psychological states in the first place. For Clarke-Doane the special kind of perception, according to Gödel, we have of the objects of set theory - as it is seen from the fact that the axioms force themselves upon us as true - scarcely helps to explain the justification of our set-theoretic beliefs let alone their reliability on the grounds that the content of such mathematical intuitions could not necessarily be an essential feature of being true.

Even as Clarke-Doane proceeds on the basis of the reliability (juxtaposed to justification) criterion for our set-theoretic beliefs to defend the argument that the pluralist is no better positioned than the universist to answer Benacerraf's challenge and therefore it is not clear how someone could epistemologically argue in favor of universe pluralism[24], he falls short, in my view, of establishing a consistent, extra-theoretical level of discourse on which to dialectically link knowledge about mathematical objects

---

[23] The Benacerraf problem, known subsequently also as the Benacerraf-Field challenge, was initially presented in Benacerraf's article on mathematical truth, (Benacerraf 1973), in which Benacerraf claimed to be in favor of "a causal account of knowledge on which for (*auth. add.*: a subject) X to know that S is true requires some causal relation to obtain between X and the referents of the names, predicates, and quantifiers of S". By this measure and on the subjectively based principle of the knowing person, Benacerraf argued that in view of the 'asymmetry' between the truth conditions of a proposition p put in formal terms and the grounds on which p is said to be known, e.g. in terms of reliability in connection with general mathematical or other knowledge "[..] makes it difficult to see how mathematical knowledge is possible". See: (Benacerraf 1973, pp. 671–673).

[24] Clarke-Doane seeks to show through various subsumed interpretations of Benacerraf-Fields' challenge, e.g., indispensability, counterfactual persistence, etc., that the pluralists do not have the edge over universists in all such cases. In his own words "if there is a reason to be a set theoretic pluralist, then it is not related to the challenge to establish a causal, explanatory, logical or even counterfactual dependence between our set-theoretic beliefs and the truths" (Clarke-Doane 2019, p. 13).

to conditions of formal truth about them. I refer in the immediately next to some prompts on the matter which are, from my standpoint, better elucidated from a subjectively rather than an ontologically founded point of view.

6 A Philosophically Inclined Argumentation in Favor of Universism

If someone, on account of Clarke-Doane's dealing with the Benacerraf challenge above, has the intention to explain the real existence of various models in set theory in connection with the set theorists' psychological states or generally the postulation of truth of a proposition P inside a logical-mathematical system in connection with the causal relation obtained between a subject X and the logical structure of P, he must have a clear view of at least the following questions: (i) the way that can be founded the meaning and truth of mathematical objects, more generally of logical-mathematical states-of-affairs, (ii) the question of whether there is an extra-logical meaning of the mathematical notions of absoluteness, well-foundedness, well-ordering, etc., (iii) the question of whether mathematical models are self-standing entities or are committally determined by corresponding formal theories and their expressional means which could be again subjected to inquiry as to their origin. Given my phenomenological motivation I offer some clues to these questions without entering deeper into a philosophical discussion to avoid going too far afield from the intended scope and the rather technical content of this article.

(i) Husserl had oriented over the years the meaning and truth of logical propositions to his predilection for the reduction of all logical-mathematical concepts, in fact of all phenomena of the external world and of mental sphere, to re-presentations in consciousness and consequently to the a priori modes prescribed by the nature of this latter. Therefore meaning in general is associated, on the soil of experience-within-the-world, in an essential way with the ways consciousness displays an a priori directedness toward objects, in the rough sense that meaning becomes each time the content of this a priori directedness called intentionality. Further, meaning associated with each actually given experience is subject to the "[..] unconditional norm that it must first comply with all the a priori 'conditions of possible experience' and the possible thinking of such experience: that is, with the conditions of its pure possibility, its representability and positability as the objectivity of a uniformly identical sense" (Husserl 1939, *Engl. transl.*, p. 353). In other words, to the extent meaning is fundamentally constrained by the a priori 'conditions of possible experience' becomes not only dependent on the constitutive mental faculties of each knowing person but it is also pre-determined and invariably the same for all humans according to eidetic attributes. In such view existence in terms of mathematical propositions can be considered an a priori possibility of existence something that may be taken as a vindication of Gödel's naively thought non-realist attitude on the question of mathematical existence in his article against Carnap's syntactical account of mathematical foundations.[25]

---

[25] In the footnote 20 of the article *Is Mathematics Syntax of Language?* Gödel offered as an example of a transfinite (i.e., non-constructive) concept the phrase 'there exists', if this phrase "means object existence irrespective of actual producibility" (Gödel 1995, p. 341).

In these terms one may define knowledge as the consciousness of the 'agreement' between an anticipatory, in eidetic sense, predicative belief and the corresponding first-hand experience of the object of the belief. Therefore truth is taken as what is experienced in the verification of the anticipatory turning toward an 'empty' predicative belief with the first-hand experience of the state-of-affairs of the object itself.

(ii) In contrast to Hamkins' and other multiversists' notion of absoluteness of mathematical entities as sensitive to a background set-theory, I propose a radical subjective reduction of the formal notion of absoluteness that links it to a subject's intentional directedness (i.e., intentionality) toward formal individuals and their categorial properties. In *Experience and Judgment* Husserl proposed a new understanding of the concept of absolute substrate in which "a 'finite' substrate can be experienced simply for itself and thus has its being-for-itself. But necessarily, is at the same time a determination, that is, it is experienceable as a determination as soon as we consider a more comprehensive substrate in which it is found. Every finite substrate has determinability as being-in-something, and this is true *in infinitum*." (ibid., p. 137).

In consequence absolute substrates may be seen as completely indeterminate from the point of view of analyticity, in virtue of being lowest-level individuals of intentionality devoid of any 'inner' analytical content themselves, thus being ultimate substrates of all first order logical activity. Consequently they exclude by their own essential being everything that may be their determination by a logical activity of a higher level. In this sense a reduction of absolute statements to atomic formulas of individuals-substrates bound by logical connectives and possibly accompanied by fundamental categorial properties (e.g., those of inclusion, order, permutability, etc.), may come to terms with a subjectively founded and invariant by any formal-mathematical transformation (including inter-model translatability) notion of absoluteness. In such radical attitude notions like well-foundedness and well-ordering associated to the one or the other degree with absoluteness may be interpreted in the same subjectively founded terms, while sticking at the same time to a notion of infinite sets as completed totalities in actuality no matter the level of infinity attained in formal terms.

(iii) In recent literature it is pretty much debated the question of a possible ontology of mathematical models and the interrelation with the mathematical theories they represent. Rather than addressing the controversy between proponents of the syntactic and the semantic account of theories, I point to the view that the status of mathematical models " is largely defined by the way models subsume a set-theoretical structure whose constraints, reducible to an extra-linguistic level of discourse, may implicitly condition the epistemic status of models as representations of axiomatic theories" (Livadas 2020, p. 13).

Further and on account of the non-categoricity of first order **ZFC** theory due to the Skolem-Löwenheim Theorem, one might argue that the inner constraints posed on the logical-mathematical level should someway be reflected in the model-theoretic one. For instance, one could not have a sound notion of isomorphism or for that matter of partial isomorphism of models if there wasn't a prior intuition of syntactical individuals as irreducible unities, or (for that matter) of the 'ontic' invariability of ordinals and ordinal definable formulas, or yet of the concept of actual infinity, e.g., as the indefinite scope of quantifiers in predicative formulas, etc. The following passage is perhaps indicative of the virtues of a subjectively based argumentation against the supposedly ontological merits of multiversism: " countability (*add of the auth.*: of models) is in fact imposed extra-theoretically in logico-linguistic and more concretely set-theoretical constructions by the way the predicative (you may prefer to call it noematic) activity, pertaining to well-meant objects of a system, is carried through by the mental activity of a subject: that is, in finitely many steps ideally extensible in infinitum, an extrapolation that can also accommodate a universal quantification over an indefinite domain." (ibid., p. 33).

There is no kind of multiversism as far as I know that, in view of my arguments in this article, can possibly accommodate the proposed subjective principles of set-theoretical construction in a way that would justify an ontological foundation of multiversism in mathematical theories.

7 Appendix

As noted in Sect. 2, par 8, this technical in character Appendix serves to show that the proof-theoretical machinery employed in the (indirectly) touching on the multiverse debate axiom $V = \text{HOD}$, and *a fortiori* to its stronger version $V \subseteq \text{HOD}^{V[G]}$, applies certain 'standard' notions without the need to appeal to radically different concepts which would in turn imply the need for alternative universes.

Woodin outlines in Woodin (2017) the proof of the following theorem which summarizes some key consequences of the axiom $V = \text{Ultimate} - L$, where the Generic-Multiverse is the generic multiverse generated by the set-theoretical universe V.

Theorem 7.1 (*V=Ultimate-L*)

- **CH** holds
- $V = \text{HOD}$
- *V* is the minimum universe of the Generic-Multiverse.

Crucial in the proof of the two latter cases of Theorem 7.1 is the following theorem which is a stronger case than $V = \text{HOD}$ and moreover establishes a set-generic extension of the set-theoretical universe V, a fact that might meet Hamkins' standards of ontological multiversism.

Theorem 7.2 (*V=Ultimate-L*) *Suppose V[G] is a set-generic extension of V. It follows*:

$$V \subseteq (\text{HOD})^{V[G]}$$

(Woodin 2017, p. 102).

The key approach to the proof of Theorem 7.2 is to fix a partial order $P \subseteq V$ with G V-generic for P and cardinal $\lambda =$ card $(P)^V$. Then for all regular cardinals $\kappa > \lambda$ one may prove that $\mathcal{P}(\kappa)^V \subseteq \text{HOD}^{V[G]}$ which will eventually prove that $V \subseteq (\text{HOD})^{V[G]}$.

The proof hinges on the following notions which in spite of their technical nature are invariant and unconstrained by the structure of extended models forged by forcing or collapsing principles.

First: It is important, on fixing a regular cardinal $\kappa > \lambda$, to have a partition of stationary sets $\mathcal{F} = <S_\alpha; \alpha < \kappa>$ inside the universal set V that is also a partition in $V[G]$. This can be done by letting $\mathcal{F}$ be a partition of the set

$$S = \{\alpha < \kappa; (\text{cof}(\alpha))^V = \omega\}$$

into stationary sets such that by definition of stationarity there is a closed unbounded set $N_o \subset \kappa$ such that $N_o \in V$ and moreover for each $\sigma \in N_o \cap S$

$$\sigma \in \cup \{S_\xi; \xi < \sigma\}$$

Now if $N \subseteq \kappa$ is a closed cofinal set such that $N \in V[G]$ then there must be a closed cofinal subset $M \subseteq N$ such that $M \in V$, having as a consequence that each S_α is stationary in $V[G]$.

So what is the trick in getting the S_αs to be stationary sets in $V[G]$? The answer is that the possibility of finding a closed cofinal subset $M \subseteq \kappa$ of N (this latter being in $V[G]$) in V that shares the same intersection properties with N_o regarding the elements of $\mathcal{F}$ is fundamentally due to the absoluteness of ω between transitive models of **ZF**, in virtue of the cofinality of the elements α of S. This would not be the case if the first limit ordinal ω was not an absolute concept (like all other ordinals).

Second: 7.2 depends on a previous theorem of Woodin's[26] which is also a consequence of $V = $ Ultimate $- L$, namely for each cardinal κ there exists an elementary embedding

$$\pi : (H(\kappa^+))^V \longrightarrow K$$

such that $K \in (\text{HOD})^{V[G]}$ and $(\pi, K) \in V$. The stationarity of the subsets $<S_\alpha; \alpha < \kappa>$ of the (regular cardinal) κ in $V[G]$ is again the decisive trick of the proof, although in the context of the elementary embedding π above into the inner model $(\text{HOD})^{V[G]}$. Of course it would be absurd to talk about inner models via elementary embeddings without a fairly absolute notion of ordinals to the extent that by definition a class N is an inner model iff N is a transitive model of **ZF** under the $\in$ predicate and contains the class of all ordinals, i.e., ON $\subseteq N$.

This is an *a fortiori* condition in the present situation given the structure of $(\text{HOD})^{V[G]}$ in terms of hereditarily ordinal definable sets whose definition is straightwardly associated with the notion of ordinals.

---

[26] See for details: Theorem 7.25, p. 101 in Woodin (2017).

Further Woodin proves that a consequence of $V = $ Ultimate $-L$ is that the universe V is the minimum universe of the Generic-Multiverse.[27] This could be of some importance for certain proponents of multiversism, yet I note that a key part of the proof depends on the use of the collapsing poset Coll (ω, δ), with δ a specially defined cardinal in V. It depends, in particular, in a substantial way on its homogeneity through a 'codification' by the countable ordinal ω such that in V

$$\text{RO } (P \times \text{Coll } (\omega, \delta)) \cong \text{RO } (\text{Coll } (\omega, \delta))$$

and in another universe V_0

$$\text{RO } (P_0 \times \text{Coll } (\omega, \delta)) \cong \text{RO } (\text{Coll } (\omega, \delta))$$

Again it would be totally impossible to reach this result without reliance to absoluteness properties, e.g. of the functions $f_\omega(\delta) : \omega \times \delta \longrightarrow \delta$ and of course the absoluteness of ω.

References

Barton N (2016) Multiversism and concepts of set: how much relativism is acceptable? In: Boccuni F, Sereni A (eds.) Objectivity, realism, and proof. FilMat studies in the philosophy of mathematics, pp. 189–209, Basel: Springer

Benacerraf B (1973) Mathematical truth. J Philos 70(19):661–679

Buzaglo M (2002) The logic of concept expansion. Cambridge University Press, Cambridge

Clarke-Doane J (2019) Set-theoretic pluralism and the Benacerraf problem. Philosophical Studies. https://doi.org/10.1007/s11098-019-01296-y

Davis P, Hersh R (1982) The mathematical experience. Houghton Miflin Co, Boston

Feferman S (1998) Why a little bit goes a long way: logical foundations of scientifically applicable mathematics. In: In the Light of Logic, pp. 284–298, Oxford: Oxford University Press

Feferman S (2011) Is the continuum hypothesis a definite mathematical problem? Text for lecture in the EFI series, Harvard University. http://math.stanford.edu/~feferman/papers/IsCHdefinite.pdf

Feferman S (1999) Does mathematics need new axioms? Am Math Mon 106(2):99–111

Gödel K (1995) Kurt Gödel: Collected Works III. In: Feferman S, et al (eds.) Oxford: Oxford University Press

Gödel K (1965) Remarks before the Princeton bicentennial conference on problems in mathematics. In: Davis M (ed) The undecidable: basic papers on undecidable propositions, unsolvable problems and computable functions. Raven Press, Hewlett, NY

Hamkins JD (2012) The set-theoretic multiverse. Rev Symb Logic 5(3):416–449

Horsten L (2019) The metaphysics and mathematics of arbitrary objects. Cambridge University Press, Cambridge

Husserl E (1976) Ideen zu einer reinen Phänomenologie und phänomenologischen Philosophie, Erstes Buch, Hua Band III/I, hsgb. K. Schuhmann, Den Haag: M. Nijhoff. Engl. transl.: (1983), Ideas pertaining to a pure phenomenology and to a phenomenological philosophy: First Book, transl. F. Kersten, The Hague: M. Nijhoff

Husserl E (1939) Erfahrung und Urteil, hsgb. L. Landgrebe, Prag: Acad./Verlagsbuch. Engl. translation: (1973), Experience and Judgment, transl. J.S. Churchill & K. Americs, London: Routledge & Kegan P

Husserl E (2019) Logic and general theory of science, transl. C. Ortiz Hill, E. Husserl, Coll. Works, ed. J. Yansen, Hua XV, Cham: Springer Nature Switzerland AG

Kunen K (1982) Set Theory. Elsevier Sc. Pub, An Introduction to Independence Proofs, Amsterdam

---

[27] See for details: Theorem 7.28, p. 103 in Woodin (2017).

Livadas S (2019) The plausible impact of phenomenology on Gödel's thoughts. Theoria. https://doi.org/10.1111/theo.12181

Livadas S (2005) The phenomenological roots of nonstandard mathematics. Rom J Inform Sci Technol 8(2):115–136

Livadas S (2013) Are mathematical theories reducible to non-analytic foundations? Axiomathes 23(1):109–135

Livadas S (2020) Talking about models: the inherent constraints of mathematics. Axiomathes 30:13–36

Maddy P (2002) Naturalism in mathematics. Clarendon Press, Oxford

Martin D (1976) Hilbert's first problem: the continuum hypothesis, in: Mathematical Developments Arising from Hilbert Problems. In: Browder FE (ed.) Proceedings of symposia in pure mathematics vol. 28, pp. 81–92, American Mathematical Society, Providence: USA

Quine VW (1947) On universals. J Symb Logic 12(3):74–84

Robinson A (1966) Non-standard analysis. North-Holland Pub. Company, Amsterdam

Steel RJ (2014) Gödel's program. In: Kennedy J (ed) Interpreting Gödel: critical essays. Cambridge University Press, Cambridge, pp 153–180

Ternullo C (2019) Maddy on the multiverse. In: Sarikaya D, Kant D, Centrone S (eds.) Reflections on the foundations of mathematics, synthese library, pp. 43–78, Cham: Springer

Tieszen R (2005) Phenomenology, logic, and the philosophy of mathematics. Cambridge University Press, Cambridge

Tieszen R (2011) After Gödel: platonism and rationalism in mathematics and logic. Oxford University Press, Oxford

Väänänen J (2014) Multiverse set theory and absolutely undecidable propositions. In: Kennedy J (ed) Interpreting Gödel: critical essays. Cambridge University Press, Cambridge, pp 180–209

Van Atten M, van Dalen D, Tieszen R (2002) Brower and Weyl: the phenomenology and mathematics of the intuitive continuum. Philos Math 10(3):203–226

Woodin HW (2011) The continuum hypothesis, the generic-multiverse of sets, and the Ω conjecture. In: Kennedy J, Kossak P (eds) Set theory, arithmetic, and foundations of mathematics: theorems, philosophies. Cambridge University Press, Cambridge, pp 13–42

Woodin HW (2017) In Search of Ultimate-L: the 19th Midrasha Mathematicae Lectures. Bull Symb Logic 23(1):1–109

Zakon E, Robinson A (1969) A set-theoretical characterisation of enlargements. In: Luxembourg WAJ (ed) Applications of model theory to algebra, analysis and probability. Holt, Rinehart and Winston, New York, pp 109–122

Is There an Ontology of Infinity?

Abstract
In this article I try to articulate a defensible argumentation against the idea of an ontology of infinity. My position is phenomenologically motivated and in this virtue strongly influenced by the Husserlian reduction of the ontological being to a process of subjective constitution within the immanence of consciousness. However taking into account the historical charge and the depth of the question of infinity over the centuries I also include a brief review of the platonic and aristotelian views and also those of Locke and Hume on the concept to the extent that they are relevant to my own discussion of infinity both in a purely philosophical and epistemological context. Concerning the latter context, I argue against Kanamori's position, in *The Infinite as Method in Set Theory and Mathematics*, that the mathematical infinite can be accounted for solely in terms of epistemological articulation, that is, in the way it is approached, assimilated, and applied in the course of the construction of mathematical hierarchies. Instead I point to a subjectively constituted immanent 'infinity' in virtue of the a priori as well as factual characteristics of subjective constitution, underlying and conditioning any talk of infinity in an epistemological sense. From this viewpoint I also address some other positions on the question of a possible ontology of the mathematical infinite. My whole approach to the question of the infinite in an epistemological sense hinges on the assumption that the mathematical infinite subsumes the infinite of physical theories to the extent that physics and science in general deal with the infinite in terms of the corresponding mathematical language and the specific techniques involved.

1 Introduction

Is there indeed an answer to the question of the title? And if so can it be a sound and well-founded one in case it does not involve a multi-level discussion across pure philosophy, starting at least from Greek antiquity, through to modern epistemology in taking into account recent advances in the entire epistemological edifice? After all such an answer would transcend the realm of absolute being in the platonic sense corresponding to the

Is there an Ontology of Infinity?

Greek term εἶναι and enter into a dialectic composition with an epistemological sense of being corresponding to the Greek term γίγνεσθαι. This is the primary intention of this article and its ultimate goal is to provide a convincing argumentation against the possibility of founding infinity in the ontological sense of εἶναι from the vantage point of phenomenological analysis, something that implies bringing into the fore the process and the a priori modes of subjective constitution.

In this motivation the concept of infinity as it is basically understood (leaving aside metaphysical idealizations), starting from the Greek classical texts to our days, may in fact be divided into two radically different subspecies: the one taken to be the 'closed' infinity conceived as the immanent[1] content of the flux of consciousness inexhaustibly extended over any conceivable boundary without any spatiotemporal and causal constraints, and the real world 'infinity' which is not really an infinity but an objective spatiotemporally founded and indefinitely extensible external reality which exists as such and such according to definite causal laws derived by human experience underlying a specific presence in the world. In short, the main argument to be defended is that it is impossible to provide a foundation of infinity in purely ontological terms insofar there exists a world, thought of in a most primitive sense, in which which human egos are included as subordinate realities and yet this world cannot be taken in an objective sense but as a secondary being posited by a constituting consciousness which 'exists' unconditionally in itself, i.e., one which "*nulla 're' indiget ad existendum*". This is done in the Sects. 1 and 3 in which I mostly rely on the original Husserlian writings, namely in *Ideas I* (Husserl 1976a), *Logical Investigations* (Husserl 1984), *Lessons on the Phenomenology of Inner Time Consciousness* (Husserl 1966), *Experience and Judgment* (Husserl 1939), *Late Texts on Time Constitution* (Husserl 2001), *On the Theory of Intersubjectivity* (Husserl 1973a), etc.

As a matter of fact Husserlian phenomenology in particular in its post-psychologistic, transcendental phase, is the backbone of my overall argumentation, though not restrictively, against an ontology of infinity and to a significant extent the *leit motiv* of the discussion of infinity as epistemologically articulated, e.g., in relation to Kanamori's (2009) views. This is mostly based on the fact that a phenomenologically motivated approach toward the concept of infinity in general not only helps unfetter infinity from idealistic illusions in an ontological sense, but can also epistemologically account for a sound meaning of the concept in view of its status in formal-mathematical theories. In these terms I give a special attention to the fact that a subjectively founded conception of infinity in the sense of an objective fulfillment in actual presentation entails both a priori and factual characteristics thus offering grounds to refute *ipso facto* any ontologically based counterarguments (Sect. 2).

Having in mind that the question of the infinite is a key philosophical preoccupation over centuries of rational thought, I thought it purposeful to briefly comment on some key ideas of Plato and Aristotle on the infinite in *Timaeus, Parmenides* (Plato), *Physics, Metaphysics I–IX*, and *Metaphysics X–XIV* (Aristotle). I have also given a special attention to the aristotelian treatment of the infinite in *Physics* in relation to my own subjectively oriented position and the possibility of a reduction within immanence. This is done in Sect. 5.

---

[1] The term immanent, widely used in phenomenological texts, can be roughly explained as referring to what is or has become correlative (or 'co-substantial') to the being of the flux of one's consciousness in contrast to what is 'external' or transcendent to it. For instance, a tree is transcendent as such to the consciousness of an 'observer' while its appearance in the modes of its appearing within his consciousness is immanent to it.

Is there an Ontology of Infinity?

Finally taking into account the literature discussion involving the epistemological aspects of the infinite I engage in Sect. 6 in a thorough treatment of the infinite principally in logical-mathematical terms, in which case I point to an implicit assumption of a kind of impredicative substratum, possibly reduced to a subjectively constituted 'closed' infinity, which circularly reproduces itself in the ascension toward higher order infinities in the context of large cardinals theory. It should be said that this particular section involves some level of knowledge of standard and higher order set theory and consequently could be skipped, at least in its strictly technical details, by the more philosophically oriented reader without losing the larger philosophical picture. Also a special mention and account is made of the work of A. Badiou on a presumed ontology of mathematical infinity in his well-known treatise *Being and Event* (Badiou 2005). One could possibly include the formal syntactical ways, along with the generated semantical content, in which various alternative mathematical theories treat the question of the infinite. But given the general intention of the paper, this would go a bit far away both in content and length and lean the balance too much toward the epistemological aspect. In any case I find nothing in the elaboration of my arguments that would not vindicate my general position also with regard to alternative mathematical theories.

The reader will find no particular discussion of the infinite in physical theories as such, for instance in general relativity theory, to the extent that physical and positive science in general deal with the issue in terms of their mathematical metatheory, in which case infinity as treated in terms of the physicalistic language alone is actually a sort of ever shifting 'horizon' of the predominant each time physical model.

2 A Phenomenologically Motivated Discussion of Infinity

Husserl had stated that what is called phenomenon has its origin a standing-flowing self-presentification, that is, the self-presenting, flowing absolute ego in its standing-flowing life, a life that is a constant living-experience, intentional and conscious apprehension, a standing-flowing validation of being (*Seinsgeltung*) in multiple modalities, a validation of being with content or meaning which inherently belong to the substance of the flowing (Husserl 2001, p. 145). This position takes into account that any phenomenon in real world terms cannot be thought of as detached from the world conceived in the sense of life-world[2] with an open ended horizon in a definite subjectively reducible sense and in relation to at least one phenomenological reduction performing subject. On these grounds, the infinity of the world, according to Husserl's views in the *Late Texts on Time-Constitution* (*Späte Texte über Zeitkonstitution*), Husserl (2001), is an open-endedness, the motivated possibility of new experiences and determinations through experience. Husserl considered that this infinity, thought of as 'external', has its counterpart in the inner infinity which 'belongs' to each particular real being. It is only bounded by the scope of my own 'I can', this latter thought of course in eidetic terms.[3] Space is constituted as a reality through my respective

---

[2] The phenomenological notion of life-world can be described in rough terms as an indefinitely extensible horizon of our special reduction-performing co-presence in the world, this latter meant as the primitive soil of our experience. A major work in which this notion is further elaborated is Husserl's well-known *Crisis of European Sciences and Transcendental Phenomenology* (Husserl 1976b).

[3] By eidetic laws or eidetic attributes in the world of phenomena one can roughly communicate to a non-phenomenologist what relates to the existence of objects or states-of-affairs as regularities by essential

all-around possibility of its unfolding and this possibility has its own subjective horizon essentially associated with inner temporality. Space is not bounded in an exact sense yet it has a finite limit (in accordance with a subject's own finiteness).[4]

For Husserl, in his final and predominant phase of transcendental phenomenology, infinity as subjectively constituted and further objectified as an immanence in consciousness is rooted in inner temporality in contradistinction to the 'external' infinity of the material world, the infinity of physical theories, which is in fact an ever receding horizon of the finiteness of the life-world, the latter being convergent but not identical to its forms of mathematization. In this temporally founded perspective a presumed ontology of infinity would be de-constructed in favor of the subjective character of inner time constitution conceived in the level of constituting and not that of constituted to which belongs the objective, scientific time. As a matter of fact this reduction of infinity, as temporally founded, to an absolute subjective source would entail in turn other questions pertaining to the impossibility of an 'ontology' of the absolute origin of temporal consciousness, But this is a deep enough question which is purely philosophical in character and, except for the original Husserlian texts, has been treated to a certain extent elsewhere.[5] In any case even though Husserl did not write much on the concept of infinity proper,[6] he had made clear this kind of subjective reduction of infinity throughout his texts even alluding to the possibility of 'men' of other planets and other galaxies, on the presupposition of sharing the same or analogous eidetic attributes, of 'co-founding' an infinite, homogenous spatiotemporal world (ibid. p. 373). At another point in the *Theory of Intersubjectivity, Third Part*, Husserl referred to the possibility of a subjective reduction of infinity in the following implicit terms:

"Meine endliche Zeit ist doch unüberschreitbar auch in dem, was ich früher hätte aktualisieren können, wie in dem, was ich künftich verwicklichen kann. Aber ich tue so, als hätte ich Zeitflügel, als hätte ich ein Vermögen der Bewegung durch alle Zeiten, als könnte ich eine Einheit der Weltanschauung, einer möglichen Welterfahrung construieren als mir eigene, in der ich in unendlicher Immanenz alle Unendlichkeiten der Erfahrung durchlaufen könnte."; (Husserl 1973b, pp. 239–240). (*Transl. of the auth.*: My finite time is thus insurmountable also in what I had prior been able to actualize, as also in what I will be able to realize in the future. Yet I do so, like I had time-wings, like I had a property of motion through all times, like I could have a unity of the intuition of the world, (like) I

Footnote 3 (continued)
necessity and not by mere facticity. One may also consult E. Husserl's *Ideas I*, (Husserl 1976a, *Engl. transl.*, pp. 12–15).

[4] "Die Unendlichkeit der Welt ist diese Offenheit, diese motivierte Möglichkeit neuer Erfahrungen und erfahrender Ausweisungen. Diese Unendlichkeit, hier als äussere gedacht, hat ihr Gegenstück in der inneren Unendlichkeit, die zu jedem einzelnen Realen gehört. Sie ist begrenzt durch den Umfang meines 'Ich kann'. Der Raum ist als realer konstituiert mit meinem jeweiligen Allseitig-ihn-erschliessen-können, und dieses Können hat seinen eigenen subjectiven Horizont, der zwar nicht voll exakt umgrenzt ist, aber doch einen endlichen Limes hat." (Husserl 2001, p. 164). *Transl. of the author*: "The infinity of the world is this openness, this motivated possibility of new experiences and determinations through experience. This infinity, here thought of as external, has its counterpart in the inner infinity which belongs to each particular real being. It is bounded by the scope of my ' I can'. The space is constituted as a reality through my respective all-around possibility of its unfolding and this possibility has its own subjective horizon which is not bounded in an exact sense, yet it has a finite limit."

[5] See, e.g., Livadas (2019).

[6] An explicit reference is found in the first paragraph of Sect. 3.

could construct a possible world experience as my own, in which I could run through all infinities of my experience in the infinite immanence).

In Husserl's view every science of being can be transformed into a 'metaphysics' insofar as it is associated with the phenomenological knowledge of essences and on this ground acquires ultimate meaning clarification and also ultimate determination of its truth-content. This is a metaphysics that owes its origin to the essence of knowledge and correlatively with it to a twofold knowledge attitude: the one purely oriented to the being itself as appearing, perceived and thought of by consciousness, the other oriented to the enigmatic essential relations between being and consciousness (*Phänomenologische Psychologie*, Husserl (1968), *Einleitung des Herausgebers*, p. xx). In the sense of being as a phenomenon Husserl associated, as said in the first paragraph, the notion of a non-reducible primordial phenomenon whose origin is the presentifying, absolute ego in its standing-flowing life. The purely subjective (factor) as reflection of a 'higher degree', as consciousness of what stands in virtue of ontological essence, is characterized as the temporalized living consciousness in the universal temporality, the temporalized infinite flux of consciousness in which are included re-presentations and appearances of what is ontological in their flowing forms and re-identifications (Husserl 2001, p. 362). Consequently questions of pure ontology are reduced to the question of the modes of an individual actual and possible experience, as part of the universal experience, appearing as 'living experience' in the stream of my inner temporality (ibid., p. 357).

Relevant to the phenomenology of inner time-consciousness, in the well-known description of the unity of the flux of consciousness in terms of the transversal and longitudinal intentionality, Husserl posed the question of whether there is an ultimate now which has no past in advance of the enactment of the a priori conjunction just passed by—original now—not yet. In case of a positive answer this would lead, on the ground of evidence, to the possibility of a de facto 'empty' time, a time which would be totally incompatible with the presence of a subject with a priori constitutional-eidetic capacities (Husserl 1985, p. 64). More than this, a subjective presence implies that there is no conceivable notion of time but time-as-fulfilled in a way that each givenness to phenomenological perception (*Wahrnehmung*) is necessarily extended in time and not simply a temporal punctuality. It is due to the temporal essence of phenomenological perception that to each necessarily prevalent now is associated a gradual 'descent' (of retentions) into a haziness which does not appear as such essentially (ibid., pp. 34–35). The allusion, on the one hand, to this de facto character of the gradual vagueness of the retentional tails to the past and, on the other, the appeal (among others) to rememoration (*Wiedererinnerung*) as an essential mode of the temporal flux of consciousness are going to be accounted for in the next, insofar as they provide strong clues to the belief that an ontology of infinity can be refuted solely on phenomenological, even simply subjectively founded grounds.

For now and in view of my intentions, I point out also from Husserl's *Lessons on the Phenomenology of Inner Time-Consciousness*, Husserl (1966), that the continuity of the modes of procession of the duration of an object is juxtaposed to the continuity of the modes of procession of each 'point' of duration itself in the sense that the former are determined by the continuity of the modes of procession of the latter. In this respect and in what may be thought a critical association of infinity as generated by inner temporality with infinity-in-spatiality, every temporal point of an object has its fulfillment, its temporal 'thisness' of content and thus as a matter of fact a spatial extension (Husserl 2001, p. 64). Husserl attributed the co-existence form of spatiality to the inner form of temporality in the sense that inner temporality makes possible that various world objects in any interval of the same temporality co-exist and in this way the same temporal points and time-intervals with the same corresponding objective contents are fulfilled. It is remarkable that in the *Late Texts on Time Constitution* Husserl gave a founding priority, concerning the self-constituting character of inner temporality, to the essential form of constituting present (or living present) which he indirectly linked to the essence of the transcendental ego (ibid., p. 4).

Talking at the level of constituted, each new now in the temporal flux is transformed into a continuous tail of retentions fading away into a hazy past and yet a durating object as immanent unity can be recalled by rememoration as an actual now which is not authentically its original presence (*Gegenwärtigung*) but its re-presented presence (*Vergegenwärtigung*) generating anew a continuous sequence of retentions and so on. Underlying the capability of presentifying a durating object as a noematic[7] one, which encloses also the continuity of its appearances over duration, is what Husserl termed the double intentionality of consciousness, namely the form of transversal intentionality in the a priori scheme retention-original presence-protention and that of longitudinal intentionality. The first one makes that each original impression is a priori tied with primary memory (i.e., retention) and a-thematic expectedness (protention) while the second one makes that the sequence of retentions, of retentions of retentions and so on as well as ultimately the temporal flux of consciousness itself are constituted as a whole in continuous unity. It turns out that longitudinal intentionality in this a priori sense invalidates *eo ipso* any talk of a possible traversability of infinity in objective terms as immanent fulfillment within consciousness.

To the extent that the double intentionality, as an a priori intentional form making possible the unity of the absolute flux of consciousness as inexhaustibly fulfilled by ever new objects as immanent appearances, may found the possibility of immanent continuous unity independently of any spatio-temporal constraints raises in turn the question of its proper objectivity in real world terms. Michalski (1997) refers to the double intentionality of temporal consciousness in these terms: It is thanks to the fact that retention is characterized by a 'double' non-objective intentionality that the consciousness of temporal succession is at all possible (Michalski 1997, p. 138). In fact as intentionality cannot be thought of independently of what is intended, and this latter even if it is simply an object of imagination cannot be but a being-in-objectivity, it is really an issue whether intentionality in general and a *a fortiori* the double intentionality of consciousness can be regarded as a priori, non-objective acts themselves or just clues on the level of constituted of an underlying absolute, subjective origin of inner temporality.

In *Experience and Judgment* Husserl stated that the back and forth passing into states of consciousness (e.g., passing to the state of rememoration spontaneously and in instantaneity) presupposes in a certain way the conception of an 'infinite' time. On this apparently 'naive' assumption he went on to conclude that the difficult problems of the apprehension of absolute temporal determinations of objects, the constitution of their location in objective time, and in general the manifestation of the continuity of absolute objective time by means of the subjective time of lived experiences, all this constitutes the great theme of a more worked out phenomenology of time-consciousness (Husserl 1939, *Engl. transl.*, p. 167).

---

[7] A noematic object, a phenomenological term, is an object as meant constituted by certain modes as a well-defined object immanent to the temporal flux of a subject's consciousness. It can then be said to be given apodictically in experience inasmuch as: (1) it can be recognized by a perceiver directly as a manifested essence in any perceptual judgement (2) it can be predicated as existing according to the descriptive norms of a language and (3) it can be verified as such (as a reidentifying object) in multiple acts more or less at will. More in Husserl's *Ideas I*: (Husserl 1976a, pp. 229–232).

Is there an Ontology of Infinity?

At this point I take advantage of the preceding discussion to point to the impasse reached in trying to found an ontology of infinity in the absolute sense of being ($\varepsilon\tilde{\iota}\nu\alpha\iota$), especially if one clings to the general position that "[..] the spatio-temporal infinity of the world requires the endlessness of the absolute consciousness", (*transl. of the author of:* "[..] die räumlich-zeitliche Unendlichkeit der Welt fordert Endlosigkeit des absoluten Bewusstseins") (Husserl 1973a, p. 17). As absolute consciousness is for Husserl the residue left over from the annihilation of the world of experience, it is therefore considered 'in advance of' objective time and may be consequently thought of as the non-objective temporal ground for the constitution of 'infinite' time and for an extended in ('infinite') time 'infinite' world.

3 Actual Infinity as Subjectively Founded

Husserl described immanent infinity, in the following terms as the unconstrained extension of any conceivable spatial and temporal stretches in imagination "The fact that we freely extend spatial and temporal stretches in imagination, that we can put ourselves in imagination at each fancied boundary of space or time while ever new spaces and times emerge before our inward gaze—all this does not prove the relative foundedness (*Fundierung*) of bits of space and time, and so does not prove space and time to be *really* infinite, or even that they could be *really* infinite, nor even that they really can be so. This can only be proved by a law of causation, which presupposes, and so requires, the possibility of being extended beyond any given boundary" (Husserl 1984, Engl. transl., p. 45).

In fact this kind of immanent infinity was recognized in a certain sense as such from Husserl's earlier so-called psychologistic stage at the time of the *Philosophy of Arithmetic*. In that work, preceding his later espousing of transcendental phenomenology, he referred to inner experience as the evident factor for the possibility of representing a multiplicity of objects as an instantaneous lived experience (Husserl 1970, p. 24). He claimed also that temporal succession[8] is what precisely characterizes multiplicity as multiplicity although this succession is attainable only to the extent that contents are found in whatever simple or complex relationship and thus can be put together as a whole in mental re-presentation (ibid., p. 25).

In his later works Husserl was increasingly intent on establishing the foundation of continuous unity, as thematically presented in reflection, on the modes of the self-constituting temporal consciousness. In *Experience and Judgment*, in particular, he explicitly referred to a special kind of constitution of unity that provides the basis for special relations, having specifically in mind formal relations (Husserl 1939, pp. 153–154 & pp. 188–189).[9] In an apparent connection to his preceding ideas on the concept of formal ontological objects in *Formal and Transcendental Logic*, he called this kind of unity a formal-ontological one and it was described as a unity extending to all possible individuals or non-individuals being originally given as objects independently of a concrete material content. The unified whole of a collection of objects as re-presented becomes thematized and therefore objective in the continuous apprehension of these objects one by one and in their totality. In this

---

[8] Temporal succession is thought of in the *Philosophy of Arithmetic* as the psychological pre-condition for the built up of number meanings and generally of the meaning of multiplicities (Husserl 1970, p. 28).
[9] This obviously refers to relations between formal-ontological objects, including such mathematical objects as sets, classes of sets, functions, domains of functions in the form of Euclidean or non-Euclidean spaces, etc.

Is there an Ontology of Infinity?

sense, one may provide a subjective foundation to universal-existential predicate formulas of an indefinite range inasmuch as a proposition of the kind *'each and every thing* (everything possible and hence everything actual) *such that....'* is possible to be intuited by consciousness as equivalent to the metatheoretical proposition: *'each and every thing such that... is, in principle, capable of being colligated'*.

As a further clue that this kind of unity might be reducible to an original form of the self-constituting temporality of the transcendental ego, Husserl characterized this collective unity as essentially founded not on material elements nor on the essence of things as this latter is taken into consideration only insofar as it makes differentiation possible (Husserl 1939, engl. transl., pp. 188–189). Rather to make a collection of objects (e.g. a set of objects or a class of sets) a thematic objectivity itself in actual presence within immanence, an act of a higher level is required not one of passive receptivity but instead one of productive spontaneity. This was termed a retrospective apprehension (*rückgreifendes Erfassen*), an act whose content is that of the thematization by the constituting ego of a collectivity, pre-constituted by the polythetic act of colligation, into an identifiable and re-identifiable object-meaning possibly posited as a substrate of judgments (ibid., pp. 246–247). On this account Husserl characterized time-consciousness as the original seat of the constitution of the unity of identity in general, making further clear that the outcome of temporal constitution is a universal form of order, of succession and coexistence of all immanent data. Talking about content, we talk about syntheses which produce the unity of a field of sense and this is meant to be a higher level of constituting activity. But this again presupposes the temporal structure of the passive field itself which precedes all acts and further the origin, in temporal terms, of the passive unity of the pregivenness of a plurality of perceived or even imagined things, that is, the absolute subjectivity thought to be the original source of self-constituting temporality. Husserl put it this way: "[..] the unity of the intuition of time is the condition of the possibility of all unity of the intuition of a plurality of objects connected in any way, for all are temporal objects; accordingly, every other connection of such objects presupposes the unity of time." (ibid., p. 182).

It is important to note that the unity originating in the being of consciousness as such not only underlies the possibility of reflecting on things in general as identical, durating unities over time but also grounds the possibility of reducing the concept of an ideal infinity in progression to an act of fulfillment and completion in the present now of consciousness. In this sense the unity of a physical thing "stands over against an ideally infinite multiplicity of noetic mental processes of a wholly determined essential content and which can be surveyed despite the infinity, all of them united by being consciousness of the 'same thing'. This unification becomes given in the sphere of consciousness itself, in mental processes which, on their side, also belong again to the group which we have delimited here." (Husserl 1976a, *Engl. transl*, p. 323). To the extent that physical objects are reducible to noematic immanent ones under certain eidetic norms, something that happens also with their unity founded in the unity of consciousness, the statement above also holds good for categorial objects corresponding to pure content-free object-forms with a priori associated, empty-of-content, specific relational forms. This latter class that includes all objects of a formal-mathematical theory, i.e., all categorial forms in general, numbers or number-theoretical forms, sets, functions of pure analysis and their Euclidean or non-Euclidean domains (ibid., p. 28).

Husserl offered a kind of metaphorical explication to account for the apparent contradiction between the all-sided infinity of continuum meant, e.g., in the sense of an ideal infinity of multiplicities of appearances of one and the same thing and the 'closed' unity of the completion of the 'running through' of appearances. Thus the idea of continuum as such and the idea of the perfect givenness prefigured by the idea of continuum are presented in an intellectual seeing (*Einsicht*) in the way an 'idea' can be intellectually seen by designating by virtue of its essence the peculiar type of intellectual content. In these terms the idea of an infinity motivated according to its essence is not itself an infinity. The fact that this infinity cannot be given in principle and *in rem*, does not preclude but rather requires the intellectually seen givenness of the idea of this infinity (ibid., p. 343). This seems to be a way out of the apparent contradiction of a 'finite infinity' even though, as with Husserl's obsessive search for a foundation of the immanent unity of consciousness in temporal terms, one can possibly raise the issue of the circular character of an endless regression of reflecting-reflected.

In this view one may have a notion of actual infinity independent, as it stands also with formal individuals, of spatio-temporal and consequently causal constraints. This kind of immanent infinity appearing in the form of a continuous whole in the actual now of reflection and possibly extended indefinitely in all 'directions' while preserving the identity and relations of any well-defined objects within it as temporal fulfillments is, in fact, what makes mathematics such an effective and inexhaustible tool to describe real world processes while by the same token conditioning (partly at least) the non-decidability of key foundational questions in axiomatic set theory.[10] This kind of infinity is not to be confused with real world causality-constrained infinity conceivable only as spatiotemporally unbounded and, phenomenologically considered, invariably extending its eidetic state-of-affairs horizon ideally *in infinitum*. It is an infinity meant in radical phenomenological reduction as a correlate of inner-time consciousness and therefore prone to the circularities and inherent impredicativity induced by its non-objective origin, namely the absolute subjectivity (i.e., the transcendental ego) of consciousness as being-in-constituting (and not constituted) *prima causa*.

In consequence infinity in this sense may open up an extra-theoretical discussion relevant to the conception of infinite sets as completed totalities especially in the case where there is no possibility to carry out a recursive enumeration on these sets or generate them by first-order predicate formulas that exclude power-set operations and certain 'external' predicates to a standard first-order system.

4 Some Prompts on Infinity in Classical Tradition

4.1 A Brief Review of Infinity in the Platonic-Aristotelian Metaphysics

In the platonic *Parmenides* a characteristic example of the contradictions that may result from ontological definitions that do not take into account a notion of subjective constitution is the person's Parmenides inference that the part (τό μόριον) "is a part, not of many nor of all, but of a single form and a single concept which we call a whole, a perfect unity created out of all; this it is of which the part is a part" (Fowler 1996: 157 E). In this case we do not come upon a relation between primary elements and their aggregate by a progression of iterative acts and their active synthesis but instead between a part and a containing

---

[10] This claim is largely associated with a subjectively based approach to the foundations of mathematics, see: Livadas (2015) and Livadas (2016). Also for a more detailed description of mathematical objects in phenomenologically motivated terms the reader may consult Livadas (2016) and Tieszen (2011).

whole which is specified as a single concept (ἰδέα) and a single form, so as to underline the different genus to which the whole belongs with respect to its parts or generally to others.

It turns out that ambiguities or contradictions found in platonic Parmenides in this and other places, e.g. in Fowler (1996): 159 B, may be due to a certain vagueness of ontological notions mainly engendered by the transformation of the objects of experience, to which we bear a specific and at least not analytically describable kind of relation, into formal objects of apophantic logic in ignoring the context established by the evidence of a constituting temporal consciousness.

If for Plato in *Timaeus* the impossibility of thinking of an all-encompassing unity in terms of plurality, even of an infinite one, is reflected in the description of the Universe as the single visible living being containing all living beings of the same natural order, Aristotle, in his part, had gone into lengths in *Metaphysics* to show that the infinite cannot exist actually nor can be an essence unto itself. On the assumption of actuality any part we might take of it would be infinite, being a substance and not an attribute of a subject, and consequently either indivisible or infinitely divisible if it is divisible. But the same thing cannot be many infinities at once just as air is part of air by being of the same genus. Consequently infinity is indivisible and impartible (ἀδιαίρετος καί ἀμέριστος). Yet what is actually infinite must be attribute of something spatio-temporally existing, therefore it must be a quantity (which is partible) and for this reason it must be an accidental attribute of that of which it is accidental which eventually means that actual infinity cannot be a self-standing essence in an ontological sense.

A still more interesting point is Aristotle's subsequent aporia as to how and in virtue of what can mathematical magnitudes be taken as a unity, more concretely, in which way a collection of mathematical unities can be regarded as a unity in its own right. Further and most important, he seems to suggest that the underlying unifying factor for objects in the world can be reasonably supposed to be the soul, or part of the soul or some other influence apart from which things are a plurality and may disintegrate. Yet even though he alluded to a subjectively founded unifying factor of an indefinite plurality of, e.g., mathematical objects, a reference which oddly enough is not substantially commented in aristotelian secondary literature, he virtually left open the question as to the cause in virtue of which mathematical magnitudes, being divisible and quantitative, are formed in unity and cohesion (Tredennick and Armstrong 1990, p. 184). In any case he did not delve further into a subjectively founded interpretation for the underlying reason of unity in terms of plurality.[11]

Concerning the apprehension of infinity in physical terms Aristotle stated in the first book of *Metaphysics* (*Metaphysics I–IX*) that even though infinity as well as void can be said to exist potentially, they cannot exist as separate states-of-being in actuality but only in knowledge in other words only as mental states-of-affairs. Views on infinity and void are more systematically taken up in Aristotle's *Physics* (resp., Book III, iv–viii and Book IV, vi–ix) where Aristotle admitted to the difficulties posed by the problem of the infinite in which many contradictions result whether we suppose it to exist or not. Therefore he

---

[11] Hellman and Shapiro have developed, in Hellman and Shapiro (2012, 2013), a formal axiomatical system to construct a 'regions based' one-dimensional continuum which follows the Aristotelian credo that continua are not composed of points (as spatially postulated). However they do not follow Aristotle in a very important aspect, namely in that they make essential use of the actual infinite rejecting the notion of potential infinity espoused, at least on epistemic grounds, by Aristotle and many other mathematicians and philosophers since then.

wondered: "If it exists, we have still to ask how it exists; as a substance or as the essential attribute of some entity? Or in neither way, yet none the less is there something which is infinite or some things which are infinitely many?" (Ross 1960, *Engl. transl.*, p. 43).

In the course of ensuing argumentations Aristotle reached the conclusion that since 'being' has more than one sense, the sense of being of the infinite is not that of an ontological being rendered unto a definite substance but consists in a process of coming to be and passing away. In particular talking about numbers, if numbers are bounded below by the least indivisible one, it is always possible in the direction of largeness to think of a larger number consequently this infinite is a potential, not an actual one. Moreover since each larger number is associated with a process of bisection with regard to the immediately smaller number, its infinity as inseparable from the process of bisection which is not a permanent actuality but consists in a process of coming to be like time and the number of time (ibid., *Engl. transl.*, p. 50).

It is noteworthy that in the last paragraph of the part viii of Book III Aristotle seems to imply that there is a possibility of an indefinite magnification of a quantity in thought[12] which however does not correspond to an infinite in real world terms adding by the same token that time, movement and also thinking are infinite in the sense that each part taken in the actual now passes in succession out of existence (ibid., *Engl. transl.*, p. 51).

I take the last statement, even if it is marginal in Aristotle's main argumentation on the nature of infinity, as an indication that the reduction of infinity to an immanence in consciousness associated in an essential way with the nature of time may point to certain aristotelian insights about the nature of infinity that run contrary to a foundation of the infinite in terms of ontological being.

4.2 Infinity in the Perspective of Locke's and Hume's Philosophies

Even though Husserl had fundamental disagreements with Locke's and Hume's views on ontology and metaphysics he had great esteem for both philosophers especially for Hume whom he regarded (along with Descartes) as a precursor of transcendental phenomenology. His primary critique concerning Locke was that he could not see that the problems of knowledge in their purity and in principle are incompatible with the objectivism of his method, that these problems require to put radically into question the whole universe of objectivity and hold it exclusively in the sphere of pure (absolute) consciousness (Husserl 1956, p. 76). In the same viewpoint, while praising Hume's *Treatise* as being the first outline of a pure phenomenology, he nevertheless remarked that it was actually in the sense of a pure sensualistic and empirical phenomenology. In this regard Hume's nominalistic reduction could not found the identity of ego, making each one the same person, out of an aggregation of constantly interconnected perceptions. Moreover Hume's inductive-empirical objectivism would be at odds with the necessity of the eidetic character of the Husserlian description of consciousness. Consequently the idea of infinity that both Locke and Hume held cannot in any way be reducible to an immanental form correlative to the intentional modes of a self-constituting temporal consciousness.

---

[12] The possibility of reaching an infinity in thought in the sense of immanence which does not correspond to a spatiotemporally founded one is also implied by the statement that "not only number but also mathematical magnitudes and what is outside the heaven are supposed to be infinite because they never give out in our thought" (Greek orig. of the underlined: διὰ γὰρ τὸ ἐν τῇ νοήσει μὴ ὑπολείπειν) (Ross 1960, *Engl. transl.*, p. 43).

Is there an Ontology of Infinity?

More specifically, Locke upheld the negativity of the ideas of infinity and infinite divisibility on the grounds of adding to the sense impressions of extension and divisibility (upon extension) the 'negativity' of unbounded or unlimited continuation in the understanding that the idea of an end is, on intuitive grounds, rather positive than negative. Yet the notion of infinity in these terms and *a fortiori* that of infinite divisibility, even in the Lockean negative sense,[13] presuppose a notion of infinite time as an *in rem* condition for the kind of conception of the negativity of an unlimited continuation,[14] thereby making the concept of infinity, as it is the case also with Hume, ultimately dependent on and derivable from a progressing series of impressions of perceptions and reflections. It follows that Locke reduced infinity to the sense Husserl precisely denied, namely to an ever extending sensual 'substratum' founded (in the Husserlian sense of *Fundierung*) on real world spatiotemporality and the accompanying causality. Evidently this would be an infinity of virtually no conceptual relevance with the formal-mathematical notion of infinity, at least as this notion has been established from the time of Cantor's introduction of the theory of transfinite numbers and has evolved since then in the development of axiomatic set theory and the theory of large cardinals, taking also into account the intuitionistic idea of infinity and the intuitive continuum. In short, the Lockean semi-empiricist position on infinity, in contrast to the Husserlian immanentization of infinity as eidetically 'constrained', cannot epistemologically account for a mathematically proper notion of infinity, for instance, of the kind generated in a non-nominalist sense by logical-mathematical formulas quantifying over an indefinite domain.

In a phenomenological perspective Hume's position can also prove faulty even if Hume discarded any argumentation based on the 'negativity' of an unlimited continuation adjoined to finitely many impressions, and espoused instead only the negativity of the vacuum, as the latter idea was entertained by the natural philosophy of the time. Yet this would leave someone clueless as to the possibility of a conception of infinity to the extent that memory, imagination and reason would be only left to elaborate on the 'materials' provided by the senses and consequently could not make more in conceptual complexity than these 'materials' would allow. This would evidently imply that the finitistic and limiting character of impressions would by necessity constrain the accessibility to any conception of infinity in an absolute sense (Jacquette 2001, p. 69).

To sum up both Locke's and Hume's account of infinity left no room for a complete riddance of the concept of infinity of the spatiotemporal and causal constraints that Husserlian phenomenology sought to abolish by treating infinity and infinite objects as categorial objects in their own eidetic characteristics and ultimately associating infinity, in terms of transcendental phenomenology, with inner temporality and its constituting subjective origin.

---

[13] In *An Essay Concerning Human Understanding*, Locke argued about the 'negativity' of the idea of infinity on the grounds of the finiteness of human mind for which an infinite extension (over time) cannot but produce a negative idea of infinity, that is, a confusing and indeterminate one out of insufficient understanding (see Jacquette 2001, p. 66).

[14] Even though Locke denied that we might have any positive idea of infinite number, space, or time he nonetheless claimed that the ideas of 'causal power' and 'unity' are found to be ubiquitous within experience (Garrett 1997, p. 18). As argued in the present article, unity (but not causality) can be integrated in the phenomenological sense of immanent infinity.

5 Is There Infinity as an Entity?

In view of the discussion of the previous sections one may reasonably claim that the possibility of an ontological foundation of infinity can be correlated with a possible ontology of intuitive continuum insofar as actual infinity, at least in phenomenological terms, can be re-presented as a complete, immanent objectivity in the form of the continuous unity of consciousness. It should be noted here that while the intuitionistic view of intuitive continuum as an impredicative, immanental substrate devoid of any quality or specification is close to the phenomenological description of internal time,[15] yet the (mathematical) infinite in Brouwer's conception of freely evolving choice sequences is associated with indefinitely processing mental processes. The fact certainly is that Brouwerian intuitionism undertook an interpretation of mathematics in terms of the notion of time which, among others, leads to the rejection of the principle of excluded middle. However it is on the grounds of the phenomenologically motivated principle of two-ity with regard to the progression of choice sequences, an intuition reducible to the intentional modes of protention-retention[16] in temporal consciousness, that Husserl's student Oskar Becker criticized Brouwer's intuitionism. In more concrete terms Becker claimed that Brouwer's thinking about time was insufficient to make sense of free-choice sequences, namely of 'lawless', non-repetitive constructions which in intuitionistic analysis were needed to introduce the real numbers.[17] Even as Becker 'deviated' from orthodox (Husserlian) phenomenology to attribute an interpretational role to the historicity of Heideggerian *Dasein*, he still endorsed the phenomenological idea of the possibility of reflecting each time upon a potentially infinite sequence of mentally implemented iterations in virtue of a whole, thus allowing finite human consciousness to grasp transfinite structures as totalities in actuality. Therefore by taking recourse to a constituting subjectivity attitude he hoped, at odds with Brouwerian intuitionism, to vindicate large parts of the Cantorian theory of transfinite numbers (Sluga 2019, pp. 577–578).

These given, an interesting and widely debated question is whether the possibility of existence of entities (in virtue of objectivities within the world), as infinity and continuum may be taken to be, can be answered empirically or categorically. The author clearly rejects the former position simply by pointing to the fact that infinity (at least as an epistemic term) is never attained empirically either in empirical physical sciences or formal logical-mathematical ones but only as an ideal limit generated by abstractions made in thought. And yet in choosing the second option and stating that the question of existence of the continuum (and infinity for that matter) is a categorial question, we face the circular inconvenience that categories are themselves categorial terms insofar as categories may not signify ontological differences but rather the ways the mind puts experience into some sort of order so that successful consequences may follow. This means that categorial distinctions are not set up by the nature of things but depend on the activity of the mind (irrespectively

---

[15] In what Brouwer described as the primordial intuition of mathematics intuitive continuum is the "substratum, divested of all quality, of any perception of change, a unity of continuity and discreteness, a possibility of thinking together several entities, connected by a 'between', which is never exhausted by the insertion of new entities" (Brouwer 1907, p. 17 in: Van Atten et al. 2002, p. 205).

[16] These specifically phenomenological terms can be roughly described as a priori forms of intentionality toward an original impression just passed-by to the past (retention) and an a-thematic 'expectation' to the future (protention). For more the reader may look at Husserl (1966).

[17] For a review of the fundamentals of the intuitionistic version of mathematical foundations, in particular the *ad hoc* continuity principles, the reader may consult (Heyting 1966).

of the content one gives to the term mind) in terms of which they are 'detached' from reality through conscious experience which is temporal and therefore continuous.

It is interesting and clearly supportive of my argumentation against an ontology of the infinite, H. Lee's view in *Are There Any entities?* that the question of whether there exist entities in a self-standing ontological sense is closely bound up with the question of whether reality is a substantial unity composed of discrete, ontologically self-standing parts, objects and classes of objects, or whether it is a process composed of continuous events. This is claimed by Lee to be perhaps the most fundamental metaphysical dispute in contemporary philosophy as it summarizes the underlying question of continuity and the relation between the continuous and the discrete (Lee 1979, p. 125). It turns out that entities as categorial terms are meaningless without some sort of constituting activity of the mind which is moreover a discursive activity if entities as such and in relation to others are going to be carriers of a meaning. Most importantly the whole approach, which in places reminds of Whitehead's 'ontology' of events in *Process and Reality*, presupposes a temporal conscious experience with respect to a reality which is a concrete continuum. The way to delineate entities as mental objects in terms of beginnings, ends, limits and boundaries is to break the continuum only in abstraction since mind "cannot actually stop process" (ibid,. p. 127). Entities, therefore, are not to be considered as existing in ontological self-sufficiency independently of the mind, yet the concept of entity becomes a fundamental categorial tool for the purpose of understanding and reaching the level of need for social communication. In short, what I find relevant here to my own approach are the following claims: (1) entities in general do not correspond to ontologically self-standing beings but are reduced to some kind of constituting-transforming activity of the mind in a way that they ultimately become hypostatizations (2) any constituting and further transforming activity of the mind is performed in terms of human experience which, conscious or unconscious, is temporal and as such it is continuous.

On these purely intuitive grounds one may have a refutation of the ontological claims for the infinite without necessarily espousing phenomenological analysis at least in a strict and constraining sense. Of course the debate of what may count as ontological entities either in metaphysical or epistemic terms is a far-reaching and evolving one especially in the light of the progressing epistemological edifice including the content one may give to the term ontology itself. A major question, for instance, is the way infinity is mediated through logico-linguistic formulation to obtain a semantic content within a formal mathematical environment. However this latter discussion would probably take us out of the scope and the limits of the present article.[18]

6 Is There an Epistemic Foundation for an Ontology of Infinity?

As already stated my argumentation is based on the assumption that the mathematical infinite subsumes the infinite of physical theories to the extent that physics and science in general deals with the infinite in terms of the corresponding mathematical metatheory and consequently through the expressional means of formal mathematical language and the specific techniques involved.

---

[18] The interested reader may look at Livadas (2020) for a detailed presentation of the issue.

Is there an Ontology of Infinity?

Modern philosophical views of infinity have, if anything else, clarified our understanding of the difficulties and questions encountered in the view of infinity as a potentiality with regard to the finiteness of the natural world, going as far as to be regarded as an 'externally' imposed disruption to the finite order. A. Badiou's epistemological approach to the question of infinity in *Being and Event* (Badiou 2005), is in fact its reconceptualization in formal-mathematical terms, more specifically in terms of set and set-forcing theories.

More concretely, axiomatic set theory is thought to revolutionize our understanding of infinity in two ways: (1) it makes possible a view of infinity as actually existing in the form of a complete, even though non-'traversable', whole and (2) it abolishes the 'naive' homogeneity of infinity by articulating a sequence of infinities of various orders. As a result in Badiou's view infinity, as actual and susceptible to articulation in thought, is made part of the world without a need to refer to an external metaphysical or 'divine' reason. In fact actual infinity in the sense of an impredicative 'substrate' upon which logical-mathematical formulas bounded by universal-existential quantifiers may lay ontological claims by generating infinite mathematical objects is implicitly present in most of foundational mathematics and logic.

Moreover as I have argued earlier actual infinity as founded in each one's temporal consciousness is indeed the only one immanently existing whose evidence is any infinite objectivity as a completed totality in reflection. Consequently, on this supposition, the known canonical scale of infinities generated by the circular notion of sets as collections of objects, the indefinite repetition of the power-set operation within infinite cardinalities or the list of large cardinals, e.g., inaccessible, supercompact and even larger ones generated by strong infinity assumptions, are in fact formal-mathematical intricacies conditioned and presupposing a temporally founded continuous unity whose 'derivative' form is actual infinity in presentational immediacy.

In a parallel situation in forcing theory[19] Badiou proposes to consider the generation of a generic set G as an indiscernible multiple out of finitistic conditions which themselves belong to a particular situation. In other words an indiscernible whole, the generic set G, is generated by means of subjective acts performed over a set of finitistic conditions. In view of this apparent incompatibility reducible to the sphere of subjectivity, Badiou wonders how "an ontological concept of the pure indiscernible multiple exists" (Badiou 2005, p. 358). In accordance and concerning the nature of a generic set as a pure indiscernible multiple, he concludes that "at base its sole property is that of consisting as pure multiple, or being. Subtracted from language, it makes do with its being." (ibid., p. 371).

This is a state of affairs which is naturally the outcome of Badiou's ontology in which the subjectivity factor is standing 'opposite' to the transcendence of the event and is deprived of the essential property of being co-constitutive with the event (be it a physical or mental one) in the modes in which it can be co-constitutive within-the-world. Yet what are thought to be essential properties of genericity, i.e., the filter and generic properties proper, are not mere subtracts of the formal language for they can be seen as abstractions presupposing subjectively founded meaning-acts as those of set formation (in terms of passive and retrospective apprehension; see Sect. 3, par. 4), of ordering, of the conservative extension of a set-theoretical structure over an indefinite horizon, etc. These can

---

[19] Forcing theory is, roughly speaking, an ingenious mathematical technique initiated by the American mathematician P. Cohen in 1963, and further developed to a full-fledged mathematical theory, mostly motivated by the interest to resolve certain key mathematical questions such as the *Continuum Hypothesis*. More can be found in Cohen's (1966) own work, and Kunen's (1982).

be considered as mathematical acts performed independently of any spatio-temporal and causal constraints, being only subjected to certain eidetic necessities of an intentional-constitutive consciousness and also mediated by previous mathematical experience in reference to the world as a ground of experience.

The fact that a generic set G retains the property of being indiscernible (in Badiou's sense), even though it does not introduce any new ordinals in the extended forcing model $M[G]$ of **ZFC** (i.e., the standard Zermelo–Fraenkel Set Theory with the Axiom of Choice), can be seen as a concrete case in the mathematics of the infinite where one can think of an infinite set in excess of constructivist steps, as having a host of desired properties even if they are not generated by definability formulas associated with Gödel's constructive universe **L**. Badiou sets a dividing line between the subject on the one side and the event (which belongs to 'that-which-is-not-being-qua-being') on the other, in the sense that "situated in being, subjective emergence forces the event to decide the true of the situation" (Badiou 2005, pp. 429–430). Infinities meant in Badiou's general ontology are associated to one or the other degree, as it happens with the extrinsic indiscernibility of a generic set G, with the transcendental character of the event which is generally thought of to be a major prerequisite of truth.

A phenomenologically motivated view could dismiss the artificial distinction between subject and event insofar as the event in the sense of implementation of a mathematical act carried out in objective time cannot be conceived independently of the self-evident presence of a consciousness endowed with specific intentional-constitutional properties within the world of experience. In this sense, referring again to the method of forcing, the subject cannot force the event to 'decide' the truthfulness of a situation existing on the ground level (by its presumed veracity in the extended model) on the supposition of existence of a generic indiscernible part of the ground model M, a position that seems to me a rather superficial interpretation of the subjective influence in shaping mathematical truths. One should rather assume that the existence of the indiscernible part G of the ground model with the presumed generic properties represents the capacity of the (mathematical) consciousness to apprehend infinite mathematical objects with specific combinatorial properties and extend or restrict them indefinitely in a consistent way eventually granting them globally desirable properties, in the fond of a continuous unity which is not as such part of the predicative universe of the formal system in question.

In the *On Ontology and Realism in Mathematics*, Gaifman (2012) has claimed that the problem of the 'natural questions' of a given area in mathematics has to do with the relations between ontological and epistemic factors. A a matter of fact major advances in the history of mathematics have been made by reorganizations of the epistemic framework which made it more transparent and thus more efficient. However, in his view, the translation of a mathematical theory into set theory is an ontological reduction that destroys the epistemic organization of the area since it is indifferent, if not counterproductive, to the mathematician who works in that area.[20] Natural questions arising in a particular

---

[20] It is questionable, though, whether the translation of a mathematical theory, be it a pure or applied mathematics theory, to the axiomatic set theory is indeed an ontological reduction properly meant or just a reduction to the meanings and methods associated with the semantics and the syntactical structure of set-theoretical models. Of course a supplementary reduction on the level of primitive logical-mathematical ideas such as an indefinite collection of abstract objects, the non-logical predicate of belonging, $\in$, etc., may lead to questions pertaining to the nature of primitive mathematical objects themselves, but then whether one chooses an ontological interpretation in a platonic context or a subjectively based one is a matter of choice and sound argumentation.

Is there an Ontology of Infinity?

mathematical area depend on the epistemic organization, and the undecidability of such a question shows to the mathematician that his grasp of the area was defective. What appeared as a well stated question that had a unique solution turns out to have more than one answer depending on the corresponding version of set theory. Speaking metaphorically, it is an undermining of the epistemic by the ontological, the latter appearing here in the form of set theory to which the given mathematical theory is reduced. An easy example to consider is any theorem or corollary in the mathematical metatheory of general relativity conditioned on the continuity of the corresponding topological structures and consequently on the solid foundation of tensor equations across space-time. These problems can be reduced to the set-theoretical question of establishing the power (cardinality) of the continuum which, as well-known, is a problem with two alternative, conflicting answers depending on the set-theoretical model one works with.

Hilbert believed that the two, epistemic and ontological, can go together. The success of Hilbert's program would guarantee that we can safely work in a given area, pretending that the actual infinities that figure in our reasoning are real and thus pretended realism is safe. And the slogan 'in mathematics there are no *ignorabimus*' would mean that our epistemic apparatus is able to solve any mathematical problem that arises in our research. After all the problem, e.g. that of determining the power of the continuum, was not forced on us by the physical world. It arose in the domain of pure thinking and therefore pure thought can possibly handle it. However, in Gaifman's view, Gödel's undecidability results introduce a wedge between the epistemic and the ontological which makes us conclude that pure thought is not enough (ibid., p. 410).

As a matter of fact immanent infinity, that is, 'infinity' as constituted in temporal consciousness in the form of an objective fulfilment exhibiting a priori eidetic characteristics, is implicitly presupposed in the treatment of the mathematical infinite even in case one discards an ontological commitment to infinity in favor of its comprehension through epistemic articulation. This is Kanamori's position in *The Infinite as Method in Set Theory and Mathematics* where "the commitment to the infinite is to what is communicable about it, to the procedures and methods in articulated contexts, to language and argument. Infinite sets are what they do, and their sense is carried in the methods we collectively employ on their behalf." (Kanamori 2009, p. 39). Yet in spite of his view that assimilation of methods along hierarchies can be viewed as commitments to the infinite in the sense that different assumptions and techniques are employed respectively in the introduction of the countably infinite of natural numbers, the continuum of real analysis, and the (empyrean) infinite of higher set theory, Kanamori urges a kind of ecumenical approach to the infinite leaving, without further specification, some clues to an irreducible semantic content of 'prior' proofs relating to the resources of the underlying elementary system of a statement (ibid., p. 40). This is a claim that leaves by itself some room for doubt concerning the claim that mathematical infinite can be accounted for only in terms of epistemic articulation, that is, in the way it is approached, assimilated, and applied in the construction of mathematical hierarchies.

On the assumption, in Kanamori's sense, that the infinite in epistemic terms can be a way out of the impasse of a purported ontology of infinity, it seems one may still stumble upon theoretical obstacles and circularities whose origin may be indeed the lack of an ontology of infinity.[21] I refer in particular to two logical paradoxes, the Russell paradox

---

[21] Of course mathematicians treat infinite in everyday mathematical practice as an ideally existing yet concrete and complete mathematical object (or rather such a collection of objects), part of the predicative universe of a formal theory. This was acknowledged as far back as Aristotle's *Physics* (Ross 1960, *Engl. transl.*, p. 50). Yet this conventional attitude, dear to logical positivism, in no way affects the question of a possible ontological treatment of the infinite.

generated by Frege's attempt of the reduction of arithmetic to logic and the Burali-Forti paradox generated by the conception of the class of all ordinals as a completed mathematical object. In both cases M. Dummett has suggested that the underlying reason is our failure to recognize and properly reason with what he calls 'indefinitely extensible concepts', a primary instance of which is the concept of ordinal numbers (Dummett 1991, p. 316). Given that for any given ordinal the position the particular ordinal occupies in the natural ordering is given by its very existence, the answer about the place occupied by a new ordinal put in the end of this ordering must presuppose the existence of a pre-existing class of all ordinals as a determinate whole which is precisely what generates the Burali-Forti paradox. Dummett sees an obvious analogy between the notion of an indefinitely extensible concept and the more philosophically familiar notion of potential infinity applied in a sense that may also include the choice sequences of intuitionistic analysis, as ever progressing ones either by a recurring formula or freely expanding, something that requires the application of intuitionistic rather than classical logic to reason about these concepts (ibid, p. 319).

Yet one knows that Cantor's well-ordering principle which corresponds to a defining characteristic of ordinals was reduced in 1904 by Zermelo to the Axiom of Choice, **AC**, namely the abstract existence assertion that for every set X there is a choice function, i.e., a function f such that for every non-empty subset $Y \in X$, $f(Y) \in Y$. In this way Zermelo showed that a set is well-orderable (in other words it can be ordered by the well-ordering of ordinals) if and only if its power set has a choice function, that is, the axiom **AC** takes hold. It turns out that the extremely important in foundational mathematics Axiom of Choice has a three-fold implication: **(a)** it is based on a meta-mathematical concept of actual infinity meant as a kind of abstract, completed infinity on which to define the choice function as indefinitely extensible **(b)** it has been proved to be independent from the rest of the axioms of the standard Zermelo–Fraenkel Set Theory, **ZF**, a result that attests, if we accept Gödel's position (about the *Continuum Hypothesis*) in the earlier version of *What is Cantor's Continuum*, to a problematic mathematical state-of-affairs and **(c)** it is, nevertheless, regarded a necessary principle "for infusing the contextualized transfinite with the order already inherent in the finite." (Kanamori 2009, p. 38). The fact is, being in principle an indefinitely extensible infusion of order, **AC** is conditioned as such on the prior existence of an abstract (completed) infinity in actuality which in turn cannot be grounded otherwise but as immanently induced in consciousness with no real space-time foundedness. By this measure it cannot be a potential infinity in Dummett's sense above in association with the concept of ordinals.

Given that the mathematical infinite is layered in degrees of complexity, starting from the countably infinite of natural numbers, it is worthwhile to show the way a metatheoretical, in fact a completed, subjectively founded infinity conditions other assumptions and circularly reproduces itself in the ascension through hierarchical levels.[22] In these terms a

---

[22] An interesting, though no further discussed on a subjective level, view of the mathematical continuum is E. Belaga's in *Halfway Up To the Mathematical Infinity I: On the Ontological & Epistemic Sustainability of Georg Cantor's Transfinite Design*. Belaga suggests that any phenomenologically and ontologically faithful axiomatization of the continuum should include a non-locality postulate (in the sense this term is understood in quantum information processing) to formally account for the following property of the continuum: All 'points', or 'elements' of the continuum are non-locally, i.e., simultaneously and at any moment, accessible. This non-local accessibility extends to all well-defined 'slices' (subsets in a set-theoretical terminology) of the continuum (Belaga 2009, pp. 34–35).

Is there an Ontology of Infinity?

question that can be raised in the study of large cardinals theory is the extent to which the assumption of a standard level of reality, more concretely the conception of the intuitive and, in abstraction, of the formal-mathematical continuum (the latter associated with the uncountably infinite of real analysis), influences in one way or another the formal-axiomatical development of the theory. We may reasonably ask whether this level of reality must be implicitly assumed, for example, in extending *ad infinitum* the domain of application of quantifiers of first-order or second-order formulas in the various stages of construction of large cardinals; e.g., in the definition of κ-complete filters and ultrafilters for $\kappa > \omega$. And of course we may raise the same question over the application, in the same context, of the Axiom of Choice or of its logical equivalents.

Over the last decades the main tool for introducing new and ever more powerful infinite cardinals is by means of ultrapowers and elementary embeddings,[23] that is, through truth-preserving injective mappings from the set-theoretical universe V into inner models M[24] equipped with structural properties associated each time with an ascending scale of infinity and reflected in the increasing resemblance between V and M. It turns out that by elementary embeddings a sense of connection with Cantor's Absolute can be obtained by increasingly enhancing the 'simulation' of M toward V thus vindicating Gödel's later position that every axiom of infinity should be derived from the extremely plausible principle that V is undefinable, where definability is to be taken in a more and more generalized and idealized sense.[25] Along the way Scott's result on measurable cardinals, obtained by the elementary embeddings approach, succeeded in transcending Gödel's delimitative universe of constructibility by contradicting the constructibility axiom $V = L$ through the postulation of existence of a measurable cardinal. Later, Vopěnka and Hrbaček generalized Scott's result by proving its generalization on the assumption of existence of a strongly compact cardinal. Both results are, characteristically, conditioned on the existential postulation of a κ-complete ultrafilter over $\kappa > \omega$ which is by itself associated with set-theoretical operations and universal quantifications on scales above $\aleph_0$ (i.e., the first infinite countable cardinal or, correspondingly, the first limit ordinal ω).

One may also argue for the implicit assumption of a standard level of reality, in the sense of an immanent continuous unity formally corresponding to the continuum of real analysis, in Woodin's research in higher set theory with the aim of acceding to Cantor's Absolute. More concretely, without entering into the tricky technical details, Woodin has tried to elaborate an inner model program which from a strategy of incremental understanding of large cardinals, with universe V forever hopelessly out of reach because of Scott's result (mentioned before) and its 'descendants', could evolve into a program for perhaps understanding V itself by approaching it closely enough. This in turn has generated an axiom for an ultimate version of Gödel's constructible universe L, namely the axiom $V = $ Ultimate-L and its accompanying conjecture, the Ultimate-L Conjecture, which

---

[23] For structures $\mathcal{M}_0 = <M_0,..>$ and $\mathcal{M}_1 = <M_1,..>$ of a language $\mathcal{L}$, an injective function $j : M_0 \longrightarrow M_1$ is an elementary embedding of $\mathcal{M}_0$ into $\mathcal{M}_1$ ($j : \mathcal{M}_0 \prec \mathcal{M}_1$) iff for any formula $\varphi(u_1,...,u_n)$ of $\mathcal{L}$ and $x_1,..,x_n \in M_0$

$$\mathcal{M}_0 \vDash \varphi[x_1,....,x_n] \text{ iff } \mathcal{M}_1 \vDash \varphi[j(x_1),....,j(x_n)].$$

[24] A class M is an inner model iff M is a transitive model of **ZF** under the $\in$ predicate and contains the class of all ordinals, i.e., $ON \subseteq M$.

[25] In fact the elementary embeddings (into inner models) approach has its inherent limitations by virtue of Kunen's fundamental result in Kunen (1971). Kunen has proved, capitalizing on the application of **AC** and the Erdös–Hajnal theorem, that if j is an elementary embedding from V into V then j must be the identity mapping. See Kunen (1971, pp. 407–408).

would supposedly prove, on the assumption of sufficiently large cardinals, that the Ultimate-L exists in close proximity to V and moreover would also settle some inherent problems in the development of set theory.[26]

Yet Woodin's axiom $V = $ Ultimate-L is based on the construction of a structural generalization of L, HOD $^{L(A,R)}$, which has been verified as such for many (yet only conjectured for all) universally Baire sets $A \subset R$.[27] This given, one can reasonably raise the following counterarguments:

First, it is at least questionable from a foundational viewpoint whether one can apply on the level of purely set-theoretical constructions topological notions inherently associated with the structure of the set of reals which is doubted in the first place to be a set at least in terms of the standard definition of a set, and the application of the power-set operation. Second, even in taking Woodin's use of topological notions in the construction of the structural generalization HOD $^{L(A,R)}$ of L as 'lawful', this can only give credit to my argument about Woodin's progression to an ultimate level of proximity to V by being conditioned on the implicit assumption of a standard prior level of reality. In other words one must rely on a formal level of reality associated with the continuum of real analysis, reducible on the subjective level to an 'infinite' continuous unity which circularly reproduces itself in the level of higher set theory.

There are other concrete instances in the axiomatization and further in the construction of mathematical theories and corresponding models in which a notion of actual infinity is applied which is not, as I have tried to show, an infinity conceivable in ontological terms. This can be *a fortiori* true for physical theories as such, independently of their mathematical metatheory, in which any conception of objective spatio-temporality may only be, at best, an unbounded 'finiteness' indefinitely extensible.

Looking back, and this could serve as a conclusion to this article, my intention was to refute an ontological conception of the infinite both on the purely philosophical level and the epistemic one, in the latter case on the assumption that the mathematical infinite underlies and conditions physical and positive science in general in terms of the predicative linguistic universe through which every empirical-'observational' science is mediated. In this viewpoint I argued, by referring to some concrete situations, against an ontology of infinity in the terms the concept of infinity is epistemologically articulated by virtue of the axiomatic and proof-theoretical machinery of mathematics. Unfettered by any platonic or generally idealist preoccupations and focusing my argumentation toward a subjective constitution on the part of a constituting temporal consciousness within-the-world, I was strongly motivated by the Husserlian writings on the matter, to a significant extent applied and commented in this paper, so as to proceed to a 'deconstruction' of the ontological foundation of the infinite at least in the sense generally espoused in philosophy and science over centuries of platonic-metaphysical tradition. Next I tried to show the ways by which a phenomenologically founded infinite can epistemologically account for the actual infinity free from spatio-temporal and causal constraints that underlies formal-mathematical theory in its own right and also as a metatheory of physics.

---

[26] To date Woodin has proved the Ultimate-L Conjecture only under certain restrictive conditions. See: Woodin (2017, p. 3). For more details on Woodin's work the interested reader can also consult Woodin (2011, 2014).

[27] A subset A of the set of reals R is universally Baire if for all topological spaces Ω and all continuous functions $\pi : \Omega \to R$, the preimage of A by π has the property of Baire (a purely topological property) in the space Ω.

Is there an Ontology of Infinity?

Needless to say, the elaboration of the foundational theories of mathematics in the last decades and the constant enrichment of the epistemological edifice in general make the discussion about the mathematical and the 'ontological' infinite ever more relevant and worthy of an interdisciplinary discussion.

References

Badiou, A. (2005). *Being and event* (O. Feltham, Trans.). London: Continuum.
Belaga, G. E. (2009). Halfway up to the mathematical infinity I: On the ontological and epistemic sustainability of Georg Cantor's transfinite design, manuscript (pp. 1–49). arXiv:0812.3207v3.
Brouwer, L. E. J. (1907). *Over de grondslangen der wiskunde*, Ph.D. thesis, Universiteit van Amsterdam. Engl. transl. Brouwer, L. E. J. (1975). On the foundations of mathematics. In A. Heyting (Ed.), *Collected works I. Philosophy and foundations of mathematics*. Amsterdam: North-Holland Publishing.
Cohen, P. (1966). *Set theory and the continuum hypothesis*. Reading, MA: W.A. Benjamin.
Dummett, M. A. E. (1991). *Frege: Philosophy of mathematics*. Cambridge, MA: Harvard University Press.
Fowler N. C. (1996). *Plato. Cratylus, Parmenides, Greater Hippias, Lesser Hippias*. Loeb Classical Library, Cambridge, MA: Harvard University Press.
Gaifman, H. (2012). On ontology and realism in mathematics. *The Review of Symbolic Logic, 5*(3), 480–512.
Garrett, D. (1997). *Cognition and commitment in Hume's philosophy*. Oxford: Oxford University Press.
Hellman, G., & Shapiro, S. (2012). Towards a point-free account of the continuous. *Iyyun: The Jerusalem Philosophical Quarterly, 61*, 263–287.
Hellman, G., & Shapiro, S. (2013). The classical continuum without points. *Review of Symbolic Logic, 6*, 488–512.
Heyting, A. (1966). *Intuitionism. An introduction*. Amsterdam: North-Holland Publisher.
Husserl, E. (1939). *Erfahrung und Urteil*, hsgb. L. Landgrebe, Prag: Acad./Verlagsbuchhandlung. Engl. translation: (1973), *Experience and judgment* (J. S. Churchill & K. Americs, Trans.). London: Routledge & Kegan Paul.
Husserl, E. (1956). *Erste Philosophie*, Erster Teil, hsgb. R. Boehm. The Hague: M. Nijhoff.
Husserl, E. (1966). *Vorlesungen zur Phänomenologie des inneren Zeibewusstseins*, Hua Band X, hsgb. R. Boehm. Den Haag: M. Nijhoff.
Husserl, E. (1968). *Phänomenologische Psychologie*, hsgb. W. Biemel. Dordrecht: Springer-Science+B.M., B.V.
Husserl, E. (1970). *Philosophie der Arithmetik*, Hua Band XII, hsgb. L. Eley. Den Haag: M. Nijhoff.
Husserl, E. (1973a). *Zur Theorie der Intersubjektivität*, Erst. Teil, hsgb. Kern, I., Hua XIII. The Hague: M. Nijhoff.
Husserl, E. (1973b). *Zur Phänomenologie der Intersubjektivität*, dritter Teil, Hua Band XV, hsgb. I. Kern. The Hague: M. Nijhoff.
Husserl, E. (1976a). *Ideen zu einer reinen Phänomenologie und phänomenologischen Philosophie*, Erstes Buch, Hua Band III/I, hsgb. K. Schuhmann, Den Haag: M. Nijhoff. Engl. transl. (1983). *Ideas pertaining to a pure phenomenology and to a phenomenological philosophy: First book* (F. Kersten, Trans.). The Hague: M. Nijhoff.
Husserl, E. (1976b). *Die Krisis der Europäischen Wissenschaften und die Transzendentale Phänomenologie*, Hua Band VI, hsgb. W. Biemel. Den Haag: M. Nijhoff.
Husserl, E. (1984). *Logische Untersuchungen*, Hua Band XIX/1, hsgb. U. Panzer, The Hague: M. Nijhoff Pub. Engl. transl.: (2001), *Logical Investigations*, transl. J.N. Findlay, New York: Routledge.
Husserl, E. (1985). *Texte zur Phänomenologie des inneren Zeitbewsstseins (1893–1917)*, hsgb. R. Bernet, Text nach Husserliana Band X. Hamburg: Meiner Verlag.
Husserl, E. (2001). *Späte Texte über Zeitkonstitution, Die C-Manuscripte*, Hua Materialien Band VIII, hsgb. D. Lohmar. Dordrecht: Springer.
Jacquette, D. (2001). *David Hume's critique of infinity*. Leiden: Brill.
Kanamori, A. (2009). The infinite as method in set theory and mathematics. *Ontology Studies, 9*, 31–41.
Kunen, K. (1971). Elementary embeddings and infinitary combinatorics. *The Journal of Symbolic Logic, 36*, 407–413.
Kunen, K. (1982). *Set theory. An introduction to independence proofs*. Amsterdam: Elsevier.
Lee, N. H. (1979). Are there any entities? *Philosophy and Phenomenological Research, 40*(1), 123–129.

Livadas, S. (2015). The subjective roots of forcing theory and their influence in independence results. *Axiomathes*, *25*(4), 433–455.
Livadas, S. (2016). What is the nature of mathematical-logical objects? *Axiomathes*, *27*(1), 79–112.
Livadas, S. (2019). The transcendence of the ego in continental philosophy: Convergences and divergences. *Horizon. Studies in Phenomenology*, *8*(2), 573–601.
Livadas, S. (2020). Talking about models. *The Inherent Constraints of Mathematics*, Axiomathes, *30*, 13–36.
Michalski, K. (1997). *Logic and time*. Dordrecht: Kluwer Academemic Publishers.
Ross, D. W. (1960). *Aristotelis Physica*, Oxonii e Typographeo Clarendoniano. Oxford: Oxford University Press. Eng. transl. (2000). *Physics by Aristotle, written 350 B.C.E.* (P. R. Hardie & K. R. Gaye, Trans.). http://classics.mit.edu/Aristotle/physics.html.
Sluga, H. (2019). Oskar Becker or the reconciliation of mathematics and existential philosophy. In I. Apostolescu (Ed.), *After Husserl: Phenomenological Foundations of Mathematics, META research in hermeneutics, phenomenology, and practical philosophy*, XI, 2 (pp. 569–588), Al. I. Cuza University of Iasi: Romania.
Tieszen, R. (2011). *After Gödel: Platonism and rationalism in mathematics and logic*. Oxford: Oxford University Press.
Tredennick, H. & Armstrong, C. G. (1990). *Aristotle. Metaphysics, X–XIV. Oeconomica, Magna Moralia*, Loeb Classical Library. Cambridge, MA: Harvard University Press.
Van Atten, M., van Dalen, D., & Tieszen, R. (2002). Brower and Weyl: The phenomenology and mathematics of the intuitive continuum. *Philosophophia Mathematica*, *10*(3), 203–226.
Woodin, H. W. (2011). The realm of the infinite. In M. Heller & H. W. Woodin (Eds.), *Infinity, new research frontiers* (pp. 89–118). New York: Cambridge University Press.
Woodin, H. W. (2014). The weak ultimate L conjecture. In S. Geschke, B. Loewe, & P. Schlicht (Eds.), *Infinity, computability and metamathematics* (Vol. 23, pp. 309–329). London: College Publications.
Woodin, H. W. (2017). In search of ultimate-L: the 19th Midrasha mathematicae lectures. *Bulletin of Symbolic Logic*, *23*(1), 1–109.

Part B

Some platonic ontological claims under a phenomenological point of view

ABSTRACT: In this article I deal with some ontological claims about unity-substance (ἕν--ὄν) in Plato's opera *Theaetetus* and *Parmenides* from a phenomenologically motivated point of view. In this respect, I try to provide a new interpretation to ontological definitions such as to a unity as substance that necessitates, in my view, the introduction of a notion of temporal constitution in a phenomenological sense prior to the sense of the ontological object as such. Moreover, in this approach, I point to a radical difference on the level of subjective evidence between the notions of unity as such and of unity as substance. In the last section of the article I point to some absurd inferences about unity in the aforementioned platonic texts, to show that reasoning about such objects in a classical ontological approach can lead to contradictions in case we do not take into account a notion of temporal constitution.

1. INTRODUCTION

There has already been some published research work on a possible connection of platonic and aristotelian philosophy with phenomenology, e.g. concerning the theory of the meaning of expressions (Niehues-Pröbstig, 1987), the theory of *eidē* (Hopkins, 2010) and the structure of inner temporality (Held, 2007) & (Kirkland, 2007). Given this, my approach towards the notion of unity in the platonic texts of *Theaetetus* and *Parmenides* may hopefully prove to be a quite original and motivating one. As it stands, in both treatises there is an extensive and meticulous examination of the notion of unity in relation to itself and to others, developing to a broad discussion which, except for the inquiry on the ontological content of the term unity as such, eventually includes also the dialectical relation between unity taken as a whole and its parts.

We may say that within the corpus of platonic works, in *Theaetetus* it is mainly dealt with the problem of the foundation of knowledge through the dialogue of Socrates and Theaetetus whereas *Parmenides* is considered as essentially an attempt by the person Parmenides to postulate unity (ἕν) as a unity in itself and also with respect to any other entity (ὄν), in affirmation and then in refutation of its existence. Given this ontological context, I will draw attention to specific arguments about the notion of unity taken first as deprived of any predicative content except for the possibility to call it as such (unity-as such) and then taken as a temporal object susceptible of predication (unity-substance), to reach certain conclusions on the necessity of introduction of an idea of temporal constitution prior to the formulation of fundamental ontological definitions.[1]

---

[1] In the following text, the ontological term unity in a non-predicable sense, meant as deprived of any categorial attributes except for the possibility to 'call' it as such (in a sense further to be clarified), will be termed a unity-as such in contradistinction to a unity-substance assumed susceptible of categorial attributes with at least that of existence. For the former and for purposes

Some Platonic Ontological Claims

In *Theaetetus* (Plato, 1996b), the person Socrates characterizes primary elements (πρῶτα στοιχεῖα) as lacking of any essence, being only susceptible of a name attribution that makes them distinguishable from any other primary element. In the relevant passage he characterizes them as unknown (ἄγνωστα) and irrational (ἄλογα), although he immediately follows by specifying them as sensible entities (αἰσθητά) (Plato, 1996b: 202 B). Of course, this runs contrary to his aforementioned designation of primary elements, as every sensible entity is not only susceptible of a name attribution but also of an attribution of substance for it is obviously a bearer of certain definite qualities (e.g. it appropriates a spatial form, certain physical properties, etc.). If we accept the authenticity of this particular passage then we must infer that in making this claim, Plato assumed that primary elements can be only approached by way of abstraction from sensible elements of the objective world. Nevertheless, primary elements are thought of in *Theaetetus* as deprived of any ontological specification since in this way they would by necessity appropriate a substance whereas there is no way to predicate anything of them including the predication of existence. In any case primary elements can intermingle among themselves and therefore become objects of predication as they become more complex and by this very process of intermingling are thought of to become bearers of sense (λόγος γεγονέναι) which finally leads (e.g. in the grammatical construction of a name out of its letters) to the paradoxical situation where one can know the whole collection yet not knowing anything of its elements. In the course of the dialogue there comes up also the question of the ontological distinction between what is termed as Everything (τό Πᾶν) and what is termed the Whole (τό Ὅλον). Do they belong to the same genus taking the former as the sum of all its constituents and the latter as an all-inclusive entity, bearer of a sense which is not found in any of its constituting elements?

It is noteworthy that in *Parmenides* (Plato, 1996a), unity in a non-predicable sense is first taken as deprived of any categorial attribute including that of existence, yet it is used in subsequent reasoning in the sense of an ontological object to reach various contradictory or even absurd conclusions e.g. the others (τά ἄλλα) taken as complementary to unity are at once not one nor many, not whole nor parts, not similar nor dissimilar, not the same nor different, etc.

In view of the above, I will deal to a certain extent with the notions of unity-as such and of unity-substance which are alternatively taken as phenomenological objects that necessarily imply a subject performing a phenomenological reduction. Further, commenting on the structure and meaning of certain statements in *Theaetetus and Parmenides*, I will point to the confusion that may result from a controversial ontological treatment of the notions above with regard to a phenomenologically motivated approach. In this view, I'll try to show how their distinct 'ontological' content can lead to a deeper question which is that of two irreducibilities of a fundamentally incompatible character; that of a unity-as such taken as a unity devoid of any predicative content except for its strictly name sense and that of a unity-substance taken as a bearer of various categorial attributes, at least those of individuality and existence. This point of view should engender a notion of temporal constitution prior to the definition of purely ontological objects. This is mainly done in Section **3,** where I try to reorient the discussion about unity-substance, taken as an ontological object, in such a way that it can be considered as a well-defined temporal objectivity in the pure immanence of consciousness after the phenomenological reduction.

This approach will be further extended to deduce the necessity of existence of a participating organic-body consciousness for which both 'ontological' entities are referred

---

of clarity I correspond the Greek term ἕν-ἕν, whereas for the latter the term ἕν-ὄν.

to specific modes of temporally constituted intentional objects; this way a phenomenology of constitution and also the principle of intersubjectivity is called to ground the subsequent structure of ontological definitions.

2. UNITIES AS INTUITIONS OF A KNOWING SUBJECT

2.1. Some prompts from the phenomenology of perception

In the following, some basic knowledge of certain phenomenological notions is assumed necessary which will prove helpful in the evaluation of my arguments in subsequent sections as they are partly associated with E. Husserl's analysis of the phenomenology of time-consciousness (Hua, X). In any case I'll use explanatory footnotes whenever deemed necessary for the reader.

Let's try to imagine a first and last point of our perception throughout our existence. Then we will certainly produce a recurring sequence of moments going as far back as our childhood until they become vague, almost impossible to recall any more, ending up in the haze of forgetfulness; yet, in any attempt to reach an 'initial point' of my past, there comes instantly attached to it a preceding point of my existence as I recollect it in the present now. Therefore, there is no way of reaching by intuition the first moment of my existence except by an indirect mode relying on other people's intersubjective definition. Almost the same happens in reverse; imagine someone projecting himself into the future pushing his existence as far in advance as he can imagine, thus reaching his death throes in a very old age. Can he postulate the moment of his death? The answer, on the same grounds, should be negative, for any moment he could imagine as that of his final end, he would be already there to instantaneously 'engender' the succeeding one. We conclude that the specification of these two extreme points of our existence is only possible by relying on some other beings' constitution of these very moments in their consciousness (Merlan, 1947: p. 37). On the same intersubjective basis, I could become a witness to someone else's first or last moment of existence (assuming that such a moment is conceivable as the first or last temporal point of a living consciousness) and sign up my part in the intersubjective signature of his moment of birth or death. Nevertheless, in view of my capacity to turn that far back in memory, it is reasonable to ask how it might be possible to recall almost at once in the present now the seemingly infinitely descending collection of my past point-like moments of existence.

As I will discuss more thoroughly next, it is basically on the condition of being bearers of the following two forms of intentionality, that we can enact our stored memory going as far back as becoming a faint mist of infantile experiences, (where any point conceived in the sense of original impression as possibly the first is automatically annulled by our being 'already there'), and yet constitute it as a whole in the present now within the homogeneous, continuous flux of our enacting consciousness. The first intentionality is that of being intentionally oriented to unities-as such as prior to any notion of constituted temporality and the second intentionality is a kind of 'post-constitutional' one, whose two distinct forms are the transversal intentionality (*Querintentionalität*) constituting each specious present now in the field-like scheme retention-original impression-protention and the longitudinal intentionality (*Längstintentionalität*) whose retentional form is the continuous unity of the objectified flux of temporal consciousness (Hua, X: pp. 76-83). These two intentionalities are of a complementary sense and it is impossible to take into account one of them without necessarily involving in one or the other way the other. In other words, to cite once more the aforementioned example, even upon relying on an intersubjective condition to specify my moments of birth and death, I would have, just to be able to approach those moments, to loose my finiteness as being only capable of enacting the intuition of each present now distinct to any succeeding or past 'present', and become 'infinite' in the sense of restituting a potentially infinite collection of already passed-by 'present nows' as an original givenness in temporal actuality within the continuous whole of the flux of temporal consciousness.

Let us further suppose that there is some kind of beings whose perceptual capacity is of such a nature that they can only discern unities-as such and moreover that these conscious beings are of a finitistic nature. This means that they can only discern among a possibly very large but finite sequence of unities-as such, taken as entities in a name sense, that is, in the sense of objects 'calling' some kind of attention on the part of a conscious being without any further possibility of categorial specification whatsoever. Let us suppose in abstraction, that these unities-as such are represented as mathematical sign-configurations corresponding to the intuition we have of natural numbers as discrete, durationless, now-points. In that case they would have the intuition, e.g. of a rational point (in the form of a fraction of natural numbers), inside the real unit interval [0, 1], in the sense of a unity-as such distinct from any other in the open horizon of intentional experience, and they could start up bisecting this interval into subintervals, this way engendering the descending sequence 1, 1/2, 1/4, 1/8,... and so on *ad infinitum*. Then they we would find out that the end-point 0 would be inaccessible to them as they would lack the possibility to retain the descending sequence of distinct original impressions within the objective unity of a continuous whole by means of a longitudinal intentionality. Then, it is only by leaving the rational part of the environment of [0,1], which means that it is only by adopting, next to the 'finitistic' situation of perceiving rational points inside [0, 1] as non-temporal point-like abstractions, the 'infinite' situation of constituting them as objects within the continuous whole of temporal consciousness, that the process of reaching the end-points 0,1 becomes the natural intuition of the real line interval [0, 1], as a continuous line segment with 'tangible' end-points. The relevance of this mathematical example with the aforementioned ideas can be appreciated to the extent that it leads to certain paradoxical situations in case we do not take into account the double intentional capacity of a potential 'observer' who is provided at once with the intentionalities as referred to on previous page.[2] Of course, in the specific case one must cling to the Husserlian view of the objects of a formal mathematical theory as abstractions through categorial intuition, reached by discarding all traits of perceptual objects relative to a material content and finally constituting an object in full generality as a formal *eidos*, an empty form with its own essential specifications, e.g. as an element of an aggregate or as an aggregate of elements with proper relational characters of its members, etc. This kind of abstraction is meant in *Ideas I* as associated with an intuition of syntactical individuals of pure logic as ultimate substrates of analytical sentences not necessarily corresponding to a material content and therefore not as by-products of a variational modification over common traits of content (Hua, III/I: pp. 33-35).

---

[2]An important result in mathematical foundations known as the Skolem Paradox has a relevant paradoxical character lying in the fact that the relativization of uncountable ordinals to a countable base model **M** of standard set theory **ZF** presupposes the intuition of both the countability and uncountability of a collection of objects ('existing' both inside and outside **M**), whereas 'existing' exclusively inside countable model **M** presupposes only the intuition of countability (Kunen, 1983: p. 141). Therefore, for the 'inhabitants' of **M** there is no way to check the uncountability of an ordinal, e.g. that of ω_1, for they presumably lack the means to constitute indefinite collections of elements as continuous wholes.

Given these prompts, I will deal more thoroughly with the notions of a unity-as such and of a unity-substance in the following section. Can the former be taken as an object having at least a deficient ontological sense (e.g. the primary elements referred to in *Theaetetus*)? Further, on what terms can the latter be taken as a lawful ontological object? In the course of the discussion I will try to prove that there is a possibility to interpret both notions by means of phenomenological analysis as objects of a different level of intentionality in view of a noetic-noematic constitution. Critical in my arguments will be that both notions cannot be properly taken as objects of ontological discussion unless there is a pre-existing notion of temporal constitution implying the presence of a subject of phenomenological reduction.[3]

2.2. Unity-as such and unity-substance

I start the discussion assuming that we possess only the intuition of a unity-as such deprived of any attribute whatsoever except for the possibility to call it as such. Then, by necessity, this would provide for the intuition of all the rest (in complementary sense) which is termed in *Parmenides* τά ἄλλα. These should be again unities-as such as we would be supposedly deprived of any other intuition of unities, e.g. unities intuited as temporal forms. Therefore, we could only conceive of collections of them belonging to the same genus as the original unity-as such and evidently there could be nothing to be predicated unto this collection of unities (exactly as it was impossible to predicate anything unto anyone of them taken separately), except for the ontologically irrelevant fact that any collection of them could be taken as the result of an *ad infinitum* aggregation of reiterated intentionalities towards an original unity-as such. This way, the universe of experience would be deprived of any object susceptible of categorial attributes and consequently would be deprived of any meaning. In the face of this absurdity we can see that a unity-as such cannot qualify even deficiently as an ontological object. Nevertheless, I propose to give it a proper meaning in the following sense.

If we regard a unity as-such as the ultimate substrate of all non-independent (*unselbständige*) categorial forms referring to it, irrespectively of whether this ultimate substrate is taken as a 'thingness' substrate (*sachhaltiges Substrat*) or as an 'empty' substrate (*Leersubstrat*) (that is, without reference to a material content whatsoever), then a unity-as such can be taken as an irreducible individual of the intentionality of experience. In analytic-syntactical terms, unities-as such can be thought of abstracted, as the last syntactical individuals of linguistic expressions which are reducible to primary evidences of experience without any further analytical content consequently without any inner syntactical form, even, according to Husserl, lacking a temporal form (Hua, XVII: pp. 210-11). Husserl's latter claim is presumably meant to refer to unity-substrates as having a pre-constitutional temporality, certainly a temporality prior to a phenomenological reduction, as they are taken to be purely intentional objects apprehended by a subject's phenomenological perception (*Wahrnehmung*). In this sense a unity-as such may be taken

---

[3] A brief reference to the meaning of noetic and noematic objects, mainly described in E. Husserl's *Ideen I* can be summed up as follows: A noematic object manifests itself as an immanence within the unity of the flux of a subject's consciousness and it is constituted by certain modes of being as such, i.e. as a well-defined object immanent to the temporal flux, which is taken further, by virtue of being registered intentionally, as a formal-ontological object of the ontological domain of a science in general. In contrast, noetic objects, described as moments of hyletic-noetic perception, can be only thought of as evident 'givennesses' of an *a priori* orientation of intentionality without referring necessarily to a temporal constitution.

as equivalent to what was termed by Husserl an *individuum*, to the extent that irrespectively of whether it is taken as a 'thingness' substrate or an empty substrate, it still represents an absolutely self-sufficient (*absolut selbständiges*) essence (Hua, III/I: p. 35), whose claim to existence and individuality may be grounded solely on its being what it 'is': an hyletic-noetic moment of intentionality whose existence is totally reduced to the certitude of existence of the intentional subject in question, whereas its individuality is derived from being concretely the particular object of intentionality in the pure evidence of its original givenness in the 'present now', eliminating by *epochë* all further claims to objectivity. What can only be generally said in this regard, is that the real moments of intentional consciousness, that is, the datum and (in each case) the intentional character of phenomenological perception are co-constitutive factors of the homogenous temporal phenomenon. Therefore, in a phenomenologically motivated view, a unity-as such can be only considered as a noetic correlate of a subject's intentional consciousness, deprived of any categorical attributes characterizing a temporal object in noematic constitution. This is the reason to deny to a unity-as such any ground to be considered (after phenomenological reduction) a well-defined object much less to be considered a properly meant ontological object in accepting moreover a notion of temporal constitution.

In contrast, a unity-substance can be taken as a full-fledged noematic object by means of a temporal constitution and my intention in the following will be to show that this term cannot be taken to represent an ontological object without prior acceptance of the principle of a constituting consciousness within an intersubjective Life-World.[4] Before this, however, I will point by some brief arguments to the fundamentally distinct character between unities as-such in the sense of lowest-level individuals of intentionality preceding constituted objective temporality and unities-substances taken as temporal objects.

In *Theaetetus* (Plato, 1996b: 201E-202A), the intermingling of primary elements among themselves in the mode they are intermingled as names in an absolute sense is thought to be the underlying reason (λόγος γεγονέναι) of their becoming more complex forms. But then again, object-forms coming into being by the intermingling of primary elements must necessarily belong to a different ontological genus than that of their constituent elements if they are to be considered as existent at all, taking into account that primary elements are defined as being solely name-symbols without any possibility of further predication. To cite an analogy, if we draw a closed curve on a piece of paper, it would be impossible to reconstruct this curve as the sum-collection of its ideally indivisible points; or yet in another example, supposing that we can enumerate to the utmost indivisible subatomic parts the tissue of a living organism and then label them by ordinal numbers, it would be impossible summing over them to equate the whole tissue with the sum of its ideally indivisible parts. Therefore, a collection of unities-as such (assuming their existence after all) is nothing more than an aggregate of its parts and further it is of the same genus as each of its constituent parts. In contrast, a unity-substance can be also conceived of as the sum of its parts, although in this case the parts are not only of the same genus as the whole but they are as irreducible to unities-as such as it is the whole to which they are parts. This might raise the question of the constitution of spatiotemporal unity as an impredicative form of existence of unities-substances in terms of which such unities, while being distinct in perception, are, in effect, embedded to unities of a higher order within the all-inclusive unity of the intentional experience. But, arguably, this leads to a mode of constitution of the world and by virtue of this to a division of a presumably 'objective' world into a pre-

---

[4] The Life-World (*Lebenswelt*), can be roughly described to a non-phenomenologist as the physical world with its ever receding horizon, including in intersubjective sense all knowing subjects in a special kind of presence in the World. More on this in E. Husserl's *The Crisis of European Sciences and Transcendental Phenomenology*, (Hua, VI).

phenomenological and a phenomenological one, the latter incorporating at least one phenomenological reduction performing ego. Consequently, the passing from the unities-as such to unities-substances (bearers of sense) is not attainable but through the intermediary of a constituting temporal consciousness which is part of the world yet it cannot perceive the world as its own immanent object. Moreover, it points the way to a shift from a static-ontological universe of discourse to a field of becoming (γεγονέναι) conceivable in a temporal sense, which can only be grasped in kinetical in-act (ἐνεργείᾳ) terms. Classical ontology cannot say much about the process of becoming itself. In *Parmenides*, for instance, the process of alteration (termed as ἐξαίφνης) i.e. the change from the state of stillness to that of motion and vice versa, is characterized as an intermediate state that cannot be conceived as a spatial or a temporal one and it is thus non-describable in the same terms as motion or stillness (Plato, 1996a: 156 D-E). Consider, for instance, the flux of a fluid. How can we possibly mentally represent a material point of the flux? Any time we reflect on it, it has already ceased to be what it was the instant we perceived it as such, and if we are to formally represent the flux, then its points can be only conceived of as ideal, not really existing points remaining identical to themselves (as unities-substances in abstraction) in the becoming of the flux.

In *Ideas I* (Hua, III/I), Husserl was led by the phenomenological reduction to an immanentisation of an object transcendent to the consciousness, thus ultimately reducing the transcendence of the object in question to the root of subjectivity of the intentional subject, while further grounding the temporally constituted object as intersubjectively the same inside the Life-World. This view can be seen to have the following consequences in relation to the ontological foundation of a unity-substance. Taking as an absolute evidence a subject's intentional consciousness towards its objects, then this intentional subjectivity seems to abolish the transcendent character of a unity-substance considered as 'external' to the immanence of consciousness, by making it its immanent object and integrating the unity-substance in question within the unique temporality of the homogenous flux of consciousness. Therefore, if there would be a properly defined object such as a unity-substance, it ought to be a correlate, after reduction, of the immanence of at least one reduction-performing consciousness and it would be defined as such from then on, irrespective of the existence or not anymore of the performing individual, as it would be now a noematic-temporal object grounded intersubjectively upon a universal mode of temporal constitution. It follows that grounding a unity-substance, on a constitutional level, as a noematic-temporal object implies its definition in kinetical terms, in the sense of a re-identifying noematic object in the ever in-act subjectivity of each one's temporal flux of consciousness.[5] In other words, we have a definition of a unity-substance, self-contradictory in classical ontological terms, leading to its 'ontification' by being constituted as a well-defined and self-identical object together with its essential categorial objectivities within the temporal flux; this is done, though, in terms of a consciousness, which in its immanent duration is not identical but a synthetic, continuous unity (Hua, III/I: pp. 230-231). This kind of 'ontification' seems to justify Husserl's view of phenomenology as a science not of a catastematical (*katastematisch*) character - a term stemming from the ancient Greek verb καθίστημι associated with 'static' being - but rather of a kinetical character which grasps unity within the flux of consciousness and in whose constant flow a unity-substance and any component, aspect or real property of it is a correlate of identity (Hua, V: p. 129).

---

[5] The description of a re-identifying noematic object as an identity within a manifold of phases is given in *Analysen zur Passiven Synthesis* (Hua, XI) and *Phänomenologie des inneren Zeitbewußtseins* (Hua, X), by means of a unity of temporal profiles of elapsed phases corresponding to each now-phase of the object in actual presence (Hua, XI: p. 322).

I now take unity-substance, intersubjectively defined in the temporal-constitutional terms under discussion, as a possible alternative phenomenological interpretation of the ontological entity (ἕν-ὄν) of reviewed platonic texts. The introduction, though, of temporal consciousness as the self-constituting foundation of any objectivity and therefore of a unity-substance taken as a temporal object, in short, the introduction of an ego of temporality as a subjectivity in whose absence the constitution of objects as such would be unthinkable, may ultimately lead to a rather obscure transcendence, derived as the 'leftover' of a new supplementary radical reduction in the immanence of consciousness itself. To this transcendence, I will refer in the immediately following section.

3. THE NECESSITY OF A NOTION OF TEMPORAL CONSTITUTION

Unities-substrates (or individual-substrates) in the sense of syntactical individuals were described by Husserl, in *Formale und Transzendentale Logik* (Hua, XVII), at the lowest possible level of reduction of analytical sentences, as direct evidences of the intentionality of experience and thus as the non-analytical foundation of a formal linguistic universe. Further, they should at least possess the attributes of their individuality and also those of their relational character with respect to any other individual or collection of individuals, consequently defining a kind of noematic nucleus (*Kernform*) for each of them (Hua, XVII: pp. 309-11). Taken then as objects of a formal ontology[6] they can generate the domain of a logical-mathematical universe in which we can reason about such individuals as objects of formulas of apophantic logic and consequently as objects of mathematical sentences within a deductive formal system. It seems improbable that E. Husserl conceived of these unities-substrates of which he denied any syntactical content, even the appropriation of a qualitative plenitude of time, as ontological objects in the sense of unities-substances (ἕν-ὄντα). Instead, we can reasonably conclude that he viewed unities-substrates as direct intentionalities of most primary experience (in a sense close to that of unities-as such of previous section), irreducible to any lower degree of evidence and noematically constituted, in a sense of Dies-da (close to the Aristotelian τόδε τι), by the retentional forms of temporal consciousness.

In an intentional approach, they could thus be taken as close to the platonic idea of primary elements in *Theaetetus* which lacked of any content except for their name 'existence', as distinctly specified from any other primary element. In final count how should primary elements be conceived of? As 'being' purely objects of an intentionality a priori directed to them without any further specification except for their being individuals-as such in original and direct self-givenness or as 'defective' ontological objects without any other specification except for the possibility of 'calling' each and everyone of them distinctly from any other? If we choose the latter option and reason about them as being 'defective' ontological objects, then we shall inevitably produce at some point a sequence of contradictory deductions e.g. in *Parmenides*, the ἕν-ὄν (unity-substance) is at once identical, similar, different, etc. from the others (τά ἄλλα).

---

[6] Husserl defined formal ontology as the a priori logical science concerned with the elaboration of formal judgements, relations and operations with respect to objects as intentionally registered. The domain of formal ontology, pertaining to the formal mathematical science, is the domain of facts and objects as registered and further apprehended by categorial intuition as 'empty' somethings in general (*Etwas-überhaupt*) and modifications of these 'empty' somethings.

These contradictions are essentially the outcome of the initial definition of a unity-as such (in the sense of ἕν-ἕν, see footnote 1), that is, as a name-term not susceptible of any predication, yet subsequently taken to be an ontological object in the structure of analytical inferences. For if it is to be predicated unto it any attribute, then given my prior arguments it should be a unity-substance which is obviously not a unity-as such as it possesses at least the attribute of existence and can be therefore conceived as a re-identifying unity in temporal constitution. In the platonic approach, however, the concept of a unity-as such without any predicative content is taken regardless of a process of temporal constitution, this way identifying as one and the same ontological object what in a phenomenological view is diverse; that is, a unity-as such taken in the sense of an hyletic-noetic moment of intentionality and co-constitutive of inner temporality,[7] and a unity-substance taken as a noematic object of temporal constitution which is a temporal object and a bearer of predicates. The latter, as it is claimed in Subsection **2.2**, can be taken as the phenomenological equivalent of the ἕν-ὄν of platonic ontology. It is worthy to refer to Husserl's own definition of a noematic-temporal object in the Analysis of Passive Synthesis (*Analysen zur Passiven Synthesis*), (Hua, XI: p. 144): *"In any case, something that is originally constituted in consciousness as an object, that is, such that the object is grasped as it is itself originaliter in consciousness, is constituted in essential necessity within original time-consciousness as continually identical and enduringly identifiable – and therefore also as identifiable beyond the sphere of the living present by means of the concatenation of remembering."* (*Engl. transl.:* Husserl, 2001a).

In the next section I intend to comment on some contradictory inferences in the text of *Parmenides* stemming from the erroneous treatment of a name-term as essentially an ontological object though it is initially defined as lacking of any ontological content. Also, by citing yet another example from *Parmenides* I will show how the 'naive' treatment of time as a pre-existing absolute objectivity regardless of which we can make ontological assumptions, can lead to false presumptions on the attributes of substances e.g. the unity-substance (ἕν-ὄν) is at the same time older and younger of itself and of the others. At this point I will proceed to complete my arguments so as to show that the phenomenology of temporal consciousness can be a firm ground to give a unity-substance its proper interpretation as a well-defined ontological object.

Summing up, it has hopefully become clear by now the underlying incompatibility in the definition of such 'objects' as unity-as such and unity-substance. A unity-substance has a temporal form by virtue of its durating presence as a re-identifying immanence in the course of the flux tied up synthetically with a multiplicity of other unities-substances and in various noematic modes (causality, contingency, etc) in time progression; to cite Husserl's own words, (Hua III/I: p. 231) *"Das Noematische sei das Feld der Einheiten, das Noetische das der 'konstituirenden' Mannigfaltigkeiten."* [The noematic is the field of unities, the noetic is the field of 'constituting' multiplicities] (*Engl. transl.:* Husserl, 1983).[8] A unity-as such as a mere givenness of consciousness co-constitutive of the temporality of its noematic immanence can only be just that, a correlate of noetic perception (by relativization of the existential term, to be, to the pre-constitutional stage), and any other description of it would lead to ambiguities and circularities in the

---

[7] It must be noted that the notion of inner time consciousness should not be confused with a notion of external or scientific time, as the former is co-constitutive of our being as organic bodies which are moreover bearers of a consciousness.

[8] The term unity employed here is the translation of the German word *Einheit* and refers to the constituted continuous unity. Therefore, it is not to be confused with the terms unity-as such or unity-substance elsewhere in the text taken in the sense of predicable or non-predicable individuals.

interpretation of linguistic existential forms. A unity-substance, on the contrary, is posterior to a notion of temporal constitution and can thus be defined as a re-identifying (in the course of the temporal flux) bearer of predicates, eidetically abstracted as the pure *eidos* of unity-substance bearing at least the attributes of existence and individuality; the latter are to be meant as temporal forms ultimately rooted in the inner temporality of the subject.

Talking however of a temporal constitution prior to the definition of ontological objects themselves might generate transcendental questions of another order. This way, a creeping, hidden transcendence may be found after all in the constitution of time itself. This transcendence can be traced in reverse order in the constitution of temporal objects, in Husserl's relevant exposition in the *Phenomenology of Inner Time Consciousness*: 1) the objects of experience within objective time, e.g. the intersubjectively identical objects such as the objects of the study of physics; 2) the multiplicities of constituting appearances in the pre-empirical time turned into immanences of the unique temporality of each one's flux after phenomenological reduction; 3) the absolute flux of consciousness which constitutes time by constituting itself.

It should be noted that Husserl explicitly reduced the qualitative continuum of the spatiotemporal presence of physical objects, of which he was able to talk extensively in *Ding und Raum* (Hua, XVI), to the continuous unity of each one's consciousness in temporal extension, in which an identical is seized in change and in complete constancy, without any leap (Hua, X: p. 244).

The absolute flux of temporal consciousness is the last possible 'stage' in the order of constitution of temporalities as it is the self-constituting objective unity of inner temporality in which all temporalities of the objects immanent to the flux are identically one. This self-constituting unity makes it possible to constitute our experience each time as a continuous whole, while at the same time tying up each present-now under a certain intentional mode with a just-passed-by past and a not-yet happened a-thematic future in time progression. Any further reduction should be a pure subjectivity evading even temporality, as inner temporality belongs to the constituted level and the absolute subjectivity of consciousness precedes the constituted level for it 'is' an ever in-act constituting factor of the continuous unity of the flux. This subjectivity reached in the extreme end of a supplementary phenomenological reduction, termed by Husserl as the absolute ego of consciousness and also referred to by the self-contradicting term *nunc-stans* (never-in-being as been), is indescribable in terms of being, unthinkable without some kind of retention, whereas any reflection on it 'instantly' produces its mirror-objectivity. It might be described metaphorically as the black hole of the most radical reduction of temporal consciousness, a transcendental pure ego whose description is beyond the expressional capacity of any linguistic universe, since any reflection on it by the same token produces its temporal ontification in terms of a static being which obviously is not itself.

Husserl left to the end the notion of absolute ego rather obscure and did not give clear answers to questions relating to the nature and role of absolute ego, drawing critiques on the part of certain philosophers that he banished the transcendence of external objective reality only to make it reappear in the immanence of consciousness. In his later work, known as the Bernau manuscripts, he still left this notion rather vague characterizing it as a primitive process (*Urprozess*) preceding any possibility of reflection, in which 'being' and 'being-in-constituting' are inseparable.[9] Consequently, it follows that the ultimate

---

[9] In a relevant passage (*Beilage V*) of Bernau manuscripts, Husserl talked about the absolute ego as a process carried out prior to any reflection, on an apperception intentionally directed to a datum,

source of any temporal objectivity within the intersubjective world, of any first-degree transcendental reflection and finally of the reflection on the absolute ego itself is not an essence, therefore any attempt to describe it in terms of being is doomed to fail. In this respect, any attempt to provide a firm foundation, in terms of the immanence of consciousness, to ontological objects such as to a unity as substance seems to be shaken by the transposition of the transcendence (with regard to a cogito) of ontological objects of classical tradition to the transcendence of the absolute ego of consciousness.

This is a tempting and still open discussion that may be carried out in depth in its own right. There are some reasons to possibly associate, in a phenomenological approach, the impredicativity of formal continuum inside logical-mathematical systems to the transcendental root of phenomenological continuum (Livadas, 2009) & (Livadas, 2010); of no less importance is the indirect emergence of a notion of self-constituting continuum of internal time in problems of quantum measurement e.g. in relation with Von Neumann's Projection Principle (see: dalla Chiara, 1977 & Grib, 1993).

In Section **4**, I will discuss certain arguments of Socratic dialogues, e.g. reasoning about time in *Parmenides,* and draw by their absurd inferences certain appropriate conclusions as to the impossibility of reasoning soundly about ontological objects without fundamentally viewing them as well-meant objects within temporal constitution.

4. REVISITING SOME ONTOLOGICAL CLAIMS IN *THEAETETUS* AND *PARMENIDES*

In *Parmenides* (Plato, 1996a: 152 A), Parmenides assumed that if unity-substance (ἕν-ὅν) exists at all then it should be temporal for "what else is ***being*** than participation of substance in the present time likewise as ***was*** (is participation) in past time and ***shall be*** (is participation) in future time?" (*transl. of the author*). Then, the reasoning goes, as time progresses unity becomes older of itself and since everything becomes older of itself by becoming (in reverse order) younger, it is deduced that unity becomes this way younger and older of itself. But in the progression of time, unity-substance has to 'intersect' the present as it leaves the past to enter the future. Therefore, whenever it 'intersects' the present by necessity ceases to become and must be instead what it is, so if it has become older in present time it is older and further since it has become older by becoming younger of itself, it is inferred that at present time unity-substance is necessarily at once older and younger of itself.

Moreover as present time is attached to a unity-substance throughout its existence we reach the conclusion that unity-substance always becomes and is at the same time older

---

similarly as the contents of phenomenological perception (*Wahrnehmung*) are constituted as temporal objects irrespective of whether we are (intentionally) directed to them (Hua, XXXIII: p. 206). In the intricate task of describing the absolute subjectivity of the flux in meaningful linguistic terms without getting trapped into the objectified temporal flux or getting out of the reflection which presents retentionality as conditioning the possibility of the absolute subjectivity, Husserl claimed elsewhere that what is in-act any time as the foundation of any reflection is not such or the other concrete 'now' and its retention in the flow but the general ego of now and the retentionality in general (Patočka, 1992: p. 167). The nature of absolute ego as well as other complex questions arising from a deeper phenomenological analysis, such as the risk of an endless regression of protentions or the possibility of an entirely 'empty' protention with regard to possible contents of its 'fulfillment' were left open in the Bernau manuscripts (see: Held, 2007).

and younger of itself; consequently, as it becomes older and younger of itself in equal time-intervals, it has accordingly the same age and it neither is nor becomes older and younger of itself in flagrant contradiction with the prior inference. It is almost trivial to see where this chain of inferences is weak and why it reaches absurdity. It assumes the present now to be a durationless point of existence totally separated from what has already passed by and what possibly follows, in whose 'domain' we can specify a unity-substance in terms of being and not becoming and predicate unto it any attribute inasmuch as it is possible to abstract it from its temporal character at least in the present now.[10] Assuming this possibility it could then be taken as an unalterable ontological object to the extent that its (temporal) existence can be taken as the sum of all its present instants.

As it turns out out, we can overcome such absurdities by a phenomenological approach insofar as we may assert the non-existence of an instantaneous and 'autonomous' present but instead of a domain of actuality (or specious present) within consciousness, intentionally correlated with a just-passed-by and a not-yet-happened. In this view, there is no way an intentional object of experience may be constituted in an a-temporal state somewhere between past and future as long as it can only be a temporal, immanent to the consciousness and re-identifying bearer of predicates that is taken as noematically and intersubjectively the same in time progression, as already described (see: Bernet, 1978 & Held, 1966). Further, it will be constituted in such a way that together with its noematic nucleus (*Kernform*) - standing for the nucleus of its a priori categorial objectivities – will be a formal-ontological object of the domain of a science in general and in complete abstraction a syntactical object of general analytical statements.

Concerning another passage of *Parmenides* (Plato, 1996a: 143 B), we note that, in the course of syllogisms, a misplaced consideration of a unity-as such as an essentially ontological object produces absurd results in analytical inferences. Parmenides initially proposes there to reflect on a name-term (in the sense of a unity-as such) as something not participating of any substance and thus not predicable of any attribute whatsoever. As a result of a sequence of logical inferences he finally comes to the contradicting conclusion that a unity-as such is in fact a number that could well be an infinite collection of beings (ὄντα) participating of substance. The evident contradiction, though, with the initial assumption that a unity-as such does not participate of any substance can be traced, in the course of reasoning, in the assumption that since unity-as such and substance are diverse then their diversity (ἑτερότης) owes not to their being unity-as such and substance respectively but to their participating in diversity which is neither unity-as such nor substance. But then if unity-as such would be predicated as diverse (since it participates in diversity) it should automatically acquire the attribute of diversity and therefore participate of substance, thus being eventually qualified as a unity-substance (ἕν-ὄν) and not a unity-as such (ἕν-ἕν) as was initially assumed in the argument. Being a unity-substance it could then be taken, in view of my arguments in Subsection **2.2**, as a well-defined temporal object and evidently not a unity-as such in the sense that the latter is attributed, that is, as a correlate of hyletic-noetic perception on a pre-constitutional temporality level.

In yet another passage from *Parmenides* (Plato, 1996a: 147 D - 148 B), we reach the contradictory conclusion that if a unity exists, then is at once diverse, similar and identical to the others (τά ἄλλα). Prior to the concatenation of inferences, Parmenides assumes this unity, as before, simply in a name sense without any predication of attributes

---

[10] Consider the intermediate situation of spatio-temporality, called in *Parmenides* ἐξαίφνης (all of a sudden) which, as already mentioned in Subsection 2.2, is characterized as the non-spatial and a-temporal state of things in which they change from motion to stillness and vice versa.

except for the possibility to call it by its name identically and distinctly with respect to any other unity of such kind.[11] By virtue of this, the argument goes, if we call something by its name irrespectively of whether we do it once or more we call always the same thing. Then, if we say that unity is diverse from others and vice-versa we call twice by the name diverse (ἕτερον) both unity and the others which implies that unity and the others are, with respect to their labelling as diverse, under the same (adjectival) designation and therefore bear on this account a 'likeness'; therefore they may be deduced as similar and ultimately through certain logical equivalences, unity-substance and the others are proved to be also identical (ταὐτόν).

The deductive process is based, however, on the premise that it is possible to specify unity invariably solely by its name discarding a necessity of existence, whereas in the course of reasoning unity it is implicitly taken as existent. Affirming, as it comes out, the attribute diverse iteratively with respect to this kind of unity cannot but be conditioned on the very existence of this unity, which nevertheless was initially defined solely by the possibility to call it by the denomination diverse. But calling a unity solely by its name irrespectively of its possible existence in terms of being, may be taken as equivalently referring to a unity-as such in the sense of a noetic object of intentionality. In such a case, its 'existence' is absolutely reduced to the intuitively unambiguous existence of the intentional consciousness whose correlate is precisely the unity bearing the name diverse distinctively from any other object in the particular intentional act. This attribution of name should be taken here certainly not in the sense of a physical act (e.g. the sonority effect of calling), but in its most fundamental and self-evident sense as a turn of the intentionality towards a certain something (*Etwas-überhaupt*) in the form of a thingness or even an 'empty' substrate, 'in advance' of its noematic-temporal constitution as a well-meant ontological object. Accordingly, the possibility to talk about this kind of unity is absolutely rooted in the intentional character of consciousness by virtue of being uniquely presented in front of it in original givenness, irrespectively of any material content and regardless of its constituted temporality.

Therefore, we may plausibly conclude that an initial assumption of a unity-as such leads in the course of analytic syllogisms into the designation of an ontological object just by assigning the attribute diverse and therefore assuming it to participate of substance. As it stands, this essentially name-attribution is presumed falsely by the person Parmenides to endow a unity-as such with an ontological sense which obviously cannot be grounded on the sole possibility of calling it as diverse, that is, in the sense of a denomination taken simply as a means to refer to that specific unity uniquely in distinction to any other in the sense described above. This kind of unity would still be claimed to be, in a phenomenological sense, a noetic correlate of intentional consciousness and thus cannot qualify as a well-meant ontological object in the sense I gave to this concept in Subsection **2.2** and in Section **3**.

A re-evaluation of Plato's notion of primary elements and of various collections of them can be drawn in essentially the same phenomenologically motivated sense. We may refer, at first, to the instance where Plato cites, in *Theaetetus*, the word Socrates (Σωκράτης) (in fact, a part of it) as being naturally a bearer of a certain sense although it is composed of a set of vocals and consonants considered to be nothing more than

---

[11]Talking in another context, unities taken solely as name attributions can be seen as close to linguistic signs in semiotic functions. In that sense a sign in a semiotic function is defined solely as a difference from other signs and ultimately to the semiotic system itself containing all possible combinations. Consequently, a sign-as such in the sense of a unique demarcated difference within a semiotic system refers only within the system which, on this account, bears no outside and it is therefore a closed system (Michalski, 1997: pp. 106-107).

sonorous effects even lacking this very effect in case they are mute symbols. Then, taking these vocals in the sense of primary elements the question that might arise is whether we can take the name Socrates as a meaningful linguistic form, that is, as a bearer of attributes and consequently knowable, yet composed of elements asserted as primary and thus not knowable (Plato, 1996b: 203 B - 204 E). My claim is that the answer to this question is dependent on the way we view the name Socrates; if we conceive it as simply an aggregate of the corresponding letters and thus of resulting vocal effects, then it is an aggregate of unities-as such (these vocals taken as bearing only the condition of distinctness in phenomenological perception) and consequently not knowable. But if we think of it as a name-substance of a radically different genus than that of its constituting parts (taken as primary elements), in other words as a unity-substance (ἕν-ὄν), bearer of predicates inside a world of senses, then it is certainly knowable and existent in an ontological sense.

Upon completing this part of dialogue the person Socrates concludes by virtue of the example above, that it is impossible to know a collection of elements, in this instance the syllables Σω-κρά, without prior knowledge of these letters themselves as (semiotic) elements, his argument being essentially that if the form is to be the aggregate of all of its parts, then they should both be by necessity knowable. In alternative case, if the collection is taken as belonging to a different genus than that of its elements, then it should stand as a new idea which is just as irreducible and impartible (ἀμερής) as primary elements themselves (Plato, 1996b: 205 C-206 C). But one could argue against this assertion, in the sense that it may not come as a necessary conclusion, in case a collection of elements belongs to another genus than that of its constituent elements, that this collection should by necessity be a new idea as impartible and not knowable as its primary elements. For any such collection of elements taken as a whole can be a bearer of substance, that is, it can be a noematic-temporal object in evident ontological distinction with its constituting primary elements (taken e.g. in the sense of syntactical individual-substrates) which can be interpreted to 'exist', in principle, only as mere intentionalities without a necessity of predication including that of temporal existence within a post-constitutional temporality. We can cite in analogy, the definition inside a formal mathematical system of a set of elements bearing a certain structure and generated meaning as a whole in contrast to the nature of its constituting $\in$-elements taken as zero-level elements (urelements) without any inner analytical structure.

It is notable that in his theory of wholes and parts, in the second volume of *Logical Investigations*, Husserl discussed the fundamental difference, on the constitutional level, between an aggregate (*Inbegriff*) of contents and a whole, in the sense that an aggregate is a purely categorial form and stands for the correlate of a certain unity of reference in relation to all relevant objects-contents with no material form of association developing among them through intentional unity. In contrast, the form of a whole is a unity due to foundation, that is, a unity through a 'thingness' co-existence determined by the material specificity of the 'founding' contents and described by synthetically a priori laws, as opposed to analytically a priori laws such as those associated with purely categorial forms, e.g. with the Form-Idea of a whole as such (Hua XIX/1: pp. 289-291). Further, to the extent that wholes are determined by the material specificity of their 'founding' contents and are, as such, subject to the causality of natural laws, associated moreover with a constituted spatio-temporality, their temporal parts are non-independent, not merely in relation to their own fulfillment but also in relation to neighbouring temporal parts and their fulfillments within a concretely fulfilled temporal unity. It is indicative that Husserl stated that the non-independence of temporal parts and their reciprocal 'foundation' is governed by laws which do not simply associate time-stretches with time-stretches but associate concretely fulfilled temporal wholes with other such temporal wholes, while at the same time cautioned that the free extension of space and time stretches in imagination is not a proof of the relative 'foundedness' of bits of space and time and therefore does not prove the real infinity of space and time which is anyway subject to the natural laws of causality (Hua XIX/1: pp. 299-300). Nevertheless, to the extent that a free extension of spatiotemporal stretches in each one's inward gaze may be ultimately associated with the objectified continuous unity of the absolute flux of consciousness, it is deducible that temporal parts are in each case non-independent and they are by essence associated as concretely fulfilled temporal wholes within the homogeneous temporality of inner time consciousness.

A characteristic example of the contradictions that may result from ontological definitions that do not take into account a notion of temporal constitution is Parmenides' inference[12] that the part (τό μόριον) "*is a part, not of many nor of all, but of a single form and a single concept which we call a whole, a perfect unity created out of all; this it is of which the part is a part*" (Plato, 1996a: 157 E). In this case, we do not come upon a relation between primary elements and their collection through a registration of iterative (intentional) acts, as in the aforementioned passage of *Theaetetus*, but instead between a part and a containing whole which is specified as a single concept (*ἰδέα*) and a single form, possibly to suggest the different genus to which the whole belongs with respect to its parts or generally to the others. As a result of analytical inferences, assuming that there exists a collection *A* of others (in fact, all of them), in the sense of primary elements, it is deduced that if a part (μόριον) *y* does not belong to this collection A, then it cannot belong to any of the elements of *A*, so it cannot belong to anything because it is proved to be nothing of nothing, consequently it must be part of an all-inclusive unity of a higher order which is the whole. Formally, this is the result of the following predicate formula inference:

Let $A = \{x: x \in A\}$.. If *y* does not belong to *A*, then *y* necessarily does not belong to any element *x* of *A* since in reverse case it would belong to at least one element of *A* and consequently would belong to A, thus contradicting the initial hypothesis; in a formal expression:

$$\neg[(\forall x \in A)(y \notin x] \equiv (\exists x \in A)(y \in x)$$

The question that might arise then is what kind of object the part should be: a primary element or a collection of primary elements, thus generating the contradictions noted in *Theaetetus* (in citing the instance of the word Σωκράτης as a sensuous object) between unknown elements and known collections of them, or it should belong to the same genus as the whole this latter taken in the sense of 'a certain entity perfectly made out of all'. Yet, the second eventuality is contradicted by the subsequent Parmenidean assertion: "Because there is nothing else besides these, which is other than one and other than the others." [Ὅτι που οὐκ ἔστι παρά ταῦτα ἕτερον, ὅ ἄλλον μεν ἔστι τοῦ ἑνός ἄλλον δε τῶν ἄλλων.] (Plato, 1996a: 159 B).

It is reasonable to hold that logical contradictions of this kind may be due to a vagueness of corresponding 'ontological' notions mainly engendered by the modification of the objects of experience, to which we bear a specific and at least not analytically describable kind of relation, into formal objects of apophantic logic in leaving aside the new ontological context established by the evidence of a constituting temporal consciousness.

---

[12] As it turns out, many of the other paradoxes in Plato's *Parmenides* come from reasoning about unity-substance (ἕν-ὄν) (e.g. equal and not equal of itself and the others) as a material, spatiotemporal body and not as an abstract eidetic form temporally constituted and bearer of predicates.

The phenomenological analysis has clearly a say in describing and clarifying this kind of a priori relationship we bear with things in the intersubjective Life-World, irrespectively of their material or non-material content, as long as their transcendent existence as original givennesses in the present now of an intentional consciousness is immanentized within the homogenous temporal flux. In this view, their existence and consequently their ontological specification is tied up with a temporality that is transposed from the bracketed objective reality to the subjective temporality of each one's consciousness.

In conclusion, my arguments served to demonstrate the radical difference between a unity-as such, meant as merely an intentionality of consciousness referring to an original givenness on the lowest possible level of phenomenological perception, and what is termed a unity-substance taken as a temporal-noematic object and - under the condition of a temporal constitution by necessity associated with a subject of phenomenological reduction - as equivalent to the notion of a well-meant ontological object.

Consequently a phenomenologically motivated approach towards 'naively' thought ontological objects in this paper is not only intended to offer in this light an alternative view of ontological objects in traditional ontology but also to clarify the dubious content of certain platonic claims in the course of the aforementioned dialogues. My belief is that there is a broad field of research ahead concerning an alternative approach to questions of classical ontology, e.g., a properly meant sense of unity as dealt with in present work, a research that would possibly involve other scientific disciplines too, for instance, the foundations of mathematical logic, the philosophy of mind, the microphysics of the brain, etc.

REFERENCES

Bernet, R. (1978), Endlichkeit und Unendlichkeit in Husserl's Phänomenologie der Wahrnehmung, *Tijdschrift voor Filosofie,* 40: 251-269.

Dalla Chiara, M. L. (1977), Logical Self Reference, Set Theoretical Paradoxes and the Measurement Problem in Quantum Mechanics, *Journal of Philosophical Logic,* 6: 331-347.

Grib, A.A. (1993), Quantum Logical Interpretation of Quantum Mechanics: The Role of Time, *Int. Jour. of Theor. Physics,* 32, 12: 2389-2400.

Held, K. (1966), *Lebendige gegenwart. Die Frage der Seinsweise des transzendentalen Ich bei Edmund Husserl, entwickelt am Leitfaden der Zeitproblematik,* The Hague: Kluwer Acad. Pub.

Held, K. (2007), Phenomenology of 'Authentic Time' in Husserl and Heidegger, *Inter. Journ. of Philosophical Studies,* 15, 3: 327-347.

Hopkins, B. (2010), *The Philosophy of Husserl,* Montreal: Mc-Gill-Queen's University Press

Husserl, E. (*1966a) Analysen zur Passiven Synthesis,* Hua XI, herausg. M. Fleischer, The Hague: M. Nijhoff.

Husserl, E. (*2001a) Analyses Concerning Passive and Active Synthesis,* transl. A. Steinbock, Dordrecht: Kluwer Acad. Pub.

Husserl, E. (1966b), Zur *Phänomenologie des inneren Zeitbewußtseins,* Hua X, herausg. R Boehm, The Hague: M. Nijhoff.

Husserl, E.(1973), *Ding und Raum,* Hua XVI, herausg. Ul. Claesges, The Hague: M. Nijhoff.

Husserl, E. (1974), *Formale und Transzendentale Logik*, Hua XVII, herausg. P. Janssen,The Hague: M. Nijhoff.

Husserl, E. (1976a), *Die Krisis der europäischen Wissenschaften und die transzendentale Phänomenologie,* Hua VI, herausg. W. Biemel, The Hague: M. Nijhoff.

Husserl, E. (1976b), *Ideen zu einer reinen Phänomenologie und phänomenologischen Philosophie,* Erstes Buch, Hua III/I, herausg. K. Schuhmann, The Hague: M. Nijhoff.

Husserl, E. (1983), *Ideas pertaining to a pure phenomenology and to a phenomenological philosophy,* First Book, transl. F. Kersten, The Hague: M. Nijhoff.

Husserl, E. (1984), *Logische Untersuchungen,* Hua XIX/1, herausg. U. Panzer, The Hague: M. Nijhoff.

Husserl, E. (1993), *Ideen zu einer reinen Phänomenologie und phänomenologischen Philosophie*, Drittes Buch: Die Phänomenologie und die Fundamente der Wissenschaften, Hua V, herausg. M. Biemel, The Hague: M. Nijhoff.

Husserl, E. (2001b), *Die Bernauer Manuscripte über das Zeitbewußtsein (1917/18)*, Hua XXXIII, herausg. R. Bernet & D.Lohmar, Dordrecht: Kluwer Acad. Pub.

Kirkland, S. (2007), Thinking in the between with Heidegger and Plato, *Research in Phenomenology*, 37: 95-111.

Kunen, K. (1983), *Set Theory. An Introduction to Independence Proofs*, Amsterdam: Elsevier Science Pub.

Livadas, S. (2009), The Leap from the Ego of Temporal Consciousness to the Phenomenology of Mathematical Continuum, *Journ. Manuscrito*, 32, 2: 321-356.

Livadas S. (2010), Impredicativity of Continuum in Phenomenology and in non-Cantorian Theories", in: *Causality, Meaningful Complexity and Embodied Cognition*, (ed.) A. Carsetti, pp. 185-199, Springer.

Merlan, P. (1947), Time Consciousness in Husserl and Heidegger, *Philosophy and Phenomenological Research*, 8, 1: 23-54.

Michalski, K. (1997), *Logic and Time. An Essay on Husserl's Theory of Meanings*, Dordrect: Kluwer Acad. Pub.

Nieheus-Pröbstig, H.: (1987), Überredung zur Einsicht: der Zusammenhang von Philosophie und Rhetorik bei Platon und in der Phänomenologie, *Philosophische Abhandlungen*, 54, Frankfurt: V. Klostermann.

Patočka, J. (1992), *Introduction à la phénoménologie de Husserl*, transl. E. Abrams, Paris: Ed. Millon.

Plato (1996a), *Cratylus, Parmenides, Greater Hippias, Lesser Hippias*, H.N. Fowler, Loeb Classical Library, Cambridge, Mass.: Harvard University Press.

Plato (1996b), *Theatetus-Sophist*, H.N. Fowler, Loeb Classical Library, Cambridge, Mass.: Harvard University Press.

THE TRANSCENDENCE OF THE EGO IN CONTINENTAL PHILOSOPHY — CONVERGENCES AND DIVERGENCES

This article deals with a core matter of continental philosophy which is the nature of the ego taken as a concept originating in the subjective idealism of the German school of the early nineteenth century and further developed in its various ramifications throughout the twentieth century. The main philosophical positions I will discuss are Husserl's phenomenology of the ego in his later transcendental phase, the Heideggerean view of the nature of *Dasein*, and Sartre's approach of the Being-for-itself as mainly exposed in *Being and Nothingness*. The central idea defended throughout this article is that self-constituting temporality as immanently induced may serve as a common foundation of the nature of the transcendental ego both in the Husserlian phenomenology and in the Heideggerean and Sartrean alternative positions; further, I will hold that, as consequence, the ultimate question about the possibility of an ontology of the pure ego is transposed to the question of the origin and foundation of inner temporality. Yet, in this case one is set to face anew the circularity of an infinite regression in terms of reflecting-reflected and the inevitability of the subjective character of the origin of temporality. Besides this key question—a primary issue of this article—I will address the issue of the convergences and differences regarding aspects of the essential nature of the Husserlian ego, the Heideggerean *Dasein*, and the Sartrean Being-for-itself, especially regarding the widely debated topic of the 'exteriority' of the latter two 'egological' concepts with regard to the world in contrast to the 'interiority' of the Husserlian absolute ego.

1. INTRODUCTION

In the philosophical literature by the term continental philosophy is generally understood the European philosophy originating mainly in the subjective idealism of Fichte, Schelling and Hegel which ultimately leads to the 20th century off shoots as are thought to be, among others, the Husserlian phenomenology, the Heideggerean theory of *Dasein* and the Sartrean existentialism. As it is known there exist certain ramifications within the broad context of continental philosophy but in the present work I will almost exclusively refer to the philosophical theories mentioned above. In this scope

I'll try to bring out some fundamental similarities with regard to the 'creeping' transcendence of the ego of consciousness, this latter taken as essentially temporally founded in the Sartrean, Heideggerean and Husserlian philosophical work. On this account I will deal to a significant extent with some key questions concerning the temporality and the place of the ego within the world taken in the broad sense of a primitive soil of experience. This given I will carry out a comparative review of the convergences and divergences in the respective philosophers' conception of the transcendental ego (taking into account the particular attitude of Heidegger and Sartre toward this concept), while addressing the possibility of founding an ontology of the pure ego. Concerning the Heideggerean view it might seem odd to include his approach in the same terms as with Husserl's and Sartre's, given his own basic categories and the sense he attributed to *Dasein*, yet as the main scope of the article is to argue for the self-constituting inner temporality as the common ground for the respective philosophical positions, I thought it especially motivating to include Heidegger's ontology of *Dasein* in this comparative study. In developing my argumentation I will mostly refer to the original works of the respective philosophers, namely to Husserl (1966, 1976), Heidegger (1986[1], 2004) and Sartre (1943, 1960). Of course there exists an extensive literature on the subject matter of this article especially with regard to the nature of absolute subjectivity[2]. However my intention is to address issues in the secondary literature to a relatively limited extent as this would require yet another paper. Instead I will focus primarily into the original texts of the aforementioned philosophers, taking of course into account current research and the general terms of the philosophical discussion on the issue.

More specifically in Section 2 I discuss the question of an infinite regression induced by the scheme reflecting-reflected and the way it is dealt with by these philosophers, taking into account that this was a prime motivation for Husserl to seek a recourse to the absolute ego in the sense of a transcendence within the immanence of consciousness. In Section 3, I discuss the relation of the Husserlian ego with the world (in the sense of a primitive soil of experience) and the respective Heideggerean view of the presence of *Dasein* within the world and its relation with the world of phenomena. A special attention will be given also to the Sartrean view of the Being-

---

[1] Mainly through its English translation (Heidegger, 1996).
[2] One may refer indicatively to the works of R. Bernet (1994), K. Held (2007), P. Keller (1999), L. Levy (2016), P. Merlan (1947), D. Zahavi (2002, 2012); also to the collective works *A Companion to Phenomenology and Existentialism* (Dreyfus & Wrathall, 2016), and *Self-Awareness, Temporality, and Alterity* (Zahavi, 1998).

for-itself (*Pour-soi*), as being in the world like any other ego, thereby refuting the Husserlian position of the existence of a non-objectifiable, extraneous to the world, a-temporal ego within consciousness. In Sections 4 and 5 I will address the question of the similarities and differences in the conception respectively of the transcendental ego and of *Dasein* between Husserl and Heidegger and in the conception of the transcendental ego and the Being-for-itself between Husserl and Sartre. Lastly in Section 6, I'll argue that temporality can stand as a unifying pole in the foundation of the transcendental ego itself (also in its alternative versions) and in its relation to the objective world, in establishing first that inner temporality should be regarded as the ultimate essential trait of the ego in general of continental philosophy. A consistent argumentation for the central position of temporality concerning the nature of the transcendental ego should be regarded as the main focus of this paper, an intention ultimately served (often in an indirect way) by the whole discussion on the character of the continental ego.

Sartre's approach will be mainly discussed in Section 5 in which case the ecstatic rapport of the Being-for-itself[3] to the past and future and the Husserlian conception of the absolute flux of consciousness will be found to imply a transcendental factor which in the case of Sartrean temporality seems to be the annihilation (*néantisation*), described as something not real, of the Being-in-itself—the source of appearance of the Being-for-itself in the world—and also of the 'ontological' nature of the Being-for-itself (Sartre, 1943, 173).

Therefore we can talk about an underlying transcendence in the Sartrean temporality inasmuch as this temporality is thought of as not existing in terms of being in objective sense but as merely the mode of 'being' of a purely subjective consciousness—Sartre's Being-for-itself—which is always ecstatically in advance of itself. In this respect, it is already 'behind' itself in present actuality and its temporality cannot be conceived but as a passing annihilation that implies by necessity a past.

The ecstatic dimension of the temporality of the Being-for-itself is described as the 'distance' to itself and this 'distance' is nothing describable in objective terms, nothing that can be predicated as being in itself. It is simply a null, an evanescence which 'is been' as a separation and it is taken to define in ecstatic unity the rapport of the Being-for-itself with its past and future, grounding this way in an endless

---

[3] The Sartrean notion of the Being-for-itself, in contrast to the Being-in-itself (*En-soi*), can be roughly taken as implying a kind of transcendental leap out of the 'inwardness' of consciousness.

regression the appearance of any consciousness as 'being already born'[4]. The past, as something not posed in front of the Being-for-itself, is ecstatically already behind and out of its thematic field to the extent that it is no more expecting to be 'clarified.' From a certain viewpoint these ideas seem to be implied by the notions of retention and protention and generally Husserl's description of the intentional forms of absolute temporal consciousness something that I will comment further along with the general Husserlian approach to the transcendental ego.

At this point it should be stated that the 'background' of the existentialist treatment of time (in Heidegger and Sartre) lies in fact in Husserl's phenomenology of inner time consciousness (Husserl, 1966). It was on the basis of Husserl's phenomenological insights about the temporal flux of consciousness that Heidegger and Sartre affirmed the priority of the future over the past and the present, even though Husserl eventually came to espouse the living present as the primary source of all living being and the mode of presence of the absolute ego in the world (Husserl, 2001b, 4). Nevertheless there is no doubt that both Heidegger's and Sartre's approaches to the treatment of temporality have Husserl's lectures on time consciousness as their basis. Yet, given the subtleties and ambivalences that come with the way these concepts are dealt with, there are cases, like V. Thomas' (Thomas, 1990) in which it is inexactly argued that existentialists developed Husserl's insights in new ways and translated his epistemological language into an existential language (Thomas, 1990, 347-348). As I will discuss and show in the sections that follow, Husserl's language on the question of the nature of transcendental ego far from having any epistemological leanings, as it is virtually a priori founded, underlies in many respects the existentialist approach.

Heidegger's approach to the nature of *Dasein* will also find its due assessment (within the scope of this article) in the coming sections, the whole undertaking leading to the position that inner temporality and its origin holds the key to clarifying the affinities and divergences in the respective positions on the character of the absolute ego. It is true that although Heidegger shared Husserl's conception of

---

[4] The last consequence may lend itself as a meaningful answer to the existentialist questions of life and death. Assuming that my consciousness is, as any other subject's, a temporal one it turns out that the finiteness of my existence is not the finiteness of myself that I experience but it is always the finiteness of others. I can never experience my own first moment (birth) and last moment (death) but only as ecstatic moments (or in Husserlian terms as intentional moments of the absolute flux of consciousness); that is, in P. Merlan's words: "*in the modus of having already forgotten birth and still expecting death... Always I have already had time, and always shall I still have time.*" (Merlan, 1947, 36-37).

time-consciousness as the framework in terms of which experience is possible, and although he also shared Husserl's commitment to the absoluteness of temporality, he relocated temporality from time consciousness to the structure of *Dasein* as 'agency' vis-à-vis the world. The finite and futural temporality of active self-understanding supplants the Husserlian infinite and now-oriented time of self-consciousness (Brough, 2006, 132-133). Yet, even though Heidegger grounded the now, as the reference point of consciousness, in the future, as the reference point of self-understanding, in contrast to Husserl's conception of the primal now as the point of orientation for our conscious lives, my intention is nevertheless to argue for a significant convergence between them in terms of inner temporality as a constituting immanent factor pointing to an essentially egological origin.

2. RECOURSE TO A TRANSCENDENCE BY INFINITE REGRESSION

A major ambivalence generated by the phenomenological attitude toward objective reality is that of the possibility of an infinite regression due to the reflecting activity of consciousness. Put in more concrete terms, one is faced with an indefinitely proceeding sequence of reflections in the mode reflecting-reflected by virtue of admitting to a self-constituting origin of phenomenological reduction. A particular instance in which Husserl took this infinite regression into account is the foundation of the irreal (not objectively real) nature of objectivities as intended senses in *Erfahrung und Urteil* (Husserl, 1973). Sense as intended content is thought, in terms of a formal ontology, to be *in extremis* an object in the sense of a 'something-in-general' possibly devoid of any 'thingness content,' or at least prone to an objectification and accordingly made substrate of a judgment and of a predicative act of identification and explication. It follows that it may acquire a sense of a second-level which means that it is objectified in having a sense and by being objectified *eo ipso* it possesses a sense. Then one is led to an infinite regression insofar as the sense of a sense (the latter as objectified) can in turn become an object, then a have a sense of its own and so on. Consequently one can deduce that sense cannot be a real (*reelles*) component of an object as it 'is' always in a non-eliminable deficiency with regard to its own ontification (Husserl, 1973, 269).

In the Bernau manuscripts (Husserl, 2001a, 184-188) Husserl was faced with the difficulties emanating from this kind of infinite regression, yet he tried to circumvent the problem by searching the possibility of talking about a process of living experiences (not of temporally constituted experiences of the first degree) which advances as a living flux (*Lebensstrom*) without being itself knowable as a temporal object and constituted through a temporal constitution. For example, talking about an incident of sound, then the living-experience flux in which the appearance of sound is given can be taken as an individual object itself having its own time-interval of duration and also its own temporal position in the phenomenological time (this latter as contrasted to objective physical or psychophysical time). Then one can talk about the flux of concrete living experiences as an individual object in terms of its givennesses which points to yet another flux through which it 'appears' in reflection which can again become a temporal object with its own modes of givennesses and this way one can enter a regression in infinitum that is obviously an absurdity. The way out of this absurdity was thought to be the arduous (and ultimately unanswerable) task of bringing into evidence a primary living process which is really not a consciousness process, at least not a consciousness process which can be known as a process in phenomenological time. In such case it is questionable what else could a primary living process be other than a first-degree immanent experience within a self-constituting temporal process in a way that even though it is thought of as irreducibly original it may be only conceivable as 1) a first-degree immanent experience in a first phenomenological time, and also as 2) a self-referring process of consciousness knowable by consciousness itself in a second phenomenological time (Husserl, 2001a, 188). Husserl had similar concerns about the absurdity of an infinite regression in considering the intentional modes of retention and protention of consciousness, the former one thought of in terms of fulfillments of previous retentions generating thereby new protentions and so long in infinitum. In the face of these absurdities Husserl took the first-degree phenomenal time as only possible by means of an inner second-degree transcendental time having as a last transcendental occurrence the infinite process itself which is by itself consciousness of a process, termed a primary living process (Husserl, 2001a, 27-30).

In the bottom line what becomes object of reflection has to be in a temporal form and has also to be identically the same in the flux of the multiplicities of its givennesses. Then if the primary process (*Urprozess*), as it is usually termed in the *Bernau Manuscripts* the equivalent of the absolute ego of consciousness, is a temporal one we might turn our reflective 'glance' to the givenness of its phases in the scheme original impression—retentional degradation, and as the givenness of these phases would stand as a temporal sequence itself upon which we could turn anew our reflection and so on in infinitum we would end up in an infinite regression of reflections each one meant as a consciousness-of.

Consequently one should plausibly seek a clarification of the essence of 'being' of an *Urprozess* as preceding reflection. Husserl asked how in such a case one can think of a primary flux, perceived as a temporal one, yet one which could nonetheless not be made consciousness of a temporal flux nor of a phenomenological perception (*Wahrnehmung*). In the face of this grave difficulty he proposed the possibility of a process in which, for example, the sequence of an event with its generated 'repercussions' may find itself in the continuous unity of consciousness and in the phenomenological time without this process having the privilege of being intentionally 'noticed' or reflected upon. In that case, except for the already apprehended temporal objectivities could be also constituted in the background fully 'unnoticed' objectivities randomly and not by necessity. In the final count the question is reduced to whether, in the strictest sense, each concrete living-ego may have the character of a consciousness-of and thus be necessarily objectivity-constituting. Further, the question is whether the living-ego can be a sort of apprehension, namely an apprehension in the usual sense of an attentive formation, or possibly an apprehension in the widest sense of forming an intentional object where this intentional object cannot be identified with the act of apprehending, namely with the intentional experience as consciousness of it (Husserl, 2001a, 198-199).

In view of these core issues Husserl asked in the *Bernau Manuscripts* whether the temporality of the subject of consciousness is, in principle, due to genetically induced apperceptions in which unknown processes incur which are not temporally constituted themselves. However this implies that even with the supposition of a succession of genetically induced apperceptions we can still reach an impasse insofar as one can hardly constitute a sequence of apperceptions in which the identity of each one could be preserved in sinking to the past without presupposing an unknown process in consciousness 'preceding' the genetically induced succession of apperceptions.

In this sense the question remains essentially open as to how a transcendental, time-constituting process can be apprehended by any other means except by reflection. Evidently if object-contents exist and flow as a continuous sequence[5] the

---

[5] In a mathematical sense the term continuous sequence is a contradiction in terms. However the term sequence must be taken here in a Husserlian meaning that involves temporal succession and the a priori intentional forms of retention-protention making possible the continuous flow of events as immanences within consciousness.

question posed in the final count concerns the founding possibility of apprehension of these contents and of their flow. This process cannot supposedly consist in phenomenological perceptions upon which we can reflect since in this way these perceptions and their hypostasized contents are to be objects in a second time-constituting process in an open-ended horizon.

It turns out that this must be a kind of process which not only cannot be presented in reflection as temporally given but there must also be the evidence that this process was constituted prior to any reflection and that being and constituted-in-being are in it inseparable, in a way that this process may be knowable just like any object of phenomenological perception as temporally constituted without the necessity of an intentionally turned 'regard' (Husserl, 2001a, 205-206). However, one may put into serious doubt the validity of a temporal expression of the kind 'this was constituted prior to any reflection,' as it seems utterly meaningless without the attentive regard of a time-constituting consciousness. It follows that it is either nonsensical to talk about the possibility of a process prior to any reflection or else generate an infinite chain of circularities founded on the very presence of a temporality-constituting consciousness. In either case there seems to be no way of eliminating the primary source of an infinite chain of regressions associated with the reflective regard of a temporal ego other than by admitting to the transcendental character of an absolute subjectivity knowable only as its 'mirror-reflection image' in temporal objectivity. As it is well-known this subjectivity was already meant by Husserl in the *Phenomenology of Inner Time Consciousness* as the absolute ego of consciousness (Husserl, 1966, 74-75).

A distinct approach in view of the trappings of an infinite regression was taken by Sartre in *Being and Nothingness* (*L' être et le néant*), by positing the act of reflection as correlative to the manifestation of the ecstatic nature of the Being-for-itself and based on an ontology of temporality (Sartre, 1943, II). On these grounds one must take account of the Being-for-itself as presenting itself to the being-in-the-world in terms of its original dispersion with regard to the Being-in-itself and in view of the implementation of the three temporal ecstasies past-present-future. As Sartre pointed out 'being' out of itself and in the most close intimacy to itself the Being-for-itself is ecstatic because it must search its being elsewhere, namely, in the reflecting which is being reflected and in the reflected which poses itself as reflecting (Sartre, 1943, 188).

In a certain sense the Being-for-itself by 'continuously' being what it is not, incorporates the quasi-duality reflecting-reflected since the motivation of reflection consists in the simultaneous tentative of objectification and interiorisation, this latter term meant as the tendency of the Being-for-itself toward the 'interiority' of its being. Sartre transposed in effect the non-eliminable residuum reflecting-reflected of a temporal ontology to the ecstatic nature of the Being-for-itself in the sense that this latter is meant as "the being which flees itself while being what it is in the mode of not-being and which flows on while being its own flow, which escapes between its proper fingers..." (Sartre, 1992, 153).

Consequently the Being-for-itself becomes a givenness which is what it is as a unity in front of a 'gaze.' Yet Sartre reached an ontological impasse in the claim that the Being-for-itself tends to be its proper foundation by capturing and dominating its proper elusiveness as an 'interiority' of itself, in other words by being its proper elusiveness instead of temporalising elusiveness as such. This would ultimately result in a failure the realisation of which is precisely the reflection (Sartre, 1992, 189), which means that Sartre could not avoid the same Husserlian trap. On the other hand, the ontological Being-in-itself cannot found anything not even itself for in that case it would render unto itself the modification of the Being-for-itself and consequently would be a foundation of itself only on condition of not further being Being-in-itself.

A phenomenologically motivated alternative would be to insist on the existence of a pre-reflective self-consciousness which, as previously argued, was thought in the *Bernau Manuscripts* as being 'excluded' from its own self-reflection, though only by a somewhat circular approach. In this regard Sartre wrote: "There is no infinite regression here, since a consciousness has no need at all of a reflecting higher-order consciousness in order to be conscious of itself. It simply does not posit itself as an object" (Sartre, 1960, 45). This means the pre-reflective self-consciousness is not transitive in relation to the state (of) which it is aware. It is, as Sartre put it, the mode of existence of consciousness itself. However, this does not mean that a higher-order representation is impossible, but merely that it always presupposes the existence of a prior non-objectifying, pre-reflective self-consciousness as its condition of possibility. Sartre thought accordingly that it is the non-reflective consciousness which renders the reflection and probably any higher-order representation of it possible.

In Heidegger's existentialist version the unfolding of an infinite regression of reflections of the Husserlian ego unto itself is addressed by reducing to the ekstatic nature of *Dasein* as a realization of its taking care within the world and it is indissolubly linked to its temporality inasmuch as

> The genuine being of Dasein is temporalness. After all, Dasein is the 'time' that exists in the mode of temporalness; the being of Dasein is temporality. In what way 'time' exists and how it is temporal, we can understand only by looking at the true being of 'time.' (Heidegger, 2011, 51)

The question of the inexhaustible possibility of reflections of *Dasein* unto itself is associated with the roughly equivalent question of the possibility of a complete accessibility of *Dasein* whose completion cannot be taken but as a moment in the 'break up' of the connecting process of experiences and events and in the cessation of the acts on account of which the being of *Dasein* is no more 'there.' In this view and true to the world-founded nature of *Dasein*, *Dasein* is taken in advance as given-in-the-world and inquired according to what still exists there as its available givenness or not. Even in taking *Dasein*'s reflection unto itself as a demonstration of anticipating resoluteness (vorlaufende Entschlossenheit), which is in turn a mode of *Dasein*'s care (Sorge), one would fall again to the trap of temporality which enables the unity of caring for, something that implies temporality may be revealed in its three ekstases past-present-future as the meaning of the caring for.

In *Being and Time* (*Sein und Zeit*) Heidegger was very cautious as to the content one might give to the temporal character of the 'glimpse' of *Dasein* (in terms of the three ecstatic directions) to a time-point and ultimately unto itself. His position was that the time-point is non-existent as an ontologically autonomous being as it is rather the 'glimpse' of *Dasein* along the three directions of view and it was essentially thought as a proper possibility of time itself. Even as the question of an 'ontology' of temporality seems inherently associated with the conception of both the Husserlian absolute ego and the Heideggerean *Dasein*, a key difference between the respective approaches seems to be that while the former reaches out for a transcendence out of this world by relying on the absolute ego of consciousness as the primary source of constituted temporality, the latter associates everything pointing to an inner transcendental source of temporality to a temporal existence within-the-world oriented to the future as a primary manifestation.

3. THE RELATION OF THE EGO TO THE WORLD AS THE PRIMITIVE SOIL OF EXPERIENCE

The relation of the transcendental ego to the world taken in its most primitive sense as the primary soil of experience is a main divergence between Husserl's notion of the ego, Heigegger's view of *Dasein*, and with some nuances the existentialist position of Sartre.

The Transcendence of the Ego

One of Husserl's earliest references to the transcendence of the ego with regard to the world at large can be found in his probably most influential purely phenomenological work, *Ideas I*, where the absolute consciousness is conceived as a residuum of the annihilation of the world, characteristically expressed in the title of the paragraph: *Das absolute Bewußtsein als Residuum der Weltvernichtung* (Husserl, 1976, 103; 1983, 109).

More specifically Husserl claimed that while the being of consciousness or of any stream of mental processes would be modified by an annihilation of the world of physical things, yet it would not be touched in its own proper existence. This means that while in an annihilation of the physical world some of the ordered concatenations of experience and consequently certain corresponding concatenations of theoretical reasoning would be eliminated, the same would not hold for concatenations of mental processes in regarding the stream of consciousness (or of any mental process) in its full generality as comprising also the mental processes of an ego. In conclusion no real being presented and legitimated in consciousness through appearances is necessary to the being of consciousness itself or generally to the being of any stream of mental processes as lived experiences.

Immanental being is therefore indubitably absolute being in the sense that by essential necessity immanental being nulla 're' indiget ad existendum. In contradistinction, the world of transcendent 'res' is entirely referred to consciousness and, more particularly, not to some logically conceived consciousness but to actual consciousness (Husserl, 1983, 110).

The Husserlian ego regarded as the ultimate foundation of temporality should not be regarded as a simple substrate in the simple sense of an unqualified immanent unity underlying the multiplicity of mental processes. Instead it must be thought of as a unity-in-act whose essential nature without its auto-alienation in the act of objectification (through reflection) is totally inaccessible. Moreover since the condition of individuality and existence is inseparable from a conception of temporality as an objectivity, one cannot attribute to the ego the predicates of existence and individuality thereby essentially banning it out of this world. It is notable though, in J. Patočka's view, that the Husserlian ego cannot be identified with the extreme idealist version of Spinoza's *intellectus Dei infinitus* nor can lead to solipsistic ambiguities as it functions in concrete terms in the flux of each individual's consciousness and intersubjectively in all existing ones (Patočka, 1992, 168). Also one should be careful enough to note that even though human ego considered in its purity is for Husserl a complex of absolute being 'impervious' or 'bounded' to anything spatio-temporal, yet it is taken along with the human being in general as subordinate single realities to the whole spatio-temporal world (Husserl, 1976, 105-106). This means that even in taking spatio-temporal world as a mere intentional being referred to the absolute existence of a consciousness by being posited in its experiences and reducible to the identity of motivated multiplicities of appearances, the existence of the absolute ego is conceived as included in the spatio-temporal world in a subordinate sense in spite of the fact that the ego by essential nature does not partake of any spatio-temporally defined objective processes.

Heidegger, on the other hand, took an approach to the origin of *Dasein* that is firmly and unquestionably rooted in the world of phenomena. In *Being and Time* it is firmly stated that certain determinations of the being of *Dasein* (i.e., authenticity, inauthenticity or the modal indifference to them) must be seen and understood as a priori grounded on that constitution of being called being-in-the-world. In this connection 'being together with' the world should be interpreted in terms of the factor of the being-in of *Dasein* which in turn cannot be understood but as something existential in a sense further to be explained and certainly not as relating to the objective presence of material things in the sense of a spatial 'in one another.' In *Der Begriff der Zeit*, Heidegger referred to the being-in as expository and as having the character of discoveredness. In a certain sense being-in is described as possessing the mode of being of a throwing into the world where in caring about the world *Dasein* cares about itself concerning its immediately next possibilities. In Heidegger's characteristic phrase the being-in of *Dasein* is in the actual present a caring encounter with the world („*Das Insein des Daseins ist ein besorgendes in die Gegenwart Begegnenlassen der Welt*") (Heidegger, 2004, 100).

It is crucial in the Heideggerean outlook to understand the facticity of one's own *Dasein* as ontologically totally different from the factual occurrence of a material-objective thing, e.g. of a metal object, in that *Dasein* may have its own 'being-in-space' based on the being-in-the-world in general but meant in the sense of its dispersion within the world. More concretely, the ways of the being-in of *Dasein* have the kind of being of 'taking care,' this latter key Heideggerean concept ontologically meant to designate the being of a possible being-in-the-world. In other words as the being-in-the-world of *Dasein* cannot be separated from its being toward the world as essentially 'taking care of,' the being of *Dasein* can be dispersed in the world in definite ways, for example, having to do with something, creating something, ordering and taking care of something, using something, giving something up, asking about something, finding out, determining, (eventually) knowing (Heidegger, 1986, 56-57).

Consequently the Heideggerean *Dasein* even in assuming an essential nature non-eliminable in terms of a spatio-temporal presence in the world, it is ontologically knit to the world in such ways that it cannot exist otherwise but in the specific modes of being 'thrown' and 'dispersed' to the world. In contrast the Husserlian ego, totally inaccessibly without some kind of retention to its objectified mirror-reflexion, is conceived as not only transcendent to any spatiotemporal reality but by essential nature as deprived of any 'empathy' with the world the letter taken in the sense of an original pre-phenomenological field of experience.

If the relation of *Dasein* to the world is established by its essential mode of being in the world, the possibility of transcendence of the Being-for-itself is founded, in the Sartrean approach, in the facticity of the world of phenomena. This means that even though the foundation of the Being-in-itself cannot be obtained through its ontological existence in the spatiotemporal world (as it is annihilated to the the Being-for-itself), the Being-for-itself is defined to exist as such, namely as a pure contingence in the world to the extent that it 'contains' something of which it is not the foundation which is its presence in the world (Sartre, 1943, 115). I will come back to these conceptual affinities in Section 5.

These taken into account we should not miss the point that for all the divergences and similarities in the respective approaches of Husserl, Heidegger and Sartre to the nature of the transcendental ego and its relation to the world there is a crucial question to be discussed in the last section which may serve, partially at least, as a unifying interpretational factor. This is the question of inner temporality and the way it may shape the discussion on the transcendental character of the absolute ego.

4. A COMPARATIVE LOOK INTO THE HUSSERLIAN EGO AND THE HEIDEGGEREAN DASEIN

As it is well-known to phenomenologists Heidegger placed the phenomenology of time and temporality at the center of the content of *Being and Time*, even if the ontology of being in general on the basis of the temporality of the being of *Dasein* is quite distinct from Husserl's doctrine: "…we need an original explication of time as the horizon of the understanding of being, in terms of temporality as the being of *Da-sein* which understands being" (Heidegger, 1996, 15). A key point of their diverging views, at least on the fundamental question of being, was Heidegger's insistence that the phenomenological clarification of being (which Husserl proposed) should be extended to the being of the transcendental subject itself in the sense that the problem of Being should be directed toward the constituting and the constituted alike. This is a question presumably left by Husserl in an ontological vacuum. Yet for all the differences in the respective approaches, particularly evident from the time of Husserl's article on Phenomenology in Encyclopaedia Britannica (1929), S. Crowell thinks in *Husserl, Heidegger, and Transcendental Philosophy: Another Look at the Encyclopaedia Britannica Article* that a significant rapprochement between Husserl and Heidegger, leaving neither totally unrevised, may become thinkable (Crowell, 1990, 518).

As mentioned in the Introduction the inclusion of the Heideggerean *Dasein* in a review of the general notion of the ego of continental philosophy might strike someone as far-reaching given that the concept of facticity associated with *Dasein*, insofar as this is inquired with respect to, on the basis of, and with a view to the character of its being, essentially leaves the concept of pure ego out of its ontological field at least in the sense the ego is conceived in Husserlian phenomenology[6].

For Heidegger there cannot exist a pure ego in isolation of the world and in his own words in *Ontology—The Hermeneutics of Facticity* it would be a fundamental misunderstanding if in the reference to *Dasein* "which is in each case our own, a directive was heard to become [...] fixated on vacantly brooding over an isolated ego-like self." (Heidegger, 1999, 25). Yet the modes of existence of *Dasein*, namely the possibility of its self-alienation within-the-world and above all the fundamental phenomenon of facticity, which is temporality as an existential condition and not as a category, provide sufficient motivation to include also the Heideggerean *Dasein* in the present discussion. Indicative of the inherent link between temporality and the essence of *Dasein* are the following two quotations of Heidegger's in *The Basic Problems of Phenomenology*. "The Dasein is intentional only because it is determined essentially by temporality. [...] How these two characters, intentionality and transcendence, are interconnected with temporality will become apparent to

---

[6] For example concerning the key phenomenological notion of intentionality, Heidegger claims in *The Basic Problems of Phenomenology* that it is not the case that intentionality is first related to the ego as its generating pole and then from there it goes to the object but rather that by means of intentionality itself is the self in its wholeness disclosed to us. To intentionality belongs not only a self-directing toward and not only an understanding of the being of the object toward which it is directed in terms of the content of this very act but also the unveiling of the essence of the self in its actual enactment. See further (Heidegger, 1982, 158-172).

us." (Heidegger, 1982, 268) and "We know, however, that this self-direction toward something, intentionality, is possible only if the Dasein as such is intrinsically transcendent. It can be transcendent only if the Dasein's basic constitution is grounded originally in ecstatic-horizontal temporality."(Heidegger, 1999, 314).

Further, *Dasein* is described as 'being' ahead of itself, that is, as projecting itself upon its potentiality-of-being before going on to any mere consideration of itself (Heideger, 1996, 373). It is 'thrown in the world' and in 'taking care of' *Dasein* is disclosed as a There. As being-in-the-world it has always expressed itself already, while being-together-with-others means that it keeps itself in average interpretedness which is articulated in discourse and expressed in language. In the final count discourse is itself temporal since all talking about.., of.., or to.., is grounded in the ecstatic unity of temporality.

Insofar as *Dasein* enters into the discussion as the ultimate bastion of the question of being we may see some fundamental similarities and also some divergences with the Husserlian ego taken as the ultimate transcendental source of the objective unity of being in the Life-World[7]. One can thus point to the advancement of *Dasein* ahead of itself as bearing a common transcendental origin with the intentionality exhibited by the Husserlian ego to the extent that intentionality as an ego-founded outward directed moment establishes itself on the basis of a reduction performing subjectivity. To the extent that the intentional moments of even a sole consciousness in the world are irreducibly self-founded in this sense, even in a complete annulment of any objects in the world being put anyway into brackets, this can be reasonably taken as implying a certain non-eliminable affinity with the sense attributed to *Dasein* by virtue of the a priori moment of the latter to project itself ahead of its potentiality-of-being-in-the world.

Clearly a convergence may be founded on a fundamental level in the possibility of grounding both *Dasein* and the Husserlian ego upon temporality, in accepting however a fundamental difference, namely that while the Husserlian ego manifests itself primarily in the actual present, time as the horizon of the self-understanding of *Dasein* is aimed toward a future for the sake of which each one acts as he does. In *Being and Time* the circumspect taking care of common sense is grounded

---

[7] The Life-World can be roughly described to a non-phenomenologist as the physical world with its ever receding horizon including in an intersubjective sense all knowing subjects in a special kind of presence in the World. More on this in E. Husserl's *The Crisis of European Sciences and Transcendental Phenomenology* (Husserl, 1962).

on temporality inasmuch as it makes possible the constitution of a present that awaits and retains. This is the way through which the advancement of *Dasein* ahead of itself is making itself 'explicit' within the world, namely in the modes of presentifying (*Gegenwärtigen*) retaining (*Behalten*) and awaiting (*Gewärtigen*). In comparison the Husserlian ego is making itself 'explicit' by being self-constituted as a 'mirror' reflexion of its ever in-act subjectivity in the actual now along with the intentional forms of not-yet and just-passed-by. After all Husserl's concept of absolute consciousness as a condition, among other intentional forms, of the possibility of the awareness with regard to any object whatsoever was accepted by Heidegger and given the new name of the ecstatic-horizonal unity of temporality which 'carries *Dasein* away' and thereby constitutes *Dasein*'s 'transcendence,' its stepping over to a world, its 'being outside itself' in a world (Brough & Blattner, 2006, 131).

In a sense Heidegger established temporality as a way through which *Dasein* is making itself expressible in addressing what it takes care of. As it turns out, this addressing and 'discussing' by which it also interprets itself is grounded in making out a present and it is only possible through it (Heidegger, 1996, 373-374). Although temporality as ecstatically open and horizontally constitutive of the clarity of the 'there' may be in these terms recognizable, nevertheless Heidegger did not preclude the possibility that primordial temporality as such as well as the origin of expressed time may remain unknown and unconceived (Heidegger, 1996, 375). Therefore we have on the one hand a temporality constitutive of the clarity of the 'there' as the means of making *Dasein* expressible in taking care of and in being-together-with things at hand, and on the other hand the origin of temporality which is only expressible by temporalizing itself in the expressed time while standing in itself virtually unknown and unconceivable. In fact the ecstatic unity of temporality, the unity of the 'outside-itself' in the raptures of the future, the having-been, and the present, is the condition of the possibility that there can be a being that exists as its 'there.' Taking the whole constitution of the being of *Dasein* as the unified ground of its existential possibility, ecstatic temporality clears the 'there' primordially and it is the prime regulator of the possible unity of all essential existential structures of *Dasein*. It is only in terms of the rootedness of *Dasein* in temporality that we can gain insight into the existential possibility grounding the fundamental constitution of the being-in-the-world.

As already discussed the corresponding Husserlian transcendental ego constitutive of temporality and consequently of spatiality (the latter meant as a temporally fulfilled objective whole) is temporalized by objectifying itself in the unity of each one's temporal consciousness. Insofar as the absolute ego can be known in objective temporality only as a mirror reflexion of its transcendental self, it is bound to remain a-temporal, unobjectifiable and for that reason absolutely impredicative[8]. Yet, while the Heideggerean *Dasein* is attributed with an ecstatic moment that projects its presence in the world as caring about its 'being' in being-with-other-beings, the Husserlian absolute ego is completely impersonalized, extraneous to the outer world and obscure and so it remained to the end in spite of Husserl's painstaking efforts in Bernau manuscripts and later to elucidate its 'ontic' character trying at the same time not to get trapped in a maze of circularities.

For Heidegger it is on the basis of the horizontal constitution of the ecstatic unity of temporality that something like a disclosed world belongs to the being which is always its 'there' (Heidegger, 1996, 334). This means temporality temporalizes itself as a future that makes present in the process of having been which is in a certain sense reminiscent of the double form of the intentionality of consciousness in Husserlian terms: On the one hand, there is the transversal intentionality as a priori binding any original impression to the attached protentions and retentions, that is, by retaining what is registered in consciousness in the present now by virtue of having been already 'anticipated,' and on the other, there is the longitudinal intentionality by which a stored memory can be retrieved by secondary memory in the present now of consciousness by having been retained as a continuously descending sequence of retentions constituted as a whole within the objective unity of the stream of consciousness. It is notable that in Heidegger temporalizing does not mean a 'succession,' in the Husserlian sense, of the ecstasies in the sense that

---

[8] It is worthwhile to mention here D. Zahavi's view (Zahavi, 2011, 322-323) and elsewhere that the Husserlian transcendental ego does not and cannot be a unifying or synthesizing actor, at least in an active way, in the unity of temporal consciousness, consequently one should talk about a continual substratum of the egoless streaming that founds it. To strengthen his argument Zahavi refers, except for certain passages in the *Phenomenology of Intersubjektivity III* and the *Formal and Transcendental Logic* where Husserl points to a pre-egoic factor grounding the passivity of the stream of consciousness, to Husserl's well-known *Phenomenology of Inner Time Consciousness* in which he purportedly gives no reference to the ego as the ultimate unifying or synthesizing agent. However this is a position that can be refuted insofar as we may take Husserl's explicit reference to an absolute subjectivity, which constitutes as a continuity of apparitions a present to which it belongs and a past which also constitutes (not constituted) and to which it also belongs, as referring precisely to the transcendental ego (Husserl, 1966, 75). Besides, there is no possible way to think of an egoless streaming in the sense of a passive streaming which is beyond the influence of the ego without generating an endless recurring sequence of reflecting-reflected which, in spite of Husserl's lasting attempts to circumvent, was and is still one of the thorny issues facing the phenomenology of temporal consciousness. See also C. Macann's views on the impossibility of a phenomenological constitution of the transcendental ego (Macann, 1991).

the future is not later than the having-been and the having-been not earlier than the present. The unity of the horizontal schemata of future, having-been and present is grounded on the ecstatic unity of temporality[9]. These given and notwithstanding the essential differences in the description of the Husserlian ego and the Heideggerean *Dasein* it is critical that in both approaches the capital issue of the original source of temporality is left in relative vagueness probably on account of the extreme difficulty in shaping a meaningful discourse on this question.

The difficulty can be seen, for instance, in Husserl's description of the essence of absolute ego as *a nunc stans* (never-in-being) which is a contradiction in terms and also in his appeal to pre-predicative intentionality structures termed so to the extent that they 'anticipate' without by essential necessity being actually oriented to temporally constituted instances, in other words without being oriented to actually existing objects of spatio-temporality. In this sense one may claim that intentionality of consciousness defines a domain of real possibility anterior to actuality (Heelan, 1988, 12; Tieszen, 2011, 114-115).

The difficulty of talking about the original source of temporality may be also found in the Heideggerean description of *Dasein* in terms of the non-ontological qualifications of 'taking care' or of 'being thrown into existence' referring to the outside-of-itself of the ecstatic unity of temporality. Both Husserl and Heidegger talked about temporality essentially in the context of constituted objectivity and of being-in-the-world respectively, considering the description of a temporal duration or of temporal unity as only a being-in-the-world discourse where any *ante* situation is virtually left as a circularities-generating, non-ontological (and therefore impredicative) state of affairs.

5. THE TEMPORALITY OF SARTRE'S BEING-FOR-ITSELF

Sartre used the terms of ecstasis and horizon as key concepts of his existential version of phenomenology, and like Heidegger before him, viewed primordial temporality as the foundation for our 'transcendence' or 'openness' to a world. However to the extent that the Heidegerrean conception of *Dasein* bore a certain

---

[9] A very interesting review of the affinities in Husserl's and Heidegger's description of the 'authentic' time (or inner time of consciousness), is presented in (Held, 2007, 336-339) through the fundamental role ascribed to the protentionality of consciousness which, by the way, refutes de facto the aristotelian notion of time as a series of still 'nows.'

influence on him he had eventually to part ways from Husserl's orientation to the lived experience of the now founded on the logic of predominance of the relation subject versus object over that of *Dasein* versus the world. Yet as it happened also with Heidegger, Sartre was largely shaped by Husserl's phenomenology even though he later came to criticize key Husserlian ideas, among them, Husserl's conception of the transcendental ego as being incompatible with Husserl's definition of consciousness as a unity in objective terms. There is even scholarly research showing the positive influence earlier Husserl's *Logical Investigations* (Husserl, 1984), played in forming Sartre's approach to basic philosophical problems such as the nature of intentionality, consciousness, and the self, even if it does not seem to me that the relevant arguments are always firmly founded.

In any case, I am going to discuss in the following certain affinities between the Sartrean version of a possible transcendental origin of consciousness and the Husserlian ego. I note at this point certain authors' views on Sartre's presumably non-egological conception of consciousness, namely Zahavi's position in (Zahavi, 2011, 323), that consciousness in Sartre is in no need of a transcendental principle of unification since it is, as such, a flowing unity and Tandon's position in (Tandon, 1998, 467) on Sartre's 'deconstruction' of the egological conception of consciousness. These views are going to be indirectly addressed and refuted in the following discussion.

Sartre's main divergences from the Husserlian perspective regarding the notion of the absolute ego appeared in *The Transcendence of the Ego* (Sartre, 1960), almost a decade earlier than the first publication of *Being and Nothingness* (1943), and concerned precisely the relation of consciousness to the transcendental ego. In more concrete terms, Sartre refused to accept anything, including in the first place the absolute ego[10], that might be interpreted as a content of consciousness while claiming in a way that sounds familiar with his subsequent clarification of the Being-for-itself in *Being and Nothingness* that consciousness is a spontaneity, a pure activity transcending and exhausting itself toward objects which is never self-contained nor

---

[10] In denying the 'existence' of the ego within consciousness Sartre stated in *The Transcendence of the Ego*: "For most philosophers the ego is an 'inhabitant' of consciousness. Some affirm its formal presence at the heart of *Erlebnisse*, as an empty principle of unification [...] We should like to show here that the ego is neither formally nor materially in consciousness: it is outside, in the world. It is a being of the world, like the ego of another." (Sartre, 1960, 31). In conclusion he accepted the 'I' (taken simply as a functional version of the ego) as existent and strictly contemporaneous with the world whose existence (that of 'I') has the same essential characteristics as the world (Sartre, 1960, 105).

it is itself a container as it is always 'outside itself.' Further, as consciousness cannot be isolated from the existing world the question of phenomenological reduction becomes problematic to the extent that such a radical reduction would contract consciousness into its own 'interiority' (Sartre, 1960, 25).

A reason invoked by Sartre for the superfluity or simply the 'non-existence' of the ego with regard to the synthetic and individual totality of each one's consciousness is that consciousness unifies itself concretely by a play of transversal intentionalities which are concrete and real retentions of past consciousness (Sartre, 1960, 39). However the validity of this argument is questionable to the extent that, first, this kind of self-constituted totality is constrained to a circular use of the notion of constituted unity through transversal and longitudinal intentionalities in the first place, and second it may also lead to an infinite regression of the kind reflecting-reflected in the reflective regard of consciousness unto itself,—in spite of Sarte's argument to the contrary. Yet even though Sartre rejected the absolute ego in the Husserlian sense, meant as a transcendental vacuity within the immanence of consciousness, and committed himself to the Being-for-itself induced to the world by the annihilation of the Being-in-itself, one may still argue that there exists no possibility to objectify let alone describe in ontological terms the process of annihilation of the Being-in-itself in its 'modification' to the Being-for-itself, this latter taken in the sense of a consciousness interwoven with the world. This means that as it happens with the Husserlian ego but in a substantially different context there persists a kind of ontological vacuum left over in the process of annihilation of the Being-in-itself toward the facticity of the Being-for-itself, something that, notably, in Sartre's view established the necessity of cogito in Descartes and Husserl. In fact, what rests from the contingency of the Being-in-itself in its transformation to the Being-for-itself is the latter's facticity and its 'unjustifiable' presence in the world in accordance with the interpretation of its existence as a necessity of fact. The result is that the Being-for-itself is the foundation of the being of consciousness but cannot in any way found by itself its presence in the world (Sartre, 1943, 120).

The question of temporality in relation to a performing subjectivity is a vital part of Sartre's analysis of the 'ontology' of the Being-for-itself in *Being and Nothingness*. In fact, he was led by a consistent critique of the views of Descartes and Bergson to the question of temporality as inherently linked to a unifying act. It is in terms of this unifying act that temporality is conceived as a quasi-multiplicity, a dissociation in terms of a unity, more precisely an irreversible succession (of moments) through temporal unity. In this sense we cannot conceive it as a content bearer whose being would be given as an objectivity, for in that case there would be no answer to the question of how this being can be fragmented into multiplicities or how the temporal minima as contents in themselves can be associated within the unity of a unique temporality (Sartre, 1943, 71). Consequently, temporality cannot be thought of in terms of a (static) being but instead should be described as the mode of being which 'is' itself in advance of itself in a way that the temporal conjunctions in advance of and after of can be intelligible for it as reciprocally defined. So long as there is an advancement (essentially an alienation) of being with regard to itself it becomes meaningful to talk in general terms about *in advance of* and *after of*. It follows that there can be no conceivable temporality but as an internal structure of the Being-for-itself in the sense that there is no ontological priority of the Being-for-itself over temporality but rather temporality is the mode of being of the Being-for-itself to the extent that the latter 'exists' ecstatically with regard to itself. In Sartre's expression, temporality does not exist (in terms of ontological being), yet the Being-for-itself temporalizes itself in existing and moreover, on account of a phenomenologically motivated view of the past, present and future, it cannot exist otherwise than in a temporal form (Sartre, 1943, 172).

Sartre distinguished the ecstatic dimensions of the Being-for-itself with the understanding that the sense of the ecstasy is taken as the distance of the Being-for-itself from itself which is not to be considered as something real not even something conceivable as being in itself. In this sense, each ecstatic dimension is a mode through which the Being-for-itself is projected in relation to itself and moreover it is a declination with regard to its being-in-itself separated by a null, something that induces (for the Being-for-itself) a shift of its 'being.' On this account, the Being-for-itself is ever either in advance of or in retard of itself and it 'is' never in the state of rest with itself. It should not be left without notice that, contrary to certain scholars' view, Sartre put the emphasis on the ecstacy of the present now as Husserl did concerning the ego of absolute consciousness but of course in another context and unlike Heidegger who insisted on the predominance of the ecstacy of the future. Sartre's claim was that it is due to its self-revelation in the present now that Being-for-itself 'is' its past and as a deficiency of its present self that it is 'haunted' by its future (Sartre, 1943, 177).

In resting on itself the Being-for-itself would 'be' in the a-temporal phase of absolute coincidence with itself, something that is reminiscent in a first reading of the Husserlian notion of a specious present within the immanence of consciousness meant as an a priori articulation at once of original impression, protention and retention which by this fact alone annuls the possibility of apprehending and objectifying time instants as ontological beings. On a deeper level it can be seen as posing in another way the question of the transcendental and a-temporal character of the origin of temporality to the extent that in the incessant interplay of reflecting-reflected whenever the Being-for-itself is determined as 'being' it is already its past while being at the same time the projection of its 'not-yet-self.' To the question whether this continual change, of a present to a past at once generating a new present, implies an internal change of the Being-for-itself, the answer is that it is the temporality of the Being-for-itself that is the foundation of change and not the change that is the foundation of temporality (Sartre, 1943, 179).

Clearly in admitting to an ecstatic nature of the Being-for-itself it is only by a presupposition of temporality that becomes meaningful a self-refutation of its spontaneity as thematically given (for otherwise it would be perpetually its being-in-itself) and also a refutation of the self-refutation, this latter taken as being-in-itself a concrete state of affairs. In this sense what is valid for the Being-for-itself as a presence in the world is also valid for temporalization in its totality. It is then a whole never completed, a totality self-refuting and self-evading meant as an extraction of its being-in-itself in the unity of the same emergence, in other words an elusive whole which at the instant of its self-givenness 'is' already beyond. In the Sartrean view temporal consciousness is conceived as the human reality temporalizing itself as a totality which cannot be described as existing but in terms of its own overpassing, meaning that it can never 'exist' as being-in-itself within the limits of an instant for in that case the Being-for-itself would be affirmed as being-in-itself which would contradict its character as never 'existing' in terms of being. These difficulties give ground, at least in part of the secondary literature, for arguing against Sartre's unfavorable position toward the transcendental ego in (Sartre, 1960), as he cannot help but eventually postulate a kind of I (Ich) even on the pre-reflective level in the sense that there must be a more fundamental structure of consciousness which recognizes the body-subject as itself.

Going a step further we may argue that even though Sartre rejected the notion of a pure ego interior to consciousness, the Sartrean Being-for-itself bears in fundamental aspects (primarily by its temporality) certain affinities with the Husserlian absolute ego of consciousness insofar as both are by essence referred to a temporality as a necessary condition of their objectification while by the same measure they are considered as themselves a-temporal yet temporally conceived only as their replicas in the ever regressing relation reflecting-reflected. Further they are thought of as the primary reason of the emergence of temporality as the 'fulfillment' of any continuous objective whole (which always refutes its being-in-instantaneity) as they ultimately establish themselves as objectively being-in-the-world, thereby laying the foundation for a deeper discussion with regard to the temporality of intuitive and possibly mathematical continuum[11]. In a phrase characteristic of the convergence of motivations Sartre kept wondering about the incomprehensibility of the intertemporal connections between before and after by asking "What is a succession which waits for unification in order to become a succession?" (Sartre, 1992, 169). Accordingly he questioned how a non-temporal 'being' can generate the unification of e.g., two isolated Being-in-itself in terms of time and place (the before and after) without losing its a-temporality and further on how a non-temporal 'being' can emanate from itself without obliterating itself.

This kind of ontological impasse naturally led Sartre to the same ambivalences faced by Husserl with regard to the endlessly regressing sequence of reflecting-reflected. This means the ontological structure of the Being-for-itself cannot be conceived otherwise but as the reflecting referred to a reflected as appearance while being at the same time the appearance of its self-reflection and in reverse mode the reflected cannot but be an appearance for a reflecting without for that reason ceasing to be its own witness. In this view the reflected cannot lay claim to a self-standing foundation inasmuch as it is profoundly altered by virtue of a reflecting consciousness whereas, in turn, the reflection as witnessing cannot be founded as such but through appearances which again deprive it of self-standing as it is necessarily defined by its functioning as reflection-of. Even as Husserl in his later Bernau writings on the phenomenology of time was arguing that the reflected may be given as already existing prior to reflection the supposedly self-standing status of the non-reflected is annulled by the phenomenon of reflection itself. In short, Sartre reduced the separation reflecting-reflected to a nothingness manifest in the 'nullifying' of the Being-for-itself upon reflection, a kind of separation leading *in extremis* to what Husserl described in quite vague terms as a retention in general interposed between the pure ego and its objectified self upon reflection.

It turns out that the transcendence of a temporally self-constituting subjectivity can, broadly conceived, lend itself as a common guiding principle of the

---

[11] For a discussion of the possibility of foundation of the intuitive and in particular of the mathematical continuum on the phenomenology of inner temporality the reader may consult (van Atten, van Dalen & Tieszen, 2002; Livadas, 2009).

respective Husserlian, Heideggerean and Sartrean views to the extent that this kind of subjectivity constitutes temporality in constantly alienating itself from its ontic 'being.' In this sense absolute subjectivity may be taken to 'be' the ultimate origin of a continuous temporal unity which is the *sine qua non* condition for the immanentization of multiplicities of discrete objects of registered-in perception [including the formal-ontological ones in the sense of *Formal and Transcendental Logic*; see Husserl (1992, §24)], passively associated within a temporal duration which is founded upon the objectified, homogenous stream of inner temporality. A temporal duration 'fulfilling' an objective continuous whole in the present now of consciousness may, in turn, generate an actual infinity meant as a non-causal, boundless immanent whole in presentational immediacy within consciousness.

6. TEMPORALITY AS THE ULTIMATE FOUNDATION OF THE EGO OF CONTINENTAL PHILOSOPHY

Let me draw attention a little more on the Sartrean approach to temporal subjectivity. Reflecting, for instance, on my self now that I draw a line in a piece of paper is in a full and complete sense already a past in terms of a state-of-affairs: I draw a line in a piece of paper whereupon as this state-of-affairs is coming over me at the present now it is already deflected to the state of already-not been (which is in deficiency of its full sense as being-in-itself) by the annihilating property of the Being-for-itself. This way the Being-for-itself is at once before and after itself. By the Sartrean definition of the past and future as ecstatic limits of the temporality of the Being-for-itself one is led to an a-temporality in the absolute coincidence of the Being-for-itself with itself.

The Sartrean a-temporality in the case of absolute coincidence with the Being-in-itself may be thought of, as already discussed, in parallel terms with the Husserlian non-existence of an absolutely self-standing temporal instant since anything intentionally perceived as original impression in present actuality is intentionally tied up to a just-passed-by in retention and a yet-to come in protention (Husserl, 1966, 31-35, 52-53). I also regard Sartre's ecstatic unity underlying the third ecstatic dimension[12] as pointing in a certain way to the intentional forms (i.e., transversal-

---

[12] A temporal transcendence underlies the third ecstatic dimension, (i.e. being what it is not and not being what it is), insofar as the Being-for-itself in a constant interplay of reflecting-reflected eludes itself in an all-encompassing ecstatic unity in which it is grounded as the ecstatic tendency toward a Being-in-itself inside its ever receding thematic field.

longitudinal intentionality) exhibited by the absolute flux of consciousness in the Husserlian phenomenology. However here is naturally raised the question of the subjectivity behind the objective unity of temporal consciousness and consequently of any form of constituted unity. It turns out that this kind of subjectivity cannot be comprehensible but as essentially associated with temporality as the form of its objective existence.

As a matter of fact an indirect clue leading to an absolute subjectivity as the original cause of inner temporality may be found in Husserl's description of longitudinal intentionality meant as an intentional form of consciousness establishing the continuous unity of retentions and ultimately the unity of the flux of consciousness as such (Husserl, 1966, 80-83). This has to do with the circular fashion in which the continuity characterizing the unity of a descending sequence of retentions is applied both on the level of constituting and that of constituted thus indirectly pointing to the non-eliminable character of an absolute subjectivity establishing the continuous unity of the flux of consciousness. Ultimately this absolute subjectivity must be a pre-reflective non-objectifiable subjectivity, the ever in-act subjectivity of the continuous unity of temporal consciousness. There is no, strictly speaking, corresponding concept to this kind of absolute subjectivity in Heidegger's analysis of the temporality of *Dasein*, for Heidegger reduced the original ecstatic temporality to quite perplexing ecstatic forms of existence of the being-in the world. Nevertheless they were both deeply concerned with the phenomenological-subjective origins of objective or scientific time (Bernet, 1994, 210).

What is of importance from my point of view is that they both reduced the temporal unity of immanent objects and finally the self-constituting unity of temporal consciousness itself to one or other source of transcendental origin. Heidegger described it as the ecstatic unity of a presentifying *Dasein* which a priori retains and anticipates (in the sense of tending toward), while Husserl except for the key radical reduction to the absolute ego suggested, on the level of constituted, the a-priori intentional forms of retention and protention of absolute consciousness to provide for the temporal identity of its immanent objects and the longitudinal intentionality for the constitution of the flux of consciousness itself. The transcendence in Heidegger's description of the temporality of *Dasein* lies, in fact, in the description of its ecstatic temporality as an impetus alienating the being-in-itself of *Dasein* from its ontological substance and transforming it into a ceaseless motivation. Temporality is for Heidegger the ecstatic unity of the ecstatic moments of *Dasein*.

On account of my arguments in the preceding two sections it follows that Heidegger's notion of ecstatic temporality may be also compatible with the Sartrean view of the ecstatic temporality of the Being-for-itself, something not strange given the influence Husserlian phenomenology had on the philosophical formation of both.

Whatever may be the differences between Sartre and Heidegger in the description of the temporality of the Being-for-itself and *Dasein* respectively and between them and Husserl concerning the character of the source of unity of temporal consciousness, I consider as most important the following common underlying factor of the respective approaches: This is the 'residual' transcendental subjectivity non-describable in ontological terms, impredicative as an objectivity, which is a constituting (and not constituted) factor of the continuous unity of each subject's temporal consciousness and intersubjectively of all beings-in-the-world.

Such convergence may be defensible insofar as their approaches are irreducibly rooted to a kind of absolute 'being' non-describable in terms of ontological being within temporal objectivity without alienating itself from its mode of 'being' as a time-constituting subjectivity-in-act. Based on the argumentation so far, the Husserlian source of the unity of temporal consciousness, the source of temporality of the Heideggerean *Dasein* and the 'essence' of the Sartrean Being-for-itself are not susceptible to an ontological postulation except by auto-alienation in objective reflection.

To the extent that we talk about an absolute subjectivity totally inaccessible as such, except in temporal objectivity, we are about to face the question of whether it should be encountered as an immanence of an embodied consciousness totally extraneous to the real objective world. Husserl had thought of the absolute subjectivity of consciousness as the residuum left after an annihilation of the world of physical things in the sense that no real being presented and legitimated in consciousness by appearances is necessary to the being of consciousness itself. This means that while the being of consciousness as an absolute immanental 'being' is by essential necessity not born out of any existing thing of the physical world, a transcendent object of physical reality, on the contrary, is entirely referred to an intentionally oriented consciousness. As claimed in Section 3 consciousness in its purity 'is' a self-contained absolute being to which nothing is spatiotemporally external and, yet, it cannot be contained within any spatiotemporality for in that case it would be temporally objectified and subjected to the laws of causation. It follows that in taking the whole spatiotemporal world, which includes the human ego in the sense of a subordinate reality, as a secondary being posited by an intentional consciousness we can reach *in extremis* the conclusion that the world is constituted by consciousness as something identical arising from motivated multiplicities of experiences beyond which there is nothing to be (Husserl, 1976, 106).

The author tends to side with the Husserlian view of the self-founded 'interiority' of the absolute ego of consciousness even though it cannot be conceived as such except as always being-in-act within the surrounding life-world. Yet if this is a point in which the views of the philosophers dealt with in this article vary, a significant part in it served to point to their convergent approaches concerning the transcendental source of any subjectivity-within-the-world and the terms under which it may be viewed as the source of constituted temporality. In the final count temporality as the ultimate form of presence of the ego in the world is argued to be a unifying contextual factor for addressing the respective philosophical positions.

REFERENCES

Bernet, R. (1994). *La vie du sujet*. Paris: PUF.
Brough, B. G., & Blattner, W. (2006). Temporality. In K. H. Dreyfus & A. M. Wrathall (Eds.), *A Companion to Phenomenology and Existentialism* (127-134). Chichester: Wiley-Blackwell.
Crowell, G. S. (1990). Husserl, Heidegger, and Transcendental Philosophy: Another Look at the Encyclopaedia Britannica Article. *Philosophy and Phenomenological Research*, 1(3), 501-518.
Dreyfus, K. H., & Wrathall, A. M. (Eds.). (2006). *A Companion to Phenomenology and Existentialism*. Chichester: Wiley-Blackwell.
Heelan, P. (1988). *Space-Perception and the Philosophy of Science*. Oakland: University of California Press.
Heidegger, M. (1982). *The Basic Problems of Phenomenology*. Bloomington: Indiana University Press.
Heidegger, M. (1986). *Sein und Zeit*. Tübingen: M. Niemeyer Verlag.
Heidegger, M. (1996). *Being and Time*. Albany: State University of New York Press.
Heidegger, M. (1999). *Ontology — The Hermeneutics of Facticity*. Bloomington: Indiana University Press.
Heidegger, M. (2004). *Der Begriff der Zeit*. Frankfurt: V. Klostermann.
Heidegger, M. (2011). *The Concept of Time*. NY: Continuum.
Held, K. (2007). Phenomenology of 'Authentic Time' in Husserl and Heidegger. *International Journal of Philosophical Studies*, 15(3), 327-347.
Husserl, E. (1962). *Die Krisis der Europäischen Wissenschaften und die Transzendentale Phänomenologie* (Hua VI). Den Haag: M. Nijhoff.
Husserl, E. (1966). *Vorlesungen zur Phänomenologie des inneren Zeibewusstseins* (Hua X). Den Haag: M. Nijhoff.
Husserl, E. (1973). *Experience and Judgment*. London: Routledge & Kegan Paul.
Husserl, E. (1976). *Ideen zu einer reinen Phänomenologie und phänomenologischen Philosophie, Erstes Buch* (Hua III/I). Den Haag: M. Nijhoff.
Husserl, E. (1983). *Ideas pertaining to a pure phenomenology and to a phenomenological philosophy: First Book*. The Hague: M. Nijhoff.
Husserl, E. (1984). *Logische Untersuchungen* (zweiter Band, erster Teil). Den Haag: M. Nijhoff.

Husserl, E. (1992). *Formale und Transzendentale Logik*, Band XVII. Hamburg: Felix Meiner Verlag.
Husserl, E. (2001a). *Die Bernauer Manuskripte über das Zeitbewusstsein (1917/18)*. Dordrecht: Kluwer Acad. Pub.
Husserl, E. (2001b). *Späte Texte über Zeitkonstitution, Die C-Manuscripte* (Hua Materialien VIII). Dordrecht: Springer.
Keller, P. (1999). *Husserl and Heidegger on Human Experience*. Cambridge: Cambridge University Press.
Levy, L. (2016). Intentionality, Consciousness and the Ego: The Influence of Husserl's "Logical Investigations" on Sartre's Early Work. *The European Legacy*, 21, 511-524.
Livadas, S. (2009). The Leap from the Ego of Temporal Consciousness to the Phenomenology of Mathematical Continuum. *Manuscrito*, 32 (2), 321-357.
Macann, C. (1991). The Impossibility of a Phenomenological Constitution of the Transcendental Ego. In *Presence and Coincidence, Phaenomenologica*, 119 (41-56). Dordrecht: Kluwer Acad. Pub.
Merlan, P. (1947). Time Consciousness in Husserl and Heidegger. *Philosophy and Phenomenological Research*, 8 (1), 23-54.
Patočka, J. (1992). *Introduction à la phénoménologie de Husserl*. Grenoble: Ed. Millon.
Sartre, J. P. (1943). *L'être et le néant*. Paris: Ed. Gallimard.
Sartre, J. P. (1960). *The Transcendence of the Ego*. New York: Hill & Wang.
Sartre, J. P. (1992). *Being and Nothingness*. NY: Washington Square Press.
Tandon, A. (1998). Sartre's Non-Egological Conception of Consciousness. *Indian Philosophical Quarterly*, 25(4), 467-476.
Thomas, C. V. (1990). The Development of Time Consciousness From Husserl to Heidegger. In T. A. Tymieniecka (Ed.) *The Moral Sense and Its Foundational Significance: Self, Person, Historicity, Community. Analecta Husserliana, 31* (347-360). Dordrecht: Springer.
Tieszen, R. (2011). *After Gödel: Platonism and Rationalism in Mathematics and Logic*. Oxford: Oxford University Press.
Van Atten, M., van Dalen, D., & Tieszen, R. (2002). Brouwer and Weyl: The Phenomenology and Mathematics of the Intuitive Continuum. *Philosophia Mathematica*, 10(3), 203-226.
Zahavi, D. (Ed.). (1998). *Self-Awareness, Temporality, and Alterity*. Dordrecht: Springer.
Zahavi, D. (2002). The Three Concepts of Consciousness in "Logische Untersuchungen". *Husserl Studies*, 18, 51-64.
Zahavi, D. (2011). Unity of Consciousness and the Problem of Self. In S. Gallagher (Ed.), *The Oxford Handbook of the Self* (316-338). Oxford: Oxford Univ. Press.
Zahavi, D. (2012). The Time of the Self. *Grazer Philosophische Studien*, 84, 143-159.

Husserl's *Sachhaltigkeit* and the Question of the Essence of Individuals

ABSTRACT: Phenomenology can be roughly described as the theory of the pure essences of phenomena. Yet the meaning of essence and of concepts traditionally tied to it (such as the concepts of *a priori* and of essential necessity) are far from settled. This is especially true given the impact modern science has had on established philosophical views and the need for revisiting certain core notions of philosophy. In this paper I intend to review Husserl's view on thingness-essence and his conception of the essence of individuals, based mainly in his writings from the time of *Logical Investigations*, *Ideas*, and later of *Experience and Judgment*. Taking account of the work of Lothar Eley in *Die Krise des Apriori*, among others, I will inquire into the ways in which phenomenology may undermine (one could even say fully "destroy") the view of essences as non-factual, as well as undermine their ontological priority. Doing so may help to shape a conception of material or formal individual essences and generally of essences as concrete objects of experience in virtue of well-defined epistemic ones.

1. INTRODUCTION

IN THIS ARTICLE[1] I INTEND TO inquire from a phenomenologically motivated viewpoint into an issue that even today is a source of controversy among phenomenologists and philosophers of science: the ontological status of essences in Husserlian phenomenology. Generally this is a discussion involving the relation that phenomenology bears to ontology,[2] understood in terms of the search for the *a priori* relations necessarily or possibly associated with the concept of an object in general (*Gegenstand-überhaupt*), considered independently of its actual existence in spatiotemporal terms. One intricacy involved in the question of the status of essences in phenomenology (putting aside the topic of their subjective constitution in relation to phenomena) is that the Husserlian emphasis on their genetic constitution and the historicity of the life-world are not reconcilable with the traditional sense of essences.[3] Claire Ortiz Hill, citing Husserl's *Introduction to Logic and Theory of Knowledge: Lectures of 1906/07*, talks about pure logic as an *a priori* discipline entirely grounded in conceptual essentialities in which all truth is nothing other

---

[1]The term *Sachhaltigkeit* is the original Husserlian term corresponding to "thingness." I left it in its original rendition in the article's title to underline the specificity of its content in Husserlian phenomenology.

[2]See Herbert Spiegelberg, "Über das Wesen der Idee: eine ontologische Untersuchung," *Jahrbuch für Philosophie und phänomenologische Forschung* 11 (1930): 1–238 at p. 8.

[3]At least according to Andrea Zhok, who speaks about the *prima facie* "unchangeable" nature traditionally attributed to essences. See Andrea Zhok, "The Ontological Status of Essences in Husserl's Thought," *The New Yearbook for Phenomenology and Phenomenological Philosophy* 11 (2012): 99–130 at p. 99.

than the analysis of essences or concepts.[4] In reference to Husserl's later view, she notes, however:

> Even the ideal Objectivity of logical formations and the *a priori* character of the logical doctrines relating to them specifically, and then again the sense of this *a priori*, are stricken with this same obscurity: since the ideal does indeed appear as located within the subjective sphere; it does indeed arise from this sphere as a produced formation.[5]

In articulating my argument I will take account of various positions on the matter in the existing literature, e.g., the article by Zohk mentioned above, J. N. Mohanty's "Individual Fact and Essence in Edmund Husserl's Philosophy,"[6] and to a significant extent Lothar Eley's *Die Krise des Apriori*,[7] which has proved quite illuminating for its review of the concept of thingness (essence) within a phenomenological context. I have to point out that my arguments concerning essence, form, and individuality are primarily articulated on the level of temporal constitution, and thus they are not grounded on any version of a Platonic theory of essences. This means that I offer no objection to the phenomenological thesis that the possibilities for the variation of essential traits in the givenness of essence-substrates are *a priori* (eidetically) "pre-determined" or of the fact that the Husserlian conception of genus (εἶδος) is meant to "determine" by itself its essence without partaking of anything else besides itself.[8]

This paper has two parts. The first deals with the question of the ontological status of essences by focusing especially on the essences of individuals. The second discusses the possibility of talking about individuals as well-defined epistemic objects according to the essential norms set up in the first part. More specifically, the discussion concerning the possibility of a "deconstruction" of the ontological status of essences (at least in the Platonic sense) helps to engender a treatment of the question of individual essences on the epistemological level.

In pursuing my topic I will take up the issue of the essence of individuals, be they essences with material content or formal essences that are empty-of-content. Based on the refutation of an ontology of essences, I will argue for the possibility of talking about these objects as "lawful" epistemic ones. My argumentation is to some extent related to Zohk's approach to the ontological status of essences from a phenomenological viewpoint, which has certain affinities with Eley's thesis concerning the view of essences as the manifestation of the "co-essential" nature of

---

[4]Claire Ortiz Hill, "Husserl and Phenomenology, Experience and Essence" in *Analecta Husserliana* CIII, ed. A-T. Tymieniecka (Berlin: Springer Science+Business Media, 2009), p. 9.

[5]Ibid., p. 10, quoting the translation of a passage from Edmund Husserl, *Formale und Transzendentale Logik*, Hua Band XVII, hsgb. E. Ströker (Hamburg: Felix Meiner Verlag, 1992), p. 35. The English translation used for this text is: *Formal und Transcendental Logic*, trans. D. Cairns (The Hague: M. Nijhoff, 1969).

[6]Jitendranath Mohanty, "Individual Fact and Essence in Edmund Husserl's Philosophy," *Philosophy and Phenomenological Research* 19 (1959): 222–30.

[7]Lothar Eley, *Die Krise des Apriori in der Transzendentalen Phänomenologie Edmund Husserls* (Den Haag: M. Nijhoff, 1962).

[8]Jean Hering, "Bemerkungen über das Wesen, die Wesenheit und die Idee," *Jahrbuch für Philosophie und phänomenologische Forschung* 4 (1921): 495–544 at pp. 505, 510–11.

consciousness and sensuous transcendence in becoming the way by which we are motivated and constitutively bound to articulate being. Yet Eley's view is far more radical in denying any attribution of an ontologically privileged status to the essence of object-individuals in an assumed scheme of *prius* and *posterius* (i.e., prior and posterior to experience). It turns out that Husserlian phenomenology provides a foundation—by the conditioning of a "thingness" (essence) to *a priori* acts and modalities of consciousness—for turning object-individuals of experience to epistemic objects, more specifically to objects of a formal theory subsumed under a physical theory or to objects of a formal mathematical theory as such. At this point, however, it seems relevant to propose some preliminary ideas concerning the essences of individuals that may further help shape my argument on the issue in the subsequent sections.

In a sentence that is a judgment, one thinks of states-of-affairs. One can say that the relation of the subject to these objectivities (the relation to them as "things") is tied to certain moments that help name them as concrete stuff. This same relation, according to Husserl, as a sense-bestowing relation to objects is made possible through other moments, that is, moments of pure form.[9] These abstract moments (characterized in a way that is totally insufficient) lack the intrinsic relatedness to a "thingness"-content (in the sense of a subject matter), yet they make that thingness-content possible in every part of a judgment. Ultimately, by way of syntactical reduction there exists a nuclear content (taken in full abstraction) that confers upon the part in question the relatedness to a "thingness"-content. The moments pertaining to these contents are called stuff-moments (*stoffliche Momente*). Accordingly, the following questions can be raised:

- What is the origin of these moments, given that they may be taken as existing in the absence of a concrete thingness-content?

- What are the essential characteristics by virtue of which one may have at any instant of reflection the conception of "something" that may be called a thingness-content (or object-matter in identical meaning)?

- Is it possible for a thingness-content to be founded independently of material and more generally of objective spatio-temporal constraints?

In Supplement I *to Formal and Transcendental Logic*, Husserl speaks of "pure stuffs" and "pure forms," not as given in advance, not as concrete objects, but instead as abstract moments in signification that make the relatedness to the object-matter possible by being susceptible to being formed at different levels. This makes the relativization at any particular level possible in a way that one may have relative stuffs and relative forms for the members of a concrete proposition or, more generally, for the members of a predicative form so long as relative stuffs and forms make the relatedness to a thingness-content (*Sachbezüglichkeit*) possible.[10]

---

[9]Husserl, *Formale und Transzendentale Logik*, pp. 301–02.

[10]This view of "pure stuffs" and "pure forms" seems to be on a metatheoretical, phenomenologically based level, consistent with the definition and properties of absolute mathematical entities in a way that is critically important in building consistent enlargements of already existing axiomatical systems and ulti-

In Husserl's discussion in *Formal and Transcendental Logic*, the lowest-level substrates of analytical sentences can be thought of as transcending the apophantic level and thus as leading to their evidence as ultimate individuals devoid of any analytically expressible content, even of the possibility of a temporal duration.[11] Given this, one may draw attention to the following. The fact that "pure forms" are thought of as lacking intrinsic relatedness to the object-matter of a proposition and therefore as not being themselves self-standing, entails as the ultimate origin of a meaningful discourse an "object-matter" that would by necessity be referred to a thingness-content in real world terms. By way of abstraction and through all sorts of possible propositional variations, one may arrive at something that identically characterizes the essential content of any "object-matter" in question, namely, the "pure stuff." "Pure stuff" is thus self-sufficient only insofar as it corresponds to concrete thingness-contents. In other words, it cannot be a pure product of imagination or of some kind of vacuous-content intentionality.

In *Ideen I* Husserl juxtaposed the materially filled essence and the "this-there" (*Dies-da*). He takes the latter in a sense that is close to the Aristotelian τόδε τι, insofar as the "this-there" is regarded as representative of a syntactically formless and devoid of any content-individual, which is consequently unsuitable to be termed an individuum insofar as the latter term has a connotation of indivisibility inherently bound to a conception of content. Yet, there is an essential connection between them since the "this-there" is thought to have a materially filled essential composition, namely, "each 'this-there' having its materially filled essential composition characterized by a substrate-essence that is formless in the sense stated."[12] In other words, it has a corresponding formless substrate-essence that is inseparable from its very conception.

In this regard one might raise doubts, in the first place, as to the possibility of contrasting them as diverse categories, that is, as belonging to essences and facts, respectively. For example, an individual fact is considered as being not only a mere "this-there" but also a "so-and-so-constituted" one, which means that there are essential predicates that hold good of it as presuppositions of accidental properties existing in real world terms.[13] However, it is questionable whether this is indeed consistent with Husserl's previous assertion in the same paragraph of *Ideas I* that substrates "empty" of content and their accompanying syntactical-categorial objectivities (taken as variations of an "empty-something") can ground the whole field of things/state-of-affairs (*Sachverhalte*) with all their derived syntactical objectivities as objects of pure logic in the sense of *mathesis universalis*. It is known that

---

mately in establishing the independence of key questions in mathematical foundations such as the Axiom of Choice and the Continuum Hypothesis; for more details, see Stathis Livadas, "What Is the Nature of Mathematical-Logical Objects?" in *Axiomathes* 27 (2016): 79–112.

[11]Husserl, *Formale und Transzendentale Logik*, p. 211.

[12]Edmund Husserl, *Ideen zu einer reinen Phänomenologie und phänomenologischen Philosophie*, Erstes Buch, Hua Band III/I, hsgb. K. Schuhmann (Den Haag: M. Nijhoff, 1976). In English translation: *Ideas Pertaining to a Pure Phenomenology and to a Phenomenological Philosophy*: First Book, translated by F. Kersten (The Hague: M. Nijhoff, 1983), p. 28.

[13]Mohanty, "Individual Fact and Essence in Edmund Husserl's Philosophy," p. 223.

a "this-there," the material essence of which is self-sufficient (i.e., a concretum), is called an individuum. In a generalization by means of an extended concept of logical variation, it becomes the prime object of pure logic, the absolute of logic to which all logical modifications refer.[14]

Given that each state-of-affairs, expressed through a formal-mathematical or simply numerical expression and within any well-defined Euclidean or non-Euclidean manifold, belongs to the class of "empty" substrates together with their associated categorial-syntactical objectivities, it becomes questionable whether one can possibly ground the existence of (at least) lowest-level mathematical objects on the evidence of an intentional orientation of consciousness independently of really existing objects-of-intentionality. Further, a question may be raised as to whether one can have a content-free intuition of mathematical-logical objects in the sense of objects of formal-axiomatical theories, given that moments of pure form (those pertaining, for instance, to the relations of identity, order, inclusion, and so on) are characterized as abstract and non-self-sufficient insofar as they may lack intrinsic relatedness to a concrete object-matter necessarily bound to a thingness-content.

These matters are extensively and thoroughly discussed in a more inclusive context in sections three and four below in view of the subtleties of a phenomenological approach to individuals in general and the impossibility of providing an ontological foundation to the essence of individuals, without being in discord with a quintessential principle of phenomenology, namely, the presence of an intentional-constituting consciousness (section two). In the last two sections I undertake a holistic approach toward both material and formal objects-individuals, motivated by the preceding argumentation on the possibility of "destruction" of an ontology of essences by way of phenomenology, along the following guidelines. The possibility of talking about physical things by virtue of appearances in consciousness as identical unities over time, the possibility of talking about individuals as re-identifying unities acquiring and preserving a sense of individuation over time independently of a thingness-content or even an empty-content (the latter ones as pure forms), and the *a priori* reasons for positing both material and formal individuals as equal-status epistemic objects that may become meaningful ones under the normative conditions of a formal language. These possibilities have largely served as the unifying link between the first and the second part of the paper (i.e., sections one to three), the former one dealing with the purely philosophical aspects of the question of individual essences.

2. THE IMPACT OF THE SUBJECTIVE FACTOR ON THE CONCEPT OF INDIVIDUAL ESSENCE

One of the most subtle questions of phenomenology, essentially from the time of *Ideas I*, is the conception of an individual as corresponding to an appropriate essence when taking into account that to every individual corresponds an essential hypostasis that is its essence. Correlatively, to every essence there corresponds a

[14]Husserl, *Ideen I*, p. 35.

range of possible individuals. In this respect one may distinguish between an individual as representative of its essence and an individual thematically posited in the sense of a "this-there", namely as an individual effectively posited by a thematic "glance" (*Blickwendung*) of consciousness.[15] Husserl talked further about the possibility of distinct judgments that refer to distinct essences, yet also of judgments that in an indefinite universality and independently of a thematic positing of individuals would refer to individuals purely as individuations of their essences in the mode of "whatsoever." In this view one might think of individuals as "whatsoever" independently both from a specification of essence and also from a "this"-thematic positing by having in mind, for instance, judgments of pure geometry referring to a straight line, an angle, a conical section, etc., not in the sense of the forms straight line, angle, conical section, etc., but in the sense of a straight line, angle, conical section, etc. as objects "whatsoever." This makes that the corresponding judgments have the character of a pure and unconditioned universality.[16]

By his own admission, Husserl had acceded to a deeper understanding of the concept of "formal" from the time of the early, psychologistic stage of the *Philosophy of Arithmetic* (1891), mainly through the ground meaning of the concepts of sets and numbers that he further developed through the analysis of the intentional-constitutive activities of a subject in which these concepts are generated as categorial objectivities in content-free intuition. In their most pure and abstract universality the concepts of set and number are respectively free of any account of the thingness-content of the colligated elements or of the enumerated unities in a way that *in Formal and Transcendental Logic* the formal character of the corresponding disciplines is founded in the relation to an "objectivity-whatsoever" or "something-whatsoever" (*Etwas-überhaupt*) conceived in its most vacuous generality in complete disregard of any thingness-content whatsoever. In this view formal mathematics with its essentially associated disciplines is seen as a science whose ground-concepts are founded on the concept of the "something-whatsoever" (or "empty-something") and on all categorial *a priori* derivative forms of the "empty-something" that make possible the emergence of ever new forms in ever new iterative constructions.[17]

On this account, however, a question to be addressed in terms of phenomenological reduction is the possibility of discerning between individuals-atoms as appearances in consciousness. Eley suggested in *The Crisis of a priori* the turn of the thematic "glance," in an intentional sense, as founding this kind of difference.[18]

---

[15] In §14 of *Ideas I* the "this-there" is associated with a formless last essence without mentioning the thematic character of the contemplation of "this." It is merely asserted that every "this-there" has its thingness-essence, which has the character of a formless substrate-substance; see Husserl, *Ideen I*, p. 34.

[16] See Husserl, *Ideen I*, pp. 17–18.

[17] These derivative forms are, for instance, next to sets and numbers (finite and infinite) such relational forms as combination, permutation, relation, order, colligation, whole and part, etc. In this approach the whole mathematics, including mathematical analysis (which is regarded as a non-apophantic mathematics in the traditional logical sense) can be founded as a formal ontology to the extent that it is an ontology in virtue of an *a priori* science of "objects" and a formal one as associated with the pure modes of "something-whatsoever." See Husserl, *Formale und Transzendentale Logik*, pp. 81–82.

[18] Eley, *Die Krise des Apriori in der Transzendentalen Phänomenologie Edmund Husserls*, p. 34.

Husserl's Sachhaltigkeit

Consequently an individual's thematization as a simply a "this" is effectuated solely by being thematically posited in the intentional "glance," whereas an individual appearing as an individuation of its essence (i.e., as a "this"-specification) is made possible only by thematically positing the corresponding eidetic association. This was clarified in Husserl's *Ideas I* in the following terms:

> No intuition of essence is possible without the free possibility of turning one's regard to a "corresponding" individual and forming a consciousness of an example—just as conversely no intuition of something individual is possible without the free possibility of bringing about an ideation and, in it, directing one's regard to the corresponding essence exemplified in what is individually sighted; but this in no respect alters the fact that the two sorts of intuitions are essentially different. . . .
> To the essential differences between the intuitions there correspond the essential relationships between "existence" (here obviously in the sense of individual factual existence) and "essence," between matter of fact and Eidos.[19]

Yet, within the next two paragraphs, Husserl also made the somewhat confusing claim that intuition of essences in which an essence is seized upon as an object, just as an individual is seized upon in experience, is not the only possible consciousness involving essences. Essences as intuitive consciousness (of essences) can be also seized upon in a certain way without becoming "objects about which."[20] This may be thought as associated with Husserl's intention to lay a foundation for regarding any judgment about essences as convertible to an equivalent unconditionally universal judgment about single particulars subsumed under essences, in fact as purely eidetic judgments (just as those of pure mathematics or logic) without the need of positing an individual factual existence even when referring to particular individuals.[21]

In view of Husserl's reference to an intuitive consciousness of essences in which essences can be seized upon in a certain way without becoming "objects about which" one is going to be faced with the subtlety of a presumably ontological *a priori* of essences in contrast with the non-eliminable "ontology," in fact the ever "in act" character of the constituting ego.

In *Ideas I* Husserl talked about essences seized upon without becoming "objects about Which" while referring all the same to eidetic judgments such as "any color whatever is different from any sound whatever" in which any individuals subsumed

---

[19] Husserl, *Ideen I*, p. 10.
[20] Ibid., p. 17.
[21] The eidetic universality of a proposition entails the possibility of transformation to individuals posited as factually existing or even to an indeterminate class of individuals posited as factually existent. This may be considered as the outcome of an eidetic necessity making the singular factually existing affair-complex (*Sachverhalt*) a necessary consequent of the eidetic universality. This kind of eidetic necessity grounds, in the same sense, the correlation between eidetic sciences and sciences of fact in establishing a connection (itself eidetic) between individual objects and essences according to which an essential "content" belongs to each individual object as its essence, just as, in reverse, to each essence correspond possible individuals as factual singularizations; see Husserl, *Ideen I*, pp. 19–20. Ultimately an eidetically universal proposition (or law) referring to one or more eidetic affair-complexes rests (in contrast to unrestricted universal laws) on what Husserl described a seeing-of-essences (*Wesenschau*), later termed an eidetic intuition.

under the essence color or under the essence sound are intuitionally "objective" owing to the distinctness of their essences in virtue of the eidetic intuition. The argumentation goes on with the claim that in this case phantasy-intuition (one implemented without positing a factual existence) and eidetic intuition are there at the same time and in a way that the latter is taken as an intuition that does not make the essence an object. It follows the ambiguous and confusing position that it is "due to the essence of the situation" that we are always free to turn to the corresponding objectivating attitude and that this kind of turning-toward is an essential possibility.[22] It seems that a reasonable way to read Husserl's last proposition is that there is always the possibility of turning the intentional regard into a thematic positing of an individual subsumed under essence as factually existing in the present now and as a concrete state-of-affairs.

However, two counterarguments can be raised here. First, if an essential state-of-affairs is considered as a pure potentiality, it cannot be turned into an actuality even in passively reflecting on it but by bringing it into factual existence and second, one may be seriously doubtful about the possibility of the existence of an intuition of essences in which an essence can be intuited without making it an "object about which." The latter holds to the extent that one cannot conceive of an intuitive consciousness except each time as thematically positing "something," even in deceptively thinking that it is not objectivity-constituting. If Husserl's assertion here is to be taken at face value there seem to be two possibilities. Either one reproduces an infinite sequence of states of consciousness in the sense of reflecting-reflected or in breaking this (ideally) infinitely proceeding chain we should negate a fundamental phenomenological tenet, namely, that no consciousness is conceivable but as a consciousness-of. In the final count one cannot perceive of an individual but as the "this-there" of an act intentionally oriented and effectuated in objective real world terms. Any other possibility of intuiting an individual as eidetically representing a proper essence without a thematic positing in terms of its effectuation in the present now is ultimately bound to entail circularities in description or arbitrary ideations.

Ultimately one has to face the capital issue of inquiring, from a phenomenological standpoint, into the very concept of *a priori* with regard to essences, intentional forms, etc., extensively employed in Husserlian texts. However, this is a quite complex and, to a significant extent, unchartered field of inquiry that may be left to a future paper.

An interesting insight to the relation of the concept of individual and the corresponding essence can be found in Eley's *The Crisis of a Apriori*. There Eley, quoting Husserl in *Ideas I* (6), claims that the "this-there" may be experienced as an individual insofar as it is *a posteriori* of its prior, that is, insofar as it becomes the "this" of its essence—in other words, insofar as it becomes the last one in a concatenation of essences in which it is the eidetic necessity of the universality of its essence. In case the prior-posterior relation is taken as more than a reciprocity of terms in a broad Aristotelian sense, meaning that one should also take into account

---

[22]Husserl, *Ideen I*, p. 18.

the intentional directedness toward "something in general," then a "this-there," in its taking aware of, is not just *a posteriori* of its prior but rather a posterior of its prior-posterior, a third "being."[23]

The whole approach in terms of prior-posterior is founded on the assumption that the relation between an object-individual as a "this-there" and its essence is of an essential and therefore not of a factual character. Only the actual thing itself upon which this relation is applied is a matter of fact.[24] However, the same argumentation as before may be used here. If the relation prior-posterior is of a constitutional character, then it must be necessarily be a factual connection (under eidetic "laws") between an individual as a "this-there" and its essence. Indeed one cannot think of any way in which a relation of prior-posterior could possibly be conceived as an essential state-of-affairs without the acting of a subject, without the enactment of an intentional "glance."[25] In Eley's approach, reality and essence become distinct complexes in the sense that an individual whose thingness substance is a Konkretum[26] "precedes" in the act of (intentional) experiencing as a concrete "this-there" its designation as the last outcome in a concatenation of essences by virtue of being a de facto posterior of its prior-posterior. In other words, the "this-there" as form of an individual in thematic positing annuls by the very act of its experiencing the transcendence of its essential relation as an individuation of its essence, meant as independent of the act of positing in the sense of a "concrete something." In the same sense the meaning of "possible to be otherwise" with regard to an intended upon individual presupposes the effectuation of the "this-there" that we experience, which entails in turn the positing of the act of "this-being" conceivable only within a spatiotemporal context. Consequently an individual corresponding to the meaning "possible to be otherwise" is the individual in its multifaceted variability and in a space-time interconnection. To the extent that the fundamental ways of knowledge of essences in Husselian phenomenology is that of variation and of free (rationally grounded) imagination, these kinds of access to essences are inconceivable but only as being acts carried out within objective spatio-temporality. In consequence this may result in the "destruction" (the term is employed by Eley) of the essential character of the relation of an individual to its essence having as a further effect the reduction of essences to pure possibilities, deprived of all facticity, hovering in "the air of absolutely pure conceivability."[27]

---

[23]Ibid., p. 36.

[24]Ibid., p. 20.

[25]The transposition of the irreducibility of essence as an eidetic universal form to the irreducibility of the intentional act of its effectuation in real objective terms implies as a natural consequence the presence of a constituting and further self-constituting absolute temporal consciousness.

[26]A *Konkretum* is characterized by Husserl an absolutely self-standing essence, in contrast to a no self-standing one called an *Abstraktum*. For instance, to the latter class belongs the formal categorial form object in general in contrast to the categorial form object with a concrete thingness substance called a *Konkretum*. A "this-there" whose thingness substance is *a Konkretum* is called an Individuum. See Husserl, *Ideen I,* p. 35.

[27]Eley, *Die Krise des Apriori in der Transzendentalen Phänomenologie Edmund Husserls,* pp. 37–38.

Husserl's Sachhaltigkeit

In this sense Husserl's conception of essences may be characterized as the outcome of its contradicting moments. In Eley's succinct expression "Husserl conceives of the universal insofar as he negates it: The essence in Husserl's sense consolidates this negation; put it otherwise: Essence in the process of its reflection becomes deprived of itself."[28] Obviously this claim stands in conflict with the position that the "this-there'" (as a thematic positing in real terms) presupposes the corresponding essence in the understanding that only then it becomes meaningful to ask about the "what" of the this-here. It is evident then that the character of this "precedence" would be one of necessity just like the eidetic specificity of a universal eidetic state-of-affairs is one of essential necessity.[29]

To face these subtleties and overcome the presumed contradictions in a phenomenological approach to the concepts of essence and *a priori*,[30] Eley had proposed (based on Husserl's views *in Ideas III*[31]) that the concept of a difference-unity (*Differenz-Einheit*) must be presupposed so that essences are the conditions of the experienced objects they "precede," in the sense of a "prior condition" that makes possible any thematization in the act of experience without being itself object of an essential intuition. Indicative of the impasse reached in talking along these lines is that Eley thought of the concept of difference-unity regarding essence and the corresponding "this-there" as a transcendental one (meant as absolutely subjective), a clue to Husserl's constant preoccupation (and belief) in a supplementary reduction toward the subjective origin of the self-constituting absolute flux of consciousness.[32]

3. THINGNESS AND FORM: CONVERGENCES AND DIVERGENCES

In this next section I will review the interconnection of the concepts of thingness and form and the necessity of subsuming the latter under the former insofar as this subsumption is established by the subjective-constitutional modes in phenomenological reduction. Moreover, I intend to open a discussion about the extent to which thingness in relation to form critically shapes the concept of an individual as an epistemic term. In this view the concept of thingness as conditioned on *a priori* constitutive-intentional forms of consciousness may provide the sound foundation for turning objects of experience to well-meant epistemic ones.

As mentioned in the previous section, if we consider Husserl's alleged conditioning of the "this-there" (as an effectuation of its essence) to the essence itself, thought of in terms of a necessary eidetic form to which any effectuation in experi-

---

[28] Ibid., p. 65 (my translation).
[29] Husserl, *Ideen I*, p. 19.
[30] As well-known the concepts of essence, essential necessity and *a priori*, among others, were postulated by Aristotle and the subsequent rational philosophy regardless of any concerns about the constitutional faculties of a subject.
[31] Edmund Husserl, *Ideen zu einer reinen Phänomenologie und phänomenologischen Philosophie. Die Phänomenologie und die Fundamente der Wissenschaften*, Hua Band V, hsgb. M. Biemel (Den Haag: M. Nijhoff, 1971). In English translation: *Ideas Pertaining to a Pure Phenomenology and to a Phenomenological Philosophy, Third Book. Phenomenology and the Foundation of the Sciences*, trans. T. Klein and W. Pohl (The Hague: M. Nijhoff, 1980).
[32] Eley, *Die Krise des Apriori in der Transzendentalen Phänomenologie Edmund Husserls*, pp. 20–21.

ence is *a priori* reducible, the notions of thingness and the corresponding universal, eidetic state-of-affairs or essence seem to be in a certain sense conflicting. Some clues are found in Husserlian writings in the following sense. Any experience is thought of as conditioned on a formal hypostasized meaning that "encloses" the idea of thing in itself wherein such a universal form in absolute sense is separate from perceptible thingness. Thingness is characterized as coincidental and as such can change over time in contrast to a universal state-of-affairs that is characterized as a pure and invariant form over time. Yet to the question of what "stands behind" the definition of a universal state-of-affairs as a pure form one must necessarily take into consideration at least the passivity of an intentional consciousness insofar as this universal form may be reduced to a system of endless processes of continuous appearances in the "background" of an *a priori* generated multidimensional continuum tied to a definite normativity.[33] This essentially means that one is faced here with the ambiguities associated with the reduction of a universal state-of-affairs to an *a priori* continuum of appearances that in a supplementary radical reduction may be further reduced to the source of inner temporality—in other terms, to the absolute subjectivity of consciousness that is essentially the Husserlian absolute ego. Consequently, in Eley's view, thingness and general objectivity themselves are irreconcilable with the continuum of appearances and the subjectivity taken as their origin. This is argued on the grounds that pure subjectivity, in the Husserlian sense, must be "out of the world," that it can be either founded solely in the realm of facticity (resulting in an endless recursion of reflections) or banished to the "beyond" of transcendence.[34]

Indicative of the contradictory character of thingness (as content) with regard to the corresponding eidetic state-of-affairs, is that Husserl referred in *Ideas III* to the *a priori* of experience essentially pointing to a notion of essence as posterior to phenomenological perception (*Wahrnehmung*). Put in simpler terms, if essence was prior in Husserl's initial position *in Ideas I*, the possibility of turning the intentional glance upon it makes that its "this-there" becomes first in terms of the phenomenological perception, and moreover a prerequisite *in rem* of the knowledge of the corresponding essence possibly abstracted as a universal. Consequently the phenomenological supposition of a constituting consciousness (the sphere of "true being") can be thought of not only as relegating essence to a "third place" in terms of prior-posterior but even as leading to its ontological doom.

If in *Ideas I* we already face the possibility of an annulment of the prevalence of an ontology of essence over its coincidental instantiations, in *Ideas III* we come closer to an argument in favor of the intentional-constitutive subject's "destruction" of essence or rather its elimination to the sort of invariants. The annulment of the *a priori* of essence means that the *a priori* "content" of an intended upon thing becomes "emptied" by means of phenomenological perception that entails the separation of form and content in the sense that the latter as thingness itself and "what it is" of

---

[33]Husserl, *Ideen I*, pp. 350–51.
[34]Eley, *Die Krise des Apriori in der Transzendentalen Phänomenologie Edmund Husserls*, p. 65.

the object is relegated to a mere factual definiteness. The result is that essence itself is made to an endless process of continuous appearances, a grouping of referential implications so that it ultimately becomes a nexus of invariants.

Let me point out that for Husserl's student Roman Ingarden, while form and content are co-existential and absolutely complementary to each other, "form" is the enduring and the "content" (matter) the mutable. In a sense that clearly points to a constituted unity which may be further reducible to a constituting subjectivity:

> Form is identified with what repeats itself continuously in many individuals, i.e., with the "common characteristics" and then with the so-called properties of the genera and the species of things, while the content becomes the unique, that which constitutes the aggregate of particular characteristics which differentiate one individual from another one.[35]

Accordingly, the relation between essence and individuality can be thought of in terms of an enacting consciousness, in a way that an individuum (i.e., a "this-there" whose thingness-essence is a Konkretum, that is, an absolutely self-standing one) deprived of a thingness content may become by eidetic intuition a logical primitive object, the purely logical absolute to which refer all logical modifications and deductions.[36] The difference between essence and "this-there" as a difference founded in the thing itself is negated by the mental process of seizing and reflecting, resulting in a rift between an "emptied" of *a priori* essence-thing and the reflecting thought. In this view the seizing upon and reflecting of an individual is originated in the pure "for-itself" of absolute consciousness, described *in Ideas I* as the residuum of the annihilation of the world, whereas by the same measure the "in itself" of the essence is annihilated to a pure "for myself" of the reflecting subjectivity making thus impossible the "in-and-for-itself" of essence. Moreover, in this way one can reduce the uniqueness and consequently the inherent discernibility of a material or formal individual to the evidence in reflection of a unique intentional enactment toward the individual each temporal now. The result is that the universal, the horizon of the meaning of the essence/"this-there," becomes subjectively conditioned, a system of endless processes of continuous appearances.

In a step further Eley considered the difference itself between essence and "this-there" a transcendental one grounded in the transcendental subjectivity.[37] Therefore one can see that while the regional difference between essence and "this-there" is eliminated and "destructed" in the seizing of an individual-object by the intentional-reflective glance of an absolute consciousness, there remains as a non-eliminable transcendental residuum the subjective origin of the absolute consciousness itself. Assuming the self-evidence of an intentional-reflective consciousness, the transcendental *a priori* of essences may be conceived of only as an ideal field of referential

---

[35]Roman Ingarden, "The General Question of the Essence of Form and Content," *The Journal of Philosophy* 57 (1960): 222–33 at p. 228.

[36]Husserl, *Ideen I*, p. 35.

[37]Eley, *Die Krise des Apriori in der Transzendentalen Phänomenologie Edmund Husserls*, pp. 53–54, 59.

implications brought to intentional apprehension in terms of a real causal being. Ultimately what seems to be a destruction *in rem* of the *a priori* of essences may "re-emerge" as the transcendence of the absolute ego, which came to be regarded as the source of self-constituting temporal consciousness, consequently of inner temporality and of all absolute subjective processes.

4. INDIVIDUALITY IN OBJECTIVE REAL-WORLD TERMS

The questions that we should now deal with concern (1) the way individual objects of phenomenological perception (immanent or transcendent to consciousness) can be turned to epistemic objects and (2) the possibility of reaching a foundation for the uniqueness of each individual, given that the ontological self-standing of essences and a fortiori their precedence in terms of prior-posterior is "annulled" by the appeal to a self-constituting temporal consciousness. Along the way and in the light of the intended approach, some attention will be given to questions pertaining to thingness-essence and individuality as well as the possibility of a contingent identity of individuals.[38]

To approach these questions, we need to make three assumptions: (a) to talk about physical things as appearances in consciousness is to take them as identical unities over time; (b) to talk about re-identifying individuals presumes the possibility of acquiring and preserving a sense of individuation over time, independently of the question of thingness-content or "empty" content (i.e., as pure forms); and (c) to assume that there are essential *a priori* reasons for positing both physical and formal (logical-mathematical) individuals as epistemic objects that may become meaningful objects under the normative conditions of a formal language.

Husserl's *Ideas I* is quite illuminating concerning the conditions underlying the regional idea of a physical thing. He writes:

> Intuiting an individual physical thing, its movements, its approaching and receding, its revolvings, its alterations in form and quality, pursuing in intuition its modes of causal relations, we effect continua of intuitings which coincide thus and so, which join together into a unity-consciousness: the regard is accordingly directed to the identical, to the X of the sense (or of the posited or neutralized positum), to the one and the same itself changing, revolving, etc. . . . And likewise, again, when we go over to the attitude of ideation and, let us say, make clear the regional idea of the physical thing.[39]

Consequently a physical thing in space is only intuitable by means of appearances in which it is and must be given in multiple but essentially pre-determined (through a fixed set of eidetic laws) perspective modes, and thus in changing orientations

---

[38] See, for instance, Stephen Yablo, "Identity, Essence, and Indiscernibility," *The Journal of Philosophy* 84 (1987): 293–314.

[39] Husserl, *Ideen I*, p. 360.

and transformations, not just for human beings but also for a supposedly supreme divinity, taken as the ideal representative of absolute cognition.[40]

In other words, the regional idea of a physical thing, as an identical noematic object,[41] implies the observance of rules underlying the multiplicities of its appearances in a pre-determined way and in accordance with the eidetic necessities proper to the essence of the thing in question. In a far reaching clue to understanding the common traits of formal and material essences as implying corresponding sorts of eidetic necessities, Husserl claims that the sequence of levels of material and formal theories of essences prescribes in a certain sense the sequence of levels of constitutive phenomenologies and determines the levels of their universality with respect to ontological and eidetic fundamental concepts and principles. Thus the fundamental ontological concepts of nature such as time, space, and matter and their immediate derivatives are indices for the strata of constituting consciousness of material thingness. In much the same way the relevant fundamental principles are indices for essential interconnections in and between the strata. The phenomenological clarification of the purely logical also makes it understandable why all "intermediate" propositions of the pure theory of time, of geometry, and of all other ontological disciplines are indices for eidetic regularities of consciousness-in-constituting.[42] As a further sign of convergent attitude toward material-thingness and formal essences on the level of constitutive consciousness and the eidetic necessities originating in its essential being, Husserl points out that each and everything is eidetically prescribed, no matter how far we widen the scope of our inquiry or no matter which level of universality or particularity we move in, even down to the lowest level concretions.

Given that the objects of phenomenological perception ought to be given as ideally inexhaustible multiplicities of their profiles, a key question to ask is about the source of their unity in virtue of being individual unities susceptible of being either objects of original impression or objects of recall (in the *a priori* mode) in primary memory or in the reproductive mode of secondary memory. Husserl unambiguously "located" the source of this kind of primordial unity within consciousness. As a next step he identified the immanent unity of consciousness as the source of inner temporality; ultimately he thought the source of inner temporality to be the absolute subjectivity of ego. Except for rendering the notion of a thingness-essence subordinate and utterly conditioned upon the evidence of the constituting-reflective ego as deconstructing the *a priori* primacy of essences, Husserl asserts that the immanent unity identifiable with the mode of being of the absolute flux of consciousness may

---

[40] See Husserl, *Ideen I*, p. 351.

[41] A noematic object, as well-known to phenomenologists, is an object said to be constituted by certain modes as a well-defined object (an object as meant) immanent to the temporal flux of a subject's consciousness. In contrast, by the term noetic are considered moments of original presentations of experience in terms of the *a priori* orientation of consciousness. See Husserl, *Ideas*, pp. 229–32.

[42] Husserl was quick to point out that this kind of relation between formal and material theories of essence, on the one side, and the corresponding levels of the constitutive phenomenologies, on the other, is in no way ontological in character for the simple reason that a phenomenologist does not judge ontologically when he makes cognizant an ontological concept or principle as a clue to constitutive eidetic states-of-affairs or to eidetic complexes. See Husserl, *Ideen I*, p. 359.

serve as a common foundation for both transcendent objectivities (e.g., perceptual objects of objective reality) and immanent ones, whether pure objects of imagination or imaginary objects bound by certain norms (e.g., of categorial intuition). It is important to note that the unity originating in the being of consciousness not only underlies the possibility of reflecting on things in general as identical and enduring unities over time but it also grounds the possibility of reducing the concept of an ideal infinity in progression to an act of fulfillment and completion in the present now of consciousness. In this sense the unity of the physical thing

> stands over against an ideally infinite multiplicity of noetic mental processes of a wholly determined essential content and can be surveyed despite the infinity, all of them united by being consciousness of the "same thing." This unification is given in the sphere of consciousness itself, in mental processes which, on their side, also belong again to the group which we have delimited here.[43]

Husserl offers a kind of metaphorical explication to account for the apparent contradiction between the all-sided infinity of the continuum, taken here in the sense of an ideal infinity of multiplicities of appearances of one and the same thing, and the "closed" unity of completion of the running through of appearances. Thus the idea of a continuum as such and the idea of perfect givenness prefigured by the idea of a continuum presents itself as an insight (*Einsicht*) into the way an "idea" can be made insightful by designating its essence as a peculiar type of insight. In these terms the idea of an infinity taken according to its essence is not itself an infinity. The intuition that this infinity cannot be given *in rem* does not preclude but rather requires the insightful givenness of the idea of such infinity.[44] This seems to be a way out of the apparent contradiction of a "finite infinity" even though, as with Husserl's obsessive search for a foundation of the immanent unity of consciousness in temporal terms, one could raise the issue of the circular character of an endless regression of reflecting-reflected. In any case, by the insightfulness mentioned above, Husserl seks to come to terms with the idea of a real thing in which it is *a priori* excluded that the fulfillment process would lead to a terminating phase so that the object would be re-presented as a full-standing appearance in all aspects brought through all its moments to intuitive givenness.[45]

In his *Logical Investigations*, Husserl describes immanent infinity in terms of a completed whole in actual presence independent of any spatio-temporal or causal constraints, in fact as a freely generating infinity in imagination in the present now of reflection. This kind of infinity does not prove the relative foundedness of bits of space and time, that is, the non-independence of time-stretches or bits of space with respect to more inclusive spatio-temporal wholes, and so does not prove space and

---

[43]Husserl, *Ideen I*, p. 323.
[44]Ibid., p. 331.
[45]Edmund Husserl, *Logische Untersuchungen*, Ergänzungsband, Erst. Teil, Hua Band XX/I, hsgb. U. Melle (Dordrecht: Kluwer Acad. Pub., 2002), p. 104.

time to be really infinite; not even that they can really be so.[46] It follows that on the level of subjective evidence actual infinity as an immanent whole cannot have any ties to objective spatio-temporality bound to causal constraints, for it is subjectively generated and is not conditioned on the possibility of being extended beyond any given objective boundary. It seems rather to be reducible to a time-constituting subjectivity capable of constituting infinity as a correlate in the form of an immanent whole by constituting its objective self.

A relevant question posed here is the possibility of talking about things as unities acquiring and preserving a sense of individuation over time independently of a thingness or "empty" content; the latter individuals are taken as purely formal objects. Given the position defended in previous sections, namely, that the thematic character of an intentional consciousness "destructs" the ontic priority of the essence of individuality as such, one may inquire into the foundation of the irreducibility of an intentional real or imaginary individual taken in the absence of a material content as a general "empty-something" of intentionality. I am inclined to believe that both the irreducibility and uniqueness of individuals in the now of reflection, taken either as transcendent or immanent objects of phenomenological perception and possibly reduced to the "lowest" possible level of apprehension, are ultimately rooted in being the content of the unique and otherwise irreducible intentional acts (e.g., in terms of hyletic-noetic moments of intentionality[47]) directed to them. Consequently they can be defined in reflection and in an objective sense as the unique noematic objects corresponding to the content of distinct enactments of intentionality. We should bear in mind that the meaning and the content of intentional acts are complementary notions. In other words, the content of an intentional act is thought of as the meaning of the act by virtue of which consciousness refers to a unique object or state of affairs as its own.

In *Experience and Judgement* Husserl considered the temporal now as origin of the uniqueness of individuals. In the actual now and in its original presentation we can know a unique actual "content" that thus grounds the uniqueness of the corresponding individual.[48] Mohanty rejects the idea that the essence of an individual can be accounted for in terms of the unique temporal character of the "now" and claimed, referring to Husserl's corresponding view in *Formal and Transcendental Logic*, that idealities (essences) cannot be temporally individuated.[49]

---

[46]Edmund Husserl, *Logische Untersuchungen*, Hua Band XIX/1, hsgb. U. Panzer (Den Haag: M. Nijhoff, 1984). In English translation: *Logical Investigations*, V. I, trans. J. N. Findlay (The Hague: M. Nijhoff, 1980), pp. 299–300.

[47]Husserl had introduced this term to argue that perceptual consciousness exhibits a kind of intentional "animation" of sensory (hyletic) data in a way that sensory data as a stuff-stratum within immanence becomes representative of a particular transcendent object or state-of-affairs.

[48]Edmund Husserl, *Erfahrung und Urteil*, hsgb. L. Landgrebe (Prague: Acad. Verlagsbuchhandlung, 1939), p. 464. In English translation, *Experience and Judgment*, translated by J. S. Churchill and K. Americs (London: Routledge & Kegan P., 1973).

[49]This is in accordance with Mohanty's general conclusion that there is a phenomenological discontinuity between facts and essences, between the real and the ideal. See Mohanty, "Individual Fact and Essence in Edmund Husserl's Philosophy," pp. 227, 229–30.

In my view, the foundation of individuality in a most inclusive sense is transposed by virtue of intentional enactments to the being of consciousness itself as intentionally oriented in the actual present to a concrete, no further reducible and unambiguous "this-there." On these grounds one can also ground the inherent discernibility of individuals as owing to the distinct character of phenomenological perceptions (*Wahrnehmungen*) that are immediately and in *a priori* mode directed to individuals in bringing them into reflection. There is, of course, certain dangers in thinking about what it really means to be an individual or generally an object in actuality, given that the "being" of its constituting source in absolute consciousness is "being-in-constituting." To do this would imply circularities in regard to time constitution. Husserl raised this issue in *Ideas I* in these terms:

> Questions about actuality enter into all cognitions as cognitions, even in our phenomenological cognitions bearing upon the possible constitution of objects: they all have, indeed, their correlates in "objects" which are meant as "actually existing." When, it may everywhere be asked, is the noematically "intended-to" [*vermeinte*] identity of X "actually the identity" of X instead of the "merely" intended-to identity, and what does this "merely intended-to" everywhere signify?[50]

This is a question relating to the thorny issue of the temporal constitution of objects in general and the reduction of the transcendence of objects to the transcendence of consciousness. As such it will not be further dealt with here, for this question is outside the scope of the present article.

Epistemologically, the issue of the relation between the identity of individuals and their indiscernibility for both classical and quantum objects has opened up a discussion among proponents of Leibniz's principle of the identity of indiscernibles[51] and those who hold that even in the case of quantum particles there should be some kind of "hidden" individuality underlying quantum non-individuality. In this context an approach toward a property-independent individuality of objects in general is one that can draw a line between discernibility of objects conditioned upon the existence of a universe in which there are at least two such objects and individuality in an "ontological" sense that is related to a non-qualitative basis of object individuality. Let me mention, in particular, Steven French's discussion of quantum individuality[52] and Robert Adams's view of individuality in general as a primitive and non-qualitative thisness (or haecceity) of objects-individuals that cannot be further analyzed.[53] Adams writes:

> A thisness is the property of being identical with a certain particular individual—not the property we all share, of being identical with some individual or other, but my

---

[50]Husserl, *Ideen I*, p. 325.

[51]Leibniz's principle of the identity of indiscernibles is usually formulated as follows: if, for every property F, the object x has F if and only if object y has F, then x is identical to y. In symbolic logic notation: $\forall F (Fx \leftrightarrow Fy) \rightarrow x = y$.

[52]Steven French, "Identity and Individuality in Quantum Theory," *The Stanford Encyclopedia Of Philosophy*, ed. E. N. Zalta, 2015 edition, https://plato.stanford.edu/archives/fall2015/entries/qt-idind/.

[53]Robert Adams, "Primitive Thisness and Primitive Identity," *The Journal of Philosophy* 76 (1979): 5–26.

property of being identical with me, your property of being identical with you, etc. These properties have been recently called 'essences', but that is historically unfortunate; for essences have normally been understood to be constituted by qualitative properties, and we are entertaining the possibility of non-qualitative thisnesses.[54]

In view of the previous discussion one may properly found thisness, in the sense of a defining non-qualitative characteristic of individuality, as a correlate of the intentional directedness of a subject. In my argumentation essences are thought to "destruct" themselves into invariants through immanent or transcendent phenomenological perceptions. In this view the *a priori* of essences is eliminated in that the intended object is "emptied" of its *a priori* content in a way that the essence, through an ideally endless process of continuous appearances, becomes their ultimate invariant. The relation between essence and individuum can then be thought of in terms of a mental process of virtual "un-thingness." In other words, it is an "unsubstantialization" of the object-individual so that the individuum may ultimately become the purely logical primitive object (*Ur-objekt*), the purely logical absolute to which all logical deductions refer. Consequently, the difference between essence and the "this-there" as a difference founded on the thing itself is negated by the very process of thematic positing of an intentionally oriented consciousness, ultimately bringing it about that this difference becomes a transcendental one in the sense that it is grounded in the modes of constitution of the absolute subjectivity of consciousness.[55]

5. OBJECT-INDIVIDUALS TURNED INTO EPISTEMIC OBJECTS

In this section I intend to show how eidetic necessities as correlates of the being of consciousness itself as well as the ego-based unity of inner temporality underlie the transformation of both physical objects-individuals of perception and abstract objects of categorical intuition into well-meant epistemic objects, taken either as objects of a physical theory (in terms of a "physicalistic language") or objects of a formal mathematical theory that conditions the former. Concerning individuals of perception, I give priority to quantum individuals insofar as they can be presented in the most evident way as intentional correlates of consciousness and further shaped as well-defined (noematic) objects in the modes implied by subjective constitutional norms.

The metatheoretical underpinnings behind the mathematical formulation of quantum phenomena consist, on the one hand, in the possibility of referring formally to quantum objects in disentangled states as well-defined syntactical individuals described by operator algebras and, on the other, in the possibility of their description across time by means of continuous transformations (e.g., by evolution operators of state vectors), which implies an "internal" continuity of the time parameter.

I reduce these fundamental possibilities, in a phenomenologically motivated approach, to the following: (1) the foundation of quantum individuals[56] as irre-

---

[54]Ibid., p. 6.

[55]Eley, *Die Krise des Apriori in der Transzendentalen Phänomenologie Edmund Husserls*, p. 57.

[56]A more focused discussion of quantum individuals and of the process of quantum "observation" in line with my general philosophical arguments is presented in Stathis Livadas, "The Expressional Limits of

ducible objects of intentionality possessing an open outer and inner horizon of noematic content[57] further conditioned on the existence of a relation of an intentional-constituting character between a knowing subject and the objects transcendent to his consciousness and (2) the continuous immanent unity of the absolute temporal flux of consciousness having an ultimate subjective origin within immanence.

In more technical terms, quantization conditions stemming from appropriate boundary conditions and the continuity of the time-evolution operator of quantum particle states may be regarded as owing to the intrinsic property of quantum objects as outcomes of sufficiently reproducible experiments to be "embeddable" in a unified meta-contextual temporal frame of probabilistic description. This is equivalent to embedding reproducible "observations" in a meta-contextual Boolean substructure associated with a homogenous internal time flux.[58]

Independently of the context that follows the preparation of a quantum experiment there should be some intrinsic way by which quantum individuals taken as intentional objects become re-identifying immanent objects of a constituting consciousness preserving invariably over time their individual essence. Eliminating all time-related modes of noematic constitution (e.g., simultaneity, succession, co-existence), there must be an underlying temporal substratum of the predicative universe of quantum mechanics whose temporality should be something radically different from the ordinary objective time meant as an internal parameter of a classical macroscopic system. In this view the unifying, meta-contextual time of the predictive tool can be seen as ultimately associated with the objectified unity of consciousness of some "observer," which is in an intersubjective sense the same objectified unity of any other potential one. Moreover, the preservation of individuality of a quantum individual over time may be no longer considered its own essential trait, for it can be reduced to the intentional-constitutive modes of a phenomenological reduction performing subject. This means that it can be reduced to a subject's *a priori* capacity to be intentionally oriented to a concrete "this-there" in actual presence in a unique and unambiguous fashion by virtue of the very "enactment" of intentionality and be able to preserve this unique original impression in primary memory (i.e., in retention) as well as in secondary memory, the latter reproducible at will.

In a further elaboration of the subjectively founded characteristics of the constitution of physical things and in a sense consistent with an epistemology of quantum individuals, Husserl states in *Ideas I* that to each physical thing and ultimately to

---

Formal language in the Notion of Quantum Observation," *Axiomathes* 22 (2012): 147–69.

[57] The question of the horizon of a noematic object *simpliciter* (i.e., simply as such) and in the how of its determinations, including undeterminatednesses "remaining open" for the time being, is a key issue in Husserl's theory of knowledge. See Husserl, *Ideen I*, p. 303. In the supplementary volume to *the Logical Investigations* (first part) Husserl refers to the notion of the "thing" that is for us what in the process of possible experience manifests itself as determinable in infinitum, a unity in multiple possible appearances in which ever new properties tied to possible real circumstances manifest themselves or can be manifested. Any appearance in actuality carries with it an open horizon of determinate indeterminacies. See Husserl, *Logische Untersuchungen*, Ergänzungsband, Erst. Teil, p. 155.

[58] Andrey Grib, "Quantum Logical Interpretation of Quantum Mechanics: The Role of Time," *International Journal of Theoretical Physics* 32 (1993): 2389–2400 at p. 2397.

the whole world of physical things there corresponds the multiplicity of noetic occurrences, the possible mental processes of singular and communal individuals related to them, mental processes that (as parallel to noematic multiplicities) have according to their essence the peculiarity to be related to the world of things in conformity with sense and positing. The unity of a (physical) thing then stands against an ideally infinite multiplicity of noetic processes of a wholly determinable and, in spite of their infinite character, surveyable essential content, all united by being consciousness of the "same" thing.[59] As has been already noted, this unity is given in the sphere of consciousness itself. And in an apparent reference to the recurring theme of the eidetic necessities underlying each thingness constitution, Husserl adds that each and every "thing" is eidetically prescribed no matter how far we stretch our field of inquiry, or to whatever level of universality or particularity we move, even to the lowest-level concretions. Insofar as each (spatial) figure inscribed in space is defined by the essence of space according to unconditionally valid laws, just as rigorously it is tied the sphere of mental processes in relation to eidetic laws and according to its transcendental essential structure, and thus there is firmly defined in it each possible essential formation according to noesis and noema. And in what may be a phenomenological clue to the dialectics of possibility vs. probability, Husserl further claims that possibility in the sense of eidetic existence is absolutely necessary possibility, "an absolutely firm member in an absolutely firm framework of an eidetic system."[60]

In view of what has preceded in the discussion, individuation in a phenomenological attitude is meant as an *a priori* intentional act independent of causality, not even of the necessity of presence of a concrete "thingness" individual. In epistemological terms and in the context of the new physics, as Husserl called quantum physics in *Crisis*, the question of individuation and identity becomes more perplexing, and on this account Husserl left a very brief indication of his views in *Beilage IV* in the German edition of *Crisis*.[61] He introduced there the term "individual type" for groups to which the real being of the last constituted elements of physical events and transformations belong. In this new physics atoms, for instance, are described as "individual type" unities, which in the being-in-itself of nature "precede" the being of their last-level elements and co-define the norms of their being as such (*Sein*) and being thus and so (*Sosein*). Consequently, the causality of such unities is meant as a norm for co-possibility in the unity of the world.[62] It may be that Husserl viewed the statistical description of quantum phenomena, in which quantum individuals are thought of as representatives of definite quantum groups by virtue of statistical

---

[59]Husserl, *Ideen I*, p. 311.

[60]Ibid., p. 323.

[61]Edmund Husserl, *Die Krisis der Europäischen Wissenschaften und die Transzendentale Phanomenologie*, Hua VI, hgb. Walter Biemel (Den Haag: M. Nijhoff, 1962), pp. 387–91. In English translation: *The Crisis of European Sciences and Transcendental Phenomenology*, trans. D. Carr (Evanston IL: Northwestern Univ. Press, 1970).

[62]Husserl, *Die Krisis der Europäischen Wissenschaften und die Transzendentale Phanomenologie*, pp. 388–90.

eidë, as a way out of the theoretical impasse reached at the time concerning the question of individuality and identity of quantum particles.[63]

On the formal-logical level Husserl thought of mathematical individuals as a special case of quasi-individuals (i.e., those that do not correspond to an absolute spatiotemporal position) in contrast to "real" individuals of physical perception, even though he considered that in both cases the individual essence[64] of the corresponding object encompasses both the identical temporal duration of each one and the identical distribution of temporal fullness over this duration. Individual essences tend toward unity in their perfect likeness (of real and quasi-individuals) and, even more, one may assume that in the noematic stock of each lived experience there is always one individual essence.[65]

Mathematical individuals as singularizations of a predicatively formed eidetic affair-complex are thought to retain their essential characteristics (regarding their "ontic" self and their relational character) in representing the corresponding eidetic affair-complex *simpliciter*.[66] In contrast, the constitution of sets as collections of individuals and also of sets of a higher order (classes) as collections of sets and so on, is conditioned on the possibility of their constituting as complete objective wholes in the immanence of consciousness and in the actual now of reflection irrespectively of whether, as in the case of infinite sets, they are formally taken as denumerable or non-denumerable ones.[67]

Another interesting question seems to be whether discernibility is an inherent property of formal individuals in the sense of being attached with a distinctive "ontological label" in the process of their appearing within immanence or whether it should be solely referred to the modes of their constitution and thus reducible to the constitutive modes of an ego-founded consciousness (see the Appendix below). To the extent that we refer to mathematical-logical individuals as non-arbitrarily constituted objects of temporal consciousness, it seems to me that their discernibility within objectivities of sense (e.g., in non-finitistic in content formulas bounded by existential-universal quantifiers) is ultimately the result of the intentional modes of consciousness orienting itself each time uniquely in an *a priori* and causality-

---

[63]The question of the individual essence of quantum elements, related historically with Pauli's exclusion principle, is still a hotly debated issue in contemporary epistemology for which there exists an interesting research literature. See, e.g., Mauro Dorato and Matteo Morganti, "Grades of Individuality: A Pluralistic View of Identity in Quantum Mechanics and in the Sciences," *Philosophical Studies* 163 (2013): 591–610, and Decio Krause and Antonio M. N. Coelho, "Identity, Indiscernibility, and Philosophical Claims," *Axiomathes* 15 (2005): 191–210.

[64]The use of the term essence here is more or less conventional in view of the position defended in this article, namely, that essences in the process of intention-reflection become ontologically "emptied" of themselves on account of the constitutive modes of the absolute subjectivity of ego.

[65]Husserl, *Erfahrung und Urteil*, p. 462.

[66]With this assertion it is by no means meant that experience in general and mathematical one in particular do not further enhance our capacity in shaping and putting in proper context mathematical objects (Husserl, *Ideen I*, p. 332).

[67]For a more detailed discussion of formal-mathematical individuals in phenomenologically motivated terms the reader may consult: Stathis Livadas, "What is the Nature of Mathematical-Logical Objects?," *Axiomathes* 27 (2016): 79–112.

Husserl's Sachhaltigkeit

independent way toward individuals-substrates as such and in the modalities of the intentional act.

Understandably this claim points to the modes of intentional apprehension of formal individuals, irrespective of any objective spatio-temporal constraints, constituted with a noematic nucleus that is thought of as their essential and unique way to be a "something-whatsoever" as such (and also with respect to, in relation to, in colligation with, etc.). It was in *Formal and Transcendental Logic* that Husserl faced squarely the question of grounding mathematics in these terms as a formal-ontological discipline, a discipline in a fully comprehensive sense whose universal domain is delimited as the range of the highest form-concept, the "object-whatsoever" (*Objekt-überhaupt*), in the emptiest generality.[68]

Husserl further describes the nature and modes of constitution of mathematical-logical objects as categorial ones in the context of transcendental phenomenology, an undertaking culminating in *Experience and Judgment*. Ultimately one may deduce in a holistically inclined view that both physical objects of perception and mathematical-logical ones as appearances within immanence are bound by phenomenological reduction to the evidence of the being of intentional-reflective consciousness whose correlates they are taken to be. Yet in view of the argumentation of the previous sections the same kind of reduction undermines the ontic character of their respective essences by reducing them to a system of "endless" processes of continuous appearances.

As a last clue, concerning the foundation provided by the phenomenological-eidetic analysis along these terms, Husserl refers to the entities determined by positive science this way: "the taking into consideration of mathematical natural science (no matter how many particular enigmas may be involved in its cognition) in no way alters our results."[69]

6. APPENDIX

The question of the discernibility of formal individuals may be associated, on the formal-mathematical level, with the definition of ordinal numbers as transitive and well-ordered by $\in$ relation sets as something that implies their "fixedness" as individuals with regard to any enlargement of a logical-mathematical structure. On these grounds urelements (roughly thought of as irreducible individuals) of an extended Zermelo-Fraenkel universe (ZFU, $\in$) taken as not identical yet indistinguishable elements, by means of the definition of A-indistinguishability within a relational structure, can be made distinguishable by associating to any collection of them an ordinal number so that it is possible to talk about a collection $\sigma_0, \sigma_1, \ldots, \sigma_{n-1}$ of such elements. This is a result of the simple proof that any ordinal as a well-ordered structure $<A, <>$ is a rigid one, which means that the only automorphism in this structure is the identity function.[70] In other words, in a rigid structure A (as

---

[68]Husserl, *Formale und Transzendentale Logik*, pp. 82–83.
[69]Husserl, *Ideen I*, p. 123.
[70]Krause et al., "Identity, Indiscernibility, and Philosophical Claims," p. 201.

it proves to be the structure of ordinals) the notions of non-identical elements and A-distinguishable elements coincide.

The question of the individuality of entities in the context of quantum mechanics has provided for much theoretical discussion on the nature of quantum objects as they are regarded by some physicists (notably by Scrödinger) as non-individuals upon which a notion of identity does not make sense, whereas by others as bearing a kind of intrinsic individuality by means of which "they might be qualitatively the same in all aspects representable in quantum mechanical models yet numerically distinct."[71] On this account Krause and Coelho claim that the mathematical structure of quantum mechanics should have a non-trivial rigid expansion (i.e., one not obtained by trivially adjoining the ordinal number structure) whose physical intuition is that quantum objects are somehow intrinsically discernible.[72] In view of the general approach of this article, the intrinsic discernibility of quantum individuals may be ultimately associated with the intentional structure of consciousness and the uniqueness of each intentional "observing" act (possibly mediated through a measuring device) founded in its very "enactment" toward a specific "this-there" and the non-eliminable evidence in reflection. This is a claim that may be also seen as an indirect argument against the position of a de facto identification of individuals defended in Yablo's *Identity, Essence, and Indiscernibility* (cited in the above).

---

[71] Bas C. Van Fraassen, *Quantum Mechanics: An Empiricist View* (Oxford UK: Clarendon Press, 1991), p. 376.

[72] Yet in J. Arenhart and D. Krause, "From Primitive Identity to the Non-Individuality of Quantum Objects," *Studies in History and Philosophy of Modern Physics* 46 (2014): 273–82, Arenhart and Krause seem to espouse the thesis that the non-individuality of quantum particles, except for accounting for certain naturalistic concerns, should be also preferred in that it fits better the claims of (quantum) theory and is better equipped on the formal level. This is a position defended against the thesis of Dorato and Morganti in "Grades of Individuality," that one may find positive reasons to assume quantum individuality as an ungrounded fact, that is, as a primitive individuality "essence" extraneous to the expressional means of the theory.

The Relevance of Phenomenological Analysis Within Current Epistemology

Abstract

This article is primarily concerned with the articulation of a defensible position on the relevance of phenomenological analysis with the current epistemological edifice as this latter has evolved since the rupture with the classical scientific paradigm pointing to the Newtonian-Leibnizian tradition which took place around the beginning of 20th century. My approach is generally based on the reduction of the objects-contents of natural sciences, abstracted in the form of ideal objectivities in the corresponding logical-mathematical theories, to the content of meaning-acts ultimately referring to a specific being-within-the-world experience. This is a position that finds itself in line with Husserl's gradual departure from the psychologistic interpretations of his earlier works on the philosophy of logic and mathematics and culminates in a properly meant phenomenological foundation of natural sciences in his last major published work, namely the *Crisis of European Sciences and the Transcendental Phenomenology* (Husserl, 1962). Further this article tries to set up a context of discourse in which to found both physical and formal objects in parallel terms as essentially temporal-noematic objects to the extent that they may be considered as invariants of the constitutional modes of a temporal consciousness.

1. Introduction

Phenomenology can generally be considered, on the one hand, as an evolution of classical continental philosophy, referring in particular to the various nuances of subjective idealism originating in the German idealist tradition of the 18th-19th century (Kant, Hegel, Fichte, Schelling) and, on the other hand, as a philosophy (in the sense of a descriptive *a priori* science as E. Husserl wanted it) open to developments in the broader epistemological edifice of the19th and 20th centuries. The latter view may be taken as associated in a definite sense with F. Brentano's and H. Lotze's theories pointing to a psychologistic reductionism of positive science in general and from a certain viewpoint with G. Frege's logical reductionism concerning mathematical foundations.

In the following, a phenomenologically motivated interpretation of certain key epistemological questions will be presented, given that the field of knowledge of phenomenology can be associated with that of epistemology insofar as the objects of epistemology taken as by-products of a process referring to the perceptual mechanisms of a subject can be considered as essentially phenomenal objects. As a matter of fact, a key part of Husserl's philosophical work was the phenomenological analysis of the experience, of judgements and of formal apophantics (e.g., in *Logical Investigations,* in *Formal and Transcendental Logic,* and in *Experience and Judgment, cf.* Husserl, 1984, 1974, and 1972, resp.), as well as the descriptive *a priori* analysis of temporal consciousness mainly elaborated in the *Phenomenology of Inner-Time Consciousness* (*Zur Phänomenologie des inneren Zeitbewußtseins,* Husserl, 1966). The phenomenological interpretation of logical laws, broadly conceived, distinguishes itself from psychologistic interpretations in that accepting as a lowest-level foundation of knowledge the pre-predicative (or pre-linguistic) experience grounding the knowledge *in rem*, it introduces moreover a special *a priori* relation we bear with things themselves which should not be regarded as solely a physical interaction though our sense organs. This *a priori* relation being essentially intentional in character may help provide a sound interpretation to the vexing epistemological question of the residuum left in the objectification of the phenomena of real world experience, these taken as presenting themselves originally 'in front' of a subject's embodied consciousness. More on this special kind of relation we bear with the objects of our physical or mental experience I will develop in the next sections.

It should not be left without notice, at this point, that E. Husserl completed his doctoral formation in mathematics at the University of Berlin under the guidance of the famous mathematician Karl Weierstrass. He continued to do research in mathematics for several years and had ample knowledge of the developments in the mathematical foundations and set theory through his exchanges with G. Cantor, G. Frege and D. Hilbert. He had also the opportunity to engage in fruitful discussions with the founder of the intuitionistic theory in mathematics, L.E.J. Brouwer, during his visit to Amsterdam in 1912. It is indicative of Husserl's mathematical background that two major works belonging to the earlier psychologistic stage of his phenomenological-transcendental philosophy are the *Philosophy of Arithmetic* (*Philosophie der Arithmetik*, Husserl, 1970) and *the Studies on Arithmetic and Geometry* (*Studien zur Arithmetik und Geometrie*, Husserl, 1983). One can note here that even though Husserl dealt in the Philosophy of Arithmetic with such basic mathematical concepts as the concepts of number and of multitude in a way that what is immediately given is restricted to what is concretely intuited and further susceptible to mental abstraction, yet in certain respects this early work bears the traces of a phenomenological-constitutional investigation (Hartimo, 2006: 328). Of course, Husserl's strong mathematical background is not by itself a vindication of the relevance of phenomenological philosophy with pure logic, the foundations of mathematics and epistemology in general. In the next, I am going to discuss in some length the arguments that make phenomenological analysis relevant with certain fundamental questions of contemporary epistemology.[1] Yet, it would be an omission to make no reference to certain phenomenology scholars who are adamantly opposed to any attempt of 'naturalizing' phenomenology and defend their position based mainly on Husserl's earlier positions around the time of *Logical Investigations* (see: Ortiz-Hill, 2013: 79).

In any case, and independently of the intentions one can ascribe to Husserl himself on the matter, phenomenology as an eidetic-descriptive science cannot and should not be 'sterilized' from what underlies its overall scope and endeavour and this is the world of phenomena unfolding within the life-world of our experience. On this account one may refer, in particular, to Husserl's views in *Cartesian Meditations* where the psychological origins of the ideas of

---

[1] Some original works on the relevance of phenomenology with current epistemology are: French (2002), Lurcat (2007), Tragesser (1977 and 1984).

space, of time, of physical things are reduced to transcendental problems of intentionality "which have their particular places among the problems of a universal genesis" (Husserl, 1960: 76). And further, the total science of the a priori, designated as the systematic unfolding of the all-embracing a priori innate in the essence of a transcendental subjectivity (and consequently in that of a transcendental intersubjectivity), would be the foundation for genuine sciences of matters of fact, for all a priori sciences without exception and for "a genuine all-embracing philosophy in the Cartesian sense: "an all-embracing science of the factually existent, grounded on an absolute foundation." (Husserl, 1960: 155).

2. A review of the evolution of the epistemological edifice

We have already passed the second decade of the 21st century and the question of the content of scientific truth and its limits is more than ever in actuality given the galloping pace of development of cutting-edge technologies, of advancing physical and cosmological theories, etc. Yet, certain questions of depth are still pending even though one might say that they are posited in a quite vague epistemological context. For example, one may ask the following questions: Is there a need of a metaphysical entity as prime reason of at least the conceivable universe? Why should there be something instead of nothing? Is there sufficient reason to expect that the widely accepted verification of the existence of the elusive Higgs particle will provide an epistemic foundation to the incompatibility of observations between the macroscopic and the quantum level of reality?[2] Further, is Bing Bang theory a complete one in the sense that it can consistently incorporate any newly acquired data (it is already doubted as 'observationally' sufficient), or is it just a theoretical model compatible up

---

2 Even in accepting the Higgs-particle's definite existence in accordance with the official announcement by CERN scientists on July 4, 2012 of the discovery of a Higgs-like particle, this fact will inevitably point to another regression of the chain of causalities within the real spatiotemporal world as it would be then raised the question of the prime underlying reason for the constitution of the Higgs particle and its associated Higgs field.

to a certain extent with the current empirical-epistemological paradigm? And given the advance of quantum theory one might also inquire into the bounds of human observational capacity regarding the microcosm and the way they are defined in the context of a quantum measurement.

Moreover one might ask whether quantum objects are ontologically self-standing, in the sense that they are they spatio-temporally hypostasized entities or whether they should be taken as co-constituted each instant of time with reference to an observer's temporal consciousness which constitutes a quantum object or state-of-affairs by constituting itself.

All these questions have been discussed in the epistemological community for over a century as positive sciences in a striking advance that was strongly motivated by the industrial-technological revolution – a case of crisis of the epistemological paradigm in the sense of T. Kuhn – were led through theoretical questioning to new radical orientations. The radical shake up in the classical epistemological edifice, which had nevertheless given theories of such breadth as the Newtonian mechanics, the electromagnetic theory of R. Maxwell, the classical mathematical analysis and the variation calculus of Cauchy-Lagrange, etc., could not but provide a new content to the historically charged relation of positive science with philosophy and analytical logic. Given the general positivist tradition showcased e.g., by the positivism of A. Compte and from a certain viewpoint by the dialectical-materialism of Marx-Engels, there was a fertile ground for the development of new philosophical approaches that would face up to the new epistemological evolution to the extent that this latter set up a context of discussion that covered the ontological-categorial field of classical philosophy almost in its entirety. It is indicative of the convergence of the evolving philosophical attitude with current epistemology the view of a major representative of the Vienna Circle, namely of Moritz Schlick in his review of R. Carnap's *The Logical Construction of the World* (*Der Logische Aufbau der Welt*), in which he claimed that the fundamental concepts of philosophy are at the same time the most general concepts of sciences (Schlick, 2008: 200). As a matter of fact, the new epistemological domain included the subatomic realm, the birth and evolution of universe, the molecular structure of living organisms, etc., extending to the psychic automatisms and the constitution of the conscious self, these being fields almost beyond the scope of positive science until the beginning of 20th century.

The Husserlian phenomenology and certain offshoots, e.g. the naturalistic version of M. Merleau-Ponty, as well as W.V. Quine's holistic empiricism and R. Rorty's neopragmatism among others, may be regarded as philosophical trends motivated by or interacting, to one or the other degree, with the aforesaid epistemological developments.

I take the occasion at this point to make, as somewhat relevant to the overall discussion, a brief reference to W. V. Quine's position which regards truth as dependent both on language construction and facts within-the-world. In Quine's view, even analytical logic and mathematics are, in final count and through a certain system of interpositions, sciences of empirical descent referred, as all knowledge in general, to psycho-physiological processes based on an empirical and biological foundation ultimately reducible to the embodied human consciousness. A significant part of these interpositions is taken to be the structure of language itself as a mode of expression and communication, independently of whether we refer to the corpus of a formal language or to a loosely formed natural language, in taking into account that the structure of the human mind and the intersubjectively founded identity of constituted objects are themselves underdetermined by language.[3]

In the next, it will be shown that among the main 20th century philosophical trends phenomenological analysis predominantly transposes the level of discussion on certain open questions of positive science to a discussion of the constitution of objects of experience as well-meant objects within constituted temporality.

In the relatively recent and contemporary evolution of natural science one can say that there have been gradually formed two distinct cognitive contexts: the one of empirical physical science as a field of 'observation' and physical interaction equipped with an appropriate physicalistic language (e.g. in quantum theory in terms of the triangle, embodied consciousness-measuring

---

3 On certain convergences of the Quinian theory of truth and knowledge as mediated by language and the Husserlian approach to the general notions of meaning and truth as 'contents' of intentional acts, see my article *The Metaphysical Source of Logic by way of Phenomenology*.

device-measured object), and that one of logical-mathematical science as a formal metatheory of empirical science and also as a formal-axiomatical theory in itself. This distinction seems to generate a two-fold inquiry summed up in the following: up to what level reach the 'observational' capabilities of an embodied consciousness endowed moreover, in M. Merleau-Ponty's view, with a reciprocal relation of a special architecture with the physical world, and at the same time, up to what point accede the expressional capabilities of a formal language by which are formalised on the level of theory the registered empirical observations-measurements? Is there a common underlying foundation to the limits of physical 'observation', on the one hand, and to the limits of formal language as a proper expressional tool, on the other? And if, indeed, there is such a common foundation, should it be found within a subject's empirical field?

Truly, if such a foundation would be found within a subject's objective spatiotemporal domain, it would then lead to a circularity to the extent that the observational-cognitive limits of reality would evidently be, in this assumption, at least co-determined by this same reality, implying therefore that they should form part of it. We could then be led to the paradoxical conclusion that the limits *de facto* imposed by our reciprocal relation with the universe of objective reality would be applied to transcend it. Consequently, the question of 'existence' of a pre-objective (or hyper-objective) 'reality' seems to be posed at this level, wherein in case such a transcendental type question could be regarded as well-posed one would then argue whether it can be a meaningful one in the absence of at least one phenomenological reduction-performing consciousness.

These given, I choose, in the next, quantum theory as the main empirical-epistemological field to refer to rather than the general theory of relativity.

The main reason is that the time parameter in quantum-mechanical processes is considered as external to the system and in a certain way as co-determining the objective existence of quantum objects/state-of-affairs, whereas time in macroscopic physical systems, irrespectively of whether they are taken as newtonian or relativistic ones, is considered as an internal parameter expressible through certain continuous mathematical transformations (e.g. in the equations of motion or generally in the field equations of relativity).

It is a predominant conviction within the community of particle physicists that quantum 'observation' is associated with a subjectivity of some kind objectifying an entangled quantum state (effectively by objectifying time) in the transition toward the corresponding disentangled state. Further, this subjectivity is mediated on the classical level by means of a measuring apparatus and it is reflected in a formal-mathematical context by the non-isomorphic projection of the holistic non-Boolean field of entangled quantum correlations into the meta-contextual Boolean field that 'disrupts' the physical unity by introducing the self-evident presence of an intentionally oriented conscious subject within the physical world. As quantum theorist A.A. Grib has claimed, the jump of truth-values in the process of measurement, due on a formal level to the absence of an isomorphism between Boolean and non-Boolean structures (in accepting the latter as the formal means of describing the 'inner' entangled state of a quantum state-of-affairs), sets upon a Boolean 'observer' the constraint of existence of an objective, continuous time in terms of which he must 'move' (Grib, 1993: 2397).

Moreover, to the extent that the objectification of an entangled quantum state implies its constitution as a temporal object/state-of-affairs with regard to a temporal consciousness, by the same token it is annulled the possibility of a complete description of its inner temporality prior to its objectification by an intentionally oriented consciousness. Therefore, it is imposed a *de facto* limit in the complete knowledge of a quantum state in the absence of its 'observation'. This *de facto* limit may provide some clues to the impossibility of a physicalistic description, that is, of a description in terms of the 'language' of the measuring apparatus of what takes place in-between the time of the performance of a quantum interaction through an experimental arrangement and the time of registration of this interaction. The impossibility of describing this part of the measurement process by the equations of quantum mechanics was clearly recognized by J. von Neumann and also prior to him by F. London and E. Bauer (Margenau *et al*, 1964: 7-8). It should not be left without due attention here that precisely von Neumann's Projection Postulate (or the 'Reduction of the Wave Function' postulate) points indirectly to the need for a self-constituting time flux by assigning to the mathematical translation $\tau((s)(t))$

of the physical state s(t) of a quantum quantity Q_i upon a first-kind measurement at time t, the same eigenvector ψ_κ as with the translation of the state $s(t_1)$ of the same quantity Q_i at time t_1 soon after the measurement.

Even if we assume von Neumann's Projection Postulate and Van Fraassen's modal interpretation of quantum mechanics as external metatheoretical conditions in a purely logical way, yet we cannot be led by any analytical linguistic means to a complete description of the 'change of states' that takes place during the measurement process in the compound system 'system + apparatus'. In fact, the question of a possible subjective source underlying the metatheoretical description of a quantum measurement had been already brought up by F. London & E. Bauer in *The Theory of Observation in Quantum Mechanics* (*La théorie de l'observation en mécanique quantique*, London & Bauer, 1939). London and Bauer formalized the critical role played by the consciousness of an observer in the transition from an entangled case to a pure one by forging a global wave function $\Psi(x,y,z)$ corresponding to the composed system [object(x) - apparatus(y) - observer(z)]. They claimed that it is not due to some kind of interaction between the apparatus and the object that produces a new ψ for the system during measurement but rather the consciousness of an 'I' (*Ich*) cutting the statistical correlations built-in in the global function $\Psi(x,y,z) = \Sigma_\kappa \psi_\kappa u_\kappa(x) v_\kappa(y) w_\kappa(z)$ and setting up a new objectivity by attributing to the object a new function $\psi'(x) = u'_\kappa(x)$. To the extent that this approach entails the constitutive non-reflective act of a temporal consciousness it raises the prospect of a more focused phenomenological approach with regard to a self-constituting temporal consciousness and the constitution of objects within it as noematic[4] correlates of the moments of its outward directed intentionality.

S. French (2002), largely motivated by London's & Bauer's assignment of a constituting role to the consciousness of a classical observer in quantum measurement, proposed a reading of the action of a 'very special character' of the ego in Husserlian terms. His approach seems close to the general position described above insofar as he refers to the domain of a potential observer in

---

[4] A noematic object manifests itself as a 'giveness' in the unity of the flux of a subject's consciousness and it is constituted by certain modes of being as such i.e., as an object immanent to the temporal flux with *a priori* categorial objectivities attached to it.

terms of a quantum mechanical description and applies the Husserlian notion of a characteristic act of reflection by means of which the phenomenological ego can reflect on its act of 'observation' and ultimately on itself. By this act of reflection the ego can separate itself from the superposition and set up a new objectivity thought not in terms of a bizarre collapse of the wave function but rather as a mutual separation of the Ego-pole and the object-pole, establishing this way a relation subject-object of an intentional character through this very act (French, 2002: 484-85). At this point one should be careful enough to properly understand the meaning attributed to the phenomenological pure ego as in Husserlian phenomenology it is commonly meant the ultimate subjective source of any conscious being-in-the-world. Which, by its non-objectifiable, a-temporal essence, should be absolutely extraneous to the world of phenomena. Yet, even though the absolute ego was left by Husserl as an obscure notion to the end of his life he was always preoccupied by the ontological vacuum that would be left as a residuum in admitting to an infinite regression reflecting-reflected in the temporal constitution of the world of objectivities. Therefore he thought of the ultimate subjectivity of consciousness (i.e., the absolute ego) as partially accessible both through its ever-in-act 'outward activity' in constituting the objectivity of phenomena and ultimately of itself, and also through the reverse activity of apodictically experiencing it in identification by iterative reflection in terms of the *Ich-bin* of phenomenological reduction (Husserl 2001b: 33-34 and 128-129).

From this standpoint the Ego-pole cannot but 'be' intentionally constantly engaged in a prima facie 'empty look' at any potential object, its act of objectification being taken in the quantum context as the attribution of a definite state to a quantum object among its distinct component-states predicted by the theory. My point, however, is that although S. French refers to the Ego-pole as something not 'substantial', in fact as an absolute subjectivity over and above its act of reflection (making reference for that matter mainly to Husserl's *Logical Investigations* and *Ideas*), he has not taken into proper consideration the temporality of the phenomenological ego in establishing new objectivities upon 'observation'. For, in accepting the constituting role of the absolute flux of consciousness, we must concede that it 'forces' its homogenous temporality upon seizing the objects of phenomenological perception, including quantum objects/states-of-affairs as intentional individuals, and transposing them in its homogenous immanent flux. But what about the origin of its own temporality, in other words, the temporality of its non-objectifiable ego? Any original act of reflection on itself will produce its objectified version and consequently will be constituted in the same objective continuous temporality as all other immanent temporal objects. In my view, this is a deep enough question which has ultimately to do with the origin of temporality itself and may be indirectly associated on an epistemic level with the time parameter in quantum mechanical processes, to the extent that it is taken as external to the quantum system and as a co-constituting factor in the decontextualization of a quantum measurement.

In this approach, quantization conditions stemming from appropriate boundary conditions and also the continuity of the time-evolution operator of quantum particle states are regarded as owing to the intrinsic property of quantum objects to be embeddable in a unified meta-contextual temporal frame of probabilistic description. This is meant as equivalent to 'embedding' reproducible quantum observations in a meta-contextual Boolean substructure associated with a homogenous internal time flux. This possibility involves at once, on a phenomenological level, a relationship subject-object of an intentional character and the noematic constitution of quantum objects as well-defined ones within the unity of consciousness. Independently of the context compatible with the preparation of a quantum experiment there should be some intrinsic way by which quantum objects taken as intentional objects become re-identifying immanent objects of a constituting consciousness invariably over homogenous temporal unity. Eliminating then all time-related modes of noematic constitution (e.g., simultaneity, succession, casual relationship) there should be an underlying temporal substratum of the predicative universe of quantum mechanics whose temporality should be something radically different from the ordinary objective time taken as an internal parameter of a classical macroscopic system. In this view the unifying, meta-contextual time of the predictive tool can be seen as ultimately reflecting the objectified unity of the absolute flux of temporal consciousness of an 'observer' which should be in an intersubjective sense the same objectified unity of any other potential one.

Yet, the origin of temporality of the pure phenomenological ego may provide ground for further research on a yet unexplored field and it is a problem that according to Husserl's own confession presented him with grave difficulties to the end. I just note that later in the *Bernau Manuscripts* he described the absolute ego in terms of an unknown primordial process (*unbewusster Urprozess*) beyond temporality, whose reflection upon itself cannot but produce its own objectification (which is obviously not itself) within objective temporal unity (Husserl, 2001a: 203-207).

3. Toward a holistic approach of epistemic objects

The argumentation above virtually reduces the question of ontification within a quantum context to a question of the origin of temporality, or more precisely to a question of constitution of temporal objectivities which should in turn be associated with a constituting subjectivity. On this account, the epistemological question of quantum existence and identification can be reduced on the level of evidence to the phenomenological analysis of temporal consciousness and the search for a no further reducible subjectivity which cannot but always 'be' the time-constituting factor and never the time-constituted objectivity. This quest ultimately led, beyond the bounds of specific *a priori* intentional structures of the constituting flux of consciousness (e.g. the transversal and longitudinal intentionality), to a rather obscure absolute (a-temporal) ego of consciousness, meant as the absolute constituting factor of the objective unity of temporal consciousness.

My point is that this absolute subjectivity of temporal consciousness, inaccessible to any kind of objectification except through its own ontic 'mirror'-reflexion, ultimately grounds as a common transcendental root both the constitution of quantum objects on the fundamental level of intentional experience and the constitution of certain mathematical objects in a sense to be further described. Concerning quantum objects/state-of-affairs the ultimate subjective factor may be seen to condition through the intentional-constituting forms of the absolute flux of consciousness their constitution as well-defined temporal objects, while its implicit presence in the constitution of objects of mathematical theories may be traceable in those objects whose formal existence implies a notion of actual infinity[5] (e.g., those of cardinality greater than countable cardinality $\aleph_0$) or those implying a notion of infinitesimality-in-actuality (e.g., the hyperreal numbers).

It should be noted that at a later stage Husserl considered objects of mathematical theories as a special class of perceptual objects which may be taken, in the sense of objects of pure logic as *mathesis universalis*, as complete mental abstractions through a particular kind of intuition (categorial intuition) independently of any material content or form by which they might be instantiated. In the more phenomenologically founded orientation initiated with the publication of *Logical Investigations*, as Husserl gradually rid himself of psychologistic preoccupations, he pointed to the *a priori* character of intentional directedness toward last individuals-substrates of analytical logic, these latter objects thought of as 'general somethings' (or objects-anyhow, *Etwas-überhaupt*), possibly 'empty' of any content taken together with devoid of content categorial objectivities such as relation, order, unity, plurality, etc. (Husserl, 1974: 81-82). It was in *Formal and Transcendental Logic* (*Formale und Transzendentale Logik*) that Husserl faced squarely the question of grounding mathematics in these terms as a formal-ontological discipline, namely a discipline in a fully comprehensive sense whose universal domain is delimited as the range of the highest form-concept, the object-anyhow; that is, the range of the object-anyhow thought of in the emptiest generality with all in this field a priori generated and hence conceivable derived forms which always give new forms in an ever iterable construction (Husserl, 1974: 82).

To this class of objects he included all those objects/states-of-affairs (*Sachverhalte*) expressible by any syllogistic or arithmetical axiom (or theorem) and by every inferential form and also every number, every numerical formation, every function of pure analysis, and every well-defined Euclidean or non-Euclidean manifold (Husserl, 1976: 33-34).

---

5 Actual infinity can be taken to be a kind of infinity freely generated in our consciousness in the sense of the unity of a whole in presentational immediacy. Consequently, it should not be identified with physical spatiotemporal infinity conditioned on the laws of causality. On the level of formal theory, it may be taken as representing any form of inexhaustible infinity apprehended as a completed whole in the actual now.

The whole approach meant a shift from the established view of logic as the exact pure science of idealized objectivities to its reassessment as fundamentally referring to the experience of being within the lifeworld,[6] this latter notion meant in a most fundamental pre-predicative sense. In this view, a genealogy of logic understood as a transcendental clarification of its origins and primarily focused in elucidating its development as an apophantic discipline should inevitably consider predicative judgements as the essential foundation of logic. This, in turn, calls for a further reduction of predication on the level of unambiguous evidence, based on the fact that the world is the universal ground of all possible substrates of predicative judgements, of all that is, in intersubjective fashion, made knowable and logically posited. It is remarkable that the lifeworld as the universal horizon of all meaning-acts was considered by Husserl as related not only to the meaning attributed to the objects as objects of possible knowledge but also to everything the natural sciences (of his time) had rendered as determination of beings. Therefore, the meaning of any objectivity is so defined that all the attributes of being as rendered by the contemporary natural sciences belong to the world (in the sense of a universal horizon) within which it is specified (Husserl, 1972: 39). In the *Analyses of Passive Synthesis* (*Analysen zur Passiven Synthesis*), and in a further elaborated notion of objects presupposing the act of rememorating, Husserl explicitly included in the class of objects the noetic and noematic structures of intuiting experience which have become scientific objects (Husserl, 1966a: 327).

In this perspective, mathematical objects as syntactical objects (with a proper semantical content) of a formal theory taken as general 'objects-anyhow' in the sense of individuals at the lowest level of intentional experience, may be considered as fundamentally temporal objects insofar as they are constituted as immanences within the homogenous flux of a subject's temporal consciousness. It follows that the intentional structure of a self-constituting temporal flux is inherently tied to the character of definite mathematical objects

---

6 The lifeworld in Husserlian phenomenology can be roughly described to a non-phenomenologist as the physical world (in a most fundamental sense) in its ever-receding horizon including in an intersubjective sense all phenomenological reduction-performing subjects in a special kind of presence in the world. More on this in E. Husserl's *The Crisis of European Sciences and Transcendental Phenomenology*, (Husserl, 1962).

as well-meant temporal ones. It determines, for instance, the essential character of a convergent sequence of natural numbers as a complete mathematical object although it is a re-iterative, finitary process of a discrete character extensible ideally *ad infinitum*.

Husserl thought of formal-mathematical individuals as a special case of quasi-individuals in contrast to 'real' individuals of physical perception (corresponding to an absolute temporal position), even though he considered that in both cases the individual essence of corresponding objects encompasses both the identical temporal duration of each one and the identical distribution of temporal fullness over this duration. This individual essence tends toward unity in their perfect likeness (of 'real' and quasi-individuals) and, even more, one may assume that in the noematic stock of each lived experience there is always one individual essence (Husserl, 1972; English translation, App. I, p. 382). In contrast, the constitution of sets as collections of individuals and also of sets of a higher order (classes) as collections of sets, etc., is conditioned on the possibility of their constituting as completed totalities in the immanence of consciousness and in the actual now of reflection irrespectively of whether infinite sets are formally postulated as denumerable or non-denumerable ones. In the case of sets or of classes of sets one should distinguish between the act of colligation or drawing together of a sequence of objects and the act of constitution of these sets as thematic objects in actual presence. In this view a set as an original objectivity is preconstituted by an act of colligation which links disjunct objects to one another and is complemented by what Husserl called a retrospective apprehension (*rückgreifendes Erfassen*), an act whose content is that of the thematization by the constituting ego of a collectivity preconstituted through the polythetic act of colligation into an identifiable and re-identifiable object possibly posited as a substrate of judgments (Husserl, 1972; English translation: 246-247).

In this view, the invariant, transtemporal, and abstract character of mathematical objects can be interpreted in a phenomenological approach that is radically different from classical or naive Platonism. And even though mathematical objects are meant and grounded as invariants of phenomena, that is, as invariants of appearances referring to our experience, yet they are taken as objects that could subsequently (i.e., in a post-constitutional sense) be taken to exist even in the total absence of subjects. For instance, the atomic predicate formula $X \in P$ or $X \notin P$ may be considered as transtemporal in the sense that it is an abstract syntactical form referring to an idealized content of a cognitive act that can be in principle realized any time by any subject in a way that it is always intersubjectively[7] the same. Richard Tieszen has worked out a conception of mathematical objects largely in this sense, namely as abstract and mind-independent. The terminology used pertains to his conception of the objects of mathematics and logic not as abstract and mind-independent$_2$ in a purely platonic sense but, in the context of his proposed constituted Platonism, as invariants of a subjective constitution which are nonetheless subjected to rationalistic constraints imposed by our living experience in the life-world and the usual mathematical practice (Tieszen, 2011: 115 and 149).

Now, I draw attention to two intentional-constitutional structures which are, in my view, critical in the interpretation of certain mathematical conjectures which involve a notion of actual infinity and also in the interpretation of the process of quantum objectification.

The first one relates to the modes of constitution of intentional objects, including both perceptual objects of the physical world and imaginary objects of our mental faculties, as temporal immanent objects within the constituting flux of temporal consciousness having as a result that their ontological being is reduced to their temporal re-identifications within the continuous unity of the flux. On this account, one can claim that the (circularly defined) continuous unity of the absolute flux of temporal consciousness and *a tergo* the transcendental character of its pure ego induce an impredicativity[8] of infinite mathematical objects meant as completed totalities in presentational immediacy within the homogenous inner temporality. For instance, such an infinite mathematical object can be considered an open interval of the real line

---

7 The notion of intersubjectivity can be said that it grounds, among other factors, the identical, invariant and thus transtemporal character of an object, irrespectively of whether it is a physical or a formal one, on the possibility of its definition as the 'common denominator' of the corresponding intentional acts of potentially all knowing subjects.

8 Generally, an impredicative notion is one that the *definiens* cannot but be defined in terms of the *definiendum* in the sense that the definition of an entity (object, concept, etc.) somehow involves or presupposes a totality that includes the entity being defined.

whose definition is regarded as impredicative as it cannot be described but in terms of its parts (i.e., in terms of basic open intervals) which are of the same genus as the whole. My view is that the essential being of all mathematical objects or concepts associated on a formal level with the notion of mathematical continuity is reducible to their subjective constitution as completed immanent totalities in presentational immediacy, which is a process further reducible to the continuous unity of a self-constituting temporal consciousness.

The second of the aforementioned intentional structures is not conditioned in its description on the notion of a constituted time, being rather an *a priori* directedness to lowest-level individuals of our pre-predicative experience. To make it clear, let us try to imagine something more fundamental in our intuition than lowest-level individuals, irrespectively of whether we talk about a quantum interaction and its registration by a classical-level apparatus or a deconstruction of a formal analytical sentence to its no further analytically reducible constituent elements. As a matter of fact, we cannot transcend this 'lowest' level of intuition meant as intuition of evidences originally presented to an intentional consciousness and apprehended as the non-reducible content of corresponding intentional acts possibly taken as close in meaning to the Aristotelian τόδε τι (this-something). These no further reducible intentional objects in the broader sense of general state-of-things (*Sachverhalte*) to the extent that they are thought of as devoid of any content that might be associated with a material or generally a thingness substance, were taken in complete abstraction by Husserl as belonging to the class of objects of universal logic and, in particular, to the domain of objects of formal mathematical structures (see, p. 9).

This 'lowest-level' intentionality which may ground what in mathematics is associated with the intuition of the concrete, finitistic and discrete can be thought to determine on the constitutional level along with certain intentional structures of the absolute flux of consciousness[9] (i.e., the transversal and longitudinal intentionalities) the conception of completed

---

[9] The absolute flux of consciousness is described as the self-constituting temporal flux of consciousness which is the field of the subjective inner temporality and the modes of constitution of immanent objects within it. Even this absolute source of temporality has a subjective ego (i.e., the absolute ego) whose objectification may be taken the absolute flux of consciousness itself upon reflection, see Husserl, 1966, §§ 34-37.

mathematical objects as, for instance, the notion of a choice sequence of natural numbers as a completed formal object or the intuition of a recursive set, etc. It is inconceivable, though, in the absence of a temporal constitution inherently associated with the objectified, continuous unity of the flux of consciousness insofar as, for instance, any generation of an infinite sequence of finite sign-configurations (think, e.g., of members of an arithmetical sequence as purely formal individuals) can be taken as a completed mathematical object only thanks to the subjective continuous unity of temporal consciousness.

This given, I consider this position on an underlying phenomenology of the mathematical continuum as pointing, in a certain sense, to the interpretation given by R. Tieszen to certain incompleteness results of mathematics and, in particular, to Gödel's second incompleteness theorem (Tieszen, 2005: 133-134). I remind that Gödel's two incompleteness theorems which are of prime importance in mathematical foundations have raised far-reaching philosophical questions as to the sound foundations of mathematics and logic in claiming (the second incompleteness theorem) that no formal-mathematical system be as simple as the system of arithmetic can prove its logical consistency with its own internal proof-theoretic means. In other words, it is shown that the semantical content of a formal mathematical system transcends the expressional capacity of the corresponding formal linguistic means.

As a matter of fact, Tieszen took as the fundamental reason of the proof of the incompleteness of formal-axiomatical theories the non-eliminable by a finitary combination of symbols (taken as sign-configurations) 'inner' meaning of non-finitary mathematical concepts. Yet, he does not seem to make any reference to a possible reduction of the impredicative character of actual infinity, or at least of the non-rigorously finitistic character of metatheoretical objects implicitly generated in incompleteness proofs, to the constitutional-intentional structure of a temporal consciousness underlying the continuous unity of its immanent objects. It looks as though this kind of phenomenological reduction of the classically viewed transtemporal objects of mathematical theories to objects immanent to consciousness each time of reflecting on them is a yet largely unexplored field in the philosophy of mathematics.

Apart from foundational mathematics, one can also find insights into how phenomenological notions can serve as an alternative interpretation of standard mathematical theories or even as the conceptual foundation of new nonstandard ones in the work of logicians and set-theorists who claim that the existence of infinitesimals and infinite cardinals has a subjective 'observational' character. This 'observational' character is essentially linked with the modes of intentionality of an 'observer's' consciousness who views the standard ZFC (Zermelo-Fraenkel Set Theory & Axiom of Choice) set-theoretical framework in a 'local' and non-Cantorian way. In this sense, the Alternative Set Theory (AST) (Vopěnka, 1979) and the Internal Set Theory (IST) (Nelson, 1986) properly interpreted, along with certain ultrafinitistic ramifications, the Nonstandard Class Theory (NCT) and the Theory of Hyperfinite Sets (THS), are generally considered as the main pillars of an alternative nonstandard mathematical approach.

More specifically, by making reference to a local and non-Cantorian way of 'observing', it is primarily meant that the actual infinity conceptually incorporated in the Cantorian ZFC theory as a metatheoretical, impredicative notion is refuted and substituted, e.g. in AST theory, by a notion of natural infinity which gradually manifests itself in the observation of macro or microscale phenomena present in very large sets. For instance, such phenomena are related to the intuition of the topological continuum in 'observing' a concrete physical surface. More specifically, the main contributor of AST theory P. Vopěnka has described the notion of countability in these terms:

'Our capacity for observation and distinction is limited by the horizon in all directions. Needless to say, this applies not only to optical observation; the horizon is understood in the sense of E. Husserl's *Krisis der europäischen Wissenschaften und die transzendentale Phänomenologie*. If a large set X is observed, then the class of all elements of X that lie before the horizon need not be infinite but may converge toward the horizon. The phenomenon of infinity associated with the observation of such a class is called countability' (Vopěnka, 1979: 39).

On the other hand, the intensional part of nonstandard analysis (mainly represented by E. Nelson's Internal Set Theory) can be metatheoretically interpreted as based on the subjective 'observations' of a potential observer realized in a local and non-Cantorian way so that that infinitesimals and infinitely large numbers do not exist in an objective way as in the extensional case (e.g. in A. Robinson's classical nonstandard analysis), but their existence has a subjective meaning and is related to the observational limitations of the interacting observer. In fact, the introduction of the undefined predicate *standard* along with three *ad hoc* axioms in the axiomatical machinery of Internal Set Theory is metatheoretically associated with a factor of vagueness in connection with a infinitely extensible series of 'observations' carried out in an essentially discrete mode (Nelson, 1986: 4-14). It is suggested, for instance, that: 'finiteness' + 'vagueness' = 'unlimited', where 'unlimited' is a non-Cantorian equivalent to (actual) infinity.

In any case, the phenomenological influence, even though somehow simplistically asserted, is more straightforward in the AST version insofar as, in Vopěnka's own account, the notions of intersubjectivity as well as those of the locality and extensibility of the observational horizon are essentially meant in the broad sense of Husserl's lifeworld in the way it is described in *Krisis* (Husserl, 1962).

In view of the discussion thus far we can say that the Husserlian reduction of the principles of analytical logic in the construction of apophantic sentences (and ultimately of formal-mathematical propositions) to subjective primary evidences of experience which refer to objects as originally registered by experience and further temporally constituted as categorial ones, may lead to the following four important claims in connection with the scope of this article:

First, the reduction of the laws of analytical logic to subjective evidences of intentional experience may be, under proper interpretation, associated with the semantical content of nonstandard mathematics. The metatheoretical content of nonstandard theories stands, in effect, in the discarding of the platonistic nature of the existing ZFC system (which formally incorporates a notion of actual infinity) and its substitution by a witnessed universe correlated with the presence of a potential 'observer' in whose extensible horizon infinities and infinitesimalities, even though axiomatically defined, refer to his subjective observations.

Second, the intentional 'observation' to lowest-level substrates of apophantic and generally of analytical statements as irreducible evidences of individuals bearing no further analytic inner structure points to a hierarchy of infinitesimals of various orders. In it, the infinitesimals of a given order appear to be points without structure to the immediately lower order until we unravel their own structure in a kind of a Russian doll game and reveal a class of infinitesimals of a still higher order playing provisionally the role of atoms-points. In nonstandard analysis this refers, for instance, to the definition of elements in the nonstandard extension R^* of the set of real numbers R, which have an inner structure as equivalence classes of infinite sequences of standard real numbers, modulo an ultrafilter $\mathscr{F}$ over the set of natural numbers. In such a case, the standard real numbers in the classical sense are the irreducible individuals of R^*.

Third, in phenomenological perspective, the aforementioned reduction of analytical statements gives the dialectical opposition between discreteness and continuity. Moreover, it motivates, on a fundamental level, a notion of actual infinity as the formal abstraction of an intuitive continuous unity, whose origin may be found within the immanence of temporal consciousness. This (impredicative) actual infinity is formalized in certain versions of nonstandard mathematics by means of *ad hoc* prolongation axioms in saturated enlargements of the domains of standard axiomatical systems.

Fourth, insofar as nonstandard extensions of the domains of classical mathematical systems – e.g., the uncountable extension of the domain of countability by the prolongation principle in AST theory (Vopěnka, 1979: 41) – presuppose the preservation of the categorial-relational properties of the individuals of the standard domain of the theory, we can associate the concept of these individuals to that of thing-like 'points' taken as 'visual atoms' in a process of fragmentation that ultimately leads to *minima visibilia*. It is notable that Husserl had pointed out the essential similarity of the visual field to itself on a large and small scale and went on to clarify that there is an immanent similarity which, as evident generic similarity, justifies the transposition of the eidetic relationships discovered, so to speak, in the macroscopic universe to the microscopic 'atoms' situated beyond divisibility (Husserl, 1973: 166).

4. The bounds of objective reality

As it is well-known, the role of a conscious, reduction-performing subject in the constitution of a co-determined 'objective' reality and the ontological context generated for that reason is of primary importance in phenomenological analysis. This way the phenomenological approach determines the breadth of the field within which a conscious subject may pose well-meant ontological questions to expect well-founded answers.

Let us consider, for instance, the concept of the phenomenological horizon taken of course not in the common meaning of the physical horizon but in the sense of a field which is co-determined by the intentional consciousness of a subject in its self-evident presence in the world and also by nature itself as a pre-phenomenological domain. The bounds of this horizon are inalienable to the extent that they refer in a reciprocal fashion to the constitutional character and the intentional modes of a subject's consciousness. Yet, they are all the same transposable inasmuch as it is transposable a subject's field of phenomenological perception (*Wahrnehmung*). In this view, current cosmological conjectures about a multiplicity of universes or even the notion of parallel universes are at least phenomenologically naive, as any hitherto 'unobserved' cosmic reality would stand for any being who is a biological carrier of a consciousness *a priori* provided with an intentional-constitutional structure simply a transposition of his 'local' phenomenological horizon.

The reference in one or other way to a consciously interacting biological subject and the special architecture of his relation with the surrounding physical world are significant factors in the predominant current interpretation of the four global (rather than universal) constants of physics, that is, of the gravitational constant G, the Planck constant $\hbar$, the velocity of light c and the Boltzmann constant κ. In a very concrete sense, these constants represent the inherent limits of human knowledge which are, on the one hand, inescapable and inalienable and, on the other, transposable just as the phenomenological horizon mentioned above. It follows that the four constants of physics articulate the existence of those 'horizon' lines that separate us from the infinitely small and the infinitely great. Accordingly, we can loosely say that the relativity constants G and c are associated with the impossibility of the definition of an absolute space and time in the universe, whereas the constants $\hbar$ and κ are associated with the bounds of the subatomic universe in discarding a well-meant and deterministic reality.

Equally important is the claim that the mode of constitution of an objective reality by a subject who is a bodily carrier of a self-constituting temporal consciousness determines not only the 'depth' of observation within physical world but also the limits of the corresponding formal metatheory. In view of the argumentation of previous sections, this is a position that can be based on Husserl's view of objects of mathematical theories, mainly in *Ideas I* and in *Formal and Transcendental Logic*, as objects founded on a categorial intuition.[10] This means: as objects associated with certain intentional acts whose content should not be necessarily identified with a material-spatiotemporal one, in such a way that these 'vacuous' objects are essentially thought of as general 'somethings' along with their specific empty of content categorial forms. Due to this reduction, lowest-level objects-individuals of analytical and consequently of formal-mathematical sentences lead to no further analytically reducible evidences of our intentional experience, evidences that cannot even have an 'inner' temporal form (Husserl, 1974: 181). Consequently, both mathematical and physical objects inasmuch as they are taken as immanent objects of consciousness and in abstraction as invariable, transtemporal objects of formal theories, can be viewed on the same terms as temporally constituted objects whose temporality is recursively founded in the following order:

(1) The absolute flux of consciousness which constitutes temporality by constituting itself.

(2) The multiplicities of appearances, or, in other words, the immanent objects as durations within the homogenous temporality of consciousness, this latter considered as the pre-empirical time and,

---

10 Categorial intuition is the kind of eidetic intuition described in Husserlian writings as reaching a purely formal object, e.g. an object of formal logic, by abstracting from an intentional content and positing the object in question regardless of a material or 'empty' content in the sense of an 'object-whatsoever' with all its essentially belonging transformations and relations. This is an intuition not to be taken as solely a process of abstraction through which we can be led by modification over content to a common invariant part of a real object, even one that is left with no traits relative to a material content. See: Husserl, 1984: 661-665.

(3) The objects of experience in objective time, that is, the objects of experience of each subject and intersubjectively the same objects identically (in constitutive mode) for all (Husserl, 1966$_a$: 73).

Further, to the extent that objects of a formal mathematical theory are categorial objects within a subject's temporal consciousness, it may become by this virtue meaningful an alternative interpretation of the undecidability of fundamental mathematical assertions concerning any higher-order than countable infinity. On this account I point, concerning the incompleteness results mentioned in Section 3, to the non-rigorously defined finitistic character of metatheoretical objects entering as formal ones in Level-2 assertions (these are assertions essentially conditioned on a universal quantification over an indefinite 'horizon'). As it is known, Level-2 formulas are critically involved in the proof of both Gödel's incompleteness theorems and Tarski's Undefinability of Truth Lemma.

If it is doubtful whether we can be sure about the validity of universal mathematical sentences especially when they express ontological claims relative to their variables as universals, it is all the more so concerning the validity of universal empirical sentences of physics in case we do not presuppose an *ad hoc* indefinite extension of the domain and 'morphology' of our constitutional experience which nevertheless we have no way to empirically prove. In set-theoretical mathematics, the negation, for instance, of a universal sentence within the set of real numbers (i.e. the Archimedean property) leads to the 'exotic' universe of nonstandard reals.

In short, there is no objective reality independent of the constitutional modes of a subjectivity referred to it; and if such a reality would indeed exist, it would not be possible to describe it but mediately and intersubjectively determined by the constituting consciousness of all biological subjects performers of (phenomenological) reduction, which means by all human beings. If science is taken, in principle, as intimately associated with the objectification of living experience, then experience eludes its scientific description in the 'residuum' of its constitution as an objectified-ontological structure within objective spatio-temporality and its subsequent abstraction by means of a formal theory. Consequently, scientific truth is conditioned on the objectification constraints posed by the constituting faculties of humans as conscious beings-in-the-world and the expressional capacity of corresponding formal theories in the language by which they are mediated.[11] It is remarkable, though, that in spite of the depth of the metatheoretical questions arising from this subjectively founded approach, mathematical models serving as theoretical idealizations of physics have proved over time particularly effective tools in the *in rem* description of the world of experience.

5. Conclusion

If the great theoretical questions on the incompleteness of mathematical theories having at least the degree of complexity of the theory of arithmetic and also those pertaining to the undecidability of critical conjectures involving mathematical (actual) infinity[12] have a common underlying root with the great open questions of contemporary subatomic physics-quantum mechanics, this might be the reduction of their context of reference to a subjective temporality constituting one. After all, the phenomenology of time was for Husserl part of an epistemological program seeking to validate natural sciences by means of a phenomenological science of the essential structures and the constitutive functions of pure consciousness. As mentioned earlier in the article, the subjective inner temporality may be further reducible to its absolute origin, the ego of temporal consciousness, paradoxically meant as a transcendental subjectivity within a surrounding concrete world susceptible of sense attribution.

The special 'architecture' of the reciprocal relation between a biological subject bearer of an intentional, time-constituting consciousness and the surrounding physical world and the concept of a transposable, yet inalienable, cosmic horizon. which is induced by this kind of 'architecture', determine the limits of scientific knowledge and the scope of well-posed questions in reference to the objective world. In this sense and taking account

---

11 The reader may consult W. V. Quine's argumentation on the matter in *Word and Object* (Quine, 1960).

12 On recent research concerning undecidable infinity statements, e.g. the Continuum Hypothesis or the existence of inaccessibly infinite cardinals, see W.H. Woodin's work in (Woodin, 2001_a), (Woodin, 2001_b) & (Woodin, 2011).

of the discussion on the place of phenomenological analysis in the interpretation of the world of science, one might not accept those questions which are commonly qualified as metaphysical or teleological as well-posed. It seems that in such cases, one should remain silent in the Wittgensteinian sense of the word.

Yet, phenomenology can prove an incisive interpretational tool in the description of the world of phenomena, as broadly conceived in the context of the lifeworld meant as the soil of primitive experience, whose apprehension and elucidation would be rather established in terms of the *Sosein* of reality as referent to the evidence of a constituting consciousness rather than in terms of a platonic mind-independent *Sein* of this very reality.

Bibliography

FRENCH, S. (2002). A Phenomenological Solution to the Measurement Problem? Husserl and the Foundations of Quantum Mechanics, *Studies in History and Philosophy of Modern Physics*, 33, pp. 467-491.

GRIB, A.A. (1993). Quantum Logical Interpretation of Quantum Mechanics: The Role of Time. *Int. Jour. Of Theoretical Physics*, 32, 12, pp. 2389-2400.

HARTIMO, M. (2006). Mathematical Roots of Phenomenology: Husserl and the Concept of Number, *History and Philosophy of Logic*, 27, pp. 319-337.

HUSSERL, E. (2001a. *Die Bernauer Manusckripte über das Zeitbewusstsein (1917/18)*. Husserliana XXIII, hsgb. R. Bernet & D. Lohmar. Dordrecht: Kluwer.

— (2001b). *Späte Texte über Zeitkonstitution, Die C-Manuscripte*, Hua Materialien Band VIII, hsgb. D. Lohmar, Dordrecht: Springer.

— (1984), *Logische Untersuchungen*, Hua Band XIX_1, (zweiter Band, erster Teil), hsgb. U. Panzer, Den Haag: M. Nijhoff.

— (1983), *Studien zur Arithmetik und Geometrie. Texte aus dem Nachlass (1886-1901)*, Hua Band XXI, hsgb. I. Strohmeyer, Den Haag: M. Nijhoff.

— (1976), *Ideen zu einer reinen Phänomenologie und phänomenologischen Philosophie*, Erstes Buch, Hua Band III/I, hsgb. K. Schuhmann, Den Haag: M. Nijhoff.

— (1974), *Formale und Transzendentale Logik*, Hua XVII, hsgb. P. Janssen, Den Haag: M. Nijhoff.
— (1973), *Ding und Raum*, Hua XVI, hsgb. U. Claesges, The Hague: M. Nijhoff.
— (1972), *Erfahrung und Urteil*, hsgb, L. Landgrebe, Hambourg: F. Meiner Verlag. Engl. transl.: (1973), *Experience and Judgment*, transl. J.S. Churchill & K. Americs, London: Routledge & Kegan.
— (1970), *Philosophie der Arithmetik. Mit erganzenden Texten (1890-1901)*, Hua Band XII, hsgb. L. Eley, Den Haag: M. Nijhoff.
— (1966a), *Zur Phänomenologie des Inneren Zeibewusstseins*, Hua Band X, hsgb. R. Boehm, Den Haag: M. Nijhoff.
— (1966b), *Analysen zur Passiven Synthesis*, Hua Band XI, hsgb. M. Fleischer, Den Haag: M. Nijhoff.
— (1962), *Die Krisis der Europäischen Wissenschaften und die Transzendentale Phänomenologie*, Hua Band VI, hsgb. W. Biemel, Den Haag: M. Nijhoff.
— (1960). *Cartesian Meditations*, engl. transl. D. Cairns, Hague: M. Nijhoff.
LONDON, F & BAUER, E. (1939). *La théorie de l'observation en mécanique quantique*, Paris : Hermann.
LURCAT, F. (2007). Understanding Quantum Mechanics with Bohr and Husserl, in: L. Boi, P. Krezberg & F. Patras (eds.), *Rediscovering Phenomenology*, pp. 229-258, Dordrect: Springer.
MARGENAU, H. & WIGNER, E. (1964). Discussion: Reply to Professor Putnam, *Philosophy of Science*, 31, 7-9.
NELSON, E. (1986). *Predicative Arithmetic*, Princeton: Princeton Univ. Press.
ORTIZ-HILL, C. (2013). The Strange Worlds of Actual Consciousness and the Purely Logical, *The New Yearbook for Phenomenology and Phenomenological Philosophy*, 13, pp. 62-83.
QUINE, V. W. (1960). *Word and Object*, Cambridge, Mass: MIT Press.
SCHLICK, M. (2008). *Moritz Schlick. Die Wiener Zeit. Aufsätze, Beiträge, Rezensionen, 1926-1936*, Wien: Springer.
TIESZEN, R. (2011). *After Gödel: Platonism and Rationalism in Mathematics and Logic*, Oxford: Oxford University Press.
— (2005). *Phenomenology, Logic, and the Philosophy of Mathematics*, Cambridge: Cambridge University Press.

TRAGESSER, R.: (1984), *Husserl and Realism in Logic and Mathematics*, Cambridge: Cambridge University Press.
— (1977), *Phenomenology and Logic*, Ithaca: Cornell University Press.
VOPĚNKA, P.: (1979) *Mathematics in the Alternative Set Theory*, Leipzig: Teubner Verlag.
WOODIN, H.W. (2001a). The Continuum Hypothesis, Part I, *Notices of the AMS*, 48, 6, pp. 567-576.
— (2001b). The Continuum Hypothesis, Part II, *Notices of the AMS*, 48, 7, pp. 681-690.
WOODIN, H.W. & HELLER, M. (eds.) (2011). *Infinity, New Research Frontiers*, N.Y.: Cambridge University Press.

The Enigma of 'Being There': Choosing Between Ontology and Epistemology

Abstract
The aim of this paper is to show, based on Heidegger's ontology of being and Husserl's ontological aspects of phenomenology, the ways in which may be highlighted the ontological turned epistemological (and vice versa) enigma of the actual presence of being-in-the-world. In such perspective the content of the philosophical term 'being there', in the sense of an original presence in the actuality of the world, is the key issue of discussion both in terms of the ontological implication of the accompanying notion of transcendence and the epistemological relevance it can have by virtue of a phenomenon within the world. Concerning the latter in particular, except for some prompts from formal-mathematical theory, a special attention is drawn to the incompleteness of quantum theory with regard to the treatment of certain 'ontological' aspects of the measurement question in a quantum context. The clarification of certain epistemological 'black box' cases as this one by virtue of a subjectively based interpretation of the 'being there' is a main goal of this article as well as the ontological foundation of the 'being there' per se.

1 Introduction

If it is true that traditional ontology was 'remolded' by the influence of German transcendental idealism of 19th century in the evolution toward the purely subjective-constitutive doctrine of phenomenology and its aftermath, then one can possibly attribute a proper content to the philosophical term 'being there'. For in this article the term 'being there' is by no means an idealistically connoted much less a naively spatial expression. It is indeed a subjectively founded expression with all that belongs to the concept of subjectivity meant further and deeper than any reductionistic or psychologistic preoccupations. Understandably, this means that my vantage point will be that of phenomenology considered in a broad sense (primarily the Husserlian and Heideggerian versions) with a critical look into the extent these versions enter into an osmotic relationship with classical ontology and foremost the way they can provide interpretational clues to a purported epistemical content of the term 'being there'.

Given that in terms of conceptual content the 'being there' is *prima facie* more affine to Heidegger's description of Dasein and its essential mode of being, that is, its transcendence toward the world (in the sense Heidegger attributes to the world), I give a certain priority to the Heideggerian views on the transcendence-within-the-world over the Husserlian conception of the absolute being of subjectivity, without favoring in fact one view over the other. Rather than contrasting their views I am more focused on finding those points of affinity that may serve my main intention, that is, the ways one can recast the ontological 'vacuities' found both in terms of empirical data and the accompanying formal theory of natural science into the ontological enigma of 'being there', the latter roughly meant in the sense of an original presence in the world. Building on this motivation I enter into a thorough discussion of the concept of transcendence as such, in both the Heideggerian and Husserlian versions, and also of the terms under which transcendence may underlie the meaning-content of 'being there' and thus provide an incisive tool to inquire into the epistemical 'gray zones' implied by a presumably hidden ontology of 'being there'. In Sections 3 and 4 I take advantage of the debate between ontology and epistemology to comment on other scholars' views concerning a presumed ontological content of epistemological questions, to show that insofar as they do not enter into a talk about transcendence *in rem*, in its 'everydayness' as Heidegger would have it, they are bound to reproduce circularities in the ontological level or get stuck in an 'act of faith' supposedly underpinned by scientific realism.

A key part of my argumentation in the discussion concerning the issue of transcendence and its purported relation to the grounding of 'being there' is the clarification of the role of subjectivity in relation to its being present-in-the-world in actuality and the ensuing implication of inner temporality. This triggers a comparative assessment of transcendence in both Heideggerian and Husserlian doctrines, more specifically of the question of its subjective or non-subjective 'substratum', of the possibility to be turned to a phenomenon that is susceptible to explication in epistemological terms, etc. Naturally that implies, on the one hand, the task of having to deal with the subtleties of Heidegger's conceptual acrobatics that reach as far as denying 'existence' to the world to the extent that transcendence as the essential character of Dasein in being-in-the-world has a temporal ecstatic character, the 'outside-of-itself', i.e., the 'overpassing' unity of future, past, present. On the other hand, one has to deal with Husserl's obscure concept of the transcendence within immanence (of consciousness), that is, with the isolated from the world pure ego and its 'personalized' ever-in-act counterpart which is the constituting source of inner temporality and all noetic-noematic acts. It is notable that while for Husserl the unity of temporality is radically reduced to the transcendental character of a non-reflective absolute ego leaving an ontological vacuum between pure ego itself and its enactment in the present 'now and there', for Heidegger the ecstatic unity of temporality, that is, the unity of the 'out-of-itself' in the raptures of future, past, present is the condition of the possibility that an existent can be as its 'there' (Heidegger (1986), *Engl. transl.*, p. 321).

The inquiry on the 'as' and 'how' more than the why of being-in-the-world is of course not limited to the aforementioned approaches. It has inspired quite a few alternative views in the domain of continental philosophy, as the privileged field of last century's subjective idealism, including Sartre's existentialism, Bergson's theory of consciousness, Merleau Ponty's naturalistic phenomenology, even O. Becker's abstruse notions of paratranscendence and paraontology, the latter evidently influenced by the insurmountable difficulties in jointly accommodating the notions of transcendence and being-in-the-world.

In the final count the discussion in this article of the Husserlian and Heideggerian versions of a phenomenology of original presence in the world is largely intended as being able to provide an appropriate context to argue on the reduction of certain epistemological issues to questions of ontological aspects of phenomenology.

2 An assessment of the 'Being There' in the Heideggerian sense

For Heidegger the interpretation of the 'being there' in terms of its thematic subject (i.e., the Dasein) points to a definite today (*das Heute*) to the extent that this reference not only must not be 'slackened off' but in order to have a full grasp of facticity one has to take it up in its utmost primordiality and follow it through to the end. Further if there is a reference of the 'being there' of Dasein 'in its public manner of having-been-interpreted in the today' to be pursued in full and to the end, this would be tied to an ontological view of the today as "the present of those initial givens which are closest to us, every-one, being-with-each-other - 'our time' " without any misunderstanding leading to the 'vacancies' of brooding over an ego-like self (Heidegger (1999), *Engl. transl.*, pp. 24-25). And yet as it happened with the Husserlian transcendental phenomenology in an unavoidable twist of a subjectively founded ontology of existence, temporality would become the 'gold standard' of acceding to a meaningful interpretation of the 'being there' of Dasein: "The 'today' can be fully defined in its ontological character as a how of facticity (existence) only when we have explicitly made visible the fundamental phenomenon of facticity: 'temporality' (not a category, but an existential)" (ibid., p. 25).

It is in being 'there' for a while in the proximity of 'today' that the Dasein can take advantage of its open space of publicness and develop a discourse 'about' itself in taking hold of and preserving itself and further assuming a definite way of having-been-interpreted and being-interpreted as essential traits of its being-in-the-world. Of course the 'being there' of Dasein (in each case our Dasein for a while at a particular time) is being in a world and largely meant as the factical life which in Heidegger's position stands by its very conception in alienation with the antithetical schema 'subject-object', i.e. consciousness vs object of knowledge, a question relegated to epistemological concerns. The ambiguities linger, however, in the way Heidegger purports to sidestep the Husserlian slipping to an 'isolated' from the world ego-self[1] by appealing, first, to temporality as a fundamental phenomenon of facticity and, second, to the how of being-of-concern and of attending to of Dasein which "shows itself as that wherefrom, out of which, and on the basis of which factical life is lived" and provides a phenomenological context for an interpretation on the most fundamental level of "the phenomenon of factical spatiality turning up there" and the phenomenon of being in a world (ibid., pp. 65-66).

Concerning the first, insofar as Dasein finds itself in a world that encounters as a series of initial givens in the now of actuality and those soon to come as closest in the awhileness (*Jeweiligkeit*) of the temporal particularity, something that implies a certain temporal 'sojourn' with respect to an actual given, it is inextricably linked with an origin of temporality for which Dasein itself can only tell from that out of which it is lived. This means of course that here lurks the not uncommon eventuality in all subjectively founded approaches to ontology of falling into an endless regression of reflecting-reflected in attempting to talk about temporality while being temporal.

Concerning the second, insofar as the being-in-the world of Dasein is associated with a 'being' itself of Dasein which is what it is in encountering the world and in such a way that in view of the world Dasein is what it is concerned about and attending to in the sense of caring (*Sorgen*), as a mode of the 'being there' of factical life, one has no way to accede to an ontological content of these alleged traits of Dasein but in its own terms. This naturally also concerns as modes of the 'being there' of Dasein, of the 'whiling', and 'sojourning' of facticity in the awhileness of its temporal particularity, such existentials as 'temporality', 'being in a world', 'dealings', 'being-interpreted' 'talk', the 'every-one', 'the world as being encountered', 'caring', 'spatiality', and in a proper sense the 'unpredictable' and 'strange' (ibid., p. 91).

In consequence the 'being there', taken as associated with the Heideggerian conception of Dasein and in no way defined in terms of an epistemological sense of spatio-temporal location, cannot but consign its ontological legitimacy to the peculiar subjectivity of Dasein and the way it constitutes the 'being there' as part and parcel of its own being-there-in-the-world. As mentioned above, the being-there-in-the-world of Dasein is largely meant in the Heideggerian sense of the 'roundabout' (*Umhaftes*) of worldly dealings with Dasein and in the modes in which it is concerned about the world, attends to it, and 'goes around' in it. In Husserlian terms the 'being there' is again reducible to a constituting subjectivity but in a quite different sense and in the context of the life-world[2] which while being a world in a

---

[1] The question of an 'isolated' from the world pure ego was, in fact, left by Husserl himself quite murky or, at least, ambivalent thus offering grounds for misinterpretations or conflicting views by the phenomenologists that followed suit. At some point Husserl regarded the construction of the eidos of transcendental ego as constituted unity unthinkable without a conception of the transcendental ego as factual, (Husserl (1973), p. 385), which makes by itself the assumption of a pure, isolated from the world ego quite problematic, while furnishing by the same token substantive credentials to the concept of the Heideggerian Dasein as essentially defined by its special kind of presence-in-the-world.

[2] For Husserl the validity of the life-world, the latter a phenomenological term describing *grosso modo* the world as the horizon of our intersubjectively defined presence, is derived out of the a priori 'constituting' intentionality of transcendental subjectivity, and accordingly life-world in its ultimate ontic meaning is immanently constituted according to the universal eidetic categories of thematic consciousness and the a priori norms of subjective (temporal) unity (Husserl (1976a), *Engl. transl.*, p. 69).

pre-predicative sense it is yet a subordinate field of the exercise of the constitutional-intentional faculties of all transcendental egos. Remarkably, in the *Late Texts on Time Constitution*, Husserl stated that the temporal present is given as a subjective spatial present that has a relationship with myself and my 'where' in various ways. In this sense the (subjective) 'how' of spatial present, although ontic, subjectifies further the temporal present and even so the temporal modes of orientation (Husserl (2001), p. 180).

Concluding here I bring to attention that concerning the ontologically critical notion of transcendence either in the sense of Dasein's 'thrownness' (*Geworfenheit*) to the world, a transcendence whose ecstatic, 'out-of-itself' temporality is a condition that Dasein can exist as its 'there', or in the sense of the Husserlian self-constitution of phenomenological ego (i.e., transcendence in immanence), Heidegger's and Husserl's views are not radically different if reduced to the origin of temporality and in a certain perspective even close[3] as will be further discussed in the next.

3 Aspects of the Debate Ontology vs Epistemology

It is a commonly accepted fact that at least since early last century there is some kind of mutual influence between ontology classically conceived and epistemology, as ever new breakthroughs in the latter, both on the level of theory and of refined experience, bear an osmotic relationship with ideas long standing as the quintessence of ontology:[4] the inquiry on the essential nature of the things the world is made of, either in the sense of extensible things (*res extensa*), or in the sense of what was thought to be thinking substance (*res cogitans*). Quantum mechanics, for example; "By emphasizing the role of man's observation and action in the very definition of reality and of truth, these conceptions do in fact reflect quite faithfully the evolution of modern science - in particular, they go a long way - it seemed to me - toward the solution of some of the conceptual difficulties of quantum mechanics, which appear as paradoxes when the transcendent reality of the things is kept, as in the older theories". And as, by the same token, the notion of localized objects in quantum theory may be just a construct this may also liberate us "from the apparent necessity of considering them (*auth add.*: individual macroscopic objects as existing independently of ourselves) as more basic than numbers, logical structures and so on." (D' Espagnat, B. (1999), *Perdo's Debate*, pp. xxii, xxix).

If a distinction along these lines between ontology and epistemology proved gradually after the 19th century to be in weak defense, it was further blurred by the introduction and advance of quantum theory in the last century to the point of talking of

---

[3] See: Moran (2014), pp. 507, 510.

[4] The term osmotic appearing twice in the text is not intended to have any ontological or other meaning except for its rather loose literary use to refer to the (existing) mutual influence ontological philosophy and epistemology have developed over the last two centuries. Yet if the author would be inclined to think in terms of the more restricted physical meaning of osmotic relation, i.e., in terms of the spontaneous vs. forced flow, he would choose philosophy, in the Husserlian sense of a universal eidetic science, over science in the conventional sense as representing the spontaneity of the flow.

an 'underdetermination' of the metaphysics by the physics,[5] an evolution that has put into doubt the realist stance in the philosophy of science insofar as quantum phenomena such as the problems of the ontological change (e.g., in the double-slit experiment) or the debate on the non-individuality of quantum objects[6] seem to fly into the face of a convinced realist. This is to say that insofar as the physics and the mathematics involved seem to be well entrenched, the situation gives extra grounds to the possibility of the wildest metaphysical assumptions in view of the data at our disposal. Of course it is known that even on the abstract theoretical level one has to face issues relating to the conception of a quantum field in terms of properties of space-time regions rather than of space-time points (this latter option excluded due to the non-locality of quantum phenomena), since a properties-based account of a quantum field 'overlaps' with a relativity based conception of space-time in the following sense: If there is indeed possible a properties-based description of a quantum field in terms of space-time regions, then insofar as the latter are reducible by relativity to relations between objects which in turn help configurate the structural properties of the field in which they are found, then obviously a 'backdoor' circularity arises. More than pointing to an incompatibility between general relativity and quantum theory proper what one may also find out here is the metaphysical distinction between things and properties (or relations) of things in the sense that properties can never be sufficient enough toward a complete and each time unique description of things inasmuch as, according to Quine, "the total field (*auth add.*: of our knowledge, or beliefs) is so undetermined by its boundary conditions, experience, that there is much latitude of choice as to what statements to reevaluate in the light of any single contrary experience" (Quine (1961), pp. 42–43). In Quine's brand of pragmatism ontological questions are indeed "on a par with questions of natural science" in the sense that total science is a system whose edges are kept squared with experience, while the rest, that is, the core of the system "with all its elaborate myths or fictions, has as its objective the simplicity of laws" (ibid., p. 45).[7]

Specific to the ontology vs epistemology debate is a debate concerning the separation between conceptual and factual in general, recognized as a rather fuzzy one from the time of Quine's *Two dogmas of empiricism* and further claimed by Marsonet to owe to a kind of 'ontological opacity' in the sense that "our ontology is characterized by the fact that the things of nature are seen by us in terms of a conceptual apparatus that is substantially influenced by mind-involving elements"

---

[5] See e.g. van Fraassen's views in van Fraasen (1985) and van Fraasen (1991).

[6] See e.g., D. Krause's views in Krause (2011), Arenhart and Krause (2014) and Krause and Arenhard (2020).

[7] In *Two dogmas of empiricism*, Quine's view of physical as well as of abstract objects essentially as convenient posits toward "working a manageable structure into the flux of experience" is primarily driven by his pragmatist concerns and correspondingly of no particular significance as to an ontological inquiry into the sense of being of objects as such. Yet his attitude of preserving an experience-independent conceptual corpus as a means to accommodate recalcitrant experience at the 'edges' is a telling sign of the ways epistemological issues may conflate with ontological concerns. This is also related with Quine's objectual interpretation of quantification, in the sense that it is not a substitutional quantification that is relevant to ontology but the quantification over the values of the variables when taken as objects in the domain over which these variables range.

(Marsonet (2018), p. 16). One could even argue according to Marsonet that on the assumption that our conceptual apparatus underlies any conception we might have of the world we live in as subordinate beings, there cannot be in principle an unconceptualized reality even as she does not deny the possibility of a mind-independent existence of unconceptualized reality (ibid., p. 17). This is a position however which, while staying clear of any phenomenological or other subjectively inclined influences, implies the relativisation of knowledge to the extent that the absoluteness of reality is at least partially ceded to our mental faculties thus making absolute truth an ideal-point 'at infinity' to which will converge all temporary truths shaped by our current mental handling of experiences. In fact an underdetermination of reality by the faculties of the mind may be thought of as in principle in accord with Husserlian phenomenology in these terms: the correlation between world-as-appearing and world-in-itself, between things-as-appearing and things-in-themselves points to an approximating ideal to which an experiencing subject can ever tend through progressing adjustments without ever reaching to it, since any factically implemented correction leaves in principle open the possibility of further adjustments (Husserl (1996), p. 52).

Whatever view one chooses to adopt the fact is that we have no way to tell how the world really is, even in recognizing that there can be a mind-independent objective reality, for we are made to encounter the natural world through our particular perceptual and conceptual capacities. In the final count the question is, and this is going to be dealt with in more detail, whether these capacities and in particular our conceptual ones can in principle be molded in such way as to provide totally different re-presentations of objective reality or whether these are a priori attributes of human subjectivity belonging to the eidetic[8] sphere rather than that of experiential contingency. The eidetically founded hypothesis based on essentially non-contingent assumptions (which in turn may ask for a revisiting of the concept of a priori) has nothing to do with the empirical limits posed by the very function of our sense organs with regard to natural stimuli, e.g., we all know that our retina is sensitive to a definite range of light wavelengths, thus giving credibility to the hypothesis that in another natural environment our perceptual capacities could be entirely different and therefore our scientific outlook of the world.

As a matter of fact the capital importance of the question of the re-presentation of reality vs. reality-in-itself may explain why the issue of the conceptual schemes we employ to constitute a coherent image of the world, on an intersubjective basis out of the contingency of real world experience, is of such importance as to be one of the foremost and at the same time most controversial issues of today's philosophy. Moreover it not only shapes the discussion on the relation between ontology and epistemology but has also a certain bearing on the question of scientific realism and the influence conceptualization schemes have on the realist vs. idealist outlook of

---

[8] By eidetic laws or eidetic attributes one can roughly determine what relates to properties of objects or states-of-affairs as regularities by essential necessity and not by mere facticity. One may consult E. Husserl's *Ideas I* in Husserl (1976b), Engl. transl., pp. 12-15.

reality (Marsonet (2018), p. 19).⁹ A case in point is the 'bundle' or the 'transcendental' view of quantum individuality, where according to the former view an individual is nothing more than its bundle of properties wherein by Leibniz's Principle of the Identity of Indiscernibles no two individuals can be absolutely indistinguishable, a thesis challenged on the grounds that individuality and distinguishability are conceptually distinct, whereas according to the latter view the principle of individuality must be 'something' beyond the properties of an object, a kind of Lockean substance, a hacceity described by Adams in Adams (1979) as 'primitive thisness'.

However, if we adopt the 'transcendental' individuality option then to the extent that a quantum state may be determined globally yet not in terms of its entangled parts due to non-separability situations, the limits according to which we can attribute to a quantum system a definite state are quite variable, in which case the controversy concerning the notion of a quantum property is transposed to the notion of the 'substrate'-bearer of such properties. It follows that given the variability of quantum states due to experimental or generally observational circumstances it is highly dubious whether one can assign to what might stand as the 'reification' of each quantum state the role of the unalterable substrate of varying determinations, something that entails its non-eligibility in terms of substance in the Aristotelian sense and consequently the non-feasibility of the attribution of predicates in a linguistic-grammatical context (Bitbol (1998), pp. 84–85).

As for the 'bundle of properties' option, in which a quantum individual (if we accept the conventional notion of individuality as applicable to quantum objects) is nothing but a bundle of properties, we may stumble upon the following problematic situations. First, one may argue that the philosophical problem of defining an object in terms of its properties in the strong sense of rendering unto it also the attribution of self-identity is bound to the following constraints: the Principle of the Identity of Indiscernibles (*PII*) to which it is traditionally associated the 'bundle of properties' option can be at best only contingently true, for, in principle, there can never be an exhaustive enumeration of the properties of an object in the real world of experience, nor is it possible to apply in such a context a universal-existential quantification where a notion of finitistic may not be rigorously defined in accepting Quine's objectual sense of quantification. Besides, *PII* clearly fails in quantum mechanics and consequently cannot guarantee individuation in terms of state-dependent properties in analogy with classical physics where at least two forms of *PII* are violated.¹⁰

---

⁹ A. Chakravartty in Chakravartty (2017) has vowed to explain why it is that any sort of scientific ontology involves at least the tacit acceptance of some metaphysical inferences, arguing that "scientific and even everyday observations are theory laden in the sense that theoretical beliefs held prior to observation significantly shape how they are experienced and described" (Chakravartty (2017), p. 56). However, in spite of Chakravartty's invocation of metaphysical inferences as having a significant a priori dimension due to their substantial conditioning on non-empirical considerations in terms of which the explanatory virtues of a given theory or hypothesis of observable phenomena are reducible to underlying objects, events, or properties, he actually nowhere proceeds to a discussion of the a priori dimension of metaphysical inferences in purely ontological terms, much less so in subjectively founded ones.

¹⁰ The three forms of *PII*, are: *PII*(1), stating that it is not possible for two individuals to possess all properties and relations in common, the form *PII*(2) that excludes spatio-temporal properties and the strongest form *PII*(3) that includes only monadic, non-relational properties alluding in a certain sense to

Second, a concept of property in terms of an observable is de facto referred to some kind of instrumentation in a way that instruments are not there only to register a property but become a de facto part of its definition. Moreover if we assimilate the quantum states to a kind of properties it seems hardly appropriate to attribute such properties to whatever physical system at whatever time owing to the well-known quantum effect of non-separability (ibid., pp. 83–84). This means that while a quantum system can be globally assigned a quantum state, this is not the case with its subsystems. As it is the case, the parts-subsystems of a global system cannot be possibly assigned a quantum state, in the course of interactions, but only through a process of disentanglement which implies in the final count the 'observation' of a subjectivity as 'being there' and moreover as being conscious of 'being there'.

Now if we stick to Quine's view that no statement can ever be free from an ultimate reference to experience, conceptual schemes like classical mechanics or quantum theory may only become primary bearers of truth to the extent that it is not solely the empirical content of the conceptual system that justifies by itself its empirical significance but also the critical presence of language that helps make our picture of reality coherent in a way that the truth of a statement significantly depends on the particular conceptual scheme adopted. For instance, talking about the individuality of quantum objects means that they can be assigned through the setup and implementation of a quantum measurement, a continuous (by re-identification) identity, a position, the possibility to be counted, etc. Then one may wonder how they could be compatible, in the sense of individuals, with quantum field realities and such quantum properties associated with quantum field theory as quantum entanglement and non-locality. This could entail, in consequence, that 'names' for quantum objects, e.g. a positron, do not correspond to some detached 'piece' of reality but to 'notations' whose use is prescribed by the structure of the corresponding theory (Putnam (1995), pp. 60–61).

A typical example of the effect a conceptual scheme has in idealizing empirically based statements, for instance, those turned by universal-existential quantification to mathematical-logical ones, is the topological definition of the closure[11] of a subset S of a topological space X in which the closure $\overline{S}$ of S does not exist in reality as it is impossible to enumerate the points x of the space X whose neighborhoods would have a non-empty intersection with S. Yet what is empirically evident only on a limited finite scale it may still acquire on an infinite scale a certain ontological status in terms of the proper formal theory, in other words in terms of the specific conceptual scheme.

We can therefore say that insofar as ontology may be found 'internal' to the language, it is internal to the conceptual scheme or world view one adopts (Marsonet

---

Footnote 10 (continued)

Leibniz's views on monadology. For details see: Identity and Individuality in Quantum Theory, (*Stanford Encyclopedia of Philosophy*): https://plato.stanford.edu/entries/qt-idind/#PII.

[11] Roughly said the closure $\overline{S}$ of a subset S of a topological space X is the union of the set S together with its limit points, the latter meant as the points of X whose neighborhoods have non-empty intersections with S.

(2018), p. 25). Talking in phenomenological-constitutional terms language can be shaped by extra-linguistic considerations which may be not ontological properly meant but nevertheless reduce to the peculiar ontology of being-in-constituting. In such view the ontological content of existential statements referring to well-meant objects of the world is reducible, on a constitutional level, to an immanent co-existence of noematic[12] objectivities conceived in turn as the unity of the (indefinite) multiplicity of their profiles something that implies also the question of a subjective origin of temporality. Even in statements in which one refers to his own self as a meaningful syntactical part "he must have already objectified his own subjectivity (in the unity of its temporal profiles) prior to any reference to himself as the singular term of a predication. It is naturally raised then the question of the origin of an ontology of being in general (including the being of logical objects) in accepting that 'being' as an object of reflection is the re-identification within the immanence[13] of consciousness of the multiplicity of its kinetic-temporal profiles" (Livadas (2018), pp. 330–331).

Consequently language as organically incorporated in our conceptual scheme not only offers a measure of autonomy with respect to the contingency of the natural world but approached in constitutional terms may be further reducible to a manifestation of the ontological aspects of a subjectivity-in-constituting. Indicative in this sense, though by no means phenomenological in proper sense, are Marsonet's arguments, drawing on Quine's insistence on "the presence and the extent of man's conceptual sovereignty in the formation of conceptual schemes", that point to a kind of transcendental shift to an immanence of the mind and lead her to the conclusion "there is, here, room for a return of the a priori on the stage. Language is something whose ultimate comprehension lies outside the domain of science" (Marsonet (2018), p. 26).

4 Why Temporality is a Prerequisite to Ontology? The Clues from Phenomenology

Understanding or interpreting ontology in terms of temporality and in reverse order the impossibility of thinking of (inner) temporality but in terms of the being in absolute sense is not what could come to the mind of an ontologist of the classical mold at least not until the crossing between the epistemological concerns of the last century and the advent of subjectively inclined philosophies paved the way to an assessment of a possible inherent connection between ontology and temporality. As known this implied the assessment of being as 'being posited' and in the ways it is being

---

[12] A noematic object is constituted by certain a priori modes as a well-defined object immanent to the temporal flux of a subject's consciousness, in simpler terms an object as meant and in the modes it is meant. More in Husserl's it Ideas I; Husserl (1976b), Engl. transl., pp. 229-232.

[13] Immanence, a properly phenomenological term, can be roughly characterized the 'interiority' of consciousness in contrast to all that is 'external' to it. An immanent object is thought of as a correlate of intentional consciousness as opposed to a transcendent to the consciousness common physical object whose objectivity is put anyway by phenomenology into brackets.

posited, a quest that would open new inroads toward a non-naturalistic comprehension of consciousness, a vital part being the modes by which it may be a bearer of temporality in the Bergsonnian sense or, in the more radical Husserlian sense a constituting factor of temporality, or yet a mode of being of Dasein in the Heideggerian sense, with all the subsequent phenomenologically inspired ramifications within the global frame of continental philosophy. One such attempt to reconcile ontology with fundamental phenomenological tenets yet without leaving aside epistemic, reductionistic concerns is Woodruff-Smith's three-facet ontology scheme in which on the basis of the three assumed aspects of every entity (form or quiddity—appearance—substrate) "ontology and phenomenology interact in our overall theory of consciousness and its place in the world" (Smith Woodruff (2004), pp. 16–26). In these terms, and notwithstanding the 'inherent' drive of most anglo-saxon philosophers to categorize concepts in a deeply entrenched analytic habit, Woodruff-Smith argues that phenomenology is ontological insofar as we use our ontology "to describe our experience, its intentional relation to objects in the world, and the things we are conscious of in perception, thought, and action" and in reverse order ontology is phenomenological insofar as "it recognizes the existence of our own consciousness, as we must in saying what exists" (ibid., pp. 16–17).

In a radical shift of view in which the question of being is transposed to a clarification of the questioning subject as being (e.g., the Heideggerian Dasein), the ontological question in a kind of Copernician inversion can reduce to the particular sense of being of the 'questioner'. Therefore in view of our being as 'questioners', we may opt along phenomenological lines either for accepting Heidegger's proposal to bring the absoluteness of the subjective factor to the level of phenomenon, so that we can draw out of the phenomenal givenness of Dasein certain basic structures that may clarify the question of being, or enter into a Husserlian spiraling regression of constituting the eidos of the transcendental ego through the transcendental ego as factual, that is, in terms of my real situation or possibility. According to Husserl, insofar as based on the apodicticity of the transcendental subjectivity and its validated world therein we proceed to the ideative construction of eidë we are found in the realm of absolute ontology and correlatively in that of mundane ontology (Husserl (1973), p. 385). In both Heideggerian and Husserlian options the 'incursion' of the temporality factor proves indeed to be ineluctable.

A telling sign of the predominance of temporality concerns in talking about the being of entities is Heidegger's assertiveness about the role time has to play in distinguishing the kinds of being so as to categorize the traditional realms of being "according to temporal, supratemporal, and extratemporal being". Heidegger argued, furthermore, that in taking up the question of being one would come across the phenomenon 'time' and accordingly be led to an explication of time in the ensuing order: (1) The description of the field in which the phenomenon of time becomes manifest which is essentially the exposition of the question of being (2) The exposition of time itself and (3) The conceptual interpretation (Heidegger (1979), *Engl. transl.*, pp. 140–141).

In fact there can hardly be found more compelling statements on the essential association between being and (inner) time than Heidegger's assertions in the *History of the Concept of Time*, that "The being, in which Dasein can be its wholeness authentically as being-ahead-of-itself, is time" and also "Not 'time is' but 'Dasein qua time temporalizes its being'" [*Nicht: Zeit ist, sondern: Dasein zeitigt qua Zeit sein Sein*] (ibid., p. 319). In other words, there is no possible Dasein which would be in its very sense otherwise meant than temporally particular (*jeweiliges*), at a concrete time, this being its inalienable characteristic.

It seems that a sense of 'integration' of the notion of temporality in purely ontological concerns is conveyed by the description of so-called dynamic ontologies in which "all beings are fundamentally related to each other in their respective processual being, their becoming, evolving, and perishing." (Röck (2019), p. 35). Somewhat akin to the Husserlian description of temporal constitution in terms of the factual, phenomenologizing ego (*faktische phänomenologisierende Ego*), T. Röck draws a demarcation line between time without 'temporality' meant as associated with building-block-ontologies in which temporality as the experienced flow of time has no intrinsic relation to the being of entities that exist, and temporality as a continuous interrelated flow in which beings are only meant as being-in-constituted. This leads to a conception of dynamic ontologies in the following sense.

"Dynamic ontologies are unified by the claim that the quality of flow in lived time, i.e. temporality, cannot be divorced from being without oversimplification. In a dynamic understanding of reality thus temporality becomes a genuine ontological feature; there is no ontological 'basis' or 'substrate' that is not fundamentally temporal. In this ontology change or being temporal is not an accident but the primary property of what there is [...] There are no a-temporal ideal entities[14] shaping the true form of existence behind the changing world of our perception. In dynamic ontologies reality is a constant flux, a process whose future is not yet decided and whose past is continuously formed by the present" (ibid., p. 36).

As a matter of fact the conception of dynamic ontologies makes for an approach that fails to consider time as self-constituting and, inquiring *a tergo*, to reach to an absolute subjective origin possible to break up the infinitely regressing chain of reflecting-reflected. In the inevitably naturalistic slipping of the dynamic ontologies approach, not only the reflection on the origin of time or simply the act of reflecting-on would be impossible but one would be deprived of any sense of retention and protention or of the double-intentionality of consciousness for evidently these are not features of consciousness belonging to the sphere of constituted. I point out that Husserl was so adamantly supportive of the absolute subjective modes of time that he declined to view time as a phenomenon, stressing instead that transcendental, egological time belongs as form to my own self, to all that is transcendentally experienceable (e.g., the transcendental specification of the I am, I was, I will be) in a way that in this temporality what is multiple is proper to me under the title subjective modes, including real spatiotemporal world and the multiplicity of transcendent 'appearances' in the broadest sense (Husserl (1973), pp. 362–363).

In consequence all talk about past, present, and future in the understanding that "sheer temporal existence incorporates, entwines and connects all of these

---

[14] For an argumentation in favor of a refutation of the notion of mathematical objects as immutable and a-temporal ones, see: Livadas (2017), sec. 3, 5.

dimensions in their constant becoming" (Röck (2019), p. 42), without taking account of inner temporal co-existence as the objectified form of some transcendental absolute origin and source of *prima causa*, leads, in my view, to the ambivalent position that: "Time as ontological temporality is inherently plural and interrelated, so there are as many temporalities as there are becoming entities that are all connected into a tapestry of temporality that we can reflect upon, but not measure. [..] The understanding of temporality in dynamic ontologies is therefore always multiple, facetted and interwoven and not linear, progressive or unified" (ibid., p. 43).

This said, one is faced with the quandary of either reducing ontology to a kind of subjectivity (say, Dasein) whose essence cannot be otherwise apprehended but as being-in-the-world in the temporal modes of its 'being there' in which case one is left without an absolute non-reflective origin as its pre-objective *prima causa* or settle for an absolute subjectivity as pure transcendence which is however unthinkable without a factual ego by necessity associated with constituted temporality. This makes that the 'being there' in general, as inextricably linked with the question of self-constituting temporality, proves to be a 'parallel narrative' of the ontology of absolute being, one whose elusiveness may be simply due to the fact that no thinking substance can think about itself in absolute terms. This state-of-affairs, as will be discussed in the next section, is reflected into some 'gray zones' when questions of ontology are re-calibrated in the form of questions about phenomena in the domain of epistemological discourse.

5 Inquiring on the Sense of 'Being There' as Epistemically Meant

A sense of being as 'being there', implying a sort of inner temporality on the part of the 'questioning entity', can possibly come up on account of logical-mathematical objects (or object generative formulas) and also physical (quantum) ones. This approach being of a holistic character, may view quantum or generally physical objects except for material ones also as objects (or relations) re-presentable in abstraction in the context of a formal-mathematical metatheory, consequently as constrained not only by their status of physical objects as such but also, in virtue of their status as formal-mathematical ones.

Taking for example a purely logical-mathematical notion, that of ω-consistency[15] of a formal system, applied in the proof of Gödel's first incompleteness theorem, we have that while, on the formal level, there could be an infinite series of provable identical formulas 'indexed' by natural number substitutes of the free variable, yet a universal quantification over an indefinite horizon over these free variables may not yield a provable formula (Kleene (1980), p. 207). An interpretation of this paradoxical situation may be found on a metatheoretical, more specifically subjectively founded level on these grounds: there is possibly "some infinity factor underlying universal quantification over an indefinite horizon which is non-eliminable by a discrete 'stepwise' approximation" (Livadas (2017), p. 99). For it is doubtful that one

---

[15] As a matter of fact ω-consistency is easily proved to imply simple consistency.

could proceed from an infinitely proceeding sequence of formulas $\neg P(0)$, $\neg P(1)$, .., $\neg P(n)$, .., which if meant as objectivities of understanding in the Husserlian sense correspond to a series of finitistic meaning-contents, to the formula $(\forall x) \neg P(x)$ whose domain of quantification is an indefinitely extending field in actual presentation, without conceding to a sort of inner temporal unity.

This temporal unity should 'cover up the vacuum' left between, say, a finitistic stepwise process ideally extensible *ad infinitum* and its 'completion' over an indefinite horizon presenting itself as an objectivity of understanding in the present now. In fact the recourse to a justification on subjectively based grounds may be implicitly needed every time a universal-existential quantification purportedly determines formal mathematical objects or states-of-affairs as well-defined ones in actual presentation.[16] In this sense both Gödel's incompleteness results in their various forms can be seen as due to the insufficiency of finitistic arithmetical means to represent meta-mathematical statements incorporating a non-rigorous finitistic content.

Mathematics had ever had to deal less with a naturalistic sense of infinity and more (at least implicitly) with infinity as a free of spatio-temporal constraints, indefinitely extensible objectivity presentable in completion in the actual now. One may argue that this 'surplus' of infinity in intuitive evidence corresponding to a state-of-affairs of consciousness itself as unity in contradistinction with finitistic, stepwise procedures, can be found in disguise under various forms in mathematical constructions over time starting from the non-definiteness of incommensurable magnitudes to the infinitesimal numbers of classical calculus to the paradoxes of Cantorian infinities reaching up to the modern theory of large cardinals. It may be even said that we can hardly enter a thorough discussion about the mathematics of infinity from an epistemological viewpoint without entering the subjective factor, say the 'questioning entity', which can verify its 'being there' as an indisputable evidence in the present now and in the modes in which it is objectivity-constituting in temporal terms. In such view one should take into account the possibility of shaping an ontology by the sheer presence of a constituting within-the-world subjectivity, possibly having epistemological implications insofar as the "mathematical form is suggestive of ontological form and the mathematical form of a piece of physical theory is integral to its content" (Smith Woodruff (2004), p. 14).

In fact nowhere in current epistemology is the impact of the subjective factor on the ontological quiddity of a physical state-of-affairs more evident than in quantum theory. There is no free pass, so to say, to a pre-determined architecture of reality inasmuch as, the classical approximative description of the macroscopic world put aside, the 'blinding' excess of proximity stands as a 'covering veil' to a complete knowledge on the part of the participatory subject (Bitbol (1998), p. 108)). Further it is known that quantum theory defies Kant's transcendental theory of knowledge

---

[16] Presentation in actuality as a general state-of-affairs should be understood in a deeper phenomenological sense as the implementation of the subjective character of the 'being there' in the world. I point out that for Husserl everything belonging to this world has its origin in the primeval flux of the living present (*lebendige Gegenwart*) which is essentially the mode of being of primeval ego (*Ur-Ego*), the *originaliter* known primeval phenomenal being, (Husserl (2001), pp. 4, 7).

in the first place since any substantive determination of objects by means of their properties in quantum measurements is undermined *in rem*, therefore making an epistemological mimesis and *a fortiori* an ontological projection problematic. In this sense it would be absurd to attribute to each quantum measurement result, irreversibly linked to a particular experimental history, a definite property that an object might have before the measurement since measurement or 'observational' tools themselves contribute to its determination (ibid., pp. 81–82). Naturally the refutation of the classical concept of property leads to a refutation of the concept of the bearer of properties, that is, of a quantum object in the sense of an invariant substrate of variable determinations, something reflected in quantum statistics for which the classical principle of counting is substituted by the principle of the interchangeability of particles (in the Bose-Einstein and the Fermi-Dirac statistical models), fueling a heated debate on the question of the individuality of quantum objects for which the field of discussion has been made wide enough to include arguments having purely philosophical or metaphysical relevance.[17]

At the level of epistemology the bizarre dissociation of being and the knowledge-about-being in quantum interactions is implied by the 'independence' of the truth-values of propositions that assign determinate values to observables in the implementation of a measuring process. Put in simpler words, independently of en eventual adoption of the alternative theory of hidden variables which is anyway contradicted as a 'local' theory by Bell's inequalities, the question about the properties a system might possess between two measurements remains high in the epistemological agenda and certainly more so in the ontological one. In fact the measurement question leads us either to the delusion of wondering what goes on 'in-between' when we concede to certain definite eigenvalues in the process of measurement or to an acceptance of the incompleteness of quantum theory to describe a physical situation on the basis of the continuity of the unitary evolution operator (Boge (2018), p. 55).

Either way one has to settle for assumptions that still leave the ontological dimension of the quantum state existence pending. On the level of theory we have, for example, to settle either for a notion of consistent quantum histories,[18] a technical term characterizing quantum processes over time in which a notion of consistence essentially stands for the counterfactual conclusion that the properties of a system between measurements are such that nothing would be changed by a checking device as to the probability of the final measurement result, or one has to concede to von Neumann's reduction postulate.

On the other hand von Neumann's reduction postulate (or 'the reduction of the wave function' postulate) can be seen as introducing indirectly the need for a self-constituting time flux by assigning to the mathematical translation $\tau(s(t))$ of the

---

[17] Arguments in favor or against quantum individuality can be indicatively found in: Dorato and Morganti (2013), Krause (2011), Arenhart and Krause (2014), Krause and Arenhard (2020), Redhead and Teller (1992).

[18] For a more detailed reference to the consistent quantum histories approach the reader can look, for example, at Isham (1994) and Griffiths (1984).

physical state $s(t)$ of a quantum system Q_i upon a first-kind measurement[19] at time t the same eigenvector ψ_κ as to the translation of the state $s(t_1)$ of the quantum system Q_i at time t_1 soon after the measurement (Livadas (2012), p. 164). Even on the supposition that the measuring device may be treated in quantum mechanical fashion and the pointer in the sense of 'pointer observable' might be in a superposition of states, von Neumann's reduction postulate reduces by a joint projection operator the sum state to a state with definite eigenvalues. Yet the question of where exactly is the spatiotemporal 'there' in which the reduction postulate comes into effect, whether it is somewhere in the broad environment of the system, or in the proximity of the measuring apparatus, or yet in the brain or mind of the observer in terms of the triangle measured system—measuring apparatus—'observer' is by all accounts left unanswered. It is known that while von Neumann and Schrödinger recognized in quantum measurement and the accompanying subjective perception a process relative to the physical environment yet not reducible to it, they nevertheless did not attribute the so-called Heisenberg cut (implied by the reduction postulate) to the consciousness of the 'observer'[20] which Wigner did by giving a special significance to the registration of the measurement result by the observer (Boge (2018), pp. 62–64).

Even if we assume von Neumann's reduction postulate or Van Fraassen's modal interpretation of quantum mechanics as 'external' metatheoretical conditions in a purely logical way we can be hardly led to a complete description on the level of theory, much less in ontological terms, of the 'change of states' that takes place during the measurement process in the compound system 'system + apparatus'. The theoretical jump of truth-values in the process of measurement, interpretable on a formal level in terms of the absence of an isomorphism between Boolean and non-Boolean structures (the latter corresponding to internal entangled states), sets the constraint, according to Grib, upon a Boolean 'observer' to concede to the existence of an objectivated, continuous time in terms of which he must proceed (Grib (1993), p. 2.397).

6 Is There a Clue to the Enigma of 'Being There'? Conclusion

If terms like being-in-constituting, intentional consciousness, constitution, a priori, inner temporality, etc. predominantly belong to the field of phenomenology, it is of no surprise to anyone well informed in the current issues of epistemology that they may be presently found possibly in variant forms in texts of the philosophy of science and the philosophy and foundations of quantum mechanics in particular. In

---

[19] A first-kind measurement is one in which the measured quantum system described by the quantum state s is taken to interact with the measuring apparatus described by the quantum state φ, so that the total wave function before the interaction is $s \cdot \varphi$.

[20] An interesting article on the purported implication of the Husserlian phenomenological ego in the quantum measurement question, giving as a matter of fact also some clues to the intricacies of the concept of pure ego itself, is S. French's *A Phenomenological Solution to the Measurement Problem? Husserl and the Foundations of Quantum Mechanics*, French (2002).

more concrete terms, except for the role of the consciousness of an 'observer' in the process of quantum measurement which is still a matter of vivid debate among quantum theorists and philosophers of science, some other *prima facie* ontologically based or even purely phenomenological notions are being recast in the mold of quantum theory proper. One such case is the recalibration of the notion of the constitutive a priori in the context of quantum theory in Boge's *Quantum Mechanics Between Ontology and Epistemology* which refers also to the works of Friedman, Friedman (1999), Reichenbach, Reichenbach (1920), and to the consciousness founded approach of the Many Worlds Interpretation[21] (**MWI**) (Boge (2018), pp. 264–269).

Drawing originally from Kant's synthetic a priori judgments as constitutive of the objects of experience, Reichenbach argues that there is a fundamental distinction between two essentially different principles within the context of any given scientific theory: the axioms of coordination and the axioms of connection, the latter being empirical laws in the usual sense involving terms and concepts that are already sufficiently well-defined by the axioms of coordination. The axioms of coordination are in their part constitutively a priori, in the sense of non-empirical principles laid down antecedently to ensure the empirical well-definedness of the objects or states-of-affairs of the theory. For instance, in general relativity the infinitesimally Lorentzian manifold structure and the space-time topology susceptible to a pseudo-Riemannian metric may be thought constitutively a priori. In particular, pseudo-Riemannian metric "realized within this framework then is determined empirically from the distribution of mass-energy, and thus the specific principles of metrical geometry now count as axioms of connection" (Friedman (1999), pp. 60–62). Yet it is true that the axioms of coordination as constitutive a priori make way for what is objectively 'there' only at a given time and relative to a particular theory. Moreover according to d'Espagnat the Kantian philosophy's constitutive a priori principles (and for that matter the axioms of coordination) may in fact become relativized a priori and as such weaken or altogether invalidate their purportedly inherent relation to the structure of our sensibility and understanding (Boge (2018), p. 334, and Friedman (1999), p. 1704).[22]

Friedman on the other hand, appealing to a theory's invariance group(s) to determine those parts of a theory having a constitutive a priori character, has suggested

---

[21] Boge refers to the decisive role attributed to consciousness in Zeh's and Wallace's interpretation of **MWI** in the sense that "only in relation to the experience of conscious beings can these (classical) 'worlds' (*auth. add.*: i.e., multiple universes) really be said to exist, because decoherence preserves one (highly entangled) state vector and never fully eliminates the off diagonal terms in a density matrix, while we (the somehow dynamically created conscious beings) do not perceive ourselves as simultaneously 'partly' in this and partly in that 'branch' " (Boge (2018), p. 269).

[22] Friedman has argued in Friedman (1999) that Kant's second tenet, namely that the (constitutive) a priori principles are given once and for all "independently of our observing and theorizing", becomes untenable by the evolution of science as the ground of prescriptive principles laid down '*à la carte*'. For instance the position that, insofar as objects are perceptible and conceivable by being embedded in a three-dimensional Euclidean space, the physical space has to be three-dimensional and Euclidean became ultimately untenable (ibid., p. 1704). The untenability in question is of course due to the general relativity theory.

that symmetries defined in terms of the invariance of an object with respect to a specified transformation group may help determine the essence of the object itself and gone as far as making a parallel with Husserl's eidetic variation in the determination of the essential being of objects.

However his argumentation seems weak in the following points: First, even as he refers to Kant's 'deduction of transcendental consciousness from invariance under different observational situations' Friedman's invariants (symmetries) as a priori definitive of objects are such only relative to a theory and consequently devoid of an ontological character unconstrained by the empirical limitations of the theory. This means that with a theory change certain 'a priori' principles may be demoted to merely factual statements that can become false under new circumstances. A typical example is general relativity in which logical-mathematical transformation rules (as L-rules) in the form of formulas containing the metric tensor in geometries of constant curvature (taken as constitutive a priori) are turned by the mass-dependent curvature of the space to rules identified with material inferences (P-rules) (Boge (2018), p. 336). The same talk can be held regarding quantum objects where what is constitutive of an object of a given kind may change with the acceptance of a new theory. Think for instance of the divergent views on the individuality of quantum objects depending on the particular version of the accompanying theory. Furthermore one can raise serious concerns whether the constitutive a priori principles in the particular sense might indeed provide what is objectively 'there' without the implication of the subjective-constitutive factor for which the determination of objects, say by symmetry-invariance, would be either eidetically founded by Husserlian doctrine or (in Heidegger's phenomenology) founded in the peculiar mode of being-in-the-world in terms of Dasein.

If we opt for the Husserlian version any conception of the essential being of objects, be they physical or abstract objects in mental re-presentation, would necessarily need to appeal to the possibility of intentional apprehension and noematic constitution on the part of a phenomenological ego on the admission that it 'belongs to the sense of anything contingent to have an essence and therefore an Eidos independently of constraints set by empirical contingency (Husserl (1976b), Engl. transl., p. 7). This in turn would do justice to the mentalistic content of Kant's second tenet properly conceived as postulating the constitutive a priori principles freed from the constraints of any particular theory. Consequently they would not be adaptable or revisable according to the broadening of our scientific outlook, even if they would remain bound to the necessities associated with a subject's presence in the life-world.[23]

Further it would be impossible to have a sound conception of the objective 'there' without a reduction to a sort of presence in the actual now as an unambiguous evidence necessarily entailing a subjective origin of actuality as a presuppositionless source of the objective 'there'. Presentification (*Vergegenwärtigung*) described in

---

[23] The a priori of the life-world, after the phenomenological Epochë, is thought to be made evident as a 'stratum' within the universal a priori of transcendental subjectivity.

Husserl's *Late texts on Time Constitution*[24] as the primordial mode of being of the transcendental ego, concretizes the enigma of 'being there' by being 'co-extended' to the immediate past and the a-thematically prospective future by means of a priori intentional forms[25] while reproducing itself at will in actuality possibly with everything stored in secondary memory. In this sense the phenomenological ego as making itself an unambiguous presence in actuality may pertain to the 'being there' of epistemology in the most general terms, in which case the reduction postulate of the quantum measurement theory may stand as a concrete demonstration of its epistemic relevance. Put in other words, the living present as form of being of the transcendental ego 'solidifies' in the actual now the temporal flux of experience, while by its very enactment nullifies the 'vacuity' between consciousness as passive receptivity (reflected) and consciousness as consciousness-of (reflecting). In epistemic terms one may therefore have, to cite the quantum measurement case, the possibility of identification of the quantum state registered by a detector with the consciousness of the same state as noematic re-presentation of a time-constituting ego.

In these terms the phenomenolo   ego (even in the lingering ambivalences of its pure self) as the subjectivity behind the 'being there' in temporal definiteness bears an inalienable affinity to the Heideggerian Dasein. As extensively discussed in Sect. 2 for Heidegger the articulation of the question of the sense of being means to exhibit the questioning (subject), meaning the Dasein itself, as an entity 'thrown' to the world in projecting itself ahead of itself. And in taking up the question of being, that is, in articulating its explication in terms of the Dasein (which we ourselves are), one ought to come across the phenomenon 'time' and accordingly be led to an explication of time (Heidegger (1979), *Engl. transl.*, pp. 148, 141). In such terms the question of being is ontologically reformulated into a question of a subjectively founded 'being-there-in-actuality', that is, into each (subjective) being's temporal particularity and the foundation of its very individuality for that matter. In that case a sense of individuality in purely subjective terms and in the specific 'being there' in objective terms would be the ultimate foundation of the definiteness of a situation/state-of-affairs in the actual present; in particular, to talk in quantum theory terms, of the disentanglement of a quantum state upon 'observation'. This calls, of course, for a relation of subject to object which has nothing to do with the supertemporal relations we know of in the ideal universe of classical ontology, for it is a relation lived out and effectively carried out by the individual beings we are, i.e., as embodied beings endowed with a constituting consciousness irreducible to objectivist, reductionistic considerations. The temporal particularity as the definiteness of being of Dasein's transcendence toward the world could be thought as Heidegger's most evident point of convergence with the Husserlian conception of the actual presence as original mode of being of the transcendental ego. It is on these grounds, one may argue, that we could find a clue to resolving the enigma of 'being there' both in

---

[24] See Husserl (2001), pp. 4, 7.

[25] These are of course the well-known to any knowledgeable with the fundamentals of phenomenology intentional forms of retention (primary memory) and protention (a-thematic expectation).

ontological and epistemological sense without following the blind alley of a reductionistic explication.

However it seems questionable that the 'being there'[26] might be eliminated to the essence of being, namely to what is implied by the consciousness-of, and yet consciousness without reference to a 'being there' (or deprived of a sense of being as 'being there') is unthinkable. In the same reasoning, inner temporality as temporality-in-constituting meant in purely subjective terms, should be also considered as subsumed to the necessity of the 'being there' for otherwise would reduce to the vacuous transcendence of an a-temporal subjective origin. In the final count this may be the riddle of the 'impermeability' of the question of a complete description of being as a phenomenon in actuality in the current scientific-epistemological edifice.

References

Adams R (1979) Primitive thisness and primitive identity. J Philos 76(1):5–26
Bitbol M (1998) L' Aveuglante Proximité du Réel. Flammarion, Paris
Boge F (2018) Quantum Mech Between Ontol Epistemol. Springer International Pub, Cham, Switzerland
Chakravartty A (2017) Scientific Ontology. Oxford University Press, New York
D'Espagnat B (1999) Conceptual foundations of quantum mechanics. Perseus Books, Reading, Mass
Dorato M, Morganti M (2013) Grades of individuality. A pluralistic view of identity in quantum mechanics and in the sciences. Philos Studies 163:591–610
French S (2002) A Phenomenological Solution to the Measurement Problem? Husserl and the Foundations of Quantum Mechanics. Studies History Philos Modern Phys 33:467–491
Friedman M (1999) Reconsidering Logical Positivism. Cambridge University Press, Cambridge
Grib AA (1993) Quantum logical interpretation of quantum mechanics: the role of time. Int J Theoretical Phys 32(12):2389–2400
Griffiths GR (1984) Consistent Histories and the Interpretation of Quantum Mechanics. J Stat Phys 36:219–272
Heidegger M (1986) Sein und Zeit, Tübingen: M. Niemeyer Verlag. Engl. transl., *Being and Time. A Translation of Sein und Zeit*, (1996), Transl. J. Stambaugh, Albany: State University of New York Press
Heidegger M (1979) Prolegomena zur Geschichte des Zeitbegriffs, Frankfurt am Main: Vit. Klostermann. Engl. transl.: (1985) History of the Concept of Time, transl. T. Kisiel, Bloomington: Indiana University Press
Heidegger M (1999) Ontology - The Hermeneutics of Facticity, engl. transl. van Buren, J., Bloomington: Indiana University Press
Husserl E (1973) Zur Theorie der Intersubjektivität, Drit. Teil, hsgb. Kern, I., Hua XV, The Hague: M. Nijhoff
Husserl E (1976a), *Die Krisis der Europäischen Wissenschaften und die Transzendentale Phänomenologie*, Hua VI, hsgb. Walter Biemel, Den Haag: M. Nijhoff. Engl. transl.: (1970), *The Crisis of European Sciences and Transcendental Phenomenology*, Transl. D. Carr, Evanston: Northwestern University Press
Husserl E (1976b) Ideen zu einer reinen Phänomenologie und phänomenologischen Philosophie, Erstes Buch, Hua Band III/I, hsgb. K. Schuhmann, Den Haag: M. Nijhoff. Engl. transl.: (1983), *Ideas*

---

[26] The notion of the 'being there' may be also thought, in terms of the discussion above, to be relevant with what Levinas described, citing Husserl's *Lessons for a Phenomenology of Inner Time Consciousness*, as the 'where' time, original impression, and consciousness conjugate, i.e., the original consciousness of time which is yet a null without sensation, more precisely without original impression (Levinas (1974), p. 40).

pertaining to a pure phenomenology and to a phenomenological philosophy: First Book, Transl. F. Kersten, The Hague: M. Nijhoff

Husserl E (1996) Erste Philosophie, (Zweiter Teil), Hua Band VIII, hsgb. R. Boehm, Dordrecht: Kluwer

Husserl E (2001) Späte Texte über Zeitkonstitution, Die C-Manuscripte, Hua Materialien Band VIII, hsgb. D. Lohmar, Dordrecht: Springer

Isham CJ (1994) Quantum Logic and the Histories Approach to Quantum Theory. J Math Phys 35:2157–2185

Kleene SC (1980) Introduction to Metamathematics. North-Holland Pub, New-York

Krause D (2011) The metaphysics of non-individuality. In: Videira AAP, Krause D (eds) Brazilian Studies in Philosophy and History of Science: An Account of Recent Works. Springer, New York, pp 125–145

Arenhart BJ, Krause D (2014) From primitive identity to the non-individuality of quantum objects. Studies History Philos Modern Phys 46:273–282

Krause D, Arenhard J (2020) Identical particles in quantum mechanics: favouring the received view, forthcoming in *Synthese Library*

Levinas E (1974) Autrement qu' être ou au-delà de l' essence. M. Nijhoff, La Haye

Livadas S (2012) The expressional limits of formal language in the notion of quantum observation. Axiomathes 22:147–169

Livadas S (2017) What is the nature of mathematical-logical objects? Axiomathes 27(1):79–112

Livadas S (2018) The transcendental source of logic by way of phenomenology. Axiomathes 28:325–344

Marsonet M (2018) On the Ontology/Epistemology Distinction. In: Wuppuluri S, Antonio Doria F (eds) The Map and the Territory. Exploring the Foundations of Science, Thought and Reality,. Springer, Cham, Switz, pp 15–35

Moran D (2014) What does Heidegger Mean by the Transcendence of Dasein? Int J Philos Studies 22(4):491–514

Putnam H (1995) Pragmatism. Blackwell, Oxford

Quine VW (1961) Two dogmas of empiricism. From a Logical Point of View. Harper & Row Pub, New York

Redhead M, Teller P (1992) Particle labels and the theory of indistinguishable particles in quantum mechanics. Brit J Phil Sci 43:201–218

Reichenbach H (1920) Relativitätstheorie und Erkenntnis Apriori. Springer, Berlin

Röck T (2019) Time for ontology? The role of ontological time in anticipation. Axiomathes 29:33–47

Smith Woodruff D (2004) Mind World. Essays in Phenomenology and Ontology. Cambridge University Press, Cambridge

van Fraasen B (1985) Statistical behaviour of indistinguishable particles: problems of interpretation. In: Mittelstaedt P, Stachow EW (eds) Recent developments in quantum logic. BI-Wissenschaftsverlag, Mannheim, pp 161–187

van Fraasen B (1991) Quantum mechanics: an empiricist view. Clarendon Press, Oxford

Is Existence an Ontologically Sound Term?

ABSTRACT: In this article I deal with a capital and perennial question of philosophy, the question of existence. Given the breadth of the question and the various angles and contexts in which it has been addressed, I have chosen to focus in the way phenomenology in general has faced the subtleties of the issue and come up with responses in dissonance with those of classical ontology. My intention to provide a convincing argumentation against the ontological certainties either of idealist or naive realist tendencies is primarily based, first, in showing the possibility of a subjective reduction of the question of existence and second, in highlighting the way the concept of existence may be `undermined' by this very reduction. Consequently this is a quest to thoroughly penetrate into the meaning of existence and possibly reach *in extremis* its ontological annihilation. A prominent place in the relevant discussion is held by the concept of infinity precisely for the motivation it gives for a radical reassessment of the content and scope of the concept of existence. The article attempts to integrate in its argumentation all main offshoots of original Husserlian phenomenology without being restrictively committed to anyone, while enriching the discussion with prompts from the realm of foundational mathematics and, marginally, even of quantum physics.

1. INTRODUCTION

It is known that over the centuries ontology was traditionally regarded as a branch of metaphysics dealing with ontological being (or the essence of being) in general, in a presuppositionless sense and in disregard of real world constraints. As ontological philosophy became more and more impregnated by the advancing progress of scientific knowledge it became subjected to influences ranging from logical or material empiricism to analytic philosophy and logicism to subjective idealism and so on. For all the diversity of these often conflicting philosophical attitudes, ontology may be assumed to basically deal with two problems more fundamental than those of epistemology, semantics or even logic: (a) What kinds of things exist? and (b) What is the nature or essence of these kinds? One may even wonder, in the bottom line, what existence means at all in which case he would either choose a possible clarification through a more encompassing philosophical or conceptual scheme or plunge into the kind of existential agony found in Sartre's *La Nausée*.

Sticking, for the moment, to the two questions above, I remind of Quine's statement in *On What There Is*:

A curious thing about the ontological problem is its simplicity. It can be put in three Anglo-Saxon monosyllables: 'What is there?' It can be answered, moreover, in a word – 'Everything' - and everyone will accept this answer as true".[1]

Of course Quine's answer to the question, that everything exists, is further refined by his application of the ontological commitment through forms of formal predication by

---

[1] W.V. Quine, *From a Logical Point of View* (New York: Harper & Row Pub, 1963), p. 1.

bounded quantifiers, a position concerning primarily the existence of genera of things, such as material objects, mental phenomena or abstract entities. If Quine's view is concordant with the Aristotelian tradition of taking the terms "existent", "being", "thing", and "object" as equivalent (which I share to a certain extent), there is another tradition, namely the one which takes "existence" as applying to concrete particulars in a more narrow Aontological sense than that, for instance, of "being" and "thing" in virtue of which one can have abstract objects that transtemporally subsist without existing, e.g., the set of all subsets of natural numbers in set theory.[2] On these grounds I agree with Glock's position, in *Does ontology exist?*, against Quine's naturalistic ontology, based on the argument that one cannot have an affirmation of existence by the sole instantiation of properties formalized in predicative formulas, a fact implying that the ontological question is largely reduced to the postulation of the types of expressions committing us to existence assumptions in the context of formal theory.[3] Ontological commitment through objectual interpretation of quantification except for contradicting common sense in the case of existence of fictional beings can simply lead to obvious paradoxes in case, for instance, one chooses the formula (∃x) [¬ x] or the well-known, self-referring formula (∃x∈ x) [$\mathcal{G}$(x)] leading to the Russell paradox.

On the other hand, I have certain reservations about Glock's view that the task of ontology

"consists not in establishing what there is, or in arguing for or against the existence of entities, but in clarifying what non-philosophical claims concerning the existence of various things amount to, and in analysing concepts like those of existence, of an object or of reality".[4]

For this means, first, that, as Glock seems to espouse, ontology would become a "second order" interpretation of the conceptual framework that "common sense and science employ in describing reality" a task more suitably assignable to the philosophy of science, and, second, that ontology would be deprived of the possibility of a priori intuitions relative to the sense of existence (or being) thus transforming itself simply to a meta-theory of science. My own argumentation will be shaped primarily along the following key prompts:
  (A) Existence as a phenomenon implying a physical presence
  (B) Existence as a phenomenon not implying by necessity a physical presence
  (C) Existence as a phenomenon reducible to the absoluteness of immanental[5] being, of which there can be no lower order reduction without "destructing" the essence of immanental being.
These will be discussed in some length in the next section in the intention of setting the terms in which to further treat the question of existence and generally of being. In the sections that follow Section 2, I will lay out the context of the discussion of the question

---

[2] H. J. Glock, "Does ontology exist?" *Philosophy*, 77 (2002): 235-256 at p. 242.
[3] In Quine's version of analytic ontologism, existence assumptions in a formal language containing only propositional connectives, predicates, the identity sign, quantifiers and their variables may be achieved through objectual interpretation of quantification; e.g., in order for the existential formula (∃x)[$\mathcal{A}$(x)∧$\mathcal{B}$(x)] to be true the domain over which the bounded variable x ranges must contain at least one object that may be substituted in both categorical forms $\mathcal{A}$ (x) and $\mathcal{B}$ (x).
[4] Ibid., p. 237.
[5] The term immanent/nce can be roughly explained to a non-phenomenologist as referring to what is or has become correlative (or "co-substantial") to the being of one's consciousness in contrast to what is "external" or transcendent to it.

of existence, by being based on phenomenology in general, especially concerning entities characterized as transcendent or even metaphysical by traditional empiricism, having in mind, for instance, the "ontology" of the infinite. This means that except for Husserlian phenomenology, I will take into account the views of philosophers who like Levinas, while being formed in the footsteps of Husserlian phenomenology, gradually demarcated themselves from Husserlian "orthodoxy" to the point of being possibly characterized as a kind of herecy. Yet to the extent that my approach and overall argumentation will be subjectively based, in other words the groundwork of the treatment of the question of existence will be about the irreducible origin of subjectivity, it is reasonable to consider also the views of such Husserlian "heretics". After all phenomenologists of every hue seem unanimous in seeking an ultimate subjective foundation of the question of existence, as they indeed seek to reduce the ontological being to a being accountable primarily in subjective terms.[6]

More precisely in Section 3 I enter into a discussion of the question of existence *in extremis* meaning that my intention is to inquire into the content of the concept of existence as deeply as possible, in my general philosophical orientation of course, without being restrictively committed to some globally encompassing philosophical doctrine even as Levinas' or Heidegger's ideas on the matter influence to a certain extent my view. My arguments of Section 3 have been put in more concrete tracks in Section 4, while the final Section 5 may be thought of as the culmination of my intended scope to attempt a reduction of the question of existence in the most ontologically fundamental sense to the question of existence as co-essential to the origin of temporality.

2. IN WHAT TERMS TO PUT THE CONCEPT OF EXISTENCE?

In what comes next I intend, as mentioned above, to discuss the following forms of existence:

(A) Existence as a phenomenon implying a physical presence
(B) Existence as a phenomenon not implying by necessity a physical presence
(C) Existence as a phenomenon reducible to the absoluteness of immanental being.

Concerning (A): it seems clear to say that no concept of existence in terms of physical presence can be founded in an absolute, self-standing sense, which means without being hetero-determined by a subjectivity to which it is transcendent. Furthermore this is a condition that may be seen as universally valid insofar as we humans may define primordial experience as eidetically prescribed. I quote below from Husserl's *Ideas I*:

> [..] when we ask about the mode of demonstration taken universally essentially determined by the positing of something transcendent - no matter how we might legitimately universalize its essence - we recognize that something transcendent necessarily must be experienceable not merely by an Ego conceived as an empty logical possibility but by any actual Ego as a demonstrable unity relative to its concatenations of experiences. But one can see [..] that what
> is cognizable by one Ego must, of essential necessity, be cognizable by any Ego. Even though it is not in fact the case that each stands, or can stand, in a relation of "empathy", of mutual understanding with every other, as e.g., not having such relationship to mental lives living on the

---

[6] D. Zahavi has argued extensively in: D. Zahavi, "Phenomenology" *in Routledge Companion to Twentieth-Century Philosophy*, ed. D. Moran, (Routledge. London, 2008), against the view that the various offshoots of Husserlian phenomenology, e.g., Heidegger's and Merleau-Ponty's versions, are mutually exclusive alternatives.

planets of the remotest stars, nevertheless there exist, eidetically regarded, essential possibilities of effecting a mutual understanding and therefore possibilities also that the worlds of experience separated in fact become joined by concatenation of actual experience to make up the one intersubjective world, the correlate of the unitary world of mental lives [..]*[7]*

More than just being a field of reference for any physical object/process constituted as such and such, the being of consciousness is self-standing in an absolute sense, meaning that while no real being by virtue of its appearances is necessary to the being of the absolute flux of consciousness this latter is an absolute being itself since by essential necessity "*nulla 're' indiget ad existendum*".[8]

Concerning (**B**): Is it meaningful to talk of existence as a phenomenon not implying by necessity a physical presence? The answer is yes, insofar as we have no difficulty to cite the instances (within immanence) of purely imaginary objects or of situations even of a surreal character. Or to cite the instances of imaginary objects as non-arbitrary re-presentations of what rational experience has taught us over time, a most common example being mathematical objects either as ideal geometrical ones or as abstract objects of mathematical theories. The question becomes trickier, though, if we ask how an object/state-of-affair's existence can be founded in the absence of its physical presence in excluding psychologically related reasons, e.g., having a rememoration from possible earlier encounters of the said object/state-of-affairs in an objective-physical sense. As it is known Husserlian phenomenology proposes a foundation in non-psychological terms, through the concept of intentional directedness (intentionality) in which nothing said about imagination or real perception as object-directed requires us to accept that such objects exist in real terms.[9]

In fact, what makes the directedness of a conscious act possible is not the existence *in rem* of the object but, except for the vacuous, non-eliminable character of the directedness itself, it is the "content" or "meaning" associated with the act, in phenomenological parlance the noema associated with the act. To take as an example logical-mathematical objects, to say that reason in mathematics and logic exhibits intentionality we intend, according to Tieszen, to say that in these fields our consciousness is directed toward mathematical and logical objects by virtue of rational mathematical experience encoded in corresponding logical-mathematical concepts.[10] Consequently without downplaying the role rational or other experience within-the-world might play in articulating what may be conceived as existence of the above class of objects, this kind of existence is however in an essential sense reducible to the immanental being, i.e., to the being and modes of absolute consciousness.

---

[7] Edmund Husserl, *Ideen zu einer reinen Phänomenologie und phänomenologischen Philosophie. Erstes Buch*, Hua Band III-I, hsgb. K. Schumann (Den Haag: M. Nijhoff, 1976). In English translation: *Ideas Pertaining to a Pure Phenomenology and to a Phenomenological Philosophy*, First Book, transl. F. Kersten, (The Hague: M. Nijhoff, 1983), p. 108.
[8] Ibid., p. 110.
[9] *In Logical Investigations*, (V. II, part I), Husserl stated that the intentional objects of mental presentation (*Vorstellung*) are the same as its real and possibly 'external' objects and that it would be nonsensical to distinguish between the two. Furthermore, irrespectively of whether we conceive of a divine creature, or of an intelligent being in itself, or of a physical thing or even a (fictional) round quadrangle, etc, these are all intentional objects, and it is irrelevant whether these objects exist, or whether they are fake or absurd . See: Edmund Husserl, E.: (1984), *Logische Untersuchungen*, Hua Band XIX/1, hsgb. U. Panzer, (Den Haag: M. Nijhoff, 1984). In Engl. translation: (2001), *Logical Investigations*, transl. J.N. Findlay, (New York: Routledge, 2001), p. 439.
[10] Richard Tieszen: *After Gödel: Platonism and Rationalism in Mathematics and Logic*, (Oxford: Oxford University Press, 2011), p. 129.

Is Existence an Ontologically Sound Term?

A special case is the way one may lay a foundation for the concept of mathematical infinity in contradistinction with real world spatiotemporal infinity, even though these options may well be thought as being in a certain sense interdependent. Attesting to this latter assertion may be taken, for instance, O. Bekker's claim in the *Mathematische Existenz* that modern developments in theoretical physics point to a genuine "transfinite" rather than to any kind of "measuring" experience as well as his reference to Weyl's contention that the sense of the transfinite in the analysis and physics can be (phenomenologically) traced to the ability of consciousness to "overpass its own shadow" for representing the transcendency[11]. As I consider the question of infinity critical for the clarification of the possibility of an absolute sense of existence I am going to deal with it more extensively in the next section.

At this point however a few words about the character of intentionality would be in order if, as above, we are going to interpret existence in general as necessarily implied by intentional directedness and only contingently (factually) by physical presence. If, in Husserlian view, intentionality is to be thought of as the vacuous, a priori trait of a consciousness to be consciousness-of, then one can pose the following two objections.

First, if intentionality is indeed an a priori attribute then how can one have accessibility to it other than through reflection which means that it would be no more a priori in the sense that it would be already objectified and re-presentable as a mirror reflexion? Obviously we could have here the not uncommon in transcendental phenomenology endless regression of reflecting-reflected which, as it is known, leads to what critics of phenomenology have characterized the transposition of the transcendency of the world to the transcendency within immanence. Further, if we accept that the a priori form of intentionality is an essential, non-presumptive attribute of an embodied consciousness it is reasonable to assume that it would be present to the subject independently of any biological or physical constraints. This being a question analogous to the one asking for an absolute start and an absolute end of presentifying consciousness (*Gegenwärtigung*), it is even by today's standards impossible to answer it without falling to reductionistic ambivalences, e.g., to the kind of uncertainties of quantum theory. Husserl had suggested in the *Late Texts on Time Constitution* (*Späte Texte über Zeitkonstitution*), that some form of intentionality starts from the mother's womb and during first infancy, yet I doubt that this could be a sufficient argument for the assumption of intentional directedness as an a priori attribute of human egos and thus as pre-objective.[12]

---

[11] Oskar Becker, "Mathematische Existenz: Untersuchungen zur Logik und Ontologie mathematischer Phänomene", *Jahrbuch für Philosophie und phänomenologische Forschung* 8 (1927): 518-519.

[12] "Aber hat das Kind in der ersten Kindheit gar kein Interesse, gar kein Seiendes? In ihm vollzieht sich seine Welt, sein Ich, und seine strömende konkrete Gegenwart ist sozusagen der Mutterleib, in dem sich aus einem embryonalen Urkeim durch embryonale Stufen hindurch schließlich die erstkindliche Welt ausbildet und zur Geburt kommt. [..] Was uns hier interessiert: am Kind erster Kindheitsperiode haben wir schon instinktive Intentionalität vor einer Interessenintentionalität in Bezug auf Seiendes im eigentlichen und vollen Sinne." (Transl. of the author: "Yet has the child of the first infancy no interest whatsoever, no being? In him is implemented his world, his ego, and his flowing concrete present is so to say his mother's body, in which from a primordial germ through embryonal stages is eventually brought to birth and is built the world of first infancy .[..] What interests us here: We have already in the child in the period of first infancy an instinctive intentionality prior to an intentionality of interest with relation to the being in full and authentic sense"), Edmund Husserl, *Späte Texte über Zeitkonstitution, Die*

Is Existence an Ontologically Sound Term?

Second, if we assume that intentional directedness at each moment of our reflection appeals, in virtue of its enactment, to an object or state-of-affairs which is unique as intended, then we can be found to be in accord with Gurwitsch's position that:

> For an object - of any description whatever - to exist means that it is inserted into a context based upon and, therefore, dominated by a specific relevancy principle. Existence means existence within a system at a certain place in the latter and, hence, in well-defined relationships with other objects pertaining to the same systematic context.[13]

This would imply in the case of mathematical objects a definite place within the system they belong, with respect to the system as a whole and also with respect to any other object of the same genus within the system (think of the set of natural numbers), while in the case of objects of the perceptual world of everyday experience, it would imply a definite place within the context of spatiotemporal relations to other real objects and events. However both implications seem to be contradicted, the mathematical one by the non-existence of a definite place and consequently of a well-meant order among the real numbers,[14] and the real world one by the Heisenberg uncertainty (position-momentum) principles holding in the quantum world. In consequence, the transposition of the question of existence from real world terms to the terms of an intentionality-exhibiting subjectivity can prove also problematic but on completely different grounds than the 'naturalistic' one.

I point out that existence in terms of fulfilled or empty intentions has been criticized by Sartre as not taking account of non-existent objects, namely objects that can never fulfill experiences, think e.g., of fictional characters. In this approach Sartre's critique of Husserl's view is that one cannot distinguish between imagined and perceived objects for two reasons. First, the notion of empty intentions and the idea that both a present "in-person" and a non-present object can fulfill them makes the distinction between imagined and perceived objects by their perceptual content, i.e., their hyle, impossible. Second, the irreal nature of the noema (insofar as noema is a re-presentation of objects and not the objects themselves) makes it also impossible to distinguish between real and non-existent objects.[15] However both Husserlian and Sartrean approaches have in common that there is a second instance needed, namely that in terms of existential judgments intentional objects must be compared to corresponding states-of-affairs in the outside world, in order to determine the existence of objects as existing in real world terms or not. Furthermore, (a) Husserl did not accept the idea that mere thoughts and (existential) judgments have different objects, arguing that the objects are the same, but presented in a different way, namely as empty or fulfilled and (b) the treatment of the question of existence in this article is broad enough to include immanent (intentional) objects as existing, albeit in a "diminished" mere intentional sense, to the extent that they may pose themselves as objects of mere thought of a subject's consciousness endowed

---

C-Manuscripte , Hua Band VIII, hsgb. D. Lohmar (Dordrecht: Springer, 2001), pp. 74-75.

[13] Aaron Gurwitsch, (1961), "The Problem of Existence in Constitutive Phenomenology", *The Journal of Philosophy* 58 (1961): 631.

[14] The real numbers are in fact provided with an order by Zermelo's well-ordering theorem but this is a rather technical *ad hoc* handling of the matter due to the assumption of the *Axiom of Choice* which in turn is proved independent of the rest of the axioms of the commonly accepted Zermelo-Fraenkel Set Theory. The interested reader may further look at any standard set theory book, e.g., T. Jech's in: Thomas Jech, *Set Theory* (Berlin: Springer-Verlag, 2006).

[15] Simon Gusman, "To the Nothingnesses Themselves: Husserl's Influence on Sartre's Notion of Nothingness", *The Journ. of the Brit. Soc. of Phenomenology* 49 (2018): 60.

Is Existence an Ontologically Sound Term?

with eidetic attributes.

Concerning (**C**): If absolute consciousness is, for Husserl, the residuum after the annihilation of the world, then is it possible to define existence, after suspending all objectivity belonging to the world, as a phenomenon solely reducible to the absoluteness of immanental being, in other words to what Husserl schematically called the (absolute) flux of consciousness? As known the most fundamental reduction, the most radical and at the same time the most intricate, indeed the limbo of phenomenology, is the reduction to the absolute subjectivity of consciousness, to what Husserl called pure or transcendental ego. As a matter of fact Husserl never achieved a complete clarification neither of the nature of the absolute ego nor of its place within the objective world of perception, except for linking it with the origin of inner temporality. A systematic attempt to describe the absolute ego of consciousness free of circularities or infinite regressions was undertaken by Husserl in the *Bernau Manuscripts*, yet with no obvious way out of the impasse. In a way that highlighted the 'slippery turf', he tried to circumscribe these difficulties by proposing the possibility of a process which may find itself in the continuous unity of consciousness and in the phenomenological time without having the privilege of being intentionally apprehended or reflected upon. On this account he wondered whether the living-ego, not being a consciousness-of, can be a sort of apprehension, possibly an apprehension in the broadest sense of forming an intentional object where this intentional object cannot be identified with the act of apprehending, namely with the intentional experience as consciousness of it.[16]

The temporal nature of the ego and more generally of being, which except for the description of the nature of Dasein itself in *Being and Time*, was also commented in the Heideggerian writings about the Kantian metaphysics[17] had E. Levinas inquire into the nature of the relation subject-object in essentially the same terms as those discussed in condition (**B**). More concretely, Levinas posed the question of clarifying the relation subject-object, in admitting to the substantiality of the temporal subject, in these terms:

This relation to the object as such is not a temporal event of which, so to speak, we could become aware. The relation points in a direction to which conscious life is bound in each moment of its passing, but in which it does not perdure. But on the other hand - and this is crucial - we cannot reduce the relation of subject to object as it persists within idealism, where the object is encompassed in consciousness, to one of these supertemporal relations we know in an ideal world. For it is a matter of a relation lived out and established effectively by the individual beings such as we are.[18]

The fact is that any philosopher or scholar who has attempted to further interpret the Husserlian ego without running the risk of getting entrapped in an infinite regression reflecting-reflected, has ended up by introducing *ad hoc* assumptions or simply by generating circularities.[19]

---

[16] Edmund Husserl, *Die Bernauer Manuskripte über das Zeitbewußsein, (1917/18)*, Hua XXXIII, hsgb. R. Bernet, D. Lohmar, (Dordrecht: Kluwer Acad. Pub., 2001), pp. 198-199. See relative comments in: Stathis Livadas, "The Transcendence of the Ego in Continental Philosophy - Convergences and Divergences", *Horizon - Studies in Phenomenology* 8 (2019): 579-581.
[17] See Martin Heidegger, *Kant und das Problem der Metaphysik* , (Frankfurt: V. Klostermann, 1991), pp. 193-194 & pp. 282-283.
[18] Emmanuel Levinas, "Martin Heidegger and Ontology", Diacritics, Transl. by the Commit. of Pub. Safety, 26 (1996): 12.
[19] Patočka, for example, had maintained that a kind of "pre-reflective" retention must exist between the self of the (atemporal) transcendental ego and its mirror reflexion so that the regression reflecting-reflected can be avoided, while leaving the ego unalienated in the reflection.

Consequently the possibility of reducing existence to the absoluteness of the pure ego of consciousness may indeed prove even more problematic than the previous cases (**A**) and (**B**).

3. HOW ONE MAY HAVE A PHENOMENOLOGICAL CLARIFICATION OF EXISTENCE?

So, one might ask, what is the point of choosing to address questions of ontology by seeking recourse to a non-reductionistic, purely subjective approach? In that case a reasonable answer could be that the ultimate foundation of objectivity in the world, conceived in the broadest sense in terms of objectivity-as-constituted, must be what is evidence beyond any doubt and this can be presumably nothing else than the (embodied) subjectivity in the present now. Even if we do not adopt the phenomenological bracketing of the objective reality (*Epochë*) anyone could possibly agree that absolute certainty in the world at large can be solely attributed to the ego-self reflecting in actuality vis-à-vis a field of experience which is by necessity thematic to the extent that we turn our attentive regard each time toward a particular something. If on these grounds a kind of subjective reduction is chosen as clearly more advantageous than classical ontological schemes, of no less importance is Husserl's unitary account of objects of every category, namely material things, objects of imagination, theoretical objects of science, ideal entities of any sort, objectivities in general, in terms of acts of consciousness in the modes these acts are carried out. This is a position that must be coupled with Husserl's account of existence as referring, in a necessary and essential way, to an order of existence in which an existent is co-defined by its essential, well-defined relationships with other existents of the same order, e.g., referring to mathematical existence one may say that an individual member of a set-collection "exists" solely in terms of "being related to" in virtue of being an irreducible member of a collection. Correspondingly in real world terms one can say that for an object or event to be real it must happen to be in definite spatiotemporal relations to other real objects and events. In fact the acts of consciousness underlie not only the modes of being of objects in general but also and above all the way they

"reveal themselves as real or existent; they present themselves as existing in a certain specific mode, viz., that mode which is characteristic of and peculiar to a certain order of existence and in which objects must exist if they are to pertain to that order under consideration".[20]

This means that there might be diverse modes of existence, e.g., of material in contradistinction to abstract, theoretical objects,[21] but ultimately the existence of all categories of objects is reducible to the certainty of existence of the reflecting ego. Of course objects in phenomenology are objects as constituted but also as experienced within

---

See: Jan Patočka, *Introduction à la phénoménologie de Husserl* (Grenoble: Ed. Millon, 1992), p. 166.

[20] Gurwitsch, p. 626.

[21] Husserl talked, for example, of actual objects as correlates of actual experience and of quasi objects as corresponding to the imaginary consciousness of quasi experience in virtue of being merely represented, yet as belonging to the same noematic stock as objects of actual experience. See, Edmund Husserl, *Erfahrung und Urteil*, hsgb., L. Landgrebe (Prag: Acad. Verlagsbuchhandlung, 1939). In English translation: *Experience and Judgment*, transl. by J.S. Churchill & K. Americs, (London: Routledge & Kegan P., 1973), p. 381.

the life-world, the latter having the broad meaning of the original soil of experience, in the sense of perceptual experience taken in its original immediacy in a boundless noematic[22] horizon independently of and prior to any conceptualization. In these steps

What phenomenology endeavors to do is to clarify the concept of existence and the different, though, perhaps, somewhat related meanings which that concept assumes with respect to the several orders of existence with which we concern ourselves: the existence of real things belonging to the perceptual world, mathematical existence, existence of propositions, and so on.[23]

By this token, namely the clarification of the concept of existence in "raw" terms, one cannot plausibly expect a radical treatment of the question of an ontology of being by "formal" procedures, that is, in terms of definitions constructed *ad hoc* to meet certain logical requirements which are set on a meta-ontological level.[24] Yet if the life-world as the fundamental order of existence and domain of pre-predicative experience is a prerequisite of derivative orders of existence like the ideative by-products of logic and mathematics, it ought nevertheless not to be taken as a self-standing, presuppositionless origin of being-in-the-world, in which case Husserl opted for an absolute subjectivity, the transcendental ego of consciousness as the residuum of the annihilation of the world. Of course mental functions, even the a priori forms of intentionality of consciousness operate upon the domain of the life-world and in this sense presuppose intuitions associated with the life-world. However, and this may make phenomenology as a systematic study of pure subjectivity a privileged doctrine over classical ontology, life-world by itself cannot eliminate absolute subjectivity as the presuppositionless origin of ontological being.

We must also have in mind a key concept of phenomenological thought, that is, the eidetic intuition primarily presented in Husserl's *Ideas I*, as a key link between real world processes and the essential forms of consciousness, in two words the realization of "it cannot essentially be otherwise". This is the kind of intuition that underlies the conception of material objects as concordant concatenations of perceptual processes originally presented as concrete appearances to consciousness and by the same mode the conception of logical-mathematical objects as completed well-defined ones in original presentation. For instance no real world processes or things would be 'perceptible' as such if they would be in disaccord with our eidetic, constitutive processes,[25] nor mathematical-logical objects could be possibly conceived that would contradict proper noetic-noematic modes of being, e.g., being an irreducible individual as such, being in relation-to, probably being a plurality in the sense of unity, being invariantly preserved in terms of certain kinds of relation-to, etc. I note however, that even as eidetic intuition and eidetic mental processes in general are meant by Husserl as a priori modes of absolute consciousness, there is a lingering ambivalence as to what can be ultimately characterized as a priori since one can plausibly argue that what is thought as an essential "cannot be

---

[22] The noematic sphere, as well-known to phenomenologists, is the realm of beings, objects or states-of-affairs with proper meanings, said to be constituted by certain a priori modes as well-defined ones (objects as meant) immanent to the temporal flux of a subject's consciousness. In contrast the moments of intentionality, e.g., as originally directed toward a "general something" are termed as noetic. More in Husserl's *Ideas I*: Husserl (1976): pp. 229-232.

[23] Gurwitsch, pp. 627-628.

[24] See e.g., U. Kriegel's Existence, Fundamentality, and the Scope of Ontology: Uriah Kriegel, "Existence, Fundamentality, and the Scope of Ontology", *Argumenta* 1 (2015): 97-108.

[25] This is why for Husserl any extra-terrestrial world would still be a world for us, a *gründende Boden*, insofar as we remain embodied subjectivities endowed with such and such a priori intentional-eidetic modes.

otherwise" could be imprinted in consciousness by the historicity of the experience of being in the world.[26] Another point of controversy could be Gurwitsch's contention that "real things have but presumptive existence" which in his view is in accord with Leibniz's claim of the essentially contingent character of factual truths related to real things and events whose contingency implies that their opposite does not generate a contradiction or absurdity (Gurwitsch, p. 631). Yet this position may be thought to run contrary to the belief that the essential traits of material objects are eidetically prescribed, as those of abstract formal objects too, in the sense that eidetic truths are beyond a spatio-temporal context and are not conditioned on spatio-temporal constraints.[27] Consequently a more sound expression would be that real things have a presumptive yet eidetically prescribed existence reducible to the essential modes of a subjective constitution.

As a matter of fact while Husserl was intent on replacing the classical ontological edifice with the new subjectively founded doctrine of phenomenology, he dedicated very little of his work to talk directly about ontological questions per se. In *Logic and General Theory of Science* he offered some aspects of his guiding attitude to ontological questions epitomized in the phrase that "[..] all ontology is for us [..] the correlate of ontological investigation", in the sense that "such and such formal or real ontological laws hold"[28] which point to the performance of proper presentations and proper thought-acts which can be valid or invalid, rational or irrational. And if we associate ontology with a system of truths, asking about the validity of thought-acts in the form of propositions about ontological systems and laws, it turns into thinking, for instance, about "numbers and number relationships, spatial figures, number systems, the Ideas 'substantiality' and 'causality', and so forth, and all that from an a priori perspective". Here is, of course, where Husserl enters his favorite field of the reduction to consciousness as ontology (in the classical sense) would not take account respectively of the consciousness of counting, of the consciousness of intuiting space as fulfillment of temporal unity, nor of spatial phenomena pertaining to the spatial intuition of phenomena with the sequences of adumbrations in the unity of their profiles. By the same measure the essence of substantiality cannot be captured without the consciousness of the unity of multiple phenomena in which substance comes to givenness, nor that of causality without the consciousness of necessity whose correlate is causality. Husserl sought therefore in virtue of subjectively founded meaning-acts to justify on what grounds that which occurs in the factual order as an empirical fact may come in human consciousness to be accorded the

---

[26] Think for a moment, to cite an instance in foundational mathematics, of the concept of a generic filter which, as a filter, is based on the intuitively evident condition of preserving the compatibility of the order relation in its unfolding, and as a generic object preserves the global character of "being everywhere" [Kenneth Kunen, *Set Theory. An Introduction to Independence Proofs*, (Amsterdam: Elsevier Sc. Pub, 1982), resp. pp. 53, 186]. These are intuitions shaped to a certain extent by our rational experience in doing mathematics over time.

[27] As Husserl asserted in *Ideas I* the unrestricted universality of natural laws are not to be confused with eidetic universality. As concrete examples he cited the proposition 'All bodies are heavy' which does not have the unconditional universality of eidetically universal propositions as it carries with it the factual positing of nature as spatiotemporal reality. On the other hand the proposition 'All material things are extended' can be taken as a purely eidetic proposition for it states something that is grounded solely in the essence of a material thing, namely to be extendible, and in the essence of the property of extension, in the way they can be given originally in presenting consciousness by freely phantasying and varying over a material thing in consciousness. See Husserl (1976), p. 15.

[28] Edmund Husserl, *Logic and General Theory of Science*, Hua XV, ed. J. Yansen, trans. C. Ortiz Hill (Cham: Springer Nature, 2019), p. 408.

status of an unconditional law with regard to what is putatively known in it. The realm of reason must therefore enter the realm of consciousness, if it is to be valid, and precisely of consciousness in relation to its meaning and object correlates. Ontological investigation in this sense aims at objects, more specifically, at objective essence and meanings so that one may rightfully ask the further question of the legitimacy of empirical-natural scientific knowledge insofar as it is not predetermined by ontological knowledge. In fact this may concern the possibility of ontological knowledge in general, and consequently the possibility of synthetic a priori knowledge, e.g., the knowledge of mathematics and pure natural science, just as the possibility of empirical a posteriori knowledge of non-ontological natural sciences, even the possibility of analytic knowledge.[29] In this view one should explain the way consciousness may immanently posit something irrespectively of physically existing as being in itself and in the form it ought to have in the sole existence of at least one other person on earth sharing the same constitutive-intentional capacities that Husserl's doctrine prescribed.

In the *Logic and General Theory of Science* Husserl offered no further clues as to the source of validity of ontological investigations in the sense that such and such formal or real ontological laws hold, except by seeking recourse to the realm of consciousness, with its object and meaning correlates, to lead to an investigation of reason if the latter is to be valid. At this stage, though, he had already unfolded an intuition for what may lie beyond consciousness thought of as a psycho-physical unit mutually dependent on the body and the bodily occurrences, in other words as something existing in terms of a spatiotemporal coming to be and going away as well as in terms of its existential patterns and causal laws. More explicitly he noted that beyond "the Idea of this basically essentially unique psycho-physical unit that I am calling 'ensouled being', with the associated Ideas of 'flow of consciousness', 'soul', 'character' and so on. [..] we have an a priori framework, an a priori form and accordingly an a priori science, the ontology of spiritual being".[30] Quite characteristically Husserl marveled at the miracle of consciousness that is called intentionality, the most primitive perception of things at all, whose naively considered obviousness is the enigma of all enigmas which hinges on the original fact that makes up the essential particularity of consciousness as such, namely, that each consciousness is an original experience attributed *eo ipso* with a sense of meaning.

Even as the goal of achieving a clarification of the concept of the absolute ego of consciousness would ultimately prove to be unattainable, Husserl's subsequent work was largely dedicated to showing that consciousness, in particular transcendental consciousness with its a priori modes of "being" and in a special relation to the life-world of phenomena is the origin of what can be a sound foundation of all regional ontologies, essentially of the question of ontological existence.

4. A TREATMENT OF THE QUESTION OF EXISTENCE *IN EXTREMIS*

If, according to Levinas, an object is considered as referring to a subject's rational activity it follows that objective knowledge is a relation to the being always passed by and in need of interpretation, in the sense that the "what is it" brings out the "this-here" (*ceci*) to the "this-there" (*cela*). This means that the being as objective knowledge related to an ego is always knowledge as historicity, of what is already done, already overpassed.

---

[29] Ibid., pp. 411-412.
[30] Ibid., p. 298.

In this respect it is always beyond its original "appearance", beyond its origin, known only in virtue of its manifestations as a phenomenon whose "reality" is already beyond reality insofar as constituted within temporality and to the extent that the temporal flow has no origin.[31] Levinas took a step further to safeguard the "autonomy" of the being, as absolute alterity to my ego manifested καθ' ἑαυτὸ, in terms of an absolute experience meant as revelation, independently of whatever position we would have in its regard. In such view the form by which the "exteriority" of the being as original manifestation presents itself cannot but alienate the originality and the authenticity of being as presentification "in person" in front of my ego.[32]

A notable example of the irreducibility of being as absolute alterity to my ego may be thought the relation entertained by the ego cogito with regard to the infinite, which the ego cogito cannot in any way "interiorize" and from which it is separate, even though infinity as *ideatum* cannot but find its origin as idea only within ourselves. In this regard, the distance between idea and *ideatum* is a "measure" of the latter's transcendence relative to the reflecting ego and represents the very content of the *ideatum* as a transcendental being absolutely "other" to the ego.

The idea of infinity has precisely this exceptionality that its *ideatum* "infinitely" surpasses its idea, whereas for things as contents-within one cannot exclude full coincidence between their objective and formal realities. The transcendence of infinity as *ideatum* makes it an absolute exteriority leading even to an overpassing of subjectivity. This is a subtlety that motivates Levinas to argue for the philosophical anteriority of existing (*étant*) to being (*être*), an exteriority which is not reducible to the interiority of the ego (e.g., through memory or any of the intentional modes of consciousness), even as the absoluteness of the ego itself is safeguarded.[33] In these terms the "distance" of the infinite with regard to the reflecting ego is a measure of its very transcendence, in other words the "distance" separating *ideatum* and (corresponding) idea constitutes the very content of the *ideatum*.

Of course Levinas' idea of the infinite is put in far more general terms than that of the respective mathematical notion, yet one may point to certain ideas of Becker's on a possible ontology of the mathematical infinite to see that both approaches are mutually mirrored on the question of the existence of infinite in ontological terms. Thus, according to Becker, both Aristotle and Kant came to rid mathematics of its mysticist vestiges and secret meanings, something that makes mathematics an abstract contemplation that is not concerned with the primary essence of things. Rather it is associated with a view of the mathematician as a finite human for whom any concept of the infinite going beyond the phenomenally demonstrable is strictly rejected.[34]

Moreover echoing Husserl's views in *Ideas I* on the impossibility of a "running through" of the infinite in no other way than the way an idea-meaning is comprehended in its completion, Becker maintained that we can reflect in each thought on all possible stages of previous reflections, in the uniformity of the sequential stages of iteration, such that in a numerical fashion we can proceed at each stage from the nth-stage as the theme of one's actual act of reflection (in finitary fashion by virtue of being temporal acts) to the next stage n+1 and thus attain a new higher level form of reflection.[35] This brings us in turn into the light of the phenomenological dimension of this process which enables the

---

[31] Emmanuel Levinas, *Totalité et Infini* (La Haye: M. Nijhoff, 1971), p. 58
[32] Ibid., pp. 60-61.
[33] Ibid., pp. 40, 44.
[34] Becker, p. 748.
[35] Ibid., p. 546.

contemplation and mastering of transfinite structures by the finite human spirit through a "law" whose content is finite just as that of each content of human consciousness. Becker allowed, by appealing to this constitutive process, to speak at least in the theory of transfinite ordinals of an ontological foundation of the theory of Cantorian transfinite numbers.[36] This is however a process phenomenologically meant as implemented within the bounds of an open, ever extensible and transposable horizon which is, nevertheless, eidetically pre-defined. The phenomenologically based accommodation of the notion of the infinite by Becker, arguably a way to salvage large parts of the Cantorian theory of transfinite numbers in contrast to the Brouwerian constructivism, seems to be, insofar as it keeps absolute infinity inaccessible by reflection, not incongruent with Levinas' total inaccessibility of the infinite meant as an *ideatùm* "infinitely" apart from its idea that "resides" within the immanence of consciousness.

More than that it may be taken as a philosophical vindication of the formal Cantorian view of infinite sets (or classes thereof) as complete totalities in actual presence, which in a phenomenological sense cannot be conceived but as constituted idealities founded, though, on the finitistic character of the intentional-reflective modes of each subjectivity. Yet, in deviation from the constitutive Husserlian position if totality for Levinas cannot be constituted in an absolute sense, it is due to the fact that infinity cannot by itself be integrated therefore it is not the insufficiency of the (phenomenological) ego that obstructs totalisation[37] but rather the nature of infinity itself as absolute "otherness".[38] In this understanding Levinas would stand against a fundamental phenomenological credo by claiming that there is no sense in talking about knowledge or ignorance (with regard to an absolute "otherness") insofar as the purest transcendence (*transcendence par excellence*) is not a (phenomenologically meant) noesis correlated to a noema.[39]

Actually Husserl did not write much about infinity as such except that he largely integrated the notion in the content and scope of transcendental phenomenology by proceeding to its immanentisation as a correlate of the objective unity of consciousness. This was done as early as in the time of *Logical Investigations* and in a more "naively" psychological sense even earlier at the time of the *Philosophy of Arithmetic*.[40] In the second volume of *Logical Investigations* he referred to infinity as a form of immanence independently of any objective, real world constraints in a way that does not prove the relative foundedness (*Fundierung*) of bits of space and time, and so does not prove space

---

[36] Hans Sluga, H., "Oskar Becker or the Reconciliation of Mathematics and Existential Philosophy" in META: *Research in Hermeneutics, Phenomenology and Practical Philosophy*, ed. Apostolescu, I. (Iasi: A. I. Cuza Univ. Press, 2019), pp. 577-578.
[37] The impossibility of the reflection of a totality (of objectivities) in the sense of complete whole is due, according to Levinas, to the "excessiveness" of the "other" (otherness) with regard to me (my own ego). This is a position that, as known, was addressed by Husserl by resorting to the self-constituting (temporal) unity originating in the transcendental ego itself.
[38] Emmanuel Levinas, *Totalité et Infini*, p. 78.
[39] Ibid., p. 89.
[40] In the *Philosophy of Arithmetic* Husserl wondered, for instance, how one could found the concept of number *in abstracto* without the possibility of thinking of an aggregation of objects (real or formal) in terms of a temporal simultaneity of content, a quandary he later proposed to resolve, in *Experience and Judgment*, and in relation to set formation by what he called the retrospective apprehension (*rückfgreifendes Erfassen*) attributed to the ego of consciousness. See resp. Edmund Husserl, *Philosophie der Arithmetik*, Hua Band XII, hsgb. L. Eley (Den Haag: M. Nijhoff, 1970), pp. 24-29 and Edmund Husserl, *Experience and Judgment*, Engl. transl., p. 246. For a more detailed discussion on the matter the reader may also look at: Stathis Livadas, "What is the Nature of Mathematical-Logical Objects?", *Axiomathes* 27(2016): pp. 79-112.

and time to be really infinite.[41]

As it happened with all other transcendencies within the bounds of the life-world, the "ontological being" of infinity would be eventually reducible to the absolute being of consciousness even if that implied the possibility of a prior annihilation of the being of the world as argued in *Ideas I*. And concerning the meaning-content of infinity this may be thought of, in the context of *Logical Investigations*, as reducible to the unity of a categorial synthesis through which phenomenological unity is expressible as a fulfillment consciousness. This way talking about the knowledge of an object and the fulfillment of the meaning-intention (*Bedeutungsintention*) express the same state of affairs in the understanding that the unity of the fulfillment consciousness is a necessary condition for the knowledge of an object.[42] Given that for Husserl to each meaning-intention corresponds an intuitiveness (*Anschauung*)[43], he proceeded in affirming that the ideal conditions of categorial intuitiveness are correlate to the conditions of the possibility of the objects of categorial intuitiveness themselves, the possibility of categorial objects in proper sense. This means that categorial syntheses and the corresponding categorial acts are realizable on the grounds of the founding intuitions concerned.[44] In short for Husserl, in contrast to Levinas, the notion of infinity as that of any other transcendency conceived in virtue of an ideatum transcending its idea, cannot be "detached" from proper categorial intuitiveness as its correlate. Then to the extent that to each meaning-intention corresponds a proper intuitiveness one has, insofar as knowledge of an object and the fulfillment of the meaning-intention express the same state of affairs, that not only the ontological being of infinity may be reducible to the being of constituting subjectivity but its signification in terms of meaning-intention may be also immanently reducible to the unity of a fulfillment consciousness.

However even in a sense of re-presentation linked with an intentionality completely different from the Husserlian original version, Levinas left no doubt of his persisting intention to leave a residuum of elusive, inconvertible through a reflective act and irreducible to presentification content which would be associated with a different non-constituting kind of intentionality, the intentionality of the "living by" (*vivre de*). And it is in virtue of this kind of impossibility of "interiorisation", of which infinity is a primary example, that Levinas criticized Husserlian phenomenology as presenting no limits to noematisation. Further, and not unexpectedly for a phenomenologist of Husserlian formation as Levinas was, the discussion would turn to the role of (inner) temporality in addressing the transcendental method in which case the consciousness of an object in terms of its thematisation is always found in a "distance" with regard to the "self" (of ego), not conceivable otherwise but in terms of time.[45]

As it happened with Husserl's inevitable descent into an endless regressing sequence of reflections, the same reservations may arise with regard to the temporal distance to the "self" of the ego as a necessary precondition for thematisation, to the extent that it rests on the consciousness of the self. The matter is, however, that for Levinas (and in a different sense for Descartes) infinity cannotbe thematised and

---

[41] Edmund Husserl, *Logische Untersuchungen*, Hua Band XIX/1, hsgb. U. Panzer (Den Haag: M. Nijhoff, 1984). In English translation, Logical Investigations, transl. J.N. Findlay, (New York: Routledge, 2001), p.45.

[42] Edmund Husserl, *Logische Untersuchungen*, Hua Band XIX/2, hsgb. U. Panzer (Den Haag: M. Nijhoff, 1984), pp. 566-567.

[43] The term *Anschauung* is a properly Husserlian term, conceived in terms of "moments" of noesis, usually rendered in English translation as intuition or intuitiveness.

[44] Edmund Husserl, *Logische Untersuchungen*, Hua Band XIX/2, pp. 718-719.

[45] Emmanuel Levinas, *Totalité et Infini*, p. 231.

therefore cannot be made accessible by the means in which well-meant objects are intuitable and attributable of a meaning-giving through a fulfillment consciousness. This is a question left by Levinas virtually unanswered even as he tried to sidestep it by appealing to vague concepts supposedly ridden of the Husserlian constituting constraints, e.g., take the substitute of intentional directedness as the *vivre de* above, or the concepts of desire (*désir*) and relishing (*jouissance*) impregnated by his distinctive literary style.

In the bottom line in the *Otherwise than Being or Beyond the Essence*, Levinas remained adamantly tied to the reduction of the essence of being (*être*) to the subjectivity of the subject, the latter in the absolute sense of what is never in the re-presenting actuality, of what is not suitable to any denomination determining beings nor of the verbs reflecting their essence but nonetheless preceding everything that can bear a name.[46] On these grounds the "otherwise than being" points to an underlying subjectivity, with the latter's being-in-itself repelling essence as ontological possession. Further the "otherwise than being" reduces to a unity of me (ego) which never coincides with nor rests upon itself,[47] in short a unity that cannot "exist" in terms of being-there, nor with the ideal identification that comes from the possibility of identifying the innumerable aspects of a being's own manifestation.[48] Consequently the inquiry on the "otherwise than being" which underlies the kind of transcendent entities, of which infinity is an outstanding example, forebodes in the hypostasis of the subject an "out of place" with absolute being, including the terms of be-ing (*étant*) as possible modulation of being (*être*) that may fill in the rupture of hypostasis.[49]

5. WHY EXISTENCE FADES AWAY IN PERFORMING REDUCTION?

In this section I argue for an origin of existence which, far from being ontologically self-standing, is constantly undermined by the process of a subjective reduction in Husserlian or generally in subjective (even in Whiteheadian) terms. I will also address the question of whether such reduction can eventually lead to a transcendence extraneous to the world or whether this transcendence is bound to circularly "re-produce" itself as part of the world. On the latter option, Whitehead's view of the Husserlian phenomenological reduction as allegedly never really getting us out of the field of nature is indicative enough.[50] As Whitehead suspended or at least relegated the role of constituting subjectivity this "led him in the first place to a reduction of the relational extensiveness to the classical question of extensive whole and extensive parts, whereas his eventual attempt in achieving a satisfactory treatment of a resulting circularity by defining a spatial point through the notion of an abstractive ensemble hurt to the problem of an infinitely regressing sequence of connecting regions".[51] Even if phenomenology at large has put squarely the question of a non-eliminable subjective residuum in a presumed ontological foundation of the world of phenomena, it is precisely the Husserlian phenomenology, in contradistinction with the Heideggerian abstruse facticity of Dasein, that clearly led to a pure subjectivity, if only

---

[46] Emmanuel Levinas, *Autrement qu' être ou au-delà de l' essence* (La Haye: M. Nijhoff, 1974), p. 233.
[47] Cf. with the Sartean being-for-itself (*pour-soi*) in contrast with the being-in-itself (en-soi).
[48] Emmanuel Levinas, *Autrement qu' être ou au-delà de l' essence*, p. 10.
[49] Ibid., p. 21.
[50] Marvin Farber, *Phenomenology and Existence: Toward a Philosophy Within Nature* (New York: Harper &Row, 1967), p. 7.
[51] Stathis Livadas, "The Notion of Process in Nonstandard Theory and in Whiteheadian Metaphysics", *Manuscrito* 36 (2013): pp. 111-112.

extraneous to the world, as a constituting origin impossible to be conceived in objective terms.

Yet for all the diverging attitudes among major figures of continental philosophy on the nature of absolute being, the common underlying factor, one could even say the common defining factor of absolute being and of existence as an essentially associated concept is, to the one or the other extent, inner temporality. For Levinas, time is not a characteristic of the essence of reality, a something, or an attribute. It is the mode of being, the expression of the fact of being. Furthermore,

> "it is that fact of being itself. In a way it is the very dimension in which the existence of being comes about. To exist is to be 'temporalized'". Consequently "To grasp time in its specificity is thus to challenge the very meaning of the word 'being' which, as 'transcendent', traditional philosophy has excluded from its domain of research. The theory of time is thus ontology, but ontology in the specific sense of the term".[52]

It follows that since ontology should take care of the being rather than of the existent (i.e., that-which-is) anyone, especially the idealists, who ignores the factor time must conclude that the subject is something which is not, except for the case that he is ready to admit to a temporal sense in the transcendence of the subject with regard to itself.

It is in distinguishing the term be-ing as that-which-is (*étant*) from the being (*être*) of be-ing that Heidegger tried to overcome such paradoxes stating that the understanding of being is the human condition of existence, as this understanding must transcend understanding through genera and specific differences which is a property of be-ing as a carrier of attributes, an eidos. Founded in a deeper sense than an act of meaning within the temporal flow of consciousness, the Heideggerian understanding of being characterizes man not as an essential attribute, but it is man's very mode of being. It determines not his essence, but his existence. No doubt, if we consider man as a be-ing, the understanding of being constitutes the essence of this be-ing. But to be precise - and this point is fundamental to Heideggerian philosophy – man's essence is simultaneously his existence. That which man is, is at the very same time his way of being, his way of being-there (*être-là*), his way of self-"temporalizing".[53] In a definite sense existence and essence of be-ing are for Heidegger overlapping if not identical meanings insofar as existence is not simply an attribution of the be-ing but precisely its mode-of-being which unconditionally and *ipso facto* underlies any conception, any clarification of being. It is existence in this sense as a mode-of-being specific to the human and not as a mere "reflexion" of his essence that entitles man to be designated by the term Dasein which is not an embodied consciousness reducible to an out-of-the world ego predominant in the Husserlian scheme.

And yet the Heideggerian analysis of Dasein is an understanding of being that essentially resumes to time itself. Time in Heidegger in contrast with Husserl's view where the origin of time is, in virtue of the pure ego, extraneous to the world, is concretized as a mode-of-being of Dasein in the sense that the authentic existence of Dasein is revealing itself in virtue of authentic, finite time. In such perspective the time we measure, the infinite scientific time achieved in principle through extrapolation from finitistic considerations, even timelessness itself, appear as temporal events of authentic time to the extent that they are non-eliminable modes-of-being of human existence. Heidegger's time is not a time conceived in terms of a succession of moments (which far from representing the originary phenomenon is a reification due to the situation of which

---

[52] Emmanuel Levinas, "Martin Heidegger and Ontology", p.13.
[53] Ibid., p. 16

the Dasein finds itself within-the-world) and also not a time-category. It is an existential time, not the unilinear unfolding of moments of acting in the sense of scientific time, it is a time that determines and at the same time is determined by the authentic presence of Dasein (say of every man) in its throwing into the world, a time indeed found in everything.

Already the fact that situations like "always already", "in retard with", "in front of", and "next to" are modes of existing and not quiddities or even a kind of Husserlian kinestheses may point to their kinship with a concept of time which is not a be-ing (*étant*) but being (*être*). The question of the "subject-object" structure, explicated by Husserl in terms of intentionality as the essential trait of a consciousness that transcends itself by existing, and the question of time itself are for Heidegger in such affine relationship that the structure of the "subject-object" relation would be a mode of time and would be rendered possible by the existential sense attributed to time.

It must be pointed out in relation to the question of infinity as related to existence, discussed in Section 4, that Levinas saw in the authenticity of the Heideggerian understanding of being, as intimately associated with the concept of time, the "very characteristic of the finitude of Dasein's existence", the foundation of the transcendence of Dasein as an event of its existence pointing to the finitude of its existence. In consequence

Finitude will become the very principle of the subject's subjectivity. It is because there is a finite existence - Dasein - that consciousness itself will be possible.[54]

It turns out that the infinite proves to be a case of existence invalidated, indeed "destructed" in appealing to the absoluteness of the subjective factor. Infinity, therefore, not only becomes negatively associated with the concept of time but it seems an "alien" feature of human existence in the sense of Dasein, accessible only through a kind of extrapolation on account of the finitude of Dasein's existence. On the other hand, Sartre's view of the contrast between consciousness and the existent in *Being and Nothingness*,[55] may be assessed in terms of the difference between finite and infinite largely interpretable as a human's self-awareness of his "infinity", in rejecting a finite image of himself (himself as an object).[56] In other words while things may have an inner, endless horizon of content (qualities), consciousness - as transcending itself throughout its existence (e.g., by exhibiting intentionality) - is everything "imaginable" at the same time. In this sense consciousness, alongside being itself, can be such as to belong to the category of the absolute, because not only there is "nothing" in it except of its sheer existence but may be also seen as the "the first being to whom all other appearances appear, the absolute in relation to which every phenomenon is relative".[57] Furthermore if, for Sartre, the being of existent is exactly what it appears, in the sense that appearance not only does not hide essence but on the contrary reveals it as a kind of concatenation of appearances in a way that rejects the dualism between appearance and essence, one can be found in front of the aforementioned dualism between the finite and the infinite. This fact in turn, if posed in

---

[54] Ibid., p. 18
[55] Jean Paul Sartre, *L'être et le néant*, (Paris: Ed. Gallimard, 1943). In English translation: *Being and Nothingness: An Essay on Phenomenological Ontology*, transl. H. E. Barnes (London: Methuen & Co, 1957).
[56] Ivan Kuzin, Alexander Drikerr & Eugene Makovetsky, "Existential aspect of Being: Interpreting J. P. Sartre's Philosophy", *Rupkatha Journal on Interdisciplinary Studies in Humanities*, 8 (2016): 225.
[57] Jean Paul Sartre, *Being and Nothingness*, p. lvii.

terms of an appearing object (to a subject) and the transcendence of the object makes that the finiteness of each appearance requires at the same time in order to be grasped as an appearance-of-that-which-appears to be surpassed toward infinity, transposes *ipso facto* the finite-infinite dualism to the a priori modes of the constituting consciousness.

Husserl, as known, largely reduced the question to the noetic-noematic modes of constituting consciousness and offered a kind of metaphorical explication to account for the apparent contradiction between the all-sided "infinity" of multiplicities of appearances of one and the same thing and the "closed" unity of the completion of the running through of its appearances. Thus the idea of the perfect givenness prefigured by the idea of continuum is presented in an intellectual seeing (*Einsicht*) in the way an "idea" can be intellectually seen "by its essence designating its own peculiar type of intellectual seeing".[58] In these terms the idea of an infinity motivated according to its essence is not itself an infinity. The fact that this infinity cannot be given *in rem*, does not preclude but rather requires the intellectually "seen" givenness of the idea of this infinity. This seems to be a way out of the apparent contradiction of a "finite infinity", insofar as infinity may be reducible to the finite nature of the subject. Yet it is through Husserl's reduction of infinity to the immanent unity of consciousness in temporal terms that one may enter the circularity of an endless regression of reflecting-reflected.

In Sartrean terms it is only through consciousness that the existent (as a general object) acquires meaning as a revelation without becoming, for that matter, either consciousness or being-in-itself (*en-soi*), the latter signified by its revelation. Unlike the existent, the being-in-itself does not become explicit through definitions and categories, but only through the meaning of being of the existent revealing itself in consciousness. For Sartre in almost parallel ways with Husserl's absolute ego-factual ego, absolute being or the being-in-itself characterized as the plenitude of existence devoid of any categorical attribution and any sense of locality or temporality is only accessible through the "regard" of the being-for-itself (*pour-soi*) which is only possible, due to the ecstatic temporality, by being "ahead of itself", in fact by being each moment what it is not. This implies that temporality must be the mode of being of a being which is by itself "out of itself" (*hors de soi*), meaning in this case the being-for-itself.[59]

As it had also happened with Heidegger, though in a somewhat different sense, the critical step for Sartre was to find a consistent way to address a twofold ontological issue: first, to deliver a concept of existence by an absolute determination, free of any supposition or of categorial attributes and spatiotemporal determination, by relying only on the evidence of its pure being. And second, to make room for a being so that existence can place a reflective regard upon itself and moreover make possible an "outward" directed transcending of itself, and yet this possibility to be a "distancing" with regard to pure existence having nothing in common to the spatiotemporal world for then one would be in need of another reflective origin and so on.[60] In this sense and in spite of the diverging paths toward a determination of absolute being against the world of phenomena both Heidegger and Sartre converge with Husserl in the way they attempt to compose the two questions above by essentially reducing existence to the consciousness existence may have of itself and the surrounding world, an undertaking inextricably linked with the

---

[58] Edmund Husserl (1976), Engl. trans., pp. 342-343.
[59] Jean Paul Sartre, *L'être et le néant*, pp. 171-173.
[60] Sartre's reflective attitude on nothingness as negation of being, yet "asymmetric" to being, has opened up the possibility of viewing nothingness as purely subjective and not a part of reality "residing" out of the sphere of human subjects. Accordingly, "nothingness is then nothing more than the conceptual unity of our negative judgements about reality" (Simon Gusman, pp. 57-58).

origin of temporality which, to cite Sartre, must have the structure of ipseity, i.e., the structure of absolute self.[61]

As the question of inner temporality (including the Heideggerian sense of the temporalizing of Dasein) and its origin has proved for phenomenologists over time a tantalizingly intricate question to deal with, I will only touch on the matter mostly in relation to the concept of existence as shaped in this article. I will do so in the next section which will be and the concluding part of the paper.

6. IS TEMPORALITY THE KEY TO UNDERSTAND THE ELUSIVENESS OF EXISTENCE?

As pointed out, phenomenologists of every particular inclination converge in seeking an ultimate subjective foundation of the question of existence. I would add that, in spite of their divergence from the original Husserlian doctrine by which they were mostly formed, they have more or less explicitly in common the reduction of the "essence" of existence to the transcendence traced in the origin of subjectivity.

To take stock, Sartre's ecstatic unity of the being-for-itself by the three ecstatic dimensions (past-present-future), by which the being-for-itself is dispersed in the incessant mirror play of reflecting-reflected, points in a certain way to the intentional forms (i.e., the double form of transversal-longitudinal intentionality) exhibited by the absolute flux of consciousness in the Husserlian phenomenology. By these forms the absolute flux, on the one hand, constitutes objects in virtue of appearances as temporal unities in internal time and, on the other, constitutes itself as a single, homogenous, progressing flow. In fact an indirect clue implying the recourse to an absolute subjective origin of inner temporality may be found in the quasi circular description of longitudinal intentionality meant as an intentional form grounding the continuous unity of retentions and in a higher order the unity of the flux of consciousness as such.[62] Ultimately this absolute subjectivity was meant to be a pre-reflective, non-objectifiable subjectivity, the ever in-act "cause" of the continuous unity of temporal consciousness by necessity alienated from any sense of temporality to avoid the infinite regression reflecting-reflected.

As known there is no, strictly speaking, a concept corresponding to Husserl's absolute subjectivity in Heidegger's description of Dasein, for Heidegger reduced the ecstatic temporality of Dasein to the quite perplexing ecstatic forms of its existence in virtue of being-in-the world and in terms of the self-constituting openness to its own existence. Temporality is for Heidegger the ecstatic unity of the ecstatic moments of Dasein in its dispersion in the world and in taking care of being-in-the-world. Nevertheless they both had to seek transcendental (i.e., non-objectifiable) forms of inner temporality and they were both deeply concerned with the subjective origins of objective or scientific time.[63]

---

[61] Jean Paul Sartre, *L'être et le néant*, p. 172.
[62] Edmund Husserl, *Vorlesungen zur Phänomenologie des inneren Zeibewußtseins*, Hua X, hsgb. R. Boehm, (Den Haag: M. Nijhoff, 1966), pp. 80-83.
[63] Brough and Blattner characterize Husserl's temporal consciousness as absolute in the following three senses: (1) it is the ultimate foundation for intentionality; (2) it is characterized by "double-intentionality" and is thereby self-constituting; and (3) it is a condition of the possibility of any awareness of any object at all. See John B. Brough, William Blattner, "Temporality" in *A Companion to Phenomenology and Existentialism*, ed. H.L. Dreyfus & M.A. Wrathall (NJ: Blackwell Pub, 2006), p. 131. They point out that Heidegger adopts these theses as well but in a

Is Existence an Ontologically Sound Term?

Sartre for his part, considered more close to the Husserlian phenomenology than Heidegger in prioritizing consciousness and using the terminology of ecstasy and horizon to account for the annihilating properties of the being-for-itself, views like Heidegger before him the primordial temporality as the foundation for our transcendence or for "reaching out" to the world.

In spite of the differences between Husserl, Heidegger and Sartre on the question of the foundation of being in general, I consider as most important in the respective approaches a common denominator, that is, the "residual" transcendence of subjectivity vis-à-vis the world, a transcendence only conceivable in temporal terms and inexpressible by any linguistic analytic means that may point to an ontological sense (i.e., τό μή λεκτὸν). Consequently if we take the whole spatiotemporal world, which includes the human ego in the sense of a subordinate reality, as a secondary being posited by an intentional consciousness we can reach *in extremis* the conclusion that the world is

"a being posited by consciousness in its experiences which, of essential necessity, can be determined and intuited only as something identical belonging to motivated multiplicities of appearances: beyond that it is nothing"[64]

Yet if we stick to this view and following the argumentation of the article opt for a not self-standing notion of existence dependent or rather reducible to an absolute subjective origin whose mode of being is a temporal one, the question that naturally follows is whether we can have a well-meant notion of existence given the ontological elusiveness of the absolute subjectivity.

Evidently, on the one hand, we cannot eliminate the transcendental ego, or the being-in-the-world of Dasein, or the Sartrean being-for-itself as a kind of essence implied by what may be conceived as consciousness-of. On the other hand, conceding to a consciousness deprived of the possibility of an "annihilating" factor, that is, of the possibility of "regarding upon itself" is unthinkable. In such terms inner temporality without an "annihilating" factor to be identified with a kind of temporality-in-constituting may be also unthinkable. Therefore if existence in the broadest sense of being-in-the-world is to transpose its ontological legitimacy to the absoluteness of subjectivity, one may well find himself lost in the maze of circularities generated by the ontological deficiency of the primordial constituting factor of being-in-the-world in actual presence. A way, though ontologically ambivalent, out of this predicament might be to turn to the constituting factor as ever presentifying itself in the actual now which, except for Husserl, Sartre also accepted insofar as in contrast with Heidegger he prioritized, regarding the being-for-itself, the ecstasy of the present as a self-revelation of its past and its 'deficiency' toward its own future.

Excluding any platonistic-metaphysical convictions, which I am not inclined to accept, I cannot think of a way to overcome the insurmountable difficulty of understanding being-in-the-world in an absolute sense while being already in the world, a

---

slightly modified form: by characterizing implicitly in *Being and Time* and explicitly in *The Basic Problems of Phenomenology*, the ecstatic unity of temporality as the final horizon of intelligibility and ontological understanding, by sharing Husserl's notion of the double intentionality and by rendering the ecstatic-horizonal unity of temporality a condition of the possibility of any awareness of any object at all. In conclusion they claim that Heidegger "shares the fundamental contours of Husserl's account of internal time-consciousness" in acknowledging however "lesser" differences, e.g., the primacy of the future in Heidegger's approach placing him at odds with both Husserl and Sartre who favored the primacy of the now.

[64] Edmund Husserl (1976), Engl. trans, p. 112.

Is Existence an Ontologically Sound Term?

difficulty stemming exactly by our situation-in-the-world. A recourse to a reductionistic approach based on epistemological arguments would not help us either as, in positive science for instance, mainstream knowledge indicates an underdetermination of the metaphysics by the physics.[65] It seems an underdetermination of the metaphysics by the underlying physics can become even more evident to the extent that the physics involved may be well-entrenched (or at least commonly accepted as such) and yet we may come across some well-known problems of ontological change and underdetermination of theories by current experimental data.[66] Such kind of experiments in the quantum world may well be taken to confirm in a certain way the conditioning of the question of existence on the absolute being of subjectivity and its constitutive modes and not the other way around insofar as the subjective "regard" (think of a measurement through the system observer-particle-measuring apparatus) may posit the mode of existence of an entangled quantum state-of-affairs while the being-in-itself of the subjectivity remains unchanged.

In view of the arguments so far the question of existence seems to be virtually undecidable especially if put in absolute ontological terms, at least in the current stage of philosophical and epistemological knowledge. We would rather be satisfied to address it as simply a question of "existence as being-there" and taking advantage of every aspect of its "being-there".

---

[65] Bas van Fraassen, *Quantum Mechanics: An Empiricist View* (Oxford: Oxford Univ. Press, 1991), pp. 454, 481.
[66] A case of underdetermination of (material) ontology by the experimental data is the well-known double-slit experiment in which quantum particles behave either as individuals or waves according to their detection or not by a measuring apparatus.

INDEX

priori, 5, 13-14, 18-19, 34, 41, 58-69, 75-79, 93, 105, 114-117, 122, 130, 136, 142, 149-151, 163, 167, 173-177, 182, 196-197, 201, 215 217, 223-225, 228, 243, 250, 257-258, 261-264, 269, 273, 285, 288, 292-296, 302, 305, 310, 313-315, 319, 323, 327-347, 352-354, 359, 362-363, 367, 372, 382, 385-388, 394-397, 402, 405, 409-411, 418

bsolute flux of consciousness, 18, 115, 130, 228, 262, 290, 295, 336, 340, 360, 362, 367, 373, 404, 419

bsolute subjectivity, 5-7, 18, 118, 159, 229, 264, 291, 300, 306, 315, 322-324, 337, 344, 347, 360-362, 391, 407-409, 419

bsoluteness, 4-5, 8, 29, 34-36, 39-42, 47-50, 75-76, 143, 189, 195-202, 207, 210, 213, 217-220, 228, 234, 238-247, 250-254, 303, 385, 389, 402-403, 407-408, 412, 417

ctual infinity, 11-13, 16-19, 26, 363, 369-371

ctual presence, 46, 58, 150-151, 218, 224, 229, 264, 287, 341, 345, 365

dams, R., 343, 386, 398

renhart, B. J., 349, 384, 393, 399

ristotle, 54, 86, 122, 131, 199, 230, 258, 266-267, 273, 278, 336, 412

Armstrong, C. G., 266, 278
Arrigoni, T., 208-215, 223-226, 231
Axiom of Choice, 29, 32, 36, 39, 42, 71, 77, 101, 125, 135, 138-143, 147, 150, 168-170, 184, 189, 192-194, 202, 213, 216-221, 227, 234, 238-239, 246-248, 272-275, 369

Badiou, A., 133, 137, 148-149, 153, 202-203, 230-231, 259, 271-272, 277
Baire space, 152, 217
Barton, N., 236, 241-242, 254
Bauer, E., 358-359, 377
Becker, O., 88, 110-112, 230-231, 269, 278, 405, 412-413
Being there, 6-8, 12, 379-399
Being-in-itself, 1-2, 14, 57, 223, 301, 306-307, 311, 318-322, 346, 415, 418
Belaga, G. E., 274, 277
Bell, L. J., 293, 393
Benacerraf, B., 233, 249-250, 254
Bergson, H., 19, 318, 381, 389
Bernet, R., 27, 132, 164, 179, 277, 292, 296-297, 300, 323-325, 376, 407
Bitbol, M., 3, 386, 392, 398
Blattner, W., 314, 325, 419
Boge, F., 393-398
Brentano, F., 352
Brough, B. G., 314, 419

Brouwer, L. E. J., 45-46, 50, 88-90, 132, 166, 177, 180, 229-231, 269, 277, 326, 353, 413
Buzaglo, M., 237, 254

Cantor, G., 4-5, 11-12, 19-21, 24-26, 38, 53, 62, 74, 89, 101, 126-128, 133-135, 142-143, 152-153, 157, 160, 166-174, 184, 197, 203-234, 238, 244-246, 268-269, 274-277, 297, 353, 369-370, 392, 413
Cardinal, 4-6, 22, 35, 40-43, 49, 63-65, 71, 77, 80, 83, 89, 109, 125-126, 133-154, 168-170, 174, 179-180, 191, 195-197, 205-231, 234-237, 240-242, 246, 253-254, 259, 268, 271-276, 363, 369, 375, 392
Carnap, R., 45, 102, 144, 158, 161, 179, 250, 355
Chakravartty, A., 187-188, 203, 386, 398
Clarke-Doane, J., 233, 249-250, 254
Cohen, P., 11, 29-40, 44-51, 71, 75, 133-136, 143, 147, 167-169, 181-183, 192-200, 203-207, 220-222, 230-231, 271, 277
Completed totality, 71, 91, 147, 153, 170, 271
Completed whole, 31-33, 36-39, 44-46, 49, 58, 71, 80, 109, 142, 146, 150-153, 159, 165, 193, 196, 202, 208, 217-221, 227, 341, 363
Concept expansion, 238-239
Consciousness, 1-7, 12-20, 23-26, 34, 37, 43-50, 53-72, 77-83, 86, 91-96, 102-110, 114-120, 123-124, 129-137, 146-153, 156-167, 170-171, 175-177, 190, 193, 196, 200-202, 224-230, 243-244, 250-251, 257-276, 282-297, 300-310, 313-326, 329-352, 355-377, 380-382, 388-398, 402-419
Constituting subjectivity, 5, 83, 129, 164, 269, 324, 338, 362, 382, 414
Constructive universe, 34, 133, 138, 149

Continuous unity, 6, 12-13, 17, 46-48, 71, 107, 123, 134, 147, 150-153, 170, 200-202, 229, 262, 269-27?, 275-276, 283, 287-290, 295, 30?, 323-324, 366-368, 371, 407, 41?
Continuum hypothesis, 4-5, 11, 29-30, 39, 42, 51, 71, 75, 126, 131, 135-136, 139, 143-144, 168-170, 190-192, 203, 206, 209, 217, 229-231, 234-239, 244, 255, 27?, 274, 277, 330, 378
Countable, 4-6, 12, 16, 21-22, 30-37, 40-47, 60, 83, 124-128, 133-136, 140, 143, 150, 153, 189-198, 20?, 212-213, 217, 221-223, 229, 23?, 239-242, 246, 254, 275, 284, 36?, 371, 374, 403
Crowell, S., 312, 325

D'Espagnat, B., 1-3, 383, 395, 398
Da Costa, N., 184-187, 190-193, 203
Da Silva, J., 55, 80-81, 88, 109-110, 111
Dalla Chiara, M. L., 291, 296
Dasein, 5-7, 269, 299-303, 307-317, 323-324, 380-383, 389-391, 396-399, 407, 415-419
Davis, P., 237, 254
Definite totality, 38, 71, 118, 126-128
Dependent logic, 247-248
Descartes, R., 267, 318, 414
Disentangled state, 344, 358
Dorato, M., 347-349, 393, 398
Dreyfus, K. H., 300, 325, 419
Drikerr, A., 417
Dummett, M. A. E., 274, 277

Ecstatic, 301-302, 306-308, 313-316, 319-324, 380, 383, 418-419
Elementary embedding, 135-136, 140-142, 150, 154, 208, 211-212, 216-221, 227, 231, 253, 275-277
Eley, L., 86, 111, 277, 327-329, 332-338, 344, 377, 413
Entity, 12, 34, 67, 122, 127, 190, 206, 230, 238, 267-270, 281-282, 288, 295, 354, 366, 389-392, 397

rdös, P., 139, 154, 216, 275

actual, 1, 12-14, 33, 37, 42-44, 67, 70-74, 106-108, 115, 122, 129, 132, 170, 225, 239, 249-250, 257-258, 310, 327, 333-335, 338, 354, 382-384, 390-393, 396, 405, 410, 418

arber, M., 415

eferman, S., 5, 37-38, 45-47, 51, 54, 70-71, 75, 83, 86-89, 98-100, 109-111, 125-128, 131, 135, 142-144, 153, 156-162, 166-169, 172-173, 176-178, 195-196, 203, 209-217, 222, 226, 229-231, 237, 245-246, 254

eist, R., 88, 111

ichte, J. G., 299, 352

initistic, 3-6, 16, 24, 284, 367-369, 374, 413, 416

øllesdal, D, 172, 178-179

orcing extension, 30-31, 185, 197, 202, 207, 221, 229, 234, 239-242

orcing model, 29, 32, 39-42, 136, 143, 181, 185, 197, 243, 246, 272

orcing theory, 29-51, 85, 132-137, 143-145, 148, 154, 169, 193, 204-207, 220, 271, 278

oundations of mathematics, 29, 50, 109, 134, 156, 167, 175, 178, 196, 206, 235, 255, 265, 277-278, 353, 368

owler, N. C., 265-266, 277, 297

ranks, C., 160, 178

rege, G., 53, 61-62, 100, 121, 161, 274, 277, 352-353

rench, S., 137, 183-187, 190-193, 203, 343, 353, 359-360, 376, 394, 398

riedman, D. S., 5, 191, 210-215, 231, 235, 395-398

Gaifman, H., 144, 272-273, 277

Garciadiego, A., 219, 231

Garrett, D., 268, 277

Generic set, 30-33, 36, 39, 42-46, 60, 143, 148-149, 169, 197, 200-202, 246, 271-272

George, A., 189, 203

Glock, H. J., 402

Gödel's incompleteness theorems, 11, 72, 113, 127-128, 192, 247, 368, 374, 391

Gödel, K., 54, 89, 101-103, 109-112, 133-135, 138-186, 192, 196-200, 203-212, 215-217, 220-223, 230-231, 272-275, 278, 326, 368, 374, 377, 391-392, 404

Goldfarb, W. D., 161, 178-179

Grib, A. A., 291, 296, 345, 358, 376, 394, 398

Griffiths, G. R., 393, 398

Gurwitsch, A., 406-410

Gusman, S., 406, 418

Hahn, H., 51, 144

Hamkins, J. D., 233, 236, 239-254

Hartimo, M., 65, 86, 353, 376

Hauser, K., 55, 80-82, 86, 134-137, 140-141, 144-146, 151-153, 157-159, 179, 199-203, 206-207, 225-227, 231

Heelan, P., 316, 325

Hegel, G. W. F., 299, 352

Heidegger, M., 5-7, 269, 296-303, 307-319, 322-326, 379-383, 389, 396-399, 403, 407, 415-419

Held, K., 21, 30, 126, 237, 267-268, 281, 291-292, 296, 300, 316, 325, 386, 396, 401

Hellman, G., 266, 277

Hering, J., 55, 241, 328

Hersh, R., 237, 254

Heyting, A., 50, 126, 132, 269, 277

Hilbert, D., 79, 88, 102, 167-168, 178, 222, 227, 230, 255, 273, 353

Hill Ortiz, C., 55, 80-82, 86, 115, 132, 254, 327-328, 353, 377, 410

Holistic, 4, 8, 11, 47, 54, 74, 109, 115, 122, 129, 188, 331, 348, 356-358, 362, 391

Hopkins, J., 86, 132, 281, 296
Horsten, L., 237, 254
Hrbaček, K., 135, 275
Hume, D, 118, 257, 267-268, 277
Husserl, E., 1-8, 11-21, 27, 34, 41-51,
    55-69, 75-83, 86-95, 102-119,
    122-123, 129-134, 137, 144,
    147-149, 153-167, 170-184,
    199-203, 223-231, 235-238, 244,
    250-251, 254, 257-264, 267-269,
    276-278, 283-291, 294-356,
    359-385, 388-419

Identity, 17-19, 35, 60-61, 69, 76, 86, 101,
    106, 118, 129, 172, 186-188,
    199-203, 221, 225, 264, 267,
    275, 287, 305, 310, 323, 331,
    339, 343, 346-349, 356, 386-387,
    398-399, 402
Immanent, 1, 4-6, 12, 17-19, 26, 37,
    44-48, 53-62, 65, 68-73, 76-77,
    80, 91-96, 102-110, 117-119,
    123, 131, 134-138, 147-151, 158,
    165, 170-171, 175, 193, 199-202,
    224-230, 257-258, 262-275,
    285-287, 290-292, 296, 299,
    303-304, 309, 322-324, 339-345,
    359-361, 366-368, 371-373, 382,
    388, 402-414, 418
Immanent infinty, 46, 138, 147, 151, 170,
    199, 227, 230, 263, 265, 268,
    273, 341, 426
Impredicativity, 19, 37, 91, 96, 265, 291,
    297, 366
Incompleteness, 4, 11, 21, 30-37, 51, 54,
    71-73, 77, 89, 113-115, 127-128,
    146, 158, 167, 192, 198, 207,
    230, 247, 368, 374-375, 379,
    391-393
Individual-substrate, 288, 294
Infinite, 6, 11-17, 22-26, 283-284, 292,
    303, 360, 363-372, 375, 403, 407,
    412-419
Infinite totality, 14-15, 37-39, 126
Infinity, 3-8, 11-26, 258-278, 295, 363,
    366-371, 374-375, 378, 401, 40,
    412-418
Ingarden, R., 163, 338
Inner model, 39, 71, 135, 139-143, 147,
    150, 168-170, 184, 198, 208-21,
    215-220, 227, 231, 253, 275
Inner time, 87, 130, 156, 159-160, 168,
    178, 200, 258-261, 289-290, 29,
    302, 306, 315-316, 398
Intentional consciousness, 17, 34, 43, 12
    162, 286-287, 293, 296, 337, 34
    367, 372, 388, 394
Intentionality, 18-20, 34, 48-50, 58, 69,
    77-79, 84, 94, 102-105, 118-119
    124, 130, 136, 159, 173-175,
    250-251, 261-262, 269, 283-289
    293, 296, 312-317, 323, 326,
    330-331, 342, 345, 354, 359,
    362, 367-369, 382, 390, 404-40
    409-411, 414, 417-419
Intuitive continuum, 5, 94, 102, 134,
    229-231, 269, 278, 326
Invariance, 20, 187, 199, 204, 395-396
Isham, C. J., 190, 202-203, 393, 399
Isomorphism, 20, 76, 183, 187-188,
    191-193, 199, 226, 236, 251, 35
    394
Iteration principle, 98, 102

Jacquette, D., 268, 277
Jech, T., 143, 154, 406
Jensen, B. R., 139, 154, 213, 217-219,
    222-223, 231

Kanamori, A., 30-31, 35, 51, 135-136,
    139, 154, 194, 203, 206-208, 21,
    215, 218-221, 229-231, 257-258,
    273-274, 277
Kant, E., 156, 160, 172, 255, 352, 392,
    395-396, 407, 412
Keisler, J. H., 139, 154, 168-169, 179,
    212, 231
Keller, P., 300, 326
Kirkland, S., 281, 297
Kleene, S. C, 72-73, 86, 98, 127-128, 132
    178, 391, 399

ause, D., 60, 86, 188, 203, 347-349, 384, 393, 399
iegel, U., 409
hn, T., 355
nen, K., 32-33, 36, 39-42, 51, 60, 71, 85-86, 127, 132, 136-140, 143, 150, 154, 198, 203, 216, 220, 229-231, 235, 241-243, 246, 254, 271, 275-277, 284, 297, 410
zin, I., 417
wenheim, L., 30, 36, 147, 182-183, 189, 196, 203, 213, 236, 251
ndgrebe, L., 86, 132, 153, 179, 203, 231, 254, 277, 342, 377, 408
rge cardinal, 5, 71, 133-150, 154, 169-170, 205-226, 231, 234-236, 246, 259, 271, 275-276, 392
vine, S., 24
wvere, F. W., 32, 51, 184, 204
besgue measure, 139
e, N. H., 1, 25-27, 35, 42, 60, 72-73, 86, 89, 92, 98, 105-107, 118, 123, 127-128, 132, 174, 178, 239, 250, 270, 277, 285, 391, 399
ibniz, G. W., 155, 166, 177, 180, 200, 238, 343, 351, 386-387, 410
vinas, E., 398-399, 403, 407, 411-417
vy, A., 139, 143-144, 154, 169, 179, 209, 221, 231
vy, L., 300, 326
cke, J., 257, 267-268, 386
hmar, D., 114, 132, 162-164, 179, 277, 297, 376, 399, 406-407
ndon, F., 358-359, 377
urcat, F., 353, 377
acann, C., 315, 326
addy, P., 5, 213-214, 221, 226, 231, 235, 255
akovetsky, E., 417
ancosu, P., 88, 112
argenau, H., 358, 377
arsonet, M., 384-388, 399
artin, D., 33, 139, 190, 219-221, 245, 255, 407, 416

Mathematical continuum, 6, 87, 91, 125, 134, 185, 274-275, 297, 321, 326
Mathematical object, 4-6, 12-13, 16, 23, 26, 30, 50, 53-58, 61-63, 68, 72-73, 78-81, 101-104, 123, 126, 136-137, 140, 143, 147-150, 156-160, 165, 168, 171-174, 177-178, 198-200, 218, 223-229, 237, 250, 265, 271-273, 331, 347, 362-368, 390-392, 404-406, 409
Maximal, 138, 142, 152, 208-211, 217-218, 222, 225
Maxwell, R., 355
Meaning-act, 25-26, 114-116, 130, 149, 165, 271, 351, 364, 410
Measurable cardinal, 135, 139-146, 154, 169, 180, 207-213, 216, 223, 231, 275
Measurement, 2, 15, 183, 291, 296, 355-361, 376, 379, 387, 393-398
Merlan, P., 283, 297, 300-302, 326
Merleau-Ponty, M., 356-357, 381, 403
Michalski, K., 50-51, 79, 86, 262, 278, 293, 297
Mill, S. J., 130-132, 297, 326, 408
Mitchell, J. W., 208, 219, 231
Mohanty, J. N., 179, 328-330, 342
Moore, H. G., 32, 51, 178, 219, 231
Moran, D., 383, 399, 403
Morganti, M., 347-349, 398
Moschovakis, J., 217, 223, 231
Multiverse, 233-255

Nagel, E., 72-73, 86, 127, 132, 154
Nelson, E., 24-27, 83, 86, 369-370, 377
Neurath, O., 144
Newman, J., 72-73, 86, 127, 132
Niehues-Pröbstig, H., 281
Noe, A., 96, 114
noema, 4, 17, 57-60, 65, 68, 78, 91, 106, 117-119, 122, 130, 149, 158, 166, 175, 200-202, 225-228, 252, 262-264, 285-289, 292-296, 340-348, 351, 359-361, 364-365, 380, 388, 397, 404-409, 413-414,

noesis, 166, 200, 346, 413-414
noetic, 17, 57, 117-119, 130, 158, 171, 175, 202, 264, 285-286, 289, 292-293, 340-342, 346, 364, 380, 409, 418
Nonstandard theories, 15, 19, 26, 185, 238

Objectivity of understanding, 73, 86, 392
Ontological multiversism, 233-236, 240-241, 247, 252
Ontology, 1-6, 14-15, 38, 47, 50, 63, 70-71, 76-77, 82, 117-118, 126, 133, 137, 144, 148-149, 152, 160, 174, 178, 181, 189, 203, 209, 223, 227, 230, 236, 251, 257-278, 287-289, 296, 299-300, 303, 306-308, 311-312, 318, 325-328, 331-333, 337, 379-391, 395-403, 407-412, 416-417
Ordinal, 4, 30-31, 34-37, 41, 46-50, 60, 63-65, 89, 134-143, 146, 149-150, 168, 188-189, 194-201, 206-208, 211-212, 216-223, 226, 234-235, 239-241, 252-254, 272-275, 284-286, 348-349, 413

Parsons, C., 4, 49-51, 54, 86, 178
Partial isomorphism, 187, 193, 199, 251
Patočka, J., 291, 297, 309, 326, 407-408
Petitot, J., 13, 20, 27
Phenomenological reduction, 17, 96, 114, 175, 259, 282, 285-287, 290, 303, 318, 345, 348, 357, 360, 364
Plato, 258, 266, 282, 293, 297
platonic, 1-3, 39, 47, 54, 133, 136, 174-176, 237, 246, 257, 265-266, 272, 276, 281-297, 328, 366, 376
platonistic, 3, 6, 11, 26, 38-39, 47, 54, 67, 70, 103, 117, 122, 161, 175, 224, 235-237, 370
Poincaré, H., 26, 89, 100, 111
Predication formula, 35, 198
Predicative activity, 65, 77-78, 202

Primitive term, 155, 161, 166, 176, 225
Putnam, H., 180, 377, 387, 399

Quantum theory, 1, 6-7, 203, 343, 355-357, 379, 383-384, 387, 392-399, 405
Quine, V. W., 4, 49-51, 54, 67-68, 86, 113-123, 132, 137, 195, 204, 247, 255, 356, 375-377, 384-385 399-402

Ramsey, F., 139-141, 144
Redhead, M., 186, 204, 393, 399
Regression, 7, 49, 56, 110, 124, 130, 16 236, 265, 291, 299-307, 318, 341, 354, 360, 382, 389, 405-4 418-419
Reichenbach, H., 395, 399
Reinhardt, W., 154, 216
Relative consistency, 29-31, 40, 44, 169 206-207, 219
Restriction principle, 109
Rittberg, J. C., 210, 231
Robinson, A., 11, 24, 238-239, 255, 370
Röck, T., 390-391, 399
Rorty, R., 356
Rosado-Haddock, E. G., 173, 179
Ross, D. W., 267, 273, 278
Rosser, B., 128, 132
Rowbottom, F., 141, 144
Russell, B., 100, 161, 273, 402
Ryckman, T., 88, 112

Sachhaltigkeit, 6, 327-349
Sartre, J. P., 299-302, 306-308, 311, 316-326, 381, 401, 406, 417-41
Schelling, F. W. J., 352
Schlick, M., 144, 355, 377
Scott, D., 51, 135, 141-142, 152, 168-16 180, 194, 211-213, 216-217, 22 223, 231, 242-243, 275
Semantic view, 181-183, 187-191, 199, 203
Set theory, 11-12, 21-27, 30, 34-36, 45, 50, 63, 89, 135-136, 139, 142, 154-157, 166-169, 173, 176-180

183-184, 187-189, 192-193, 198,
203, 206-212, 218-222, 226, 231,
235, 241, 246-249, 255-259, 265,
268, 271-277, 284, 297, 353,
369-370, 378, 402, 406, 410

…apiro, S., 266, 277

…er, G., 53-55, 74-76, 86, 99, 122,
277-278

…olem, T., 30, 35-36, 51, 147, 182-183,
189, 193-196, 203-204, 213, 236,
241-242, 251, 284

…olem-Löwenheim Theorem, 30, 36,
147, 182-183, 189, 196, 236, 251

…uga, H., 269, 278, 413

…nyth, B. M., 152-154

…lovay, R., 30, 33-35, 51, 139-144, 154,
169, 178-179, 194, 209, 231

…piegelberg, H., 327

…teel, R. J., 5, 210, 213, 219, 231-233,
236, 240, 246, 255

…tone space, 152-153

…ubjective, 1-7, 11-26, 29-51, 55, 61, 70,
73, 76-85, 91, 97, 101-105, 108,
111, 114-120, 125, 128-134,
137-140, 146-154, 159, 162,
165-178, 181-184, 188, 193-205,
208-211, 214, 219-221, 224-230,
233-252, 257-268, 271-278,
281-292, 296, 299-301, 309, 313,
323-324, 327-328, 331, 336-339,
342-345, 352, 356, 359-370,
374-375, 379-398, 401-404,
408-410, 415-419

…ubjective origin, 7, 11, 17, 20, 26, 33,
43-45, 114-115, 153, 159, 230,
262, 323, 336-338, 345, 390,
396-398, 419

…ubjectivity, 1-7, 13, 18, 46, 64, 77-78,
82-83, 94-95, 104, 113-114,
117-120, 124, 127-133, 148,
159, 164, 196, 229, 258-260, 264,
269-271, 283, 287-291, 300, 306,
313-315, 318, 322-325, 337-340,
344, 347, 354, 358-362, 366, 370,
374-375, 379-382, 385, 388-392,

396-397, 403, 406-409, 412-419
Supercompact, 109, 139-141, 148, 170,
208-210, 216, 220-221, 271
Suppes, P., 154, 183-185, 188, 204

Tandon, A., 317, 326
Tarski, A., 75, 127, 139, 154, 168-169,
179, 193, 212, 231, 248, 374
Teller, P., 393, 399
Temporal consciousness, 4-5, 18-19, 23,
48, 56-57, 71, 79-81, 107, 119,
129-130, 134, 147, 153, 159, 164,
170, 202, 244, 260, 263, 266-269,
276, 283-284, 287-290, 297, 302,
315, 320, 323-326, 335, 339, 347,
351-352, 355, 358-362, 366-368,
371-374, 419
Temporal ego, 81-82, 301, 306
Temporal particularity, 6, 382, 397
Temporal unity, 73, 151, 158, 164, 229,
286, 294, 316-318, 322-323, 362,
392
Ternullo, C., 234-235, 240, 255
Thomas, C. V., 406
Tieszen, R., 27, 37-39, 44-48, 51-55,
74-82, 86, 89, 103-105, 112, 132,
136, 151, 154, 175-176, 180, 231,
246, 255, 265, 278, 316, 321,
326, 366-368, 377, 404
Time-point, 93, 107, 308
Toader, I., 89, 112
Tragesser, R., 353, 378
Transcendence, 5-8, 81-82, 95, 131, 148,
159, 171, 205-206, 209, 271, 278,
287-291, 299-326, 329, 335-339,
343, 379-383, 391, 397-399, 407,
412-419
Transcendental ego, 5, 17, 77, 81, 114,
159, 262-265, 299-302, 308, 311,
314-317, 320, 326, 382-383, 389,
397, 407-409, 413
Transcendental phenomenology, 15, 23,
39, 54-57, 82, 114, 155-156, 159,
165, 259-260, 263, 268, 286, 313,
346-348, 351, 364, 381, 398, 413

Tredennick, H., 266, 278
Turney, P., 188, 204
Tzouvaras, A., 27

Unity, 1, 4-6, 12-20, 23-26, 42, 45-50,
    57-59, 64-73, 77-80, 86, 91-94,
    102-110, 115-119, 123, 129-131,
    134, 137, 147, 150-153, 157-165,
    170-171, 175, 197, 200-202,
    219, 224-230, 234, 244, 260-272,
    275-276, 281-296, 301, 305-309,
    313-326, 336-341, 344-347,
    353-355, 358-368, 371, 380-382,
    388, 392, 403, 407-410, 413-415,
    418-419
Universal-existential quantification, 48,
    67, 71, 115, 119, 121-126, 140,
    146-147, 170, 386-387, 402
Universe of sets, 21-23, 192, 195, 211,
    215, 226, 235, 240

Väänänen, J., , 233, 247–249, 255
van Atten, M., 46, 51, 151, 154-156, 166,
    177, 180, 229-231, 244, 269, 278,
    321, 326
van Dalen, D., 51, 147, 154, 191, 204,
    231, 278, 321, 326

van Fraassen, B. C., 183-185, 188-193,
    204, 349, 359, 384, 394
Vitali, G., 143
Vopěnka, P., 11, 19-22, 27

Wang, H., 80, 86, 135, 154-160, 164, 16*
    172, 180, 223, 232, 326
Weierstrass, K., 62, 121, 124, 353
Weyl, H., 19, 25-27, 61-62, 86-112, 132,
    231, 255, 278, 326, 405
Whitehead, N. A., 118, 125, 132, 222,
    270, 415
Wigner, E., 377, 394
Wittgenstein, L., 114, 118, 132, 376
Woodin, H. W., 71-72, 86, 134-137,
    140-141, 145-148, 153-154,
    170-171, 180, 208-210, 214-216
    219-220, 231-235, 239-240,
    245-246, 252-255, 275-278, 375
    378
Woodruff Smith, D., 389, 392, 399
Wrathall, A. M., 300, 325, 419

Yablo, S, 339, 349

Zahavi, D., 300, 315-317, 326, 403
Zakon, E., 238-239, 255
Zhok, A., 327

www.ingramcontent.com/pod-product-compliance
Lightning Source LLC
Chambersburg PA
CBHW051031160426
43193CB00010B/904